NBER Macroeconomics Annual 2020

NBER Macroeconomics Annual 2020

Edited by
Martin Eichenbaum and Erik Hurst

The University of Chicago Press
Chicago and London

NBER Macroeconomics Annual 2020, Number 35

Published annually by The University of Chicago Press.
www.journals.uchicago.edu/MA/

Subscriptions: Individual subscription rates are $95 print + electronic and $45 e-only ($23 for students). Institutional print + electronic and e-only rates are tiered according to an institution's type and research output: $148 to $312 (print + electronic), $129 to $271 (e-only). For additional information, including back-issue sales, classroom use, rates for single copies, and prices for institutional full-run access, please visit www.journals.uchicago.edu /MA/. Free or deeply discounted access is available in most developing nations through the Chicago Emerging Nations Initiative (www.journals.uchicago.edu/ceni/).

Please direct subscription inquiries to Subscription Fulfillment, 1427 E. 60th Street, Chicago, IL 60637-2902. Telephone: (773) 753-3347 or toll free in the United States and Canada (877) 705-1878. Fax: (773) 753-0811 or toll-free (877) 705-1879. E-mail: subscriptions @press.uchicago.edu.

Standing orders: To place a standing order for this book series, please address your request to The University of Chicago Press, Chicago Distribution Center, Attn. Standing Orders/Customer Service, 11030 S. Langley Avenue, Chicago, IL 60628. Telephone toll free in the U.S. and Canada: 1-800-621-2736; or 1-773-702-7000. Fax toll free in the U.S. and Canada: 1-800-621-8476; or 1-773-702-7212.

Single-copy orders: In the U.S., Canada, and the rest of the world, order from your local bookseller or direct from The University of Chicago Press, Chicago Distribution Center, 11030 S. Langley Avenue, Chicago, IL 60628. Telephone toll free in the U.S. and Canada: 1-800-621-2736; or 1-773-702-7000. Fax toll free in the U.S. and Canada: 1-800-621-8476; or 1-773-702-7212. In the U.K. and Europe, order from your local bookseller or direct from The University of Chicago Press, c/o John Wiley Ltd. Distribution Center, 1 Oldlands Way, Bognor Regis, West Sussex PO22 9SA, UK. Telephone 01243 779777 or Fax 01243 820250. E-mail: cs-books@wiley.co.uk.

The University of Chicago Press offers bulk discounts on individual titles to Corporate, Premium and Gift accounts. For information, please write to Sales Department—Special Sales, The University of Chicago Press, 1427 E. 60th Street, Chicago, IL 60637 USA or telephone 1-773-702-7723.

This book was printed and bound in the United States of America.

ISSN: 0889-3365
E-ISSN: 1537-2642
ISBN: 978-0-226-80268-8 (pb.:alk.paper)
eISBN: 978-0-226-80271-8 (e-book)

Relation of the Directors to the Work and Publications of the NBER

1. The object of the NBER is to ascertain and present to the economics profession, and to the public more generally, important economic facts and their interpretation in a scientific manner without policy recommendations. The Board of Directors is charged with the responsibility of ensuring that the work of the NBER is carried on in strict conformity with this object.

2. The President shall establish an internal review process to ensure that book manuscripts proposed for publication DO NOT contain policy recommendations. This shall apply both to the proceedings of conferences and to manuscripts by a single author or by one or more coauthors but shall not apply to authors of comments at NBER conferences who are not NBER affiliates.

3. No book manuscript reporting research shall be published by the NBER until the President has sent to each member of the Board a notice that a manuscript is recommended for publication and that in the President's opinion it is suitable for publication in accordance with the above principles of the NBER. Such notification will include a table of contents and an abstract or summary of the manuscript's content, a list of contributors if applicable, and a response form for use by Directors who desire a copy of the manuscript for review. Each manuscript shall contain a summary drawing attention to the nature and treatment of the problem studied and the main conclusions reached.

4. No volume shall be published until forty-five days have elapsed from the above notification of intention to publish it. During this period a copy shall be sent to any Director requesting it, and if any Director objects to publication on the grounds that the manuscript contains policy recommendations, the objection will be presented to the author(s) or editor(s). In case of dispute, all members of the Board shall be notified,

and the President shall appoint an ad hoc committee of the Board to decide the matter; thirty days additional shall be granted for this purpose.

5. The President shall present annually to the Board a report describing the internal manuscript review process, any objections made by Directors before publication or by anyone after publication, any disputes about such matters, and how they were handled.

6. Publications of the NBER issued for informational purposes concerning the work of the Bureau, or issued to inform the public of the activities at the Bureau, including but not limited to the NBER Digest and Reporter, shall be consistent with the object stated in paragraph 1. They shall contain a specific disclaimer noting that they have not passed through the review procedures required in this resolution. The Executive Committee of the Board is charged with the review of all such publications from time to time.

7. NBER working papers and manuscripts distributed on the Bureau's web site are not deemed to be publications for the purpose of this resolution, but they shall be consistent with the object stated in paragraph 1. Working papers shall contain a specific disclaimer noting that they have not passed through the review procedures required in this resolution. The NBER's web site shall contain a similar disclaimer. The President shall establish an internal review process to ensure that the working papers and the web site do not contain policy recommendations, and shall report annually to the Board on this process and any concerns raised in connection with it.

8. Unless otherwise determined by the Board or exempted by the terms of paragraphs 6 and 7, a copy of this resolution shall be printed in each NBER publication as described in paragraph 2 above.

Contents

Editorial   xi
Martin Eichenbaum and Erik Hurst
Abstracts   xix

1 **Imperfect Macroeconomic Expectations: Evidence and Theory   1**
George-Marios Angeletos, Zhen Huo, and Karthik A. Sastry

Comments   87
Jessica A. Wachter
Ricardo Reis

Discussion   112

2 **Diverging Trends in National and Local Concentration   115**
Esteban Rossi-Hansberg, Pierre-Daniel Sarte, and Nicholas Trachter

Comments   151
Jan Eeckhout
Robert E. Hall

Discussion   173

3 **What Do We Learn from Cross-Regional Empirical Estimates in Macroeconomics?**   175

Adam Guren, Alisdair McKay, Emi Nakamura, and Jón Steinsson

Comments   224

Gabriel Chodorow-Reich
Valerie A. Ramey

Discussion   242

4 **Innovative Growth Accounting**   245

Peter J. Klenow and Huiyu Li

Comment   296

John Haltiwanger

Discussion   308

5 **The Glass Ceiling and the Paper Floor: Changing Gender Composition of Top Earners since the 1980s**   309

Fatih Guvenen, Greg Kaplan, and Jae Song

Comments   374

Paola Sapienza
Raquel Fernández

Discussion   388

6 **Sources of US Wealth Inequality: Past, Present, and Future**   391

Joachim Hubmer, Per Krusell, and Anthony A. Smith, Jr.

Comments   456

Owen Zidar
Benjamin Moll

Discussion   480

Editorial

Martin Eichenbaum, *Northwestern University,* United States of America, *and NBER,* United States of America

Erik Hurst, *University of Chicago,* United States of America, *and NBER,* United States of America

The NBER's 35th Annual Conference on Macroeconomics brought together leading scholars to present, discuss, and debate six research papers on central issues in contemporary macroeconomics. In addition, Jeremy Stein, former governor of the Federal Reserve, led a thought-provoking discussion on whether the financial system is safer now than it was prior to the Great Recession. Given the pandemic, the conference took place via Zoom. Video recordings of the presentations of the papers and the after-dinner talk are all accessible on the web page of the NBER Annual Conference on Macroeconomics. These videos make a useful complement to this volume and make the content of the conference more widely accessible.

This conference volume contains edited versions of the six papers presented at the conference. With one exception, each paper is followed by two written discussions by leading scholars and a summary of the debates that followed each paper. In the exception, there is only one written discussion.

In their paper "Imperfect Macroeconomic Expectations: Evidence and Theory," George-Marios Angeletos, Zhen Huo, and Karthik Sastry tackle a central question in macroeconomics: How should we model people's expectations? For many years the answer to this question was widely viewed among mainstream macroeconomists as a settled issue. The answer was that people have rational expectations and common knowledge about the state of the economy. That consensus shattered under the weight of a large literature testing rational expectations, based in part on survey-based data. But what should we replace our simple benchmark model of expectations with? The paper by Angeletos et al.

brings to bear new econometric evidence on this question. Their key empirical result is that, in response to the main shocks driving the business cycle, expectations underreact initially but eventually overshoot. In their view, this evidence, and results in the survey-based empirical literature, favors models in which there is dispersed, noisy information across people and overextrapolation of expectations. The paper develops and analyzes such a model.

The first discussant, Jessica Wachter, provides a valuable summary of the difficulties involved in interpreting survey-based evidence on expectations. She then brings to bear insights from psychology and behavioral economics to provide an alternative interpretation of the evidence. Her interpretation gives less weight to "private information" and more weight to the idea that agents filter common information differently through the lens of their experiences.

The second discussant, Ricardo Reis, provides a thorough analysis of the statistical evidence and the model proposed by Angeletos et al. Reis then raises a different set of puzzles about expectations that the paper abstracts from. These puzzles revolve around the fact that people disagree in their forecasts about critical macro variables. Significantly, the extent and nature of that disagreement changes in predictable ways. The model proposed by Angeletos et al. does not account for the stylized "disagreement" facts. Reis displays a perturbation of that model that succeeds in doing so.

There is a large literature documenting the rise in firm concentration within the United States over the last few decades. The top few firms in each industry are producing a larger share of aggregate output. Some researchers have associated the rising firm concentration with a fall in competition and an increase in firm market power. Yet most product markets are local. Individuals consume retail products and services often close to their residence or place of work. The change in local competition, therefore, is an interesting object to study above and beyond trends in aggregate competition.

In their paper, "Diverging Trends in National and Local Concentration," Esteban Rossi-Hansberg, Pierre-Daniel Sarte, and Nicholas Trachter contrast the patterns of rising aggregate firm market concentration with falling market concentration over time at the local level. Using data from the National Establishment Time Series (NETS), the authors show that Herfindahl-Hirschman indices (HHI) have been falling within states, metropolitan statistical areas, and zip codes despite rising in the aggregate. The paper documents that these patterns are pervasive within most industries, with declining local concentration being larger in the service and retail industries. In addition, the paper highlights that when a large firm in a given industry—like Walmart—enters a local area, the total number of firms in that industry increase. Although it is true that large firms like Walmart may drive out some competitors, the effect is less than one-for-one such that the number of firms increases on net.

The paper uses these findings to suggest that local competition is actually increasing given that local firm concentration is falling. Both discussants caution against this interpretation. First, as highlighted by the remarks of Jan Eeckhout, HHIs are a poor proxy for market competition. Both Jan Eeckhout and Bob Hall, the second discussant, stress that one needs to think hard about what constitutes a local market. They both suggest that measuring how markups have evolved at the local level would be more informative of whether competitive forces have changed. Finally, both discussants provide areas for future research within the literature. Despite their comments, the discussants praise the authors for documenting the novel dichotomy that the paper has uncovered showing that local concentration has fallen despite rising national concentration.

There has been an explosion of research in the last decade using regional data to learn about macroeconomic forces. One common criticism of this literature is that many of the general equilibrium forces of interest to macroeconomists get differenced out from cross-region regressions. However, it may be possible to recover meaningful structural parameters by exploiting cross-region variation. In the paper "What Do We Learn from Cross-Regional Empirical Estimates in Macroeconomics?" Adam Guren, Alisdair McKay, Emi Nakamura, and Jón Steinsson develop a novel econometric procedure to recover structural parameters of interest to macroeconomists using cross-region variation.

The example highlighted in the paper for their econometric procedure is to recover micro estimates of the direct effect of housing wealth changes on individual household consumption. This is a parameter of interest in many macro models assessing the effects of housing booms and busts on the macroeconomy. When econometricians exploit regional variation to assess the effect of local housing price changes on local consumption, the estimates confound both the direct effect of wealth effects on household consumption as well as the indirect effect of local multipliers from the initial consumption response. Guren et al. propose a methodology to isolate the direct effect of house price changes on consumption by using other estimates of demand multipliers from the local government spending literature to deflate estimates of the total effect of local consumption on local house prices. The paper shows that their methodology is approximately correct under a wide array of model assumptions. The paper also discusses other examples where their methodology is applicable.

Overall, the paper provides future researchers with a road map of how to use cross-region variation to isolate parameters of interest to macroeconomists. Gabriel Chodorow-Reich and Valerie Ramey provide excellent discussions highlighting how this paper fits into the recent literature of macroeconomists exploiting cross-region variation as well as pointing out other potential methods to estimate structural parameters using micro data.

There is widespread agreement that productivity growth has declined. But the sources of this slowdown are not well understood. In "Innovative Growth Accounting," Peter Klenow and Huiyu Li tackle the closely related questions: What form does innovation take, and which firms do most of the innovation? Their analysis decomposes growth into three types of innovation: creative destruction, brand-new varieties, and innovation by incumbents on their own products. The authors further decompose each of these sources into contributions by firm age and size.

The authors base their decomposition on (1) a growth accounting framework that is motivated by a quality ladder model of innovation, and (2) plant-level data across all firms in the nonfarm business sector over the period 1982–2013. Their main findings can be summarized as follows. First, young firms generate roughly 50% of productivity growth. Most of this growth comes from new variety introduction. Second, most of the surge in productivity during the mid-1990s and the subsequent slowdown is accounted for by older firms. Third, a majority of growth takes the form of quality improvements by incumbents on their own products.

The discussant, John Haltiwanger, notes that quantifying the contribution of innovation to economic growth for the entire private sector is a major step forward. He also writes that the authors have developed a rich framework that enables researchers to explore many issues on a much broader basis than existing research that uses alternative approaches. However, he cautions that the authors' empirical approach imposes a number of strong assumptions that are inconsistent with empirical evidence. In his view, the associated limitations of the analysis are likely to be quantitatively important.

It has been well documented that the share of income accruing to top earners has been growing over time. In their paper, "The Glass Ceiling and the Paper Floor: Changing Gender Composition of Top Earners since the 1980s," Fatih Guvenen, Greg Kaplan, and Jae Song use detailed micro panel data from the Social Security Administration (SSA) to assess the progress women have made into the top 1% and top 0.1% of the income distribution over time.

The paper provides a plethora of interesting facts gleaned from the SSA data. In the early 1980s, women comprised roughly 3% of top 0.1% of the annual income distribution. By the 2012, that share had increased to about 10%. Women are dramatically underrepresented in the top income distribution, albeit less in the 2000s compared to the 1980s. The panel nature of the authors' data allows them to measure multiyear average of income. A key finding is that individuals—both men and women—are more likely to remain within the top 0.1% of the income distribution in the 2000s relative to the 1980s. Despite the total share of earnings accruing to the top percentiles remaining relatively stable during the last decade, top earnings are being spread among a decreasing share of the overall population. Moreover, even relative to men, women are more likely to remain top earners during the 2000s than they were during the 1980s. Finally, the panel data allow for a new analysis of the life-cycle profile of top earners and how those profiles differ by gender. The gender gap in top earning shares is smallest for individuals in their 20s and individuals close to retirement.

Overall, this paper provides a detailed taxonomy of how the gender composition of top earners in the United States has evolved over time. The paper should serve as a launching-off point for other researchers who are interested in explaining why the gender composition of top earners has changed during the 1980s and 1990s and also why those changes have stalled during the 2000s. The discussants, Paola Sapienza and Raquel Fernández, both praise the authors for marshaling together such important and interesting data. Both, also provide suggestions to the literature about further potential explorations. For example, Paola Sapienza comments that it would be interesting to see how the gender patterns of top earners change when incorporating broader measures of earnings that also include interest, dividends, and rents earned by owners of firms. Raquel Fernández discusses the importance of exploring how differential entry and exit from the labor force by gender interacts with the life-cycle patterns documented in the paper.

Few topics are as important or as controversial as the reasons for growing wealth inequality across the developed world. In "Sources of US Wealth Inequality: Past, Present, and Future," Joachim Hubmer, Per Krusell, and Anthony A. Smith Jr. tackle this difficult issue, focusing on the modern

US experience. They do so using an incomplete, heterogeneous-agent model in which inequality is determined by individual households' reactions to changes in their environment and the equilibrium resulting from those interactions. Critically, the authors depart from standard versions of that model by introducing portfolio heterogeneity across and within wealth. This type of heterogeneity receives clear support from the data and helps their model match a key feature of wealth and earnings distributions: the former is much more highly concentrated than the latter.

Using their model, Hubmer et al. argue that the significant drop in tax progressivity starting in the late 1970s was the most important source of growing wealth inequality in the United States. Strikingly, the sharp observed increases in earnings inequality and the falling labor share cannot account for the bulk of the increase in wealth inequality.

The first discussant, Owen Zidar, reviews and brings to bear new evidence to support the view that tax progressivity, portfolio heterogeneity, and return heterogeneity are quantitatively important drivers of wealth inequality in the United States. In addition to providing valuable caveats about the model calibration, Zidar highlights three other forces that are not emphasized in the paper: (1) life cycle and demographic trends, (2) falling interest rates and concomitant asset price growth, and (3) inherited wealth and family firms.

According to the second discussant, Benjamin Moll, the Hubmer et al. paper provides the best quantitative assessment to date of a number of plausible drivers of the rise in wealth inequality in the United States. Like the other discussant, Moll notes that a key element in the model's ability to account for many US wealth trends is the rich stochastic process for asset returns. Moll summarizes other corroborating evidence that heterogeneity of portfolio and asset returns are key drivers of the wealth inequality. Like the authors, Moll notes that return premia in the model are exogenous in both the time series and cross section. So like them, Moll emphasizes the need to understand the reasons for that heterogeneity. To make the point concrete, he uses a series of insightful examples to clarify the relationship between wealth and welfare inequality.

As in previous years, the editors posted and distributed a call for proposals in the spring and summer prior to the conference and some of the papers in this volume were selected from proposals submitted in response to this call. Other papers are commissioned on central and topical areas in macroeconomics. Both are done in consultation with the advisory board, whom we thank for their input and support of both the conference and the published volume.

The authors and the editors would like to take this opportunity to thank Jim Poterba and the National Bureau of Economic Research for their continued support for the *NBER Macroeconomics Annual* and the associated conference. We would also like to thank the NBER conference staff, particularly Rob Shannon, for his continued excellent organization and support. Financial assistance from the National Science Foundation is gratefully acknowledged. We also thank the rapporteurs, Riccardo Bianchi Vimercati and Marta Prato, who provided invaluable help in preparing the summaries of the discussions. And last but far from least, we are grateful to Helena Fitz-Patrick for her invaluable assistance in editing and publishing the volume.

For acknowledgments, sources of research support, and disclosure of the authors' material financial relationships, if any, please see https://www.nber.org/books-and-chapters/nber-macroeconomics-annual-2020-volume-35/editorial-nber-macroeconomics-annual-2020-volume-35.

Abstracts

1 Imperfect Macroeconomic Expectations: Evidence and Theory
George-Marios Angeletos, Zhen Huo, and Karthik A. Sastry

We document a new fact about survey expectations: in response to the main shocks driving the business cycle, expectations of unemployment and inflation underreact initially but overshoot later on. We show how previous, seemingly conflicting, evidence can be understood as different facets of this fact. We finally explain what the cumulated evidence means for macroeconomic theory. There is little support for theories emphasizing underextrapolation or two close cousins of it, cognitive discounting and level-K thinking. Instead, the evidence favors the combination of dispersed, noisy information and overextrapolation.

2 Diverging Trends in National and Local Concentration
Esteban Rossi-Hansberg, Pierre-Daniel Sarte, and Nicholas Trachter

Using US National Establishment Time Series data, we present evidence that the positive trend observed in national product market concentration between 1990 and 2014 becomes a negative trend when we focus on measures of local concentration. We document diverging trends for several geographic definitions of local markets. Standard Industrial Classification (SIC) 8 industries with diverging trends are pervasive across sectors. In these industries, top firms have contributed to the amplification of both trends. When a top firm opens a plant, local concentration declines and remains lower for at least 7 years. Our findings, therefore, reconcile the increasing national role of large firms with falling local concentration and a likely more competitive local environment.

3 What Do We Learn from Cross-Regional Empirical Estimates in Macroeconomics?
Adam Guren, Alisdair McKay, Emi Nakamura, and Jón Steinsson

Recent empirical work uses variation across cities or regions to identify the effects of economic shocks of interest to macroeconomists. The interpretation of such estimates is complicated by the fact that they reflect both partial equilibrium and local general equilibrium effects of the shocks. We propose an approach for recovering estimates of partial equilibrium effects from these cross-regional empirical estimates. The basic idea is to divide the cross-regional estimate by an estimate of the local fiscal multiplier, which measures the strength of local general equilibrium amplification. We apply this approach to recent estimates of housing wealth effects based on city-level variation and derive conditions under which the adjustment is exact. We then evaluate its accuracy in a richer general equilibrium model of consumption and housing. The paper also reconciles the positive cross-sectional correlation between house price growth and construction with the notion that cities with larger price volatility have lower housing supply elasticities using a model in which housing supply elasticities are more dispersed in the long run than in the short run.

4 Innovative Growth Accounting
Peter J. Klenow and Huiyu Li

Recent work highlights a falling entry rate of new firms and a rising market share of large firms in the United States. To understand how these changing firm demographics have affected growth, we decompose productivity growth into the firms doing the innovating. We trace how much each firm innovates by the rate at which it opens and closes plants, the market share of those plants, and how fast its surviving plants grow. Using data on all nonfarm businesses from 1982 to 2013, we find that new and young firms (ages 0–5 years) account for almost one-half of growth—three times their share of employment. Large established firms contribute only one-tenth of growth despite representing one-fourth of employment. Older firms do explain most of the speedup and slowdown during the middle of our sample. Finally, most growth takes the form of incumbents improving their own products, as opposed to creative destruction or new varieties.

5   The Glass Ceiling and the Paper Floor: Changing Gender Composition of Top Earners since the 1980s
Fatih Guvenen, Greg Kaplan, and Jae Song

We analyze changes in the gender structure at the top of the earnings distribution in the United States from the early 1980s to the early 2010s using a 10% representative sample of individual earnings histories from the US Social Security Administration. The panel nature of the data set allows us to investigate the dynamics of earnings at the top and to consider definitions of top earners based on long-run averages of earnings, ranging from 5 years to 30 years. We find that, despite making large inroads, women still constitute a small proportion of the top percentile groups—the glass ceiling, albeit a thinner one, remains. In the early 1980s, there were 29 men for every woman in the top 1% of the 5-year average earnings distribution. By the late 2000s, this ratio had fallen to 5. We measure the contribution of changes in labor force participation, changes in the persistence of top earnings, and changes in industry and age composition to the change in the gender composition of top earners. We find that the bulk of the rise is accounted for by the mending of the *paper floor*—the phenomenon whereby female top earners were much more likely than male top earners to drop out of the top percentiles. We also provide new evidence on the top of the earnings distribution for both genders: the changing industry composition of top earners, the relative transitory status of top earners, the emergence of top earnings gender gaps over the life cycle, and the life-cycle patterns and gender differences for lifetime top earners.

6   Sources of US Wealth Inequality: Past, Present, and Future
Joachim Hubmer, Per Krusell, and Anthony A. Smith Jr.

This paper employs a benchmark heterogeneous-agent macroeconomic model to examine a number of plausible drivers of the rise in wealth inequality in the United States over the last 40 years. We find that the significant drop in tax progressivity starting in the late 1970s is the most important driver of the increase in wealth inequality since then. The sharp observed increases in earnings inequality and the falling labor share over the recent decades fall far short of accounting for the data. The model can also account for the dynamics of wealth inequality over the period—in particular the observed U shape—and here the observed variations in asset returns are key. Returns on assets matter because portfolios of households differ systematically both across and within wealth groups, a feature in our model that also helps us to match, quantitatively, a key long-run feature of wealth and earnings distributions: the former is much more highly concentrated than the latter.

1

Imperfect Macroeconomic Expectations: Evidence and Theory

George-Marios Angeletos, *MIT,* United States of America, *and NBER,* United States of America

Zhen Huo, *Yale University,* United States of America

Karthik A. Sastry, *MIT,* United States of America

I. Introduction

The rational expectations hypothesis is a bedrock of modern macroeconomics. It is often combined with a strong, complementary hypothesis that all data about the state of the economy are common knowledge. But an explosion of recent theoretical and empirical work has questioned both premises. This has pushed the discipline back toward reckoning with the "wilderness" of alternative models for expectations formation and equilibrium (as Sargent 2001, paraphrasing Sims 1980, famously put it).

One strand of the literature emphasizes informational frictions, which are sometimes rich enough to blur the boundary between the rational and nonrational.[1] Moving strictly beyond the rational model, some authors emphasize biases to overextrapolate the past (Fuster, Laibson, and Mendel 2010; Gennaioli, Ma, and Shleifer 2015; Guo and Wachter 2019), whereas others advocate for two close cousins of underextrapolation, cognitive discounting and level-k thinking (Iovino and Sergeyev 2017; Farhi and Werning 2019; García-Schmidt and Woodford 2019; Gabaix 2020). Another strand emphasizes overconfidence in various information sources, or prioritization of those that seem "representative "(Bordalo, Gennaioli, and Shleifer 2017; Kohlhas and Broer 2019).

What does survey evidence on expectations tell us within the space of these alternative hypotheses? And what kind of evidence is most useful for building macroeconomic models and providing guidance about counterfactual scenarios?

In the hopes of answering these questions and helping identify "where we are in the wilderness," this paper uses a simple but flexible framework to accomplish the following goals: to draw a variety of recent theoretical and empirical contributions under a common umbrella; to guide a new, more informative, empirical strategy; and to select among competing theories of "imperfect expectations" in macroeconomics.

Our main empirical finding is initial underreaction of beliefs in response to shocks followed by delayed overreaction. Both unemployment and inflation expectations have an initially sluggish response to the shocks that drive most of the business-cycle variation in these variables. But over medium horizons, forecasts tend to overshoot the actual outcomes.

This pattern speaks in favor of models that combine two key mechanisms: dispersed, noisy information and overextrapolation. The former leaves room for theories emphasizing higher-order beliefs. The latter points in the opposite direction of cognitive discounting and level-k thinking, two concepts that, at least for our purposes, are close cousins of underextrapolation.

We also demonstrate why our empirical strategy is more informative, at least vis-à-vis the class of theories under consideration, than previous alternatives. And we explain how our findings help resolve the apparent inconsistency between three previous empirical findings, which indeed serve as our starting point.

Understanding prior, seemingly conflicting, evidence. Previous empirical studies of expectations have often relied on simple regressions or correlations between actual outcomes and their forecasts in surveys.[2] In Section III, we revisit three such previously documented facts, henceforth referred to as facts 1–3:

> F1. For both unemployment and inflation, aggregate forecast errors are positively related to lagged aggregate forecast revisions, as in Coibion and Gorodnichenko (2015), or CG hereafter. This pattern suggests that aggregate forecasts underreact to aggregate news.

> F2. The opposite pattern is often present at individual-level forecasts: as previously shown in Bordalo, Gennaioli, Ma, and Shleifer (2020), or BGMS hereafter, individual forecasts appear to overreact to their own revisions (in the case of inflation, although not in the case of unemployment).[3]

> F3. Finally, the following pattern, first noted in Kohlhas and Walther (2018), or KW hereafter, points toward overreaction even at the aggregate level: aggregate forecast errors are positively correlated with the actual levels of unemployment and inflation.

These facts elude a simple, unified explanation. Do beliefs in the data underreact to innovations, as predicted by theories emphasizing informational frictions, higher-order uncertainty, cognitive discounting, and level-k think-ing? Or do they overreact, suggesting an entirely different mechanism?

To provide a clearer picture, we turn to theory. In Section IV, we in-troduce the "PE version" of our framework. Like the related empirical literature, this abstracts from the equilibrium fixed point between expec-tations and outcomes. But it allows for two key mechanisms: dispersed noisy information and overextrapolation. A third mechanism, overcon-fidence, is also nested but turns out to be rather inessential.

The combination of dispersed information and overextrapolation makes a sharp prediction for the impulse response functions (IRFs) of the average forecasts and forecast errors to aggregate shocks. In the first few periods after a shock occurs, the informational friction guarantees that forecasts underreact. But as time passes and learning kicks in, this friction dies out and overextrapolation takes over, guaranteeing that forecasts eventually overreact. The most telling feature of the combina-tion of the two mechanisms is therefore a reversal of sign in the IRF of the average forecast errors.

The regressions underlying facts 1 and 3 can be described as different weighted averages of this IRF. The one in CG happens to put more weight on the early portion of this IRF, where errors are positively cor-related with past revisions due to dispersed information, whereas that in KW happens to put more weight on the later portion, where errors are negatively correlated with outcomes due to overextrapolation. This resolves the apparent conflict between the form of underreaction docu-mented in CG and the form of overreaction documented in KW, but per-haps most importantly underscores the difficulty in interpreting and us-ing this kind of evidence. A similar point applies to the BGMS evidence, or fact 2.

Focusing on IRFs. Under the lens of our analysis, a superior empirical strategy emerges: the IRFs of the average forecasts and the average fore-cast errors to aggregate shocks provide strictly more information than the aforementioned empirical strategies and are also more easily inter-pretable. This leads to our main empirical contribution, which appears in Section V and which is to show that the hypothesized pattern of "sign reversal" in the response of forecast errors holds true in the data. We summarize this below as fact 4:

> F4. Consider two shocks, one that accounts for most of the business-cycle variation in unemployment and other macroeconomic quantities and an-other that accounts for most of the business-cycle variation in inflation.[4]

Construct the IRFs of the average forecasts of unemployment and inflation to the corresponding shocks. In both cases, average forecasts are initially underreacting before overshooting later on, or predicting larger and longer-lasting effects of the shock than those that occur.

For the reasons already explained, fact 4 alone helps nail down the "right" combination of frictions under the lens of our framework: to match this fact, it is necessary and sufficient to combine overextrapolation with a sufficiently large informational friction. And because this combination implies facts 1–3, fact 4 subsumes them and serves as a "sufficient statistic" for the counterfactuals of interest (more on this below).

We provide additional evidence for each of the two mechanisms as follows. First, we show that the subjective persistence, as revealed by the term structure of subjective expectations, is larger than the objective persistence, as measured by the impulse response of the outcome. And second, we show that the forecast revisions of one agent help predict the forecast errors of other agents. The former fact speaks directly to overextrapolation, the latter to not only noisy but also dispersed, or private, information.

From partial equilibrium (PE) to general equilibrium (GE). In Section VI, we incorporate a GE feedback between expectations and outcomes. This part of our paper, which builds on the methods of Angeletos and Huo (2020), lets us accomplish four goals. First, we extend our lessons about the "right" model of beliefs to a broader GE context.[5] Second, we connect level-k thinking and cognitive discounting to the GE implications of underextrapolation and spell out the empirical content of these theories vis-à-vis expectations data. Third, we clarify how the causal effect of the belief distortions on macroeconomic outcomes depends on parameters that determine the relative strength of PE and GE effects, such as the marginal propensity to consume (MPC). Finally, we quantify these distortions in a three-equation New Keynesian model.

The bottom line. The combination of old and new evidence we marshal in this paper offers not only support for theories emphasizing informational frictions and higher-order uncertainty, but also guidance on what type of departure from full rationality seems most relevant in the business cycle context. In particular, we argue that overextrapolation is needed to not only reconcile the previous, seemingly conflicting evidence of CG, KW, and BGMS, but also account for the eventual overshooting in the response of the average forecasts we have documented here.

Conversely, we have ruled out theories that rely heavily on underextrapolation of the present to the future, whether in the simple PE form of underestimating the persistence of an exogenous fundamental or in the related GE forms of cognitive discounting and level-k thinking. These mechanisms are at odds both with the dynamic overshooting of the average forecasts documented here and with the overreaction of individual forecasts documented in Bordalo et al. (2020) and Kohlhas and Broer (2019).

The same is true for adaptive expectations insofar as the latter means systematic anchoring of current expectations to past outcomes. Adaptive expectations can generate a similar "stickiness" or sluggishness in the response of average forecasts to aggregate shocks as that generated by dispersed, noisy information. But only the latter helps account for why such stickiness is absent in the response of individual forecasts to individual news or why individual forecast errors are predictable by the past information of others. This echoes a broader lesson of our analysis, which is to highlight how the similarities or differences of the properties of the individual and average forecast errors help disentangle mechanisms.

Overextrapolation in finance and macro. Our main empirical finding echoes a literature in finance documenting a similar pattern—slow initial reaction and subsequent overreaction—in individual stock prices (De Bondt and Thaler 1985; Cutler, Poterba, and Summers 1991; Lakonishok, Shleifer, and Vishny 1994). Theoretical work such as Barberis, Shleifer, and Vishny (1998), Daniel, Hirshleifer, and Subrahmanyam (1998), and Hong and Stein (1999) provide parsimonious interpretations that combine tentative initial reactions with medium-run overreaction due to overextrapolation. More recently, Greenwood and Shleifer (2014) and Gennaioli, Ma, and Shleifer (2015) demonstrate patterns in survey expectations of stock returns and firm earnings that are also suggestive of overextrapolation.

We complement these works in three ways. First, we provide the first (to the best of our knowledge) evidence of overextrapolation in expectations of unemployment and inflation. Second, we propose and implement a new empirical strategy, in terms of the IRFs of forecast errors to identified aggregate shocks, and explain why this strategy is best suited to guide theory. And third, we show how to combine overextrapolation and dispersed, noisy information in a GE setting. Both our empirical strategy and our GE tools could find applications in finance in the future.

Other related literature. Our emphasis on the IRFs of forecast errors (fact 4) instead of unconditional moments (facts 1–3) is shared by Coibion and Gorodnichenko (2012). But there are two key differences. First, we focus on different kinds of shocks, which have more "power" in terms of explaining a larger share of the business-cycle volatility in outcomes and forecasts. And second, we use different econometric methods, which, unlike that used in that paper, allow the detection of the eventual over-shooting in forecasts.[6] Kucinskas and Peters (2019) also suggest that IRFs are a more informative way to understand the nature of expectation formation. They further show that the dynamics of forecast errors at the aggregate level differ from that at the individual level. But they do not contain the specific IRF evidence provided here (fact 4) and our reconciliation of seemingly conflicting findings in the literature (facts 1–3).

We distill the essence of a diverse set of theories of expectation formation and use survey evidence to evaluate their potential relevance for business cycles. But we do not address related laboratory evidence (e.g., Nagel 1995; Dean and Neligh 2017; Landier, Ma, and Thesmar 2019) and field experiments (Coibion, Gorodnichenko, and Kumar 2018; Coibion, Gorodnichenko, and Ropele 2019).

We leave out of the analysis a variety of other plausible theories, which help explain different types of data. These include wishful thinking (e.g., Brunnermeier and Parker 2005; Caplin and Leahy 2019), overweighting of personal experience (e.g., Malmendier and Nagel 2016; Das, Kuhnen, and Nagel 2020; D'Acunto et al. 2021), adaptive learning (e.g., Evans and Honkapohja 2001; Sargent 2001; Eusepi and Preston 2011), uncertainty shocks (e.g., Bloom 2009; Baker, Bloom, and Davis 2016), robustness and ambiguity (e.g., Hansen and Sargent 2012; Ilut and Schneider 2014; Bhandari, Borovička, and Ho 2019), non-Bayesian belief contagion (e.g., Carroll 2001; Burnside, Eichenbaum, and Rebelo 2016), and other plausible departures from the fully rational model (e.g., Adam and Woodford 2012; Woodford 2018; Gabaix 2019; Molavi 2019).

Another angle that we do not consider is disagreement in the sense of dogmatic heterogeneous priors and/or heterogeneous interpretation of public information. Models with these features have been profitably applied to explain professional forecast heterogeneity (Giacomini, Skreta, and Turen 2020), disagreement between policy makers and markets (Caballero and Simsek 2019; Sastry 2020), and disagreement among financial market participants (Geanakoplos 2010; Caballero and Simsek 2020). But it is an open question whether they can help explain the evidence considered in this paper.

II. Data and Measurement

We focus on two macroeconomic outcomes: unemployment and inflation. We now review the exact data sources we use for forecasts and realized outcomes of these variables.

Forecasts from the Survey of Professional Forecasters. Our main data set for forecasts is the Survey of Professional Forecasters (SPF), a panel survey of about 40 experts from industry, government, and academia, currently administered by the Federal Reserve Bank of Philadelphia. Every quarter, each survey respondent is asked for point-estimate projections of the civilian unemployment rate and the gross domestic product (GDP) deflator, among several macro aggregates. Our main sample runs from Q4 1968 to Q4 2017.

Whenever our analysis requires aggregate (or "consensus") forecasts, we use the median forecast of the object of interest (e.g., unemployment or inflation at a given horizon). Using the median instead of the mean is standard in the related empirical literature. The rationale is that it alleviates concerns about outliers and/or data entry errors, which could be quite influential in the 40-forecaster cross section, driving the results. That said, our main empirical finding is robust to using the mean instead of the median.

For the individual-level results, where concerns about outliers are even more relevant, we always trim observations in forecast errors and revisions that are plus or minus four times the interquartile range from the median, where both reference values are calculated over the entire sample.[7]

Other survey sources. Although our main analysis focuses on the SPF, we provide corroborating evidence from two additional survey data sets. The first is the Blue Chip Economic Indicators Survey, a privately operated professional forecast with a similar scale and scope to the SPF. We use Blue Chip data from 1980 to 2017 and focus on the reported "consensus forecast" for unemployment and GDP deflator.[8] The second source is the University of Michigan Survey of Consumers, which is (for our purposes) a repeated cross section of about 500 members of the "general public" contacted by phone. Like with the Blue Chip survey, we focus on end-of-quarter waves. We take the Michigan survey inflation forecast as the median response to the question about price increases.[9] We also code a forecast for the growth rate of unemployment based on a question about whether unemployment will increase or decrease over the coming 12 months.[10] For this measure we take the cross-sectional mean, which corresponds to a "consensus forecast" about the sign of the growth rate of unemployment.

Macro data (and vintages thereof). Our unemployment measure u_t is the average US Bureau of Labor Statistics (BLS) unemployment rate in a given quarter t. Our inflation measure π_t is the annualized percentage increase in GDP or GNP deflator over the 4 quarters up to t.[11] For the corresponding forecast data, our "default" choice of horizon is $k = 3$, in line with the main specification of CG, but we explore other choices for robustness.

In our replication of CG, BGMS, and KW in Section III, we use first-vintage macro data for consistency with these works.[12] However, such measurement is not necessarily the right one vis-à-vis theory. If agents are forecasting the actual levels of unemployment and inflation, the econometrician should use the final-release data. We will thus verify the robustness of the relevant facts to the use of final-release data.

We finally use final-release data in our study of IRFs in Section V both for the above reason and for consistency with the main macro time-series literature. But once again, we consider the opposite measurement (in this case, first-vintage data in place of final-release data) for robustness.

Shocks. Our study of IRFs requires the use of identified shocks. For our main exercises, we borrow two such shocks from Angeletos et al. (2020): Their "main business cycle shock," which accounts for the bulk of the business-cycle comovements in unemployment, hours worked, output, consumption, investment; and a nearly orthogonal shock that accounts for most of the fluctuations in inflation. A description of these shocks and the rationale for using them are provided in Section V. For robustness, we also consider other, more "standard," shocks, such as a technology shock identified as in Galí (1999).

III.   A Puzzling Empirical Backdrop: Underreaction or Overreaction?

This section reviews three stylized facts about macroeconomic forecasts. One of them suggests that expectations underreact to news. The other two point in the opposite direction. The apparent contradiction paves the way for the theoretical exercise and the empirical strategy we undertake in the subsequent sections: We will eventually argue that there is a "better" way to think about the issue both in the theory and in the data.

A.   Fact 1: Under-reaction in Average Forecasts

Coibion and Gorodnichenko (2015), henceforth CG, test for a departure from full-information rational expectations by estimating the predictability of professionals' aggregate ("consensus") forecast errors using information in previous forecast revisions.

Let $\overline{\mathbb{E}}_t[x_{t+3}]$ denote the median expectation of variable x_{t+3} (either unemployment or inflation) measured at time t. Let $\overline{\mathbb{E}}_{t-1}[x_{t+3}]$ be the median forecast at time $t-1$.[13] The associated forecast error from time t is $\text{Error}_t \equiv x_{t+3} - \overline{\mathbb{E}}_t[x_{t+3}]$, suppressing notation for the variable x and the forecast horizon, and the forecast revision is $\text{Revision}_t \equiv \overline{\mathbb{E}}_t[x_{t+3}] - \overline{\mathbb{E}}_{t-1}[x_{t+3}]$. CG run the following regression that projects aggregate forecast errors onto aggregate forecast revisions:

$$\text{Error}_t = \alpha + K_{CG} \cdot \text{Revision}_t + u_t, \tag{1}$$

where K_{CG}, in shorthand notation that references the authors, is the main object of interest.

Table 1 reports results from estimating regression (eq. [1]) at the horizon $k = 3$ for both unemployment and inflation in our data. We report results over the full sample 1968–2017 (columns 1 and 3) and also over a restricted sample after 1984 (columns 2 and 4). We may believe a priori that the latter is a more consistent and "stationary" regime for the US macroeconomy (i.e., after the oil crisis and Volcker disinflation).

Like the original authors, we find in all specifications a point estimate of $K_{CG} > 0$: when professional forecasters, in aggregate, revise upward their estimation of unemployment or inflation, they on average always "undershoot" the eventual truth. For inflation, we find the predictability is considerably lower on the restricted sample, which underscores the large influence of the aforementioned key events for US inflation expectations. Table A1 shows robustness along a number of dimensions including (i) using different forecast horizons, (ii) putting final release data in

Table 1
Predicting Aggregate Forecast Errors with Revisions, from Regression (eq. [1])

	Unemployment		Inflation	
	(1)	(2)	(3)	(4)
	1968–2017	1984–2017	1968–2017	1984–2017
Revision$_t$ (K_{CG})	.741	.809	1.528	.292
	(.232)	(.305)	(.418)	(.191)
R^2	.111	.159	.278	.016
N	191	136	190	135

Note: The data set is the Survey of Professional Forecasters and the observation is a quarter between Q4 1968 and Q4 2017. All regressions include a constant. The forecast horizon is 3 quarters. Standard errors are heteroskedasticity and autocorrelation robust, with a Bartlett kernel and lag length equal to 4 quarters. The data used for outcomes are first release ("vintage").

place of the vintage data, and (iii) using forecasts from the Blue Chip Economic Indicators Survey. All findings, including the differences across older and newer samples, are very similar to those reported in table 1.

The finding of $K_{CG} > 0$ rejects full-information rational expectations: because Revision$_{t,k}$ is necessarily known to the representative agent at time t, it should not systematically predict that agent's forecast error at $t + 1$ if that agent is rational.[14] But note that it provides ambiguous evidence on the separate hypotheses of informational frictions versus nonrationality. In particular, the fact is just as consistent with a population of rational but heterogeneously informed agents (as indeed Coibion and Gorodnichenko 2015 propose in their paper) as it is with a representative irrational agent who systematically underreacts to news because of a behavioral bias (as indeed Gabaix 2020 proposes in his own paper). Similarly, an "old-fashioned" model of adaptive expectations can also generate the fact. It is only by combining this fact with the additional fact reported next that we can start disentangling the role of informational frictions and misspecified beliefs.

B.   Fact 2: Overreaction in Individual Forecasts

To probe further the need for irrationality to explain the data, recent papers by Bordalo et al. (2020), Fuhrer (2018), and Kohlhas and Broer (2019) have studied forecast error patterns at the individual level in the professional forecasts. Let Error$_{i,t} \equiv x_{t+3} - \mathbb{E}_{i,t}[x_{t+3}]$ and Revision$_{i,t,} \equiv \mathbb{E}_{i,t}[x_{t+3}] - \mathbb{E}_{i,t-1}[x_{t+3}]$ denote forecast errors and revisions for a particular forecaster, indexed by i, at the baseline horizon $k = 3$. Each of the aforementioned studies estimates the following regression that translates regression (eq. [1]) to the individual level:

$$\text{Error}_{i,t} = \alpha + K_{BGMS} \cdot \text{Revision}_{i,t} + u_{i,t}, \qquad (2)$$

where the object of interest K_{BGMS}, named in shorthand reference to the authors of Bordalo et al. (2020), is the individual-level analogue to K_{CG}. Regardless of the information structure, individual-level rationality imposes $K_{BGMS} = 0$.

In columns 1 and 3 of table 2, we provide estimates of the individual-level regression (eq. [2]) in the SPF over the full sample for our two variables of interest, unemployment and inflation. Columns 2 and 4 of the same table conduct the analysis on the subsample from 1984 to the present. Results for different horizons and data choices (vintage versus final) are similar and reported in table A2.

Table 2
Predicting Individual Forecast Errors with Revisions, from Regression (eq. [2])

	Unemployment		Inflation	
	(1)	(2)	(3)	(4)
	1968–2017	1984–2017	1968–2017	1984–2017
Revision$_{i,t}$ (K_{BGMS})	.321	.398	.143	−.263
	(.107)	(.149)	(.123)	(.054)
R^2	.028	.052	.005	.025
N	5,383	3,769	5,147	3,643

Note: The observation is a forecaster by quarter between Q4 1968 and Q4 2017. The forecast horizon is 3 quarters. Standard errors are clustered two-way by forecaster ID and time period. Both errors and revisions are winsorized over the sample to restrict to 4 times the interquartile range away from the median. The data used for outcomes are first release ("vintage").

For unemployment, we find substantial evidence that $K_{BGMS} > 0$ over the full and restricted sample period. And for inflation, we find imprecise evidence that $K_{BGMS} > 0$ over the full sample, which includes the 1970s and Volcker disinflation, but strong evidence of $K_{BGMS} < 0$ in the "more stationary" environment post-1984.

BGMS argue that a negative relation between revisions and subsequent errors, or $K_{BGMS} < 0$, is a robust feature of the forecasts of various macroeconomic variables. A closer look at their findings yields a more nuanced picture. But if we take for granted their thesis, we have that macroeconomic forecasts appear to overreact at the individual level at the same that they appear to underreact at the aggregate level.

We reinforce this apparent contradiction below. But we also invite the reader to keep the following basic insight in mind: whereas the CG evidence confounds the effects of informational frictions and nonrationality, the BGMS evidence speaks exclusively to the latter. We will leverage on this insight later to argue that the gap between the CG and the BGMS evidence speaks to the role of informational frictions.

C.   Fact 3: Overreaction in Aggregate Forecasts

Facts 1 and 2 by themselves may suggest that going to the individual-level data is necessary, if not sufficient, to see evidence of overreaction. But a recent paper by Kohlhas and Walther (2018) calls into question this view by presenting an additional moment: the slope of forecast errors in current realizations of the variable, as measured in the following regression:

$$\text{Error}_t = \alpha + K_{\text{KW}} \cdot x_t + u_t. \tag{3}$$

In our implementation, Error_t is the error in 3-quarter-ahead forecast of unemployment or annual inflation, and x_t is the current (forecasting) period's realization of one or the other.

Clearly, $K_{\text{KW}} \neq 0$ is inconsistent with full-information rational expectations. It is also hard to square with the CG evidence. More heuristically, in a world of "sluggish" expectations, we may expect $K_{\text{KW}} > 0$, or a positive correlation between today's realization and the direction of the forecast error k periods out.

Table 3 reports results from estimating regression (eq. [3]). For unemployment we find weak evidence supporting the hypothesis that $K_{\text{KW}} < 0$. The results for inflation depend once again on whether we want to consider data from the 1970s and early 1980s. In the whole sample, the evidence is more supportive of $K_{\text{KW}} > 0$. But in the more recent sample period, for inflation too we find weak evidence of $K_{\text{KW}} < 0$. Table A3 probes robustness to different data choices and subsamples and uncovers broadly consistent results. KW provide evidence of $K_{\text{KW}} < 0$ for forecasts of other variables, such as GDP growth.[15]

All in all, there is a good case for $K_{\text{KW}} < 0$ in the data. This is consistent with a world of overreactive expectations: as an example, if agents are forecasting unemployment to be too high in recessions (high x_t, negative forecast error) and too low in booms (low x_t, positive forecast error), then

Table 3
Predicting Aggregate Forecast Errors with Recent Outcomes, from Regression (eq. [3])

	Unemployment		Inflation	
	(1)	(2)	(3)	(4)
	1968–2017	1984–2017	1968–2017	1984–2017
x_t (K_{KW})	−.061	−.036	.111	−.068
	(.056)	(.038)	(.075)	(.068)
R^2	.016	.007	.058	.012
N	194	136	193	135

Note: The data set is the Survey of Professional Forecasters and the observation is a quarter between Q4 1968 and Q4 2017. All regressions include a constant. The forecast horizon is 3 quarters. Standard errors are heteroskedasticity and autocorrelation robust, with a Bartlett kernel and lag length equal to 4 quarters. The data used for outcomes are first release ("vintage").

we may naturally get $K_{KW} < 0$. But in such a world we would also expect $K_{CG} < 0$, which is not what we found earlier. This reinforces the puzzle: the picture for over- or underreaction is unclear even if we focus on the properties of aggregate forecasts.

IV. A Simple Model

In this section we introduce a simplified version of our framework, which combines dispersed noisy information with misspecified beliefs but abstracts from the fixed point between expectations and outcomes. We use this to reconcile facts 1–3, but also, and more importantly, to pave the way to our preferred empirical strategy, which we in turn implement in the next section.

A. Primitives

Let $\{x_t\}$ be a stochastic process that a group of agents, indexed by $i \in [0, 1]$, are trying to forecast (e.g., unemployment or inflation). Ideally we want to think of x_t as endogenous to the agents' behavior. But for now, to put the focus only on the expectations formation process, we assume that x_t follows an exogenous AR(1) process with Gaussian errors. That is,

$$x = \frac{1}{1 - \rho \mathbb{L}} \varepsilon_t, \tag{4}$$

where $\rho \in (0, 1)$ parameterizes the persistence of the process, $\varepsilon_t \sim N(0, 1)$ is a Gaussian innovation, and $\mathbb{L}$ denotes the lag operator (i.e., $\mathbb{L}x_t = x_{t-1}$).

An agent's observation of x_t is contaminated with idiosyncratic noise. That is, each agent in period t observes a signal $s_{i,t}$ given by

$$s_{i,t} = x_t + \frac{u_{i,t}}{\sqrt{\tau}}, \tag{5}$$

where τ measures precision and $u_{i,t} \sim_{iid} N(0, 1)$ is idiosyncratic Gaussian noise. As in a large literature, we can think of this noise either literally, as the product of dispersed noisy information (Lucas 1972; Morris and Shin 2002), or metaphorically, as a representation of rational inattention and imperfect perception (Mankiw and Reis 2002; Sims 2003, 2010; Woodford 2003).

We depart from this literature by adding two forms of irrationality, or belief misspecification. First, whereas the true process of the private signal is given by equation (5), agents perceive this process to be

$$s_{i,t} = x_t + \frac{u_{i,t}}{\sqrt{\hat{\tau}}} \tag{6}$$

for some perceived precision $\hat{\tau} > 0$ that may differ from τ. And second, whereas the true process from x_t is given by equation (4), agents perceive this process to be

$$x_t = \frac{1}{1 - \hat{\rho}\mathbb{L}} \varepsilon_t \tag{7}$$

for some perceived persistence $\hat{\rho}$ which may differ from ρ.

The case $\hat{\tau} > \tau$ captures overconfidence: Each agent thinks their information is better than it truly is. The opposite case, $\hat{\tau} < \tau$, captures underconfidence. Moore and Healy (2008) provide a representative review of the experimental psychological evidence for such biases. Their broad conclusion is that overconfidence is consistently prevalent for reported beliefs in the laboratory, but that the extent of effects can be context-specific. Kohlhas and Broer (2019) and Bordalo et al. (2020) use, respectively, $\hat{\tau} > \tau$ and a close variant of it to reconcile facts 1 and 2.[16] We will nest this possibility in the subsequent analysis but also show that $\hat{\rho} > \rho$ serves the same goal while also matching fact 3. And we will provide additional evidence in favor of $\hat{\rho} > \rho$ in the form of our (not yet introduced) fact 4 about dynamic overshooting.

The case $\hat{\rho} > \rho$ encodes an overextrapolation of today's state to tomorrow, whereas $\hat{\rho} < \rho$ encodes underextrapolation. Both narratives are appealing in different economic contexts. On the one hand, Greenwood and Shleifer (2014) and Gennaioli et al. (2015) argue that overextrapolation is evident both in stock market expectations and in expectations of firms' sales forecasts; see also Guo and Wachter (2019) for how a simple model with overextrapolation over dividend growth can explain a variety of asset-price phenomena. On the other hand, level-k thinking (Farhi and Werning 2019; García-Schmidt and Woodford 2019) and cognitive discounting (Gabaix 2020) are "close in spirit" to the opposite scenario, $\hat{\rho} < \rho$, because they cause agents to underestimate the (endogenous or exogenous) response of future outcomes to current innovations. We will make this connection formal in Subsection VI.D, once we extend the analysis to a GE context and properly nest these models.

As anticipated in the introduction and as will become clear in the sequel, only the second type of misspecification ($\hat{\rho} \neq \rho$) is strictly needed for our main purposes. The first type ($\hat{\tau} \neq \tau$) is nevertheless useful for two complementary reasons: It enlarges the set of theories nested in, or proxied by, our framework; and it helps clarify which evidence is most directly relevant in the GE context of Section VI.

B. Facts 1, 2, and 3 in the Model

The structure introduced above yields a highly tractable, finite auto-regressive moving average (ARMA) representation of the individual and average forecasts, which can be found in lemma 1. This in turns allows a simple, closed-form characterization of the theoretical counterparts of the regressions reviewed in Section III.

Proposition 1 (Regression coefficients in the theory). The theoretical counter-parts of the coefficients of regressions (eqs. [1–3]) are given by the following:

$$K_{CG} = K_{CG}(\hat{\tau}, \rho, \hat{\rho}) \equiv \kappa_1 \hat{\tau}^{-1} - \kappa_2(\hat{\rho} - \rho) \tag{8}$$

$$K_{KW} = K_{KW}(\hat{\tau}, \rho, \hat{\rho}) \equiv \kappa_3 \hat{\tau}^{-1} - \kappa_4(\hat{\rho} - \rho) \tag{9}$$

$$K_{BGMS} = K_{BGMS}(\tau, \hat{\tau}, \rho, \hat{\rho}) \equiv -\kappa_5(\hat{\tau} - \tau) - \kappa_6(\hat{\rho} - \rho) \tag{10}$$

for some scalars $\kappa_1, ..., \kappa_6$ that depend on the deeper parameters but are necessarily positive. In particular, $\kappa_1, \kappa_2, \kappa_3,$ and κ_4 are functions only of $(\hat{\tau}, \rho, \hat{\rho})$, whereas κ_5 and κ_6 depend also on τ.

Let us unpack these expressions. First of all, note that the actual pre-cision, τ, enters only the BGMS coefficient. That is, the moments of the average forecasts do not depend on the true level of noise, conditional on the perceived noise. The latter dictates how each agent's forecasts responds to her information, and hence also how the average forecasts respond to the underlying shocks. The actual idiosyncratic noise, instead, washes out at the aggregate level.

Consider next condition (eq. [8]), which characterizes the CG coeffi-cient. With rational expectations, which herein means $\hat{\tau} = \tau$ and $\rho = \hat{\rho}$, K_{CG} is merely a monotone transformation of the level of noise. In particular,

$$K_{CG} = \frac{1 - g}{g}, \tag{11}$$

where $g \in (0, 1)$ is the Kalman gain.[17] This is the structural interpretation given in CG.

Our result qualifies this structural interpretation in two ways. First, if we maintain $\rho = \hat{\rho}$ but allow $\hat{\tau} \neq \tau$, we get an analogue of equation (11) with a subjective Kalman gain $\hat{g}$ in place of its objective counterpart. That is, even in the absence of overextrapolation, the CG coefficient tells us something about the subjective level of noise, which does not have to co-incide with the objective level. Second, if we allow $\hat{\rho} \neq \rho$, we now have that K_{CG} confounds two mechanisms: a high value for K_{CG} could be evidence of either large informational friction or large underextrapolation, or a low value for K_{CG} could hide a large information friction if there is also large overextrapolation. Indeed, K_{CG} could even be negative.

Consider next condition (eq. [9]), which characterizes the KW coefficient. The informational friction and the overextrapolation enter this coefficient in a qualitatively similar way as they enter the CG coefficient. The former contributes toward $K_{KW} > 0$, the latter toward $K_{KW} < 0$. The logic is exactly the same as that for the CG coefficient. What is subtle is the possibility that the two forces balance out in such a way that the one coefficient is negative at the same time that the other is positive, a point we revisit below.

Finally, consider condition (10), which characterizes the BGMS coefficient. When $\hat{\tau} = \tau$ and $\rho = \hat{\rho}$, $K_{BGMS} = 0$. This is an example of the more general property that, under rational expectations, an individual's forecast error is unpredictable by his own past information. Away from this benchmark, both overconfidence ($\hat{\tau} > \tau$) and overextrapolation ($\hat{\rho} > \rho$) contribute toward $K_{BGMS} < 0$. In the presence of overextrapolation, agents overestimate the effect of any given innovation today on future outcomes. In the presence of overconfidence, they get this effect right but overestimate the precision of the signal they receive about the innovation. In both cases, they make a systematic mistake in the direction of overestimating the informational content of their current signal about the future outcome, and this mistake manifests as $K_{BGMS} < 0$. The converse is true for underconfidence or underextrapolation.

C. The Right Combination of Belief Distortions

Let us summarize the lesson for two versions of our model that are familiar from the literature but fail to match facts 1–3:

Corollary 1. The following two cases are inconsistent with facts 1–3:

    (i) Noisy but rational expectations: $\hat{\tau} = \tau < \infty$ and $\hat{\rho} = \rho$ implies $K_{CG} > 0$, $K_{KW} > 0$, and $K_{BGMS} = 0$.

    (ii) Noiseless but extrapolative expectations: $\tau = \hat{\tau} \to \infty$ and $\hat{\rho} \neq \rho$ implies $\text{sign}(K_{CG}) = \text{sign}(K_{KW}) = \text{sign}(K_{BGMS}) = \text{sign}(\rho - \hat{\rho})$.

The first case stylizes a large literature on informational frictions, and it is precisely the case considered in Coibion and Gorodnichenko (2015). This case counterfactually forces K_{CG} and K_{KW} to be the same sign, a restriction first pointed out in Kohlhas and Walther (2018), because there is only a single "dampening" force coming from noisy expectations. Moreover, this case cannot accommodate $K_{BGMS} \neq 0$ because forecasters remain individually rational.

The second model is an entirely "behavioral" one that admits a mis-calibrated representative agent, as in Gabaix (2016, 2020). But switching from an underextrapolative model ($\hat{\rho} < \rho$) to an overextrapolative model ($\hat{\rho} > \rho$) must necessarily flip all three signs for the aforementioned moments. Thus it too cannot match the patterns observed so far.

Let us now turn to the scenario that best accounts for the evidence.

Corollary 2 (Matching Facts 1–3). The combination of informational friction and overextrapolation is necessary and sufficient for all three facts in the following sense:

(i) $K_{CG} > 0$ and $K_{KW} < 0$ only if $0 < \hat{\tau} < \infty$ and $\hat{\rho} > \rho > 0$,
(ii) There exists an open set of parameter values, with $0 < \tau \le \hat{\tau} < \infty$ and $\hat{\rho} > \rho > 0$, such that $K_{CG} > 0$, $K_{KW} < 0$, and $K_{BGMS} < 0$.

Figure 1 illustrates this by plotting the model's "sign predictions" for the three coefficients in the $(\hat{\tau}, \hat{\rho})$ space. For this picture, we set $\rho = 0.90$, which is illustrative but immaterial to the overall pattern. We also restrict $\tau = \hat{\tau}$, that is, we assume away both over- and underconfidence. The

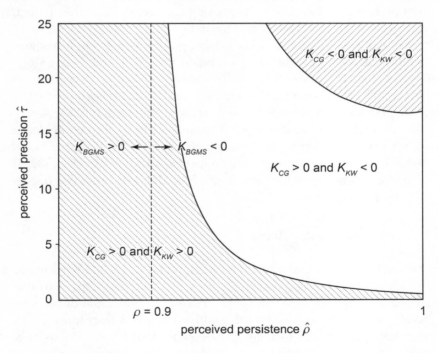

Fig. 1. The regression coefficients K_{CG}, K_{KW}, and K_{BGMS} in the theory. A color version of this figure is available online.

center region identifies the combinations of $\hat{\tau}$ and $\hat{\rho}$ that match all three facts qualitatively.

What happens if we let $\tau \neq \hat{\tau}$? The left, center, and right regions remain intact, and so does the mapping from the specific values of K_{CG} and K_{KW} to the corresponding values of $\hat{\tau}$ and $\hat{\rho}$. This is because the stochastic properties of the average forecasts depend merely on the perceived level of noise and the degree of overextrapolation, not on the actual level. What changes as we vary τ, or equivalently the degree of overconfidence, is only the position of the vertical line, and along with it the specific value of this "free" parameter needed to match a specific value for K_{BGMS}.

This suggests a simple, recursive, identification strategy: first, calibrate ρ to actual process of unemployment or inflation; next, identify $\hat{\tau}$ and $\hat{\rho}$ jointly from K_{CG} and K_{KW}; finally, identify τ from K_{BGMS}. Table A4 implements this strategy and reports the specific values of the model parameters that quantitatively match the evidence reported before. But both this identification strategy and corollary 2 suffer from the same basic problem: It is unclear how the theory produces at once underreaction in the sense of $K_{CG} > 0$ and overreaction in the sense of $K_{KW} < 0$. We cut the Gordian knot in the next subsection by proposing a different, more transparent, way of connecting the theory and the data.

We end this subsection with a bibliographical note. Kohlhas and Walther (2018) offer a different resolution to facts 1 and 3 (i.e., $K_{CG} > 0 > K_{KW}$) than that presented here. This alternative preserves rational expectations by allowing for asymmetric attention to procyclical and countercyclical components of the forecasted outcome. But it imposes $K_{BGMS} = 0$, failing to match fact 2, and it does not square with fact 4, the new evidence we provide in Section V. Kohlhas and Broer (2019), on the other hand, match fact 2 by introducing overconfidence, and Bordalo et al. (2020) achieve the same with a formally similar bias. But neither of these papers addresses facts 3 and 4.

D.   *A More Informative Approach: IRFs*

Our intuition about the various forces behind facts 1–3, and particularly the tension between K_{CG} and K_{KW}, had a dynamic flavor that was collapsed to essentially static moments. Indeed our derivation of proposition 1 quite literally involved starting with a moving-average form of each stochastic process and then computing static correlations. Let us now explore more directly what we would learn from observing directly the dynamic response of forecast errors in response to shocks.

Proposition 2 (IRF of Forecast Errors). Let $\{\varsigma_k\}_{k=1}^{\infty}$ be the IRF of the average, one-step-ahead, forecast error. That is, for all $k \geq 1$,

$$\varsigma_k \equiv \frac{\partial(x_{t+k} - \overline{\mathbb{E}}_{t+k-1}[x_{t+k}])}{\partial \varepsilon_t}$$

is the kth coefficient in the moving-average representation of the average forecast error.[18]

(i)   If $\hat{\rho} < \rho$, or agents underextrapolate, then $\varsigma_k > 0$ for all $k \geq 1$.

(ii) If $\hat{\rho} > \rho$ and $\hat{\tau}$ is small enough relative to $\hat{\rho} - \rho$, or agents overextrapolate and learning is slow enough, then $\varsigma_k > 0$ for $1 \leq k < k_{\mathrm{IRF}}$ and $\varsigma_k < 0$ for $k > k_{\mathrm{IRF}}$, for some $k_{\mathrm{IRF}} \in (1, \infty)$.

(iii) Finally, if $\hat{\rho} > \rho$ but $\hat{\tau}$ is large enough relative to $\hat{\rho} - \rho$, or agents overextrapolate but learning is fast, then $\varsigma_k < 0$ for all $k \geq 1$.

Corollary 3 (Delayed Overshooting). The IRF of the average forecast errors starts positive but eventually switches negative if and only if there is both overextrapolation and sufficiently large informational friction.

A sign switch in the impulse response of forecast errors to a macro shock is "smoking-gun" evidence for a combination of noise and overextrapolation. A complementary lesson is that the point at which the sign switch occurs provides a gauge of the relative importance of the two mechanisms: the slower the learning relative to overextrapolation, the longer it takes for the sign switch to occur.

This is, in our view, easier to interpret than the previous strategy of comparing K_{CG} with K_{KW} because it gets to the heart of the economic question: at what point are economic agents sufficiently informed about an economic event (i.e., particular shock) such that their model misspecification becomes the dominant explanation for any errors?

Figure 2 illustrates these patterns by plotting the IRFs of outcomes and forecasts (left column) and forecast errors and revisions (right column) in two scenarios: a benchmark without overextrapolation (top row) and a variant with overextrapolation (bottom row). The key observation is that only with the combination of slow learning and overextrapolation can the theory generate a sign reversal for the aggregate forecast errors, or average forecasts that undershoot initially and overshoot later on.

Now, to drive home the connection to K_{CG} and K_{KW}, consider the moving average (MA) representations of the forecast errors, the forecast revisions, and the actual outcome:

$$\mathrm{Error}_{t,t+1} = \sum_{k=0}^{\infty} \varsigma_k \varepsilon_{t+1-k} \qquad \mathrm{Revision}_t = \sum_{k=0}^{\infty} f_k \varepsilon_{t-k} \qquad \mathrm{Outcome}_t = \sum_{k=0}^{\infty} \rho^k \varepsilon_{t-k}.$$

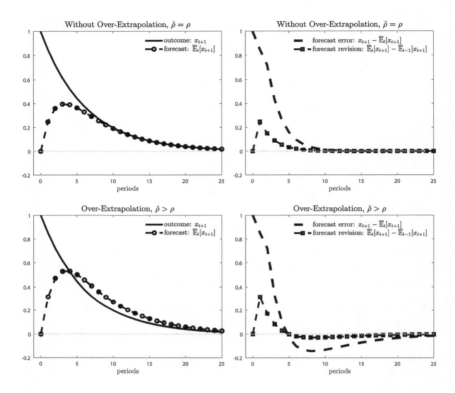

Fig. 2. Impulse response functions of aggregate forecasts and errors in the theory. A color version of this figure is available online.

where $\{\zeta_k\}$ and $\{f_k\}$ are the IRFs of, respectively, the average forecast errors and the average forecast revisions. Using these representations, the coefficient of regression (eq. [1]) can be expressed as

$$K_{\mathrm{CG}} = \frac{\mathrm{Cov}(\mathrm{Error}_{t,t+1}, \mathrm{Revision}_t)}{\mathrm{Var}(\mathrm{Revision}_t)} = \frac{\sum_{k=0}^{\infty} \zeta_{k+1} \cdot f_k}{\sum_{k=0}^{\infty} f_k^2}, \qquad (12)$$

and similarly the coefficient of regression (eq. [3]) can be expressed as

$$K_{\mathrm{KW}} = \frac{\mathrm{Cov}(\mathrm{Error}_{t,t+1}, \mathrm{Outcome}_t)}{\mathrm{Var}(\mathrm{Outcome}_t)} = \frac{\sum_{k=0}^{\infty} \zeta_{k+1} \cdot \rho^k}{\sum_{k=0}^{\infty} \rho^{2k}}. \qquad (13)$$

This makes clear that K_{CG} and K_{KW} are, up to rescaling, equal to the dot products of the IRF of the forecast errors with the IRF of, respectively, the revisions and the outcome.

What does this look like? Consider the bottom row of figure 2, which corresponds to the combination of noise and overextrapolation. The dynamic response of the forecast errors, or the solid IRF in the bottom-right subfigure, exhibits the reversal property we noted earlier: forecast errors switch from positive to negative after a while. A similar reversal is also present in the forecast revisions; see the dashed line in the same subfigure. It follows that the dot product of these two IRFs contains more positive terms than the dot product of either one of them with that of the outcome, which is given by the solid line in the bottom-left subfigure. This helps explain why $K_{CG} > 0$ at the same time that $K_{KW} < 0$.

Apart from resolving the "mystery" behind the different signs of K_{CG} and K_{KW}, this exercise also underscores that the IRFs of the forecast errors contain strictly more information about the dynamic properties of beliefs than any of the these regression coefficients. Either one of these coefficients offers a confusing picture by averaging under- and overreaction across different horizons. The IRFs let one see when exactly beliefs undershoot and when exactly they overshoot.[19]

V.   A New Fact: Delayed Overshooting

We now go after what the theory has identified as the most useful moment to characterize imperfect expectations: the dynamic response of forecasts and forecast errors to shocks. Here we corroborate the hypothesis derived above and uncover a consistent pattern of initial underreaction and delayed overshooting in the response of forecast errors to shocks. This, at least in the context of the last section's analysis, is "smoking-gun" evidence of a combination of noisy information and overextrapolation.

A.   Methodology

We start with the details of the empirical implementation.

Identified shocks. As anticipated in Section II, we consider two empirical shocks, both borrowed from Angeletos et al. (2020).[20]

The first shock, which these authors call "main business cycle shock," is constructed by maximizing its contribution to the business-cycle variation in unemployment and is found to have the following properties: it encapsulates strong positive comovement in employment, output, investment, and consumption only over the business cycle; it is nearly indistinguishable, in terms of IRFs and variance contributions, to the shocks identified by targeting any of the aforementioned variables; it has a negligible footprint on total factor productivity (TFP) at all horizons; and it has a small to modest footprint on inflation. It can thus be interpreted as a non- or mildly inflationary demand shock, which drives the bulk of the business cycle in the data.[21]

The second shock is identified by maximizing its contribution to the business-cycle variation in inflation, and it is found to have a negative but very small footprint on real quantities and zero footprint on TFP. It is thus akin to the kind of markup or cost-push shocks the dynamic stochastic general equilibrium (DSGE) literature uses to account for the bulk of the inflation fluctuations in the data.[22]

We denote the two shocks, respectively, as $(\varepsilon_t^D, \varepsilon_t^S)$ for "demand" and "supply." Whether these shocks, or any other SVAR-based (structural vector autoregression) shocks, are "truly" structural is largely a philosophical question and certainly beyond the scope of the present paper. For our purposes, the appeal of the particular shocks compared with others found in the literature (e.g., Gali 1999; Sims and Zha 2006) is that they drive a significant component of the business-cycle variation in macroeconomic activity and inflation. There is thus a good chance that they also drive a significant component of the corresponding variation in real-world expectations.

Main specification: ARMA-IV. To estimate dynamic responses to the aforementioned shocks, we consider two different empirical strategies.

The first is to estimate the IRFs via a parsimonious, instrumental variables ARMA(P, K) representation. In particular, we estimate the following regression:

$$z_t = \alpha + \sum_{p=1}^{P} \gamma_p \cdot z_{t-p}^{\text{IV}} + \sum_{k=0}^{K} \beta_k \cdot \varepsilon_{t-k} + u_t. \tag{14}$$

Depending on the variable whose dynamic response we want to look at, z_t is the actual outcome (unemployment or inflation), the relevant forecast, or the corresponding forecast error. In all cases, $\varepsilon_t \in \{\varepsilon_t^D, \varepsilon_t^S\}$ is one of the aforementioned two shocks drawn from Angeletos et al. (2020). Finally, for $p \in \{1, \dots, P\}$, z_{t-p}^{IV} are the lagged values of z_t instrumented by the lagged values of ε_t.[23] This instrumental variables (IV) approach recovers the conditional dynamic responses to the structural shock under consideration—intuitively, how z_t moves when driven by the shock process of interest. We will call this method the "ARMA-IV" estimation.

By estimating equation (14) for outcomes (e.g., z_t equal to that quarter's unemployment rate or the past 4 quarters' inflation rate), we can generate dynamic impulse response coefficients $(\beta_{\text{out},h})_{h=0}^{H}$ as functions of $(\beta_0, (\gamma_p)_{p=1}^{P})$. For forecasts, we can do the same thing with z_t equal to the forecast in period t (e.g., $\overline{\mathbb{E}}_t[u_{t+3}]$ and $\overline{\mathbb{E}}_t[\pi_{t+3,t-1}]$): estimate the impulse response coefficients $(\tilde{\beta}_{\text{fc},h})_{h=0}^{H}$ and then "reindex" these coefficients to line up with the realized outcomes. More specifically, we generate $(\beta_{\text{fc},h})_{h=0}^{H}$ such that $\beta_{\text{fc},h} = 0$ for $h < 3$ (effectively imposing unpredictability of the shocks), and $\beta_{\text{fc},h} = \tilde{\beta}_{\text{fc},h-3}$ for $h \geq 3$. Finally, we can construct the IRF of the forecast errors either by taking the difference between the IRF of the outcome and the forecasts or by repeating the aforementioned procedure with x_t being the average forecast error.

In all cases, we construct standard errors for the coefficients that are heteroskedasticity and autocorrelation robust (HAC) with a 4-quarter Bartlett kernel, and we then use the delta method to calculate standard errors for the IRFs. All reported error bands are 68% confidence intervals $(\pm 1 \cdot \text{SE})$.

Local projection. Our main strategy strives for parsimony by requiring the IRFs to accept a low-dimension ARMA representation as in equation (14). But we can also estimate impulse responses directly using the projection method of Jordà (2005). In this case, the estimating equation, for each horizon $0 \leq h \leq H$, is the following:

$$z_{t+h} = \alpha_h + \beta_h \cdot \varepsilon_t + \gamma' W_t + u_{t+h}, \tag{15}$$

where $(\beta_h)_{h=0}^{H}$ traces out the dynamic response of the outcome, W_t is a vector of control variables, and γ are the coefficients on these controls. Consistently, across specifications, we include the lagged outcome x_{t-1} and the lagged forecast $\overline{\mathbb{E}}_{t-k-1}[x_{t-1}]$ as control variables. Conceptually, as long as these controls are orthogonal to the shock ε_t, these should not affect the population estimate we get of the impulse response parameters; but their inclusion may help with small-sample precision. We find overall that results are not sensitive to choices of controls. Standard errors are constructed in the same aforementioned way.

Finally, we set $k = 3$ quarters as the forecast horizon, in line with what we did in Section III, and we set $H = 20$ quarters as the maximum period for tracing out IRFs.

B.   The Fact: Dynamic Overshooting

Figure 3 shows, in a two-by-two grid, the main impulse response estimates.[24] In the first column, we show the dynamic response of unemployment and median forecasts thereof to the demand shock ε_t^D. The first

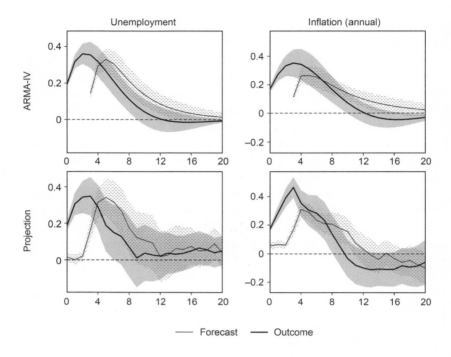

Fig. 3. Dynamic responses: outcomes and forecasts. ARMA = autoregressive moving average. The sample period is Q1 1968–Q4 2017. The shaded areas are 68% confidence intervals based on heteroskedasticity and autocorrelation robust standard errors with a Bartlett kernel and four lags. The x-axis denotes quarters from the shock, starting at 0. In the first column the outcome is u_t and the forecast is $\overline{\mathbb{E}}_{t-3}[u_t]$; in the second column the outcome is $\pi_{t,t-4}$, or annual inflation, and the forecast is $\overline{\mathbb{E}}_{t-3}[\pi_{t,t-4}]$. A color version of this figure is available online.

row shows the instrumented ARMA method of equation (14), and the second row shows the projection method of equation (15). For both methods, we "align" the forecast responses such that, at a given vertical slice of the plot, the outcome and forecast responses are measured over the same horizon, and the difference thereof is a measure of the response of forecast errors. In the second column, we plot the same for the response of 1-year-average inflation to the supply shock ε_t^S.

The consistent pattern across specifications is an initially delayed and then overpersistent response of forecasts to the shock. Consider, as an illustration, the response of unemployment and forecasts thereof to ε_t^D. Unemployment spikes around quarter 3 in both estimation methods before reverting back to its long-run mean. The point estimate is extremely close to zero by $t = 12$ in both cases.

Now consider the response of forecasts at $t = 3$ in the plot. These are forecasts made at $t = 0$, when the very first macro data (e.g., BLS reports) from $t = 0$ become available. Forecasted unemployment immediately spikes and begins to decay over the next 5–6 quarters. Forecasters remain convinced there are adverse demand conditions, when in reality conditions have reverted back to the mean. A similar, and indeed more dramatic, pattern is visible in the response of inflation to the supply shock (second row). And these patterns look qualitatively and quantitatively quite similar with both the smooth, ARMA estimates (top row) and the unrestricted projection regression estimates (bottom row).

Figure 4 shows this overshooting pattern more clearly in terms of the impulse response of forecast errors. For both the ARMA and projection methods, this is obtained by taking the difference of the previous estimates for outcomes and forecasts. For both unemployment and inflation, we find evidence that forecast errors start positive and then turn negative at longer horizons. The estimated "crossing points" of the forecast errors response with 0, using the ARMA method, are $K_{IRF}^u = 4.14$ and $K_{IRF}^\pi = 6.43$, respectively.[25]

Finally, in the left panel of figure A1, we complete the picture with the "off-diagonal" impulse responses of inflation to the demand shock and unemployment to the supply shock. The former is weakly inflationary at

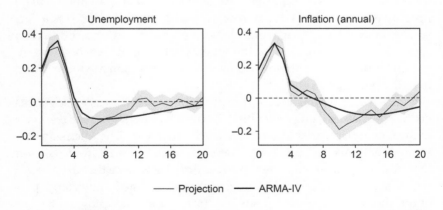

Fig. 4. Dynamic responses: forecast errors. ARMA = autoregressive moving average. The sample period is Q1 1968–Q4 2017. The shaded areas are 68% confidence intervals based on heteroskedasticity and autocorrelation robust standard errors with a Bartlett kernel and four lags. The x-axis denotes quarters from the shock, starting at 0. In the first column the outcome is u_t and the forecast is $\overline{\mathbb{E}}_{t-3}[u_t]$; in the second column the outcome is $\pi_{t,t-4}$, or annual inflation, and the forecast is $\overline{\mathbb{E}}_{t-3}[\pi_{t,t-4}]$. A color version of this figure is available online.

longer horizons and the latter weakly contractionary at medium horizons. And in both cases we have modest evidence of the overshooting pattern of interest.

C.   *Robustness and Extensions*

Sample choice. We conduct a number of initial robustness checks, mirroring those in Section III, related to measurement and sample choice. The middle panel of figure A1 recreates the regression results in the SPF, back again with modern data, in the sample 1984–2017. As discussed previously, we might think of the post-Volcker and post-oil-crisis data as a more "consistently stationary" regime for forecasters trying to model the world. We find largely the same patterns in forecast errors. The right panel of figure A1 recreates the main analysis with forecast data from Blue Chip Economic Indicators over the shorter available sample (1980–2017) and again finds the same patterns.[26]

General public. Carroll (2003) and others have argued that the forecasts of professional forecasters are in general good proxies for those of the general public. But does this apply to our particular finding?

To address this question, we look at the University of Michigan Survey of Consumer Sentiment and construct an "unemployment expectation" using the survey's question about whether unemployment will go up, stay the same, or go down over the next 12 months. We code a variable $\overline{\mathbb{E}}_t[\text{UnempUp}_{t+4}]$ that averages the "up" responses, and code a data equivalent UnempUp_{t+4} using the Bureau of Economic Analysis unemployment rate.[27] For inflation, we use the survey's estimate for inflation over the next 12 months.[28]

Figure A2 shows the results from projecting our business-cycle shocks on these variables using equation (15). The left panel shows the response of the UnempUp variable and forecasts thereof to ε_t^D. The Michigan survey expectations perk up slightly before the shock hits (i.e., for $t < 4$) and then spike 1 quarter "too late." We see further evidence that the general public is also particularly unable to forecast the "mean-reverting" part of the shock, or the eventual downward trend in unemployment.

The right panel shows the response of the GDP deflator and the annual inflation expectation of the Michigan survey to ε_t^S. Here, responses are much too noisy to pick out an obvious "peak response." Again, there is some weak evidence of anticipation, and at quarters 10 and onward evidence of some overextrapolation of recent price trends.

Other shocks of interest. An appealing feature of using projections and the ARMA-IV method is that it is easy to combine with auxiliary identification techniques, without fully specifying a multivariate model and considering the problem of jointly identifying many shocks. To illustrate this property, and probe the robustness of our results to other candidate "supply and demand" shocks from the macroeconomics literature, figure A3 replicates our main analysis for three different shocks: a technology shock à la Galí (1999), normalized here to be inflationary and contractionary; an oil price shock à la Hamilton (1996); and the investment-specific shock extracted from the DSGE model of Justiniano et al. (2010). The former two are variations of "supply shocks" (to productivity or input costs), and we show the response of inflation; the last is like a demand shock, and we show the response of unemployment. In all cases we see evidence of the overshooting pattern.

Methods for estimating dynamics. Our ARMA-IV method resembles the method suggested by Romer and Romer (2004) and applied by Coibion and Gorodnichenko (2012) in their study of how forecast errors respond to structural shocks. That method estimates an empirical ARMA process like equation (14) via ordinary least squares ("ARMA-OLS"). It therefore uses unconditional autocovariance properties to pin down dynamics. Our prior is that, in a world of very different, shock-specific dynamics (induced, for instance, by differential persistence in the driving process or differential ability to learn about these shocks), the ARMA-OLS method could give misleading results. Indeed, in our replication of a key result from Coibion and Gorodnichenko (2012), the response of inflation and forecast errors thereof to technology shocks, we find evidence of our overshooting patterns when we use both our ARMA-IV method and a local projection. Appendix B unpacks the differences in methodology and demonstrates why the particular implementation in Coibion and Gorodnichenko (2012) makes it impossible to see the overshooting patterns uncovered here: the forecast errors are therein restricted to be uniformly positive.

Two complementary SVARs. Another option for estimating complex dynamics, of course, is to jointly estimate a multivariate model. We estimate a 13-variable VAR comprised of the 10 key macroeconomic variables from Angeletos et al. (2020) plus 3 forecast variables of interest: the 3-period-ahead unemployment forecast, the 3-period-ahead annual inflation forecast, and the 3-period-ahead quarterly inflation forecast.[29] We apply the same Bayesian inference procedure as that paper, including

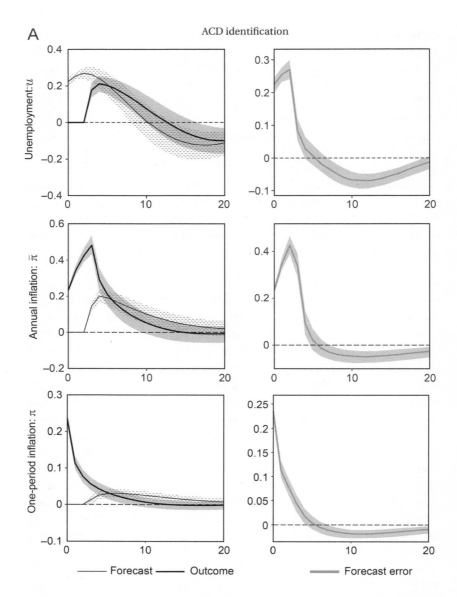

Fig. 5. Dynamic responses in a structural vector autoregression. Part (*A*) shows results from a "max share" identification as in Angeletos et al. (2020) and part (*B*) shows results from a triangular identification. The sample period is Q4 1968–Q4 2017. The *x*-axis denotes quarters from the shock (starting at 0). The shaded areas are 68% high-posterior-density regions and the point estimate is the posterior median. In the first row the outcome is u_t and the forecast is $\overline{\mathbb{E}}_{t-3}[u_t]$; in the second row the outcome is $\pi_{t,t-4}$, or annual inflation, and the forecast is $\overline{\mathbb{E}}_{t-3}[\pi_{t,t-4}]$; and in the last row, the outcome is $\pi_{t,t-1}$, or one-quarter inflation, and the forecast is $\overline{\mathbb{E}}_{t-3}[\pi_{t,t-1}]$. See the main text for details. A color version of this figure is available online.

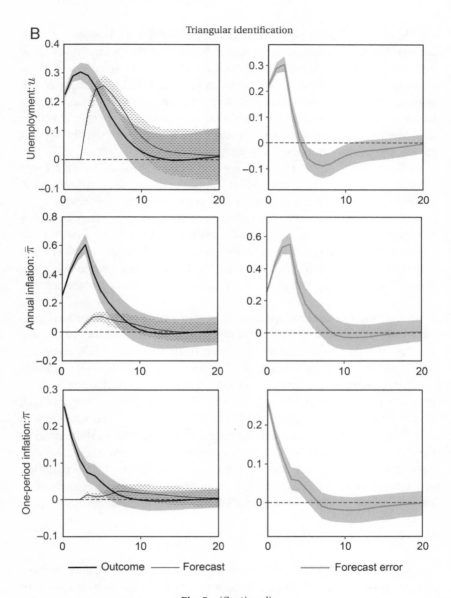

Fig. 5. (*Continued*)

prior specification and posterior sampling procedures, and replicate their identification of shocks that target the "max share" of the business-cycle variation in unemployment and inflation.[30]

The left panel of figure 5 shows the results. In the first row, we show the response of unemployment, forecasts thereof, and forecast errors to the "unemployment shock." This can be compared directly to the first column of figures 3 and 4, and largely agrees about the potential for large and persistent "overshooting" in forecast errors. The second and third rows show the response of outcomes and forecasts to the inflation shock in the same SVAR model, but with different forecast horizons and transformations of the outcome variable (annual averages in row 2 versus quarter-to-quarter rates in row 3). Here we find quantitatively smaller effects per period, but also very persistent ones.[31]

In the right panel of figure 5, we show the results of two different "Cholesky" identifications based on triangular short-run restrictions (ordering unemployment or inflation first). We find strong corroborating evidence of overshooting for unemployment but only very weak evidence for inflation. Hence, fact 4 for inflation seems to rely on filtering the "right" variation in the data. A related point is made below in the context of fact 3, where we show that this fact is reinforced when we focus on the shock that drives the variation of inflation at business-cycle frequencies.

Dispersions, not means. Motivated by our framework, which emphasizes only mean forecasts, we have not looked at the dynamics of the dispersion in forecasts. In figure A5, we reestimate equation (15) using the cross-sectional interquartile range of forecasts as the outcome.[32] There is a rough pattern of dispersion spiking on impact of shocks, particularly in the "diagonal" responses. A "cheap" way to accommodate this fact, which echoes Mankiw, Reis, and Wolfers (2004), in our framework is to let τ be time-varying while maintaining $\hat{\tau}$ fixed; this allows dispersion to vary without affecting at all the joint dynamics of average forecasts and aggregate outcomes. The more interesting possibility that time variation in the levels of uncertainty and disagreement influence aggregate behavior (e.g., Bloom 2009; Bloom et al. 2018) is left outside our analysis.

D. Three Complementary Tests

The impulse response evidence, combined with the discussion in Section IV, suggest we are heading toward a model that includes both incomplete information and overextrapolation. Here, before proceeding to determine the implications of such a theory, we organize three additional tests that independently corroborate our main story.

The "term structure" of forecasts. The IRFs plotted show forecasts of a constant horizon at different dates after the shock. But they do not show a forecaster's belief at any fixed date about how macro outcomes will behave in the future, which could perhaps offer the most direct evidence of over- or underextrapolation.

We can estimate a version of this in the SPF data, for forecasts up to 4 quarters out; forecasts of longer horizons are unavailable for the full sample. We thus consider the following "slice" of the projection regressions for forecasted variable and the realized outcome at horizons $k \in \{0, ..., 4\}$:

$$\overline{\mathbb{E}}_t[x_{t+k}] = \alpha_k + \beta_k^f \cdot \varepsilon_t + \gamma \cdot W_t + u_{t+k} \tag{16}$$

$$x_{t+k} = \alpha_k^o + \beta_k^o \cdot \varepsilon_t + \gamma^o \cdot W_t + u_{t+k} \tag{17}$$

We run these specifications for x equal to unemployment and inflation, and for ε equal to the corresponding shock. For consistency, we use the same control as those used earlier in projection (eq. [15]).

The coefficients of interest are (β_k^f, β_k^o), which reveal the persistence of outcomes and forecasts. If $\beta_k^f < \beta_k^o$, which we have already verified for $k = 3$, we know agents underreact on impact. If β_k^o is much more persistent across k than β_k^f, this is also evidence of overextrapolation right at the impact of the shock—that is, agents end up being more correct about impacts further in the future because their overextrapolation partially cancels out their underreaction.

Figure 6 plots the results, showing the values of β_k^o and β_k^f on the left and right scales, respectively. By comparing the left and right scales, we see that forecasts at all horizons underreact. But by comparing the dark line to the light one, we also see that, in the case of unemployment, agents expect the effect of the shock to persist longer than it actually does.

A "structural" version of facts 1 and 3. Now that we have committed to some notion of what "business-cycle variation" we want to map to the model's shocks, we should recognize that a more precise analogue to facts 1 and 3 (and our argument linking these facts to the IRFs) would involve subsetting to this particular variation. We thus revisit those regressions with an appropriate IV strategy.[33] Concretely, we estimate versions of regressions (eq. [1]) and (eq. [3]) using the current and six lags of the corresponding shock as an instrument for, respectively, Revision$_t$ and x_t. Table 4 reports the results.

For fact 1, we find similar values to the OLS estimates for unemployment, but slightly larger, and more stable, values for inflation. This is consistent with the relative stability of our IRFs, as demonstrated in the

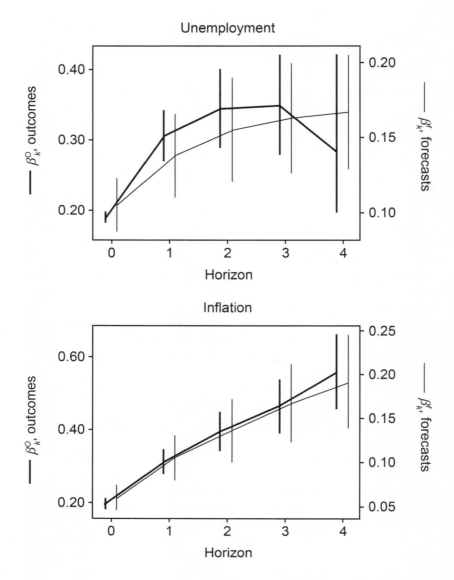

Fig. 6. The term structure of forecasts and outcomes. The sample period is Q4 1968–Q4 2017. The x-axis denotes quarters from the shock or horizon of forecast (starting at 0). The lines are one-standard-error bars. The light lines plot the terms structure of forecasts, or β_k^f from equation (16), and the dark lines show the response of outcomes, or β_k^o from equation (17).

Table 4
Forecast Error Predictability with Business-Cycle Variation

Regression		Unemployment		Inflation	
		1968–2017	1984–2017	1968–2017	1984–2017
Equation (1)	Revision$_t$ (K_{CG})	.585	.867	1.460	.511
		(.393)	(.270)	(.521)	(.358)
	First-stage F	7.527	4.736	3.517	5.047
	N	189	130	188	130
	OLS Estimate	.741	.809	1.528	.292
Equation (3)	x_t (K_{KW})	−.260	−.073	.085	−.642
		(.144)	(.086)	(.125)	(.328)
	First-stage F	2.671	5.560	1.697	1.513
	N	191	136	190	135
	OLS Estimate	−.061	−.036	.111	−.068

Note: The data set is the Survey of Professional Forecasters and the observation is a quarter between Q4 1968 and Q4 2017. All regressions include a constant. The forecast horizon is 3 quarters. Standard errors are heteroskedasticity and autocorrelation robust, with a Bartlett kernel and lag length equal to 4 quarters. The data used for outcomes are first release ("vintage"). The F values are a multivariate extension of the Kleibergen and Paap (2006) rk statistic and can be compared with critical values reported in Stock and Yogo (2005) for given levels of tolerated bias. OLS = ordinary least square.

comparison of the left and middle panels of figure A1. For fact 3, we find more negative values that the OLS estimates. This underscores that the aspect of overshooting that is picked up in the KW regression is more pronounced when focusing on the relevant business-cycle variation.

Auxiliary support for dispersed, private information. By embracing overextrapolation, we have committed to a model in which some noisy perception is necessary to capture the initial sluggishness in expectations and the related fact 1. Appendix C shows more clearly how to use a hybrid regression of individual and aggregate predictability (facts 1 and 2) to test for noisy signals in this class of models. The underlying idea is that the difference between the CG and BGMS regression coefficients speaks directly to dispersed private information per se: if aggregate forecast errors are strongly positively related to past aggregate revisions, and if in addition one's forecast errors are negatively, or less positively, related to one's own past revision, it has to be that one's forecast error is positively related to others' past revision. In other words, there is evidence supporting the hypothesis of "forecasting the forecasts of others."[34]

VI.   Imperfect Expectations in GE

We now put the accumulated evidence about expectations to work in an
equilibrium macroeconomic model. This serves four purposes. First, we
verify that our main conclusions about identifying specific frictions via
survey data are robust to considering the GE fixed point. Second, we
demonstrate how our evidence can speak intrinsically to equilibrium theories of expectations formation, which had no place in our earlier PE analysis. Third, we clarify how the causal effects of the imperfect expectations
in such a context depend on parameters that regulate GE feedbacks, such
as the MPC, or the slope of the Keynesian cross. And finally, we offer a
proof-of-concept calibration exercise which demonstrates how our evidence can offer not only theoretical but also quantitative guidance.

A.   Primitives

Consider the New Keynesian model with no capital and rigid prices. Let
y_t be output and c_t be consumption, where all quantities are in log deviations. The market clearing condition is $y_t = c_t$, and output is purely
demand-determined given a fixed path of nominal interest rates (which
also equal real interest rates).[35]

When agents have different and potentially irrational expectations,
aggregate demand can no longer be represented by the Euler equation
of a representative consumer. Following the same steps as in Angeletos
and Lian (2018), one can instead obtain the following "modern" version
of the Keynesian cross:

$$c_t = \beta \sum_{k=0}^{\infty} \beta^k \overline{\mathbb{E}}_t[\xi_{t+1}^d - \varsigma r_{t+k}] + (1 - \beta) \sum_{k=0}^{\infty} \beta^k \overline{\mathbb{E}}_t[y_{t+k}], \qquad (18)$$

where $\overline{\mathbb{E}}_t$ denotes the average expectation in period t, β is the subjective
discount factor, ς is the elasticity of intertemporal substitution (EIS), r_t is
the nominal (also real) interest rate, and ξ_t^d is a demand (preference) shock.
This condition follows from aggregating the log-linearized optimal consumption function. The second term captures the consumers' present discounted value income, as in the permanent income hypothesis (PIH).

To see more clearly how equation (18) captures the Keynesian cross,
let $Y = \Sigma_{k=0}^{\infty} \beta^k \overline{\mathbb{E}}_t[y_{t+k}]$ be the average, possibly irrational, expectation of
permanent income. We can then read equation (18) as $c = a + bY$, where
$a \equiv \Sigma_{k=0}^{\infty} \beta^k \overline{\mathbb{E}}_t[\xi_t^d - \varsigma r_t]$ is the intercept of the Keynesian cross and $b \equiv$
$(1 - \beta)$ is its slope, or equivalently the MPC out of income.

For our purposes, it is therefore best to replace β in condition (eq. [18]) with $1 - $ mpc, treat mpc as a primitive parameter, and think of mpc ≈ 0.3 as an empirically plausible benchmark. This is further justified in Angeletos and Huo (2020) by drawing a connection between a heterogeneous-agent variant of the present framework and the Heterogenous Agent New Keynesian (HANK) literature.[36]

Let $\xi_t \equiv \xi_t^d - \varsigma r_t$ denote the "total demand shock" relative to steady state; formally, this is a rescaling of the deviation of interest rates from the natural rate. We close the model by letting ξ_t be an exogenous AR(1) process with persistence ρ and Gaussian one-step-ahead innovations ε_t:

$$\xi_t = \frac{1}{1 - \rho\mathbb{L}} \varepsilon_t. \tag{19}$$

A positive ε_t can be either an expansionary monetary policy or an expansionary demand shock.

Like in Section IV, we let each consumer observe only a noisy Gaussian private signal of ξ_t, the true precision of which is given by $\tau > 0$:

$$s_{i,t} = \xi_t + \frac{u_{i,t}}{\sqrt{\tau}} \qquad u_{i,t} \sim_{iid} N(0, 1). \tag{20}$$

And we let consumers' subjective perception of the precision of their information and of the persistence of the underlying impulse be, respectively, some $\hat{\tau} > 0$ and some $\hat{\rho} \in (0, 1)$, which may differ from the objective counterparts.

B.   Solving and Characterizing the Fixed Point

As already mentioned, Angeletos and Huo (2020) have solved the fixed point of a similar model as ours, under the restrictions $\hat{\rho} = \rho$ and $\hat{\tau} = \tau$. The following two propositions extend their results to the present environment and offer a simple description of how the frictions influence macro dynamics.

Proposition 3.   An equilibrium to this model exists, is unique, and admits a finite ARMA representation for the aggregate outcome and the average forecasts.

Proposition 4 (As-If Representation).   There exist functions Ω_f and Ω_b such that the unique equilibrium dynamics of the imperfect-expectations economy is the same as that of a perfect-expectations counterpart with the following Euler equation:

$$c_t = -\varsigma r_t + \omega_f \mathbb{E}_t^* [c_{t+1}] + \omega_b c_{t-1} + \xi_t^d, \tag{21}$$

where $\omega_f = \Omega_f(\hat{\tau}, \rho, \hat{\rho}, \text{mpc})$, $\omega_b = \Omega_b(\hat{\tau}, \rho, \hat{\rho}; \text{mpc})$, and $\mathbb{E}_t^*$ is the rational, full-information, expectation operator. Furthermore, $\omega_b > 0$ if and only if $\hat{\tau} < \infty$, and $\omega_f < 1$ if and only if either $\hat{\rho} < \rho$ or $\hat{\tau}$ is small enough relative to $\hat{\rho} - \rho$.

This result offers a bridge to simple representative-agent macro models: ω_b resembles habit persistence, ω_f represents a form of myopia (if $\omega_f < 1$) or hyperopia (if $\omega_f > 1$). The economy with noisy perception ($\hat{\tau} < \infty$ and $\tau < \infty$) but no overextrapolation ($\hat{\rho} = \rho$) features both myopia ($\omega_f < 1$) and anchoring ($\omega_b > 0$). At the other extreme, if we shut down noisy perception (i.e., take $\hat{\tau} = \tau \to \infty$), we find that overextrapolation alone maps to hyperopia ($\omega_f > 1$) and underextrapolation alone maps to myopia ($\omega_f < 1$), but neither by itself produces anchoring ($\omega_b = 0$).

The case of most interest, overextrapolation combined with sufficiently large noise, maps to $\omega_f < 1$ and $\omega_b > 0$. The former dampens the economy's response to innovations and to news about the future. The latter plays a similar role as habit persistence in consumption—or, if we translate the results to other contexts, as adjustment costs to investment, price indexation in the New Keynesian Phillips curve (NKPC), or momentum in asset prices (see Angeletos and Huo 2020, and references therein). Finally, compared with the versions of these mechanisms found in the DSGE literature, the ones obtained here have two distinctive qualities. First, they are endogenous to policy, market structures, and GE multipliers. And second, they are disciplined by the provided evidence on expectations.[37]

C.   Facts 1–4 in GE

Let us next focus on the connection with the data, which is the main contribution of our paper. The following result verifies that all our main insights from Section V go through modulo additional dependence on GE feedback:

Proposition 5 (Facts 1–4 in GE).   Corollaries 1, 2, and 3 go through in the GE context, but all moments now depend also on the MPC.

That is: (i) we can still show that the pure noisy rational expectations and pure misspecification models are insufficient to describe the observed moments; (ii) we can still select the combination of noise and overextrapolation as the "right" model; and (iii) we still have that delayed overshooting in IRFs is smoking-gun evidence of the combination of noise and overextrapolation; but (iv) we now must condition all inference on additional information about the extent of GE feedback in the economy.

D. *Imperfect Reasoning versus Imperfect Expectations*

A claim we have made earlier, and now have the tools to formalize, is that certain models of imperfect reasoning in equilibrium work in similar ways as our more mechanical model of underextrapolation and are therefore not a good fit for the data. We consider, in particular, three such models:

1. **Dogmatic higher-order doubts.** Assume that each consumer observes ξ_t with probability 1 but attaches only probability $q \in (0, 1)$ that any other consumer also observes ξ_t; with the remaining probability, any other agent is expected to have her belief about ξ_t reset to the prior. Such a model is the main specification in Angeletos and Sastry's (2020) work on forward guidance at the zero lower bound (ZLB). It captures the same kind of inertia in forward-looking higher-order beliefs and the same consequent forms of myopia and GE attention as those featured in Angeletos and Lian (2018) and our own GE setting, but it replaces the informational friction with a systematic bias in beliefs. It therefore builds a bridge to the following two models, which introduce similar biases.

2. **Level-k thinking.** Assume that a consumer of "level 1" perfectly observes ξ_t but assumes all others consumers a default action $c_{i,t}^d = 0$; an agent of level 2 also perfectly observes ξ_t but assumes all other agents play the level-1 action; and this definition recursively extends up to order K, for some finite $K > 2$. Such models have been used to explain the sluggish, and often incomplete, convergence to Nash equilibrium play in laboratory settings (e.g., Nagel 1995) and, more recently, agents' expectations formation about "unconventional" policy (e.g., Iovino and Sergeyev 2017; Farhi and Werning 2019; García-Schmidt and Woodford 2019).

3. **Cognitive discounting (Gabaix 2020).** Agents have misspecified priors about the processes of the exogenous state and the endogenous aggregate spending. In particular, whenever the actual laws of motion are

$$\xi_t = \rho\xi_{t-1} + \varepsilon_t \quad \text{and} \quad y_t = Ry_{t-1} + D\varepsilon_t,$$

for some constants R and D (to be determined as part of the solution), the agents believe that

$$\xi_t = m\rho\xi_{t-1} + \varepsilon_t \quad \text{and} \quad y_t = mRy_{t-1} + D\varepsilon_t,$$

for some exogenous scalar $m \in (0, 1)$ that represents the degree of "cognitive discounting" applied when the consumers contemplate the future.

These models have different methodological underpinnings. But they induce essentially the same distortion in beliefs. In particular, it is easy to show that all three models impose that the average subjective expectation and the corresponding rational expectation are connected by the following restriction:

$$\overline{\mathbb{E}}_t[y_{t+1}] = d \cdot \mathbb{E}_t^*[y_{t+1}],$$

where $d \in (0, 1)$ is a scalar that depends on the "deep" parameter $\zeta \in \{q, K, m\}$ of the respective model. This scalar measures how much consumers underestimate the future response in the behavior of others and, equivalently, the future response of y_t. What differs is the reason for $d < 1$: underestimating the knowledge of others (model 1), underestimating the rationality of others (model 2), or applying a behavioral discount to the future (model 3).

Now note that the form of underextrapolation accommodated in our framework plays the same role as well. Indeed, if we shut down noisy perception, we can show that

$$\overline{\mathbb{E}}_t[y_{t+1}] = \frac{\hat{\rho}}{\rho} \mathbb{E}_t^*[y_{t+1}].$$

It follows that, for any of the aforementioned three models, we can find a value of $\hat{\rho}$ less than ρ such that our model implies the same effective friction in the expectations. The next proposition verifies that this logic carries over to the entire set of predictions about outcomes and forecasts. The corollary spells out the relevant empirical implications.

Proposition 6. For any of the three models described above and any value for the corresponding parameter $\zeta \in \{q, K, m\}$, there exists some $\hat{\rho} = f(\rho, \zeta, \text{mpc}) < \rho$, such that the outcome of the original model is observationally equivalent to our own model without noise ($\tau = \hat{\tau} = \infty$) and underextrapolation ($\hat{\rho} < \rho$).

Corollary 4. For any of the three models described above, the following properties hold: $K_{CG} = K_{BGMS} > 0$, $K_{KW} > 0$, and the IRF of the average forecast errors is uniformly positive. That is, these models are at odds with facts 2, 3, and 4.

All these models have consumers underestimate the future response of others, which in turn affects behavior in a similar way as an underestimation of the persistence of ξ_t. The only subtle difference between them is whether the belief misspecification operates through both PE and GE considerations, or only through GE. For the first two models (noiseless higher-order doubts and level-k thinking), because the extent of the friction is tied closely to the extent of strategic interaction, the replicating $\hat{\rho}$ will be a function of the MPC.

Our observation that pure underextrapolation cannot explain the business-cycle macro data on imperfect expectations (corollary 1 and proposition 5) thus extends to the aforementioned GE dampening models as well. First, each model restricts $K_{CG} = K_{BGMS}$, or it fails to provide a reason why the forecast errors of one are predictable by the information of others. And second, even in variants that add some noisy perception and that could thus help match the CG and BGMS evidence, none of these theories could explain the observed overextrapolation in IRFs.[38]

The obvious caveat to this conclusion is that it only applies to the particular evidence we have considered here and may not extend to other contexts. Another caveat is that this conclusion is modulated by parsimony: given the evidence at hand, we cannot reject the hypothesis that agents overextrapolate the aggregate shocks and at the same time are shallow thinkers with respect to GE.

E. A Quantitative Assessment

Let us now illustrate how our empirical findings can help quantify the GE effects of the documented mechanisms, using the New Keynesian model as our laboratory economy.[39]

To speak jointly to data on output (unemployment) and inflation, let us first extend the model to allow for partially flexible prices. This involves adding a block of noncompetitive intermediate goods firms who operate a linear technology and reset prices with probability $1 - \theta \in (0, 1)$ and a final goods firm that competitively combines these goods with a constant-returns-to-scale technology. As in Angeletos and Lian (2018) and Angeletos and Huo (2020), the model's three equations can be expressed as follows:

$$c_{i,t} = \mathbb{E}_{i,t}\left[\sum_{k=0}^{\infty}(1 - \text{mpc})^{k+1}\left[\xi_{t+k}^{d} - \varsigma(i_{t+k} - \pi_{t+k+1})\right] + \text{mpc}\sum_{k=0}^{\infty}(1 - \text{mpc})^{k}c_{t+k}\right]$$

$$\pi_{i,t} = \mathbb{E}_{i,t}\left[\theta\sum_{k=0}^{\infty}(\beta\theta)^{k}\kappa(c_{t+k} + \xi_{t+k}^{s}) + (1 - \theta)\sum_{k=0}^{\infty}(\beta\theta)^{k}\pi_{t+k}\right]$$

$$i_t = \phi_{\pi}\pi_t$$

The first equation is the dynamic IS (investment-saving) curve, modified to allow for informational frictions and misspecified beliefs along the lines discussed earlier. The parameter i_t is the nominal interest rate, π_t is inflation, and ξ_t^d is a preference shock, which maps to our empirical demand shock. The second equation is the corresponding modification of the NKPC. The parameter κ is its slope with respect to the real marginal cost, θ is the Calvo parameter (one minus the probability of resetting prices), and ξ_t^s is a cost-push shock, which maps to our empirical supply shock. The third and final equation is the rule for monetary policy, in which ϕ_π is the slope in current inflation.

We close the model by specifying the shock processes and the belief structures in the same way as before. Using the methods of Angeletos and Huo (2020), we then analytically solve for the equilibrium responses of inflation and consumption as functions of two sets of parameters: the "familiar" parameters (ς, mpc, β, θ, κ, ϕ_π); the actual and perceived persistence of the shocks (ρ, $\hat{\rho}$); and the perceived precision ($\hat{\tau}$). For the reasons already explained, the actual precision (τ) does not enter the determination of either the aggregate outcomes or the average expectations thereof.

To connect the model to the data, we interpret π_t as the quarterly rate of inflation and the negative of y_t as the quarterly rate of unemployment. The first choice requires no justification. The second one is based on the logic that, in our model, y_t coincides with the output gap, which in turn is closely related to unemployment both in richer models and in the data. We next fix the model's behavioral and policy parameters to conventional values, as shown in top panel of table 5. We finally pick, for each shock, the values of ρ, $\hat{\rho}$, and $\hat{\tau}$ so as to match as well as possible the key

Table 5
Model Parameters

(a) Exogenously Fixed		
Parameter	Description	Value
θ	Probability of price reset	.6
κ	Slope of Phillips curve	.02
β	Discount factor	.99
mpc	Marginal propensity to consume	.3
ς	Elasticity of intertemporal substitution (EIS)	1.0
ϕ	Policy rule slope	1.5
(b) Calibrated		
	ρ	$\hat{\rho}$	$\hat{\tau}$
Demand shock	.80	.95	.36
Supply shock	.57	.82	.15

evidence reported in Section V—that is, the IRF of outcomes and forecasts in figures 3 and 4 (ARMA-IV method) as well as the "term structure" of forecasts in figure 6. These moments provide the most direct evidence of the forces we have in mind, as discussed in Section IV. This procedure yields the parameters values seen in the bottom panel of table 5.

Figure 7 illustrates the model's fit vis-à-vis the empirical IRFs seen earlier in figure 3. The fit is quite good in the context of the demand shock, but mediocre in the context of the supply shock. This underscores that, although the model has the right qualitative ingredients, its quantitative performance is not automatic: there is no abundance of degrees of freedom.

We henceforth focus on the demand shock and study two counterfactuals. In the one, we shut down the overextrapolation, isolating the role of the information friction. In the second, we shut down both frictions, recovering the textbook New Keynesian model. These counterfactuals are illustrated in, respectively, the second and third columns of figure 8. The first column is the full model, with both frictions.

By comparing the second column to the third one, we see that the informational friction alone is the source of both significant dampening and significant persistence relative to the frictionless benchmark. Compared with the textbook model, the informational friction—calibrated to the evidence presented in this paper—decreases the impact of the demand shock on the output gap by about 50% and its impact on inflation by about 75%. As for the induced persistence, it is quantitatively comparable to that obtained in the richer DSGE model with the use of habit persistence in consumption and the hybrid version of the NKPC.

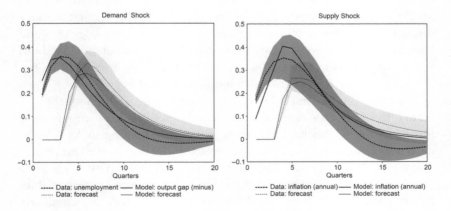

Fig. 7.   Model versus data. A color version of this figure is available online.

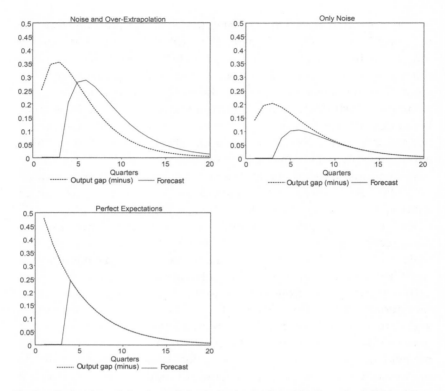

Fig. 8.   Counterfactuals for demand shock. A color version of this figure is available online.

This echoes the common message of a large literature on information frictions (e.g., Woodford 2003; Mankiw and Reis 2007; Nimark 2008; Maćkowiak and Wiederholt 2015). The added value here is that we have disciplined the theory with expectations evidence (as in Angeletos and Huo 2020) and that we have accommodated overextrapolation. Without it, the model fails to capture fact 4: as seen in the second column of figure 8, the forecasts in the noise-only model do not overshoot.

By comparing the first column to the second one, we then see that the main effect of overextrapolation on actual outcomes is to amplify their responses to the shock. And although the overshooting looks "small" in terms of the size of the forecast errors, the aforementioned amplification is sizable for two reasons. First, a small difference between $\hat{\rho}$ and ρ translates to a large difference in the kind of discounted present values that determine consumer spending and firm pricing. And second, any such mistake gets amplified at the aggregate level by GE feedback.

Needless to say, these counterfactuals should not be taken too seriously. They do, however, illustrate the potential value of accommodating the mechanisms and the evidence presented here in richer models.

We close this section with the following note. So far, we have utilized only evidence on average forecasts, ignoring the kind of individual-level evidence that was the focus of BGMS. This is because the BGMS regression coefficient only helps pin down a "residual" parameter (τ) that does not enter the dynamics of either the aggregate outcomes or the average forecasts. The BGMS evidence therefore has no (independent) effect on the counterfactuals conducted above.[40] As for the CG and KW evidence, they were subsumed by our evidence about IRFs.

VII.   Conclusion

Where are we in the "wilderness" of imperfect expectations? This paper organized theory and survey evidence to answer this question, taking into account both the possibility for multiple competing distortions in expectations formation and the equilibrium fixed point between expectations and outcomes.

We proposed and implemented a new empirical strategy: estimation of the IRF of the average forecast errors of unemployment and inflation to the shocks that drive most of the business-cycle variation in these variables. We explained why in theory this strategy is both more informative and more easily interpretable than alternatives found in previous empirical studies. And we demonstrated in practice how the information extracted via our strategy helps achieve three goals: resolve the apparent conflict between the empirical findings of previous works, help select among multiple competing theories of expectation formation, and serve as a "sufficient statistic" for quantitative purposes.

The main empirical finding was a form of delayed overshooting in expectations: following any shock, forecasts appear to underreact for the first few quarters but overshoot later on. The main lesson for theory was that, at least with the class of models considered, the data require the combination of a sizable informational friction and a behavioral tendency to overextrapolate the macroeconomic dynamics.

Theories that emphasize underextrapolation or closely related mechanisms, such as cognitive discounting and level-k thinking, were shown to be at odds not only with the new fact documented here but also with the individual-level evidence on expectations documented by Bordalo et al. (2020). At the same time, we echoed Angeletos and Huo's (2020) point that such individual-level evidence may not be strictly needed for the purpose of quantifying the overall effect on the macroeconomic dynamics: in the class of models considered, our evidence about average forecasts served as "sufficient statistics" for the counterfactuals of interest.

We conclude with a few notes on future research that would further solidify our understanding of macro belief dynamics and further the research program outlined in this paper.

Learning foundations. A question we have not tried to answer, at any point in this paper, is where agents' subjective model of the world comes from. More specifically, why would agents think that business-cycle shocks to demand or marginal costs have a higher persistence than they really do?

Our analysis simplifies the matter greatly by having agents put a dogmatic belief that the true persistence is $\hat{\rho}$. One might hypothesize that standard results on the learning foundations of rational expectations equilibria, extended to our setting, would rule out convergence of beliefs to $\hat{\rho} \neq \rho$ given a reasonable (nondegenerate) prior on $\hat{\rho}$ (Marcet and Sargent 1989; Evans and Honkapohja 2001). That said, if we extended the model to make the one-dimensional, AR(1) representation of fundamentals only an imperfect approximation of a richer underlying truth, we may observe convergence to $\hat{\rho} \neq \rho$ (Molavi 2019).

A variant story involves rational confusion between transitory and permanent shocks. Such confusion may cause agents to respond to the transitory shock as if they incorrectly perceive its persistence to be higher than is true. That is, such confusion can produce a rational form of overextrapolation. But it also predicts that agents ought to underextrapolate the effects of the permanent shock. Of course an auxiliary prediction is that agents underreact to the permanent changes. We found no support for this prediction when we looked at the dynamic responses of forecasts to a technology shock identified as in Galí (1999). But a more thorough quantitative analysis along these lines is an interesting angle for future work.

Nonstationary environments. Agents may also be using the wrong model because the underlying structure of the economy is changing underneath them. Two examples of this stick out.

The first involves the long-run changes in the behavior of US inflation, especially after the 1970s and early 1980s. The empirical findings in Section III suggest more severe overextrapolation for inflation in the modern period, in which inflation itself is less persistent. This could be consistent with agents' perceiving some "shadow" of the more ferocious shocks and/or timid policy response of the earlier period.[41]

A second important event in our sample is the extended stint at the ZLB during the Great Recession. A number of authors have postulated that this unfamiliar and extreme event may have caused agents to "throw out" their conventional models, justifying more dramatic departures from rational expectations (Iovino and Sergeyev 2017; Farhi and Werning 2019; Garcia-Schmidt and Woodford 2019; Angeletos and Sastry 2020; Gabaix 2020). We are sympathetic to this view and not insistent that our conclusions need to apply for expectations at the ZLB. There is more work to be done in investigating exactly for what counterfactuals and policy changes our empirical findings may provide good guidance.

The "right" expectations data. This paper, like much of the related empirical literature, has relied primarily on surveys of professional forecasters and analysts, because of data availability and quality. We provided corroborating evidence from the University of Michigan Consumer Sentiment Survey, but the imprecise measure of the relevant expectations in that survey precluded an equally sharp exercise as that based on SPF and Blue Chip data. The ideal implementation of our approach, which we leave for the future, requires sufficiently long time series of the expectations of consumers and firms, not only about macroeconomic outcomes, but also about the objects that matter more directly to their behavior, such as consumers' own income and firms' own sales.

Applications to finance. The coexistence of underreaction and overextrapolation is a classic fact for many asset prices (De Bondt and Thaler 1985; Cutler et al. 1991; Lakonishok et al. 1994). Our findings thus represent a step toward unifying our understanding of imperfect expectations in both macroeconomics and finance. An interesting possibility for future work is to replicate our impulse response evidence with dividends or earnings and expectations thereof, to determine if a similar structural interpretation (noise plus overreaction) holds true in this domain and also provides useful predictions for stock price dynamics.

Appendix A

Extra Tables and Figures

Table A1
Regression (eq. [1]), Robustness to Data Choices and Horizons

Sample	Horizon =	Unemployment			Inflation		
		1	2	3	1	2	3
Full, Vintage, SPF	Revision$_t$ (K_{CG})	.384	.606	.741	.649	1.048	1.528
		(.128)	(.178)	(.232)	(.290)	(.337)	(.418)
	R^2	.111	.143	.111	.122	.200	.278
	N	196	196	191	195	195	190
Post-1984, Vintage, SPF	Revision$_t$ (K_{CG})	.385	.657	.809	−.100	.160	.292
		(.203)	(.255)	(.305)	(.159)	(.174)	(.191)
	R^2	.116	.195	.159	.002	.005	.016
	N	136	136	136	135	135	135
Full, Final, SPF	Revision$_t$ (K_{CG})	.411	.612	.731	.578	.991	1.403
		(.127)	(.180)	(.233)	(.215)	(.261)	(.334)
	R^2	.135	.147	.108	.104	.200	.249
	N	199	198	192	199	198	192
Post–1980, Vintage, BC	Revision$_t$ (K_{CG})	.310	.544	.804	.024	.378	.618
		(.129)	(.213)	(.231)	(.204)	(.188)	(.205)
	R^2	.091	.132	.149	.000	.033	.067
	N	151	151	150	150	150	149

Note: All regressions include a constant. Standard errors are heteroskedasticity and autocorrelation robust, with a Bartlett kernel and lag length equal to 4 quarters. SPF = Survey of Professional Forecasters; BC = Blue Chip Economic Indicators Survey.

Table A2
Regression (eq. [2]), Robustness to Data Choices and Horizons

Sample	Horizon =	Unemployment			Inflation		
		1	2	3	1	2	3
Full, Vintage, SPF	Revision$_{i,t}$ (K_{BGMS})	.186	.300	.321	−.100	.024	.143
		(.077)	(.094)	(.107)	(.084)	(.098)	(.123)
	R^2	.029	.042	.028	.004	.000	.005
	N	5,808	5,699	5,383	5,496	5,458	5,147
Full, Final, SPF	Revision$_{i,t}$ (K_{BGMS})	.200	.296	.321	−.100	.056	.179
		(.075)	(.090)	(.106)	(.075)	(.091)	(.122)
	R^2	.035	.042	.028	.004	.001	.006
	N	5,831	5,728	5,419	5,571	5,520	5,226

Note: All regressions include a constant. Standard errors are clustered two-way by forecaster ID and time period. Both errors and revisions are winsorized over the sample to restrict to four times the interquartile range away from the median. SPF = Survey of Professional Forecasters.

Table A3
Regression (eq. [3]), Robustness to Data Choices

		Forecast Error			
		Unemployment		Inflation	
Sample	Data for Error =	Vintage	Final	Vintage	Final
Full, Vintage, SPF	x_t (K_{KW})	−.061	−.061	.111	.097
		(.056)	(.056)	(.075)	(.066)
	R^2	.016	.016	.058	.047
	N	194	195	193	195
Full, Final, SPF	x_t (K_{KW})	−.058	−.058	.117	.115
		(.056)	(.056)	(.078)	(.069)
	R^2	.014	.009	.062	.063
	N	194	195	192	194

Note: All regressions include a constant. Standard errors are heteroskedasticity and autocorrelation robust, with a Bartlett kernel and lag length equal to 4 quarters. SPF = Survey of Professional Forecasters.

Table A4
Calibrating with Unconditional Moments

	Unemployment		Inflation	
	1968–2017	1984–2017	1968–2017	1984–2017
ρ	.91		.89	
K_{CG}	.741	.809	1.528	.292
K_{BGMS}	.321	.398	.143	−.263
K_{KW}	−.061	−.036	.111	−.068
$\hat{\rho}$	.972	.966	.893	.947
$\hat{\tau}$	.449	.418	.335	1.850
T	2.028	2.231	.464	.693

Note: The persistence values come from band-pass filtered data on final outcomes over our sample.

Table A5
First-Stage F Statistics

	Unemployment		Inflation	
	Outcomes	Forecasts	Outcomes	Forecasts
N	188		188	
F	1.686	2.941	2.077	2.381
Endogenous regressors	3	3		
Instruments	8	8		

Note: The F (F-statistic) values are a multivariate extension of the Kleibergen and Paap (2006) rk statistic and can be compared with critical values reported in Stock and Yogo (2005) for given levels of tolerated bias.

Sample		Unemployment			Inflation		
		1	2	3	1	2	3
Full	$\Delta\text{Revision}_{i,t,k}$ ($-K_{\text{noise}}$)	−.183	−.189	−.166	−.422	−.427	−.346
		(.035)	(.043)	(.043)	(.047)	(.036)	(.042)
	$\text{Revision}_{t,k}$ (K_{agg})	.441	.6421	.745	.675	1.108	1.550
		(.114)	(.138)	(.173)	(.209)	(.245)	(.278)
	R^2	.120	.147	.103	.168	.194	.211
	N	5,808	5,699	5,383	5,496	5,458	5,147
Post-1984	$\Delta\text{Revision}_{i,t,k}$ ($-K_{\text{noise}}$)	−.217	−.264	−.162	−.517	−.481	−.410
		(.039)	(.043)	(.053)	(.034)	(.035)	(.041)
	$\text{Revision}_{t,k}$ (K_{agg})	.462	.722	.841	−.070	.179	.412
		(.159)	(.183)	(.210)	(.185)	(.178)	(.180)
	R^2	.136	.195	.152	.106	.085	.072
	N	3,986	3,918	3,769	3,779	3,745	3,643

Note: The observation is a forecaster by quarter between Q4 1968 and Q4 2017. Standard errors are clustered two-way by forecaster ID and time period. Both errors and revisions are winsorized over the sample to restrict to four times the interquartile range away from the median. The data used for outcomes are first release ("vintage").

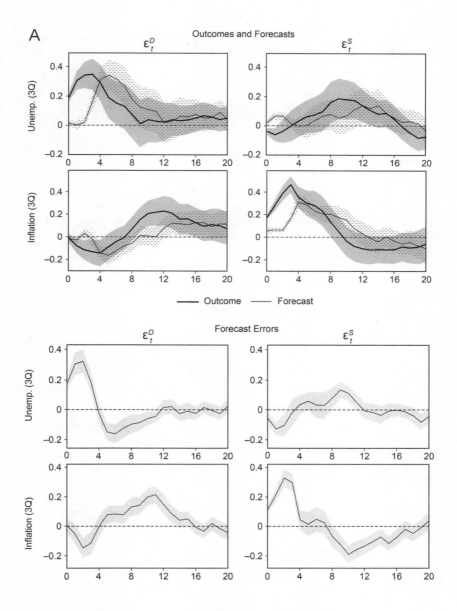

Fig. A1. The dynamic response of unemployment and inflation, robustness. Each sub-figure (A)–(C) corresponds, as indicated, to a different choice of data and time period. The sample period is Q4 1968–Q4 2017. The shaded areas are 68% confidence intervals based on heteroskedasticity and autocorrelation robust standard errors with a Bartlett kernel and four lags. In the first row of each panel, the outcome is u_t and the forecast is $\overline{\mathbb{E}}_{t-3}[u_t]$; in the second row, the outcome is $\pi_{t,t-4}$, or annual inflation, and the forecast is $\overline{\mathbb{E}}_{t-3}[\pi_{t,t-4}]$. A color version of this figure is available online.

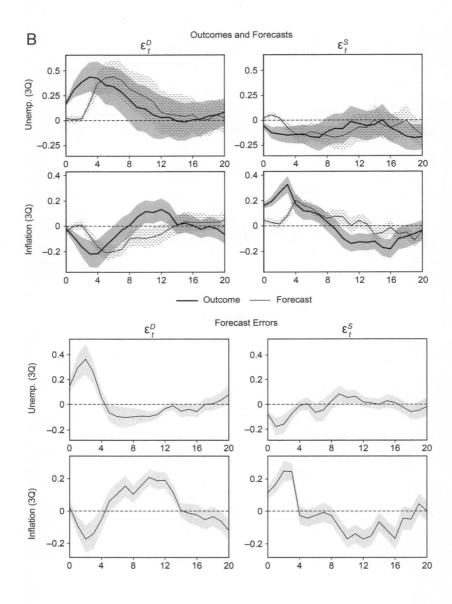

Fig. A1. (*Continued*)

50

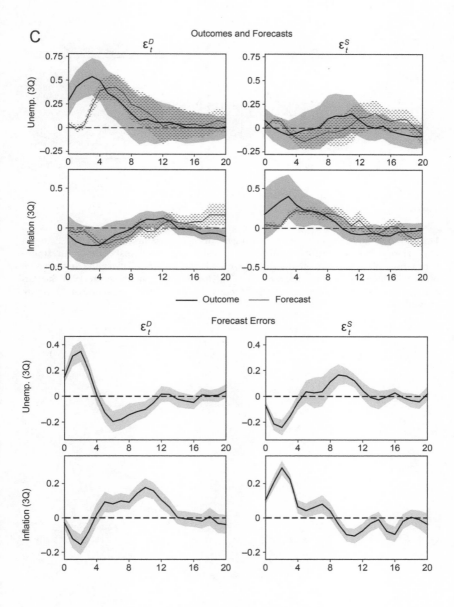

Fig. A1. (*Continued*)

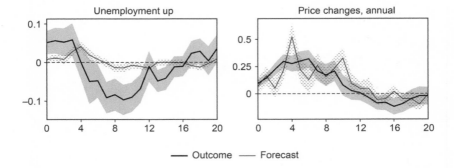

Fig. A2. Dynamic responses in the Michigan survey. The sample period is Q1 1968–Q4 2017. The shaded areas are 68% confidence intervals based on heteroskedasticity and auto-correlation robust standard errors with a Bartlett kernel and four lags. In the first plot, the outcome is $\text{UnempUp}_{t,t-4}$ and the forecast is $\overline{\mathbb{E}}_{t-4}[\text{UnempUp}_{t,t-4}]$; in the second plot, the outcome is $\pi_{t,t-4}$, or annual inflation, and the forecast is $\overline{\mathbb{E}}_{t-4}[\pi_{t,t-4}]$. A color version of this figure is available online.

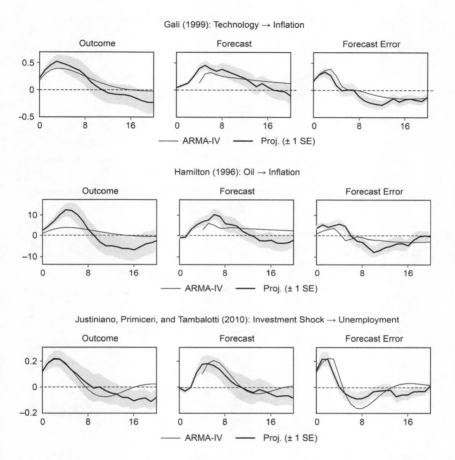

Fig. A3. Responses to other structural shocks. The sample period is Q4 1968–Q4 2017. The *x*-axis denotes quarters from the shock (starting at 0). The shaded areas are 68% confidence intervals based on heteroskedasticity and autocorrelation robust standard errors with a Bartlett kernel and four lags. The first shock is a technology shock à la Galí (1999), as obtained from Coibion and Gorodnichenko (2012) and normalized to be inflationary and contractionary. The second is an oil shock à la Hamilton (1996), again obtained from Coibion and Gorodnichenko (2012). The third is the investment-specific shock of Justiniano et al. (2010), updated to cover the full sample until 2017. Proj. = projection. See appendix B for details. A color version of this figure is available online.

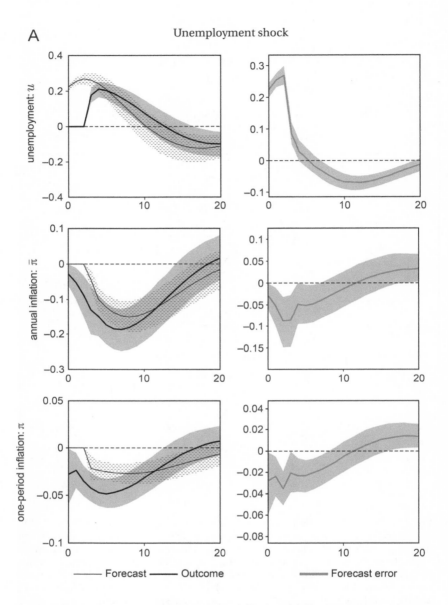

Fig. A4. Dynamic responses in the Angeletos, Collard, and Dellas (2020) structural vector autoregression, all responses. The sample period is Q4 1968–Q4 2017. The x-axis denotes quarters from the shock (starting at 0). The shaded areas are 68% high-posterior-density regions and the point estimate is the posterior median. In the first row the outcome is u_t and the forecast is $\overline{\mathbb{E}}_{t-3}[u_t]$; in the second row the outcome is $\pi_{t,t-4}$, or annual inflation, and the forecast is $\overline{\mathbb{E}}_{t-3}[\pi_{t,t-4}]$; and in the last row, the outcome is $\pi_{t,t-1}$, or one-quarter inflation, and the forecast is $\overline{\mathbb{E}}_{t-3}[\pi_{t,t-1}]$. Panel ($A$) shows the response to a shock that maximizes the business-cycle variation in unemployment; panel (B) shows the response to a shock that maximizes the business-cycle variation in gross domestic product deflator inflation. A color version of this figure is available online.

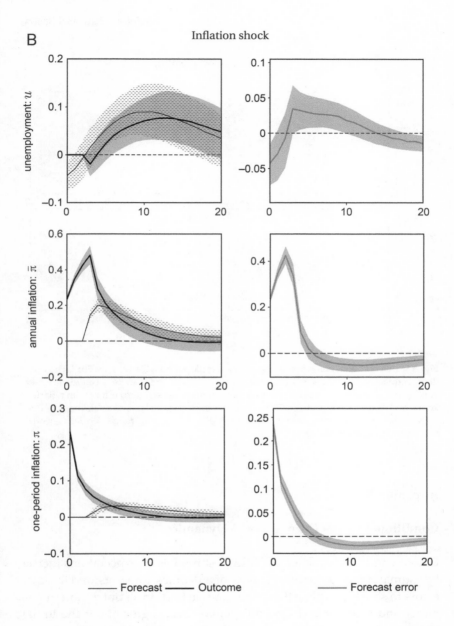

Fig. A4. (*Continued*)

Forecast Dispersion (IQR)

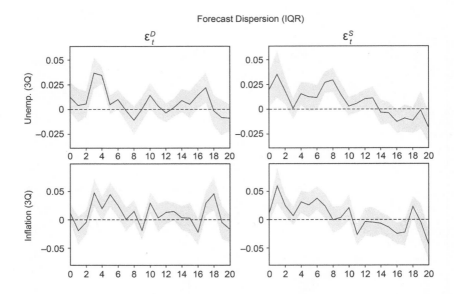

Fig. A5. Dynamic response of dispersion. The sample period is Q4 1968–Q4 2017. The *x*-axis denotes quarters from the shock (starting at 0). The shaded areas are 68% confidence intervals based on heteroskedasticity and autocorrelation robust standard errors with a Bartlett kernel and four lags. The outcome variable is the cross-sectional interquartile range of forecasts in the Survey of Professional Forecasters. IQR = Interquartile range. A color version of this figure is available online.

Appendix B

Conditional versus Unconditional Dynamics

Coibion and Gorodnichenko (2012) test models of expectations inertia by estimating the dynamic response of outcomes, forecasts, and forecast errors to shocks, just like this paper does in Section V. But although this paper and Coibion and Gorodnichenko (2012) agree about the initial underreaction of professional forecasters to economic shocks, only the present paper finds robust evidence of the "overshooting" that we characterize as fact 4. What explains the differences in results, given that our analyses study similar data over a similar time period?

   In this appendix, we will show that a major difference is estimation methodology—and we will argue that our approach is preferable.

To this goal, we will focus on one main result from Coibion and Gorodnichenko (2012): that inflation expectations respond sluggishly to an inflationary negative supply shock. We will recreate this fact using the data directly provided in that paper for the strongest comparability, although these data are of course essentially identical to those used in our own main analysis.[42]

To identify a technology shock, the authors run a four-lag, three-variable VAR with labor productivity, the change in labor hours, and the (1-quarter-ahead) GDP deflator inflation and apply the long-run restrictions introduced by Galí (1999).[43] Finally, to make the shock inflationary like our main example shock is, we take the negative shock that corresponds to a technological contraction.

Their method. To estimate impulse responses, Coibion and Gorodnichenko (2012) apply the following method due to Romer and Romer (2004). For a given variable z_t (e.g., forecast errors), they estimate the empirical ARMA process via OLS:

$$z_t = \alpha + \sum_{p=1}^{P} \gamma_p \cdot z_{t-p} + \sum_{k=0}^{K} \beta_k \cdot \varepsilon_{t-k} + u_t, \tag{B1}$$

where $(\varepsilon_{t-k})_{k=0}^{K}$ are the identified shocks. The authors use information criteria to pick an optimal lag length combination (P, K). In the empirical application, for estimating the response of inflation, forecasts, and forecast errors to the technology shocks, they find that $K = 1$ and $P = 1$ uniformly fit the data the best subject to their chosen penalty for extra parameters.

But now note that $P = 1$ effectively imposes that the IRF of forecast errors cannot switch signs. Indeed, abstracting from MA term (which after all turns out to be small in their estimation), their method effectively imposes that the IRF of the average forecast error to the technology shock is that of the AR(1) process that best describes the unconditional dynamics of the average forecast errors.

Our method. The approach we take in Section V has two key differences. First, we fix a larger value of P (in our preferred specification, $P = 3$), in anticipation of the fact that the model may demand more complex dynamics than an AR(1). Second, we instrument for lagged values of z_t using past shocks. Intuitively, this isolates the possibility that dynamics may be "shock-specific" and not informed entirely by the unconditional autocovariance patterns in z_t. This is to be expected if the data-generating process does in fact involve multiple shocks and/or variables, so thinking of the model as exactly a single-shock ARMA could be very inaccurate.

For comparability with (B1), we will estimate the following system of equations with two-stage least squares. The reduced-form equation is exactly (B1) with $K = 1$ and $P = 3$ (to capture higher-order dynamics):

$$z_t = \alpha + \sum_{p=1}^{3} \gamma_p z_{t-p} + \sum_{k=0}^{1} \beta_k \varepsilon_{t-k} + u_t. \tag{B2}$$

The first-stage relates the lags of z_t with shocks before $t - 1$. In vector form,

$$Z_{t-1} = \eta + \mathcal{E}'_{t-2} \Theta + e_t, \tag{B3}$$

with $Z_{t-1} = [z_{t-1}, z_{t-2}, z_{t-3}]$ and $\mathcal{E}_{t-2} = [\varepsilon_{t-j}]_{j=2}^{J}$. Like in the main text, we have $J = 9$, which means there are eight instruments. Armed with these IV estimates of the γ and β coefficients, we can calculate an alternative impulse response.

Local projections. Finally, we can also run the following local projection regression separately for each horizon h:

$$z_{t+h} = \alpha_h + \beta_{h,d} \cdot \varepsilon_t + \gamma' W_t + u_{t+h}. \tag{B4}$$

For controls W_t we will use the four lags each of labor productivity, the change in labor hours, and inflation that entered the original VAR. This is necessary, in the smaller sample, to make the estimated shock series truly orthogonal to lagged macro conditions.

Results. Figure A6 compares the results, extended out to 28 quarters. Plotted in the dotted line, with a shaded 68% confidence interval, is the projection estimate of impulse responses for outcomes (left), forecasts (middle), and forecast errors. Plotted in the light line is the point estimate of the Coibion and Gorodnichenko (2012) method, or the estimate that comes from (B1). Plotted in the dark line are the estimates from the IV method, or the combination of (B2) and (B3). And plotted in the dashed line is the difference between the dark lines for outcomes and forecasts, which is a different estimator for the response of forecast errors.

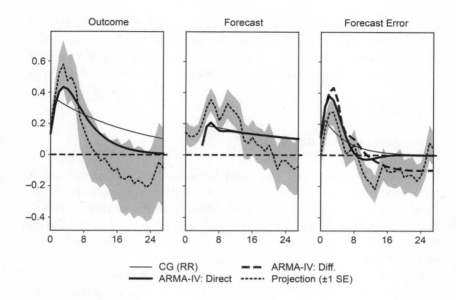

Fig. B1. Comparison of IRF methods for response to technology shock. RR = Romer and Romer (2004). A color version of this figure is available online.

The thin lines in all cases are much more persistent than the projection responses. In the first and third case, in particular, the thin lines smoothly and slowly converge back to zero. The unrestricted projection estimator, however, suggests that the response of inflation eventually turns negative (slightly, but not completely, offsetting the effects on the price level) and that the response of forecast errors also turns negative.

The ARMA-IV estimator, compared with the Coibion and Gorodnichenko (2012) method, gives a very similar response of forecast errors but a much less persistent response of the outcome. This estimation of the outcome IRF more closely matches the projection estimates. As such the "difference" estimator, or the dashed line in the third panel, shows evidence of overextrapolation in the point estimate at moderate (>10 quarter) horizons. The ARMA-IV estimator directly applied to forecast errors, on the other hand, shows only modest evidence of overshooting.

Bottom line. A method that imposes uniform dynamics as if the data-generating process involved only one shock, like that introduced by Romer and Romer (2004) and adopted by Coibion and Gorodnichenko (2012), may provide a distorted picture of the conditional dynamics. The possible solutions include the "shock-specific" IV approach introduced here, a flexible local projection, or a more structured multivariate model. The tradeoffs between these models involve robustness and small-sample efficiency.

Appendix C

Noise and a Hybrid Regression

Proposition 1 underscored that, away from rational expectations, the CG regression coefficient is no longer a measure of the informational friction alone: It is "contaminated" by the departure from the rationality. But the BGMS coefficient isolates the role of the latter. This suggests that the gap between the two coefficients ought to say something about the actual level of noise.

We next show how one can arrive at essentially the same answer with a "hybrid" of the CG and BGMS regressions. Let $(\mathcal{V}_{ind}, \mathcal{V}_{agg})$ respectively denote the variances of the idiosyncratic and aggregate forecast revisions.

Lemma. The following regression holds in the theory:

$$\text{Error}_{i,t,k} = K_{CG} \cdot \text{Revision}_{t,k} - K_{noise} \cdot \frac{\mathcal{V}_{agg}}{\mathcal{V}_{idio}} \cdot \Delta\text{Revision}_{i,t,k} + u_{i,t,k}, \qquad (C1)$$

where $\Delta\text{Revision}_{i,t,k} \equiv \text{Revision}_{i,t,k} - \text{Revision}_{t,k}$ and

$$K_{noise} \equiv K_{CG} - \frac{\mathcal{V}_{ind}}{\mathcal{V}_{agg}} K_{BGMS} = \kappa_1 \tau^{-1}. \qquad (C2)$$

From the perspective of this regression, K_{CG} measures the predictability in individual forecast errors attributed to the common component of the lagged forecast revisions, and K_{noise} the one attributed to the purely idiosyncratic components of the lagged forecast revisions. As already explained, the former confounds the effects of misspecification and information. The latter, which is again the gap between K_{CG} and K_{BGMS} appropriately rescaled, isolates the effect of the idiosyncratic noise.[44]

Table A6 shows results from estimating the hybrid regression over the full and restricted samples for all horizons of forecast. Across these margins, the estimated value of K_{noise} is positive (and statistically different from zero). This is lines up with the following observation: if we go back to the results presented in Section III and the appendix regarding facts 1 and 2, we can readily verify that K_{BGMS} was consistently lower that K_{CG}, even in specifications where both were positive.[45]

Of course, as evident from the previous discussion, the hybrid regression does not provide independent information compared with facts 1 and 2. The coefficients of the hybrid regression can be inferred from the original CG and BGMS regressions, and vice versa, up to small-sample differences between some moments.[46] What this regression however accomplishes is to combine facts 1 and 2 in a way that more clearly illustrates how the gap between K_{CG} and K_{BGMS}, or more precisely the object K_{noise} described above, provides the needed "correction" of the original CG coefficient. With rational expectations, K_{noise} coincides with K_{CG}. Away from that benchmark, K_{noise} partials out from K_{CG} the component due to irrationality. In both cases, K_{noise} isolates the effect of idiosyncratic noise.[47]

Appendix D

Proofs

The following lemma, which is proved below, will help in proving the results in the main text:

Lemma 1. The one-step-ahead forecasts obey

$$\mathbb{E}_{i,t}[x_{t+1}] = \hat{\rho}\mathbb{E}_{i,t}[x_t] = (\hat{\rho} - \hat{\lambda})\frac{1}{1 - \hat{\lambda}\mathbb{L}}s_{i,t} = (\hat{\rho} - \hat{\lambda})\frac{1}{1 - \hat{\lambda}\mathbb{L}}\left(\frac{1}{1 - \rho\mathbb{L}}\varepsilon_t + \tau^{-\frac{1}{2}}u_{i,t}\right).$$

The corresponding forecast errors obey

$$\text{Error}_{i,t} = x_{t+1} - \mathbb{E}_{i,t}[x_{t+1}] = \frac{1 - \hat{\rho}L}{(1 - \rho L)(1 - \hat{\lambda}L)}\varepsilon_{t+1} - \frac{\hat{\rho} - \hat{\lambda}}{1 - \hat{\lambda}\mathbb{L}}\tau^{-\frac{1}{2}}u_{i,t}.$$

And finally the forecast revisions obey

$$\text{Revision}_{i,t} = \mathbb{E}_{i,t}[x_{t+1}] - \mathbb{E}_{i,t-1}[x_{t+1}] = \frac{(\hat{\rho} - \hat{\lambda})(1 - \hat{\rho}L)}{(1 - \rho L)(1 - \hat{\lambda}L)}\varepsilon_t + \frac{(\hat{\rho} - \hat{\lambda})(1 - \hat{\rho}L)}{1 - \hat{\lambda}\mathbb{L}}\tau^{-\frac{1}{2}}u_{i,t}.$$

Proof. The perceived signal process can be represented as

$$s_{i,t} = \mathbf{M}(\mathbb{L})\begin{bmatrix}\varepsilon_t \\ u_{i,t}\end{bmatrix}, \qquad \text{with} \qquad \mathbf{M}(\mathbb{L}) = \left[\frac{1}{1 - \hat{\rho}\mathbb{L}} \quad \hat{\tau}^{-\frac{1}{2}}\right].$$

Let $B(\mathbb{L})$ denote the fundamental representation of the perceived signal process,[48] which is given by

$$B(\mathbb{L}) = \hat{\tau}^{-\frac{1}{2}}\sqrt{\frac{\hat{\rho}}{\hat{\lambda}}\frac{1-\hat{\lambda}\mathbb{L}}{1-\hat{\rho}\mathbb{L}}}, \quad \text{where} \quad \hat{\lambda} = \frac{1}{2}\left(\hat{\rho} + \frac{1+\hat{\tau}}{\hat{\rho}} + \sqrt{\left(\hat{\rho} + \frac{1+\hat{\tau}}{\hat{\rho}}\right)^2 - 4}\right).$$

It is useful to note that $\hat{\lambda} < \hat{\rho}$, and $\hat{\lambda}$ is decreasing in $\hat{\tau}$. By the Wiener-Hopf prediction formula, the individual forecast about x_t is

$$\mathbb{E}_{i,t}[x_t] = \left[\frac{1}{1-\hat{\rho}\mathbb{L}}\mathbf{M}'(\mathbb{L}^{-1})B(\mathbb{L}^{-1})^{-1}\right]_+ B(\mathbb{L})^{-1}s_{i,t} = \left(1 - \frac{\hat{\lambda}}{\hat{\rho}}\right)\frac{1}{1-\hat{\lambda}\mathbb{L}}s_{i,t}.$$

Alternatively, this forecast rule can be written as

$$\mathbb{E}_{i,t}[x_t] = (1-\hat{g})\hat{\rho}\mathbb{E}_{i,t-1}[x_{t-1}] + \hat{g}s_{i,t},$$

which is a weighted average of the prior $\rho\mathbb{E}_{i,t-1}[x_{t-1}]$ and the new signal $s_{i,t}$, where the weight on the signal is the Kalman gain $\hat{g} = 1 - (\hat{\lambda}/\hat{\rho})$. In the equations above, note that only perceived $\hat{\rho}$ and $\hat{\tau}$ matter for how agents use their signals. The actual ρ and τ matter for how the signal $s_{i,t}$ evolves over time.

Proof. Accordingly, the 1-period-ahead forecast is

$$\mathbb{E}_{i,t}[x_{t+1}] = \hat{\rho}\mathbb{E}_{i,t}[x_t] = (\hat{\rho} - \hat{\lambda})\frac{1}{1-\hat{\lambda}\mathbb{L}}s_{i,t} = (\hat{\rho} - \hat{\lambda})\frac{1}{1-\hat{\lambda}\mathbb{L}}\left(\frac{1}{1-\rho\mathbb{L}}\varepsilon_t + \tau^{-\frac{1}{2}}u_{i,t}\right).$$

The individual forecast error and revision are then straightforward to obtain:

$$\text{Error}_{i,t} = x_{t+1} - \mathbb{E}_{i,t}[x_{t+1}] = \frac{1-\hat{\rho}L}{(1-\rho L)(1-\hat{\lambda}L)}\varepsilon_{t+1} - \frac{\hat{\rho} - \hat{\lambda}}{1-\hat{\lambda}L}\tau^{-\frac{1}{2}}u_{i,t},$$

$$\text{Revision}_{i,t} = \mathbb{E}_{i,t}[x_{t+1}] - \mathbb{E}_{i,t-1}[x_{t+1}] = \frac{(\hat{\rho} - \hat{\lambda})(1-\hat{\rho}L)}{(1-\rho L)(1-\hat{\lambda}L)}\varepsilon_t + \frac{(\hat{\rho} - \hat{\lambda})(1-\hat{\rho}L)}{1-\hat{\lambda}L}\tau^{-\frac{1}{2}}u_{i,t}.$$

$\square$

Proof of Proposition 1

Let $\mathcal{V}_{\text{ind}}$ denote the variance of Revision$_{i,t}$ and $\mathcal{V}_{\text{agg}}$ denote the variance of Revision$_t$. First consider the calculation of K_{CG}. We have

Cov(Error$_t$, Revision$_t$)

$$= \text{Cov}\left(\frac{1 - \hat{\rho}L}{(1 - \rho L)(1 - \hat{\lambda}L)}\varepsilon_{t+1}, \frac{(\hat{\rho} - \hat{\lambda})(1 - \hat{\rho}L)}{(1 - \rho L)(1 - \hat{\lambda}L)}\varepsilon_t\right)$$

$$= (\hat{\rho} - \hat{\lambda})\left(\frac{\hat{\lambda}}{1 - \hat{\lambda}^2} + (\rho - \hat{\rho})\frac{(1 + \hat{\lambda}^2)(1 - \rho^2) + (\hat{\lambda} + \rho)(\rho - \hat{\rho})}{(1 - \hat{\lambda}^2)(1 - \rho^2)(1 - \hat{\lambda}\rho)}\right)$$

$$= \hat{\tau}^{-1}\frac{(\hat{\rho} - \hat{\lambda})^2(1 - \hat{\lambda}\hat{\rho})}{1 - \hat{\lambda}^2} + (\rho - \hat{\rho})(\hat{\rho} - \hat{\lambda})\frac{(1 + \hat{\lambda}^2)(1 - \rho^2) + (\hat{\lambda} + \rho)(\rho - \hat{\rho})}{(1 - \hat{\lambda}^2)(1 - \rho^2)(1 - \hat{\lambda}\rho)},$$

which leads to

$$K_{\text{CG}} = \kappa_1 \hat{\tau}^{-1} - \kappa_2(\hat{\rho} - \rho),$$

where

$$\kappa_1 = \frac{1}{\mathcal{V}_{\text{agg}}}\frac{(\hat{\rho} - \hat{\lambda})^2(1 - \hat{\lambda}\hat{\rho})}{1 - \hat{\lambda}^2},$$

$$\kappa_2 = \frac{1}{\mathcal{V}_{\text{agg}}}(\hat{\rho} - \hat{\lambda})\frac{(1 + \hat{\lambda}^2)(1 - \rho^2) + (\hat{\lambda} + \rho)(\rho - \hat{\rho})}{(1 - \hat{\lambda}^2)(1 - \rho^2)(1 - \hat{\lambda}\rho)}.$$

As $1 > \hat{\rho} > \hat{\lambda} > 0$, $\kappa_1 > 0$. To show that $\kappa_2 > 0$, it is equivalent to show that $(1 + \hat{\lambda}^2)(1 - \rho^2) + (\hat{\lambda} + \rho)(\rho - \hat{\rho}) > 0$. Given that $\hat{\rho} < 1$, it follows that

$$(1 + \hat{\lambda}^2)(1 - \rho^2) + (\hat{\lambda} + \rho)(\rho - \hat{\rho}) > (1 + \hat{\lambda}^2)(1 - \rho^2) + (\hat{\lambda} + \rho)(\rho - 1)$$

$$= (1 - \rho)(1 - \hat{\lambda} + \hat{\lambda}^2(1 + \rho)) > 0.$$

Now turn to the calculation of K_{BGMS}. We have

Cov(Error$_{i,t}$, Revision$_{i,t}$)

$$= \text{Cov}\left(\frac{1 - \hat{\rho}\mathbb{L}}{(1 - \rho\mathbb{L})(1 - \hat{\lambda}\mathbb{L})}\varepsilon_{t+1}, \frac{(\hat{\rho} - \hat{\lambda})(1 - \hat{\rho}\mathbb{L})}{(1 - \rho\mathbb{L})(1 - \hat{\lambda}\mathbb{L})}\varepsilon_t\right)$$

$$+ \text{Cov}\left(-\frac{\hat{\rho} - \hat{\lambda}}{1 - \hat{\lambda}\mathbb{L}}\tau^{-\frac{1}{2}}u_{i,t}, \frac{(\hat{\rho} - \hat{\lambda})(1 - \hat{\rho}\mathbb{L})}{1 - \hat{\lambda}\mathbb{L}}\tau^{-\frac{1}{2}}u_{i,t}\right)$$

$$= -(\hat{\rho} - \hat{\lambda})\frac{\hat{\lambda}}{(1 - \hat{\lambda}^2)}\frac{\hat{\tau} - \tau}{\tau} + (\rho - \hat{\rho})(\hat{\rho} - \hat{\lambda})\frac{(1 + \hat{\lambda}^2)(1 - \rho^2) + (\hat{\lambda} + \rho)(\rho - \hat{\rho})}{(1 - \hat{\lambda}^2)(1 - \rho^2)(1 - \hat{\lambda}\rho)}.$$

It follows that

$$K_{\text{BGMS}} = -\kappa_5(\tau^{-1} - \hat{\tau}^{-1}) + \kappa_6(\rho - \hat{\rho}),$$

where κ_5 and κ_6 are

$$\kappa_5 = \frac{1}{\mathcal{V}_{\text{ind}}}(\hat{\rho} - \hat{\lambda})\frac{\hat{\lambda}}{\tau(1 - \hat{\lambda}^2)},$$

$$\kappa_6 = \frac{1}{\mathcal{V}_{\text{ind}}}(\hat{\rho} - \hat{\lambda})\frac{(1 + \hat{\lambda}^2)(1 - \rho^2) + (\hat{\lambda} + \rho)(\rho - \hat{\rho})}{(1 - \hat{\lambda}^2)(1 - \rho^2)(1 - \hat{\lambda}\rho)}.$$

Lastly, we look at K_{KW}. We have

$$\text{Cov}(\text{Error}_t, x_t) = \text{Cov}\left(\frac{1 - \hat{\rho}\mathbb{L}}{(1 - \rho\mathbb{L})(1 - \hat{\lambda}\mathbb{L})}\varepsilon_{t+1}, \frac{1}{1 - \rho\mathbb{L}}\varepsilon_t\right)$$

$$= \frac{\hat{\tau}^{-1}(\hat{\rho} - \hat{\lambda})(1 - \hat{\lambda}\hat{\rho})(1 - \rho^2) + \rho - \hat{\rho}}{(1 - \hat{\lambda}\rho)(1 - \rho^2)},$$

which leads to

$$K_{\text{KW}} = \kappa_3\hat{\tau}^{-1} - \kappa_4(\hat{\rho} - \rho),$$

where κ_3 and κ_4 are

$$\kappa_3 = \frac{\hat{\rho} - \hat{\lambda}}{1 - \rho^2}, \quad \kappa_4 = \frac{1}{(1 - \hat{\lambda}\rho)(1 - \rho^2)^2}.$$

Proof of Corollary 1

As $\hat{\tau} = \tau$ and $\hat{\rho} = \rho$, we have

$$\text{Cov}(\text{Error}_t, \text{Revision}_t) = \hat{\tau}^{-1}\frac{(\hat{\rho} - \hat{\lambda})^2(1 - \hat{\lambda}\hat{\rho})}{1 - \hat{\lambda}^2} > 0$$

$$\text{Cov}(\text{Error}_{i,t}, \text{Revision}_{i,t}) = 0 \quad \text{and} \quad \text{Cov}(\text{Error}_t, x_t) = \hat{\tau}^{-1}(\hat{\rho} - \hat{\lambda}) > 0,$$

which together imply

$$K_{\text{CG}} = \kappa_1\hat{\tau}^{-1} > 0, \quad K_{\text{BGMS}} = 0, \quad K_{\text{KW}} = \kappa_3\hat{\tau}^{-1} > 0.$$

As $\tau = \hat{\tau} \to \infty$, $\hat{\lambda} \to 0$, and it follows that

$$\kappa_1 \to \frac{\hat{\rho}^2}{\mathcal{V}_{\text{agg}}}, \quad \kappa_2 = \frac{1}{\mathcal{V}_{\text{agg}}}\hat{\rho}\frac{1 - \rho\hat{\rho}}{1 - \rho^2}, \quad \kappa_3 \to \frac{\hat{\rho}}{1 - \rho^2},$$

$$\kappa_4 = \frac{1}{(1 - \rho^2)^2}, \quad \kappa_5 \to 0, \quad \kappa_6 = \frac{1}{\mathcal{V}_{\text{agg}}}\hat{\rho}\frac{1 - \rho\hat{\rho}}{1 - \rho^2}.$$

As a result, the signs of the three regression coefficients are the same as the sign of $\rho - \hat{\rho}$.

Proof of Corollary 2

With $\hat{\rho} \leq \rho$, $K_{KW} > 0$, and therefore $\hat{\rho} > \rho$ is necessary to make $K_{KW} < 0$. With $\hat{\tau} = \infty$ and $\hat{\rho} > \rho$, both $K_{CG} < 0$ and $K_{KW} < 0$. Therefore, it is necessary to have both $\hat{\tau} < \infty$ and $\hat{\rho} > \rho$ to allow $K_{CG} > 0$ and $K_{KW} < 0$. The sufficiency part is established by the numerical example and a standard continuity argument.

Proof of Proposition 2

The law of motion of the average forecast error is given by

$$\text{Error}_t = \frac{1 - \hat{\rho}\mathbb{L}}{(1 - \rho\mathbb{L})(1 - \hat{\lambda}\mathbb{L})} \varepsilon_{t+1} = \left(\frac{\rho - \hat{\rho}}{\rho - \hat{\lambda}} \frac{1}{1 - \rho L} + \frac{\hat{\rho} - \hat{\lambda}}{\rho - \hat{\lambda}} \frac{1}{1 - \hat{\lambda}L} \right) \varepsilon_{t+1}.$$

Suppose $\rho > \hat{\rho}$, then $\rho > \hat{\lambda}$. The coefficients of the two AR(1) terms are both positive, and the responses are therefore all positive.

Suppose $\rho < \hat{\rho}$. Consider the following continuous time version of the response

$$g(t) = \frac{\rho - \hat{\rho}}{\rho - \hat{\lambda}} \rho^t + \frac{\hat{\rho} - \hat{\lambda}}{\rho - \hat{\lambda}} \hat{\lambda}^t,$$

and $g(t) = \zeta_k$ when $t = k \in \{0, 1, \dots \}$. Note that (i) $g(t)$ is negative when t is large enough (no matter $\rho > \hat{\lambda}$ or $\rho < \hat{\lambda}$); (ii) when $t = 0$, $g(0) = 1 > 0$; (iii) there is at most one root of $g(t)$. As a result, $\{\zeta_k\}_{k=1}^{\infty}$ eventually stay negative, but they might be positive or negative for k small enough.

The root of $g(t)$ is

$$k_{IRF} = \frac{\log(\hat{\rho} - \rho) - \log(\hat{\rho} - \hat{\lambda})}{\log \hat{\lambda} - \log \rho}.$$

To have $\{\zeta_k\}_{k=1}^{\infty}$ switch signs, it is necessary that $g(1) > 0$ and $\hat{\rho} > \rho$, which correspond to $g(1) = \rho + \hat{\lambda} - \hat{\rho} > 0$ and $\hat{\rho} > \rho$, or

$$\hat{\lambda} > \hat{\rho} - \rho \quad \text{and} \quad \hat{\rho} > \rho.$$

Finally, note that k_{IRF} is decreasing in $\hat{\rho}$ for given $\hat{\lambda}$, which verifies the claim in the main text that the magnitude of k_{IRF} reveals information about the relative importance of the two mechanisms.[49]

When $\hat{\rho} > \rho$ but $\hat{\lambda} > \hat{\rho} - \rho$, $g(1) < 0$ and the sequences $\{\varsigma_k\}_{k=1}^{\infty}$ stay negative all the time.

Proof of Corollary 3

Follows directly from proposition 2.

Proof of Proposition 3

Aggregate consumption satisfies the fixed-point restriction

$$c_t = \sum_{k=0}^{\infty}\beta^k\overline{\mathbb{E}}_t[\xi_{t+k}] + (1 - \beta)\sum_{k=0}^{\infty}\beta^k\overline{\mathbb{E}}_t[c_{t+k+1}],$$

where we have used the market clearing condition $y_t = c_t$, and the assumption that agents observe y_t but do not extract information from it. This aggregate outcome is the outcome of the following beauty-contest game

$$c_{i,t} = \mathbb{E}_{i,t}[\xi_t] + \beta\mathbb{E}_{i,t}[c_{i,t+1}] + (1 - \beta)\mathbb{E}_{i,t}[c_{t+1}].$$

Denote the agent's equilibrium policy function as

$$c_{i,t} = h(\mathbb{L})s_{i,t}$$

for some lag polynomial $h(\mathbb{L})$. The actual law of motion of aggregate outcome can then be expressed as follows

$$c_t = h(\mathbb{L})\xi_t = \frac{h(\mathbb{L})}{1 - \rho\mathbb{L}}\varepsilon_t.$$

However, the perceived law of motion by consumers is

$$c_t = \frac{h(\mathbb{L})}{1 - \hat{\rho}\mathbb{L}}\varepsilon_t.$$

As in the case where the outcome is given by the exogenous AR(1) process, the forecast about the fundamental is

$$\mathbb{E}_{i,t}[\xi_t] = \left(1 - \frac{\hat{\lambda}}{\hat{\rho}}\right)\frac{1}{1 - \hat{\lambda}\mathbb{L}}s_{i,t} \equiv G_1(\mathbb{L})s_{i,t}.$$

Consider the forecast of the future own and average actions. The perceived law of motion of $c_{i,t+1}$ and c_{t+1} are

$$c_{t+1} = \begin{bmatrix} \dfrac{h(\mathbb{L})}{\mathbb{L}(1 - \hat{\rho}\mathbb{L})} & 0 \end{bmatrix} \begin{bmatrix} \varepsilon_t \\ u_{i,t} \end{bmatrix}, \quad c_{i,t+1} - c_{t+1} = \begin{bmatrix} 0 & \hat{\tau}^{-\frac{1}{2}}\dfrac{h(\mathbb{L})}{\mathbb{L}} \end{bmatrix} \begin{bmatrix} \varepsilon_t \\ u_{i,t} \end{bmatrix},$$

and the forecasts are

$$\mathbb{E}_{i,t}[c_{t+1}] = G_2(\mathbb{L})s_{i,t}, \quad G_2(\mathbb{L}) \equiv \frac{\hat{\lambda}}{\hat{\rho}}\hat{\tau}\left(\frac{h(\mathbb{L})}{(1 - \hat{\lambda}\mathbb{L})(\mathbb{L} - \hat{\lambda})} - \frac{h(\hat{\lambda})(1 - \hat{\rho}\mathbb{L})}{(1 - \hat{\rho}\hat{\lambda})(\mathbb{L} - \hat{\lambda})(1 - \hat{\lambda}\mathbb{L})} \right),$$

$$\mathbb{E}_{i,t}[c_{i,t+1} - c_{t+1}] = G_3(\mathbb{L})s_{i,t}, \quad G_3(\mathbb{L}) \equiv \frac{\hat{\lambda}}{\hat{\rho}}\left(\frac{h(\mathbb{L})(\mathbb{L} - \hat{\rho})}{\mathbb{L}(\mathbb{L} - \hat{\lambda})} - \frac{h(\hat{\lambda})(\hat{\lambda} - \hat{\rho})}{\hat{\lambda}(\mathbb{L} - \hat{\lambda})} - \frac{\hat{\rho}}{\hat{\lambda}}\frac{h(0)}{\mathbb{L}} \right)\frac{1 - \hat{\rho}\mathbb{L}}{1 - \hat{\lambda}\mathbb{L}}.$$

Recall that fixed-point problem that characterizes the equilibrium is

$$c_{i,t} = \mathbb{E}_{i,t}[\xi_t] + \beta\mathbb{E}_{i,t}[c_{i,t+1}] + (1 - \beta)\mathbb{E}_{i,t}[c_{t+1}].$$

We can replace the left-hand side with $h(\mathbb{L})s_{i,t}$. Using the results derived above, on the other hand, we can replace the right-hand side with $[G_1(\mathbb{L}) + G_2(\mathbb{L}) + \beta G_3(\mathbb{L})]s_{i,t}$. It follows that in equilibrium

$$h(\mathbb{L}) = G_1(\mathbb{L}) + G_2(\mathbb{L}) + \beta G_3(\mathbb{L}).$$

Equivalently, we need to find an analytic function $h(z)$ that solves

$$h(z) = \frac{\hat{\lambda}}{\hat{\rho}}\hat{\tau}\frac{1}{1 - \hat{\rho}\hat{\lambda}}\frac{1}{1 - \hat{\lambda}z} + \frac{\hat{\lambda}}{\hat{\rho}}\hat{\tau}\left(\frac{h(z)}{(1 - \hat{\lambda}z)(z - \hat{\lambda})} - \frac{h(\hat{\lambda})(1 - \hat{\rho}z)}{(1 - \hat{\rho}\hat{\lambda})(z - \hat{\lambda})(1 - \hat{\lambda}z)} \right)$$

$$+ \beta\frac{\hat{\lambda}}{\hat{\rho}}\left(\frac{h(z)(z - \hat{\rho})}{z(z - \hat{\lambda})} - \frac{h(\hat{\lambda})(\hat{\lambda} - \hat{\rho})}{\hat{\lambda}(z - \hat{\lambda})} - \frac{\hat{\rho}}{\hat{\lambda}}\frac{h(0)}{z} \right)\frac{1 - \hat{\rho}z}{1 - \hat{\lambda}z},$$

which can be transformed as

$$\tilde{C}(z)h(z) = d(z; h(\hat{\lambda}), h(0))$$

where

$$\tilde{C}(z) \equiv z(1 - \hat{\lambda}z)(z - \hat{\lambda}) - \frac{\hat{\lambda}}{\hat{\rho}}\{\beta(z - \hat{\rho})(1 - \hat{\rho}z) + \hat{\tau}z\}$$

$$d(z; h(\hat{\lambda}), h(0)) \equiv \frac{\hat{\lambda}}{\hat{\rho}}\hat{\tau}\frac{1}{1 - \hat{\rho}\hat{\lambda}}z(z - \hat{\lambda}) - \frac{1}{\hat{\rho}}\left(\hat{\tau}\frac{\hat{\lambda}}{1 - \hat{\rho}\hat{\lambda}} + \beta(\hat{\lambda} - \hat{\rho}) \right)z(1 - \hat{\rho}z)h(\hat{\lambda})$$

$$- \beta(z - \hat{\lambda})(1 - \hat{\rho}z)h(0).$$

Note that $\tilde{C}(z)$ is a cubic equation and therefore contains three roots. We will verify later that there are two inside roots and one outside root. To make sure that $h(z)$ is an analytic function, we choose $h(0)$ and $h(\hat{\lambda})$ so that the two roots of $d(z; h(\hat{\lambda}), h(0))$ are the same as the two inside roots of $\tilde{C}(z)$. This pins down the constants $\{h(0), h(\hat{\lambda})\}$, and therefore the policy function $h(\mathbb{L})$ is

$$h(\mathbb{L}) = \left(1 - \frac{\vartheta}{\hat{\rho}}\right)\frac{1}{1 - \hat{\rho}}\frac{1}{1 - \vartheta\mathbb{L}},$$

where ϑ^{-1} is the root of $\tilde{C}(z)$ outside the unit circle.

Now we verify that $\tilde{C}(z)$ has two inside roots and one outside root. $\tilde{C}(z)$ can be rewritten as $\hat{\lambda}C(z)$ where

$$C(z) = -z^3 + \left(\hat{\rho} + \frac{1}{\hat{\rho}} + \frac{1}{\hat{\rho}}\hat{\tau} + \beta\right)z^2 - \left(1 + \beta\left(\hat{\rho} + \frac{1}{\hat{\rho}}\right) + \frac{1}{\hat{\rho}}\hat{\tau}\right)z + \beta,$$

$$= -z^3 + \left(\hat{\rho} + \frac{1}{\hat{\rho}} + \frac{1}{\hat{\rho}}\hat{\tau} + 1 - \text{mpc}\right)z^2$$

$$- \left(1 + (1 - \text{mpc})\left(\hat{\rho} + \frac{1}{\hat{\rho}}\right) + \frac{1}{\hat{\rho}}\hat{\tau}\right)z + 1 - \text{mpc}.$$

With the assumption that $1 > \text{mpc} > 0$, it is straightforward to verify that the following properties hold:

$$C(0) = 1 - \text{mpc} > 0, \quad C(\hat{\lambda}) = -\text{mpc}\frac{\hat{\tau}}{\hat{\rho}} < 0, \quad C(1) = \text{mpc}\left(\frac{1}{\hat{\rho}} + \hat{\rho} - 2\right) > 0.$$

Therefore, the three roots are all real, two of them are between 0 and 1, and the third one, ϑ^{-1}, is larger than 1.

To show that ϑ is less than $\hat{\rho}$, it is sufficient to show that

$$C\left(\frac{1}{\hat{\rho}}\right) = \frac{\hat{\tau}(1 - \hat{\rho})}{\hat{\rho}^3} > 0.$$

Because $C(\vartheta^{-1}) = 0$, it has to be that ϑ^{-1} is larger than $\hat{\rho}^{-1}$, or $\vartheta < \hat{\rho}$. Similarly, to show that ϑ is larger than $\hat{\lambda}$, it is sufficient to show that

$$C\left(\frac{1}{\hat{\lambda}}\right) = -\frac{\hat{\tau}(1 - \text{mpc})\text{mpc}}{\hat{\rho}\hat{\lambda}^2} < 0.$$

Therefore, it has to be that $\vartheta > \hat{\lambda}$. In the proof of the properties of the expectations, we will utilize the fact that $\vartheta \in (\hat{\lambda}, \hat{\rho})$.

In Angeletos and Huo (2020), the equilibrium policy rule is derived under $\rho = \hat{\rho}$ and $\tau = \hat{\tau}$. In the derivation above, note that $h(\mathbb{L})$ does not depend on ρ nor τ. The actual law of motion of $y_t = c_t$ will depend on ρ:

$$y_t = \frac{1}{1-\hat{\rho}} \left(1 - \frac{\vartheta}{\hat{\rho}}\right) \frac{1}{1-\vartheta\mathbb{L}} \frac{1}{1-\rho\mathbb{L}} \varepsilon_t.$$

On the other hand, the frictionless case is given by

$$y_t^* = \frac{1}{1-\rho} \frac{1}{1-\rho\mathbb{L}} \varepsilon_t.$$

Combining these two leads to

$$y_t = \left(1 - \frac{\vartheta}{\hat{\rho}}\right) \left(1 + \frac{\hat{\rho}-\rho}{1-\hat{\rho}}\right) \left(\frac{1}{1-\vartheta\mathbb{L}}\right) y_t^*.$$

Turn to the forecast of the future outcome. By the Wiener-Hopf prediction formula, the individual forecast is

$$\mathbb{E}_{i,t}[y_{t+1}] = \left[\frac{1}{1-\hat{\rho}} \left(1 - \frac{\vartheta}{\hat{\rho}}\right) \frac{1}{1-\vartheta L} \frac{1}{1-\rho\mathbb{L}} \mathbf{M}'(\mathbb{L}^{-1}) B(\mathbb{L}^{-1})^{-1}\right]_+ B(\mathbb{L})^{-1} s_{i,t},$$

$$= \frac{1}{1-\hat{\rho}} \left(1 - \frac{\vartheta}{\hat{\rho}}\right) \left(1 - \frac{\hat{\lambda}}{\hat{\rho}}\right) \frac{1}{1-\vartheta\hat{\lambda}} \frac{\hat{\rho}+\vartheta-\hat{\rho}\vartheta(\mathbb{L}+\hat{\lambda})}{(1-\vartheta\mathbb{L})(1-\hat{\lambda}\mathbb{L})} s_{i,t},$$

and the average forecast is

$$\overline{\mathbb{E}}_t[y_{t+1}] = \left(1 - \frac{\hat{\lambda}}{\hat{\rho}}\right) \frac{1}{1-\vartheta\hat{\lambda}} \frac{\hat{\rho}+\vartheta-\hat{\rho}\vartheta(\mathbb{L}+\hat{\lambda})}{(1-\vartheta\mathbb{L})(1-\hat{\lambda}\mathbb{L})} \left(1 - \frac{\vartheta}{\hat{\rho}}\right) \left(1 + \frac{\hat{\rho}-\rho}{1-\hat{\rho}}\right) y_t^*.$$

Proof of Proposition 4

Denote $\kappa \equiv [1 - (\vartheta/\hat{\rho})][1 + (\hat{\rho}-\rho)/(1-\hat{\rho})][1/(1-\rho)]$. If $c_t = \kappa[1/(1-\vartheta\mathbb{L})(1-\rho\mathbb{L})]\varepsilon_t$ is the perfect-information outcome, it has to be that

$$c_t = \xi_t + \omega_f \mathbb{E}_t^*[c_{t+1}] + \omega_b c_{t-1}$$

$$= \frac{1}{1-\rho\mathbb{L}} + \omega_f \kappa \frac{\vartheta+\rho-\vartheta\rho\mathbb{L}}{(1-\vartheta\mathbb{L})(1-\rho\mathbb{L})} + \omega_b \kappa \frac{\mathbb{L}}{(1-\vartheta\mathbb{L})(1-\rho\mathbb{L})},$$

where the right-hand side is simply the perfect information expectation of the behavioral equilibrium. This leads to

$$\omega_f = \frac{\hat{\rho}^2 - \vartheta}{(\vartheta + \rho)(\hat{\rho} - \vartheta)} \quad \text{and} \quad \omega_b = \frac{\vartheta(\rho(\hat{\rho} - \vartheta) + \vartheta\hat{\rho}(1 - \hat{\rho}))}{(\vartheta + \rho)(\hat{\rho} - \vartheta)}.$$

In the absence of informational friction ($\hat{\tau} \to \infty$), we have $\vartheta = 0$ and therefore $\omega_b = 0$ and $\omega_f = \hat{\rho}/\rho$. In its presence ($\hat{\tau} < \infty$), we have that $\vartheta > 0$ and $\omega_b > 0$ necessarily. When $\hat{\rho} < \rho$, we have

$$\omega_f = \frac{\hat{\rho}^2 - \vartheta}{(\vartheta + \rho)(\hat{\rho} - \vartheta)} < \frac{\hat{\rho}^2 - \vartheta}{(\vartheta + \hat{\rho})(\hat{\rho} - \vartheta)} < \frac{\hat{\rho}^2 - \vartheta^2}{(\vartheta + \hat{\rho})(\hat{\rho} - \vartheta)} = 1.$$

Note that ϑ is decreasing in $\hat{\tau}$. With a very high level of informational friction ($\hat{\tau} \to 0$), we have $\vartheta = \hat{\rho}$. Particularly when $\vartheta \in (\hat{\rho}^2, \hat{\rho})$, ω_f is negative. Therefore, to show that $\omega_f < 1$ when $\hat{\tau}$ is small, it is sufficient to show that ω_f is decreasing in ϑ. Note that

$$\frac{\partial \omega_f}{\partial \vartheta} = \frac{\rho(\hat{\rho}^2 - \hat{\rho}) - \vartheta^2 - \hat{\rho}^3 + 2\hat{\rho}^2\vartheta}{(\rho + \vartheta)^2(\hat{\rho} - \vartheta)^2},$$

where the numerator is linear in ρ with a negative slope. To verify $\partial \omega_f / \partial \vartheta < 0$, we only need to show that the numerator is negative when $\rho = 0$, or $g(\vartheta) \equiv -\vartheta^2 - \hat{\rho}^3 + 2\hat{\rho}^2\vartheta < 0$. Note that $g(\vartheta)$ is maximized at $\vartheta = \hat{\rho}^2$, and $g(\hat{\rho}^2) = \hat{\rho}^4 - \hat{\rho}^3 < 0$, which completes the proof.

Proof of Proposition 5

Properties of average forecast errors. The average forecast error is given by

$$y_{t+1} - \overline{\mathbb{E}}_t[y_{t+1}] = \frac{1}{1 - \hat{\rho}}\left(1 - \frac{\vartheta}{\hat{\rho}}\right)\frac{1}{1 - \vartheta\mathbb{L}}\xi_{t+1}$$

$$- \frac{1}{1 - \hat{\rho}}\left(1 - \frac{\vartheta}{\hat{\rho}}\right)\left(1 - \frac{\hat{\lambda}}{\hat{\rho}}\right)\frac{1}{1 - \vartheta\hat{\lambda}}\frac{\hat{\rho} + \vartheta - \hat{\rho}\vartheta(\mathbb{L} + \hat{\lambda})}{(1 - \vartheta\mathbb{L})(1 - \hat{\lambda}\mathbb{L})}\xi_t$$

$$= \frac{1}{1 - \hat{\rho}}\left(1 - \frac{\vartheta}{\hat{\rho}}\right)\left(\frac{\omega_1}{1 - \vartheta\mathbb{L}} + \frac{\omega_2}{1 - \rho\mathbb{L}} + \frac{\omega_3}{1 - \hat{\lambda}\mathbb{L}}\right)\varepsilon_{t+1},$$

where

$$\omega_1 = \frac{\hat{\lambda}\vartheta(\hat{\rho} - \vartheta)(1 - \hat{\rho}\vartheta)}{\hat{\rho}(\vartheta - \hat{\lambda})(1 - \hat{\lambda}\vartheta)(\rho - \vartheta)} \qquad \omega_2 = \frac{(\rho - \hat{\rho})(\hat{\lambda}\vartheta(1 - \rho\hat{\rho}) + \hat{\rho}(\rho - \vartheta))}{\hat{\rho}(\rho - \hat{\lambda})(1 - \hat{\lambda}\vartheta)(\rho - \vartheta)},$$

$$\omega_3 = 1 - \omega_1 - \omega_2.$$

We use $\{\varsigma_k\}_{k=0}^{\infty}$ to denote the IRF. The following properties hold:

1. When $\rho > \hat{\rho}$, $\varsigma_k > 0$ for all $k \geq 0$.
   Note that if $\rho > \hat{\rho}$, it is also the case that $\rho > \hat{\rho} > \vartheta > \hat{\lambda}$. As a result, $\omega_1 > 0$ and $\omega_2 > 0$. Also note that $\varsigma_k = \omega_1 \vartheta^k + \omega_2 \rho^k + \omega_3 \hat{\lambda}^k$. It follows that

$$\varsigma_k > (\omega_1 + \omega_2)\vartheta^k + \omega_3 \hat{\lambda}^k = (\omega_1 + \omega_2)(\vartheta^k - \hat{\lambda}^k) + \hat{\lambda}^k > 0.$$

2. When $\rho < \hat{\rho}$, $\varsigma_k < 0$ for k large enough.
   When k large enough, the sign of ς_k will be the same as the sign of ω_1 if $\vartheta > \rho$, and it will be the same as the sign of ω_2 if $\vartheta < \rho$. If $\vartheta > \rho$, $\omega_1 < 0$. If $\vartheta < \rho$, $\omega_2 < 0$. Therefore, the forecast error is negative in the long run.

3. When $\rho < \hat{\rho}$, there exists a threshold $\bar{\lambda}$ such that only if $\hat{\lambda} > \bar{\lambda}$, $\varsigma_1 > 0$. That is, the forecast error does not immediately switch to negative only if learning is slow enough.
   A straightforward calculation yields

$$\varsigma_1 = \omega_1 \vartheta + \omega_2 \rho + \omega_3 \hat{\lambda} = \frac{D(\hat{\lambda})}{\hat{\rho}(1 - \hat{\lambda}\vartheta)}, \quad \text{where}$$

$$D(\hat{\lambda}) = \frac{(-\hat{\rho}\vartheta)\hat{\lambda}^2 + (\hat{\rho}^2\vartheta - \hat{\rho}\vartheta^2 - \rho\hat{\rho}\vartheta + \hat{\rho} + \vartheta)\hat{\lambda} - \hat{\rho}^2 + \rho\hat{\rho}}{\hat{\rho}(1 - \hat{\lambda}\vartheta)}.$$

The sign of ς_1 is the same as the numerator $D(\hat{\lambda})$. Because $D(0) = \hat{\rho}(\rho - \hat{\rho}) < 0$, and $D(\hat{\rho}) = \hat{\rho}(\rho + \vartheta)(1 - \hat{\rho}\vartheta) > 0$, there exists $\bar{\lambda} \in (0, \hat{\rho})$ such that $D(\hat{\lambda}) > 0$ only if $\hat{\lambda} > \bar{\lambda}$.

Regression coefficients. We now study the theoretical counterparts of K_{CG}, K_{BGMS}, and K_{KW}.

Case 1: $\tau = \hat{\tau}$ and $\rho = \hat{\rho}$. We have already proved that the IRF of the forecast error is always positive. Because the IRF of the outcome is always positive, K_{KW} has to be positive. By individual rationality, K_{BGMS} has to be zero. What remains is to prove that K_{CG} is positive.

As the outcome follows an AR(2) process, the individual forecast error and forecast revision are given by

$$y_{t+1} - \mathbb{E}_{i,t}[y_{t+1}] = \frac{1}{1-\rho}\left(1 - \frac{\vartheta}{\rho}\right)(g_1^\varepsilon(\mathbb{L})\varepsilon_{t+1} + g_1^u(\mathbb{L})u_{i,t}),$$

$$\mathbb{E}_{i,t}[y_{t+1}] - \mathbb{E}_{i,t-1}[y_{t+1}] = \frac{1}{1-\rho}\left(1 - \frac{\vartheta}{\rho}\right)(g_2^\varepsilon(\mathbb{L})\varepsilon_t + g_2^u(\mathbb{L})u_{i,t}),$$

where

$$g_1^\varepsilon(\mathbb{L}) = \frac{1}{(1 - \vartheta\mathbb{L})(1 - \rho\mathbb{L})} - \left(1 - \frac{\hat{\lambda}}{\rho}\right)\frac{1}{1 - \vartheta\hat{\lambda}}\frac{\rho + \vartheta - \rho\vartheta(\mathbb{L} + \hat{\lambda})}{(1 - \vartheta\mathbb{L})(1 - \hat{\lambda}\mathbb{L})(1 - \rho\mathbb{L})}\mathbb{L},$$

$$g_2^\varepsilon(\mathbb{L}) = \left(1 - \frac{\hat{\lambda}}{\rho}\right)\frac{1}{1 - \vartheta\hat{\lambda}}\left(\frac{\rho + \vartheta - \rho\vartheta(\mathbb{L} + \hat{\lambda})}{(1 - \vartheta\mathbb{L})(1 - \hat{\lambda}\mathbb{L})(1 - \rho\mathbb{L})}(1 - (\vartheta + \rho)\mathbb{L})\right.$$
$$\left. + \frac{\rho\vartheta(1 - \rho\vartheta\hat{\lambda}\mathbb{L})}{(1 - \vartheta\mathbb{L})(1 - \hat{\lambda}\mathbb{L})(1 - \rho\mathbb{L})}\mathbb{L}\right),$$

$$g_1^u(\mathbb{L}) = -\left(1 - \frac{\hat{\lambda}}{\rho}\right)\frac{1}{1 - \vartheta\hat{\lambda}}\frac{\rho + \vartheta - \rho\vartheta(\mathbb{L} + \hat{\lambda})}{(1 - \vartheta\mathbb{L})(1 - \hat{\lambda}\mathbb{L})}\tau^{-1},$$

$$g_2^u(\mathbb{L}) = \left(1 - \frac{\hat{\lambda}}{\rho}\right)\frac{1}{1 - \vartheta\hat{\lambda}}\left(\frac{\rho + \vartheta - \rho\vartheta(\mathbb{L} + \hat{\lambda})}{(1 - \vartheta\mathbb{L})(1 - \hat{\lambda}\mathbb{L})}(1 - (\vartheta + \rho)\mathbb{L})\right.$$
$$\left. + \frac{\rho\vartheta(1 - \rho\vartheta\hat{\lambda}\mathbb{L})}{(1 - \vartheta\mathbb{L})(1 - \hat{\lambda}\mathbb{L})}\mathbb{L}\right)\tau^{-1}.$$

The covariance between individual forecast error and individual forecast revision is

$$\text{Cov}(\text{Error}_{i,t}, \text{Revision}_{i,t}) = \left(\frac{1}{1-\rho}\left(1 - \frac{\vartheta}{\rho}\right)\right)^2(\text{Cov}(g_1^\varepsilon(\mathbb{L})\varepsilon_{t+1}, g_2^\varepsilon(\mathbb{L})\varepsilon_t)$$
$$+ \text{Cov}(g_1^u(\mathbb{L})u_{i,t}, g_2^u(\mathbb{L})u_{i,t})),$$

and a long but straightforward calculation yields the following expression:

$$\text{Cov}(g_1^u(\mathbb{L})u_{i,t}, g_2^u(\mathbb{L})u_{i,t}) = -\tau^{-1}\left(\left(1 - \frac{\hat{\lambda}}{\rho}\right)\frac{1}{1 - \vartheta\hat{\lambda}}\right)^2\frac{1 - \hat{\lambda}\rho}{(1 - \hat{\lambda}\vartheta)(1 - \hat{\lambda}^2)}\Delta,$$

where

$$\Delta \equiv (\vartheta^3\hat{\lambda}(1 - \hat{\lambda}^2) - 3\vartheta\hat{\lambda}(1 - \vartheta\hat{\lambda}) + (1 - \vartheta^2))\rho^2 - (\vartheta^3(1 - \hat{\lambda}^2) + \vartheta(3\vartheta\hat{\lambda} - 2))\rho + \vartheta^2.$$

With $\tau = \hat{\tau}$ and $\rho = \hat{\rho}$, agents are rational and $K_{\text{BGMS}} = 0$. That is, $\text{Cov}(\text{Error}_{i,t}, \text{Revision}_{i,t}) = 0$. Let us assume momentarily that $\Delta > 0$. It follows that

$$\text{Cov}(\text{Error}_t, \text{Revision}_t) = \left(\frac{1}{1-\rho}\left(1-\frac{\vartheta}{\rho}\right)\right)^2 \text{Cov}(g_1^\varepsilon(\mathbb{L})\varepsilon_{t+1}, g_2^\varepsilon(\mathbb{L})\varepsilon_t)$$

$$= -\left(\frac{1}{1-\rho}\left(1-\frac{\vartheta}{\rho}\right)\right)^2 \text{Cov}(g_1^u(\mathbb{L})u_{i,t}, g_2^u(\mathbb{L})u_{i,t}) > 0,$$

which implies that $K_{CG} > 0$.

The argument is completed by the lemma below, which verifies that $\Delta > 0$ by mapping ρ to x, ϑ to y, and λ to z.

Lemma. When $x, y, z \in (0, 1)$, the following inequality holds

$$(y^3 z(1 - z^2) - 3yz(1 - yz) + (1 - y^2))x^2 - (y^3(1 - z^2) + y(3yz - 2))x + y^2 > 0.$$

Proof. Recast the left-hand side of the above inequality as a quadratic in x:

$$C(x) \equiv (y^3 z(1 - z^2) - 3yz(1 - yz) + (1 - y^2))x^2 - (y^3(1 - z^2) + y(3yz - 2))x + y^2.$$

This has two real roots, $x = x_1$ and $x = x_2$, given by

$$x_1 = -\frac{y}{1 - yz} \qquad \text{and} \qquad x_2 = -\frac{y}{y^2 z^2 - 2yz - y^2 + 1}.$$

Clearly, given the assumption that $y, z \in (0, 1)$, x_1 is negative and $C(0) = y^2 > 0$. If x_2 is negative, then $C(x)$ is positive when $x \in (0, 1)$. If x_2 is positive, to guarantee that $C(x)$ is positive when $x \in (0, 1)$, we need to show that $x_2 > 1$, which is equivalent to show that

$$y^2 z^2 - 2yz + (y - y^2 + 1) > 0.$$

Define the following quadratic equation in z:

$$D(z) = y^2 z^2 - 2yz + (y - y^2 + 1).$$

Its discriminant is $-4y^3(1 - y)$, which is negative given that $y \in (0, 1)$. Therefore, $D(z)$ is always positive, which in turn verifies that $x_2 > 1$. $\qquad \square$

Case 2: $\tau = \hat{\tau} = \infty$ **and** $\rho \neq \hat{\rho}$. If $\hat{\tau} = \tau = \infty$, then $\hat{\lambda} = \vartheta = 0$. In this case, all agents receive the same signal, and there is no distinction between $\mathbb{E}_{i,t}[\cdot]$ and $\overline{\mathbb{E}}_t[\cdot]$. It follows that $K_{CG} = K_{BGMS}$.

To derive the K_{BGMS}, note that

$$y_{t+1} - \mathbb{E}_{i,t}[y_{t+1}] = \frac{1}{1-\hat{\rho}}(\varepsilon_{t+1} + (\rho - \hat{\rho})y_t)$$

$$\mathbb{E}_{i,t}[y_{t+1}] - \mathbb{E}_{i,t-1}[y_{t+1}] = \frac{1}{1-\hat{\rho}}\hat{\rho}(y_t - \hat{\rho}y_{t-1})$$

It follows that

$$K_{BGMS} = \frac{\hat{\rho}(1 - \rho\hat{\rho})(\rho - \hat{\rho})}{(\hat{\rho}^2 + \hat{\rho}^4 - 2\rho\hat{\rho}^3)}.$$

Clearly, the sign of K_{BGMS} is the same as the sign of $\rho - \hat{\rho}$. The sequence of the forecast error IRF $\{\varsigma_k\}_{k=1}^{\infty}$ is given by

$$\varsigma_k = \frac{1}{1-\hat{\rho}}\rho^{k-1}(\rho - \hat{\rho}),$$

which are either all positive or all negative. Because the IRF of the outcome is always positive, the sign of K_{KW} is the same as $\rho - \hat{\rho}$.

Case 3: $0 < \hat{\tau} < \infty$ **and** $\hat{\rho} > \rho > 0$. With $\hat{\tau} = \infty$, the signs of $K_{CG} > 0$ and $K_{KW} < 0$ are always the same as $\rho - \hat{\rho}$. Therefore, $0 < \hat{\tau} < \infty$ is necessary to allow $K_{CG} > 0$ and $K_{KW} < 0$.

With $\hat{\rho} \leq \rho$, the average forecast error is always positive, the IRF of the forecast error is always positive. Together with the fact that the IRF of the outcome is always positive, we have $K_{KW} > 0$. Therefore, $\hat{\rho} > \rho$ is necessary to allow $K_{KW} < 0$.

Proofs of Proposition 6 and Corollary 4

We first consider the case with "higher-order doubts." The recursive formulation of individual consumer i's consumption choice is

$$c_{i,t} = \mathbb{E}_t[\xi_t] + \beta\mathbb{E}_t[c_{i,t+1}] + (1 - \beta)\mathbb{E}_t[c_{t+1}].$$

As ξ_t is perfectly observed by consumer i, we guess the policy function is

$$c_{i,t} = a\xi_t,$$

for some constant a.

Under the assumption that agent i believes that other agents observe the fundamental shock with probability q, it follows that

$$\mathbb{E}_{i,t}[c_{i,t+1}] = \mathbb{E}_{i,t}[a\xi_{t+1}] = a\rho\xi_t, \quad \mathbb{E}_{i,t}[\overline{\mathbb{E}}_t[\xi_t]] = q\xi_t, \quad \mathbb{E}_{i,t}[c_{t+1}] = \mathbb{E}_{i,t}[\overline{\mathbb{E}}_t[a\xi_{t+1}]] = aq\rho\xi_t.$$

Substituting these expectations into consumers' optimal response leads to

$$a\xi_t = \xi_t + \beta a\rho\xi_t + (1-\beta)aq\rho\xi_t,$$

which further verifies our guess by setting the constant a as

$$a = \frac{1}{1 - (\beta\rho + (1-\beta)q\rho)} < \frac{1}{1-\rho}.$$

In the economy without higher-order doubts but with misperceived $\hat{\rho}$, the aggregate outcome is

$$c_t = \frac{1}{1-\hat{\rho}}\xi_t.$$

The outcomes in the two economies are observationally equivalent iff

$$\frac{1}{1-\hat{\rho}} = \frac{1}{1 - (\beta\rho + (1-\beta)q\rho)} \quad \rightarrow \quad \hat{\rho} = \rho - (1-\beta)\rho(1-q) < \rho.$$

In terms of forecasts, in the economy with higher-order doubts,

$$\mathbb{E}_{i,t}[c_{t+1}] = \overline{\mathbb{E}}_t[c_{t+1}] = q\mathbb{E}_t^*[c_{t+1}],$$

where $\mathbb{E}_t^*[\cdot]$ is the perfect-information rational expectation operator.

Next, we consider the level-k thinking. The agents are assumed to observe the fundamental and to have the correct prior about its process but a misspecified prior about the behavior of others: They are "level-k thinkers" for some finite integer $k \geq 0$. Level-0 agents are assumed to play $c_t = c_t^0 \equiv 0$, for all t and for all ξ^t. Level-1 agents believe that other agents are level 0. They therefore play $c_t = c_t^1$, where c_t^1 is given by the solution to

$$c_t^1 = \xi_t + \beta\mathbb{E}_t[c_{t+1}^1].$$

Level-2 agents believe that other agents are level 1. They therefore choose $c_t = c_t^2$, where c_t^2 is given by the solution to

$$c_t^2 = \xi_t + \beta\mathbb{E}_t[c_{t+1}^2] + (1-\beta)\mathbb{E}_t[c_{t+1}^1].$$

Similarly, the aggregate outcome for level-k agents when $k > 0$ satisfies

$$c_t^k = \xi_t + \beta \mathbb{E}_t[c_{t+1}^k] + (1 - \beta)\mathbb{E}_t[c_{t+1}^{k-1}].$$

We proceed by a guess-and-verify approach. Suppose that $c_t^k = a_k \xi_t$. Then for $k > 0$, a_k has the following recursive structure

$$a_k = 1 + \beta \rho a_k + (1 - \beta)\rho a_{k-1}.$$

Using the fact $g_0 = 0$, we have for $k > 0$,

$$a_k = \frac{1}{1 - \rho}\left(1 - \left(\frac{(1 - \beta)\rho}{1 - \beta\rho}\right)^k\right),$$

which has proved the conjecture.

Compared with the economy with misperceived $\hat{\rho}$, the aggregate outcomes are equivalent iff

$$\frac{1}{1 - \hat{\rho}} = \frac{1}{1 - \rho}\left(1 - \left(\frac{(1 - \beta)\rho}{1 - \beta\rho}\right)^k\right).$$

Because $(1 - [(1 - \beta)\rho/(1 - \beta\rho)]^k) < 1$, we have $\hat{\rho} < \rho$. In terms of the forecast, in the level-k economy,

$$\mathbb{E}_{i,t}[c_{t+1}] = \overline{\mathbb{E}}_t[c_{t+1}] = a_{k-1}\rho\xi_t = \frac{a_{k-1}}{a_k}\mathbb{E}_t^*[c_{t+1}],$$

where $a_{k-1}/a_k < 1$.

Lastly, consider the cognitive discounting economy. We still proceed by a guess-and-verify approach. Suppose that the actual law of motion of c_t is

$$c_t = Rc_{t-1} + D\varepsilon_t,$$

and the perceived law of motion is

$$c_t = mRc_{t-1} + D\varepsilon_t.$$

Meanwhile, the perceived law of motion of ξ_t is

$$\xi_t = m\rho\xi_{t-} + \varepsilon_t.$$

Recall that the aggregate outcome is given by

$$c_t = \sum_{k=0}^{\infty}\beta^k\overline{\mathbb{E}}_t[\xi_{t+k}] + (1 - \beta)\sum_{k=0}^{\infty}\beta^k\overline{\mathbb{E}}_t[c_{t+k+1}].$$

Using the misspecified priors, we have

$$c_t = \frac{1}{1 - \beta m \rho} \xi_t + (1 - \beta) \frac{mR}{1 - \beta mR} c_t,$$

which leads to the actual law of motion of c_t as

$$c_t = \rho c_{t-1} + \frac{1 - \beta mR}{1 - mR} \frac{1}{1 - \beta m \rho} \varepsilon_t.$$

To be consistent with our guess, we have

$$R = \rho, \quad D = \frac{1}{1 - m\rho}.$$

Compared with the economy with misperceived $\hat{\rho}$, the aggregate outcomes are equivalent iff

$$\frac{1}{1 - \hat{\rho}} = \frac{1}{1 - m\rho}, \quad \rightarrow \quad \hat{\rho} = m\rho < \rho.$$

In terms of the forecast, in the cognitive discounting economy,

$$\mathbb{E}_{i,t}[c_{t+1}] = \overline{\mathbb{E}}_t[c_{t+1}] = m\mathbb{E}_t^*[c_{t+1}].$$

In all three economies (higher-order doubts, level-k, and cognitive discounting), the individual forecast is the same as the average forecast about the aggregate outcome, and it follows that $K_{CG} = K_{BGMS}$. In addition, in all three economies,

$$c_t = \varphi \xi_t, \quad \text{and} \quad \overline{\mathbb{E}}_t[c_{t+1}] = \varsigma \mathbb{E}_t^*[c_{t+1}] = \varsigma \rho \varphi \xi_t,$$

for some constant φ and $\varsigma \in (0, 1)$. Therefore, we have

$$\text{Cov}(\text{Error}_t, \text{Revision}_t) = \text{Cov}(\varphi \xi_{t+1} - \varsigma \rho \varphi \xi_t, \varsigma \rho \varphi \xi_t - \varsigma^2 \rho^2 \varphi \xi_{t-1})$$
$$= \varphi^2 \rho^2 \varsigma (1 - \varsigma) \frac{1 - \varsigma \rho^2}{1 - \rho^2},$$

which implies $K_{CG} = K_{BGMS} > 0$.

In addition, the law of motion of the forecast error is

$$\text{Error}_t = \varphi \frac{1 - \varsigma \rho \mathbb{L}}{1 - \rho \mathbb{L}} \varepsilon_{t+1} = \varphi \left((1 - \varsigma) \frac{1}{1 - \rho L} + \varsigma \right) \varepsilon_{t+1},$$

and the corresponding IRF is always positive given $\varsigma \in (0, 1)$.

Given that in all these economies the IRFs of the outcomes are always positive and that the IRF of the forecast error is always positive, we know that K_{KW} in all of these economies has to be positive as well.

Proof of Lemma in Appendix C

We consider the case with $k = 1$. Note that average revision, Revision_t, and the idiosyncratic component of individual revision, ($\text{Revision}_{i,t} - \text{Revision}_t$), are independent of each other. Therefore, the regression coefficient on the average forecast revision remains K_{CG}.

The covariance between individual forecast error and idiosyncratic revision component is

$$\text{Cov}(\text{Error}_{i,t}, \text{Revision}_{i,t} - \text{Revision}_{i,t})$$

$$= \text{Cov}\left(-\frac{\hat{\rho} - \hat{\lambda}}{1 - \hat{\lambda}\mathbb{L}}u_{i,t}, \frac{\hat{\rho} - \hat{\lambda}}{1 - \hat{\lambda}\mathbb{L}}(\tau^{-\frac{1}{2}}u_{i,t} - \hat{\rho}\tau^{-\frac{1}{2}}u_{i,t-1})\right)$$

$$= -\tau^{-1}\frac{(\hat{\rho} - \hat{\lambda})^2(1 - \hat{\lambda}\hat{\rho})}{1 - \hat{\lambda}^2}$$

$$= -\kappa_1 V_{\text{agg}}\tau^{-1}.$$

Denote the regression coefficient on ($\text{Revision}_{i,t} - \text{Revision}_t$) as β. It follows that

$$\beta = \frac{\text{Cov}(\text{Error}_{i,t}, \text{Revision}_{i,t} - \text{Revision}_t)}{V_{\text{idio}}}$$

$$= \frac{\text{Cov}(\text{Error}_{i,t}, \text{Revision}_{i,t}) - \text{Cov}(\text{Error}_t, \text{Revision}_t)}{V_{\text{idio}}}$$

$$= \frac{V_{\text{ind}}}{V_{\text{idio}}}K_{\text{BGMS}} - \frac{V_{\text{agg}}}{V_{\text{idio}}}K_{\text{CG}},$$

and hence

$$K_{\text{noise}} = -\beta\frac{V_{\text{idio}}}{V_{\text{agg}}} = K_{\text{CG}} - \frac{V_{\text{ind}}}{V_{\text{agg}}}K_{\text{BGMS}}.$$

Using the definitions of K_{CG} and K_{BGMS}, we then also have $K_{\text{noise}} = \kappa_1\tau^{-1}$. Because κ_1 is independent of τ, K_{noise} is decreasing in τ, and vanishes when $\tau \to \infty$.

Endnotes

Author email addresses: Angeletos (angelet@mit.edu), Huo (zhen.huo@yale.edu), Sastry (ksastry@mit.edu). This paper was prepared for the 2020 NBER Macroeconomics Annual. We owe special thanks to our discussants, Ricardo Reis and Jessica Wachter, and the organizers, Martin Eichenbaum and Erik Hurst. We also thank Fabrice Collard for help with some of the material in Section V. We finally thank Jeffrey Campbell, Olivier Coibion, Nicola Gennaioli, Cosmin Ilut, Yueran Ma, and Alp Simsek for useful comments. Angeletos acknowledges the financial support of the National Science Foundation (Award #1757198). For acknowledgments, sources of research support, and disclosure of the authors' material financial relationships, if any, please see https://www.nber.org/books-and-chapters/nber-macroeconomics-annual-2020-volume-35/imperfect-macroeconomic-expectations-evidence-and-theory.

1. This includes works on rational inattention (Sims 2003, 2010; Maćkowiak and Wiederholt 2009; Matĕjka 2015), sticky information (Mankiw and Reis 2002; Kiley 2007), and higher-order uncertainty (Morris and Shin 2002, 2006; Woodford 2003; Nimark 2008; Angeletos and Lian 2016, 2018).

2. This applies to the papers cited below, as well as Andrade and Le Bihan (2013), Gennaioli et al. (2015), Kohlhas and Broer (2019), and Fuhrer (2018). See also the discussion of Coibion and Gorodnichenko (2012) in Section V and appendix B.

3. For inflation forecasts, the same pattern has been independently documented in Kohlhas and Broer (2019). BGMS offer a comprehensive investigation across variables, surveys, and empirical methods.

4. These shocks are described at the end of Section II and are obtained from Angeletos et al. (2020).

5. This echoes lessons from Angeletos and Lian (2018), Angeletos and Huo (2020), and Farhi and Werning (2019).

6. For a detailed discussion of this difference, see the end of Section V and the accompanying appendix B.

7. For context, in a Gaussian distribution, the probability of an observation so far in the tails is about 6.8×10^{-8}. Nonetheless, in the sample of three-quarter-ahead inflation forecast errors, there are 57 such observations out of 7,438 forecaster-quarter observations, or about 10^6 times the aforementioned probability. All of these outliers involve forecast errors greater than 5.37 percentage points and often appear to be typos (an extra digit).

8. This data set is available at the monthly frequency, so we use end-of-quarter forecasts (i.e., those made in March, June, September, and December) for comparability with the SPF. The reported inflation forecasts in the Blue Chip consensus are actually quarter-to-quarter, so we construct the consensus estimate of longer-horizon inflation as the "chained consensus" rather than the "consensus of chained inflation."

9. The exact question is the following: "By about what percent do you expect prices to go (up/down) on the average, during the next 12 months?" Respondents can key in a response rounded to the nearest whole number.

10. The exact question is the following: "How about people out of work during the coming 12 months. Do you think that there will be more unemployment than now, about the same, or less?" There are three responses, as indicated in the question.

11. The ambiguity between GDP and GNP matches the fact that the SPF changed its main target variable from GNP (and the deflator thereof) to GDP (and the deflator thereof) starting in 1992.

12. We take all vintage data series from the Philadelphia Fed's website: https://www.philadelphiafed.org/research-and-data/real-time-center/survey-of-professional-forecasters.

13. In the data, we prefer to use the median to limit the influence of outliers and/or data entry errors. But results with the mean are essentially identical. In the theory, means and medians coincide because we let all variables and signals be normally distributed.

14. An auxiliary assumption in this context, which we will not question throughout the analysis, is "perfect recall": a rational Bayesian agent who forgets past information (like last period's forecast) could make such a predictable error.

15. One discrepancy between our implementation of KW and the original one is that these authors apply a Hodrick-Prescott filter to x_t. We prefer not to do so because it complicates the mapping to the theory: as the filtered value of x_t is a function of realizations after t, finding $K_{KW} \neq 0$ does not necessarily reject full-information, rational expectations under their approach, whereas it does under ours. That said, the big picture is the same. And in Subsection V.D and table 4 we will use an instrumental variables method that conditions on predetermined data (identified shocks) to achieve a similar goal of extracting the business-cycle component of variation in x_t.

16. The variant used in Bordalo et al. (2020) is motivated by a broader concept, "diagnostic expectations," the precise formal content of which varies across applications. It is the specific formalization employed in Bordalo et al. (2020) that is very similar to overconfidence; this similarity is evident in the modified Kalman filter that is at the core of that paper.

17. As in the textbook version of the Kalman filter, g is such that $\mathbb{E}_{i,t}[z_t] = (1-g)\mathbb{E}_{i,t-1}[z_t] + gs_{i,t}$ and is an increasing and continuous function of τ, with $g \to 0$ as $\tau \to 0$ and $g \to 1$ as $\tau \to \infty$.

18. We exclude ζ_0 from this statement because it is mechanically 1. Also, all our theoretical statements focus on one-step-ahead forecasts for expositional simplicity, but our empirical implementations of the theory use the exact counterparts of the objects constructed in the data (e.g., as the 3-quarter-ahead forecasts of annualized inflation).

19. The idea that the IRFs of forecast errors contain superior information is also emphasized in Kucinskas and Peters (2019), although for different purposes than those pursued here.

20. The empirical strategy taken in that paper builds on the max-share approach (Uhlig 2003; Barsky and Sims 2011) but is guided by the following goal: providing a parsimonious representation of the business cycle in terms of one dominant shock. To this goal, Angeletos et al. (2020) run a vector autoregression (VAR) on a set of 10 or more key macroeconomic variables that includes the two variables we focus on here, the rate of unemployment and the rate of inflation. They then compile a collection of multiple shocks, each identified by maximizing its contribution to the volatility of a particular variable over a particular frequency band, and they draw lessons from comparing the empirical footprint of all these shocks.

21. Angeletos et al. (2020) further show that this shock in the data is closely related to the following counterparts in models: the investment-specific demand shock in Justiniano, Primiceri, and Tambalotti (2010), the risk shock in Christiano, Motto, and Rostagno (2014), and the confidence shock in Angeletos, Collard, and Dellas (2018).

22. The two shocks are not constructed to be orthogonal to one another, but they are very close to being so in the data.

23. The first-stage equation is given, in vector form, by $Z_{t-1} = \eta + \mathcal{E}_{t-K-1'}\Theta + e_t$, where $Z_{t-1} \equiv (z_{t-p})_{p=1}^{P}$, $\mathcal{E}_{t-K-1} \equiv (\varepsilon_{t-K-j})_{j=K+1}^{J}$ and $J - K \geq P$. Our main specifications use $P = 3$, $K = 1$, and $J = 9$ (i.e., eight instruments for three regressors). But the results are robust to $P = 2$ and $P = 4$, as well as to different J and K.

24. We report first-stage F statistics for the ARMA-IV estimates in table A5. These are low with respect to the reference values suggested by Stock and Yogo (2005), which is part of the reason that we also consider alternative estimation methods including the linear projection and multivariate linear model.

25. The corresponding estimates from the projection regressions are 4.87 and 7.79.

26. We also replicate all SPF and Blue Chip findings with vintage data and find similar results (not reported for brevity).

27. Results are similar if we treat a different portion (e.g., 1/2 or all) of the "about the same" responses as corresponding to "up."

28. For consistency with the previous analysis, we compare this to data on the GDP deflator, even though this is almost certainly not a perfect match for the price variable households have in mind when answering the survey.

29. The 10 macro variables are the following: real GDP, real investment, real consumption, labor hours, the labor share, the Federal Funds Rate, the rate of change in the GDP deflator, labor productivity in the nonfarm business sector, unemployment rate, and utilization-adjusted TFP. Full variable descriptions and data construction discussion are in Angeletos et al. (2020). The sample period is Q4 1968–Q4 2017.

30. We are grateful to Fabrice Collard for help with this replication.

31. In figure A4, we show the "off-diagonal" impulse responses of unemployment to the supply shock and inflation to the demand shock. They, too, show evidence of the over-shooting.

32. Results are similar using cross-sectional standard deviations, but the interquartile range method seems safer in the presence of outliers.

33. Note, of course, that there is no clear "filtered" or "shock-specific" version of fact 2 that can be estimated in the data. Once one subsets to aggregate variation, the BGMS regression essentially replicates the CG regression.

34. Another strand of evidence comes from recent field experiment work in Coibion, Gorodnichenko, and Kumar (2018) and Coibion et al. (2019).

35. For completeness, assume that labor is supplied to meet final demand, and that a competitive, representative firm operates a linear production technology with constant productivity to produce the homogeneous final good.

36. See also the related overlapping generations (OLG) versions of the New Keynesian model in Piergallini (2007), Del Negro, Giannoni, and Patterson (2015) and Farhi and Werning (2019).

37. Maćkowiak and Wiederholt (2015) and Afrouzi and Yang (2019) argue a version of the first point by focusing on the endogeneity of attention, or of τ in our framework. Here, we instead emphasize the endogeneity of ω_f and ω_b on the MPC and other GE parameters for given τ, as in Angeletos and Huo (2020).

38. Furthermore, in a survey of firms designed to shed light on related issues, Coibion, Gorodnichenko, Kumar, and Ryngaert (2021) find support for informational frictions but no relation between measured level-k thinking and expectations.

39. Previous works such as Mankiw and Reis (2007), Maćkowiak and Wiederholt (2015), and Melosi (2016) have also sought to quantify the macroeconomic effects of informational frictions in the baseline New Keynesian model but have not disciplined the exercise with the expectations evidence we consider here. Bordalo et al. (2019), on the other hand, quantify the role of overextrapolation in an real business cycle (RBC) model with credit friction, but they abstract from informational frictions and do not address the particular patterns of the expectations of inflation and unemployment on which we focus.

40. The BGMS evidence was nevertheless useful in corroborating the case for overextrapolation and, conversely, in ruling out theories that resemble underextrapolation. In this sense, it remains useful for selecting the "right" model of beliefs. But it could be dispensed with in our counterfactuals.

41. This explanation relates to a rich literature looking for statistical break points in volatility and/or policy in modern history (Sargent 2001; Primiceri 2005; Sargent, Williams, and Zha 2006; Sims and Zha 2006). It is also natural within the GE theory presented here and in Angeletos and Huo (2020): in this context, the information-driven persistence in inflation is modulated by policy and, more specifically, decreased by a steeper Taylor rule.

42. There are only three salient differences. The first is that Coibion and Gorodnichenko (2012) use forecast means rather than medians as a measure of the aggregate. The second is that Coibion and Gorodnichenko (2012) measure expected annual inflation with the forecast of the 4-quarter-ahead price level relative to the now-cast of the (unreleased) current-quarter price level; whereas our main analysis uses 3-quarter-ahead relative to the previous quarter. And the third is that their sample period runs from Q4 1974 to Q4 2007.

43. The estimation period they use for this VAR covers Q2 1952–Q3 2007.

44. To the best of our knowledge, the particular regression we propose here and the offered structural interpretation are novel. However, Fuhrer (2018) and Kohlhas and Broer (2019) contain a few empirical specifications that have a similar spirit, namely the separately test of the extent to which aggregate-level and individual-level variables help predict forecast errors.

45. The same seems to be true for almost all the specifications considered in Bordalo et al. (2020), including those regarding a variety of interest rates and spreads.

46. To be precise, one also needs to compute V_{idio} and V_{agg}, the variances of, respectively, the individual and aggregate forecast revisions. But these variances are already implicit in the calculation of K_{BGMS} and K_{CG}.

47. The following caveat applies to the adopted interpretation of K_{noise}. In the model we work with in this paper, idiosyncratic noise is the sole source of heterogeneity in beliefs:

irrationality is a (possibly time-varying) fixed effect in the cross section of the population. Without this restriction, K_{noise} may confound the effects of "rational" noise (due to idiosyncratic information) and "irrational" noise (due to idiosyncratic misspecification).

48. $B(\mathbb{L})$ satisfies the requirement $B(\mathbb{L})B'(\mathbb{L}^{-1}) = M(\mathbb{L})\hat{M}'(\mathbb{L}^{-1})$, and $\hat{B}(\mathbb{L})$ is invertible.

49. On a more technical level, note that, as written, k_{IRF} need not be an integer. It is indeed obtained from the continuous-time limit of the ARMA process that describes the average forecast error. But the result, as stated, holds for the true, discrete-time process. Also, a small caveat is that in the model with overextrapolation ($\hat{\rho} > \rho$) but no noise ($\hat{\tau} \to \infty$), right after $t = 0$, the forecast error switches sign from positive (by construction, given that the data were hit by an unpredictable innovation) to negative (as a result of flawed reasoning). That is, $\zeta_0 = 1$ always, but we can have $\lim_{h \downarrow 0} \zeta_h < 0$. In the data, given that we properly observe some average of forecast errors between $t = 0$ and $t = 1$ as the "observation" at $t = 0$, we would expect to see impulse responses of uniform sign.

References

Adam, Klaus, and Michael Woodford. 2012. "Robustly Optimal Monetary Policy in a Microfounded New Keynesian Model." *Journal of Monetary Economics* 59 (5): 468–87.

Afrouzi, Hassan, and Choongryul Yang. 2019. "Dynamic Rational Inattention and the Phillips Curve." Mimeo.

Andrade, Philippe, and Hervé Le Bihan. 2013. "Inattentive Professional Forecasters." *Journal of Monetary Economics* 60 (8): 967–82.

Angeletos, George-Marios, Fabrice Collard, and Harris Dellas. 2018. "Quantifying Confidence." *Econometrica* 86 (5): 1689–726.

———. 2020. "Business Cycle Anatomy." *American Economic Review* 110 (10): 3030–70.

Angeletos, George-Marios, and Zhen Huo. 2020. "Myopia and Anchoring." *American Economic Review*, forthcoming.

Angeletos, George-Marios, and Chen Lian. 2016. "Incomplete Information in Macroeconomics: Accommodating Frictions in Coordination." In *Handbook of Macroeconomics*, vol. 2, ed. John B. Taylor and Harald Uhlig, 1065–240. Amsterdam: Elsevier.

———. 2018. "Forward Guidance without Common Knowledge." *American Economic Review* 108 (9): 2477–512.

Angeletos, George-Marios, and Karthik A. Sastry. 2020. "Managing Expectations: Instruments vs. Targets." *Quarterly Journal of Economics*, forthcoming.

Baker, Scott R., Nicholas Bloom, and Steven J. Davis. 2016. "Measuring Economic Policy Uncertainty." *Quarterly Journal of Economics* 131 (4): 1593–636.

Barberis, Nicholas, Andrei Shleifer, and Robert Vishny. 1998. "A Model of Investor Sentiment." *Journal of Financial Economics* 49 (3): 307–43.

Barsky, Robert B., and Eric R. Sims. 2011. "News Shocks and Business Cycles." *Journal of Monetary Economics* 58 (3): 273–89.

Bhandari, Anmol, Jaroslav Borovička, and Paul Ho. 2019. "Survey Data and Subjective Beliefs in Business Cycle Models." Working Paper no. 19-14, University of Minnesota, New York University, and Federal Reserve Bank of Richmond.

Bloom, Nicholas. 2009. "The Impact of Uncertainty Shocks." *Econometrica* 77 (3): 623–85.

Bloom, Nicholas, Max Floetotto, Nir Jaimovich, Itay Saporta-Eksten, and Stephen J. Terry. 2018. "Really Uncertain Business Cycles." *Econometrica* 86 (3): 1031–65.

Bordalo, Pedro, Nicola Gennaioli, Yueran Ma, and Andrei Shleifer. 2020. "Over-reaction in Macroeconomic Expectations." *American Economic Review* 110 (9): 2748–2782.

Bordalo, Pedro, Nicola Gennaioli, and Andrei Shleifer. 2017. "Diagnostic Expectations and Credit Cycles." *Journal of Finance* 73 (1): 199–227.

Bordalo, Pedro, Nicola Gennaioli, Andrei Shleifer, and Stephen J. Terry. 2019. "Real Credit Cycles." Mimeo.

Brunnermeier, Markus K., and Jonathan A. Parker. 2005. "Optimal Expectations." *American Economic Review* 95 (4): 1092–118.

Burnside, Craig, Martin Eichenbaum, and Sergio Rebelo. 2016. "Understanding Booms and Busts in Housing Markets." *Journal of Political Economy* 124 (4): 1088–147.

Caballero, Ricardo J., and Alp Simsek. 2020. "A Risk-Centric Model of Demand Recessions and Speculation." *Quarterly Journal of Economics* 135 (3): 1493–1566.

———. 2019. "Monetary Policy with Opinionated Markets." MIT mimeo.

Caplin, Andrew, and John V. Leahy. 2019. "Wishful Thinking." Working Paper no. 25707, NBER, Cambridge, MA.

Carroll, Christopher D. 2001. "The Epidemiology of Macroeconomic Expectations." Working Paper no. 8695, NBER, Cambridge, MA.

———. 2003. "Macroeconomic Expectations of Households and Professional Forecasters." *Quarterly Journal of Economics* 118 (1): 269–98.

Christiano, Lawrence J., Roberto Motto, and Massimo Rostagno. 2014. "Risk Shocks." *American Economic Review* 104 (1): 27–65.

Coibion, Olivier, and Yuriy Gorodnichenko. 2012. "What Can Survey Forecasts Tell Us about Information Rigidities?" *Journal of Political Economy* 120 (1): 116–59.

———. 2015. "Information Rigidity and the Expectations Formation Process: A Simple Framework and New Facts." *American Economic Review* 105 (8): 2644–78.

Coibion, Olivier, Yuriy Gorodnichenko, and Saten Kumar. 2018. "How Do Firms Form Their Expectations? New Survey Evidence." *American Economic Review* 108 (9): 2671–713.

Coibion, Olivier, Gorodnichenko, Yuriy, Kumar, Saten, and Ryngaert, Jane. 2021. "Do You Know That I Know That You Know . . . ? Higher-Order Beliefs in Survey Data." *Quarterly Journal of Economics*, forthcoming.

Coibion, Olivier, Yuriy Gorodnichenko, and Tiziano Ropele. 2019. "Inflation Expectations and Firm Decisions: New Causal Evidence." *Quarterly Journal of Economics* 135 (1): 165–219.

Cutler, David M., James M. Poterba, and Lawrence H. Summers. 1991. "Speculative Dynamics." *Review of Economic Studies* 58 (3): 529–46.

D'Acunto, Francesco, Ulrike Malmendier, Juan Ospina, and Michael Weber. 2021. "Exposure to Grocery Prices and Inflation Expectations." *Journal of Political Economy*, forthcoming.

Daniel, Kent, David Hirshleifer, and Avanidhar Subrahmanyam. 1998. "Investor Psychology and Security Market Under- and Overreactions." *Journal of Finance* 53 (6): 1839–85.

Das, Sreyoshi, Camelia M. Kuhnen, and Stefan Nagel. 2020. "Socioeconomic Status and Macroeconomic Expectations." *Review of Financial Studies* 33 (1): 395–432.

De Bondt, Werner F. M., and Richard Thaler. 1985. "Does the Stock Market Overreact?" *Journal of Finance* 40 (3): 793–805.

Dean, Mark, and Nate Leigh Neligh. 2017. "Experimental Tests of Rational Inattention." Working paper, Columbia University.

Del Negro, Marco, Marc P. Giannoni, and Christina Patterson. 2015. "The Forward Guidance Puzzle." FRB of New York mimeo.

Eusepi, Stefano, and Bruce Preston. 2011. "Expectations, Learning, and Business Cycle Fluctuations." *American Economic Review* 101 (6): 2844–72.

Evans, George W., and Seppo Honkapohja. 2001. *Learning and Expectations in Macroeconomics*. Princeton, NJ: Princeton University Press.

Farhi, Emmanuel, and Iván Werning. 2019. "Monetary Policy, Bounded Rationality, and Incomplete Markets." *American Economic Review* 109 (11): 3887–928.

Fuhrer, Jeffrey C. 2018. "Intrinsic Expectations Persistence: Evidence from Professional and Household Survey Expectations." Working Papers 18-9, Federal Reserve Bank of Boston.

Fuster, Andreas, David Laibson, and Brock Mendel. 2010. "Natural Expectations and Macroeconomic Fluctuations." *Journal of Economic Perspectives* 24 (4): 67–84.

Gabaix, Xavier. 2016. "Behavioral Macroeconomics Via Sparse Dynamic Programming." Working Paper no. 21848, NBER, Cambridge, MA.

———. 2019. "Behavioral Inattention." In *Handbook of Behavioral Economics: Foundations and Applications*, vol. 2, ed. B. Douglas Bernheim, Stefano DellaVigna, and David Laibson, 261–343. Amsterdam: North-Holland.

———. 2020. "A Behavioral New Keynesian Model." *American Economic Review* 110 (8): 2271–327.

Galí, Jordi. 1999. "Technology, Employment, and the Business Cycle: Do Technology Shocks Explain Aggregate Fluctuations?" *American Economic Review* 89 (1): 249–71.

Garcia-Schmidt, Mariana and Michael Woodford. 2019. "Are Low Interest Rates Deflationary? A Paradox of Perfect-Foresight Analysis." *American Economic Review* 109 (1): 86–120.

Geanakoplos, John. 2010. "The Leverage Cycle." *NBER Macroeconomics Annual* 24:1–65.

Gennaioli, Nicola, Yueran Ma, and Andrei Shleifer. 2015. "Expectations and Investment." *NBER Macroeconomics Annual* 30:379–431.

Giacomini, Raffaella, Vasiliki Skreta, and Javier Turen. 2020. "Heterogeneity, Inattention, and Bayesian Updates." *American Economic Journal: Macroeconomics* 12 (1): 282–309. https://www.aeaweb.org/articles?id=10.1257/mac.20180235.

Greenwood, Robin, and Andrei Shleifer. 2014. "Expectations of Returns and Expected Returns." *Review of Financial Studies* 27 (3): 714–46.

Guo, Hongye, and Jessica A. Wachter. 2019. "'Superstitious' Investors." Working Paper no. 25603, NBER, Cambridge, MA.

Hamilton, James D. 1996. "This Is What Happened to the Oil Price-Macroeconomy Relationship." *Journal of Monetary Economics* 38 (2): 215–20.

Hansen, Lars Peter, and Thomas J. Sargent. 2012. "Three Types of Ambiguity." *Journal of Monetary Economics* 59 (5): 422–45.

Hong, Harrison, and Jeremy C. Stein. 1999. "A Unified Theory of Underreaction, Momentum Trading, and Overreaction in Asset Markets." *Journal of Finance* 54 (6): 2143–84.

Ilut, Cosmin L., and Martin Schneider. 2014. "Ambiguous Business Cycles." *American Economic Review* 104 (8): 2368–99.

Iovino, Luigi, and Dmitriy Sergeyev. 2017. "Quantitative Easing without Rational Expectations." 2017 Meeting Papers 1387, Society for Economic Dynamics, Stonybrook, NY.

Jordà, Òscar. 2005. "Estimation and Inference of Impulse Responses by Local Projections." *American Economic Review* 95 (1): 161–82.

Justiniano, Alejandro, Giorgio E. Primiceri, and Andrea Tambalotti. 2010. "Investment Shocks and Business Cycles." *Journal of Monetary Economics* 57 (2): 132–45.

Kiley, Michael T. 2007. "A Quantitative Comparison of Sticky-Price and Sticky-Information Models of Price Setting." *Journal of Money, Credit and Banking* 39 (s1): 101–25.

Kleibergen, Frank, and Richard Paap. 2006. "Generalized Reduced Rank Tests Using the Singular Value Decomposition." *Journal of Econometrics* 133 (1): 97–126.

Kohlhas, Alexandre, and Tobias Broer. 2019. "Forecaster (Mis-)Behavior." IIES mimeo.

Kohlhas, Alexandre, and Ansgar Walther. 2018. "Asymmetric Attention." IIES mimeo.

Kucinskas, Simas, and Florian S. Peters. 2019. "Measuring Biases in Expectation Formation." Mimeo.

Lakonishok, Josef, Andrei Shleifer, and Robert W. Vishny. 1994. "Contrarian Investment, Extrapolation, and Risk." *Journal of Finance* 49 (5): 1541–78.

Landier, Augustin, Yueran Ma, and David Thesmar. 2019. "Biases in Expectations: Experimental Evidence." https://doi.org/10.2139/ssrn.3046955.

Lucas, Robert E., Jr. 1972. "Expectations and the Neutrality of Money." *Journal of Economic Theory* 4 (2): 103–24.

Maćkowiak, Bartosz, and Mirko Wiederholt. 2009. "Optimal Sticky Prices under Rational Inattention." *American Economic Review* 99 (3): 769–803.

———. 2015. "Business Cycle Dynamics under Rational Inattention." *Review of Economic Studies* 82 (4): 1502–32.

Malmendier, Ulrike, and Stefan Nagel. 2016. "Learning from Inflation Experiences." *Quarterly Journal of Economics* 131 (1): 53–87.

Mankiw, N. Gregory, and Ricardo Reis. 2002. "Sticky Information versus Sticky Prices: A Proposal to Replace the New Keynesian Phillips Curve." *Quarterly Journal of Economics* 117 (4): 1295–328.

———. 2007. "Sticky Information in General Equilibrium." *Journal of the European Economic Association* 5 (2–3): 603–13.

Mankiw, N. Gregory, Ricardo Reis, and Justin Wolfers. 2004. "Disagreement about Inflation Expectations." *NBER Macroeconomics Annual* 18:209–70.

Marcet, Albert, and Thomas J. Sargent. 1989. "Convergence of Least Squares Learning Mechanisms in Self-Referential Linear Stochastic Models." *Journal of Economic Theory* 48 (2): 337–68.

Matějka, Filip. 2015. "Rationally Inattentive Seller: Sales and Discrete Pricing." *Review of Economic Studies* 83 (3): 1125–55.

Melosi, Leonardo. 2016. "Signalling Effects of Monetary Policy." *Review of Economic Studies* 84 (2): 853–84.

Molavi, Pooya. 2019. "Macroeconomics with Learning and Misspecification: A General Theory and Applications." MIT mimeo.

Moore, Don A., and Paul J. Healy. 2008. "The Trouble with Overconfidence." *Psychological Review* 115 (2): 502.

Morris, Stephen, and Hyun Song Shin. 2002. "Social Value of Public Information." *American Economic Review* 92 (5): 1521–34.

———. 2006. "Inertia of Forward-Looking Expectations." *American Economic Review* 96 (2): 152–57.

Nagel, Rosemarie. 1995. "Unraveling in Guessing Games: An Experimental Study." *American Economic Review* 85 (5): 1313–26.

Nimark, Kristoffer. 2008. "Dynamic Pricing and Imperfect Common Knowledge." *Journal of Monetary Economics* 55 (2): 365–82.

Piergallini, Alessandro. 2007. "Real Balance Effects and Monetary Policy." *Economic Inquiry* 44 (3): 497–511.

Primiceri, Giorgio E. 2005. "Time Varying Structural Vector Autoregressions and Monetary Policy." *Review of Economic Studies* 72 (3): 821–52.

Romer, Christina D., and David H. Romer. 2004. "A New Measure of Monetary Shocks: Derivation and Implications." *American Economic Review* 94 (4): 1055–84.

Sargent, Thomas, Noah Williams, and Tao Zha. 2006. "Shocks and Government Beliefs: The Rise and Fall of American Inflation." *American Economic Review* 96 (4): 1193–224.

Sargent, Thomas J. 2001. *The Conquest of American Inflation*. Princeton, NJ: Princeton University Press.

Sastry, Karthik A. 2020. "Disagreement about Monetary Policy." MIT mimeo.

Sims, Christopher A. 1980. "Macroeconomics and Reality." *Econometrica* 48 (1): 1–48.

———. 2003. "Implications of Rational Inattention." *Journal of Monetary Economics* 50 (3): 665–90.

———. 2010. "Rational Inattention and Monetary Economics." *Handbook of Monetary Economics* 3:155–81.

Sims, Christopher A., and Tao Zha. 2006. "Were There Regime Switches in U.S. Monetary Policy?" *American Economic Review* 96 (1): 54–81.

Stock, James H., and Motohiro Yogo. 2005. "Testing for Weak Instruments in Linear IV Regression." In *Identification and Inference for Econometric Models: Essays in Honor of Thomas Rothenberg*, ed. Donald W. K. Andrews and James H. Stock, 80–108. New York: Cambridge University Press.

Uhlig, Harald. 2003. "What Moves Real GNP?" Mimeo.

Woodford, Michael. 2003. "Imperfect Common Knowledge and the Effects of Monetary Policy." In *Knowledge, Information, and Expectations in Modern Macroeconomics: In Honor of Edmund S. Phelps*, ed. Philippe Aghion, Roman Frydman, Joseph Stiglitz, and Michael Woodford. Princeton, NJ: Princeton University Press.

———. 2018. "Monetary Policy Analysis When Planning Horizons Are Finite." *NBER Macroeconomics Annual* 33:1–50.

Comment

Jessica A. Wachter, Wharton School, University of Pennsylvania, United States of America, *and NBER,* United States of America

I. Introduction

The authors build a quantitative framework, broad enough to nest different types of ideas proposed in behavioral macroeconomics, to help make sense of the survey evidence on expectations. The goal is not so much to understand survey evidence for its own sake, though that might be interesting. Nor is it to decide between a class of competing models, all of which work fairly well. Rather, the goal is to inform future directions for research in a field that at the moment seems a bit lost in a "wilderness." In the end, using their approach, the authors are able to say that the weight of the evidence favors some types of models rather than others.

The focus on survey evidence comes at a time of uncertainty about future directions in macroeconomics. Many, including some of the authors in prior work, have noted serious failings with benchmark models. These failings have a solution, perhaps, within a different class of models, ones that do not impose rational expectations. But rational expectations are a powerful disciplining device, and this broader class seems impossibly large.

The literature has, for several years, recognized the potential of survey evidence to itself be a disciplining device, filling some of the role that rational expectations used to, and do still, play. Barberis et al. (2015), for example, argue for using survey evidence to decide between competing models in financial economics. In macroeconomics, Coibion and Gorodnichenko (2015) argue that one need not have a model to interpret survey evidence: a positive sign in regressions of forecast errors on forecast revisions is model-free evidence of underreaction in macroeconomics, relative to a rational expectations benchmark.

Coibion and Gorodnichenko (2015) indeed find evidence for such underreaction. Their preferred interpretation is one of dispersed private information. The authors discuss a substantial literature in macroeconomic theory that proposes other types of underreaction operating at the level of the individual. Indeed, dispersed private information is a form of individual underreaction because it requires some individuals to persist in having different views than others in what would seem in principle to be the same data.

In fact, underreaction might be the first model that would come to mind if one moved away from the rational expectations benchmark. Suppose that some process interfered with agents' encoding of information (one could call it limited attention), or that agents forgot information with some probability (formalized by Mullainathan 2002). In either type of model, beliefs would display persistent changes due to the fact that it takes several "tries" for new information to enter the agent's database.

II. Summary of the Evidence

To understand the results in this paper and the related literature, it is first helpful to review the terminology. Agents forecast a macroeconomic series x_t. Let $\mathbb{E}_t$ denote the forecast as of time t—note that, like the authors, I assume by use of this notation that the forecast is an expectation (and not, say, a median)—so that $\mathbb{E}_t[x_{t+k}] - \mathbb{E}_{t-1}[x_{t+k}]$ is the revision in expectation as of time t, whereas $x_{t+k} - \mathbb{E}_t[x_{t+k}]$ is the forecast error. The idea behind the Coibion and Gorodnichenko (2015) regressions is to attempt to forecast the error with the revision. Thus the revision in the forecast is used to forecast the forecast error. This is a mouthful, so I will simply refer to the right-hand side variable as the revision and the left-hand side variable as the error.

Assuming $\mathbb{E}_t$ is a true expectation, namely it obeys the laws of conditional probability, then the error should be unforecastable by any variable available to the agent at time t. Presumably, this should include the agent's own revision. After all, if something can forecast the error, it follows that it can be used to improve the expectation and should be part of the revision.

What if, however, there is information at time t not captured in the forecast? Bordalo et al. (2018) argue for running the regression on individual-level data. They point out, as do Coibion and Gorodnichenko (2015), that forecastability of errors from median forecasts is compatible with individual rationality (at least in a narrow sense). If some individuals lack information that goes into the median forecast, what looks like predictability will appear to be a surprise to these investors, who are late in the game. This situation is called "dispersed private information," and although it is compatible with Bayesian updating, it requires artificially restricting the data, or manipulation of the priors.

Indeed, it is hard to argue that regressions with $\mathbb{E}_t$ representing an individual forecast do not represent rationality, at least if we consider rationality as equivalent to Bayesian updating (and if we assume that the forecast is a mean and not, say, a median). Bordalo et al. (2018) show that the individual-level forecasts are a mix of over- and underreaction, but with overreaction dominating. The importance of this result is best understood in light of the goals in the first paragraph. Bordalo et al. (2018) argue that overreaction is the trace we see of the representativeness heuristic at work. The representativeness heuristic, though it has no agreed-upon cognitive foundation, is a candidate for a unifying principle in behavioral macroeconomics.

The authors rerun the regressions from these prior papers (tables 1 and 2). Confirming results from the prior literature, they find that the coefficient in median-level forecasts (K_{CG}) for unemployment and inflation is positive—consistent with underreaction.[1] They find a similar result for the coefficient on individual-level forecasts (K_{BGMS}) for unemployment, but not for inflation. For inflation, results for K_{BGMS} are inconclusive for the full sample and strongly negative—indicating overreaction—for a subsample beginning in 1984.

III. Summary of Novel Findings

One message of the paper is that the survey data are indeed informative, but not in the way we might first think. The paper offers a summary of evidence and additional tests, then a model that reconciles seemingly contradictory findings in the survey evidence, taking the data-generating process (DGP) as given.

Finally, the authors go a step further and derive what the DGP would be in a New Keynesian model in which agents' beliefs followed the specified form. The authors then have a truly general equilibrium model of survey evidence, perhaps the first of such a kind. Although this is impressive, I can't help but wonder if this second part of the paper may have less of an impact than the first. After all, the first part potentially speaks to anyone with an interest in how beliefs are formed, whereas the second part does require subscribing to the New Keynesian framework. Yes, the first part does formally require specification of a DGP; yet here the authors make a fairly natural and parsimonious choice. Moreover, their approach could be applied to other DGPs.

A.   New Evidence

The authors augment the survey evidence with evidence from a vector autoregression (VAR) using shocks to unemployment and inflation. Consider

$$x_t = \alpha + \sum_{i=1}^{I}\gamma_i x_{t-i}^{IV} + \beta_0\varepsilon_t + u_t,$$

where x_t could be the underlying series or its median forecast, and ϵ_t is a shock, and x_{t-i}^{IV} are instrumented regressors, so γ_i correctly measures the response of x_t to x_{t-i}.

Figure 3 in the paper shows the results: the forecasts clearly lie below the outcome at the start (underreaction) and then above the outcome at the end. It looks like underreaction and then overshooting. This is true for both unemployment and inflation. The degree of overshooting (the fact that expectations start out below the realized and then end up above) is captured in a coefficient K_{IRF}, which is greater than one if overshooting occurs. The goal of the model will be to jointly match K_{CG}, K_{BGMS}, and the novel VAR evidence (K_{IRF}).

Already, however, a tension appears. Though estimated on the same data as Coibion and Gorodnichenko (2015), the authors have found evidence for a type of overreaction in expectations, namely overshooting. Coibion and Gorodnichenko (2015) show that median forecasts underreact. Figure 3 shows that median forecasts overshoot. How can both be true?

A careful look at figure 3 does reveal pervasive underreaction. At the start, the forecast lies below the outcome. Both the forecast and the outcome are rising. But the forecast does not rise fast enough, and so, in the short term, errors are positive. Then the forecast crosses the outcome. Now the outcome is below the forecast. Both the outcome and the forecast are falling. But the forecast does not fall fast enough. Thus the forecast does underreact in the short term. One contribution of the paper is the finding that there are situations in which a negative coefficient in

Coibion and Gorodnichenko (2015) regressions is consistent with long-run overreaction.

B. The Model Confronts the Evidence

The model can easily be described in a few short equations. Assume the following DGP for x_t:

$$(1 - \rho L)x_t = \epsilon_t \sim N(0, 1).$$

Agent i observes signal $s_{i,t}$, equal to x_t plus normally distributed noise:

$$s_{i,t} = x_t + \frac{u_{i,t}}{\sqrt{\tau}}.$$

This is dispersed private information: agents observe their own signals and cannot share them with others. The agent will form beliefs using a standard Kalman filter, except that the agent's beliefs are misspecified. In particular, the agent believes

$$(1 - \hat{\rho} L)x_t = \epsilon_t$$

and understands that the signal is noisy, but misjudges the noise of the signal:

$$s_{i,t} = x_t + \frac{u_{i,t}}{\sqrt{\hat{\tau}}}.$$

Under this model, the coefficient for individual forecasts, up to a constant of proportionality, equals

$$K_{BGMS} \propto -\kappa_1(\tau^{-1} - \hat{\tau}^{-1}) + \kappa_2(\rho - \hat{\rho}).$$

The evidence is that this is < 0 for inflation and > 0 for unemployment. Given the coefficient for individual forecasts, the coefficient for the aggregate forecast is proportional to

$$K_{CG} \propto \kappa_1 \tau^{-1} + V_{ind} K_{BGMS}.$$

The evidence is that that is > 0. Finally, the measure of overshooting equals

$$K_{IRF} = \frac{\log(\hat{\rho} - \rho) - \log(\hat{\rho} - \hat{\lambda})}{\log \hat{\lambda} - \log \rho}.$$

The evidence says that this is > 1.

In light of the model, how can we interpret this evidence? First, $K_{CG} > 0$ indicates dispersed private information. Unlike other types of underreaction that the literature has proposed, dispersed private information is compatible with beliefs overshooting. Second, $K_{IRF} > 0$ implies overextrapolation, not overconfidence. Although $K_{BGMS} < 0$ by itself might imply overconfidence, overconfidence operates on impact, and one needs some mechanism that operates on long-run expectations.

Thus dispersed private information becomes the primary mechanism for $K_{CG} > 0$, and overextrapolation, the primary mechanism for $K_{BGMS} < 0$. Because overextrapolation is doing the work of fitting both K_{BGMS} and K_{IRF} (overshooting), "confidence" (over- or under-) then becomes the "plug" for which one fits K_{BGMS} if necessary. If one wonders whether this extra degree of freedom—confidence—means that we cannot identify K_{CG}, one need not worry, because confidence and dispersed private information can then be separately identified from the differences in K_{CG} and K_{BGMS}.

C. Comments on the Model

A general comment is that these agents are fairly rational in that their beliefs are governed by the Bayes rule. Putting them into an economy with asset prices implies that asset prices would obey no-arbitrage. They do not, however, display rational expectations in the sense of "communism of models" (Hall and Sargent 2018). The true DGP does not equal the subjective DGP, and moreover, agents cannot learn the true DGP because they have, in a sense, dogmatic priors over $\hat{\tau}$ and $\hat{\rho}$. I give several specific comments below.

What Is the Correct Null Hypothesis?

The equations for K_{CG}, K_{BGMS}, and K_{IRF} have the required interpretation only if the agents are running the same Kalman filter as the authors. On one level, this is a restatement of the fact that they are Bayesian. But they are required to solve a complicated filtering problem in which mistakes are possible. For example, the agents may make suboptimal use of the previous signal (or may fail to use this signal entirely). If the agent simply bases today's forecast on today's information, which does not, intuitively, seem that far from optimality, then $K > 0$.

More generally, mistakes would seem to point to $K < 0$. All that is needed is that large deviations from a fundamental are more likely to be wrong.

This is because large deviations are likely to be on the same side of both the truth and previous forecast. If the agent suddenly forecasts a high value for unemployment, say, this will be coded as an upward revision. When unemployment turns out to be low relative to the forecast, the error is negative. Potential sources of error are numerous: They could be cognitive (the agent has the wrong model), perhaps a computer bug, perhaps an error in the agent's own data, or perhaps an error in reporting the forecast or in entering the forecast into the database.[2] As does the field at large, the authors accept the existence of such errors when following the common practice of winsorizing the data. But at what point is something an "outlier" that must be removed versus an error indicating, say, overconfidence or overextrapolation? The answer is not obvious.

Confidence: Over or Under?

The situation is further complicated by the fact that the cited evidence for over- or underconfidence does not support the usual interpretation of these terms in economics. Moore and Healy (2008) show that, in difficult tasks, subjects overestimate their own performance, while at the same time believing that they are worse than others at the tasks. For easy tasks, subjects underestimate their own performance but believe they are better than others. One interpretation is that agents are sometimes over- and sometimes underconfident.

But a more parsimonious interpretation is that agents shade their own judgments toward the mean. When they perform badly, they interpret the feeling of "performing badly" as in part that the task was difficult for them (they are worse than others), but also in part that they performed better than they thought (namely, they understand that their sense of performing badly is subject to error). When they perform well, they interpret that subjective feeling as the task being easy (they are better than others), but also that their own judgment may be in error. Agents are doing what we say they should under a model where they receive a noisy signal—weighting that signal toward the mean.

One might object: Why can't the agents correctly sense their own performance and also simply accept that the tasks are hard or easy for everyone? But in the Moore and Healy (2008) experiment, the agents do not know the "true" difficulty of the task. In the world we are trying to model, agents may not know the true dispersion of private information, which would correspond to the true task difficulty. But there is no particular reason to believe that they would not try to learn it, or even eliminate said private information. From a cognitive point of view, under- or overconfidence as a parameter is suspect.

What Is Overextrapolation?

In the model, overextrapolation is $\hat{\rho} > \rho$. The literature on behavioral economics has proposed two very different foundations for this behavior. The first is simply: extrapolation. Extrapolation could arise from recency effects (agents are more likely to remember recent events). This is well established in laboratory experiments. It is also well established in the data when it comes to understanding stock returns, a setting where it is distinctly suboptimal (Greenwood and Shleifer 2014). In any case, it is clear that the recent past matters in decision-making beyond what it should in a Bayesian model.

A second proposed mechanism, and the focus of Bordalo et al. (2018), is the representativeness heuristic. The idea behind the representativeness heuristic comes from a literature on judgment and decision-making in psychology, and in particular from Tversky and Kahneman (1973). In their work, agents, when asked to make a probabilistic judgment (e.g., how likely is it that an individual, given certain information, works in a certain occupation), will give a high value if the individual "matches" the category—represents essential features of the category—and ignore the base rate of the occupation. Bordalo et al. (2018) apply representativeness to the problem of detecting an underlying process given a signal. In their work, the signal becomes representative of a latent state, and agents overestimate its value in saying something about that state. In the present paper, the representativeness heuristic is overconfidence: the agent updates too much on impact. The paper firmly rejects this viewpoint of "overreaction on impact."

Evidence of some type of overextrapolation is present in asset prices.[3] Figure 1 is from recent work (Guo and Wachter 2019). This figure shows the time series of prices and dividends. Updating work of Shiller (1981) and Campbell and Shiller (1988) to the present, this figure shows at least graphical evidence that when prices and dividends diverge, it is prices that fall to meet dividends and not the other way around.

Interpreting the Inflation Series

Figure 2 shows the median forecast from the Survey of Professional Forecasters as well as realized inflation from the data. Recall that the initial interpretation of expectations was underreaction (Coibion and

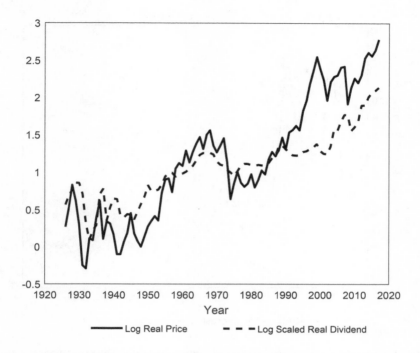

Fig. 1. Log real dividend and log real price level of the aggregate market, full sample. This figure plots the annual frequency log price level and log dividend of the US stock market in the post-1926 era. The log real dividend is multiplied by 27.43, the mean price/dividend ratio post-1926. The dividend and the price are adjusted for inflation.

Gorodnichenko 2015). Then, it became overreaction (Bordalo et al. 2018), via the representativeness heuristic. The current paper interprets it as overshooting (agents overestimate the persistence). Looking at the figure reveals the potential for confusion.

The figure reveals that the forecast clearly missed the high inflation in the 1970s, nor did it catch up sufficiently quickly. Then it missed the speed of the downturn, and again, it did not catch up sufficiently quickly. Remarkably, there was a period over a decade long—the early 1980s until the late 1990s—in which for almost every month, the median forecast lay above the actual realized inflation.

One could interpret this as overshooting: agents were slow to react to the shock, and then, in the face of much evidence, continued to believe that inflation would be high. Figure 2 suggests, however, that the VAR is misspecified.[4] The problem plaguing much research in expectations comes in full force. To interpret behavior as irrational, we need a benchmark model. If the benchmark model is misspecified, however, our interpretation is subject to error and beliefs may be more rational than

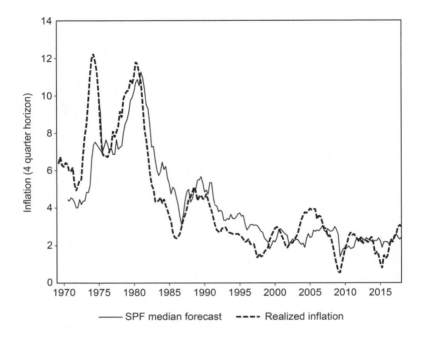

Fig. 2. Forecasted and realized inflation. The figure shows the median inflation forecast from the Survey of Professional Forecasters (SPF), as well as realized inflation.

the economists' specifications. This way of thinking can lead to an infinite regress because (i) one always needs a model to interpret expectations and (ii) *any* model is wrong. There is no solution to this problem except perhaps to remember that terms like "rationality" are ultimately technical (Bayes law, for example, or "communism of beliefs"), and should not carry their normal English-language associations.

This state of confusion would be unimportant if one could just lay aside the forecasts of inflation. However, expectation formation of inflation has been a central agenda in macroeconomics since the very beginning of the field. Accounts of Federal Reserve decision-making suggest that it operates with implicit knowledge of expectations formation (Tarullo 2017). Closing the gap between this implicit knowledge and formal knowledge through science seems important.

IV. Conclusion: What Should a Model Eventually Look Like?

This paper stresses dispersed private information, underconfidence, and overextrapolation. But the underlying parameters, τ, $\hat{\tau}$, and $\hat{\rho}$, must be estimated series-by-series. Why might these differ in different series? Do these parameters, for instance, form the correct explanation for, say, the failure of forward guidance?

Here is an alternative view of what a model could look like: First, a growing body of literature suggests experience effects persist for far longer than they should.[5] The series itself suggests that forecasters were permanently influenced by the high inflation in the 1970s. A benefit of a model of experience effects is that it endogenizes "private information." It is not so much that information is private, but rather that agents filter that information differently through the lens of their experiences.

Second, results in this paper suggest a slow updating to new information, with eventual overshooting. In recent work (Wachter and Kahana 2020), Michael Kahana argues that experience effects and slow updating to new information, with overshooting, can be captured by incorporating principles of association, together with encoding and retrieval of a persistent contextual state. Laboratory tasks on free recall show that agents possess a persistent mental context. Context and an endogenous set of associations influence what comes to mind. Context then responds to features of the environment based on these associations (Howard and Kahana 2002). Incorporating these ideas into a model of financial decision-making, we show that agents can initially underreact to novel features of the environment. If the novel features display some permanence, beliefs will update too much (overshooting) in that agents will forget the previous features. Perhaps most importantly, though, the model incorporates long-run experience effects through prior associations. These associations continue to influence how the agent sees the data.

This paper has indeed helped to show the way with new results and a new theoretical framework. If one loses something of the cognitive foundations, one certainly gains in terms of tractability and generality.

Endnotes

Author email address: Wachter (jwachter@wharton.upenn.edu). For acknowledgments, sources of research support, and disclosure of the author's material financial relationships, if any, please see https://www.nber.org/books-and-chapters/nber-macroeconomics-annual-2020-volume-35/comment-imperfect-expectations-theory-and-evidence-wachter.

1. A positive coefficient indicates underreaction because the agents do not update enough, given whatever information made them revise their estimates.

2. One might respond: but this error is exactly what we are trying to pick up! But in fact this is not the case. The ultimate goal is to model economic behavior, because this is what matters for macroeconomic aggregates. Evidence suggests that individuals do not take their own beliefs seriously (Giglio et al. 2019).

3. One can of course think of asset prices as a type of survey data because they reflect the (risk-neutral) forecasts of investors. Although much attention has been paid to the difference between risk-neutral and physical forecasts, it is not obvious that the actual difference warrants the attention. Moreover, conceivably survey evidence also suffers from this problem, as forecasters may be reporting what agents most worry about.

4. An interesting area for further work is the interpretation of the impulse response functions in light of such misspecification. Much research has shown a bias in autocorrelations stemming from uncertainty in the mean. It may be that the results from figure 3 are sensitive to whether one imposes that the forecast and the actual data have the same mean. Moreover, if either is nonstationary, then the figure is uninterpretable. A Monte Carlo study under various plausible DGPs would answer that question.

5. On inflation, see, e.g., Malmendier and Nagel (2016).

References

Barberis, N., R. Greenwood, L. Jin, and A. Shleifer. 2015. "X-CAPM: An Extrapolative Capital Asset Pricing Model." *Journal of Financial Economics* 115 (1): 1–24.

Bordalo, P., N. Gennaioli, Y. Ma, and A. Shleifer. 2018. "Over-reaction in Macroeconomic Expectations." Working Paper no. 24932, NBER, Cambridge, MA.

Campbell, J. Y., and R. J. Shiller. 1988. "The Dividend-Price Ratio and Expectations of Future Dividends and Discount Factors." *Review of Financial Studies* 1 (3): 195–228.

Coibion, O., and Y. Gorodnichenko. 2015. "Information Rigidity and the Expectations Formation Process: A Simple Framework and New Facts." *American Economic Review* 105 (8): 2644–78.

Giglio, S., M. Maggiori, J. Stroebel, and S. Utkus. 2019. "Five Facts about Beliefs and Portfolios." Working Paper no. 25744, NBER, Cambridge, MA.

Greenwood, R., and A. Shleifer. 2014. "Expectations of Returns and Expected Returns." *Review of Financial Studies* 27 (3): 714–46.

Guo, H., and J. Wachter. 2019. "'Superstitious' Investors." Working Paper no. 25603, NBER, Cambridge, MA.

Hall, R. E., and T. J. Sargent. 2018. "Short-Run and Long-Run Effects of Milton Friedman's Presidential Address." *Journal of Economic Perspectives* 32 (1): 121–34.

Howard, M. W., and M. J. Kahana. 2002. "A Distributed Representation of Temporal Context." *Journal of Mathematical Psychology* 46 (3): 269–99.

Malmendier, U., and S. Nagel. 2016. "Learning from Inflation Experiences." *Quarterly Journal of Economics* 131 (1): 53–87.

Moore, D. A., and P. J. Healy. 2008. "The Trouble with Overconfidence." *Psychological Review* 115 (2): 502–17.

Mullainathan, S. 2002. "A Memory-Based Model of Bounded Rationality." *Quarterly Journal of Economics* 117 (3): 735–74.

Shiller, R. J. 1981. "Do Stock Prices Move Too Much to Be Justified by Subsequent Changes in Dividends?" *American Economic Review* 71:421–36.

Tarullo, D. K. 2017. "Monetary Policy without a Working Theory of Inflation." Working Paper no. 33, Hutchins Center on Fiscal and Monetary Policy, Washington, DC.

Tversky, A., and D. Kahneman. 1973. "Availability: A Heuristic for Judging Frequency and Probability." *Cognitive Psychology* 5 (2): 207–32.

Wachter, J. A., and M. J. Kahana. 2020. "A Retrieved-Context Theory of Financial Decisions." Working Paper no. 26200, NBER, Cambridge, MA.

Comment

Ricardo Reis, London School of Economics, United Kingdom

I. Introduction

I have been doing research on expectations in macroeconomics for 20 years. When I started, back in the year 2000, almost every model assumed rational expectations. There were no alternative assumptions that were simultaneously (i) tractable across models, (ii) consistent within each model, and (iii) with few parameters to set. At the same time, most empirical studies of survey data rejected the null hypothesis of rational expectations. In the data, people's stated forecast errors turned out to be sometimes biased, often persistent, and always inefficient.

At the time, I felt that progress required new models to fill this gap. So this is what I did, writing models of sticky information and inattentiveness that only had one parameter to calibrate, that could be inserted as assumptions in any model of dynamic decisions, and that were as easy to solve as models with rational expectations (Mankiw and Reis 2002, 2010). Many others were in the same pursuit, and in these 2 decades the theoretical literature has flourished with models of expectations that are as good or better in satisfying these criteria, including dispersed private information (Woodford 2003; Angeletos and Lian 2016), rational inattention (Sims 2003; Mackowiak, Matejka, and Wiederholt 2018), adaptive learning (Evans and Honkapohja 2001; Eusepi and Preston 2018), ambiguity and a desire for robustness (Hansen and Sargent 2010; Ilut and Schneider 2014), memory (Malmendier and Nagel 2016), misspecification and overextrapolation (Fuster, Hebert, and Laibson 2012; Bordalo et al. 2018), coarseness (Stevens 2019), news selection (Chahrour, Nimark, and Pitschner 2019), and cognitive discounting and overconfidence (Gabaix 2020).

Just as impressive has been the progress in empirically analyzing survey data on expectations. Research moved far beyond just computing measures of central tendency in the data or just testing the null hypothesis of rational expectations. Exciting new results have come from looking at the dynamics of expectations (Coibion and Gorodnichenko 2012; Andrade et al. 2019), their revisions and reaction to news (Coibion and Gorodnichenko 2012; Bordalo et al. 2018), disagreement within surveys (Mankiw, Reis, and Wolfers 2004), disagreements across surveys (Carroll 2003), information and regime treatments (Capistran and Ramos-Francia 2010; Coibion, Gorodnichenko, and Weber 2019), differences across horizons (Andrade et al. 2016), uncertainty (Binder 2017), and the link from expectations to actions (Bachmann, Berg, and Sims 2015; Coibion, Gorodnichenko, and Ropele 2020) and to inflation dynamics (Coibion, Gorodnichenko, and Kamdar 2018).

Today, in 2020, we have a wealth of insights from this literature. Researchers are making progress across many dimensions and, understandably, they spend their energy debating the often-subtle ways in which these models differ and marginally improve our understanding. From the perspective of outsiders, however, what stands out too often is a bewildering wilderness of alternatives. Today, few wince at a researcher making an alternative assumption on expectations in a seminar, but at the same time, few also teach anything but rational expectations in a core macroeconomics class. The core knowledge that gets passed in textbooks and classes consists of some key insights in a few parsimonious models. The literature on nonrational expectations has not yet produced its own basic model.

A comparison with two other building blocks of macroeconomic models may help clarify what I mean by this. Every macroeconomist knows that the Cobb-Douglas production function is wrong. It is easy to reject the null hypothesis that one can aggregate multiple inputs into only capital and labor, and the elasticity of substitution between them is surely not constant, let alone equal to one. Yet decades of research on production and technology have convinced most that the Cobb-Douglas specification is a good starting point. Wrong, yes, but useful, capturing fundamental principles of a technology frontier, of substitution between factors, or of the link between average and marginal products. When a researcher sits to write a paper focusing on expectations, she feels confident in assuming a Cobb-Douglas function in the production side of the economy, aware that she is missing some features, but confident that she is capturing the basics of production. The same could be said for assuming expected utility, a constant relative risk aversion utility function, or

Calvo price rigidity. We have learned, through hundreds of research papers, that these baseline specifications capture basic features of behavior that are fundamentally important. The nonrational expectations literature is missing such an off-the-shelf model.

II. Yes, One Parsimonious Model of Expectations

Angeletos, Huo, and Sastry (2020) propose such a parsimonious model. Consider only macroeconomic models that are *linear and stationary*, in the sense that their endogenous variables z_t depend on a set of exogenous disturbances ε according to a Wold representation:

$$z_t = R(L)\varepsilon_t. \tag{1}$$

The lag polynomial $R(L) = R_0 + R_1L + R_2L^2 + ...$ is the solution of the model, with sparse R_i matrices whose many elements depend on only a few economic parameters. Most dynamic macroeconomic models fit into this description.

Equilibrium is, as always, a fixed point between beliefs and outcomes. For concreteness assume that there is a continuum of individuals i that each form some subjective belief on some or all of the macroeconomic variables: $\hat{E}_{i,t}[z_t]$. At this level of generality, just write equilibrium as

$$z_t = f(\{\hat{E}_{i,t}[z_t]\}_{i\in[0,1]}), \tag{2}$$

where $f(.)$ is the function mapping agents' expectation to their behavior and to market clearing conditions, which in turn determine the actual macroeconomic outcomes.

The nonrationality of expectations comes from two ingredients. First, agents in the model perceive macroeconomic dynamics to be given by a different model that has $\hat{R}(L) \neq R(L)$. Many behavioral biases can map into different specifications for this perceived process. For instance, agents that overextrapolate into the future are those that perceive the variable to be more persistent than what it is. Agents that use heuristics may neglect cross correlations but perceive each macroeconomic variable as being a univariate process. Agents that are scarred by their younger formative years may put a larger Wold weight on the disturbances realized during their 20s.

Second, conditional on this misperceived process, agents receive noisy individual signals of the macroeconomic variables and use Bayesian signal extraction to form their expectation. In particular, agents observe

$z_t + \tau^{-1/2}u_{i,t}$ where the $u_{i,t}$ is a vector of idiosyncratic noises, each one of mean zero and unit variance, so that τ measures the inverse precisions of these signals. This captures the incomplete and dispersed nature of information that comes out of the literature on inattention. Angeletos et al. (2020) also explore the possibility that the actual precision τ may be lower than the perceived precision, namely because agents may be overconfident. This does not seem to play a large role, according to their estimates, so I ignore it.

Letting $\mathbb{E}_t(.)$ denote a Bayesian expectation, then the parsimonious model of beliefs is

$$\hat{E}_{i,t}[z_t] = \mathbb{E}_t\left[z_t|\hat{R}(L)\varepsilon_t + \tau^{-1/2}u_{i,t}\right]. \tag{3}$$

This is a promising setup. It is simple, easy to explain, and flexible.

This approach still has too many free parameters. But with some discipline so that $R(L) - \hat{R}(L)$ depends only on a couple of parameters, and a reasonable restriction that τ is diagonal, then one gets closer to the goal. For instance, consider a very simple flexible-price model where inflation follows an AR(1) in equilibrium with parameter ρ, and agents receive noisy signals on its realizations. Then, there are only two expectational parameters: the perceived persistence $\hat{\rho}$ and the precision of the signals τ. Moreover, the rich empirical literature has provided strong guidance on how to set these two parameters.

III. Evidence on Over- and Underreaction and Sluggishness

A simple panel-data regression nicely captures two of the main insights of the literature that has looked at survey expectations over the last decade. Take the case where z_t is a scalar, namely inflation, to take advantage of the available good long panels of data on inflation expectations. Then, define the following variables:

$$\text{Error}_{i,t} = z_{t+1} - \hat{E}_{i,t}[z_{t+1}] \tag{4}$$

$$\text{Revision}_{i,t} = \hat{E}_{i,t}[z_{t+1}] - \hat{E}_{i,t-1}[z_{t+1}] \tag{5}$$

$$\text{AvRevision}_t = \int \text{Revision}_{i,t}di \tag{6}$$

The regression is

$$\text{Error}_{i,t} = \kappa\text{AvRevision}_t - \chi(\text{Revision}_{i,t} - \text{AvRevision}_t) + u_{i,t}. \tag{7}$$

With monthly or quarterly data on a panel of people reporting their expectations of inflation over the next year, as we for instance have in the Survey of Professional Forecasters, we can estimate this regression.

The typical estimates are $\kappa > 0$ and $\chi < 0$, and they reveal two salient features of the data. First, imagine one averaged both sides of the regression equation across people. The $\chi < 0$ would drop out, and the regression of average forecast errors on average forecast revisions would capture the stickiness of expectations. When a shock raises inflation, people, on average, increase their expectations by less than the new reality. The positive κ reflects this underreaction over time. It produces a positive serial correlation of forecast errors, a fact that study after study has found in the data (Coibion and Gorodnichenko 2015).

Second, imagine that one only had cross-sectional data to estimate this equation, so that only the χ was identified. A negative estimate then indicates that those that revise their expectations by more overdo it and so end up making forecast errors in the opposite direction. A negative χ captures the *overreaction* in the cross section, which may be attributable to overconfidence on current data being overrepresentative of what the future will be like. The data on forecasts of financial variables, in particular, show strong evidence of this behavior (Bordalo et al. 2018)

The literature has often struggled with these two facts, with some studies finding overreaction, and others underreaction. The panel regression makes clear that these apparently disparate results are explained by either leaving out one of the two variables on the right-hand side or by having the variation in the data be dominated by the cross section or the time-series dimension. People on average underreact over time but, conditionally on that, individually overreact in the cross section.

Macro models are often evaluated not by regression coefficients, but rather by their Wold representation $R(L)$. Figure 1 shows it for inflation, where, as in Angeletos et al. (2020), I use a particular reduced-form shock that accounts for a large share of business-cycle variation in a few macroeconomic series. The estimates of these impulse response functions come from local projections and data on the gross domestic product deflator between Q4 1968 and Q4 2017. Inflation follows familiar sluggish and hump-shaped dynamics after a shock.

The figure shows also the impulse response of survey forecasts using the average forecast in the Survey of Professional Forecasters for inflation in the year ahead. It is important to be precise about what this measures. It is the change in the subjective forecasts of agents, as expected by the econometrician forming rational expectations according to her statistical

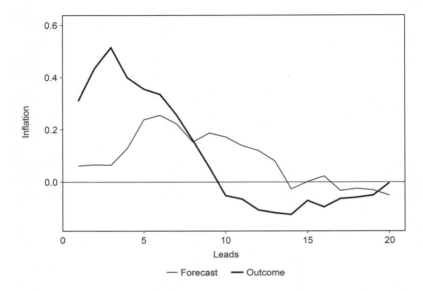

Fig. 1.   The response of 1-year ahead inflation and its expectations to a shock

model. These are not the actual changes in those subjective expectations. Mathematically,

$$\mathbb{E}_t\left[\frac{\partial}{\partial\varepsilon_t}\hat{E}_{i,t+h}(z_{t+h+4})\right] \neq \frac{\partial}{\partial\varepsilon_t}\hat{E}_{i,t}(z_{t+h+4}) \tag{8}$$

because the law of iterated expectations need not hold across the expectations operators.

The sluggishness of expectations is clear. Following a shock, expectations are sticky, only catching up to reality 8 quarters after the shock. Forecast errors are positive not just on impact, but for a prolonged period. It is this stickiness of expectations that, in varied ways, the models of the last two decades have tried to make sense of.

IV.   The Delayed Overshooting of Expectations

Angeletos et al. (2020) highlight another feature of figure 1. The impulse response of forecasts crosses that of the actual variable from below after 8 quarters, and stays above it afterward. Although average forecast errors are positive initially, they become negative after some periods. This reversal of the sign of the forecast error pins down a very particular pattern for the expectational parameters. The initial sluggishness reflects the noisy and imperfect information that people have on current shocks. The later negative forecast errors reflect an overextrapolation that makes people expect the shocks' effects to persist longer than they do. In terms of the simple AR(1) model: $z_t = \rho z_{t-1} + r\varepsilon_t$ where agents perceive $\hat{\rho}$ and get signals $z_t + \tau^{-1/2}u_{i,t}$, the initially positive forecast errors point to a small τ whereas the later negative errors point to $\hat{\rho} > \rho$.

This proposed fact is promising. However, for now, to my eyes, it is only suggestive rather than definitive. Two points give me pause before taking figure 1 and its many variants that Angeletos et al. (2020) put forward as establishing delayed overshooting of expectations as a solid fact. First, the standard errors associated with these impulse response functions are wide, especially at longer horizons. Statistical tests at conventional significance levels can reject the null hypothesis that the forecast errors are zero in the first few quarters, against the alternative that they are positive. But rejecting the null hypothesis of zero for longer horizons is much harder. From a Bayesian perspective, if one starts with a prior for the average forecast error at horizons 10–20 centered at zero, the evidence in figure 1 and in Angeletos et al. (2020) would tilt the posterior toward being more inclined to the forecast errors being negative rather than positive, but not by a lot. The difference between the two curves in figure 1 after 10 quarters is not so large, and the estimation uncertainty is plentiful.

Second, consider a different way to look at the problem of figuring out what is $\hat{\rho}$ and whether it is larger than ρ. Recall that according to the parsimonious model, agents perceive that $z_t = \hat{\rho} z_{t-1} + r\varepsilon_t$. It then follows that, no matter what the signals are, the agent's expectations at long and short horizons will be linked by $\mathbb{E}_{i,t}(z_{t+T}) = \hat{\rho}^T \mathbb{E}_{i,t}(z_t)$. Fortunately, the same survey that asks people what their expectations are for inflation over the next year also asks for their expected inflation on average over the next 5 years. The ratio of long-horizon and short-horizon expectations is

$$\frac{\sum_{h=1}^{H} \mathbb{E}_{i,t}(z_{t+h})/H}{\mathbb{E}_{i,t}(z_{t+1})} = \frac{1}{H}\frac{1-\hat{\rho}^H}{1-\hat{\rho}}, \tag{9}$$

which reveals what is the implicit $\hat{\rho}$.

By taking the ratio of the impulse responses of long-horizon and short-horizon forecasts to the same shock, we can use the formula on the right-hand side of this equation to back out the $\hat{\rho}$ in people's minds. Intuitively, if that ratio is close to 1, it must be that people expect the

long-run impact to be as large as the short-run one, and thus that the series is very persistent: a $\hat{\rho}$ close to 1. Instead, if the ratio is small, then people think that the impact of the shocks on inflation dies off quickly so $\hat{\rho}$
is close to 0. In the Survey of Professional Forecasters data, this ratio reveals $\hat{\rho} = 0.81$. Using the actual inflation data and the estimates in figure 1 suggests $\rho = 0.26$, consistent with people *overextrapolating*.

Following precisely the same procedure used to produce figure 1, estimate instead the impulse response of outcomes and forecasts for 5-year
inflation and 5-year-ahead forecasts. The results are in figure 2. Because
annual inflation has a large transitory component, estimates of ρ based
on figure 1 point to a low ρ. But, when one looks at 5-year averages, as
in figure 2, the permanent component stands out, and it reveals that the
right inference at longer horizons is that ρ is close to 1. More precisely,
the largest autoregressive root of the inflation process is close to one,
whereas the serial correlation at an annual frequency is close to zero. By
comparison, the forecast estimates in figure 2 are always below the actual
ones. Although the forecasts decline toward zero, the outcomes do not.
People behave as if inflation is a transitory process, in spite of the permanent component visible in outcomes. According to figure 2, we see people *underextrapolating*.

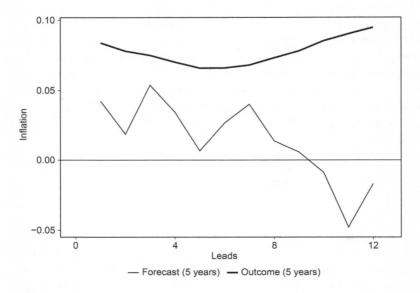

Fig. 2. The response of 5-year ahead inflation and its expectations to a shock

There is a blunter way to state the story these estimates are telling. US history teaches us that inflation can sometimes drift away, but only does so rarely. When asked in surveys about what they expect at long horizons, people at first respond too much to shocks but then quickly revert to answering 2% no matter what the shock was. Is this over- or underextrapolation?

For now, at least, the jury is still open on the direction of how $\hat{R}(L)$ differs from $R(L)$, that is, on what is the best baseline choice of parameters for the parsimonious model of expectations.

V. Missing Disagreement

Accusing a parsimonious model of missing some features misses the point of what parsimony is for. At the same time, for a model to clear the high bar that I set at the start—to become the Cobb-Douglas, the constant relative risk aversion, or the Calvo of expectations—then it should capture the central features that we have learned from surveys of expectations. The proposal by Angeletos et al. (2020) captured by equation (3) in Section II does very well, but it misses in one important dimension: disagreement and communication.

A large literature has studied the extent of disagreement in expectations, and how communication policies affect it. In theory, this has led to important insights on the role of strategic complementarities and the effects of transparency (Morris and Shin 2002; Haldane and McMahon 2018). In policy, it has spurred insights on how to steer this disagreement and have a real effect on macroeconomic outcomes (Coibion et al. 2019; Coibion et al. 2020). In the data, it has led to a focus on the second moment of expectations surveys (Mankiw et al. 2004; Dovern, Fritsche, and Slacalek 2012).

My reading of this literature is that a benchmark model should try to capture three important facts about disagreement on inflation:

1. Shocks, positive or negative, raise disagreement temporarily.

2. Policy communication lowers the disagreement that results from a shock.

3. Regime changes that raise transparency can permanently lower disagreement.

Within the framework of Section II for a scalar fundamental, a measure of disagreement is the cross-sectional variance:

$$V_t = \int (\hat{E}_{i,t}(z_{t+1}) - \int \hat{E}_{i,t}(z_{t+1})di)^2 di. \tag{10}$$

Then, assuming an AR(1) with normal shocks for the fundamental $z_t = \rho z_{t-1} + r\varepsilon_t$, noisy normal signals $z_t + \tau^{-1/2}u_{i,t}$ and letting L denote the lag operator, a few steps of algebra show that

$$(1 - \hat{\lambda}L)^2 V_t = (\hat{\rho} - \hat{\lambda})^2 \tag{11}$$

where $\hat{\lambda}$ is the root in $(0, \hat{\rho})$ of the quadratic: $(\hat{\lambda} + 1)/\hat{\lambda} = [\hat{\rho} + (1 + \tau)]/\hat{\rho}$. Crucially, the shocks ε_t do not show up. This is a deterministic equation with a stable steady state. If disagreement starts at the steady state, it will stay constant forever. It therefore follows that in the Angeletos et al. (2020) setup:

1. Disagreement does not respond to shocks.

2. Communication, understood as lowering r so that shocks are not as intense, has no effect on disagreement.

3. An increase in transparency, understood as more precise signal τ, raises disagreement as it lowers λ.

In short, the model does not capture the endogeneity of disagreement in this literature.

VI.   Disagreeing Constructively

A small modification of the model delivers an alternative parsimonious model that can capture disagreement. It adds one parameter θ, although because I had earlier removed another parameter, $\hat{\tau}$, the model is arguably just as parsimonious. The modification works as follows: a fraction $1 - \theta$ of agents form expectations precisely according to equation (3). But, a fraction θ instead happens to have full information, and so they know the current state z_t, making forecasts according to: $\mathbb{E}_t(z_{t+1}) = \rho z_t$. Whether this fraction θ is endogenous, or how it is drawn from the population, matters for dynamics. Different articles have explored how and why this matters, but in a simple parsimonious model θ can just be taken as a given constant. Likewise, assuming that these agents have perfect information is just a simple way to capture heterogeneity in the population over their signal precision τ. Assuming different groups, each with a different τ, would simply be less parsimonious than assuming that a fraction has infinite precision, and the other fraction has a finite τ precision.

A little bit of algebra shows that, in this model, the law of motion for disagreement is instead

$$(1 - \hat{\lambda}L)^2 V_t = \theta(1 - \theta)\hat{\lambda}^2\varepsilon_t^2 + (1 - \theta)(\hat{\rho} - \hat{\lambda})^2. \tag{12}$$

Note that if $\theta = 0$, then equation (12) becomes equation (10).

In this parsimonious model, the under- and overreaction of expectations, the sluggishness in adjustment to shocks, and potentially the delayed overshooting are all still present. But disagreement is now endogenous, and it has properties that fit the lessons from the data:

1. Disagreement varies over time and is affected by shocks, as it follows an AR(2) after a shock ε_t.

2. Policy communication lowers disagreement, because a lower r lowers disagreement both on impact and in the steady state.

3. Transparency in the sense of a higher θ lowers disagreement. The effect of a higher τ on disagreement depends, as it changes both the reliance of agents on their signals, as well as the dispersion of these signals.

VII. Conclusion

The literature on expectations in macroeconomics needs a simple canonical model, which can be used for teaching in core classes and as a benchmark assumption that replaces rational expectations. Angeletos et al. (2020) propose one such benchmark, with few parameters, that is easy to solve, and that can be incorporated in most dynamic macroeconomic models. Their model captures the under- and overreaction of forecasts, as well as the sluggish response of average expectations to shocks, that are the staple results of this literature. It also can capture a candidate new fact on delayed overshooting of expectations through overextrapolation. It fails to capture one important dimension of the literature, on disagreement and communication, but a modification of it can easily fix this problem. This modified imperfect expectations model meets all the criteria for the desired benchmark model. I hope teachers and researchers will use it, so that imperfect expectations soon become as routinely used as rational expectations have been so far.

Endnote

Author email address: Reis (r.a.reis@lse.ac.uk). I am grateful to Adrien Couturier and José Alberto Ferreira for research assistance. This project has received funding from the European Union's Horizon 2020 research and innovation program, INFL, under Grant No. GA: 682288. For acknowledgments, sources of research support, and disclosure of the author's material financial relationships, if any, please see https://www.nber.org/books-and -chapters/nber-macroeconomics-annual-2020-volume-35/comment-imperfect-expectations -theory-and-evidence-reis.

References

Andrade, Philippe, Richard K. Crump, Stefano Eusepi, and Emanuel Moench. 2016. "Fundamental Disagreement." *Journal of Monetary Economics* 83 (C): 106–28.

Andrade, Philippe, Gaetano Gaballo, Eric Mengus, and Benoît Mojon. 2019. "Forward Guidance and Heterogeneous Beliefs." *American Economic Journal: Macroeconomics* 11 (3): 1–29.

Angeletos, George-Marios, Zhen Huo, and Karthik Sastry. 2020. "Imperfect Macroeconomic Expectations: Evidence and Theory." *NBER Macroeconomics Annual* 35:1–114.

Angeletos, George-Marios, and Chen Lian. 2016. "Incomplete Information in Macroeconomics: Accommodating Frictions in Coordination." In *Handbook of Macroeconomics*, vol. 2, ed. John B. Taylor and Harald Uhlig, 1065–240. Amsterdam: Elsevier.

Bachmann, Rüdiger, Tim O. Berg, and Eric R. Sims. 2015. "Inflation Expectations and Readiness to Spend: Cross-Sectional Evidence." *American Economic Journal: Economic Policy* 7 (1): 1–35.

Binder, Carola C. 2017. "Measuring Uncertainty Based on Rounding: New Method and Application to Inflation Expectations." *Journal of Monetary Economics* 90 (C): 1–12.

Bordalo, Pedro, Nicola Gennaioli, Yueran Ma, and Andrei Shleifer. 2018. "Overreaction in Macroeconomic Expectations." Working Paper no. 24932, NBER, Cambridge, MA.

Capistran, Carlos, and Manuel Ramos-Francia. 2010. "Does Inflation Targeting Affect the Dispersion of Inflation Expectations?" *Journal of Money, Credit and Banking* 42 (1): 113–34.

Carroll, Christopher D. 2003. "Macroeconomic Expectations of Households and Professional Forecasters." *Quarterly Journal of Economics* 118 (1): 269–98.

Chahrour, Ryan, Kristoffer Nimark, and Stefan Pitschner. 2019. "Sectoral Media Focus and Aggregate Fluctuations." Working Papers in Economics 987, Boston College.

Coibion, Olivier, and Yuriy Gorodnichenko. 2012. "What Can Survey Forecasts Tell Us about Information Rigidities?" *Journal of Political Economy* 120 (1): 116–59.

———. 2015. "Information Rigidity and the Expectations Formation Process: A Simple Framework and New Facts." *American Economic Review* 105 (8): 2644–78.

Coibion, Olivier, Yuriy Gorodnichenko, and Rupal Kamdar. 2018. "The Formation of Expectations, Inflation, and the Phillips Curve." *Journal of Economic Literature* 56 (4): 1447–91.

Coibion, Olivier, Yuriy Gorodnichenko, Saten Kumar, and Mathieu Pedemonte. 2020. "Inflation Expectations as a Policy Tool?" *Journal of International Economics* 124 (C): Article 103297.

Coibion, Olivier, Yuriy Gorodnichenko, and Tiziano Ropele. 2020. "Inflation Expectations and Firm Decisions: New Causal Evidence." *Quarterly Journal of Economics* 135 (1): 165–219.

Coibion, Olivier, Yuriy Gorodnichenko, and Michael Weber. 2019. "Monetary Policy Communications and Their Effects on Household Inflation Expectations." Working Paper no. 25482, NBER, Cambridge, MA.

Dovern, Jonas, Ulrich Fritsche, and Jiri Slacalek. 2012. "Disagreement among Forecasters in G7 Countries." *Review of Economics and Statistics* 94 (4): 1081–96.

Eusepi, Stefano, and Bruce Preston. 2018. "The Science of Monetary Policy: An Imperfect Knowledge Perspective." *Journal of Economic Literature* 56 (1): 3–59.

Evans, George, and Seppo Honkapohja. 2001. *Learning and Expectations in Macroeconomics*. Princeton, NJ: Princeton University Press.

Fuster, Andreas, Benjamin Hebert, and David Laibson. 2012. "Natural Expectations, Macroeconomic Dynamics, and Asset Pricing." *NBER Macroeconomics Annual* 26 (1): 1–48.

Gabaix, Xavier. 2020. "A Behavioral New Keynesian Model." *American Economic Review* 110 (8): 2271–327.

Haldane, Andrew, and Michael McMahon. 2018. "Central Bank Communications and the General Public." *AEA Papers and Proceedings* 108:578–83.

Hansen, Lars Peter, and Thomas J. Sargent. 2010. "Wanting Robustness in Macroeconomics." In *Handbook of Monetary Economics*, vol. 3, ed. Benjamin M. Friedman and Michael Woodford, 1097–157. Amsterdam: Elsevier.

Ilut, Cosmin L., and Martin Schneider. 2014. "Ambiguous Business Cycles." *American Economic Review* 104 (8): 2368–99.

Mackowiak, Bartosz, Filip Matejka, and Mirko Wiederholt. 2018. "Survey: Rational Inattention, a Disciplined Behavioral Model." Discussion Paper no. 13243, CEPR, London.

Malmendier, Ulrike, and Stefan Nagel. 2016. "Learning from Inflation Experiences." *Quarterly Journal of Economics* 131 (1): 53–87.

Mankiw, N. Gregory, and Ricardo Reis. 2002. "Sticky Information versus Sticky Prices: A Proposal to Replace the New Keynesian Phillips Curve." *Quarterly Journal of Economics* 117 (4): 1295–328.

———. 2010. "Imperfect Information and Aggregate Supply." In *Handbook of Monetary Economics*, vol. 3A, ed. Benjamin Friedman and Michael Woodford, 183–230. Amsterdam: Elsevier.

Mankiw, N. Gregory, Ricardo Reis, and Justin Wolfers. 2004. "Disagreement about Inflation Expectations." *NBER Macroeconomics Annual* 18:209–48.

Morris, Stephen, and Hyun Song Shin. 2002. "Social Value of Public Information." *American Economic Review* 92 (5): 1521–34.

Sims, Christopher A. 2003. "Implications of Rational Inattention." *Journal of Monetary Economics* 50 (3): 665–90.

Stevens, Luminita. 2019. "Coarse Pricing Policies." *Review of Economic Studies* 87 (1): 420–53.

Woodford, Michael. 2003. "Imperfect Common Knowledge and the Effects of Monetary Policy." In *Knowledge, Information, and Expectations in Modern Macroeconomics: In Honor of Edmund S. Phelps*, ed. Phillipe Aghion, Roman Frydman, Joseph Stiglitz, and Michael Woodford, 25–58. Princeton, NJ: Princeton University Press.

Discussion

Following up on Ricardo Reis's discussion, Martin Eichenbaum asked a question on disagreement in models with heterogeneous beliefs, which sparked a general discussion on the topic. In practice, disagreement between agents seems to be very persistent. He asked whether the authors' model and the modification suggested by the discussant were consistent with this observation. Alp Simsek seconded Eichenbaum's comment, pointing out that most models with dispersed information, including the authors', have the implication that if an individual were to elicit other agents' expectations, she would account for this new information. In other words, if average beliefs were part of the current information set, individuals would update their own beliefs in response. This does not seem to be supported by the data, he claimed. Simsek's own empirical analysis of the Blue Chip Financial Forecasts in Ricardo Caballero and Alp Simsek ("Monetary Policy with Opinionated Markets" [Working Paper no. 27313, NBER, Cambridge, MA, 2020]) finds evidence in support of *confident disagreement*: past individual forecasts are a better predictor for future individual forecasts than past consensus forecasts. This fact seems to indicate that forecasters have dogmatic beliefs and do not consider the other agents to have useful information when forming expectations for the future. It is important to take this into account for understanding how agents respond to new information, he claimed.

The authors answered to the remarks on the role of disagreement among agents arguing that it does not have material consequences for the implications of their theory. There are two arguments that support this conclusion. First, the actual level of information precision is irrelevant for shaping aggregate outcomes. It is the *perceived* level of precision of the signals received by agents that determines their reaction. Hence, an arbitrary time-varying level of actual noise, combined with agents' perception of a fixed level of noise, would result in observationally equivalent aggregate outcomes and arbitrary time-varying levels of disagreement. Formally, their paper shows how aggregate outcomes do not depend on the parameter governing belief dispersion. Second, the response of individual beliefs to aggregate shocks in their model is independent of the degree of heterogeneity in prior beliefs. For example, an agent believing that her signal is not informative would never update expectations after observing a signal, regardless of the true level of precision of information, they argued. Taken together, these two facts indicate that disagreement among agents does not play a role in determining aggregate dynamics in the class of linear models considered in the paper. For this reason, they emphasized that empirical evidence on individual expectation revision based on Pedro Bordalo, Nicola Gennaioli, Yueran Ma, and Andrei Shleifer ("Over-reaction in Macroeconomic Expectations" [Working Paper no. 24932, NBER, Cambridge, MA, 2018])—whose theoretical counterpart is shown to directly depend on the actual level of noise—does not offer any discipline for model-implied aggregate outcomes in their setting. Reis further clarified that the goal of the parsimonious model he presented in the discussion was to have time variation in disagreement. The persistent disagreement in that model (or in the authors' model) likely falls short of the average disagreement we observe in the data. Introducing multiple priors could fix this through ex ante disagreement and may actually make little difference to the aggregate responses to macro shocks.

Jeffrey Campbell asked the authors to clarify the role of discounting in their modified IS curve. The model could exhibit a high degree of forward-looking behavior, despite the presence of informational frictions, he pointed out. The authors clarified that, although theoretically possible, the case of exacerbated forward-looking behavior is not empirically supported. Informational frictions generate myopic behavior, which dampens the feedback effects of forward-looking variables. Such dampening is stronger the more powerful general equilibrium forces are, in line with other behavioral models like Emmanuel Farhi and Iván Werning ("Monetary Policy, Bounded Rationality, and Incomplete Markets," *American Economic Review* 109, no. 11 [2019]: 3887–928). However, the presence of some degree of extrapolation introduces a countervailing element that exacerbates forward-looking behavior, they claimed. When calibrating the model to conditional moments observed in the data, the former dampening effect prevails on the amplification introduced by extrapolation.

Yueran Ma offered a comment on Jessica Wachter's discussion regarding the role of persistence in beliefs. Experimental evidence shows that the relationship between subjective and objective persistence depends on the underlying process. In particular, the gap between the two is higher when the process is more transitory. Ma made a case in favor of carefully modeling the underlying foundations of how beliefs are formed. This would make models with heterogeneous beliefs immune to Lucas's critique and allow the researcher to understand how beliefs vary with the environment, she concluded.

The authors concluded the general discussion with comments on data availability. They first addressed a comment by Cosmin Ilut, who pointed out that firms' and households' expectation data would be a precious source of information to complement the evidence from professional forecasters. They endorsed Ilut's suggestion, adding that the quality of such data is lower than for professional forecasters. They then answered a comment offered by Reis during the discussion, who suggested analyzing 5-year-ahead expectation data on top of the 1-year-ahead evidence they already showed. Ideally, one would want to use all intermediate horizons for a thorough analysis, but such data are not available. Moreover, for the purpose of business-cycle analysis, looking at longer horizons would provide increasingly less important evidence, they argued.

2

Diverging Trends in National and Local Concentration

Esteban Rossi-Hansberg, *Princeton University,* United States of America, *and NBER,* United States of America

Pierre-Daniel Sarte, *Federal Reserve Bank of Richmond,* United States of America

Nicholas Trachter, *Federal Reserve Bank of Richmond,* United States of America

I. Introduction

Most product markets are local. The reason is simply that the transportation of goods and people is costly so firms set up production plants, distribution centers, and stores close to customers. In turn, individuals locate in areas where they can obtain the goods they desire. A coffee shop or restaurant in Manhattan does not compete with similar establishments in Seattle and probably not even in Brooklyn. The wedge in prices created by the inconvenience and monetary cost of buying a product far away from the desired consumption point shields companies in different locations from direct competition. Of course, the size of these costs and, therefore, the geographic extent of the market vary by product. Markets are also product specific. Producers of a particular product are shielded from competition by producers of distinct but related goods and services to the degree that their consumption requires households to move away from their ideal variety.

Much has been written recently about the increase in national market concentration observed over the last 2 decades and the role that large national firms have played in driving this trend. The evidence for the rise in concentration is uncontroversial; the shares of the largest firms and the Herfindahl-Hirschman Index (HHI), among other measures of concentration, have increased consistently in most sectors since 1990.[1] A narrative has emerged whereby this increase in national concentration is perceived as the cause of lower product-market competition. This fall in competition is then viewed as the culprit of other apparent trends, such as rising markups and market power (Gutiérrez and Philippon 2017; Hall 2018; De Loecker,

Eeckhout, and Unger 2020), the increasing profits of large firms (Barkai 2020), declining labor market dynamism and firm entry (Decker et al. 2017), and declining wages and declining labor share (e.g., Autor et al. 2017).[2] Some studies have called into question the interpretation of these facts as evidence of increasing market power (see Hopenhayn, Neira, and Singhania 2018; Syverson 2019), and the empirical robustness and validity of some of these trends have also been contested in recent work.[3] However, the uncontroversial rise in national market concentration remains as the main empirical foundation of this central narrative.

In this paper, we use the National Establishment Time Series (NETS) data set to document four main facts regarding national and local product-market concentration in the US economy between 1990 and 2014. The first fact is that the observed positive trend in market concentration at the national level has been accompanied by a corresponding negative trend in average local market concentration. We measure concentration using the HHI, but our findings hold for a variety of statistics. We observe an increase in concentration at the national level overall across the vast majority of sectors and industries but a fall in concentration when it is measured at the core-based statistical area (CBSA), county, or ZIP code levels.[4] The narrower the geographic definition, the faster is the decline in local concentration. This is meaningful because the relevant definition of concentration from which to infer changes in competition is, in most sectors, local and not national.

The second fact shows that local concentration is falling across Standard Industrial Classification (SIC) 8 industries that together account for 78% of employment and 72% of sales. Furthermore, conditioning on industries where national concentration is rising, industries where local concentration has declined account for the majority of employment overall (72% of employment and 66% of sales) across all major sectors. The presence of these diverging trends is always large but more pronounced in Services, Retail Trade, and Finance, Insurance, and Real Estate (FIRE) sectors relative to Wholesale Trade and Manufacturing. This ordering is natural given that transport costs are less relevant in the latter two sectors. Together, these first two facts underscore an unmistakable decline in local concentration on average that is pervasive across all sectors.

How does one reconcile a positive trend in national concentration with a negative trend in local concentration? The third fact shows that, among SIC 8 industries exhibiting this pattern, top firms have accelerated these trends. That is, excluding the top firm in each industry (in terms of national sales in their SIC 8 industry in 2014), the national increase in concentration becomes naturally less pronounced. Perhaps more surprisingly, the decline in local concentration also becomes less pronounced. Put another way, large firms have materially contributed to the observed decline in local concentration.[5] Among industries with diverging trends, large firms have become bigger but the associated geographic expansion of these firms, through the opening of more plants in new local markets, has lowered local concentration thus suggesting increased local competition. In the considerably smaller set of industries where we observe increases in both national and local concentrations, top firms have also been responsible for both forms of concentration.

The fourth fact establishes that among industries with falling local concentration, the opening of a plant by a top firm is associated with a decline in local concentration at the time of the opening and that this lower level of concentration persists for at least 7 years. This observation provides further evidence that in those industries, large enterprises do not enter and dominate the local market but instead lower its concentration, either by competing with the previous local monopolist or by simply adding one more establishment that grabs a proportional market share from other local establishments. In any case, the notion that entry by large firms eliminates local producers to the point of increasing concentration is certainly not supported in the vast majority of industries where most of US employment resides.

Consider the much publicized case of Walmart. Most of Walmart's establishments are in the discount department stores industry, an industry with declining local concentration. Consistent with the fourth fact listed earlier, when Walmart opens a store, the HHI falls by 0.15 in the associated ZIP code. In contrast, computing the HHI without taking into account the opening of a Walmart establishment, concentration remains constant. One can also consider the effect of Walmart on the number of firms in a market. When Walmart enters an area, the total number of establishments in the ZIP code increases, though by less than one to one (i.e., about three to four). In other words, Walmart generates some exit but the net result of opening a Walmart store is a greater number of competitors in the market for at least 7 years after entry.[6] This case is paradigmatic, but there are many others across all major sectors. For example, the expansion of Cemex, the top firm by sales in 2014 in the ready-mixed concrete industry, led to a similar decline in local concentration and an expansion in the local number of establishments in the industry.[7]

Our findings challenge the view that product-market concentration is increasing in the United States. They do so not by challenging the evidence that national concentration has increased—we actually provide additional evidence to that effect across many industries—but by observing that this national trend does not imply a positive local trend in concentration. In fact, we show that it implies the opposite in most industries, a declining trend in concentration. Ultimately, concentration matters because it can lead to less competition. Hence, measures of concentration have to be aligned with product markets as well as their geographic and industrial scope. In particular, for the majority industries, concentration is likely more relevant to firm pricing and other strategic behavior at a more local level. Our findings are also consistent with the mixed evidence found in recent literature regarding secular changes in markups across individual industries. If local competition matters, we should not see increases in markups or profits in the markets where local competition is increasing. The measurement of markups in local markets associated with particular industries depends on important assumptions and requires very detailed data. The NETS data do not allow us to calculate these local statistics, but there exists evidence of flat markups over time in specific industries with declining concentration (Anderson, Rebelo, and Wong 2018) and in the aggregate (Traina 2018). Finally, our results are also consistent with recent papers contending that labor market concentration is falling in the US economy (Rinz 2018; Berger, Herkenhoff, and Mongey 2019; Hershbein, Macaluso, and Yeh 2019).[8] In contrast to these studies, we demonstrate the contribution of top firms, including in specific examples such as Walmart, to the divergence between the national and local concentration measures.

The NETS data set covers the universe of US firms and their plants.[9] The data set includes sales and employment numbers of all plants at different levels of geographic and industrial disaggregation down to the SIC 8 product code. Neumark, Zhang, and Wall (2006) and Barnatchez, Crane, and Decker (2017) provide thorough discussions of the advantages and disadvantages of this data source relative to US Census data. The next section discusses many of these and the extent to which they are relevant for our findings. In particular, we show that for the industries covered in our study, the geographic distribution of employment in the data is very highly correlated with that in the US Census and, moreover, that this correlation is stable over time. Our findings, therefore, cannot be driven by changes in data coverage, accuracy, or the speed of updates. The small discrepancies we find between NETS and standard Census data sources can evidently not explain the variety of consistent patterns revealed in the data. In addition, a critical feature of the NETS data integral to our analysis is that the data set allows researchers to explore and share the role of individual enterprises in shaping changes in industry concentration. This defining characteristic of NETS, therefore, permits explorations that would otherwise be infeasible with Census data.

The facts we document are directly relevant to the design of antitrust policy and other policies that can prevent successful firms from growing at the national level. We document heterogeneous trends across industries and, in some industries, concentration is clearly rising both at the national and local levels. However, our results should provide pause for policy makers who worry about increases in market power. On the whole, and in most industries, large firms are lowering local concentration and, therefore, most likely increasing product-market competition. Carl Shapiro, a former deputy assistant attorney general at the Antitrust Division of the Department of Justice and member of the President's Council of Economic Advisers (CEA) under Barack Obama, makes a similar argument. Discussing evidence on the positive trend in national market concentration, he observes: "So, while these data do reflect the fact that large, national firms have captured an increasing share of overall revenue during the past 20 years in many of these 893 'industries,' they do not, in and of themselves, indicate that the relevant local markets have become more concentrated" (Shapiro 2018). In this paper, we provide the empirical evidence supporting the notion that, in the face of rising national concentration, local markets have indeed become on average significantly less concentrated.[10]

The rest of the paper is organized as follows. Section II describes our data, the way we use the data, and our benchmark measures of national and local concentrations. Section III presents our main four facts and describes their implications. Section IV studies the quality of the NETS data among various dimensions and Section V concludes. An online appendix presents a large variety of additional calculations using other concentration statistics and provides additional detail regarding the data and the results in the main text.[11]

II. Data and Concentration Statistics

Our analysis uses data from the NETS provided by the firms Walls & Associates and Dun and Bradstreet and comprises annual observations on specific lines of business at unique locations over the 1990–2014 period. In particular, NETS data allow us to observe sales and employment of 8–19 million lines of business each year in our sample. Each line of business is assigned a data universal numbering system (DUNS) identifier that makes it possible to track its sales and employment over time at the SIC 8 level and at specific latitudes and longitudes. Industries can be mapped into broader SIC 2 classifications or divisions, and locations can be mapped into ZIP codes, counties, or CBSAs. In addition, each line of business is also assigned a headquarters (HQ) number that gives the particular enterprise to which it reports. Thus, the NETS data encompass the universe of establishments operating in the United States, as well as the enterprise to which each belongs, between 1990 and 2014.

To better illustrate the nature of the NETS data, consider the case of Walmart as an example of an enterprise. It is headquartered in Bentonville, Arkansas, and in 2014, it is associated with approximately 4,700 establishments across all 50 states. Each of these 4,700 establishments is assigned its own eight-digit primary SIC code, with 3,718 establishments operating mainly as discount department stores (SIC 53119901), 603 establishments operating mainly as warehouse club stores (SIC 53999906), 241 establishments operating primarily as grocery stores (SIC 54110000), and the remaining establishments scattered mostly across various retail classifications.

Because each establishment in the NETS data is assigned a unique DUNS identifier, it is possible to track when an establishment enters our sample (for those that enter after 1990) and, if applicable, when it exits. In addition, the DUNS identifier follows each establishment over time even if it is sold from one enterprise to another or becomes included in a merger of enterprises, so that sales and employment of particular establishments may be tracked irrespective of corporate-level changes.

Approximately a quarter of enterprises in the NETS data have only one employee. This feature of the data is typically not accounted for by alternative government sources of local employment as estimated by the County Business Patterns (CBP) or the Quarterly Census of Employment and Wages (QCEW).[12] Because these establishments nevertheless report positive sales, we include them in our benchmark analysis. In an online appendix to this paper, we show that our results are robust to excluding enterprises with only 1, fewer than 5, or fewer than 10 employees.

At the two-digit SIC code, the data are classified in terms of 11 divisions, including Manufacturing, Services, Retail Trade, Wholesale Trade, and Finance, Insurance and Real Estate (FIRE), that together account for approximately 85% of sales and 80% of employment in 2014. Because our analysis centers on the relationship between market concentration and the geographic expansion of enterprises, we exclude from our benchmark exercises industries that are intrinsically tied to specific locations because of weather or endowments of natural resources. These industries include mining; agriculture, forestry, and fishing; construction; and transportation and public utilities. We also exclude from our benchmark analysis any government establishment including establishments belonging to enterprises whose HQs are associated with a public administration SIC code and establishments associated with education, nonprofit endeavors, and central banking.

Throughout the analysis, we consider different levels of industrial and geographic disaggregation. The most basic level of disaggregation we consider is defined as an SIC 8-ZIP code pair. The NETS data cover 18,000 SIC-8 industries and about 40,000 ZIP codes. Because we omit particular industries whose operations have intrinsic ties to geographic endowments, our sample includes 15,305 industries. In each year, we only use SIC 8-ZIP code pairs that have reported both positive sales and positive employment. This leaves us with around 6 million SIC 8-ZIP code pairs for each year on average that we aggregate in different ways. Because we only consider in each year SIC 8-ZIP code pairs that have at least one establishment with positive sales and employment, the number of industry-geography pairs at a given level of aggregation (e.g., SIC 4-County) can vary from year to year. Below and in the online appendix, we show that our results are robust to exercises that only consider industry-geography pairs that have at least one establishment with positive sales and employment in every year. In the latter exercises, the number of industry-geography pairs is constant across time.

Finally, a key advantage of NETS is that it allows researchers to bypass restrictive confidentiality rules accompanying Census micro data. For example, NETS allows researchers to study the role of top firms, such as Walmart or Cemex, something not feasible when working with Census data. As we show below, this feature of NETS allows us to highlight the key role of large firms in driving the diverging trends between national and local market concentration measures. In Section IV, we explore the quality of the NETS data set along various dimensions. We establish that, once appropriately confined to the sample of industries used in this study, NETS compares favorably with the Census data.

Establishments in our data set are indexed by industry, i, location, ℓ, and year, t. Industries are defined by SIC 8 codes. Locations are defined by a latitude-longitude pair. We denote collections of industries into broader classifications (e.g., SIC 2 or divisions) by d. We denote collections of locations into broader geographies (ZIP codes, CBSAs, counties, states, or the whole United States) by g. When defining locations at the CBSA level, counties that are not within CBSAs are not represented, which amount to 5%–10% of establishments in any given year.

Let $S_{e,i,\ell,t}^{I,G}$ denote the nominal sales of enterprise e in industry i at location ℓ in year t, and $S_{e,i,g,t}^{I,G} = \Sigma_{\ell \in g} S_{e,i,\ell,t}^{I,G}$ its sales in the broader geography g (i.e., the sum of all its establishments' sales across all latitude-longitude pairs ℓ in geography g). The index I refers to the industrial level of aggregation (i.e., by SIC 2, SIC 4, SIC 6, or SIC 8). The index G indicates the geographic level of aggregation (i.e., by ZIP code level, CBSA level, county level, or the whole United States) that we use to define a location ℓ. We then denote by $s_{e,i,g,t}^{I,G}$ this enterprise's share of all sales in industry i located in geography g at date t for the levels of aggregation I and G. We adopt as our benchmark measure of market concentration the HHI,

$$C_{i,g,t}^{I,G} = \sum_e (s_{e,i,g,t}^{I,G})^2,$$

where $C_{i,g,t}^{I,G} \in [1/N_{i,g,t}^{I,G}, 1]$ is the sales concentration, and $N_{i,g,t}^{I,G}$ the number of enterprises in industry i and geography g at time t. In the online appendix to this paper, we also consider alternative measures of concentration, such as the sales share of the top firm, or the adjusted HHI, and show that all of our findings are robust to these other measures. In particular, to the degree that the number of small firms in an industry differs between NETS and CBP data, and that this difference were to have an increasing trend that materially reduces the lower bound of the HHI, the range of the adjusted HHI index no longer depends on the number of firms.[13]

III. National and Local Market Concentration: The Facts

We organize the discussion of our findings into four main facts. The first two facts document the diverging trends in national and local concentrations and their importance across sectors and geographic definitions of a "local" market. The third and fourth facts document the role that large firms have played in these trends. As a form of corollary to the last fact, we also present evidence specific to Walmart, a firm that has featured prominently in the debate on the evolution of market concentration.

A. Fact 1: Diverging Trends on Average

Fact 1 is summarized in figures 1 and 2. Figure 1 shows a weighted average of the change in concentration, $\Delta C_t^{I,G}$, across all industry-geography pairs (i, g) for different definitions of geography G, namely, ZIP code, county, CBSA, and the whole United States,

$$\Delta C_t^{I,G} = \sum_{i,g} w_{i,g,t}^{I,G} \Delta C_{i,g,t}^{I,G},\tag{1}$$

where the weights $w_{i,g,t}^{I,G}$ are given by the employment shares of industry-geography (i, g) in aggregate employment in year t, and $\Delta C_{i,g,t}^{I,G}$ denotes the change in market concentration between year t and the first year for which we observe sales in the location-industry pair (i, g). As mentioned in Section II, all findings presented in this paper are robust to excluding enterprises with 1, fewer than 5, and fewer than 10 employees. In part, this is because, by construction, our employment-weighted measures of concentration already assign small weights to industry-geography pairs that contain mostly small enterprises.[14]

As indicated in the 2016 CEA report, Barkai (2020), Gutiérrez and Philippon (2017), and others find market concentration at the national level has been steadily increasing since 1990. However, the exact opposite is true for less aggregated measures of concentration. Figure 1 shows that the more geographically disaggregated the measure of concentration,

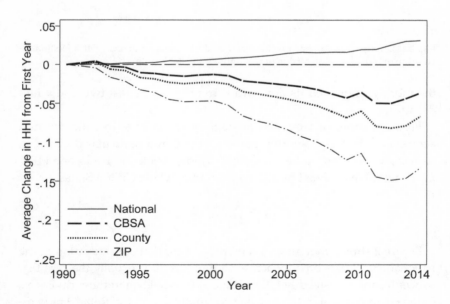

Fig. 1. Diverging economy-wide national and local concentration trends. A color version of this figure is available online.

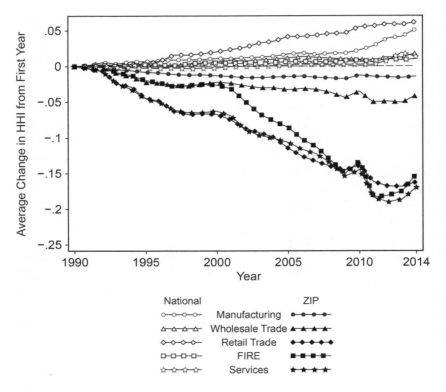

Fig. 2. Diverging division-level national and local concentration trends. HHI = Herfindahl-Hirschman Index. A color version of this figure is available online.

the more pronounced its downward trend over the last two and a half decades.

Figure 2 shows a weighted average of the change in concentration across all industry-geography pairs (i, g) within a particular division, d, namely, Manufacturing, Services, Retail Trade, Wholesale Trade, and FIRE, for geographies defined by ZIP code and the whole United States,

$$\Delta C_{t,d}^{I,G} = \sum_{i \in d, g} w_{i,g,t,d}^{I,G} \Delta C_{i,g,t}^{I,G}.$$

Figure 2 shows that although increasing market concentration at the national level holds broadly across all divisions, it is equally the case that concentration has steadily fallen at the ZIP code level in these divisions. Observe, in particular, that market concentration in the Retail Trade division has been increasing nationally more than in any other division. However, Retail Trade is also among the divisions that show the steepest decline in concentration at the ZIP code level. This fact is especially striking given that physical retail establishments in our data set are likely to have very local markets.

Concentration by Industrial Classification and Employment

Figure 3 depicts the divergence between national and local concentrations at the ZIP code level for different degrees of industrial aggregation, I. This growing divergence between national and local concentrations is most pronounced at the SIC 8 level but clearly present at lower levels of industrial aggregation as well, including the coarsest SIC 2 classification. Thus, we explore below in more detail how these diverging trends between national and local concentrations are related to industrial classification.

Figure 4 repeats the exercise in figure 3 but focuses on employment rather than sales. As the figure shows, using employment rather than

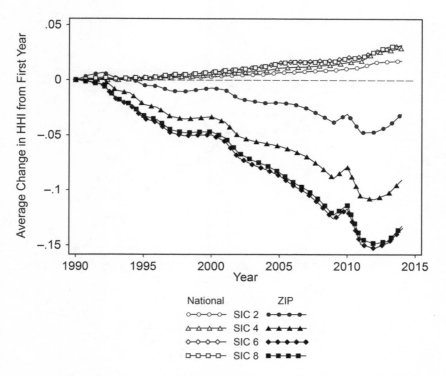

Fig. 3. Diverging economy-wide trends in sales concentration. HHI = Herfindahl-Hirschman Index; SIC = Standard Industrial Classification. A color version of this figure is available online.

sales is immaterial for the growing divergence between national and local concentrations.[15] In the online appendix, we show that all of our other findings regarding diverging trends between national and local concentrations also hold for employment as well as sales.

In summary, figures 1–4 indicate a growing divergence in national and local concentrations that holds for broad levels of industrial and geographic definitions. In the online appendix, we carry out and present a large number of exercises that highlight the robustness of our findings.[16]

Concentration and Sample Selection

Before proceeding with the analysis and an exploration of the roots underlying our basic fact 1, we discuss an important aspect of this fact related to sample selection. In particular, because we omit in each year industry-geography pairs with no establishments, the resulting unbalanced panel can create situations where an industry-geography pair with

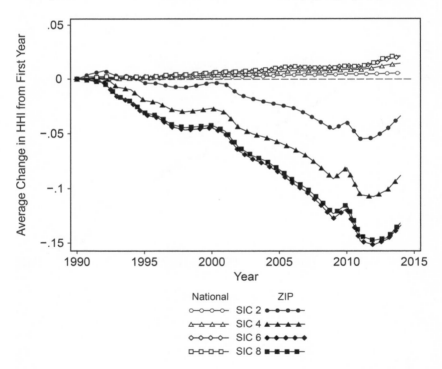

Fig. 4. Diverging economy-wide trends in employment concentration. HHI = Herfindahl-Hirschman Index; SIC = Standard Industrial Classification. A color version of this figure is available online.

a single establishment is dropped from one year to the next. Because the omitted observation is one with a single establishment, and thus associated with high concentration, local concentration decreases simply as a result of losing the observation. Conversely, of course, entry has the opposite effect whereby new establishments in markets without a previous incumbent raise local concentration.[17]

Figures 5 and 6 repeat the exercises in figures 1 and 2 but only considering industry-geography pairs where at least one establishment is present in every year. The resulting panel, therefore, is balanced. Though slightly less pronounced, the divergence between national and local concentration trends remains unequivocal. Furthermore, it is still the case that this divergence becomes more pronounced when moving toward more disaggregated definitions of local markets. It is also still the case that the divergence in concentration trends is particularly evident in service industries, such as Retail and FIRE, which make up the bulk of the US economy.

In the online appendix, we show that these balanced-panel findings also hold for other measures of concentration such as the share of the largest firm or the adjusted HHI. It is worth noting that, for more

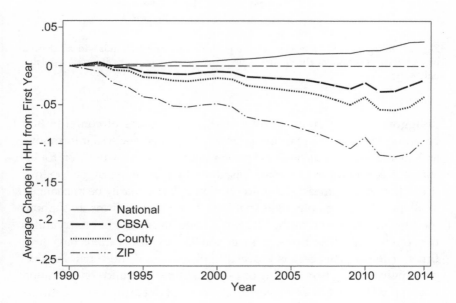

Fig. 5. Diverging economy-wide national and local concentration trends with a balanced panel. HHI = Herfindahl-Hirschman Index; CBSA = core-based statistical area. A color version of this figure is available online.

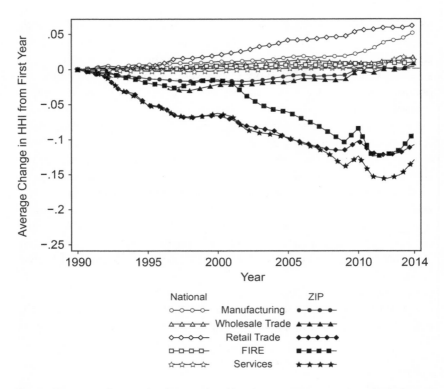

Fig. 6. Diverging division-level national and local concentration trends with a balanced panel. HHI = Herfindahl-Hirschman Index. A color version of this figure is available online.

disaggregated definitions of local markets, measures of concentration based on the sales share of the largest X firms become less informative as X increases. The reason lies in strong selection issues. Consider, for instance, a concentration measure based on the sales share of the top four firms. In that case, measured concentration will necessarily be unchanged in all industry-geography pairs that have four or fewer firms throughout the sample. However, at the SIC 8-ZIP code level, 90% of observations turn out to have three firms or fewer and 93% of observations have four firms or fewer. This case is especially misleading if those pairs are increasingly moving from having one firm to three firms and concentration is actually falling. For example, in the discount department store industry (which includes Walmart), of the ZIP codes that had one firm in 1990 and at least one firm in 2014, 56% had at least two firms competing in 2014 but only 5% of those ZIP codes had more than four firms.

It emerges, therefore, that we have to be cautious when measuring concentration at local levels. Because industry-geography pairs with four or fewer firms represent the large majority of local markets, any study that attempts to measure market concentration in disaggregated sectors and highly disaggregated geographies using the share of the largest four firms faces strong measurement problems. Such studies (e.g., Ganapati 2018) do not challenge the results in our paper or their interpretation.

B. Fact 2: Pervasive Diverging Trends

Fact 2 is presented in figure 7. Within each SIC 2 classification, the figure gives a breakdown of employment in industries with different market concentration trends. In particular, for a given SIC 2 classification, the height of each bar gives the percentage of employment in all industries within that classification that have rising market concentration at the national level between 1990 and 2014. For each SIC 8 industry i within an SIC 2 classification, we compute in each year $\Delta C_{i,t}^{I,G} = \Sigma_g w_{i,g,t}^{I,G} \Delta C_{i,g,t}^{I,G}$, where both g and G denote the whole United States, and regress $\Delta C_{i,t}^{I,G}$ on t. The height of the bar then represents the percentage of labor, within that SIC 2 and across all years, employed in all SIC 8 industries with positive national concentration time trends. Thus, the major part of US employment resides in industries with rising national concentration across all SIC 2 classifications. Within a bar associated with a given SIC 2 classification in figure 7, the colors red, blue, and black represent, respectively,

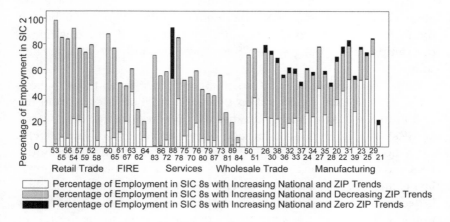

Fig. 7. Pervasive diverging trends across two-digit sectors. SIC = Standard Industrial Classification. A color version of this figure is available online.

the percentage of employment that resides in industries with declining, rising, and flat market concentrations at the ZIP code level.[18]

Figure 7 shows the pervasiveness of SIC 8 industries with diverging trends.[19] That is, a substantive share of employment resides in industries with rising market concentration at the national level and declining market concentration at the ZIP code level. It also shows the heterogeneity in this share across SIC 2 divisions. For example, in SIC 2 53, which includes General Merchandise Stores, virtually all employment resides in SIC 8 industries with diverging trends (96.38%). In contrast, in SIC 2 21, which includes Tobacco Products, none of the SIC 8 industries exhibit a positive national trend and a negative local trend. Diverging trends are more pronounced in Retail, FIRE, and Services than in Wholesale Trade and Manufacturing, though still very much present in the latter two divisions.

The proportion of aggregate US employment located in all SIC 8 industries with increasing national market concentration and decreasing ZIP code level market concentration is 43%. Thus, given that some industries have also had declining concentration at both the national and ZIP code levels, 78% (or over three-fourths) of US employment resides in industries with declining local market concentration.[20]

C. *Fact 3: The Role of Top Firms*

Fact 3 explores the contribution that top firms in terms of sales share have made to the diverging trends in each SIC 8 industry. Figures 8 and 9 focus on just those industries whose market concentration has increased at the national level since 1990, represented by the height of the bars in figure 7. Those industries account for roughly half of all industries in our sample, 61% of aggregate US employment, and 67% of aggregate sales.

Within that set of SIC 8 industries, figure 8 focuses on those that exhibit negative local concentration trends. These industries account for 72% of total employment in industries with positive national trends (66% of sales). The figure presents in solid orange and solid red, respectively, the national HHI and the local ZIP code level HHI among these industries. Given our industry selection, the national concentration (orange) line is increasing by construction and the local concentration (red) line is decreasing by construction. The dashed orange and dashed red lines in that figure depict the same objects but exclude the top enterprise in each SIC 8 industry as measured by sales in 2014.[21] We consider only

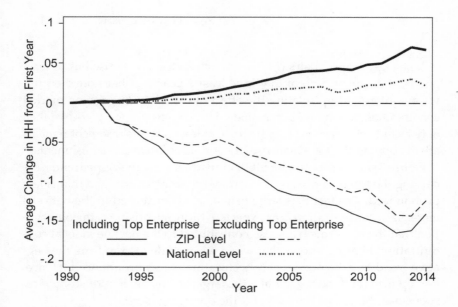

Fig. 8. The role of top enterprises in national and local concentration trends in diverging industries. HHI = Herfindahl-Hirschman Index. A color version of this figure is available online.

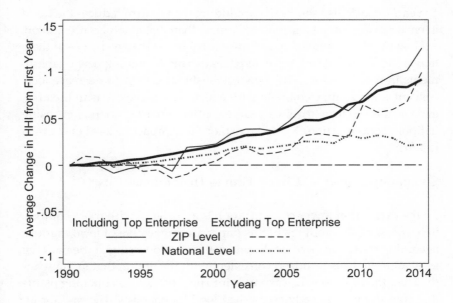

Fig. 9. The role of top enterprises in national and local concentration trends in concentrating industries. HHI = Herfindahl-Hirschman Index. A color version of this figure is available online.

industry-geography pairs (i, g) for which i's top enterprise has at least one establishment present in g in at least 1 year. Furthermore, because we are interested in isolating the effect of the top enterprise on market concentration, among those remaining industry-geography pairs, we then only include observations (i, g, t) where at least one establishment remains after dropping the top enterprise in i and its associated establishments.[22]

Figure 8 shows that among SIC 8 industries with diverging trends, excluding the top firm results in a national concentration trend that is less pronounced. The fact that large firms have contributed to the national increase in concentration is as expected. More surprising is the observation that the top firms have also contributed to the decline in local concentration. Figure 8 shows that when we exclude the top firm, the negative trend in ZIP-code-level concentration is less pronounced. Hence, the top firm (and more generally the largest firms) in an industry are responsible (though not entirely) for the diverging trends.

Figure 9 is constructed exactly as figure 8 but uses the SIC 8 industries with increasing national trends that are not depicted in figure 8. In other words, it uses the SIC 8 industries with positive national and local trends. The figure shows that for this set of industries, excluding the top firm lowers both the national and the local trends in concentration. Over the last 10 years or so, it also shows that excluding the top firm reduces the trend in national concentration significantly more than that in local concentration.

How can the growth of large firms contribute to the divergence in these trends? To a large extent, top enterprises expand by adding new establishments in new locations. The new establishments tend to decrease local concentration as they compete with existing establishments in the area, even as the top firm acquires a larger national market share, increasing national concentration. Next, we explore the impact of local entry by a top firm.

Comparing Industries' Largest Firm to Their Runner-Ups

To the extent that lower concentration is associated with more competitive markets, the findings in this paper are suggestive of local markets becoming more competitive despite concentration rising at the national level. Our analysis is indeed consistent with the notion that in many industries, the top enterprise expands into new markets by opening plants that compete with already established local monopolists. The case for increasing competition, however, is less clear if the observed fall in concentration is the result of a few firms entering several markets. As discussed in Bernheim and Whinston (1990) and Bond and Syropoulos (2008), when firms compete in multiple markets simultaneously, the potential for collusion can grow because these firms' ability to punish any deviation can be enhanced by their multiple "contacts" across markets. Hence, increasing national concentration resulting from the increasingly large positions of two or three enterprises in an industry can result in declines in local concentration, more local contacts between competitors, and a rise in the ability to collude and thus the effective market power of the largest firms. If, in contrast, increasing national concentration results from the gradual expansion of a single top firm competing with local firms, a decline in local concentration will be associated with reductions in market power in those local markets.

To gain insight into the role of the largest enterprise in a given industry relative to that of the largest two or three enterprises, figure 10 repeats the exercise in figure 8 but excludes the second and third largest enterprises instead of the top enterprise. For industries where national and local concentration trends diverge, excluding the second and third largest enterprises results in an increase in concentration at the local level as in figure 8. Thus, as with the top enterprise, when the second and third largest enterprises enter new geographical markets, local concentration falls.

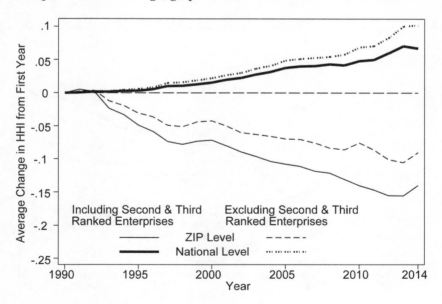

Fig. 10. The role of the second and third largest enterprises in diverging industries. HHI = Herfindahl-Hirschman Index. A color version of this figure is available online.

However, unlike figure 8, excluding the second and third largest enter-prises increases national concentration. Put another way, unlike the top en-terprise, the second and third largest enterprises contribute to reducing concentration at the national level. This finding is inconsistent with the view that the largest two or three enterprises are responsible for a simul-taneous rise in national concentration and decline in local concentration as they expand in new untested markets. Instead, figure 8 shows that entry of the second and third largest enterprises leads to overall declines in con-centration as with any other less dominant firm.

Analogous to figure 10, figure 11 repeats the exercise in figure 9 for cases where both national and local concentrations have been rising but excludes the second and third largest enterprises instead of the top enter-prise. Comparisons with figure 9 make it even more apparent that the second and third largest firms have an impact that on average differs from that of the most dominant enterprise across industries. In figure 11, we see that the second and third largest enterprises contribute to lowering con-centration both at the national and local levels whereas the most domi-nant enterprise in figure 9 contributes to higher concentration nationally.

Figure 12 helps further contrast the way in which, across industries, the dominant enterprises have expanded geographically relative to the

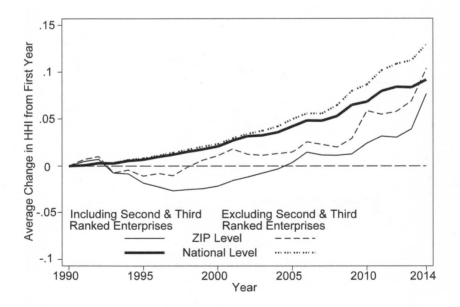

Fig. 11. The role of the second and third largest enterprises in concentrating industries. HHI = Herfindahl-Hirschman Index. A color version of this figure is available online.

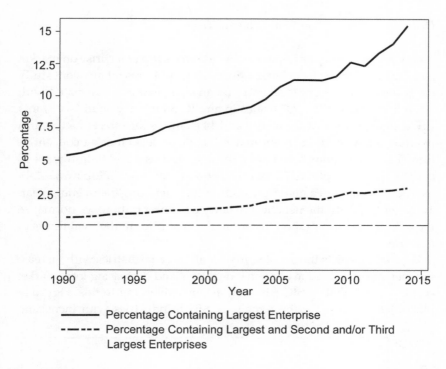

Fig. 12. Expansion of top enterprises into ZIP codes. A color version of this figure is available online.

next two largest enterprises. Specifically, the solid line in figure 12 shows the proportion of SIC 8-ZIP code pairs, weighted by employment associated with that pair, where the dominant enterprise has at least one establishment. This proportion steadily increased from 5.4% in 1990 to 15.5% in 2014. In other words, on average across industries, the largest enterprise has unambiguously and steadily expanded into new local markets over the last 25 years. The dashed line in figure 12 depicts the proportion of SIC 8-ZIP code pairs where not only the largest enterprise but also the second and third largest enterprises have at least one establishment. Although the dashed line has gradually increased over the last 25 years, it has done so at a considerably slower rate than the solid line. Put differently, the difference between the two lines represents the proportion of SIC 8-ZIP code pairs in the United States where the top enterprise is competing with smaller firms rather than its next two largest competitors, and this difference has itself gotten markedly larger over the last 3 decades.

D.   Fact 4: When a Top Firm Comes to Town

To further illustrate the impact of an industry's top enterprise on market concentration at the local level, figures 13 and 14 present an event study describing the effect of local entry by an establishment associated with a top firm (defined by 2014 sales in an SIC 8 industry as in fact 3) in a ZIP code. Specifically, figures 13 and 14 examine the effect of a top firm opening a new establishment in a ZIP code on local market concentration. The calculations here mimic those in figures 9 and 8. In figures 13 and 14, the x-axis plots a 10-year window surrounding a top firm establishment opening in a given ZIP code, with 0 denoting the opening year. To better highlight the net effect of entry on concentration, we normalize the change in concentration to zero in the year prior to the establishment opening.

Figure 13 depicts the event study for all SIC 8 industries with increasing market concentration at the national level and decreasing local market concentration, that is, SIC 8 industries with diverging trends. Figure 14 illustrates findings for the remaining SIC 8 industries with increasing

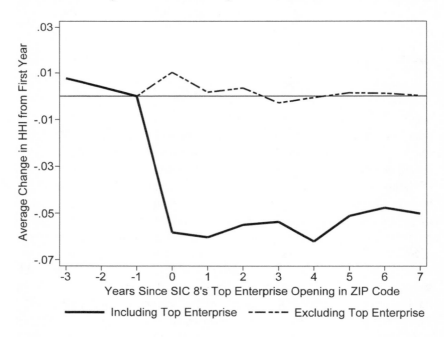

Fig. 13.   Effect on concentration when a top enterprise enters a local market in diverging industries. HHI = Herfindahl-Hirschman Index; SIC = Standard Industrial Classification. A color version of this figure is available online.

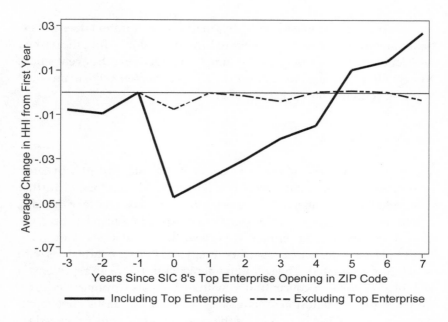

Fig. 14. Effect on concentration when a top enterprise enters a local market in concentrating industries. HHI = Herfindahl-Hirschman Index; SIC = Standard Industrial Classification. A color version of this figure is available online.

national concentration: those where both national and local trends are positive over our sample period. The solid lines in both figures present the evolution of the HHI when the entering establishment is included; the dashed lines illustrate the same object when excluding the opening establishment owned by the top enterprise within each industry.

Among industries with diverging trends, the opening of an establishment in a ZIP code is associated with a fall in market concentration. Moreover, this fall persists at about the same size for at least 7 years after the event. In contrast, among industries with increasing local market concentration, the opening of an establishment leads to a temporary decrease in market concentration but one that reverses quickly. After 4–5 years, concentration is higher than it would have been absent the opening. Hence, in the former case, the establishment owned by the top enterprise does not become dominant, whereas in the latter case it eventually dwarfs the establishments of other firms. The data suggest that, on the whole, the case where the top firm does not become dominant at the local level is markedly more relevant.[23]

The dashed lines in both figures 13 and 14 suggest that when all shares are recalculated excluding sales of the opening establishment belonging to the top enterprise in each industry, market concentration does not exhibit a significant trend over the entire 10-year window. Thus, the dashed lines lend credibility to a central assumption underlying the event study, namely, that entry by a top enterprise in a local market is the main event affecting concentration in each market.

The Case of Walmart

The event study presented in fact 4 averages the effect of entry by a top enterprise across many markets. It is informative, therefore, to further delve into the data within a particular sector. In the last couple of decades, one of the most widely studied cases of an expanding firm has been the case of Walmart.[24] Hence, here we repeat the calculations underlying fact 4 but for the particular case of Walmart and the SIC 8 industries with which it is associated. The solid line depicted in figure 15 represents a weighted average of concentration within Walmart's primary industry (discount department stores) across all ZIP codes. The dashed line represents the same object but excludes the opening establishment owned by

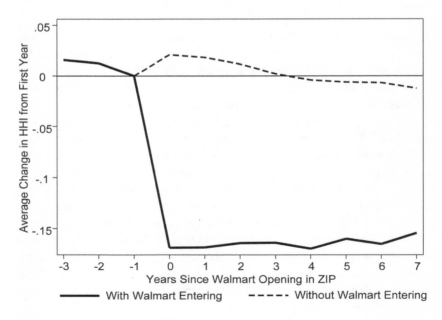

Fig. 15. Effect on concentration when Walmart enters a local market. HHI = Herfindahl-Hirschman Index. A color version of this figure is available online.

Walmart (i.e., all shares are recalculated excluding Walmart's sales from the new establishment).

Our findings for Walmart are qualitatively similar to those in fact 4 for industries with diverging trends (as is the case for Walmart's industries). Absent a Walmart opening, there is no trend in concentration, but there is a significant fall in the HHI of a ZIP code in which Walmart opens a new establishment. This lower level of concentration remains about constant for at least 7 years.

One advantage of considering a particular firm and its industries is that we can also show, and easily interpret, the effect of entry on the number of establishments in the local market. To do so, figure 16 illustrates the effect of a Walmart establishment opening in a given ZIP code on the number of establishments in that ZIP code. The solid line in the figure indicates that, when averaged across all ZIP codes (weighted by geography-SIC 8 employment, as in all other figures), the opening of a Walmart establishment is associated with an increase in the number of local establishments. This increase is somewhat less than one for one (roughly 0.75), which suggests that the entry of Walmart is associated with some establishment exits across ZIP codes. Consistent with this observation,

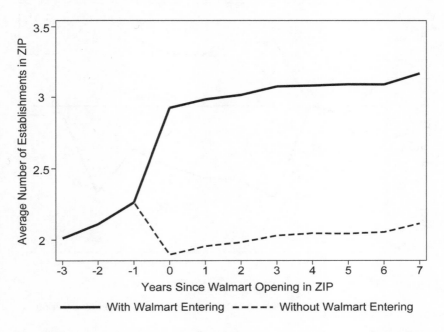

Fig. 16. Effect on number of establishments when Walmart enters a local market. A color version of this figure is available online.

the dashed line indicates that when the newly established Walmart is excluded from the calculation, the number of establishments falls somewhat across ZIP codes.[25]

The Case of Cemex

Figure 7 suggests that a very high share of employment in Retail Trade
resides in industries with diverging national and local trends, while this
phenomenon is much less prevalent in Manufacturing and Wholesale
Trade. However, the sector level of aggregation presented in figure 7
obscures considerable heterogeneity within industries in a given sector.
It is still the case that many manufacturing industries have diverging
trends and see declining local concentration following the arrival of their
largest enterprise in a ZIP code. To use one example, figures 17 and 18
highlight the SIC 8 code 32730000, Ready-Mixed Concrete, whose top
enterprise by sales in 2014 is Cemex, a building materials company. Figure 17 shows that the arrival of Cemex into a ZIP code reduces concentration in its industry by about 0.1. Although this effect dissipates after

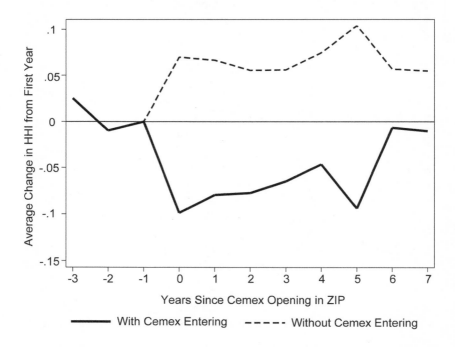

Fig. 17. Effect on concentration when Cemex enters a local market. HHI = Herfindahl-
Hirschman Index. A color version of this figure is available online.

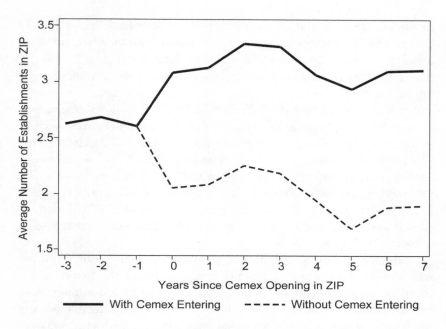

Fig. 18.   Effect on number of establishments when Cemex enters a local market. A color version of this figure is available online.

7 years, concentration measured excluding Cemex remains higher than it otherwise would when included so that this company is still contributing to lower local concentration. Figure 18 shows that, as with the case of Walmart, although some existing establishments do exit when Cemex opens a plant, the overall number of establishments in the ZIP-industry pair rises on average. Although Syverson (2008) documents increasing national concentration within this industry, consistent with our findings, Syverson (2004, 2008) also argues that high transport costs make local measures of concentration more relevant. In this paper, we show that these more local measures exhibit a downward trend.

IV.   The NETS Data

One important advantage of the NETS data is that it covers every establishment in the United States at an exceptionally high level of disaggregation both by industry and geographic area. Unlike the comparable microdata available from the Census Bureau that produce the CBP data, NETS does not require that a research proposal be approved describing how the data are to be used. It also does not require that an approved researcher travel to the location of a Federal Statistical Research Data Center (FSRDC) for secure access or compliance with the disclosure process to protect sensitive information. NETS data only require a subscription fee and can be easily accessed on any machine without undergoing a formal review process.

A critical feature of the NETS data is that NETS allows researchers to examine and illustrate the impact of individual enterprises, such as Walmart in the discount department stores industry, or Cemex in the ready-mixed concrete industry. This feature of NETS is integral to our analysis in that it permits us to explore and disclose the extent to which findings on concentration are driven by specific and large enterprises in individual industries. This defining characteristic of NETS, which we exploit in this paper, thus permits explorations that would otherwise be infeasible with Census data.

Evidently, to the degree that NETS allows us flexibility not permitted with Census data, it is important to benchmark how the two data sets compare. Barnatchez et al. (2017) note that NETS includes many nonemployer establishments not covered by the CBP, which tend to be very small establishments. When removing establishments with one employee or fewer than five employees, they find that overall trends in employment and establishments counts are closely aligned with the CBP. They suggest, therefore, verifying that findings using NETS data are robust to these sample restrictions. Barnatchez et al. (2017) also observe that differences between NETS and Census data are largely related to discrepancies in Agriculture, Mining, and Construction. In particular, in the latter two sectors, NETS appears to not have captured the full extent of recent employment changes. These include changes resulting from the boom-bust cycles associated with the shale oil and gas expansion in the early 2000s for mining and the bursting of the housing bubble in 2007 for construction. As mentioned above, our analysis excludes these sectors in any case because their activity is intrinsically tied to local geographic characteristics.

To get an idea of the differences between NETS and the CBP, figure 19 illustrates standardized (i.e., set to 1 in 1990) aggregate employment in the NETS database and the CBP. Unlike Barnatchez et al. (2017), we remove from both data sets the set of industries described above and, thus, we are restricted to the five major sectors used in this study: FIRE, Manufacturing, Retail, Services, and Wholesale Trade. Consistent with their observations, in the NETS data, we plot standardized employment when including all enterprises as well as when excluding, in each year,

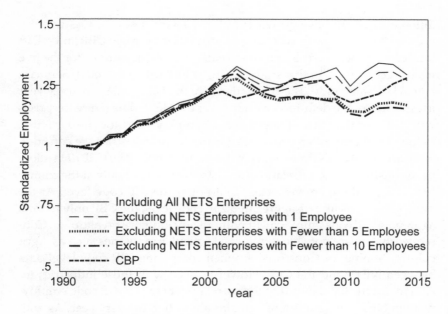

Fig. 19. Standardized national employment in County Business Pattern and National Establishment Time Series data. A color version of this figure is available online.

enterprises with 1, fewer than 5, and fewer than 10 employees. As shown in the figure, the NETS data line up almost identically with the CBP data up to around 2002.[26] Small differences arise after that year though all series appear to flatten out. Of note, almost throughout the sample, CBP employment lies in between employment excluding one and fewer than five employees in the NETS data. The difference in the sampling of small firms between NETS and the Census noted in Barnatchez et al. (2017), therefore, appears bounded by these two cases. In an online appendix, we show that all findings in this paper hold for all NETS cases shown in figure 19. Moreover, as described above, all weighted average estimates in this study are weighted by employment so that, by construction, any differences in the sampling of small firms after 2002 are also given small weight. Observe also that higher-frequency changes in Census data, such as the dip in employment following the Great Recession, are present in the various NETS cases shown in figure 19. Evidently, differences in sampling between NETS and the Census manifest themselves mainly as a level effect after 2002.

Although differences between NETS and the CBP primarily result from the sampling of small firms, a question arises as to whether these differences might have grown over time. To explore this question, figure 20a illustrates the cross-sectional correlation between CBP and NETS total employment across counties in each year of our sample, for the five major sectors used in this study: FIRE, Manufacturing, Retail, Services, and Wholesale Trade. The correlation is high at above 0.98 in every year irrespective of the definition we adopt for the NETS data (i.e., enterprises with 1, fewer than 5, and fewer than 10 employees). More importantly, to the extent that differences exist, for the set of industries we consider, there are no obvious time trends in those differences. The CBP data allow us to construct these correlations industry by industry only at the county level, where these are very close, but not at the ZIP code level. At the more geographically disaggregated ZIP code level, the CBP only reports aggregate ZIP code employment without any industry breakdown. Consequently, we are not able to remove particular industries such as Agriculture, Mining, or Construction when comparing ZIP code level data between NETS and the CBP. However, even with those industries included, figure 20b shows that the correlation between ZIP code employment in NETS versus the CBP remains above 0.85 in every year. As with the county-level data, to the extent that this correlation is not exactly 1 and to the extent that differences exist between the two data sets, there is no trend in the way that ZIP code employment differs between NETS and the CBP.

In summary, our findings are consistent with those of Barnatchez et al. (2017) who find differences between NETS and Census data related to the sampling of small firms. As the authors suggest, these differences appear to be bounded by exercises that remove small firms. Specifically, we find that standardized CBP employment is bounded by cases that remove firms with one and fewer than five employees in the NETS data. Moreover, our analysis removes industries identified by Barnatchez et al. (2017) as those least closely matching employment in the CBP, though we remove them for different reasons as explained above. Finally, although there appears to be an increase in the difference between CBP and NETS employment starting in 2002, this discrepancy emerges mainly as one time change with no visible trends after 2002. All of these observations, therefore, suggest that any findings related to aggregate or industry-wide estimates that we discuss above cannot be driven by the scope or coverage of the two data sets.

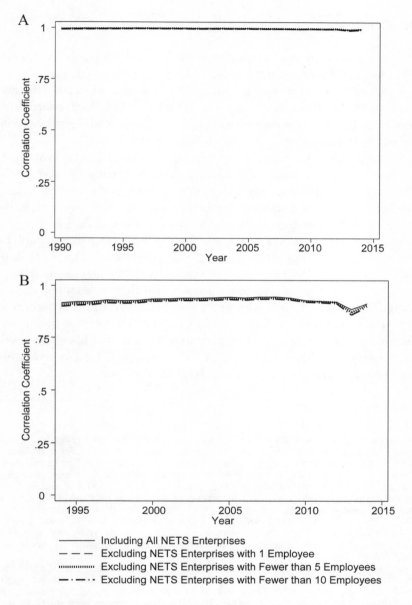

Fig. 20. County-level (*a*) and ZIP-level (*b*) correlations between National Establishment Time Series and County Business Pattern employment. HHI = Herfindahl-Hirschman Index. A color version of this figure is available online.

V. Conclusions

We have shown by way of four main facts that the increase in market concentration observed at the national level over the last 25 years is being shaped by enterprises expanding into new local markets. This expansion into local markets is accompanied by a fall in local concentration as firms open establishments in new locations. These observations are suggestive of more, rather than less, competitive markets.[27]

The findings in this paper potentially help reconcile the observation of increasing concentration at the national level and the more mixed evidence on increasing markups and profits. Almost no theory of product-market competition associates decreasing concentration with either increasing markups or increasing profits. One exception resides in theories of multimarket collusion where a few firms competing in many markets can have enhanced opportunities to collude. Although this form of collusion could be important in specific industries, we show that an expanding top firm competing with local producers is a much more common occurrence. Thus, our facts indicate that the rising trend in national concentration is not, in and of itself, necessarily a concern for antitrust policy. By decreasing local concentration, the growth of top firms has likely increased local competition in many industries and, therefore, helped improve the quality and reduce the prices of much of what we buy.

Endnotes

Author email addresses: Rossi-Hansberg (erossi@princeton.edu), Sarte (pdgs4frbr@gmail .com), Trachter (trachter@gmail.com). We thank Ryan Decker, Jan Eeckhout, Francois Gourio, Bob Hall, and Huiyu Li for formal discussions. We also thank Simcha Barkai, Tom Holmes, Erik Hurst, Greg Kaplan, Simon Mongey, Steve Redding, and participants at numerous seminars and conferences for their feedback. We thank Eric LaRose, Reiko Laski, and Sara Ho for outstanding research assistance. The views expressed herein are those of the authors and do not necessarily represent the views of the Federal Reserve Bank of Richmond or the Federal Reserve System. For acknowledgments, sources of research support, and disclosure of the authors' material financial relationships, if any, please see https://www.nber.org/books -and-chapters/nber-macroeconomics-annual-2020-volume-35/diverging-trends-national-and -local-concentration.

1. A 2016 report by the CEA, for instance, finds that the national revenue share of the top 50 firms has increased across most North American Industry Classification System (NAICS) sectors between 1997 and 2012. The report can be found at https://obamawhitehouse .archives.gov/sites/default/files/page/files/20160414_cea_competition_issue_brief.pdf. Gutiérrez and Philippon (2017) show that this increase in US-wide market concentration is not uniform across all sectors and has been most pronounced in nonmanufacturing sectors. Barkai (2020) and Autor et al. (2017) find that the national sales share of top firms has also been rising since 1997 and, in fact, helps explain the decline in the labor share over the same period.

2. Other examples are Azar, Marinescu, and Steinbaum (2019); Benmelech, Bergman, and Kim (2018); and Qiu and Sojourner (2019).

3. Although rising market concentration at the national level is relatively undisputed, the evidence regarding markups is more mixed. De Loecker et al. (2020) show evidence of rising markups since the 1980s among publicly traded firms. However, Traina (2018) points out that the evidence on markups depends crucially on the measurement of variable costs. When variable costs include marketing and management costs, as well as other indirect costs of production, markups have been relatively flat since the mid-1980s. Hall (2018) also finds essentially constant markups at the sectoral level using KLEMS productivity data. Similarly, Karabarbounis and Neiman (2018) find generally flat markups over time when also accounting for selling, general, and administrative expenses. Anderson et al. (2018) focus on the retail sector and find stable markups since 1979 using scanner data on the price of transactions and measuring marginal costs as replacement costs at the store level. Edmond, Midrigan, and Xu (2018) show that when weighted by costs rather than sales, as implied by the microfoundations they lay out, aggregate markups have increased only modestly.

4. In the main text, we focus mostly on ZIP codes as our geographic definition of a local market. An online appendix presents results with other geographic units.

5. This finding also holds when we exclude the top three firms in each industry instead of just the top firm.

6. Jia (2008) studies competition by Walmart and other discount retail stores. She proposes a structural model of this competition and argues that the profits of previously available retailers decrease when "Walmart comes to town." This is consistent with our view that Walmart lowers concentration by taking market share away from local competitors. Moreover, the exit of firms we observe is also consistent with those observed by Jia (2008) when measured at the county level. Holmes (2011) studies the expansion strategy of Walmart and, in particular, its geographic expansion strategy. Our findings are exactly consistent with this view of geographic expansion and provide related facts concerning its impact on local concentration. In contrast to these studies, our empirical findings extend to most US industries in addition to the discount retail sector.

7. This industry was singled out in Syverson (2008) as an example of an industry with a local market.

8. Berger et al. (2019) also develop an equilibrium model of the US labor market and find that, although there are large welfare gains from increasing competition, in their framework market power is unable to explain the decline in the labor share.

9. Throughout the paper, we interchangeably use the terms "plant" and "establishment." We also treat firm and enterprise as synonymous.

10. De Loecker and Eeckhout (2018) also argue that to measure concentration in a way that is meaningful as an indicator of market power, this measurement has to be carried out for specific goods and local markets using the universe of firms. This is exactly what we do in this paper using the NETS data.

11. The online supplementary appendix to this paper is available at http://www .princeton.edu/~erossi/DTNLC_Appendix.pdf.

12. Many enterprises with one employee are nonemployer enterprises or, in other words, have no paid employees. Although employment at those enterprises may at times be the result of imputations, Barnatchez et al. (2017) show that taking out those imputations leaves measures of local employment that are generally highly correlated with those in the CBP across industries.

13. The adjusted HHI is given by $\tilde{C}_{i,g,t}^{l,G} = \frac{\left[C_{i,g,t}^{l,G} - \left(1/N_{i,g,t}^{l,G} \right) \right]}{\left[1 - \left(1/N_{i,g,t}^{l,G} \right) \right]} \in [0, 1]$ when $N_{i,g,t}^{l,G} > 1$ and $\tilde{C}_{i,g,t}^{l,G} = 1$ when $N_{i,g,t}^{l,G} = 1$.

14. Given differences in the number of firms and other industry characteristics, we study changes in the HHI instead of the level of the HHI, so that we can compare trends in concentration across industries. This is why we aggregate changes in the HHI instead of aggregating levels of the HHI. Using sales shares instead of employment shares as weights yields similar results.

15. In the NETS data, establishment sales numbers are more frequently imputed than employment numbers. However, given that the CBP data do not report sales figures, the similarities in national and local concentration trends for sales and employment in NETS are consistent with the notion that, for a given enterprise, increasing sales by opening new establishments in local markets requires hiring labor in those markets.

16. We also consider county and CBSA geographies, as well as the SIC 4 industrial classification code, highlighting respectively the importance of local markets and well-defined industries.

17. See, e.g., the argument and evidence presented in Ganapati (2018).

18. Specifically, in the calculation of $\Delta C_{i,t}^{I,G} = \Sigma_g w_{i,g,t}^{I,G} \Delta C_{i,g,t}^{I,G}$, both g and G now represent a ZIP code.

19. We reserve the use of the term "diverging trends" for a case of positive national trend and a negative local trend. The case of a negative national trend and a positive local trend is also possible, though much less common in virtually all industries.

20. The share of national sales in sectors with decreasing local market concentration is 72%.

21. We show in the online appendix that we obtain similar results when we exclude the top three firms rather than only the top firm.

22. We also exclude industry-geography pairs whose first year of observed sales results from only one establishment belonging to the top enterprise, because the change in market concentration cannot be computed in that case.

23. Neumark et al. (2006) and Barnatchez et al. (2017) argue that the NETS data set might at times be slow in reporting the entry and exit of small firms. Given their findings, one might question the extent to which our results are driven by the exit of small firms not being reported accurately. However, the fact that the fall in the HHI persists for up to 7 years diminishes this potential concern.

24. See, e.g., Basker (2007); Jia (2008); Zhu, Singh, Manuszak (2009); Ailawadi et al. (2010); and Holmes (2011).

25. Consistent with the findings in Jia (2008) and Basker (2007), carrying out these calculations at the county level reveals a more pronounced effect of Walmart's entry on firm exit. Nevertheless, the decline in the HHI is still large on impact and still negative after 7 years.

26. Barnatchez et al. (2017) also raise the issue of imputation in the NETS. As a practical matter, this issue is a more general one that can arise even in Census data. For example, White, Reiter, and Petrin (2018) indicate that in the 2002 Census of Manufactures, more than three-fourths of observations have imputed data for at least one variable used to compute total factor productivity. For robustness, however, we show in the technical appendix that the results herein are robust to using only nonimputed NETS data, which in this case consist of employment for a subset of establishments.

27. Hsieh and Rossi-Hansberg (2019) show, using Census data, that these and other complementary patterns are particularly pronounced in service sectors. They argue that this evolution is the result of a new "Industrial Revolution in Services" that has allowed top service firms to replicate in space and access smaller, more marginal, markets at a lower cost.

References

Ailawadi, Kusum L., Aradhna Krishna, Michael W. Kruger, and Jie Zhang. 2010. "When Wal-Mart Enters: How Incumbent Retailers React and How This Affects Their Sales Outcomes." *Journal of Marketing Research* 47 (4): 577–93.

Anderson, Eric, Sergio Rebelo, and Arlene Wong. 2018. "Markups Across Space and Time." Working Paper no. 24434, NBER, Cambridge, MA.

Autor, David, David Dorn, Lawrence F. Katz, Christina Patterson, and John Van Reenen. 2017. "The Fall of the Labor Share and the Rise of Superstar Firms." Working Paper no. 23396, NBER, Cambridge, MA.

Azar, Jose, Ioana Marinescu, and Marshall Steinbaum. 2019. "Labor Market Concentration." Working Paper no. 24147, NBER, Cambridge, MA.

Barkai, Simcha. 2020. "Declining Labor and Capital Shares." *Journal of Finance, American Finance Association* 75 (5): 2421–2463.

Barnatchez, Keith, Leland D. Crane, and Ryan A. Decker. 2017. "An Assessment of the National Establishment Time Series (NETS) Database." Finance and Economics Discussion Series 2017–110, Federal Reserve Board, Washington, DC.

Basker, Emek. 2007. "The Causes and Consequences of Wal-Mart's Growth." *Journal of Economic Perspectives* 21 (3): 177–98.

Benmelech, Efraim, Nittai Bergman, and Hyunseob Kim. 2018. "Strong Employers and Weak Employees: How Does Employer Concentration Affect Wages?" Working Paper no. 24307, NBER, Cambridge, MA.

Berger, David, Kyle Herkenhoff, and Simon Mongey. 2019. "Labor Market Power." Working Paper no. 25719, NBER, Cambridge, MA.

Bernheim, B. Douglas, and Michael D. Whinston. 1990. "Multimarket Contact and Elusive Behavior." *RAND Journal of Economics* 21 (1): 1–26.

Bond, Eric W., and Constantinos Syropoulos. 2008. "Trade Costs and Multimarket Collusion." *RAND Journal of Economics* 39 (4): 1080–104.

De Loecker, Jan, and Jan Eeckhout. 2018. "Global Market Power." Working Paper no. 24768, NBER, Cambridge, MA.

De Loecker, Jan, Jan Eeckhout, and Gabriel Unger. 2020. "The Rise of Market Power and the Macroeconomic Implications." *Quarterly Journal of Economics* 135 (2): 561–644.

Decker, Ryan A., John Haltiwanger, Ron S. Jarmin, and Javier Miranda. 2017. "Declining Dynamism: Allocative Efficiency, and the Productivity Slowdown." *American Economic Review: Papers and Proceedings* 107 (5): 322–26.

Edmond, Chris, Virgiliu Midrigan, and Daniel Yi Xu. 2018. "How Costly Are Markups?" Working Paper no. 24800, NBER, Cambridge, MA.

Ganapati, Sharat. 2018. "Growing Oligopolies, Prices, Output, and Productivity." Working Paper no. 18–48, Center for Economic Studies, U.S. Census Bureau.

Gutiérrez, Germán, and Thomas Philippon. 2017. "Declining Competition and Investment in the U.S." Working Paper no. 23583, NBER, Cambridge, MA.

Hall, Robert E. 2018. "New Evidence on the Markup of Prices over Marginal Costs and the Role of Mega-Firms in the US Economy." Working Paper no. 24574, NBER, Cambridge, MA.

Hershbein, Brad, Claudia Macaluso, and Chen Yeh. 2019. "Concentration in U.S. Local Labor Markets: Evidence from Vacancy and Employment Data." 2019 Meeting Paper no. 1336, Society for Economic Dynamics.

Holmes, Thomas J. 2011. "The Diffusion of Wal-Mart and Economics of Density." *Econometrica* 79 (1): 253–302.

Hopenhayn, Hugo, Julian Neira, and Rish Singhania. 2018. "From Population Growth to Firm Demographics: Implications for Concentration, Entrepreneurship and the Labor Share." Working Paper no. 25382, NBER, Cambridge, MA.

Hsieh, Chang-Tai, and Esteban Rossi-Hansberg. 2019. "The Industrial Revolution in Services." Working Paper no. 25968, NBER, Cambridge, MA.

Jia, Panle. 2008. "What Happens When Wal-Mart Comes to Town: An Empirical Analysis of the Discount Retailing Industry." *Econometrica* 76 (6): 1263–316.

Karabarbounis, Loukas, and Brent Neiman. 2018. "Accounting for Factorless Income." Working Paper no. 24404, NBER, Cambridge, MA.

Neumark, David, Junfu Zhang, and Brandon Wall. 2006. "Employment Dynamics and Business Relocation: New Evidence from the National Establishment Time Series." Working Paper no. 11647, NBER, Cambridge, MA.

Qiu, Yue, and Aaron Sojourner. 2019. "Labor-Market Concentration and Labor Compensation." IZA Discussion Paper 12089, Institute of Labor Economics, Bonn.

Rinz, Kevin. 2018. "Labor Market Concentration, Earnings Inequality, and Earnings Mobility." Working Papers 2018-10, Center for Administrative Records Research and Applications, US Census Bureau, Washington, DC.

Shapiro, Carl. 2018. "Antitrust in a Time of Populism." *International Journal of Industrial Organization* 61:714–748.

Syverson, Chad. 2004. "Market Structure and Productivity: A Concrete Example." *Journal of Political Economy* 112 (6): 1181–222.

———. 2008. "Markets: Ready-Mixed Concrete." *Journal of Economic Perspectives* 22 (1): 217–33.

———. 2019. "Macroeconomics and Market Power: Facts, Potential Explanations and Open Questions." Brookings Institution Report (January), Washington, DC.

Traina, James. 2018. "Is Aggregate Market Power Increasing? Production Trends Using Financial Statements." New Working Paper Series 17 no. 26, Stigler Center for the Study of the Economy, Chicago.

White, T. Kirk, Jerome P. Reiter, and Amil Petrin. 2018. "Imputation in U.S. Manufacturing Data and Its Implications for Productivity Dispersion." *Review of Economics and Statistics* 100 (3): 502–9.

Zhu, Ting, Vishal Singh, and Mark D. Manuszak. 2009. "Market Structure and Competition in the Retail Discount Industry." *Journal of Marketing Research* 46 (4): 453–66.

Comment

Jan Eeckhout, *UPF Barcelona,* Spain

There is a rapidly growing recent literature that analyzes the rise of market power over the last 4 decades in the United States and in many other economies. The study of market power is, of course, not new and is arguably as old as the study of economics itself.[1] But the renewed interest is its scope, particularly the role for macroeconomics. Much of the recent literature focuses on measuring market power throughout the economy and on its quantitative macroeconomic implications. Many macroeconomic models from monetary economics, over trade and urban economics, to labor have predictions that hinge on the degree of market power that firms have. The monetary transmission mechanism in the New Keynesian models, for example, crucially depends on markups and the extent to which the market power of firms is pervasive throughout the economy. The challenge, therefore, is to find appropriate ways to measure market power for a representative sample of the universe of firms in the economy.

The paper by Esteban Rossi-Hansberg, Pierre Sarte, and Nico Trachter draws attention to an important and hitherto understudied issue in this literature, the dichotomy between national and local measures of concentration. The main idea is that the degree of concentration of firms at the national level is very different than what it is at a local level, be it the state, the metropolitan area, or the ZIP code. They find a baffling fact: all measures of local concentration show a declining trend, whereas measures of national concentration show an increasing trend.

This is an important observation and I sympathize with the premise of investigating market power at different levels of aggregation and for different subeconomies of the macro economy. After all, to understand the macro economy we need to understand the micro origins. The paper also makes a noteworthy contribution in attempting to rationalize this dichotomy by investigating the role of superstar firms and firms with multiple establishments such as national chains in retail and big box stores. There is no doubt that the technological transformation of distribution and logistics has had a significant impact on concentration. The paper's main conclusion is that large national firms may exhibit market power at the national level, but they do so by inducing competition in local markets. The authors deduce that the increased competition in local markets is the result of more market power nationally. Therefore, the rise of national market power may raise consumer welfare.

Unfortunately, the paper does not fully deliver on this ambitious research agenda. The reason why it fails to do so is of interest to the research community in macroeconomics that focuses the role of market power for the aggregate economy. The approach in this paper is instructive because it highlights the particular challenges that macroeconomic analysis faces once we take the micro origins with due consideration. The reason why the paper fails is because it has overlooked 3 decades of research in industrial organization (IO) that has repeatedly shown the shortcomings of the concentration measures on which the analysis here is based. Following the influential contribution of Bresnahan (1989), the IO literature has moved away from concentration measures toward alternative approaches to measure market power. What this paper highlights is not simply that concentration measures are inadequate tools and that the authors have ignored the insights from the IO literature. This paper shows that in addition to the shortcomings in a traditional IO analysis, the challenges of a macro setting with diverse sectors and long time series completely incapacitate concentration measures as a tool in macro. This paper does provide a clear illustration where concentration measures go wrong.

In the remainder of this short comment I provide some remarks that I hope help guide the discussion for future research. I illustrate the shortcomings of concentration measures when used in macro, I revisit the four main facts of the paper in the light of that discussion, and I propose some alternative methodology to think about market structure in the macro economy.

I. Concentration Measures

Market power is canonically defined as "the ability of a firm to profitably raise the market price of a good or service over marginal cost." This is typically expressed as the markup, the ratio of the price the firm charges over the marginal cost. As such, it is a statement about the behavior of an individual firm. Of course, what makes the measurement of market power conceptually a challenge is the fact that except in the case of a monopoly, the firm behavior is determined strategically and in equilibrium with the behavior of competitors in the market.

The problem that any researcher on market power faces is how to measure the marginal cost of a firm or of a product. An alternative is to focus on the measurement of profits instead, which includes not just the marginal cost but also overhead and fixed costs. Unfortunately, the fact that accounting profits are typically not equal to economic profits raises an additional hurdle.

Therefore, an alternative route is to obtain indirect measures. To that effect and inspired by the one-to-one relationship between market power of a firm and its market share of revenue in a Cournot (1838) model, concentration measures inform us about the distribution of market power in a well-determined market. The most popular of the concentration measures is the Herfindahl–Hirschman Index (HHI). It is defined as sum of squared market shares s_i of all firms i in a market: $HHI = \Sigma_i s_i^2 \in [0; 10,000]$. It is typically expressed as a number from 0 to 10,000 where the market share is expressed in percentages. The HHI is effectively a measure of inequality, just like the Gini coefficient or the variance. It turns a complex distribution of market shares with possibly infinite moments into a scalar that has an easy interpretation. Under monopoly (or a dominant firm with the entire market share), the market share is 100, which when squared yields an HHI of 10,000. Under perfect competition with all market shares equal to zero, the HHI is zero. Its simplicity is part of the broad appeal of HHI, as are the readily available measures of revenue to calculate market shares.

There are, however, two long recognized shortcomings. First, the reliance on market shares as a measure of market power is not always suitable. There is indeed a direct positive relationship between markups and market share in the Cournot model, but in many models that relationship is not so direct and the HHI only imprecisely measures markups. What is even worse, however, is that in some models the market share is declining in the markup (e.g., Melitz 2003; Melitz and Ottaviano 2008). A higher HHI, therefore, indicates lower market power, not higher!

Second, the HHI crucially depends on the definition of a market: Who are the competitors? If we wrongly determine the participants in the market, we get an incorrect measure of the HHI and, therefore, an incorrect measure of market power.

Are concentration measures a good tool to measure market power? Policy makers who review mergers at the Federal Trade Commission (FTC) and the Department of Justice (DoJ) still rely heavily on measures of concentration. The magic number there is 3,000, where merger review is automatically activated when the HHI in a market crosses this 3,000 watermark. It continues to be a transparent measure that is successful in convincing nonspecialized judges who rule over merger cases.

However, following an influential article by Bresnahan (1989), the academic IO literature that studies market power seems to have veered toward a rejection of the HHI. Instead, the literature has opted for a structural approach. The most celebrated is the demand approach pioneered by Berry, Levinsohn, and Pakes (1995), which specifies a model of consumer demand over goods with different degrees of substitutability, of a market structure with well-defined competitors and how they compete (e.g., quantity versus price competition), and with a specified production technology. This approach has been successful in determining market power in markets such as cars, breakfast cereal, cement, beer, and so on. Because this so-called demand method is enormously demanding in terms of data requirements, in recent years the production approach has gained traction, especially because the data requirements are far less stringent, thus lending itself better to the analysis of market power in macroeconomics with broad cross sections and long time series.[2]

Concentration measures in macro. So what are the prospects of concentration measures in macro? There is no doubt that the HHI is easy to calculate, that data on revenue are relatively widely available, and that this permits for data on broad cross sections and long time series. That is exactly what this paper exploits. The Achilles' heel, however, is the market definition. What constitutes a market in the macro sense?

Here, macro faces even taller obstacles than IO. Two sets of reasons for the taller obstacles are reasons based on the cross-sectional comparison and reasons based on intertemporal comparison. The fundamental problem is that the HHI is mechanically related to how a market is defined, typically the intersection of an industry classification and a geographical area. There are some 6 million firms and nearly 7 million establishments in the United States. Each of them belongs to an industry (e.g., Standard Industrial Classification 8 [SIC-8]) and a geographical area (e.g., ZIP code or metropolitan statistical area [MSA]). It is precisely that ad hoc definition that does not correspond well to the true market definition—namely, who competes with whom.

First, consider the cross-sectional comparison. A typical SIC × Geo definition may be a close enough description of the true market, but it cannot be for all markets. For example, the ZIP code may be a more or less accurate description of a market for coffee shops or dry cleaners, but it is not for furniture retailers such as IKEA. For those companies, the MSA is the more accurate market definition. And for yet other manufacturers, such as car assembly plants, the adequate market definition is national. The problem is that the HHI is calculated for the same SIC × Geo definition for all firms, say, either ZIP code or MSA. Therefore, either the SIC × Geo definition is not appropriate for furniture or car assembly (when ZIP code, as most car manufacturers in a ZIP code are monopolists and virtually all ZIP codes have zero car manufacturers) or it is not appropriate for coffee shops (when MSA). Inherently in the field of macro, there is never one size that fits all. If the set of sectors was reduced to tailor all industries to the same definition, it would be so product specific that it becomes IO and not macro.

But even at the ZIP code level, the size of the SIC × Geo definition is typically still too large for most products. The DoJ considers there to be a lack of competition starting at an HHI of larger than 3,000 or three similar firms. Having more than 10–15 firms is considered perfect competition in any model of oligopoly for any set of reasonable preferences. Some of these market definitions have more than 10,000 establishments. The national measures have millions. Rather than an HHI of thousands, those definitions whip up HHIs that are in the decimals. This is very far away from the interpretation of what constitutes a market that exhibits limited competition. Using the SIC × Geo definition poses serious difficulties in the cross-sectional measurement of market power in macro, much more so than in IO.[3]

Second, consider the intertemporal comparisons. The ad hoc SIC × Geo definitions of what constitutes a market are an even bigger challenge because those definitions are fixed. In the presence of demographic changes, these fixed definitions induce a mechanical change in concentration measures such as the HHI. As the number of establishments in these SIC × Geo cells change for demographic reasons, so does the HHI.

For the purpose of understanding what drives the results in this paper, I show that four premises that are borne out in the data lead to the dichotomy of diverging concentration measures locally and nationally. The four premises are the following:

1. Population growth: Figure 1A shows that the employment population in the United States has grown from around 70 million in the early 1980s to nearly 120 million now.

2. Constant average establishment size (fig. 1*B*): The average size of establishments in the United States is fairly constant at around 17 workers per establishment, hovering between 16 and 18 workers over the same period.

3. The ratio of establishments to firms has increased from 1.22 in 1980 to 1.33 most recently (fig. 1*C*).

4. The industry-location grid (the SIC × Geo cell definition) is constant.

The insight is that as the population grows for a given location, so does the number of establishments. The firm size is constant, so with a growing employment pool, there must be more establishments in which those employees work. For example, in Manhattan there used to be 4 supermarkets every 10 blocks; now there are 6 every 10 blocks. Before we turn to what this tells us about competition, we look at the effect this has on the HHI. To do so, consider the following stylized example laid out in table 1.

In our stylized economy there are two SIC × Geo areas, say coffee shops in the Philadelphia and Boston metro areas. All firms are identical and there are 1,000 of them in each area. The local HHI in both areas is

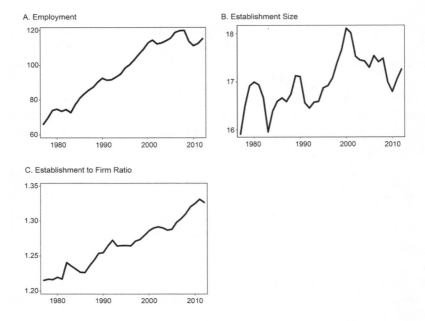

Fig. 1.   Demographics of employment, establishments, and firms

Table 1
Stylized Example of the Mechanical Source of the Dichotomy between National and Local Concentration

	SIC × Geo 1	SIC × Geo 2	Aggregate	
			Local	National
		1980		
		Baseline Economy		
	1,000 establishments	1,000 establishments	2,000 establishments	
Local HHI: HHI$_{SIC×Geo}$	10	10	10	5
		2020		
	Increase Population; Constant Firm Size; Multi-establishment Firms			
	1,500 establishments	1,500 establishments	3,000 establishments	
Local HHI: HHI$_{SIC×Geo}$	6.7	6.7	6.7	6.7

Note: HHI = Herfindahl–Hirschman Index; SIC = Standard Industrial Classification.

equal to 10. The local market share of each identical firm is 0.1%, squared and times 1,000 gives an HHI of 10. When we take a weighted average over the HHI in both local markets, the aggregate local HHI is 10. Now at the national level, there are 2,000 establishments and suppose for the sake of argument that the establishment to firm ratio is 1. Then the HHI nationwide is 5.

Fast-forward to 2020, and the population has increased by 50%, and the firm size is still constant. Therefore, there are 1,500 establishments in Philadelphia and in Boston, giving an HHI of 6.7, which is also the aggregate of the two identical local HHIs. Now let us assume for the sake of argument that the establishment to firm ratio has gone up to 2. Each firm has two establishments, so there are 1,500 firms in the entire economy. Therefore, even though there are 3,000 establishments, only 1,500 can be considered independent competitors. As a result, the national HHI is equal to 6.7. If all two establishments of the same firm are the two different markets, then the local HHI is also 6.7. The national HHI increases while the local HHI decreases: hence, the dichotomy.

This simple example shows that under the four premises, we obtain the dichotomy for purely mechanical reasons. The mechanism stems from demographic changes on a fixed definition of what constitutes a SIC × Geo unit. This does not tell us anything about what has happened to competition in the many markets within these units. If competition among coffee shops in each market of the unit goes up and we now have 15 shops competing instead of 10, then the increase in population is competition enhancing. That translates in a decline in markups and of the true HHI. Instead, if the number of competing shops per market goes down from 10 to 5, then we see an increase in market power. In both cases, the HHI goes down locally and up nationally.

The problem that this exercise highlights is that it is extremely difficult, if not impossible, to observe the boundaries of a market. As the number of supermarkets goes from 4 to 6 on 10 blocks in Manhattan, does that mean there is more competition? Maybe. We don't know until we identify who competes with whom or if we measure markups directly. Inferring competition from a geographical definition is tricky because the definition varies with population density. Because it is 50 miles from one Whole Foods to the next in rural New Jersey and only 25 blocks from one to the next in Manhattan does not necessarily mean that the market in Manhattan is more competitive than New Jersey. Firms compete differently in denser areas. In fact, the evidence using markups instead of concentration measures seems to suggest that market power is higher in denser areas (Anderson, Rebelo, and Wong 2018), areas where there are more competitors per block! Therefore, as population grows, the market definition changes. And with higher population density, New Jersey starts to look a bit more like Manhattan did 50 years ago.

I come to two conclusions. First, considering the HHI over time for a fixed grid does not inform us about a change in competition. Second, the dichotomy between national and local HHI is mechanical and does not inform us about whether indeed there is a dichotomy between national and local market power.[4]

Simulation in an Atkeson and Burstein (2008) economy. I now reproduce the same mechanical findings in a more realistic economy simulated under demographics that satisfy the four premises. In our model economy, we obtain the dichotomy in national and local HHI, while market power increases both nationally and locally.

The model is based on De Loecker, Eeckhout, and Mongey (2018) with market power in the output market and where the input market for labor is competitive. There is no free entry. The production function is linear, $Y_{ij} = A_{ij}L_{ij}$, where productivity A_{ij} is drawn from $\log(A_{ij}) \sim \mathcal{N}(\mu, \sigma^2)$. In each market, there are N firms that compete à la Cournot.[5]

Let the number of competitors in 1980 be $N = 10$, so there are 100 markets, 10 in each cell. In 1980, the size of the labor force is normalized to 1. For the 2020 economy, the population increases to 1.5 (premise 1) and the number of establishments grows to 1,500, which keeps the average establishment size constant between 1980 and 2020 (premise 2). In 2020, we consider that there is an increase in market power, where the number of competitors declines to $N = 3$. As a result, there are 500 markets, 50 in each cell. To this setup, we add a distinction between firms and establishments. There are two types of firms; single-establishment (SE) firms and multi-establishment (ME) firms. In an attempt to capture the rise of national chains (and superstar firms), I assume that in 1980 the ME firms each have two establishments, while in 2020 the ME firms each have 10 establishments. We adjust for the number of SE firms F_1 and ME firms F_m to ensure that the establishments-to-firms ratio in the economy r is 1.2 in 1980 and 1.3 in 2020 (premise 3).[6] For simplicity, let each of the establishments belonging to a single ME firm be in different locations; let there be 10 SIC $\times$ Geo cells in 1980, which remain the same in 2020 (premise 4).

Figure 2 and table 2 summarize the results of this thought experiment. In both panels of figure 2, the straight lines simply connect the two observations for the model economies in 1980 and 2020. Both scenarios generate a divergence in the local and national HHIs. This is due to the mechanical increase in the number of establishments in a fixed grid of SIC $\times$ Geo cells. Having more establishments implies a lower local HHI. Still, the national HHI moves in the opposite direction because multiple establishments of the same firm are counted as one firm. Due

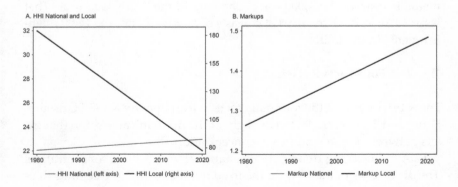

Fig. 2. Herfindahl–Hirschman Index (HHI) and markups in simulated Atkeson and Burstein (2008) economy.

Table 2
HHI for Different Atkeson and Burstein (2008) Economies

	Aggregate HHI		Markup	
	Local	National	Local	National
	1,000 establishments $r = 1.2$			
1980:				
Low Market Power $N = 10$	185	22	1.27	1.27
	1,500 establishments $r = 1.3$			
2020:				
High Market Power $N = 3$	78	23	1.48	1.48

Note: The SIC × Geo grid is fixed at 10 in all economies. HHI = Herfindahl–Hirschman Index; SIC = Standard Industrial Classification.

to the rise of the establishment-to-firm ratio, together with how these establishments are distributed over firms, there is an increase in the national HHI.

Table 2 reports the numerical values for these HHIs and markups. The level of the local HHI is notably larger than the national HHI, simply because locally there are fewer firms. Over time, there is a decline in the local HHI from 185 to 78. The national HHI increases from 22 to 23.

Most striking is that this divergence is completely independent of the change in markups. Aggregate markups increase from 1.27 to 1.48. They are identical for local and aggregate markets. In the Atkeson and Burstein (2008) model of Cournot competition, the markup depends directly on the number of competitors N. And in Cournot, the markup is also related to the HHI, only it is the HHI within a market with $N = 10$ establishments instead of the 1,000 establishments in the SIC × Geo unit. That is for 1980; in 2020, the market consists of $N = 3$ and not the 1,500 establishments in the unit.

II. The Four Facts Revisited

I now briefly revisit the four main facts in the paper by Rossi-Hansberg, Sarte, and Trachter (2021) in the light of the mechanical relation that exists between national and local concentration.

Fact 1: Diverging trend between national versus local concentration. The divergence of the HHI for the fixed number of SIC × Geo units does not imply there is divergence in market power at the national and local levels. In the simulation of the Atkeson and Burstein (2008) economy, market power depends on the number of competitors N within the market, which can increase or decrease even if the number of firms within a SIC × Geo unit increases.

Fact 2: Pervasive diverging trends. The paper finds a significant role for this trend across different sectors, which is very pronounced in the services sector. The paper does a wonderful job drawing attention to the role of national chains and big box retailers such as Walmart. The development in services shows that the third premise I outlined (i.e., the ratio of establishments to firms has risen) is most acutely present in the services sector. We expect therefore to find the biggest national versus local dichotomy in the HHI there.

Fact 3: The role of top firms. Large national firms make the mechanical force behind the dichotomy stronger. This also raises the question of reallocation of market share from low-markup firms to high-markup, superstar firms. That reallocation is large and accounts for two thirds of the rise in market power (see Autor et al. 2017; De Loecker, Eeckhout, and Unger 2020). This also raises the question of the efficiency-increasing effect of reallocation to which I turn below.

Fact 4: When a top firm comes to town. Using case studies, the paper shows that the entry of large firms in local markets leads to an increase of competition, not a decline. In the light of our four premises, as population grows we must see an increase in the number of establishments. Yet at the same time, with the SIC × Geo units constant, there is a decline in the HHI due to an increase in the number of establishments. Because some of those entrants will be top firms like Walmart, it is no surprise that entry is accompanied by a decline in the local HHI. Equally important, the strategy of top firms in which location to open new stores is not random. They will open where the demand is growing fastest and where, as a result, the HHI declines fastest. This is indeed what Holmes (2011) finds: Walmart selectively opens where the demand in its distribution network grows fastest. Houde, Newberry, and Seim (2017) find similar results for Amazon's strategy to develop its distribution network of fulfillment centers. This selection further reinforces the perception that entry of top firms leads to a decline in the local HHI, through the mechanical effect of population growth on the HHI.

III. Unobserved Market Structure in Macro

Using an invariant SIC × Geo definition of a market on which to calculate the HHI is not an adequate method to measure market power. In macro, the obstacles related to the vast heterogeneity across sectors and technologies and the desire to analyze long time series make it substantially more problematic than in IO. If it does not work for cement and breakfast cereal, it is unlikely that the HHI will inform us for the entire macro economy over a long period of time. This then begs the question what we can do in macro to study the evolution of market power.

In the absence of observing who competes with whom, what the market boundaries are, and what the preferences and technology are, there are existing methods to measure market power in the macro economy. The demand method of Berry et al. (1995) has been enormously successful in IO, but it is unlikely that we will have the data and the computational power to extend beyond their specifically defined markets, such as the markets for cars, breakfast cereal, beer, and cement.

The production approach building on Hall (1988), but now applied to firm-level data instead of aggregate data, shows that we can obtain reliable estimates at the firm or establishment level for a large set of firms in the economy with limited data requirements (for the United States, see De Loecker et al. 2020). This enables us to evaluate the evolution of the distribution of market power at different levels of (dis)aggregation and local markets, including the global economy (see De Loecker and Eeckhout 2018).

But the ambition in macroeconomics goes one step further beyond mere measurement. We want to perform welfare analysis, do counterfactuals, and evaluate the impact of policy interventions. To that effect, I suggest that we approach market structure in the same way we approach total factor productivity (TFP). A scholar in management might enter a BMW factory and literally measure the production function, that is, how the factory transforms quantities of inputs (e.g., materials, labor, management, capital, or patents) into quantities of output (how many cars roll off the assembly belt every day).

Because of the shortcomings of measurement and data, and because of the huge heterogeneity in production technologies, this method is impossible to measure TFP in the macro economy. Instead, as macroeconomists we collect information on aggregate inputs and outputs and impose a structural model of production (with or without heterogeneity) to infer TFP as the residual. This is the celebrated Solow residual approach to measuring productivity. The information is highly aggregated and by no means as detailed as the micro-level production function the management scholar at BMW estimates, but it does allow us to estimate welfare and counterfactual experiments. And most importantly, it informs us about the evolution of TFP throughout the economy.

Likewise, even if the IO economist can infer the structure from a narrowly defined market, the macroeconomist has neither the data nor the tools to do that. So I suggest we treat the market structure as the residual that we estimate through the lens of a model. We observe the quantities of inputs, prices, and wages, and we observe revenues and profits. Then in a model with oligopolistic markets, we can use those observables—either those moments from the aggregate distribution or micro-level observations—to match the model-generated moments with the moments we observe in the data. We do not observe who competes with whom, but we know that the revenue and markups that we observe in the data are consistent with the number of competitors, the entry costs that determine the selection of firms that enter, and so on.

Matching the aggregate moments of the data on markups and fixed costs, De Loecker et al. (2018) find that the entry costs in 1980 were a lot lower than in 2016 and, most importantly, that the number of competitors has decreased substantially between 1980 and 2016.[7] The IO economist, rightly, complains that this approach is too broad, just like the management researcher in the BMW factory complains that the TFP measures using the Solow residual lack detail and precision. And I agree. But it is the only alternative we have if we want to make statements regarding market power in the aggregate economy. The benefit of this approach is that we can analyze why markups change, we can do counterfactuals, and we can evaluate policy interventions.

For example, the approach to back out the market structure as the residual allows us to address the major issue that the paper under discussion set out to answer in the first place: Is the rise of dominant, national firms that are highly productive welfare improving? Those firms are dominant because they are more productive. The most important implication is that those productive firms can set lower prices and thus obtain a larger share of the market. This leads to the reallocation of revenue share toward highly productive firms and is positive for consumers because prices are lower. But those dominant firms also exert market power. The deadweight loss that results from the rise in market power is detrimental for the consumer. In addition to the effect of selection of which firms enter and stay in the market, an effect that is ambiguous, we can calculate the overall effect on welfare. In De Loecker et al. (2018) we find that the net effect is negative. The negative effect of the deadweight loss dominates the positive effect from reallocation, while the selection effect is small. Technological change whereby national chains enter local markets to compete and drive down prices is on average anticompetitive.

IV. Conclusion

This paper draws attention to an important issue in macroeconomics: the evolution of market power over time and across the entire economy. The macroeconomics dimension of market power is as important as the detailed microeconomic and market-specific aspects that inform policy, such as merger review. Instead, economy-wide changes in market power have general equilibrium effects on the labor market, on wages and on wage inequality, as well as on all other realms of the economy. The paper deserves all the credit for putting this issue in the spotlight.

Unfortunately, the paper does not deliver on answering the question of whether there is indeed divergence in national versus local market power, as opposed to concentration. Nor does it answer the question of whether dominant national chains are welfare improving. I show that HHI measures are not adequate tools to study market power in the macro economy. In particular, there is a mechanical relation between the HHI and demographic change. The nature of the macro economy poses even bigger challenges than those already faced by IO. Based on solid grounds, the IO literature has resolutely decided to dispense with HHI measures. In macro we cannot ignore 30 years of research progress in IO, especially because the macro difficulties are even bigger than those in IO.

I propose that to study market power in the macro economy, we instead rely on firm-level measures of markups and profits rather than concentration measures. And to measure the market structure we need to give up on the detailed description of markets that micro studies can measure. Instead, I propose that we treat the market structure in the same way we treat TFP. We back out TFP as a Solow residual in the context of a model, and in the same manner, I suggest we back out the market structure (the number of competitors, entry costs, etc.) using firm-level data for the macro economy.

All the same, the thought-provoking findings in this paper have been instrumental in stimulating research into the macroeconomics of market power. I am optimistic that other work will take on the challenges in this paper and further our understanding of this important issue.

Endnotes

Author email address: Eeckhout (jan.eeckhout@upf.edu). ICREA-GSE-CREi. I would like to thank Jan De Loecker and Shubhdeep Deb for discussions and comments. This research received financial support from the ERC, advanced grant 339186, and from

ECO2015-67655-P. For acknowledgments, sources of research support, and disclosure of the author's material financial relationships, if any, please see https://www.nber.org /books-and-chapters/nber-macroeconomics-annual-2020-volume-35/comment-diverging -trends-national-and-local-concentration-eeckhout.

1. In historical times, enterprises such as the Dutch and the British East India Company were built on the premise of exclusive trading rights that effectively granted them monopoly power. And even in ancient Greece writings there are mentions of monopoly power that derives from patents. More formally, as early as 200 years ago, Cournot (1838) derived a mathematical formulation of what is now known as the Cournot-Nash oligopoly equilibrium.

2. See Hall (1988) for the initial contribution proposing to use the firm's cost minimization decision to back out marginal cost and hence markups. Although Hall (1988) uses aggregate data, De Loecker and Warzynski (2012) and De Loecker et al. (2020) have used firm-level data to calculate firm-level markups and generate an economy-wide distribution of markups.

3. Another well-known issue is the problem of missing data. Clearly, the HHI changes if observations are missing. This is a well-known issue that affects the National Establishment Time Series (NETS) data in particular.

4. This spurious dichotomy does not only apply to market power in the output market. In the case of market power in the labor market, frictions to mobility between local markets lead to monopsony and hence markdowns on wages. Based on measures of the HHI in local labor markets, one would also erroneously conclude that monopsony power has been declining. Instead, Deb, Eeckhout, and Warren (2020) find that wage markdowns have been constant since the 1980s.

5. We maintain the parameter configuration: within-sector elasticity $\eta = 10$; between-sector elasticity $\theta = 1.5$; mean of log productivity $\mu = 1$; variance of log productivity $\sigma^2 = 0.2$.

6. Define E and F as the total number of establishments and firms in the economy, where $E/F = r$ is the average establishment-to-firm ratio. Let $N_s F_1$ be the number of SE firms and F_m is the number of ME firms. Let $E_1 = 1$ and E_m be the number of establishments of the two types of firms. Then $F_1 + F_m = E/r$ and $F_1 + E_m F_m = E$, implying that $F_m = (E - F)/(E_m - 1)$.

7. See also Deb et al. (2020) and Eeckhout, Patel, and Warren (2020) for estimation of the market structure using micro data.

References

Anderson, E., S. Rebelo, and A. Wong. 2018. "Markups across Space and Time." Technical report, NBER, Cambridge, MA.

Atkeson, A., and A. Burstein. 2008. "Pricing-to-Market, Trade Costs, and International Relative Prices." *American Economic Review* 98:1998–2031.

Autor, D., D. Dorn, L. F. Katz, C. Patterson, and J. Van Reenen. 2017. "The Fall of the Labor Share and the Rise of Superstar Firms." Technical report, Centre for Economic Performance, LSE, London.

Berry, S., J. Levinsohn, and A. Pakes. 1995. "Automobile Prices in Market Equilibrium." *Econometrica* 63:841–90.

Bresnahan, T. F. 1989. "Empirical Studies of Industries with Market Power." *Handbook of Industrial Organization* 2:1011–57.

Cournot, A. A. 1838. *Researches into the Mathematical Principles of the Theory of Wealth*. New York: Macmillan.

De Loecker, J., and J. Eeckhout. 2018. "Global Market Power." Working Paper no. 24768, NBER, Cambridge, MA.

De Loecker, J., J. Eeckhout, and S. Mongey. 2018. "Quantifying Market Power." Mimeo.

De Loecker, J., J. Eeckhout, and G. Unger. 2020. "The Rise of Market Power and the Macroeconomic Implications." *Quarterly Journal of Economics* 135:561–644.

De Loecker, J., and F. M. P. Warzynski. 2012. "Markups and Firm-level Export Status." *American Economic Review* 102:2437–71.

Deb, S., J. Eeckhout, and L. Warren. 2020. "The Macroeconomics of Market Power and Monopsony." UPF mimeo.

Eeckhout, J., A. Patel, and L. Warren. 2020. "The Contribution of Market Power to Wage Inequality." UPF mimeo.

Hall, R. 1988. "The Relation between Price and Marginal Cost in U.S. Industry." *Journal of Political Economy* 96:921–47.

Holmes, T. J. 2011. "The Diffusion of Wal-Mart and Economies of Density." *Econometrica* 79:253–302.

Houde, J.-F., P. Newberry, and K. Seim. 2017. "Economies of Density in E-Commerce: A Study of Amazon's Fulfillment Center Network." Technical report, NBER, Cambridge, MA.

Melitz, M. 2003. "The Impact of Trade on Aggregate Industry Productivity and Intra-Industry Reallocations." *Econometrica* 71:1695–725.

Melitz, M. J., and G. I. Ottaviano. 2008. "Market Size, Trade, and Productivity." *Review of Economic Studies* 75:295–316.

Comment

Robert E. Hall, *Stanford University,* United States of America, *and NBER,* United States of America

Authors Rossi-Hansberg, Sarte, and Trachter have delivered a focused, definitive paper, part of a broader research program on structural change in US product and labor markets. The subject of the paper is concentration. Measurement of concentration starts from the market definition. Concentration depends on the pattern of market shares within a market, defined by a product, a geographic region, and a time period. A market is a specification of the product, region, and time such that a hypothetical monopolist would have market power—it could elevate its price substantially above marginal cost. The connection to concentration is the general belief that the actual market power of the firms selling in a market depends on the number and importance of the competitors selling in that market.

The most widely used measure of concentration—and the one used in this paper—is the Herfindahl-Hirschman Index (HHI), the sum of the squared market shares of the sellers in a market. This measure is sensitive to both the number of sellers and their market shares, and it is a sufficient statistic for the elevation of price over marginal cost in certain oligopoly models. However, other models, especially those involving collusion, predict substantial exercise of market power with prices marked up well above marginal cost, in the face of HHI measures suggesting rather less price elevation.

Some markets are national or international. The products in these markets have low transport cost across the country relative to price. A substantial body of research has found high and rising concentration in many national markets, primarily for manufactured goods. The paper confirms that finding. The paper does not pursue the key question of price elevation associated with rising concentration but does cite much of the recent literature on that subject, such as Berger et al., De Loecker et al., Syverson, Traina, and this writer. That literature tends to find rising markups of price over marginal cost, though with substantial disagreements about the level and growth rates of the markups.

Two quite different approaches have evolved in this literature to find the level and growth of markups. Berger and coauthors build an oligopoly model that predicts how much a firm thinks its sales will fall if it increases its price—the slope of the residual demand facing the firm net of the supply response of its rivals. If the residual demand is highly elastic, the market disciplines any price increase and the market price is not far above marginal cost. If not, the equilibrium price is well above marginal cost. The other researchers listed above measure marginal cost directly and then calculate the ratio of price to marginal cost.

The big contribution of Rossi-Hansberg et al.'s paper is to explore concentration in markets that are presumptively local rather than national. A threshold question in this line of research is how to set the boundaries of local markets. In principle, the boundaries, based on transport costs and similar factors, differ across products. For some products, notably beer and transit-mix concrete, a good deal of research has been done on this topic. But research covering all products, such as Rossi-Hansberg et al.'s contribution, is limited to the use of data using existing boundaries to define the spatial markets. Figure 5 of the paper shows results for a variety of choices of spatial aggregation: national, metropolitan area, county, and ZIP code. None of these really makes the grade. National misses the whole point of the paper. Metropolitan areas are far too big for many products, as the authors' example of a restaurant in Brooklyn demonstrates. Counties are ridiculously heterogeneous and the great majority of counties are tiny. ZIP codes are reasonably homogeneous in population but not in square mileage. An acute problem for many products is that ZIP codes flunk the basic test for spatial boundaries, because many of them lack any sellers of products that are widely consumed. The paper is candid about the challenge of these ZIP codes with zero sellers, especially for measuring trends in concentration, where modest increases can result in ZIP codes disappearing from the sample. All things considered, however, the authors make a reasonable case that ZIP codes are the best of the available but flawed approaches to spatial market definition.

Similar comments apply to the boundaries of product markets. Figures 3 and 4 in Rossi-Hansberg et al. show that the downward trend of concentration across ZIP codes is weak when product boundaries are coarse (two-digit Standard Industrial Classification [SIC] codes) and much stronger when they are fine (eight-digit SIC codes). The paper does not make a case that demand and supply substitution patterns favor the eight-digit boundaries. The paper by Berger et al., as mentioned above, does undertake such measurement on the demand side but not the supply side.

As a believer in measuring market power by calculating the ratio of price to correctly defined and measured marginal cost, I believe that measuring concentration has a limited role in diagnosing market power. The posture of Rossi-Hansberg et al. is that concentration has become a controversial issue on its own and thus worthy of study even apart from any direct numerical connection between concentration and market power. The procedures of the two main competition authorities in the United States, the Antitrust Division of the Department of Justice and the Federal Trade Commission, straddle this issue in an interesting way. Concentration, measured by the HHI, has a fully specified role in their screening of challenges to antitrust misconduct, especially mergers. But, once a challenge has survived screening, the agencies turn to direct analysis of price elevation (or wage depression, in some cases).

In another interesting paper on a related subject, "The Industrial Revolution in Services," Rossi-Hansberg and Chang-Tai Hsieh pursue the idea that services, broadly defined, are going through a revolution typified by Walmart's expansion in competition with local supermarkets. Whereas the Rossi-Hansberg et al. paper emphasizes the general importance of the process across all industries, the Rossi-Hansberg and Hsieh paper places the revolution primarily in service-type industries where markets are local. Figure 7 in the paper by Rossi-Hansberg et al. shows that the truth lies in between.

In what Rossi-Hansberg and Hsieh call the New Industrial Revolution (NIR), firms use advanced information technology (IT) to standardize products and production methods across thousands of nearly identical establishments. Firms may own all these establishments (Starbucks) or franchise smaller firms to deliver products (McDonald's). The sectors most influenced are finance, insurance, real estate, retail trade, wholesale trade, and services. Sectors undergoing the revolution grow faster than other sectors, refuting market power stories and supporting productivity stories.

The NIR view emphasizes the role of computerization and broadband communication. The fixed asset tables of the National Income and Product Accounts report stocks of intellectual property (IP) by sector. I define the

IP intensity of a sector as the ratio of the value of its IP to the value of its structures. I show the ratio of the IP intensity of the NIR sector (trade, health, accommodation, and food services) to the non-NIR sector (fig. 1).

Franchise contracting is a powerful tool for accomplishing the revolution. The US Economic Census began gathering data on franchise status by establishment in 2007 and continued in 2012 and 2017. So far, only the 2012 survey has been published. The results are sharp: only 3% of sales economy-wide arise in franchised establishments, but 26% of sales arise in franchised establishments in the NIR sectors.

In five North American Industry Classification System (NAICS) six-digit industries, more than half of total sales occurred in franchised establishments:

- New car dealers
- Limited-service restaurants (fast food)
- Private mail centers
- Diet and weight reducing centers
- Optical goods stores

All of these are in the NIR sector.

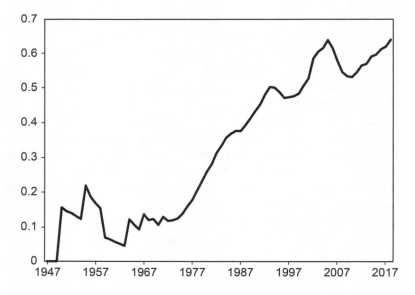

Fig. 1. IP intensity of New Industrial Revolution industries as a ratio to other industries. A color version of this figure is available online.

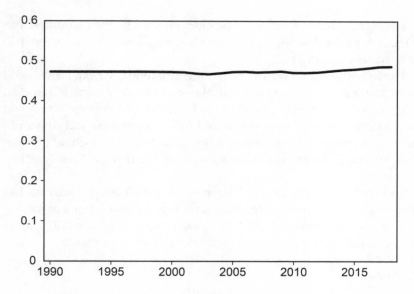

Fig. 2. Ratio of fast-food employment to total restaurant employment. A color version of this figure is available online.

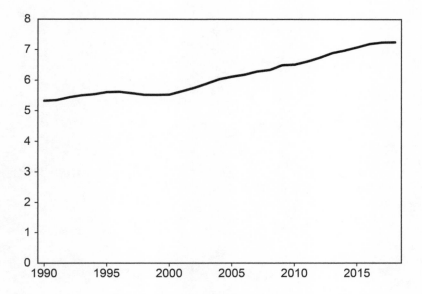

Fig. 3. Restaurant employment has risen substantially as a fraction of total non-farm employment. A color version of this figure is available online.

I thought that fast food might be more affected by the revolution, but the employment fraction of fast food among all restaurants is remarkably stable (see fig. 2).

The hypothesis that sectors benefiting differentially from NIR should grow faster is sustained in the case of restaurants (a leading NIR sector, it appears). The growth of out-of-the-household food preparation and consumption relative to in-household food preparation and consumption has been noted in the context of the modeling of household production, but the paper offers a new explanation: the rising efficiency of restaurants (fig. 3).

To conclude, the team producing the papers I have discussed has made major contributions to understanding the interactions of market power, concentration, and product characteristics. There is still a lot more to do, including more intensive study of individual industries.

Endnote

Author email address: Hall (rehall@gmail.com). For acknowledgments, sources of research support, and disclosure of the author's material financial relationships, if any, please see https://www.nber.org/books-and-chapters/nber-macroeconomics-annual -2020-volume-35/comment-diverging-trends-national-and-local-concentration-hall.

Discussion

John Haltiwanger opened the discussion by bringing attention to the data used in the paper. The analysis used data from the National Establishment Time Series (NETS). The authors argued that the NETS is a reliable source because it aligns on several dimensions with another data set, the County Business Patterns (CBP). However, Haltiwanger argued that NETS overstates employment because of imputations. Further, NETS sales data are not reliable, as documented by Barnatchez, Crane, and Decker ("An Assessment of the National Establishment Times Series [NETS] Database," *Finance and Economics Discussion Series* 2017 [2017]: 110). The authors recognized that there are imputations in NETS. However, they emphasized that their findings are validated by several robustness checks. In addition, they noted that similar results hold when using a different data set, the Longitudinal Business Database (LBD).

The next comments were related to the suitability of the Herfindahl-Hirschman Index (HHI) as a measure of market power at different levels of geographic aggregation. Jeffrey Campbell pointed out that the HHI is not a reliable measure of market power for large cities, where there are many firms in the market and there is substantial variation across neighborhoods. He encouraged the authors to repeat their analysis for small towns. The authors responded that they replicated their results for different measures of concentration and that their findings are robust regardless of the measure considered. Erik Hurst questioned why the authors decided to start the analysis at the smallest area of aggregation, the ZIP-code level, as opposed to a larger area of aggregation, such as the county level. Seconding Campbell's remark, the authors responded that the measurement of market power is more reliable for smaller geographical areas, where it is easier to avoid problems that arise when many firms are active in the market.

The authors then addressed some of the concerns raised by the discussants. First, they focused on comments regarding the correct interpretation of the facts described in the paper. They argued that the goal of the paper is to document new facts rather than to offer an interpretation of them. For the latter, a fully specified structural model is needed to capture the underlying forces that explain why the economy has evolved in the observed direction. Second, they addressed concerns about the endogeneity of the fourth fact presented in the paper, which illustrates the effect of the entrance of a top enterprise in a local market on concentration. Although there are some pre-trends in the event studies, the authors argued that they are not of great importance. They offered the case study of Walmart as corroborating evidence, citing the study of Holmes ("The Diffusion of Wal-Mart and Economies of Density," *Econometrica* 79, no. 1 [2011]: 253–302). The expansion strategy of Walmart was to enter locations neighboring its existing establishments, rather than targeting locations with special features, providing some evidence of the exogeneity of the location choice for new establishments to local concentration trends.

3

What Do We Learn from Cross-Regional Empirical Estimates in Macroeconomics?

Adam Guren, *Boston University,* United States of America, *and NBER,* United States of America

Alisdair McKay, *Federal Reserve Board of Minneapolis,* United States of America

Emi Nakamura, *University of California, Berkeley,* United States of America, *and NBER,* United States of America

Jón Steinsson, *University of California, Berkeley,* United States of America, *and NBER,* United States of America

I. Introduction

A growing literature uses variation across cities or regions to identify the effects of economic shocks of interest to macroeconomists.[1] What exactly these estimates identify is often complicated by the fact that metropolitan and regional outcomes reflect both the partial equilibrium effects of the shock in question as well as local general equilibrium responses to the shock. In this paper we propose an approach by which applied researchers can isolate the partial equilibrium effect of the shock. The partial equilibrium effect is useful for several reasons. First, it has a clear theoretical interpretation and speaks more directly to specific economic mechanisms. In contrast, estimates that include local general equilibrium effects reflect a combination of several economic mechanisms and are more difficult to interpret as a result. Second, the partial equilibrium effect can more easily be matched with a theoretical counterpart for calibration purposes. The method we propose allows researchers to avoid formulating and solving a multi-region general equilibrium macroeconomic model to be able to compare their empirical results to analogous concepts in a model.

The easiest way to describe our approach is in the context of a concrete application. The application we focus on is the analysis of so-called housing wealth effects. The US housing boom and bust in the 2000s focused attention of economists on the effect of changes in home prices on consumer spending. Prominent recent papers in this literature use regional data to estimate the effect of changes in house prices on outcomes such as spending, car registrations, and employment (e.g., Mian, Rao, and Sufi 2013;

Mian and Sufi 2014). The appropriate interpretation of these estimates is not straightforward. House prices are endogenous at the level of a city and a shock that changes home prices surely alters consumption through other channels. The shock may affect consumption directly. In addition, the increased spending triggered by higher house prices will raise wages and incomes locally, which will lead to more local spending (a local general equilibrium effect). For these reasons, it is not immediately clear what we can learn from the response of city-level consumption to a change in local house prices.

We show how existing empirical estimates of the housing wealth effect on consumption can be decomposed into the partial equilibrium effect of house prices on consumption and local general equilibrium effects. We start by drawing a distinction between prices that are determined nationally and prices that are determined locally. For example, financial markets are highly integrated at a national level, whereas labor markets and markets for nontradable goods are quite local. This distinction is important because variation in national prices will be absorbed by the constant in a cross-sectional regression or the time fixed effect in a panel regression and will therefore not affect cross-regional estimates of the housing wealth effect.

Local general equilibrium effects that operate through local markets will, however, not be captured by the constant or time fixed effects in cross-regional regression analysis. The key insight in our paper is that estimates of the local fiscal multiplier can be used to gauge the strength of these local general equilibrium effects. In particular, we derive conditions under which one can remove local general equilibrium effects from a city-level estimate of the housing wealth effect simply by dividing that estimate by an estimate of the local fiscal multiplier. The logic underlying this result is that the equilibrium response to an increase in local demand will be the same whether that demand comes from private consumption as a result of the housing wealth effect or from a fiscal shock. Dividing by the local fiscal multiplier yields an estimate of the partial equilibrium housing wealth effect that corresponds to the effect of a change in home prices holding fixed wages and other nonhousing prices. This partial equilibrium effect has a simple interpretation and it can be used to discipline a partial equilibrium model of housing and consumption.

In recent complementary work, we estimate the housing wealth effect based on city-level variation in house prices and using retail employment as a proxy for local consumption (Guren et al. 2020). We estimate an elasticity of retail employment with respect to house prices of 0.072. We furthermore show in that paper that retail employment has approximately a unit elasticity with respect to consumption in the aggregate and across cities, which allows us to interpret the retail employment response as a consumption response. To convert the elasticity we estimate into a marginal propensity to consume out of housing wealth (MPCH), we divide by the housing consumption ratio, which averaged 2.17 from 1985 to 2016. This yields an MPCH of 3.3 cents on the dollar. For the reasons discussed above, this estimate reflects both the partial equilibrium and local general equilibrium responses of consumption to housing. To isolate the partial equilibrium effect, we divide it by an estimate of the local fiscal multiplier. Nakamura and Steinsson (2014) estimate the local fiscal multiplier to be approximately 1.5. Dividing our housing wealth effect estimate by the local fiscal multiplier yields a partial equilibrium MPCH of 2.2 cents on the dollar.

Our approach of combining several reduced-form estimates to identify a structural parameter is an application of the general method of simultaneous equations identification. The identification challenge is that multiple structural systems can give rise to the same reduced-form estimates. For example, the cross-regional housing wealth effect may be large because the partial equilibrium effect of house prices on consumption is large or because local general equilibrium effects are large. Identification requires making restrictions on the system. In our example, the restrictions are exclusion restrictions: for example, shocks to government spending do not directly affect consumption demand (they affect consumption through income). The key point in our argument is that allowing for more sources of exogenous variation (government spending shocks) helps identify the system even though it enlarges the system. We discuss how the identification problem and solution are closely related to structural vector autoregression (VAR) methods. A general lesson is that researchers who use regional variation can benefit from approaching their estimates as components of a system of simultaneous equations. In this context, shocks to government purchases are particularly useful in identifying local general equilibrium effects because the direct effect of the shock on demand is known. We discuss how this simultaneous equations approach is valuable in many situations where the object of interest is the direct effect of a change in demand whether it arises from housing wealth effects, credit supply shocks, foreign demand, or other sources.

We present several refinements of the basic idea of dividing by the local fiscal multiplier. The most important refinement from a quantitative perspective is to allow for the fact that an increase in house prices stimulates local construction activity. This is a separate channel from the standard consumption multiplier because the initial partial equilibrium increase in demand is not consumption but residential investment. We derive a simple formula for isolating the partial equilibrium effect of house prices on consumption in the presence of effects on local construction activity. To evaluate this formula, we need an estimate of the response of construction activity to house prices. We present such an estimate using an analogous research design to that used in Guren et al. (2020). The refined formula yields an estimate of the partial equilibrium housing wealth elasticity of 0.040 or a partial equilibrium MPCH of 1.8 cents on the dollar.

A second important refinement is to allow for dynamics. In a dynamic context, there is no single fiscal multiplier. Rather there is an entire impulse response of output to a fiscal shock. For the dynamic case, we develop a matrix version of the simple formula that applies in the static case. For example, the dynamic version of our formula involves the inverse of a matrix with the (i, j) element giving the effect of a fiscal shock at date j on output at date i (a matrix version of dividing by the local fiscal multiplier). Using simulations, we explore how well our static formula performs when the data are generated by a dynamic model. We show that under some conditions it holds almost exactly. In the richest dynamic structural model we consider, our simple static formula accounts for the bulk of the needed adjustment but somewhat underestimates it.

In our analysis, we address Davidoff's (2016) critique of the use of heterogeneous supply constraints—such as those captured by the Saiz (2010) housing supply elasticity estimates—as instruments for home prices. Davidoff points out that if housing markets experience a common demand shock but move along different supply curves, then prices and quantities should be negatively correlated: the most constrained cities should see the largest housing price responses but the smallest housing quantity responses. However, Davidoff shows that there is a positive relationship between housing price growth and the growth of housing units. Our construction employment estimates confirm Davidoff's critique applies at business cycle frequencies.[2]

We show that a model that allows for differences between short-run and long-run housing supply elasticities can address Davidoff's critique. We consider a version of our dynamic model in which short-run housing supply elasticities are low in all cities, but housing supply elasticities are more heterogeneous in the long run. This distinction reflects both the time it takes to plan and develop new housing units (which makes short-run elasticities low in all cities) and differences in constraints on land supply that are not binding in the short run but may bind in the long run as in Nathanson and Zwick (2018). House prices, like other asset prices, are forward-looking in nature and, as a result, are primarily determined by the long-run elasticity of housing supply even in the short run. The short-run construction response, on the other hand, reflects the short-run constraints faced by housing developers. Consider two cities that have the same short-run supply elasticity but differ in the long-run supply elasticity. A common shock to expected future housing demand will move prices differently across the two cities due to expectations about future housing supply responses. Furthermore, expectations about larger future capital gains (or smaller future capital losses) will imply that the shock results in a larger change in current housing demand in the city with a less elastic long-run housing supply curve. In terms of construction, both cities move along the same short-run housing supply curve but by different amounts. The upward-sloping short-run supply curve yields a positive correlation between prices and quantities even though the changes in prices are generated primarily by a common demand shock moving the cities along different (long-run) supply curves.

The idea of dividing cross-regional estimates of housing wealth effects by estimates of the local fiscal multiplier to arrive at an estimate of the partial equilibrium effect of changes in house prices on consumption implicitly assumes that existing evidence on the local fiscal multiplier is stronger than for the partial equilibrium effect of house prices on consumption. However, if the reverse is true, our method is just as useful. In this case, we can use our method to infer the size of the local fiscal multiplier from the combination of cross-regional estimates of housing wealth effects and estimates of the partial equilibrium effect of house prices on consumption. More generally, in the context of housing wealth effects, our method implies that cross-regional estimates can provide information about some combination of the local fiscal multiplier and the strength of partial equilibrium effects.

The key idea we explore in this paper is that the general equilibrium adjustment to a change in private consumption is equivalent to the general equilibrium adjustment to a government spending shock. This demand equivalence idea is also explored in several contemporaneous papers. In the context of a two-period model of the stock market wealth effect, Chodorow-Reich, Nenov, and Simsek (2020) derive a demand equivalence result that links the direct spending response to the change in the local wage bill. Wolf (2019a) lays out conditions under which demand equivalence holds exactly for the impulse responses of a dynamic model and Wolf (2019b) applies those results to cross-regional comparisons and local general equilibrium. In our analysis, the relationship between impulse responses is expressed in terms of the matrix relationship described above.[3] Applying this result directly is challenging because it requires that the researcher observe the full dynamic response to the shock of interest and a fiscal spending shock that has the same dynamics as the (as yet unknown) partial equilibrium response of interest. However, we show that the simpler static adjustment works fairly well across several alternative specifications of a fully dynamic model. As each of these papers considers a different application, taken together, they demonstrate that the demand equivalence logic that is common among them is useful in a variety of contexts.[4]

Interpreting cross-regional estimates is tricky because of general equilibrium effects. On the one hand, these estimates include local general equilibrium effects. The focus of this paper is getting from the cross-regional estimates to partial equilibrium effects by removing local general equilibrium effects. On the other hand, cross-regional estimates difference out national general equilibrium effects. This implies that cross-regional estimates do not directly answer questions about aggregate effects (e.g., what is the aggregate effect of fiscal stimulus, the China shock, or the 2000s rise and fall of house prices). A rapidly growing recent literature has used multi-region general equilibrium models to assess what cross-regional estimates imply about these macro questions (e.g., Nakamura and Steinsson 2014; Beraja, Hurst, and Ospina 2019; Herreno 2020). One way to do this type of analysis is to use the cross-regional estimate to distinguish among competing general equilibrium models and then see what the favored general equilibrium model implies about the macroeconomic question of interest (Nakamura and Steinsson 2018).

The paper is organized as follows. Section II lays out the challenge the paper seeks to address. Section III presents adjustments of cross-sectional estimates of the housing wealth effect for local general equilibrium effects in simple static environments. Section IV explains that our adjustment of the housing wealth effect is an application of estimating one equation in a system of simultaneous equations. Section V provides a fully structural, multi-region macro model of the housing wealth effect on consumption. Section VI derives the matrix adjustment for local general equilibrium effects in the dynamic model presented in Section V. Section VII discusses the importance of distinguishing between the short-run and long-run housing supply elasticities. Section VIII conducts a Monte Carlo analysis of the fully structural model to evaluate the accuracy and robustness of the simple adjustment used in Section III. Section IX concludes.

II.   Interpreting Cross-Regional Regressions

To address the issue of how to interpret cross-regional regression coefficients, it is useful to consider a concrete example. The example we focus on is the estimation of the housing wealth effect. A relatively standard estimating equation for a regional estimate of the housing wealth effect is

$$\Delta c_{i,t} = \psi_i + \xi_t + \beta \Delta p_{i,t} + \varepsilon_{i,t}, \tag{1}$$

where i indexes cities, t indexes time, $\Delta c_{i,t}$ is the first difference of log consumption in city i, $\Delta p_{i,t}$ is the first difference of log house prices in the city, ψ_i is a city fixed effect, ξ_t is a time fixed effect, and $\varepsilon_{i,t}$ captures unmodeled influences. The coefficient of interest is β, which gives the elasticity of local consumption with respect to local house prices.

To identify the causal effect of local house prices on local consumption, researchers must confront the twin challenges of reverse causation and measurement error. A common approach to overcoming these challenges is premised on the view that house prices differentially respond to aggregate housing demand shocks across cities due to differences in housing supply elasticities. This approach is, for example, used by Mian et al. (2013), Mian and Sufi (2014), and Guren et al. (2020). Let's suppose we have used such a shift-share approach to form a causal estimate of β. The question we ask is, How should we interpret this estimate?

Let's suppose for simplicity that the consumption function of households in the regional economies under consideration is a linear function of household income $y_{i,t}$, house prices $p_{i,t}$, interest rates R_t, and the source of aggregate variation that drives house prices; call it Ω_t

$$c_{i,t} = C_y y_{i,t} + C_p p_{i,t} + C_R R_t + C_\Omega \Omega_t, \tag{2}$$

where C_y, C_p, C_R, and C_Ω are the coefficients in this linearized consumption function. Later in the paper, we describe an example of a model where such an equation arises, although in a dynamic model consumption will depend not only on current income and prices but also on future income and prices. In this consumption function, the coefficient C_p has a straightforward interpretation as the amount consumption changes when house prices rise holding incomes and other prices fixed. In other words, C_p summarizes a partial equilibrium experiment.

Let's now suppose that regression equation (1) is estimated on data generated by equation (2). In this case, what is the interpretation of the coefficient β? First, the variation in consumption coming from $C_R \Delta R_t + C_\Omega \Delta \Omega_t$ and any other aggregate factors that may enter the consumption function is common across cities and will be absorbed by the time fixed effect ξ_t. Notice that this means that the direct effect of the shock on consumption and any national general equilibrium effects that are mediated by national prices will not be captured by the coefficient β.

What about effects that the shock may have on local income $\Delta y_{i,t}$? To the extent that $\Delta y_{i,t}$ is correlated with $\Delta p_{i,t}$, our estimate of β in equation (1) will not only reflect the partial equilibrium housing wealth effect, C_p, but also the response of consumption to changes in local income. Unfortunately, there is a compelling reason to expect $\Delta y_{i,t}$ and $\Delta p_{i,t}$ to be correlated even when a sophisticated identification strategy is employed. The partial equilibrium housing wealth effect $C_p \Delta p_{i,t}$ will itself raise demand for locally produced goods and thereby bring about an increase in local incomes. This implies that β will reflect not just the partial equilibrium effect C_p but also local general equilibrium effects induced by the initial partial equilibrium effect.

An alternative, more direct, approach to estimating the partial equilibrium effect of house prices on consumption is to regress an individual-level consumption measure on changes in house prices and a control for individual-level income by ordinary least squares (OLS; e.g., Campbell and Cocco 2007) or instrumenting for changes in house prices (e.g., Aladangady 2017). It is important to note, however, that these studies use city-level house price variation. Without the individual-level income control, the coefficient on house prices in this type of regression will therefore include local general equilibrium effects. Furthermore, as Campbell and Cocco (2007) and Aladangady (2017) stress, there are several reasons why including individual-level income as a control is unlikely to purge the regression coefficient on changes in house prices of the local general equilibrium effects. First, individual-level income is likely measured with error. If so, changes in house prices may be a useful proxy for changes in income and the resulting omitted variable bias will include some component of the local general equilibrium effect. Second, changes in overall individual-level income are likely to have different statistical properties (e.g., less persistence) than changes in income induced by changes in house prices. This means that the marginal propensity to consume (MPC) out of these different sources of income is likely different, which implies that controlling for individual-level income would not accurately capture the local general equilibrium effects of house price changes. Third, there are likely other local general equilibrium channels that would not be controlled for by including individual-level income such as changes in the local price level.

This logic applies more generally outside the context of housing wealth effects. Although there are some situations where individual-level variation allows the direct estimation of a partial equilibrium effect, in many situations the most convincing identification strategies rely on regional variation. In other situations, all variations are by definition regional. In these cases, one must remove the local general equilibrium effects to obtain an estimate of the partial equilibrium effect.

III. A Simple Adjustment for Local General Equilibrium Effects

In this section we derive a simple adjustment of cross-sectional regression estimates of the housing wealth effect for local general equilibrium effects. The idea is that researchers who have constructed estimates of the housing wealth effect using cross-sectional regressions at the metropolitan or state level, can use this adjustment to recover a rough estimate of what their regression results imply about the partial equilibrium effect of house prices on consumption. The simple formulas we derive in this section are based on several approximations and simplifying assumptions. In Sections V and VI, we then present a fully specified multi-region general equilibrium model and an exact adjustment formula for this model. Later in the paper we show that the simple adjustment derived in this section is very close to the exact adjustment in certain cases and reasonably close in others.

A. The Fiscal Multiplier as a Measure of Local General Equilibrium Effects

Our central idea is that estimates of the local fiscal multiplier can be used to gauge the strength of local general equilibrium effects. We start by illustrating this in a very simple static case. The economy consists of two equally sized regions: "home" and "foreign." Each region has three markets: a goods market, a housing market, and a labor market. In the home region, the two relative prices are the real wage w and the price of housing p, both denominated in goods. Suppose goods are produced with labor according to the production function $Y = N$, where Y is goods produced and N is labor supply. Labor supply is given by a function $N(w, p, T)$ that depends on the wage, the price of housing, and taxes T. Household demand for goods is given by $C(w, p, T)$. In addition to this private consumption demand, goods are used for public consumption in amount G, where G is exogenous. We assume that taxes are set at the national level and satisfy a government budget constraint. It is important to our argument that both regions face the same taxes.

In this simplest case, we ignore trade across regions and across time; these features are added in Subsection III.C and Section V, respectively. The aggregate resource constraint is then $Y = C(w, p, T) + G$. Although this resource constraint is very standard, it embeds the important assumption that an increase in demand from private consumption requires the exact same supply response as an increase in demand from the government. For housing, we specify an excess demand function $H(w, p, T, s)$, where s is an exogenous shock. Because we only use data on the price of housing and not on the quantity of housing, we do not need to specify housing supply and demand separately.

Given these assumptions, the equilibrium level of wages and house prices in this home region is given by the solution to the following two equations:

$$C(w, p, T) + G = N(w, p, T) \tag{3}$$

$$H(w, p, T, s) = 0, \tag{4}$$

taking G and T as given.

The foreign region mirrors the home region with relative prices denoted w^* and p^*. These prices satisfy equations

$$C(w^*, p^*, T) + G^* = N(w^*, p^*, T) \tag{5}$$

$$H(w^*, p^*, T, s^*) = 0. \tag{6}$$

There are two important assumptions here. First, note that these are the same functions C, N, and H as in the home region but with different arguments. Second, in the foreign region the government spending differs from the home region, but the taxes do not.

We make two additional simplifying assumptions. First, there are no wealth effects on labor supply, $N_p \equiv \partial N / \partial p = 0$. This assumption implies that changes in housing wealth are not supply shocks in addition to being demand shocks. We view this assumption as being a reasonable approximation to reality in the short run. Second, we assume that house prices are independent of income, $H_w = 0$. This assumption is less likely to hold in reality. We relax it in Subsection III.D. It is, however, helpful to make this assumption in this first pass to simplify the exposition.

Suppose we observe an instrumental variables (IV) estimate of the housing wealth effect based on regional variation. In our notation, this is

$d\hat{Y}/d\hat{p} = (d\hat{Y}/ds)/(d\hat{p}/ds)$, where s is the shock (instrument) used to estimate $d\hat{Y}/d\hat{p}$ and a hat denotes a cross-regional difference: $\hat{Y} = Y - Y^*$. The trouble is that this IV estimate is the total derivative of consumption with respect to house prices, not the partial derivative C_p. The total derivative includes local general equilibrium effects; for instance, the initial shock may raise wages and lead to an increase in local consumption, which will further raise wages and increase local consumption, and so on. To get from the IV estimate to the partial equilibrium effect of house prices on consumption C_p, we need to adjust for these local general equilibrium effects.

To this end, take the total derivatives of equations (3) and (5) with respect to G and take the difference across regions of the resulting expressions to arrive at

$$C_w \frac{d\hat{w}}{dG} + C_p \frac{d\hat{p}}{dG} + 1 = N_w \frac{d\hat{w}}{dG}. \tag{7}$$

Note that the effect of taxes does not appear because $\hat{T} = 0$ as both regions face the same taxes. This lines up well with the empirical estimates, which include a constant term or time fixed effects and are therefore estimated off of cross-regional differences that omit factors that affect all regions equally. Taking total derivatives of equations (4) and (6) with respect to G and rearranging yields $d\hat{p}/dG = 0$. Then equation (7) implies $d\hat{w}/dG = 1/(N_w - C_w)$.

Taking total derivatives of equations (3)–(6) with respect to s and performing similar manipulations yields the response of prices to s. In summary, we have the following matrix of the price response to the two shocks:

$$\begin{pmatrix} \dfrac{d\hat{w}}{dG} & \dfrac{d\hat{w}}{ds} \\[2ex] \dfrac{d\hat{p}}{dG} & \dfrac{d\hat{p}}{ds} \end{pmatrix} = [N_w - C_w]^{-1} \begin{pmatrix} 1 & -\dfrac{H_s}{H_p} C_p \\[2ex] 0 & \dfrac{H_s}{H_p}(C_w - N_w) \end{pmatrix}. \tag{8}$$

We similarly differentiate the resource constraint. This yields the response of $\hat{Y}$ to the two shocks:[5]

$$\frac{d\hat{Y}}{dG} = C_w \frac{d\hat{w}}{dG} + C_p \frac{d\hat{p}}{dG} + 1 \tag{9}$$

$$\frac{d\hat{Y}}{ds} = C_w \frac{d\hat{w}}{ds} + C_p \frac{d\hat{p}}{ds}. \tag{10}$$

Combining equations (8) and (10) yields

$$\frac{d\hat{Y}}{ds} = -C_p \frac{H_s}{H_p} \frac{N_w}{N_w - C_w}$$

$$\frac{d\hat{p}}{ds} = -\frac{H_s}{H_p},$$

which in turn yields the regional IV estimate of the housing wealth effect

$$\frac{d\hat{Y}}{d\hat{p}} = \frac{d\hat{Y}/ds}{d\hat{p}/ds} = (1 - C_Y)^{-1}C_p, \tag{11}$$

where $C_Y \equiv C_w/N_w$ is the MPC out of income. From this we see that the regional IV estimate of the housing wealth effect is equal to the partial equilibrium response of consumption to house prices C_p multiplied by a local general equilibrium feedback factor $(1 - C_Y)^{-1}$.

Notice also that equations (8) and (9) imply that the local fiscal multiplier is equal to

$$\frac{d\hat{Y}}{dG} = 1 + \frac{C_w}{N_w - C_w} = (1 - C_Y)^{-1}. \tag{12}$$

The local fiscal multiplier is, thus, exactly equal to the local general equilibrium factor in equation (11). Intuitively, an increase in home prices of one unit spurs an extra C_p of spending, which then triggers local adjustments in wages with accompanying consumption effects. These same local adjustments occur when the initial spending is due to a government spending shock.

An important feature of government spending shocks is that their size is known: the dollar amount of the government spending is observed (or the dollar amount that is explained by whatever instrument we are using to identify exogenous variation in government spending). This is why the "direct effect" in equation (12) is equal to 1 as opposed to some unknown scaling factor. This feature makes the local fiscal multiplier estimates particularly useful as measures of local general equilibrium effects.

Combining these last two equations, we get that

$$C_p = \frac{d\hat{Y}/d\hat{p}}{d\hat{Y}/dG}. \tag{13}$$

In other words, the partial equilibrium effect of house prices on consumption, C_p, is equal to the cross-regional IV estimate of the housing wealth effect, $d\hat{Y}/d\hat{p}$, divided by the local fiscal multiplier, $d\hat{Y}/dG$. An estimate of the local fiscal multiplier can therefore be used to convert a cross-regional IV estimate of the housing wealth effect into an estimate of the partial equilibrium effect of house prices on consumption.

In Guren et al. (2020), we estimate an MPCH of 3.3 cents on the dollar. This estimate corresponds to the total effect captured by $d\hat{Y}/d\hat{p}$. Nakamura and Steinsson (2014) estimate a local fiscal multiplier of about 1.5.[6] Equation (13) then implies that the partial equilibrium MPCH is 2.2 cents on the dollar.

B. Residential Investment

A potentially important channel that we abstract from above is the response of residential investment to changes in house prices: an increase in house prices may induce an increase in residential investment, which then induces local general equilibrium effects. We now augment the simple model above to allow for this channel. In this case, the equilibrium level of wages and house prices in the home region are given by the solution to the following two equations:

$$C(w, p, T) + I(p, T) + G = N(w, T) \tag{14}$$

$$H(p, T, s) = 0. \tag{15}$$

Relative to the previous example, we have added demand for local goods coming from residential investment $I(p)$. We maintain the "one good" setup in which output produced with labor can be converted into consumption, government purchases, and residential investment. This implies that an increase in residential investment leads to a supply response and a general equilibrium response on wages and incomes that unfolds in the same way as changes in demand coming from private or public consumption. We will have to account for this response to recover the partial equilibrium response of consumption to house prices. In addition, we assume that residential investment is independent of income conditional on house prices, $I_w = 0$.

The foreign region again mirrors the home region. In an approach similar to the approach used in Subsection III.A, manipulation of the equilibrium conditions and resource constraints shows the regional IV estimate of the housing wealth effect for this case is

$$\frac{d\hat{Y}}{d\hat{p}} = \frac{d\hat{Y}/ds}{d\hat{p}/ds} = (1 - C_Y)^{-1}(C_p + I_p). \tag{16}$$

The difference from the approach used in Subsection III.A is that there are two partial equilibrium effects: one for consumption and another for residential investment.

The addition of residential investment does not affect the regional fiscal multiplier (as we have assumed that $I_w = 0$). The regional fiscal multiplier $(1 - C_Y)^{-1}$ can, therefore, again be used to adjust for local general equilibrium effects, which yields

$$C_p = \left(\frac{d\hat{Y}/d\hat{p}}{d\hat{Y}/dG} \right) - I_p.$$

Because $I_w = 0$, $I_p = d\hat{I}/d\hat{p}$. We must, however, also take account of the fact that the increase in residential investment contributes to $d\hat{Y}/d\hat{p}$. In this case, we have $d\hat{Y}/d\hat{p} = (d\hat{C}/d\hat{p}) + (d\hat{I}/d\hat{p})$. Using these expressions, we can rewrite the above equation as

$$C_p = \left[\frac{(d\hat{C}/d\hat{p}) + (d\hat{I}/d\hat{p})}{d\hat{Y}/dG} \right] - \frac{d\hat{I}}{d\hat{p}}. \tag{17}$$

In this case, we need a regional estimate of the response of residential investment to a change in house prices in addition to the regional housing wealth effect and fiscal multiplier estimates. We use changes in construction and real estate employment as a proxy for residential investment. Using a quarterly panel of core-based statistical area (CBSA)-level employment and house prices covering 1990–2017, we estimate an analogous specification to the housing wealth effect estimate we present in column 2 of table 1 of Guren et al. (2020). Results are reported in table 1 and we focus on our preferred "sensitivity" instrument. Our estimated elasticity is 0.362 (with a standard error of 0.053). To convert this to a simple derivative, we must divide by the ratio of housing wealth to residential investment H/I, which we estimate to be 28.2.[7] This yields 0.013 as our estimate of $d\hat{I}/d\hat{p}$. Plugging in this estimate along with our estimates of the housing wealth effect and fiscal multiplier into equation (17) yields a partial equilibrium MPCH estimate of 1.8 cents on the dollar.

C.   Demand Leakage Due to Trade

The analysis above ignores the fact that the data used to estimate the regional housing wealth effect come from regional economies that are open to trade with other regions. This implies that some of the extra demand induced by higher house prices "leaks out" to other regions. Let ϕ

Table 1
Elasticity of Construction and Real Estate Employment to
Home Prices

Sample Period	1990–2017
Ordinary least squares	.470***
	(.025)
Sensitivity instrument	.362***
	(.053)
Saiz instrument	.500***
	(.102)

Note: The specification is the same as the specification used for
table 1 in Guren et al. (2020) except that the dependent variable
is construction and real estate employment rather than retail employment. "Ordinary least squares" uses no instrument. "Sensitivity instrument" uses the sensitivity instrument described in Guren
et al. (2020). Saiz uses an instrument that interacts Saiz's elasticity
with the national change in house prices. All three approaches use
the same control variables: two-digit industry shares with date-
specific coefficients, the cyclical sensitivity control described in Guren et al. (2020), and the analogously constructed controls for differential city exposure to interest rates and the Gilchrist-Zakrajsek
excess bond premium along with CBSA and division-time fixed
effects. Standard errors are two-way clustered at the time and
CBSA level.
***Indicates statistical significance at the 0.1% level.

be the expenditure share on local goods. Households display home bias
when $\phi > 1/2$. Here, again, we maintain the "one good" assumption,
which in this case implies that the real exchange rate between the regions is fixed and equal to one. We relax this assumption in Section V.
Building on equations (14)–(15), we have the following system:

$$\phi[C(w, p, T) + I(p, T)] + (1 - \phi)[C(w^*, p^*, T) + I(p^*, T)] + G = N(w, T),$$

$$(1 - \phi)[C(w, p, T) + I(p, T)] + \phi[C(w^*, p^*, T) + I(p^*, T)] + G^* = N(w^*, T),$$

$$H(p, s, T) = 0,$$

$$H(p^*, s^*, T) = 0.$$

In this case, it is important to distinguish between local expenditures
and local output. We define $E = C(w, p, T) + I(p, T)$ to be home expenditures. Regional IV estimates of the housing wealth effect measure the
response of expenditures to house prices, not the response of output
to house prices. With this definition of local expenditures, we can use

similar manipulations of the equilibrium conditions and resource constraints as in Subsections III.A and III.B to derive the regional IV estimate of the housing wealth effect:

$$\frac{d\hat{E}}{d\hat{p}} = \frac{d\hat{E}/ds}{d\hat{p}/ds} = (1 - \Phi C_Y)^{-1}(C_p + I_p), \tag{18}$$

and the local fiscal multiplier:

$$\frac{d\hat{Y}}{dG} = (1 - \Phi C_Y)^{-1}, \tag{19}$$

where $\Phi \equiv 2\phi - 1$. Once again, we see that the cross-regional housing wealth effect $d\hat{E}/d\hat{p}$ is equal to a partial equilibrium effect ($C_p + I_p$) multiplied by a local general equilibrium effect, which is exactly equal to the local fiscal multiplier $d\hat{Y}/dG$.

The strength of the local general equilibrium effect is tempered by the degree of openness of each regional economy. Trade linkages attenuate the differences in activity across regions because some of the extra spending in the home region spills over onto the foreign region. In our simple model, this is captured by the factor Φ in the denominator on the right-hand side of equation (19). This factor runs from zero to one depending on the degree of home bias of demand. In a more complex model with movements in the relative prices of home and foreign goods, the elasticity of substitution between home and foreign goods would also play a role in determining the size of this attenuation.

Combining the last two equations, using the fact that $d\hat{E}/d\hat{p} = (d\hat{C}/d\hat{p}) + (d\hat{I}/d\hat{p})$, the fact that $I_p = d\hat{I}/d\hat{p}$, and rearranging yields

$$C_p = \left[\frac{(d\hat{C}/d\hat{p}) + (d\hat{I}/d\hat{p})}{d\hat{Y}/dG}\right] - \frac{d\hat{I}}{d\hat{p}}, \tag{20}$$

which is no different from equation (17). In other words, the attenuation due to openness has no impact on our analysis because it only shows up in the size of the local general equilibrium effect, which we measure in the data. There is, however, some subtlety to this outcome. The housing wealth effect is measured in terms of an expenditure response whereas the fiscal multiplier is measured in terms of a production response and normally we would think that production is more attenuated than expenditure. However, in specifying the model we assumed that the government buys a purely local good, not a mix of home and foreign goods. So, the production response to a government spending shock is no more attenuated than the expenditure response to house prices.

D. Income Effects on Housing

We now allow for an income effect on the price of housing. In this case, the housing market equilibrium conditions become

$$H(w, p, s, T) = 0,$$
$$H(w^*, p^*, s^*, T) = 0,$$

where housing demand now responds to wages. The goods market equilibrium conditions are the same as in Subsection III.C. We can again use similar manipulations of the equilibrium conditions and resource constraints as in earlier sections to derive the regional IV estimate of the housing wealth effect:

$$\frac{d\hat{E}}{d\hat{p}} = \frac{d\hat{E}/ds}{d\hat{p}/ds} = (1 - \Phi C_Y)^{-1}(C_p + I_p), \tag{21}$$

and the local fiscal multiplier:

$$\frac{d\hat{Y}}{dG} = \left(1 - \Phi C_Y + \Phi \frac{C_p + I_p}{N_w} \frac{H_w}{H_p}\right)^{-1}. \tag{22}$$

Derivations of these equations, which encompass all the derivations in this section as special cases, are presented in appendix A.

Notice that the housing wealth effect is the same in this case as in Subsection III.C: equation (21) is the same as equation (18). However, the local fiscal multiplier is different: equation (22) is different than equation (19). This means that the addition of income effects on house prices breaks the exact equivalence between the local fiscal multiplier and the local general equilibrium effects induced by a change in house prices. The reason for this is that part of the response to the government spending shock comes through house prices and the housing wealth effect, but we would like to isolate only the part of the fiscal multiplier that relates to wage adjustments.

To this end, suppose we observe an estimate of the response of house prices to income $d\hat{p}/d\hat{Y}$.[8] Some further manipulation of the equilibrium conditions yields

$$C_p = \left[\frac{(d\hat{C}/d\hat{p}) + (d\hat{I}/d\hat{p})}{d\hat{Y}/dG}\right]\left[1 - \Phi\left(\frac{d\hat{C}}{d\hat{p}} + \frac{d\hat{I}}{d\hat{p}}\right)\frac{d\hat{p}}{d\hat{Y}}\right]^{-1} - \frac{d\hat{I}}{d\hat{p}}. \tag{23}$$

This expression, which we derive in appendix A, differs from equation (20) by the term in the large bracket. This term represents the adjustment to the local fiscal multiplier estimate that is needed to focus on the part of general equilibrium effect that comes from change in wages.

We need two extra pieces of data to be able to evaluate equation (23). First, we need an estimate of $\Phi = 2\phi - 1$. We use Nakamura and Steinsson's (2014) estimate of $\phi = 0.69$, which implies $\Phi = 0.38$.[9] Second, we need an estimate of the response of house prices to income $d\hat{p}/d\hat{Y}$. Lamont and Stein (1999) provide a set of short-run estimates of the income elasticity of house prices, which implies that it is less than 0.8 and more likely near 0.3. We use 0.3 as our estimate, but our conclusions are little changed by using 0.8. This estimate must be divided by the ratio of housing wealth to total expenditures of 2.02 to yield a value of 0.149 for the derivative $d\hat{p}/d\hat{Y}$ in equation (23).

Together, these numbers imply that the term inside the large bracket in equation (23) is 0.998. In other words, allowing for income effects on housing implies that the simple idea of dividing the housing wealth effect by the local fiscal multiplier is off by only a minuscule amount. Taking this effect into account does not affect the implied partial equilibrium MPCH to the precision we are reporting.

IV. Identification in a System of Equations

The arguments we made in the previous section may seem special. In fact, they are applications of a general method for identification that is used pervasively in economics: simultaneous equations estimation. To see this and to see how cross-regional estimates can be used in other settings to identify partial equilibrium responses, it is useful to recast what we have done as an application of the general method of identification when variables are determined by a system of equations. In doing this, we see that our approach to identifying partial equilibrium responses from cross-regional estimates is mathematically closely related to identification of structural VARs (another prominent example of simultaneous equations identification in macroeconomics).

Using this simultaneous equations perspective, it is easy to verify whether we have the necessary sources of variation to identify the partial equilibrium effect of interest. We see formally that the partial equilibrium housing wealth effect is not identified by cross-regional housing wealth effect estimates alone but is identified with the help of cross-regional responses to government spending shocks.

To keep things as simple as possible, we focus on the example from Subsection III.A. Appendix B shows that the same argument applies for the more complicated system considered in Subsection III.D. Appendix B furthermore provides other examples of systems of equations—namely, one involving local credit supply shocks and another involving foreign demand shocks—where government spending shocks are again useful to identify the direct (partial equilibrium) effect of the shock.

Consider equations (3)–(6) from Subsection III.A. Linearizing these equations and using $Y = N(w)$ and its inverse, $w = N^{-1}(Y)$, we can write this as a system of three equations

$$\hat{C} = C_p\hat{p} + C_Y\hat{Y}$$

$$\hat{Y} = \hat{C} + \hat{G}$$

$$0 = H_p\hat{p} + H_s\hat{s},$$

where $C_Y = C_w/N_w$ as before. This system has three endogenous variables $\hat{C}$, $\hat{Y}$, and $\hat{p}$ and two exogenous variables $\hat{G}$ and $\hat{s}$. The exogenous variables $\hat{G}$ and $\hat{s}$ are the "structural shocks" affecting this system.

We can rewrite this system as

$$X\Gamma = z\Delta, \tag{24}$$

where X and z are row vectors given by $X = (\hat{C}, \hat{Y}, \hat{p})$ and $z = (\hat{G}, \hat{s})$; Γ and Δ are matrices of coefficients. Let's now postmultiply the system by Γ^{-1} to obtain the reduced-form representation of the system:

$$X = z\Delta\Gamma^{-1}. \tag{25}$$

Our goal is to estimate C_p (an element of Γ). However, what we estimate using the reduced-form response of $\hat{C}$ to $\hat{s}$ is an element of $\Delta\Gamma^{-1}$, which is influenced by other aspects of the system such as the response of $\hat{C}$ to $\hat{Y}$.

Formally, the identification challenge is that multiple structural systems (eq. [24]) can give rise to the same reduced form (eq. [25]). We can see this by postmultiplying equation (24) by an arbitrary 3×3 matrix F. This yields $X(\Gamma F) = z(\Delta F)$. The reduced form of this system is

$$X = z(\Delta F)(\Gamma F)^{-1} = z\Delta\Gamma^{-1}.$$

The F and F^{-1} cancel out implying that this alternative structural system yields the same reduced-form system. For example, the same reduced-form response of C to s can arise if C_p is small and C_Y is large or vice versa.

To identify the system, we need to place restrictions on the system (on Γ and Δ) such that there is no scope to transform the system with an F

without violating one or more of the restrictions. To be more precise, we need restrictions so that the only allowable F is the identity matrix.

Note the analogy to structural VARs. A structural VAR is $A(L)Y_t = u_t$ (with $A(0) = I$) and $Ru_t = \epsilon_t$, where u_t are the reduced-form errors and ϵ_t are the structural errors. Equation (25) in our application is analogous to $Ru_t = \epsilon_t$ in the structural VAR setting. In structural VARs, identification involves placing restrictions on R, just as in our setting identification involves placing restrictions on Δ and Γ. However, there are some differences. In structural VARs, the typical assumption is that ϵ_t is not observed but has the same dimension as u_t (same number of shocks as variables). Researchers place restrictions on R (and use the variance-covariance matrix of u_t) to identify the remainder of R (and ϵ_t). In our case, the structural shocks z are observed, but z may have a smaller dimension than X. We are interested in identifying an element of Γ but can only observe elements of $\Delta\Gamma^{-1}$. Our case is more analogous to identification of structural VARs with observed external instruments.

As our interest is in identifying the partial equilibrium housing wealth effect, we focus on whether the coefficients in the first equation of our system—the linearized consumption function—are identified. This is less demanding than identifying the whole system because we can allow for transformations of the system that change the other equations as long as they do not change the first equation. In other words, we need only be sure that the first column of any transformation F is the first column of the identity matrix.

In general, identification of (parts of) a system of equations requires a certain number of restrictions. Intuitively, the number of observed facts must equal the number of unknown parameters of interest. In the simultaneous equations literature, this is known as the "order condition" (see, e.g., Wooldridge 2010, section 9.2.2). In addition, the restrictions must result in a system that has certain rank. Intuitively, the facts must each provide information about the system that is independent of any linear combination of the other facts. This is known as the "rank condition." Finally, identification requires a normalization.

We begin by discussing the order condition for our case. As our system contains three endogenous variables, we need two restrictions on the system to satisfy the order condition. In our example, these restrictions are that neither G nor s appears directly in the consumption function. These restrictions are similar to the exclusion condition in an IV regression. Without excluding G from the consumption function, we would not be able to tell if a large fiscal multiplier reflects a large C_Y or a large direct effect of G on

C. But to understand the local general equilibrium amplification of the housing wealth effect we specifically want to know C_Y. Notice that if we dropped $\hat{G}$ from the system, we would have only one restriction and we would not be able to satisfy the order condition for identification of C_p without making a direct assumption about C_Y.

We now turn to the rank condition. Our restrictions can be represented by the matrices

$$R_\Gamma = \begin{pmatrix} 0 & 0 & 0 \\ 0 & 0 & 0 \end{pmatrix} \qquad R_\Delta \begin{pmatrix} 1 & 0 \\ 0 & 1 \end{pmatrix},$$

such that

$$\underbrace{(R_\Gamma \Gamma + R_\Delta \Delta)}_{\equiv \mathcal{R}} e_1 = 0, \tag{26}$$

where $e_1 \equiv (1, 0, 0)'$ selects the first column of $\mathcal{R}$.

Now suppose we transform the system by postmultiplying it by F. As we want the first columns of Γ and Δ to be identified, we want to make sure that only an F with the first column e_1 can satisfy the restrictions on the system. In this case, F does not transform the first column of Γ and Δ, which houses the coefficients of the first equation in the system. To satisfy the restrictions on the system, F must satisfy

$$(R_\Gamma \Gamma F + R_\Delta \Delta F)e_1 = \mathcal{R}Fe_1 = \mathcal{R}f_1 = 0, \tag{27}$$

where $f_1 \equiv Fe_1$ is the first column of F.

Our goal is that F does not transform the first equation in the system so its first column is the first column of the identity matrix, that is, $f_1 = e_1$. So the question is what must be true of $\mathcal{R}$ such that f_1 can only satisfy equation (27) if $f_1 = e_1$? To answer that, we want to make sure that $\mathcal{R}$ maps any vector other than e_1 to a nonzero vector. This requires that all of the columns of $\mathcal{R}$ other than the first one are linearly independent. Or equivalently, the rank of $\mathcal{R}$ must be one less than the number of equations, which means two in our case. This is the rank condition. It is easily verified for our system.

The final requirement for identification is a normalization. The rank condition only requires that $f_1 = e_1$ up to a scalar multiple and so a normalization is needed to pin down this scalar. In our system, the first equation has a natural normalization: when we write $\hat{C} = C_p\hat{p} + C_Y\hat{Y}$ we have imposed that the coefficient on $\hat{C}$ is 1. Together, these conditions—the rank condition with a normalization—are necessary and sufficient for identification (Wooldridge 2010, Thm. 9.2).

Clearly if there are fewer than two restrictions, the rank of $\mathcal{R}$ cannot be two because $\mathcal{R}$ has fewer than two rows. (This is the order condition.) Suppose that G did not appear in the second equation and was therefore absent from the system altogether. In this case, we would only have one restriction to place on Δ and Γ and the order condition would fail. Introducing a second exogenous source of variation (G) is therefore crucial for identification in our application.

One potentially useful piece of prior knowledge we have about G is that the coefficient on G in the resource constraint is 1 (i.e., we know the direct demand effect of the G shocks). However, the argument above does not make use of this information. Suppose we introduce an unknown parameter Y_G such that the second equation becomes

$$\hat{Y} = \hat{C} + Y_G \hat{G}.$$

Even though we do not know Y_G, we can still identify C_p by the argument above. The reason is that in our reduced form we are implicitly assuming that we observe both $d\hat{Y}/d\hat{G}$ and $d\hat{C}/d\hat{G}$. Differentiating the resource constraint gives

$$\frac{d\hat{Y}}{d\hat{G}} = \frac{d\hat{C}}{d\hat{G}} + Y_G.$$

The parameter Y_G can then be found from the difference between $d\hat{Y}/d\hat{G}$ and $d\hat{C}/d\hat{G}$.

However, if we instead assume that we are not able to observe the consumption response $d\hat{C}/d\hat{G}$ directly, then we do need to use the prior knowledge that $Y_G = 1$. To see this, eliminate $\hat{C}$ from the system so we have a system of two endogenous variables in two unknowns $\hat{Y}$ and $\hat{p}$:

$$(1 - C_Y)\hat{Y} = C_p\hat{p} + Y_G\hat{G}$$

$$0 = H_p\hat{p} + H_s\hat{s}.$$

Our goal is still to identify C_p. So, we are interested in identifying the first equation. We can impose the restriction that $\hat{s}$ does not appear in the first equation. This suffices for the order and rank conditions to be satisfied. The knowledge that $Y_G = 1$ then provides the crucial normalization we need to complete the identification. This shows that one aspect of government spending shocks that can make them more valuable for identification of partial equilibrium responses than other shocks is the fact that we know the size of the shock.

V. Dynamic Model

We now present a microfounded, dynamic model of multiple regions. After presenting the model, we show how the arguments laid out in Sections III and IV can be applied in the context of this model.

Demographics. There are two regions: "home" and "foreign." The population of the entire economy is 1 with a share n in the home region. All variables are expressed in per capita terms.

Preferences. Households maximize

$$\mathbb{E}_0 \sum_{t=0}^{\infty} \beta^t u(C_t, N_t, H_t; \Omega_t),$$

where the arguments are consumption, labor supply, units of housing H_t chosen at date t and held to date $t + 1$, and an aggregate housing demand shock Ω_t. The period utility function is given by

$$u(C, N, H; \Omega) = \frac{\left\{ \left[\left(C - \frac{N^{1+\nu}}{1+\nu} \right)^\kappa (H - \Omega)^{1-\kappa} \right]^{1-\sigma} - 1 \right\}}{(1 - \sigma)}.$$

Note that consumption and leisure are substitutable in the style of Greenwood, Hercowitz, and Huffman (1988), which eliminates wealth effects on labor supply, an assumption we maintained in Section III. We model the housing demand shock using a Stone-Geary formulation, but this exact specification is unimportant. What matters is that there is a shock that changes the marginal rate of substitution between housing and nondurables.[10]

Commodities and technology. Consumption C_t is a Cobb-Douglas bundle of final goods produced in both home and foreign regions:

$$C_t = \phi^{-\phi}(1 - \phi)^{-(1-\phi)} C_{H,t}^\phi C_{F,t}^{1-\phi},$$

where $C_{F,t}$ is the consumption in the home region of the good produced in the foreign region.[11] We use * to denote foreign variables. So, $C_{H,t}^*$ is the consumption in the foreign region of the good produced in the home region. We assume

$$C_t^* = \phi^{*-\phi^*}(1 - \phi^*)^{-(1-\phi^*)} C_{F,t}^{*\phi^*} C_{H,t}^{*(1-\phi^*)}.$$

The parameters $\phi > n$ and $\phi^* > 1 - n$ capture the degree of home bias in demand for goods. The price index for the consumption bundle in the home region is $\mathcal{P}_t = \mathcal{P}_{H,t}^{\phi}\mathcal{P}_{F,t}^{1-\phi}$, where $\mathcal{P}_{H,t}$ and $\mathcal{P}_{F,t}$ are the prices of the final goods produced in the home and foreign regions, respectively.

Each region produces a final good using a continuum of intermediate inputs. The production of the final good satisfies

$$Y_t = \left(\int_0^1 y_t(z)^{\frac{\eta-1}{\eta}}dz \right)^{\frac{\eta}{\eta-1}}.$$

Each intermediate good is produced linearly with labor according to $y_t(z) = N_t(z)$.

Housing supply. The supply of housing satisfies

$$H_t = (1 - \delta)H_{t-1} + I_t^{\alpha}M_t^{1-\alpha}. \tag{28}$$

Here we assume that the construction of new residential housing units requires two inputs: residential investment I_t and construction permits M_t, which are sold by the federal government. The construction permits are a tractable way to represent a variety of factors that limit housing supply including zoning regulations and limits to new land supply. The elasticity of supply of the construction permits may differ across regions giving rise to different housing supply elasticities. Residential investment requires a mix of local and imported inputs analogous to the mix used for consumption:

$$I_t = \phi^{-\phi}(1 - \phi)^{-(1-\phi)}I_{H,t}^{\phi}I_{F,t}^{1-\phi}.$$

Markets. The two regions share the same money, which serves as the numeraire. Final goods markets are competitive and completely integrated across regions. The prices of intermediate-goods firms are sticky. These firms receive an opportunity to change their price each period with $1 - \chi$ as in Calvo (1983). The labor markets are local to each region and competitive with real wages denoted w_t. Units of housing trade at relative price p_t. Households trade a nominal bond that pays interest i_t between t and $t + 1$. Let $\mathcal{P}_t B_t$ be the nominal value of bond holdings in the home region at the end of period t. We consider two cases for asset markets. In the "incomplete markets" economy, there is only trade in risk-free nominal bonds. In the "complete markets" economy, the regions also trade state-contingent assets in quantities A_t at prices $\Xi_{t,t+1}$. In the complete markets economy, the bond is redundant, but it can still be priced and this price will enter our monetary policy rule.

Intermediate-goods firms produce profits, which are rebated to the households in the region. We use D_t to denote the real profits received. We impose a portfolio holding cost in the style of Schmitt-Grohé and Uribe (2003) whereby holding bond position B_t incurs a flow cost ζB_t^2. This portfolio cost implies that steady-state wealth holdings in each region are determinate. This can be viewed as a crude approximation to precautionary savings motives that decline with wealth.

Government. The government purchases goods, sells construction permits, and sets monetary policy. Let G_t and G_t^* be per capita spending in home and foreign regions, respectively. The government buys local goods in each region. The exogenous process for G_t is

$$G_t = (1 - \rho_G)\bar{G} + \rho_G G_{t-1} + \epsilon_{G,t}. \tag{29}$$

G_t^* is independent of G_t but follows the same process.

The government's monetary policy may be described by a rule for the nominal interest rate:

$$1 + i_t = \beta^{-1} + \varphi_\pi(\pi_t^n \pi_t^{*1-n} - 1) + \varphi_y \left[n \log \left(\frac{Y_t}{\bar{Y}} \right) + (1 - n) \log \left(\frac{Y_t^*}{\bar{Y}} \right) \right], \tag{30}$$

where policy responds to the population-weighted averages of inflation and output.

The government sells construction permits according to the rule

$$M_t = \bar{M} p_t^\gamma. \tag{31}$$

The parameter γ is the elasticity of construction permits granted with respect to the price of housing. This parameter is meant to reflect some combination of the stringency of zoning regulations and the availability of suitable vacant land. The government sets the relative price of a permit, q_t, equal to its marginal product in construction of new housing units. It is fairly standard to model housing supply as combining a flow of new land or permits with residential investment. We assume that the supply of permits is price elastic whereas the literature typically assumes it is constant (Davis and Heathcote 2005; Favilukis, Ludvigson, and Van Nieuwerburgh 2017; Kaplan, Mitman, and Violante 2020). Later, we allow the regions to differ in their permit supply elasticities (i.e., $\gamma \neq \gamma^*$) in the spirit of identification schemes that follow Saiz (2010).

The government imposes lump-sum taxes in nominal amounts $\mathcal{P}_t T_t$ and $\mathcal{P}_t^* T_t^*$. The national government budget constraint is

$$n\mathcal{P}_{H,t}G_t + (1 - n)\mathcal{P}_{F,t}^* G_t^* = n\mathcal{P}_t T_t + (1 - n)\mathcal{P}_t^* T_t^* + n\mathcal{P}_t q_t + (1 - n)\mathcal{P}_t^* q_t^*.$$

We assume that the government taxes each region equally (per capita) in nominal terms.

Market clearing. The market for home goods clears if

$$Y_t = \phi\left(\frac{\mathcal{P}_{H,t}}{\mathcal{P}_{F,t}}\right)^{\phi-1}(C_t + I_t) + \frac{1-n}{n}(1-\phi^*)\left(\frac{\mathcal{P}_{H,t}}{\mathcal{P}_{F,t}}\right)^{-\phi^*}(C_t^* + I_t^*) + G_t, \quad (32)$$

where $\mathcal{P}_{H,t}/\mathcal{P}_{F,t}$ is the real exchange rate. This expression involves local and home expenditures on the bundles of home- and foreign-produced goods. The cost-minimizing bundle depends on the degree of home bias and the real exchange rate. Similarly, the market for foreign goods clears if

$$Y_t^* = \frac{n}{1-n}(1-\phi)\left(\frac{\mathcal{P}_{H,t}}{\mathcal{P}_{F,t}}\right)^{\phi}(C_t + I_t) + \phi^*\left(\frac{\mathcal{P}_{H,t}}{\mathcal{P}_{F,t}}\right)^{1-\phi^*}(C_t^* + I_t^*) + G_t^*. \quad (33)$$

Bond market clearing requires

$$nB_t + (1-n)B_t^* = 0.$$

Decision problems. Under incomplete markets and assuming certainty equivalence so that the real return on bonds is treated as known, $R_t \equiv (1 + i_t)/\pi_{t+1}$, the household maximizes

$$\sum_{t=0}^{\infty}\beta^t u(C_t, N_t, H_t; \Omega_t),$$

subject to the budget constraint

$$p_t H_t + C_t + B_t + \zeta B_t^2 = W_t N_t + D_t + R_{t-1}B_{t-1} + p_t H_{t-1}(1 - \delta),$$

where R_t is the gross real interest rate between t and $t + 1$.[12] The intratemporal optimality conditions of the household's problem imply

$$\tilde{H}_t = x_t \tilde{C}_t$$

$$N_t^\nu = w_t$$

where

$$\tilde{C}_t \equiv C_t - \frac{N_t^{1+\nu}}{1+\nu}$$

$$\tilde{H}_t \equiv H_t - \Omega_t$$

$$x_t \equiv \frac{1-\kappa}{\kappa}\left(p_t - \mathbb{E}_t\left[p_{t+1}(1-\delta)\beta\frac{u_{C,t+1}}{u_{C,t}}\right]\right)^{-1}.$$

Abstracting from the portfolio holding cost, we have

$$\tilde{C}_t = \kappa \frac{R_{t-1}B_{t-1} + p_t H_{t-1}(1-\delta) + \sum_{\tau=t}^{\infty} R_{t,\tau}^{-1}\left[Y_\tau - \frac{1-\kappa}{\kappa x_\tau}\Omega_\tau - \frac{N_\tau^{1+\nu}}{1+\nu}\right]}{\sum_{\tau=t}^{\infty} R_{t,\tau}^{-1} X_{t,\tau}}, \qquad (34)$$

where

$$R_{t,\tau} \equiv R_{t,\tau-1}R_{\tau-1} \qquad \forall \tau > t$$

$$X_{t,\tau} \equiv \left[\beta^t R_{t,\tau}\left(\frac{x_\tau}{x_t}\right)^{(1-\kappa)(1-\sigma)}\right]^{1/\sigma},$$

and $R_{t,t} = 1$. See appendix C.1 (apps. C–E are available online) for the derivation.

Turning to construction, a representative competitive real estate developer maximizes revenue from new houses less material and permit costs:

$$\max_{I_t, M_t} \left\{ p_t I_t^\alpha M_t^{1-\alpha} - I_t - q_t M_t \right\}.$$

The first-order condition of this problem with respect to I_t and equation (31) implies

$$I_t = \alpha^{\frac{1}{1-\alpha}} \bar{M} p_t^{\gamma+\frac{1}{1-\alpha}}, \qquad (35)$$

so the supply of new housing is

$$I^\alpha M_t^{1-\alpha} = (\alpha p_t)^{\frac{\alpha}{1-\alpha}} M_t.$$

Finally, intermediate-goods producers set their reset prices, $\tilde{P}_t$, to solve

$$\max_{\tilde{P}_t} \mathbb{E}_t \sum_{\tau=t}^{\infty} \chi^t \lambda_{t,\tau} \left[\left(\frac{\tilde{P}_t}{P_\tau} - w_\tau\right) y_\tau\right]$$

where $\lambda_{t,\tau}$ is the discount factor between τ and t and subject to the demand curve for their variety $y_\tau = Y_\tau(\tilde{P}_t/P_{H,\tau})^{-\eta}$. This problem gives rise to a forward-looking inflation response to variations in the real wage and the real exchange rate (see app. D.1).

VI. Adjusting for Local General Equilibrium Effects in the Full Model

We now show how the static relationships derived in Section III relate to dynamic relationships in the context of the dynamic model. We consider a perfect foresight transition lasting $\mathcal{T}$ periods. We assume that the two regions are equally open to trade. Given their unequal sizes, this implies $1 - \phi^* = n/1 - n(1 - \phi)$. We define $\Phi \equiv \phi + \phi^* - 1$. Furthermore, to keep the expressions in this section as simple as possible, we assume that prices are perfectly rigid. This implies that the real exchange rate is constant at one.

Taking a cross-regional difference of the market-clearing conditions (eqs. [32] and [33]) yields

$$\hat{Y} = \Phi(\hat{C} + \hat{I}) + \hat{G}, \tag{36}$$

where $\hat{Y}$ is a column vector of length T that gives values of $Y_t - Y_t^*$ for all $t \in \{1, \dots, T\}$. $\hat{C}, \hat{I},$ and $\hat{G}$ are defined similarly.

Linearizing the consumption function shown in equation (34) around a symmetric steady state and taking a cross-regional difference yields

$$\hat{C} = \mathbf{C}_p \hat{p} + \mathbf{C}_Y \hat{Y}, \tag{37}$$

where $\mathbf{C}_Y$ is a $T \times T$ matrix where the $[t, s]$ element gives the coefficient of the response of C_t to Y_s and the matrix $\mathbf{C}_p$ is defined similarly. $\mathbf{C}_Y$ is the intertemporal MPC matrix highlighted by Auclert, Rognlie, and Straub (2018). Notice that Ω, taxes, and interest rates do not appear in this expression because these variables are common across regions and drop out when we take the difference.

Linearizing the residential investment response (eq. [35]) around a symmetric steady state and taking a cross-regional difference yields

$$\hat{I} = \mathbf{I}_p \hat{p}, \tag{38}$$

where we abstract (for now) from regional heterogeneity in land supply.

Combining equations (36), (37), and (38) yields

$$\hat{Y} = \Phi \mathbf{M}(\mathbf{C}_p + \mathbf{I}_p)\hat{p} + \mathbf{M}\hat{G} \tag{39}$$

where $\mathbf{M} \equiv [I - \Phi \mathbf{C}_Y]^{-1}$. Using equations (37), (38), and (39), local expenditure is given by

$$\hat{C} + \hat{I} = \mathbf{M}(\mathbf{C}_p + \mathbf{I}_p)\hat{p} + \mathbf{C}_Y \mathbf{M}\hat{G}, \tag{40}$$

where we have used the definition of $\mathbf{M}$ to note that $I + \mathbf{C}_Y \Phi \mathbf{M} = \mathbf{M}$.

From this last equation, we can calculate the impulse response of expenditures to home prices as

$$\frac{d\hat{E}}{d\hat{p}} = \mathbf{M}(\mathbf{C}_p + \mathbf{I}_p), \tag{41}$$

where $\hat{E} \equiv \hat{C} + \hat{I}$ and $d\hat{E}/d\hat{p}$ is a $\mathcal{T} \times \mathcal{T}$ matrix in which the (t, s) element gives the response of expenditure in period t to a change in house prices in period s. This is the dynamic analog to our static (scalar) IV estimate $d\hat{E}/d\hat{p}$ from the setting discussed in Section III.

Notice that, just as in Section III, the regional impulse response is equal to the partial equilibrium response $\mathbf{C}_p + \mathbf{I}_p$ multiplied by a local general equilibrium feedback factor $\mathbf{M}$. Our next task is to relate this local general equilibrium feedback factor to observables. To this end, we linearize housing demand, $H(p, Y, T, R, \Omega)$, and housing supply (eq. [28]) and equate them, which yields

$$\mathbf{H}_p p + \mathbf{H}_R R + \mathbf{H}_Y Y + \mathbf{H}_T T + \mathbf{H}_\Omega \Omega = \mathbf{H}_p^S p.$$

Taking a cross-regional difference and rearranging yields

$$\hat{p} = \mathbf{p}_Y \hat{Y}, \tag{42}$$

where

$$\mathbf{p}_Y \equiv (\mathbf{H}_p^S - \mathbf{H}_p)^{-1} \mathbf{H}_Y,$$

and $\mathbf{H}_Y$ is the response of housing demand to income. Substituting equation (42) into equation (39) and rearranging yields

$$\hat{Y} = \left[I - \Phi \mathbf{M}(\mathbf{C}_p + \mathbf{I}_p)\mathbf{p}_Y\right]^{-1} \mathbf{M}\hat{G}. \tag{43}$$

From equation (43) the impulse response of output to government spending is:

$$\frac{d\hat{Y}}{dG} = \left[I - \Phi \mathbf{M}(\mathbf{C}_p + \mathbf{I}_p)\mathbf{p}_Y\right]^{-1} \mathbf{M}. \tag{44}$$

Here again, $d\hat{Y}/d\hat{G}$ is a $\mathcal{T} \times \mathcal{T}$ matrix in which the (t, s) element gives the response of output in period t to a change in government spending in period s. This is the dynamic equivalent of the static (scalar) local fiscal multiplier from the setting discussed in Section III.

Rearranging equation (44) and using the fact that $d\hat{p}/d\hat{Y} = \mathbf{p}_Y$ we have that

$$\mathbf{M} = \left(I - \Phi \frac{d\hat{E}}{d\hat{p}} \frac{d\hat{p}}{d\hat{Y}}\right) \frac{d\hat{Y}}{dG}.$$

Plugging this expression for $\mathbf{M}$ into equation (41) and rearranging yields

$$\mathbf{C}_p = \left[\frac{d\hat{Y}}{dG}\right]^{-1} \left(I - \Phi \frac{d\hat{E}}{d\hat{p}} \frac{d\hat{p}}{d\hat{Y}}\right)^{-1} \left(\frac{d\hat{E}}{d\hat{p}}\right) - \mathbf{I}_p. \tag{45}$$

This result is a dynamic analog to the main result in Subsection III.D (see eq. [23]). As we note above, in this dynamic setting, the components $d\hat{E}/d\hat{p}$, $d\hat{Y}/dG$, and so on are matrices rather scalars. If these matrices have important off-diagonal elements, then the logic of our static examples is complicated by dynamic responses of the economy. However, if the contemporaneous responses are large relative to the dynamic responses (i.e., the matrices are close to diagonal), then the logic of the static economy goes through because in that case equation (45) reduces to the same scalar relationship as equation (23).

VII.   Long-Run Heterogeneity in Housing Supply

To provide a convincing assessment of the accuracy of the simple adjustment formula that we present in Section III, we need a model that can roughly match our empirical estimates for the observables that enter that adjustment formula: the local housing wealth effect, the local fiscal multiplier, and the local effect of house prices on construction. Our estimates of the local housing wealth effect and local effect of house prices on construction rely on an identification strategy that exploits heterogeneity in housing supply curves across cities interacted with aggregate home price changes as an instrument. Research using this identification strategy has proxied for city-level housing supply elasticities with topographic features of the cities (Saiz 2010) or equilibrium sensitivity of local house prices to regional house price variation (Guren et al. 2020).

We can introduce heterogeneity in housing supply elasticities into the model we present in Section V and assess whether this model can match our empirical estimates. When we do this, we find that the response of residential investment to house prices is far from our empirical estimates. In fact, this response is negative in the model: when we calibrate the model to have γ and γ^* equal to the 10th and 90th percentiles, respectively, of the elasticities estimated by Saiz (2010), the model implies an elasticity of residential investment to house prices of -12. In contrast, the empirical estimates we present in Section III are positive, ranging from 0.36 to 0.50.

The left panel of figure 1 illustrates the economics behind this counterfactual prediction of the model. The panel plots housing supply curves for two cities with different supply elasticities. In response to a common demand shock, the less elastic city (represented by line S) has a larger price response but a smaller quantity response.[13] Davidoff (2016) has

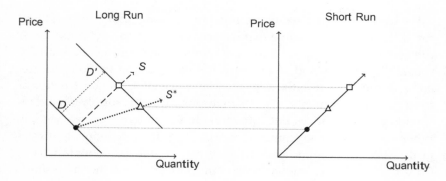

Fig. 1. Long-run and short-run housing supply curves. A color version of this figure is available online.

critiqued estimates of the housing wealth effect based on the identification strategy described above on the grounds that quantity growth has been larger for inelastic cities than elastic cities. Our finding that construction employment responds positively to changes in house prices is another piece of evidence on quantities that is at odds with the simple view of heterogeneous housing supply curves discussed above.

However, it is relatively simple to remedy this empirical failing of our model by allowing for differences between short-run and long-run housing supply elasticities. Suppose, in particular, that housing supply is inelastic in all cities in the short run but becomes more elastic in the long run in one of the cities. The two panels of figure 1 illustrate this with the right panel depicting the short run and the left panel depicting the long run. The equilibrium price of housing is forward looking as current housing demand depends on expectations of all future capital gains on housing. As a result, the equilibrium housing price is largely determined by long-run forces in the housing market. However, the incentives to construct and sell new houses depend on the current availability of inputs to construction and the current price of houses. Therefore, the construction response depends much more on short-run forces in the housing market. The short-run equilibrium in the housing market reflects different endogenous changes in housing demand across regions reflecting the different expected capital gains going forward. Short-run housing demand will increase more in the region in which a larger capital gain is expected and this moves that region further up the common short-run supply curve. This logic generates a positive response of construction to house prices even though regional house price fluctuations reflect differences in (long-run) housing supply elasticities.

We use a regime-switching formulation to model short-run and long-run differences. We assume that the economy is currently in the short-run regime and is expected to switch to the long-run regime with 2% probability each period after which it will remain in the long-run regime. In the short run, the supply of land available for construction is fixed in both regions ($\gamma = \gamma^* = 0$). In the long run, the supply of land responds to house prices but differentially in the two regions ($\gamma < \gamma^*$). When we simulate the economy, we assume that the economy is always in the short-run regime and the long-run regime never materializes. Construction in both regions reflects movements along the same short-run supply curve whereas house prices are differentially affected by aggregate changes in housing demand that move expectations along the heterogeneous long-run housing supply curves.

VIII. Monte Carlo Analysis

We are now ready to use the dynamic model developed in Sections V and VII to assess the accuracy of the simple adjustment for local general equilibrium effects that we derived in Section III (eq. [23]). We do this by presenting results from a series of Monte Carlo simulations of different versions of the dynamic model. Recall that discrepancies between the appropriate size of the adjustment in our full model and the simple adjustment formula arise from the nondiagonal elements in equation (45).

We will work with equation (23) rewritten in terms of elasticities:

$$\frac{\partial \log C}{\partial \log p} = \left[\frac{e}{\frac{d\hat{Y}}{dG}\left(1 - \Phi e \frac{C}{Y}\frac{d\log \hat{p}}{d\log Y}\right)} \right] - \frac{\bar{I}}{\bar{C}}\frac{d\log \hat{I}}{d\log \hat{p}} \tag{46}$$

where

$$e \equiv \frac{d\log \hat{C}}{d\log \hat{p}} + \frac{\bar{I}}{\bar{C}}\frac{d\log \hat{I}}{d\log \hat{p}}$$

and we define $\log \hat{X} = \log X - \log X^*$.

The left-hand side of equation (46) is the partial equilibrium response of consumption to changes in house prices. In a dynamic setting, this depends not only on current house prices but also on the entire future excepted path of house prices. In our model, we compute the partial equilibrium effect using the analytical consumption function (eq. [34]), and the exact dynamics of house prices implied by the model. Specifically, we first simulate the general equilibrium model. Then for each period of this simulation, we feed the resulting current house price and expected future path for house prices into the household's analytical consumption function and calculate the household's consumption (holding everything other than the path for house prices constant). This yields a series for consumption in the home and foreign regions. Finally, we regress the cross-regional difference in consumption on the simulated cross-regional difference in house prices and take the regression coefficient from this regression as the partial equilibrium response of consumption to house prices. See appendix C for additional details.

To calculate the right-hand side of equation (46) in our model, we perform two simulations of the model. First, we simulate the model with only aggregate housing demand shocks. The output from this simulation allows us to calculate $d \log \hat{C}/d \log \hat{p}$ and $d \log \hat{I}/d \log \hat{p}$. We do this simply by running an OLS regression of the change in $\log C$ and $\log I$, respectively, on the change in $\log p$ in the model and including time fixed effects. By limiting the shocks to aggregate housing demand shocks in this simulation, we are estimating using the same variation that we isolate with our sensitivity instrument in Guren et al. (2020). Next, we simulate the model with only region-specific government purchases shocks. The output from this simulation allows us to calculate $d\hat{Y}/d\hat{G}$ and $d \log p/d \log Y$ in a similar fashion. Conceptually, when we calculate $d \log \hat{p}/d \log \hat{Y}$ from the output of this simulation, we are implicitly using government purchases as an instrument for changes in local output. Finally, $\bar{C}/\bar{Y}$ and $\bar{I}/\bar{C}$ are steady-state ratios and $\Phi \equiv \phi + \phi^* - 1$ is a measure of home bias all of which we assume are known to the analyst.

A. Model Calibration

We calibrate the model as follows. A time period is a quarter. We set the population share of the home region to be 2% with the interpretation that the home region is a city and the foreign region is the rest of the country. We set the home-bias parameter $\phi = 0.4$ based on the share of shipments in the Commodity Flow Survey that goes to the same metro area. We set the elasticity of substitution between varieties to be $\eta = 6$.

We normalize the steady-state supply of construction permits, $\bar{M}$, so that the steady-state relative price of a unit of housing is one. We set the depreciation rate on housing to 3% annually. We target a 4.4% share of residential investment to gross domestic product (GDP), which is the average ratio over the period 1970–2019. This implies that the residential investment share in the construction of new houses (i.e., one minus the land share) is $\alpha = 0.38$. The home and foreign regions differ in their land (construction permit) supply elasticities, γ. We set them to match the 10th and 90th percentiles of the elasticity estimates from Saiz (2010), which are 1.05 and 4.39. The Saiz estimates reflect the response of housing units, which we interpret as the change in H_t. The (long-run) price elasticity of housing supply in the model is $[\alpha/(1 - \alpha)] + \gamma$. Therefore, we set $\gamma = 0.45$ and $\gamma^* = 3.78$.

Turning to preferences, we set the subjective discount factor $\beta = 0.99$, and we set $\kappa = 0.58$ to target a 25% expenditure share on housing, which is the average housing expenditure in the Consumer Expenditure Survey (CEX) in 2018. We set the labor supply elasticity to $\nu = 1$ and the coefficient of risk aversion to $\sigma = 2$. We set a steady-state G/Y ratio of 20% and we use standard interest rate rule parameters $\varphi_\pi = 1.5$ and $\varphi_y = 0.125$.

Regional government purchases follow independent AR(1) processes with quarterly persistence of 0.95. The housing demand shock follows an AR(1) with the same persistence. We set the scale of the portfolio holding cost to $\zeta = 10^{-4}$. We set the quarterly Calvo adjustment probability to 11% to target the point estimate of 0.030 of the inflation response to local government spending shocks reported by Nakamura and Steinsson (2014). We consider the robustness of our results to our parameter choices in Subsection VIII.F.

B. Complete Markets

As a starting point, we consider a complete-markets version of our model. In this version, the consumption response to house prices is a function of the current user cost only. We also start with a specification in which prices are fully rigid ($\chi = 1$), houses are produced entirely from land with no material inputs ($\alpha = 0$), and the land supply elasticities are fixed at their long-run values. The partial equilibrium housing wealth effect is particularly simple to compute in this case. Equating the marginal utility of consumption between regions yields

$$\frac{C_t - \psi \frac{L_t^{1+\nu}}{1+\nu}}{C_t^* - \psi \frac{L_t^{*1+\nu}}{1+\nu}} = \left(\frac{p_t - \mathbb{E}_t[\omega_{t+1} p_{t+1}(1 - \delta)]}{p_t^* - \mathbb{E}_t\left[\omega_{t+1} p_{t+1}^*(1 - \delta)\right]} \right)^{\frac{(1-\kappa)(\sigma-1)}{\sigma}}, \tag{47}$$

where ω_{t+1} is the stochastic discount factor for payoffs at $t + 1$. The region with a higher user cost will consume more nondurables and less housing. With mean-reverting house price dynamics, a higher price of housing is associated with a larger user cost, which induces a positive relationship between nondurable consumption and house prices.

Results for this version of our model are shown in the first column of table 2. The first four rows of this table report the components of the right-hand side of equation (46). We describe above how these are calculated from the Monte Carlo simulation. The first row reports the measured housing wealth effect ($d \log \hat{C}/d \log \hat{p}$) in this version of the model is 0.022. The second row reports the local fiscal multiplier ($d\hat{Y}/dG$) is 1.477. The third row reports the construction response ($d \log \hat{I}/d \log \hat{p}$), which in this version of the model we assume to be zero. Finally, the fourth row reports the income elasticity of house prices ($d \log \hat{p}/d \log \hat{Y}$) is small with complete markets (−0.004).

Using equation (46), we can combine these four responses from the model to calculate the partial equilibrium housing wealth effect implied by our simple formula. The fifth row in the table reports that for the complete-markets model this turns out to be 0.015. Row (6) then reports the actual partial equilibrium housing wealth effect for this version of the model, which also turns out to be 0.015. In other words, in this version of the model, our simple adjustment formula is very accurate. Because there is no construction response and the income elasticity of house prices is small, our formula boils down to dividing the measured housing wealth effect by the local fiscal multiplier. Finally, row (7) reports the magnitude of the error associated with the implied housing wealth effect relative to the error associated with the measured housing wealth effect defined as |Row 5 − Row 6|/|Row 1 − Row 6|.

Table 2
Monte Carlo Analysis of Housing Wealth Elasticity

	(i)	(ii)	(iii)	(iv)
Complete markets	✓			
Rigid prices	✓	✓		
Construction				✓
Long-run housing supply heterogeneity				✓
(1) Measured housing wealth effect	.022	.121	.151	.144
(2) Local fiscal multiplier	1.477	1.499	1.451	1.465
(3) Construction response	0	0	0	1.613
(4) Income elasticity of home prices	−.004	.032	.151	.167
(5) Implied partial equilibrium housing wealth effect	.015	.081	.104	.072
(6) Actual partial equilibrium housing wealth effect	.015	.063	.078	.041
(7) Relative error	.000	.306	.368	.295

C. Incomplete Markets

The second column of table 2 reports results for a version of our model with incomplete markets but maintains the assumption that prices are rigid and that no resources are used in constructing houses. With incomplete markets the determination of the consumption response to house prices is more complicated as it is affected by expectations of future incomes and user costs (see eq. [34]). In this case, the off-diagonal elements of the matrices in equation (45) become more important and it need not be the case that these dynamic relationships can be summarized by simple regressions. We find that the measured housing wealth effect is 0.121. Using equation (46) to adjust for local general equilibrium effects yields an implied partial equilibrium housing wealth effect of 0.081. However, the actual partial equilibrium housing wealth effect is a bit lower at 0.063. In this case, the adjustment implied by our formula goes in the right direction but does not go far enough. Here the relative error is about 1/3 as large after applying our formula.

D. Incorporating Price Responses

The assumption of rigid prices implies that both regions face the same real interest rate. When prices respond differentially in the two regions, real interest rates differ across regions. Suppose that the home region experiences a larger increase in activity. It will then also experience a larger increase in inflation, which reduces the real interest rate and further stimulates demand in the home region. However, the differential price response changes the real exchange rate, which reduces the demand for goods from the home region and increases the demand for goods from the foreign region. On one hand, these differential price responses affect the fiscal multiplier, so in principle, adjusting the measured housing wealth effect by the fiscal multiplier may fully account for these effects. On the other hand, the price responses further complicate the dynamics of the responses in ways that may not be fully captured by our approach.

The third column in table 2 allows for some degree of price flexibility. Specifically, we set the quarterly Calvo adjustment probability to 11% to target the response of inflation to local government spending shocks of 0.030 reported by Nakamura and Steinsson (2014). In this case, we find that the measured housing wealth effect rises to 0.151. The local fiscal multiplier is reduced due to the expenditure switching effect. The combination of these two changes raises the implied housing wealth effect to 0.104. Even though real interest rates do not change in the partial equilibrium calculation, the partial equilibrium housing wealth effect depends on the particular dynamics of house prices that we feed into the calculation and the house price dynamics change as a result of price adjustments. As a result, the actual partial equilibrium housing wealth effect is somewhat larger in this case rising to 0.078. Again, our simple adjustment formula somewhat underestimates the needed adjustment. The relative error is 0.368 in this case.

E. Adding Construction

The fourth column of table 2 presents results for a version of the model in which we allow for resources to be used in the construction of housing; that is, we set α equal to its calibrated value of $\alpha = 0.38$. To generate a positive response of residential investment to changes in house prices, we also introduce the regime-switching dynamics for γ and γ^* described in Section VII. This version of the model yields a construction response of 1.613, which is somewhat higher than the value we estimate in the data (0.363). If we instead assume that the housing supply elasticities γ and γ^* differ in the short run, the model generates a construction response of −12. The short-run/long-run distinction reverses the sign of the construction response even though the heterogeneous response of house prices still reflects differences in supply curves across regions.

The measured housing wealth effect in this case is 0.144. Taking account of the construction response and using the local fiscal multiplier to adjust for the local general equilibrium effect yields an implied housing wealth effect of 0.072. The actual partial equilibrium housing wealth effect is 0.041. As in the previous two cases, our simple adjustment somewhat understates the needed adjustment. The relative error is 0.295 in this case.

F. Robustness

Table 3 reports results for several variants of the model specification in column (iv) of table 2. We focus our robustness analysis on this model specification because it is the richest one in table 2 and the one that comes closest to the magnitudes of the measured housing wealth effect and construction response. Each column in table 3 reports results for a version of the model in which we vary one or two parameters and leave

Table 3
Monte Carlo Analysis of Housing Wealth Elasticity: Robustness

	(i)	(ii)	(iii)	(iv)
			$\chi = .75$	
	$\rho_G = .9$	$\rho_\Omega = .9$	$\varphi = .7$	$\sigma \rightarrow 1$
Measured housing wealth effect	.144	.167	.341	.262
Local fiscal multiplier	1.449	1.465	2.318	1.466
Construction response	1.613	1.613	1.613	1.613
Income elasticity of home prices	.082	.167	.208	.165
Implied partial equilibrium housing wealth effect	.073	.088	.104	.154
Actual partial equilibrium housing wealth effect	.041	.041	.074	.110
Relative error	.305	.372	.111	.287

the remaining parameters at their baseline values. Column (i) reduces the quarterly persistence of the government spending shocks from its baseline value of 0.95 to 0.90. This change has little effect on our results. Column (ii) reduces the persistence of the aggregate housing demand shock from the baseline of 0.95 to 0.90. This change slightly raises the measured housing wealth effect and implied partial equilibrium housing wealth effects, while leaving the actual housing wealth effect virtually unchanged. Overall, columns (i) and (ii) are reassuring that the exact details of the dynamics of the changes in house prices and changes in government spending are not crucial to the performance of our adjustment.

Column (iii) of table 3 considers a case with more price flexibility and less openness. Making prices more flexible leads to a smaller fiscal multiplier due to expenditure switching after a government purchases shock while making the economies less open raises the fiscal multiplier. The combination of parameters considered here is close to those used by Nakamura and Steinsson (2014). In this case, we see a large increase in the measured and actual housing wealth effect and fiscal multiplier relative to our baseline. Our simple adjustment still yields an implied housing wealth effect much closer to the true partial equilibrium effect with the relative error now falling to about 1/9 on account of the larger role of the fiscal multiplier.

Column (iv) considers a case where $\sigma \rightarrow 1$. In our baseline model with $\sigma = 2$, housing demand shocks (changes in Ω_t) raise the marginal utility of consumption due to the interaction in the utility function between consumption and housing. This leads to a strong direct response of consumption to Ω shocks. As Ω is an aggregate shock, this force affects both regions equally and is differenced out in the cross section, but it implies a very strong response of aggregate consumption to Ω in the time series. This does not occur in the case with $\sigma \to 1$ as the utility function becomes additively separable between consumption and housing and the time-series housing wealth effect is more comparable in magnitude to the cross-sectional housing wealth effect. Despite the very different behavior of aggregate consumption with $\sigma \to 1$, the cross-sectional results are similar to our baseline.

G. Summary

The analysis we present in this section shows that the simple static formula we derive in Section III to adjust estimates of housing wealth effects for local general equilibrium effects tends to somewhat underestimate the needed adjustment. In our richest specification, column (iv) of table 2, the adjustment yields an estimate of the housing wealth effect that has an error that is $1/3$ as large as that associated with the measured housing wealth effect. More fully accounting for the dynamics of the responses to house prices as in the matrix relationships discussed in Section VI may yield a more accurate estimate of the partial equilibrium effect. However, the much simpler approach of using our static formula seems to account for the bulk of the needed adjustment (roughly $2/3$).

IX. Conclusion

Cross-regional empirical estimates have become part of the macroeconomist's toolkit, but the appropriate interpretation of these estimates can be difficult as they often blend together partial equilibrium responses with local general equilibrium effects. We argue that researchers can benefit from approaching cross-regional estimates as part of a system of simultaneous equations that also integrates other sources of evidence on the magnitude of local general equilibrium effects, such as evidence on the magnitude of fiscal multipliers.

This approach allows researchers to decompose the effects they estimate into the components arising from the direct partial equilibrium effect and those arising from local general equilibrium effects. We apply this methodology to analyzing regional estimates of housing wealth effects and show that an important part of the estimated regional effects likely arise from local general equilibrium effects. Gauging the relative importance of the partial and local general equilibrium components of these effects is crucial to developing appropriate microfoundations for the housing wealth effect.

In our analysis of housing, we also address a recent critique by Davidoff (2016), who points out that if housing markets experience a common demand shock but move along different supply curves, then prices and quantities should be negatively correlated. The relationship in the data is the opposite. We show, however, that a model that allows for differences between short-run and long-run housing supply elasticities can address Davidoff's critique. In such a model, expectations about future capital gains imply that the common aggregate shock results in a larger change in current housing demand in the city with a less elastic long-run housing supply curve.

Appendix A

Derivation of Key Equations in Section III

Here we derive the key equations in Subsection III.D. The derivations of the corresponding equations in earlier subsections of Section III are special cases of this derivation. To get the results in Subsection III.C, set $H_w = 0$. To get the results in Subsection III.B, set $\Phi = 1$. Finally, to get the results in Subsection III.A, set $I_p = 0$.

We start by taking derivatives of the first two equations in Subsection III.C with respect to G—these equations represent the goods market equilibrium conditions in Subsection III.D as well as Subsection III.C. This yields

$$\phi(C_p + I_p)\frac{dp}{dG} + \phi C_w \frac{dw}{dG} + (1-\phi)(C_p + I_p)\frac{dp^*}{dG} + (1-\phi)C_w \frac{dw^*}{dG}$$
$$+ (C_T + I_T)\frac{dT}{dG} + 1 = N_w \frac{dw}{dG},$$

$$(1-\phi)(C_p + I_p)\frac{dp}{dG}$$
$$+ (1-\phi)C_w \frac{dw}{dG} + \phi(C_p + I_p)\frac{dp^*}{dG} + \phi C_w \frac{dw^*}{dG}$$
$$+ (C_T + I_T)\frac{dT}{dG} = N_w \frac{dw^*}{dG}.$$

Subtracting the second of these equations from the first and rearranging, we get

$$(N_w - \Phi C_w)\frac{d\hat{w}}{dG} - \Phi(C_p + I_p)\frac{d\hat{p}}{dG} = 1, \tag{A1}$$

where $\Phi = 2\phi - 1$ and hatted variables denote cross-regional differences, for example, $\hat{p} = p - p^*$.

Next, we take derivatives of the first two equations in Subsection III.D with respect to G. This yields

$$H_w \frac{dw}{dG} + H_p \frac{dp}{dG} + H_T \frac{dT}{dG} = 0,$$

$$H_w \frac{dw^*}{dG} + H_p \frac{dp^*}{dG} + H_t \frac{dT}{dG} = 0.$$

Subtracting the second of these equations from the first yields

$$H_w \frac{d\hat{w}}{dG} + H_p \frac{d\hat{p}}{dG} = 0. \tag{A2}$$

Similarly, we now take derivatives of the goods market and housing market equilibrium conditions with respect to s and then take cross-regional differences to arrive at

$$(N_w - \Phi C_w) \frac{d\hat{w}}{ds} - \Phi(C_p + I_p) \frac{d\hat{p}}{ds} = 0, \tag{A3}$$

$$H_w \frac{d\hat{w}}{ds} = H_p \frac{d\hat{p}}{ds} = -H_s. \tag{A4}$$

We can now solve equations (A1)–(A4) for the relative response of house prices and wages to the two exogenous shocks:

$$\begin{pmatrix} \dfrac{d\hat{w}}{dG} & \dfrac{d\hat{w}}{ds} \\[2ex] \dfrac{d\hat{p}}{dG} & \dfrac{d\hat{p}}{ds} \end{pmatrix} = M \begin{pmatrix} 1 & -\Phi(C_p + I_p)\dfrac{H_s}{H_p} \\[2ex] -\dfrac{H_w}{H_p} & -(N_w - \Phi C_w)\dfrac{H_s}{H_p} \end{pmatrix}, \tag{A5}$$

where

$$M = \left(N_w - \Phi C_w + \Phi(C_p + I_p)\frac{H_w}{H_p} \right)^{-1}.$$

Define total home expenditures as $E = C(w, p, T) + I(p, T) + G$. The derivative of total home expenditures with respect to s is

$$\frac{dE}{ds} = (C_p + I_p)\frac{dp}{ds} + C_w \frac{dw}{ds} + C_T \frac{dT}{ds}.$$

Taking the difference between this equation and the foreign version of this equation yields

$$\frac{d\hat{E}}{ds} = (C_p + I_p)\frac{d\hat{p}}{ds} + C_w\frac{d\hat{w}}{ds}.$$

Using equation (A5) we then get that

$$\frac{d\hat{E}}{ds} = -(C_p + I_p)N_w M \frac{H_s}{H_p}$$

and

$$\frac{d\hat{E}}{d\hat{p}} = \frac{d\hat{E}/ds}{d\hat{p}/ds} = \frac{C_p + I_p}{1 - \Phi C_Y}, \qquad (A6)$$

where, again, $C_Y \equiv C_w/N_w$. Next, we differentiate home output and foreign output with respect to G and take the difference to get

$$\frac{d\hat{Y}}{dG} = \Phi(C_p + I_p)\frac{d\hat{p}}{dG} + \Phi C_w\frac{d\hat{w}}{dG} + 1.$$

Using equation (A5) we then get that

$$\frac{d\hat{Y}}{dG} = N_w M. \qquad (A7)$$

Taking the ratio of equations (A6) and (A7) yields

$$\frac{d\hat{E}/d\hat{p}}{d\hat{Y}/d\hat{p}} = (C_p + I_p)\frac{1 - \Phi C_Y + \Phi \frac{C_p + I_p}{N_w}\frac{H_w}{H_p}}{1 - \Phi C_Y}.$$

Manipulation of this equation yields

$$\frac{d\hat{E}/d\hat{p}}{d\hat{Y}/d\hat{p}} = (C_p + I_p)\left(1 - \Phi\frac{d\hat{E}/d\hat{p}}{d\hat{Y}/d\hat{p}}\frac{d\hat{p}}{dG}\right),$$

which can be manipulated further to yield equation (23) in the main text.

Appendix B

Additional Examples of Identification in Systems of Equations

This appendix presents three example systems of equations and demonstrates that in each of them the government spending shock is needed to identify the coefficient of interest.

B.1.   *Example from Subsection III.D*

We start by showing that the argument regarding identification in Section IV applies to the richer setting considered in Subsection III.D.

Linearize the equations of the model and take the difference across regions to yield

$$\hat{C} = C_p \hat{p} + C_Y \hat{Y}$$

$$\hat{I} = I_p \hat{p}$$

$$\hat{Y} = \Phi(\hat{C} + \hat{I}) + \hat{G}$$

$$0 = H_Y \hat{Y} + H_p \hat{p} + H_s \hat{s}$$

where we have substituted out for wages using $\hat{w} = N_w^{-1} \hat{Y}$ and defined $C_Y = C_w N_w^{-1}$ and $H_Y = H_w N_w^{-1}$ as in Section IV. There are four endogenous variables $(\hat{C}, \hat{I}, \hat{Y}, \hat{p})$ and two exogenous variables $(\hat{G}, \hat{s})$. We will write the system as $(\hat{C}, \hat{I}, \hat{Y}, \hat{p})\Gamma = (\hat{G}, \hat{s})\Delta$, where the coefficient matrices are

$$\Gamma = \begin{pmatrix} -1 & 0 & \Phi & 0 \\ 0 & -1 & \Phi & 0 \\ C_Y & 0 & -1 & H_Y \\ C_p & I_p & 0 & H_p \end{pmatrix} \qquad \Delta = \begin{pmatrix} 0 & 0 & -1 & 0 \\ 0 & 0 & 0 & -H_s \end{pmatrix}.$$

The restrictions on the first equation are

$$R_\Gamma = \begin{pmatrix} 0 & 1 & 0 & 0 \\ 0 & 0 & 0 & 0 \\ 0 & 0 & 0 & 0 \end{pmatrix} \qquad R_\Delta = \begin{pmatrix} 0 & 0 \\ 1 & 0 \\ 0 & 1 \end{pmatrix}$$

such that $(R_\Gamma \Gamma + R_\Delta \Delta)e_1 = 0$. The three restrictions are exclusion restrictions that exclude I, G, and s, respectively, from appearing directly in the consumption function. To check the rank condition, form $\mathcal{R} = R_\Gamma \Gamma + R_\Delta \Delta$:

$$\mathcal{R} = \begin{pmatrix} 0 & -1 & \Phi & 0 \\ 0 & 0 & -1 & 0 \\ 0 & 0 & 0 & -H_s \end{pmatrix},$$

which has rank 3 provided that $H_s \neq 0$ so the rank condition is satisfied. The first equation has a natural normalization as the coefficient on C is

−1. If we drop G from the system, we lose one restriction and the order
condition fails.

B.2. Local Credit Supply Example

The spirit of this example is that credit markets for investment spending
are (partially) segmented across space perhaps due to banking relationships. The credit supply shock could represent a shock to the banks serv-
ing a given region that affects the supply of credit to the region leading
to a change in local interest rates. We first argue that fiscal shocks are
needed to identify the investment demand curve, and then we solve
for the coefficients from the investment demand curve as a function of
the reduced form estimates. Here, we focus on a single regional economy and the variables can be interpreted as deviations from national
averages that are absorbed by time fixed effects.

The system is

$$Y = C + I + G$$
$$I = I_r r + I_y Y$$
$$C = C_y Y$$
$$b = b_I I$$
$$b = b_s s + b_r r$$

where the endogenous variables (Y, I, C, b, r) correspond to output, investment, consumption, credit quantity, and interest rates. The exogenous variables (s, G) correspond to a credit supply shifter and government purchases. In order, the equations are the resource constraint, an
investment demand curve, a consumption function, credit demand, and
credit supply.

The consumption and investment equations are both identified in that
they satisfy the rank condition and have a natural normalization. Without the shock to G, the investment demand curve is not identified as the
order condition fails: there are three excluded variables and five endogenous variables. Intuitively, the problem is that the reduced form shows
that investment reacts after a shock to s, but we do not know if I_r is small
and I_Y is large or vice versa. The fiscal shocks provide information about
the magnitude of I_y.

With the reduced form estimates in hand, we can solve for I_r as follows. Define the following IV estimates:

$$\frac{dY}{dG} = \frac{-b_iI_r + b_r}{b_iC_yI_r - b_iI_r - b_rC_y - b_rI_y + b_r}$$

$$\frac{dr}{dY} \equiv \frac{dr/dG}{dY/dG} = -\frac{b_iI_y}{b_iI_r - b_r}$$

$$\frac{dC}{dY} \equiv \frac{dC/dG}{dY/dG} = C_y$$

$$\frac{dI}{dr} \equiv \frac{dI/ds}{dr/ds} = \frac{I_r(C_y - 1)}{C_y + I_y - 1}.$$

The reduced forms are expressions involving structural parameters given by (ratios of) the appropriate elements of $\Delta\Gamma^{-1}$. Manipulating these expressions yields

$$I_r = \frac{\frac{dI}{dr}}{M}$$

$$M \equiv \frac{dY}{dG}\left(1 - \frac{dr}{dY}\frac{dI}{dr} - \frac{dC}{dY}\right).$$

(B1)

Here M is our "adjusted" fiscal multiplier as we need to adjust the fiscal multiplier in a similar manner to what we did in Section IV. The IV regression dI/dr measures how much investment responds to a given change in local interest rates. When we measure the local fiscal multiplier, we capture the channels operating through I_y, C_y, and the effect on local interest rates as credit demand rises. We need to remove the effect on interest rates just as we removed the effect of fiscal shocks on house prices in Section IV. We also need to adjust for the role of consumption in the fiscal multiplier. Specifically, we are interested in how a unit movement in investment is amplified. The direct effect, first round, second round, and so on are given by

Output response $\quad 1,\ I_y + C_y,\ (I_y + C_y)^2,\ \cdots$

Investment response $1,\quad I_y,\quad I_y(C_y + I_y),\quad \cdots$

The investment response is therefore $1 + [I_y/(1 - C_y - I_y)] = M$. It is then straightforward to solve for I_y. Rearranging M yields

$$I_y = \frac{(M - 1)\left(1 - \frac{dC}{dY}\right)}{M}.$$

B.3. Foreign Demand Example

Consider the system

$$Y = C + G + X_s s$$
$$C = C_Y Y$$

where there are two endogenous variables Y and C and two exogenous variables G and s where s is an instrument for foreign demand. X_s is an unknown coefficient that gives the direct output effect of a change in s. For example, s could be China exposure, but we do not know how China exposure translates to a change in local demand because there may be more or less scope for local production to transition to other goods for which demand is still strong after the China shock. The goal is to estimate X_s. Substitute the second equation into the first,

$$Y = MG + MX_s s,$$

where $M \equiv 1/(1 - C_Y)$. In the absence of the fiscal shock, we only identify the product MX_s. With the fiscal shock, we can determine M. One way to relate this to the discussion of identification in Section IV is to write the equation with the coefficient of interest on s,

$$(C_Y - 1)Y + G + X_s s = 0,$$

and note that without G we lack a normalization.

Endnotes

Authors' email addresses: Steinsson (jsteinsson@berkeley.edu), Nakamura (enakamura@berkeley.edu). An earlier version of this paper previously circulated as an appendix to "Housing Wealth Effects: The Long View" by the same authors. We thank Joao Fonseca Rodrigues for excellent research assistance. We thank Adrien Auclert, Gabe Chodorow-Reich, Erik Hurst, and Valerie Ramey for helpful comments and discussions. Guren thanks the National Science Foundation (grant SES-1623801) and the Boston University Center for Finance, Law, and Policy. Nakamura thanks the National Science Foundation (grant SES-1056107). Nakamura and Steinsson thank the Alfred P. Sloan Foundation for financial support. The views expressed herein are those of the authors and not necessarily those of the Federal Reserve Bank of Minneapolis or the Federal Reserve System. For acknowledgments, sources of research support, and disclosure of the authors' material financial relationships, if any, please see https://www.nber.org/books-and-chapters/nber-macroeconomics-annual -2020-volume-35/what-do-we-learn-cross-regional-empirical-estimates-macroeconomics.
   1. Prominent examples include Autor, Dorn, and Hanson (2013), Chodorow-Reich (2014), Mian and Sufi (2014), Nakamura and Steinsson (2014), and Martin and Philippon (2017). See Nakamura and Steinsson (2018) and Chodorow-Reich (2019) for further discussion of this literature.
   2. Davidoff (2016) shows that the change in housing units from 1980 to 2010 was negatively correlated with Saiz's housing supply elasticity across cities. The long-horizon

quantity response is less worrisome than the business cycle quantity response because differential demand trends across cities can be absorbed by city-level fixed effects in a panel specification (Guren et al. 2020).

3. Wolf describes his results in terms of addition and subtraction of impulse response functions. To understand the connection, a simplified version of our result is $C_{PE} = F^{-1}E$, where F is the matrix in which the (i, j) element gives the response of output at horizon i to a change in government spending at horizon j and the column vector E is the measured housing wealth effect impulse response. Wolf expresses his result as $C_{PE} + (F - I)C_{PE} = E$ where $(F - I)C_{PE}$ is the private consumption response to the fiscal shock that has the same dynamic profile as the partial equilibrium housing wealth effect.

4. Groundwork for these papers was provided by Auclert and Rognlie (2020) who show that the general equilibrium effects of a shock to consumption can be separated into a partial equilibrium path of consumption and a general equilibrium multiplier matrix that does not depend on the shock that perturbs consumption.

5. Here we use the demand side of the economy to form the quantity responses (eqs. [9] and [10]). As we are analyzing equilibrium changes in quantities, we can use either the demand response or supply response to the equilibrium prices and arrive at the same answer.

6. Nakamura and Steinsson find larger multipliers in regional data than in state data. As the analysis of the housing wealth effect is undertaken at the city (CBSA) level, it may be appropriate to use a fiscal multiplier somewhat below 1.5.

7. We construct this estimate as $(H/C)(C/I)$. Between 1985 and 2016, the average ratio of H/C was 2.17, where H is measured as the market value of owner-occupied real estate from the Flow of Funds and C is measured as total personal consumption expenditures (PCE) less PCE on housing services and utilities from the National Income and Product Accounts. Over this same period, I/C was 0.077, where I is residential investment from the National Income and Product Accounts.

8. Think of this as an IV estimate. For example, in the current model $d\hat{p}/d\hat{Y}$ can be estimated as a ratio of responses to exogenous variation in government spending: $(d\hat{p}/dG)/(d\hat{Y}/dG)$.

9. Nakamura and Steinsson estimate the local fiscal multiplier based on state-level data, whereas Guren et al. estimate the housing wealth effect on consumption at the CBSA level. Incorporating trade linkages into our analysis is accounting for the fact that the local fiscal multiplier is attenuated by trade linkages so it makes sense to use a value of φ consistent with the geographic unit used to estimate the fiscal multiplier.

10. In addition to changing the marginal rate of substitution between housing and nondurables, a shock to Ω_t also affects the marginal utility of consumption as the extra demand for housing is not fully satisfied in equilibrium. This can lead to a strong consumption response to Ω_t in the aggregate time series, but it equally affects both regions and therefore does not influence our cross-sectional analysis.

11. Including the term $\phi^{-\phi}(1 - \phi)^{-(1-\phi)}$ in the definition of the bundle simplifies the expression for the price index.

12. This case applies to the steady-state, perfect foresight transitions and first-order accurate solutions to stochastic economies.

13. Appendix E describes this negative relationship between quantities and prices in econometric terms and shows that our adjustment formula from Section III remains valid with heterogeneous housing supply curves.

References

Aladangady, A. 2017. "Housing Wealth and Consumption: Evidence from Geographically-Linked Microdata." *American Economic Review* 107:3415–46.

Auclert, A., and M. Rognlie. 2020. "Inequality and Aggregate Demand." Working paper, Stanford University.

Auclert, A., M. Rognlie, and L. Straub. 2018. "The Intertemporal Keynesian Cross." Working paper, Stanford University.

Autor, D. H., D. Dorn, and G. H. Hanson. 2013. "The China Syndrome: Local Labor Market Effects of Import Competition in the United States." *American Economic Review* 103:2121–68.

Beraja, M., E. Hurst, and J. Ospina. 2019. "The Aggregate Implications of Regional Business Cycles." *Econometrica* 87:1789–833.

Calvo, G. A. 1983. "Staggered Prices in a Utility-Maximizing Framework." *Journal of Monetary Economics* 12:383–98.

Campbell, J. Y., and J. F. Cocco. 2007. "How Do House Prices Affect Consumption?" *Journal of Monetary Economics* 54:591–621.

Chodorow-Reich, G. 2014. "The Employment Effects of Credit Market Disruptions: Firm-Level Evidence from the 2008–9 Financial Crisis." *Quarterly Journal of Economics* 129:1–59.

———. 2019. "Geographic Cross-Sectional Fiscal Multipliers: What Have We Learned?" *American Economic Journal: Policy* 11:1–34.

Chodorow-Reich, G., P. T. Nenov, and A. Simsek. 2020. "Stock Market Wealth and the Real Economy: A Local Labor Market Approach." *American Economic Review*, forthcoming.

Davidoff, T. 2016. "Supply Constraints Are Not Valid Instrumental Variables for Home Prices Because They Are Correlated with Many Demand Factors." *Critical Finance Review* 5:177–206.

Davis, M. A., and J. Heathcote. 2005. "Housing and the Business Cycle." *International Economic Review* 46:751–84.

Favilukis, J., S. C. Ludvigson, and S. Van Nieuwerburgh. 2017. "The Macroeconomic Effects of Housing Wealth, Housing Finance, and Limited Risk Sharing in General Equilibrium." *Journal of Political Economy* 125:140–223.

Greenwood, J., Z. Hercowitz, and G. W. Huffman. 1988. "Investment, Capacity Utilization, and the Real Business Cycle." *American Economic Review* 78 (3): 402–17.

Guren, A. M., A. McKay, E. Nakamura, and J. Steinsson. 2020. "Housing Wealth Effects: The Long View." *Review of Economic Studies*, forthcoming.

Herreno, J. 2020. "The Aggregate Effects of Bank Lending Cuts." Working paper, Columbia University.

Kaplan, G., K. Mitman, and G. L. Violante. 2020. "The Housing Boom and Bust: Model Meets Evidence." *Journal of Political Economy* 128 (9): 3285–3345.

Lamont, O., and J. Stein. 1999. "Leverage and House-Price Dynamics in US Cities." *RAND Journal of Economics* 30:498–514.

Martin, P., and T. Philippon. 2017. "Inspecting the Mechanism: Leverage and the Great Recession in the Eurozone." *American Economic Review* 107:1904–37.

Mian, A., K. Rao, and A. Sufi. 2013. "Household Balance Sheets, Consumption, and the Economic Slump." *Quarterly Journal of Economics* 128:1687–726.

Mian, A., and A. Sufi. 2014. "What Explains the 2007–2009 Drop in Employment?" *Econometrica* 82:2197–223.

Nakamura, E., and J. Steinsson. 2014. "Fiscal Stimulus in a Monetary Union: Evidence from US Regions." *American Economic Review* 104:753–92.

———. 2018. "Identification in Macroeconomics." *Journal of Economic Perspectives* 32:59–86.

Nathanson, C. G., and E. Zwick. 2018. "Arrested Development: Theory and Evidence of Supply-Side Speculation in the Housing Market." *Journal of Finance* 73:2587–633.

Saiz, A. 2010. "The Geographic Determinants of Housing Supply." *Quarterly Journal of Economics* 125:1253–296.

Schmitt-Grohé, S., and M. Uribe. 2003. "Closing Small Open Economy Models." *Journal of International Economics* 61:163–85.

Wolf, C. 2019a. "The Missing Intercept: A Demand Equivalence Approach." Working paper, Princeton University.

———. 2019b. "The Missing Intercept in Cross-Regional Regressions." Working paper, Princeton University.

Wooldridge, J. M. 2010. *Econometric Analysis of Cross Section and Panel Data.* Cambridge, MA: MIT Press.

Comment

Gabriel Chodorow-Reich, Harvard University, United States of America, *and NBER,* United States of America

In this paper, Guren, McKay, Nakamura, and Steinsson (Guren et al.) advocate using regional cross-sectional empirical estimates to measure microeconomic parameters such as the marginal propensity to consume out of housing wealth. The "divide-by-multiplier" method recovers the microeconomic parameter by dividing the regional response to a shock by a "demand multiplier" estimated separately as the regional response to a government spending shock. This method has many potential applications in regional data. (Full disclosure: in Chodorow-Reich, Nenov, and Simsek [2019] I use it to measure the stock market wealth effect on consumption.) Guren et al. provide a comprehensive yet accessible theoretical exposition and a numerical evaluation in the context of a model of housing wealth.

I divide my comments into four parts. First, I provide background on literatures using regional data in macroeconomics and on demand multipliers. Second, Guren et al. apply the method to a shock to preferences for housing. This choice introduces complications because housing is both part of wealth and an expenditure item, and both construction and consumer spending may respond to changes in house prices. I illustrate the relationship using a simpler yet still fully microfounded model with pure wealth shocks. Third, I use this model to make my main critique of the paper or, more accurately, of the paper's title. A casual reader might infer that the divide-by-multiplier method provides the only valid way to interpret regional empirical estimates. My simple model illustrates an additional property of regional effects of demand shocks, namely, that they provide a lower bound for the appropriately defined aggregate effect of the shock. I conclude by reviewing other recent approaches to interpreting regional regressions and their applicability to different sources of regional variation.

Comment I: Context. Researchers have come up with many creative approaches to measuring shocks at the regional level, for example, variation in the location of government spending or in sensitivity to the aggregate housing cycle that is orthogonal to other local variables. Chodorow-Reich (2020) counts 50 articles published in top field or general interest journals between 2012 and 2018 using regional data to address macroeconomic questions. This explosion reflects the rich variation across subnational regions and the availability of long regional time series. The question identified in Guren et al. is what structural parameters or causal effects these regional shocks can help to identify.

To understand the appeal of the divide-by-multiplier method, it helps first to state the problem with the usual interpretation of cross-sectional regressions. The Rubin (1978) potential outcomes model provides the canonical framework for interpreting cross-sectional regressions in applied microeconomics. In this model, unit i receives treatment W and has a potential outcomes function $Y_i(W)$ that relates the outcome to the treatment. Identifying a causal effect requires "as good as random" assignment of the treatment (conditional on covariates) with respect to the potential outcomes function, expressed in the examples in the preceding paragraph as the orthogonality of regional treatment to other local variables. Furthermore, in applied microeconomic settings researchers typically assume the potential outcome of unit i is independent of the treatment applied to all units $j \neq i$, known as the stable unit treatment value assumption (SUTVA). Under these conditions, a cross-sectional regression consistently identifies the average treatment effect (ATE) of changing from treatment W to W', defined as the population expectation $E[(Y_i(W') - Y_i(W))/(W' - W)]$.

The problem is that SUTVA almost certainly fails in a regional context. For example, a positive spending shock in region i causes output in region j to increase because some of the spending of people in i naturally falls on goods produced in j and prices in i rise relative to prices in j, leading to expenditure switching. This failure does not necessarily invalidate the ATE interpretation; if the impact on each j of a shock to i is sufficiently small, a cross-sectional regional regression can still consistently identify the average effect of the shock to i on region i. However, macroeconomists typically want to know the impact of a shock on all regions, which requires summing over the spillovers to each other region j. Even if the SUTVA violation to each individual region is *de minimus*, the sum of many small spillovers can drive a quantitatively important wedge between the treatment effect on i that is identified from the cross-sectional regression and the effect on the total economy.[1]

Guren et al. propose to circumvent this difficulty by instead using demand multipliers to relate regional estimands to microeconomic objects. By demand multiplier, I mean the proposition that the same general equilibrium multiplier applies to different components of demand. This idea goes back at least to the Keynesian cross, which is a market-clearing condition where consumption depends on income. Formally, one substitutes into the (for simplicity, closed economy) market-clearing condition $Y = C + I + G$ the consumption function $C = C_y(Y - T) + C_xX$ relating consumption C to disposable income $Y - T$ via the marginal propensity to consume out of income C_y and to any other determinant of consumption such as housing wealth X via the marginal propensity to consume out of that determinant C_x. Then the government purchases multiplier is $dY/dG = 1/(1 - C_y)$, whereas for any other determinant of consumption such as housing wealth, the output multiplier dY/dX is the direct propensity to consume out of that component, C_x, multiplied by the demand multiplier dY/dG: $dY/dX = C_x dY/dG$.[2]

Government and professional forecasters have long made use of demand multipliers. For example, the Congressional Budget Office (CBO) describes its procedure for estimating the output effects of different policies as follows (Reichling and Whalen 2012):

Direct effects consist of changes in purchases of goods and services by federal agencies and by the people and organizations who are recipients of federal payments or payers of federal taxes. The size of the direct effects of a change in policies depends on the behavior of those recipients and payers. The indirect effects can be summarized by a demand multiplier. CBO's analysis applies the same demand multiplier to any $1 of direct effect from a change in fiscal policies. The product of a direct effect and a demand multiplier is sometimes referred to as an output multiplier. A change in federal purchases has a direct effect of 1, so the output multiplier for federal purchases equals the demand multiplier; most other changes in fiscal policies have direct effects that are less than 1 (because recipients of benefits and payers of taxes tend to adjust their spending less than one-for-one with changes in their income).

Thus, for example, CBO would estimate the output effects of tax rebates to individuals by multiplying their estimate of the direct marginal propensity to consume out of tax rebates, the direct effect, by their estimate of the government purchases multiplier.

Academic economists have historically made less use of demand multipliers, perhaps reflecting a discomfort with the absence of proper microfoundations or dynamic considerations in the traditional Keynesian cross. Auclert, Rognlie, and Straub (2018) broke through this barrier by deriving an intertemporal version of the Keynesian cross, with the scalar C_y replaced by a matrix with the response of consumption in period s to income in period t. Guren et al. and their companion paper (Guren et al. 2020) extend the demand multiplier structure to the regional level and, crucially, recognize that it can be used in reverse to go from regional effects to the direct, microeconomic effect. By changing the object of interest from the national effect of a shock to the microeconomic effect, this approach sidesteps the cross-regional SUTVA violation.

Two additional aspects merit amplification. First, the method has power only if regional fiscal multipliers are strongly identified. Although no single study may be perfect, Chodorow-Reich (2019) reviews the recent proliferation of empirical estimates of the output effects of the federal government spending more in one region than another and finds support for a multiplier in the neighborhood of 1.8, close to the value of 1.5 used in Guren et al. Furthermore, the theoretically correct regional fiscal multiplier should not be adjusted for the fact that federal spending in a local region does not raise the relative tax burden in that region, making the empirical multipliers the proper analog for the regional demand multiplier. Second, as stressed in Guren et al. as well as in contemporaneous work by Wolf (2019), the dynamic considerations require a fiscal multiplier based on the same persistence of government spending as the direct spending effects of the shock. Numerical results in Guren et al., based on a dynamic, microfounded model, provide some assurance that the static adjustment gets the magnitude roughly correct. Of course, whether acknowledging a reasonable range of uncertainty over the magnitude of the demand multiplier or the bias of the static multiplier still allows for meaningful conclusions about microeconomic effects will depend on the application.

Comment II: Demand multiplier in a simpler model. The application to housing wealth in Guren et al. complicates their analysis because housing is both part of wealth and an expenditure item, and both construction and consumer spending respond to changes in house prices. I now describe a simpler yet still microfounded model of wealth effects on consumption and derive an exact version of the regional divide-by-demand-multiplier result. I then use this model to illustrate another use of regional data in macroeconomics, which I call the lower bound result.

The environment is a simplified version of the model in Chodorow-Reich et al. (2019). I describe the key equations and direct the reader to that paper for additional details. A continuum of areas indexed by a produce a tradable and nontradable good each period with technologies $Y_{a,t}^T = L_{a,t}^T$, $Y_{a,t}^N = L_{a,t}^N$. A national retailer aggregates the tradable output into a final good Y_t^T using the technology $\ln Y_t^T = \int_a \ln Y_{a,t}^T da$. A representative agent in each area has preferences across the tradable and nontradable goods of $C_{a,t} = (C_{a,t}^N)^{1-\phi}(C_{a,t}^T)^\phi$ and maximizes intertemporal utility $\Sigma_{t=0}^\infty 1/(1+\tilde{\rho})\ln C_{a,t}$. At time 0, each area a experiences an unexpected change in wealth of $\Delta_a = \bar{\Delta} + \tilde{\Delta}_a$, where $\int_a \tilde{\Delta}_a da = 0$. This wealth increase stems from the sudden blooming of a Lucas tree, which starting in period 1 will produce fruit that is a perfect substitute for the composite tradable good Y_t^T. Thus, the only shock at time 0 is to wealth.

The effect on period 0 log nominal expenditure illustrates the demand multiplier:

$$(p_{a,0} + c_{a,0}) = \frac{dP_{a,0}C_{a,0}}{P_{-1}C_{-1}} = \frac{\mathcal{M}_a\rho\Delta_a}{P_{-1}C_{-1}}, \tag{1}$$

where $z_{a,0} = dZ_{a,0}/Z_{a,-1}$ denotes the log deviation of a variable z from the pre-shock value, $P_{a,t}$ the ideal consumption price index, and $\rho = \tilde{\rho}/(1+\tilde{\rho})$. Wealth goes up by Δ_a, which, with log preferences, causes a direct, household-level increase in expenditure of $\rho\Delta_a$. This increase gets multiplied by the demand multiplier $\mathcal{M}_a$, given by $\mathcal{M}_a = 1/[1-(1-\phi)\rho]$. This demand multiplier coincides exactly with the open-economy (nominal) government spending multiplier.

Comment III: Lower bound result. Aggregating over all local areas yields the aggregate response to the wealth shock when interest rates do not change:

$$(w_0 + \ell_0) = (p_0 + c_0) = \frac{\mathcal{M}\rho\bar{\Delta}}{P_{-1}C_{-1}}, \tag{2}$$

where $\mathcal{M} = 1/(1-\rho)$. The aggregate economy is closed, so the change in nominal output equals the change in expenditure. This expression also takes the form of a direct consumption response multiplied by a demand multiplier, where now the multiplier is the closed-economy multiplier $\mathcal{M}$.

Comparing equation (2) to the response of local output to the shock yields the lower bound result. The response of local output, equal to the response of local labor income $W_{a,t}L_{a,t}$ (because there is a single factor of production), is

$$(w_{a,0} + \ell_{a,0}) = (1-\phi)(p_{a,0} + c_{a,0}) = \frac{\mathcal{M}_a(1-\phi)\rho\Delta_a}{P_{-1}C_{-1}}. \tag{3}$$

The aggregate output response $(w_0 + \ell_0)$ in equation (2) exceeds the local output response $(w_{a,0} + \ell_{a,0})$ in equation (3) for two reasons. First, local output responds only to the part of the increase in local demand that falls on nontradable goods. As a result, the local output response is a fraction $(1 - \phi)$ of the local expenditure response. In the aggregate closed economy, everything is nontradable, so the aggregate response also includes the increase in production of tradable goods. Second, $\mathcal{M}_a < \mathcal{M}$; the local demand multiplier is smaller than the closed-economy demand multiplier, precisely because of trade leakages at the local level to other areas.

This lower bound result for output turns out to hold across many economic environments under certain conditions. First, the result applies to demand shocks. Second, it requires making a proper comparison to the closed-economy case; the comparison should hold fixed endogenous responses to the shock, such as monetary policy, that do not vary across regions. Although this condition sounds restrictive, in practice we often want to know the aggregate impact of a shock while holding as much else constant as possible. Third, the result depends on factors of production not moving across local areas insofar as these factors, such as population, are fixed nationally. Finally, it applies to output, not necessarily to absorption. Under these conditions, regional analysis directly informs about the aggregate effect of a demand shock by providing a lower bound.

Just as the divide-by-multiplier method will perform better in some settings than others, these conditions show that the lower bound result is not universal. Indeed, it does not necessarily hold in the structural model in Guren et al. It is informative to understand why. The primitive shock in their environment is not a pure wealth shock that raises demand, but rather it is a shock to the demand for housing relative to the consumption good, which increases the relative price of housing. In the version of their model without produced construction, and under Cobb-Douglas aggregation of the housing and consumption contributions to utility and log preferences across time, the increase in demand for housing has no effect on either utility from consumption or the economy-wide resources to produce the consumption good. Therefore, the aggregate response of output is zero in this case.[3]

Conclusion. The divide-by-multiplier method has many potential applications. Guren et al. exposit the method in both a simple, static setting and a fully specified, microfounded, dynamic setting and show that the simple version can work pretty well as an approximation.

I do not, however, view this method as offering the only kosher use of regional data in macroeconomics. I gave an example where regional estimates provide a lower bound for an aggregate response of interest. I briefly mention two other recent approaches. Beraja, Hurst, and Ospina

(2019) show how the response of regional wage inflation to regional employment can identify microeconomic wage rigidity parameters if labor markets do not spill across regions. Huber (2018), Berg, Reisinger, and Streitz (2020), and Egger et al. (2019) use research designs with multiple levels of randomization to estimate directly a part of the spillovers to other units, an approach that offers the possibility of more tightly characterizing the aggregate response at the cost of greater demands on the cross-regional variation. Each of these methods has virtues and limitations. It is a promising development that macroeconomists now have many tools to incorporate regional data. Context should dictate the tool used in a particular application.

Endnotes

Author email address: Chodorow-Reich (chodorowreich@fas.harvard.edu). For acknowledgments, sources of research support, and disclosure of the author's material financial relationships, if any, please see https://www.nber.org/books-and-chapters/nber-macroeconomics-annual-2020-volume-35/comment-what-do-we-learn-cross-regional-empirical-estimates-macroeconomics-chodorow-reich.

1. See Chodorow-Reich (2020) for further discussion of the potential outcomes framework as applied to regional data.

2. This exposition assumes that investment I does not depend on income, but the formulas extend straightforwardly to that case.

3. I follow Guren et al. here in defining aggregate output as the sum of the consumption good and government purchases. National income accountants would also include in output and consumption the rental value of owner-occupied housing. Valuing the change in the rental value in the presence of preference shocks poses further complications.

References

Auclert, Adrien, Matthew Rognlie, and Ludwig Straub. 2018. "The Intertemporal Keynesian Cross." Working Paper no. 25020, NBER, Cambridge, MA.

Beraja, Martin, Erik Hurst, and Juan Ospina. 2019. "The Aggregate Implications of Regional Business Cycles." *Econometrica* 87 (6): 1789–833.

Berg, Tobias, Markus Reisinger, and Daniel Streitz. 2020. "Handling Spillover Effects in Empirical Research." October 29. https://ssrn.com/abstract=3377457.

Chodorow-Reich, Gabriel. 2019. "Geographic Cross-Sectional Fiscal Spending Multipliers: What Have We Learned?" *American Economic Journal: Economic Policy* 11 (2): 1–34.

———. 2020. "Regional Data in Macroeconomics: Some Advice for Practitioners." *Journal of Economic Dynamics and Control* 115:103875.

Chodorow-Reich, Gabriel, Plamen Nenov, and Alp Simsek. 2019. "Stock Market Wealth and the Real Economy: A Local Labor Market Approach." *American Economic Review*, forthcoming.

Egger, Dennis, Johannes Haushofer, Edward Miguel, Paul Niehaus, and Michael Walker. 2019. "General Equilibrium Effects of Cash Transfers: Experimental Evidence from Kenya." Working Paper no. 26600, NBER, Cambridge, MA.

Guren, Adam M., Alisdair McKay, Emi Nakamura, and Jón Steinsson. 2020. "Housing Wealth Effects: The Long View." *Review of Economic Studies* rdaa018. https://doi.org/10.1093/restud/rdaa018.

Huber, Kilian. 2018. "Disentangling the Effects of a Banking Crisis: Evidence from German Firms and Counties." *American Economic Review* 108 (3): 868–98.

Reichling, Felix, and Charles Whalen. 2012. "Assessing the Short-Term Effects on Output of Changes in Federal Fiscal Policies." Technical report, Congressional Budget Office, Washington, DC.

Rubin, Donald B. 1978. "Bayesian Inference for Causal Effects: The Role of Randomization." *Annals of Statistics* 6 (1): 34–58.

Wolf, Christian. 2019. "The Missing Intercept: A Demand Equivalence Approach." https://scholar.princeton.edu/sites/default/files/ckwolf/files/missing_intercept.pdf.

Comment

Valerie A. Ramey, University of California, San Diego, United States of America, *and NBER,* United States of America

I. Introduction

This insightful paper by Guren, McKay, Nakamura, and Steinsson (Guren et al.) contributes to the literature that seeks to translate effects estimated on data at one level of geographic aggregation to another level of geographic aggregation. It can also be seen as a companion paper to their paper on the effects of variations of housing wealth on consumption (Guren et al. forthcoming). The current paper develops a very clever method for recovering "partial equilibrium" effects from regressions using variation across subnational units, such as cities and states. It then applies this method to estimating the marginal propensity to consume out of housing wealth. Separately, it offers a solution to a puzzle that has arisen with respect to the widely used Saiz (2010) instrument used for house prices.

II. Linking Estimates at Different Levels of Aggregation

Identifying causal effects is particularly difficult in macroeconomics because of general equilibrium, dynamics, and expectations. Macroeconomists were slow to adopt the new methods developed in applied microeconomics during its "credibility revolution." The diffusion of applied micro methods to macro accelerated, however, at the start of the Great Recession, when researchers interested in macroeconomic questions began to estimate causal effects of fiscal policy, housing price changes, and so on, using cross-state or cross-city data. Initially, many thought that we could simply apply microeconometric methods to answer macro questions. The fiscal literature quickly realized, however, that the intercepts in cross-state (or city) regressions or time fixed effects in state panel regressions netted out the macroeconomic effects we were trying to estimate.

This realization has led me to conclude that there is no "applied micro free lunch" for macroeconomists. Identification of macroeconomic effects can only be accomplished with macroeconomic identifying assumptions. As I outlined in Ramey (2019), there are two broad categories of methods for identifying macro causal effects: (i) using aggregate data in conjunction with time series identification or dynamic stochastic general equilibrium (DSGE) identification to estimate macroeconomic effects directly and (ii) estimating micro or subnational effects and translating them to macroeconomic effects using macroeconomic theory, such as a DSGE model. Guren et al.'s method is related to the latter but with an important twist.

Figure 1 represents the effects at different levels of aggregation and how Guren et al.'s exercise differs from the standard exercise.

The rest of the literature has focused on determining the relationship between causal effects estimated at the state or local level (what Guren et al. call "local general equilibrium effects") to the aggregate general equilibrium effects. That is, they seek to translate the effects estimated for the middle circle to the downstream effects at the aggregate. Guren et al. instead seek to translate the local general equilibrium (GE) effects upstream to what they call "partial equilibrium" (PE) effects. As they make clear, what they are calling the "PE" effect is the effect of housing prices on consumption, holding other variables constant.

I think that the phrase "partial equilibrium" is misused here, as well as in numerous other places in the recent macroeconomics and public finance literature. Partial equilibrium refers to the equilibrium in one market, taking as exogenous prices in other markets as well as agents' incomes. The partial equilibrium effect of an exogenous shock is the change

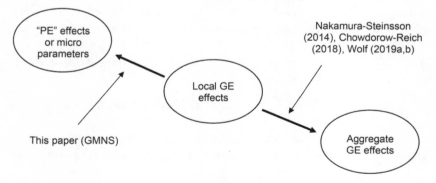

Fig. 1.   Relationship between micro, local, and aggregate estimates

in equilibrium price and quantity in that market. In contrast, the response of household or city-level average household consumption to a change in house prices, with other conditions remaining the same, represents the optimal responses of individual households. It is a parameter of a best response function and it is based on the outcome of a constrained maximization problem for households. It is not a partial equilibrium outcome. Therefore, I refer to the parameters they are trying to identify as micro parameters.

III.   Guren et al.'s Method for Identifying Micro Parameters

Guren et al. explain their idea very clearly, first in a simple model and then in progressively more general models. To illustrate a later point I wish to make, I explain their idea in a simple introductory macroeconomics Keynesian cross model. In particular, suppose the economy takes the following very simple form:

$$Y = C + G \quad \text{NIPA identity} \tag{1}$$

$$C = \alpha \cdot Y + \beta \cdot H \quad \text{Consumption function} \tag{2}$$

where Y is output (and income), C is consumption, G is government purchases, H is housing wealth, α is the marginal propensity to consume (MPC) out of income, and β is the marginal propensity to consume out of housing wealth (MPCH).

Suppose we observe an exogenous increase in housing wealth in a city. How will consumption change? Guren et al.'s insight is that estimates across cities do not reveal the micro (what they call "partial equilibrium") parameter β because the response estimated across cities contains endogenous feedback. To demonstrate their point, I solve the simple Keynesian cross (which assumes that output is demand determined) to find equilibrium income and consumption in the city:

$$Y = \frac{\beta \cdot H + G}{1 - \alpha} = \frac{1}{1 - \alpha}[\beta \cdot H + G] \quad \text{City equilibrium output/income} \tag{3}$$

$$C = \frac{\beta}{1 - \alpha}H + \frac{\alpha}{1 - \alpha}G \quad \text{City equilibrium consumption} \tag{4}$$

These equations make clear that looking at the effects of exogenous changes in housing wealth across cities yields the following estimates:

$$\frac{dY}{dH} = \frac{dC}{dH} = \frac{\beta}{1 - \alpha} \tag{5}$$

As Guren et al. point out, the city consumption response to an exogenous increase in housing wealth confounds two effects: the MPCH, β, and the Keynesian multiplier, $1/(1 - \alpha)$, which captures the local spillovers of one household's consumption on other households' income and consumption.

How then do we identify the MPCH from estimates that use city variation? Guren et al.'s insight is to identify the MPCH using an estimate of the government spending multiplier; that is,

$$\frac{dY}{dG} = \frac{1}{1 - \alpha} \tag{6}$$

Thus, we can identify the MPCH (β) if we take a second step and divide the city estimate of the effect of an exogenous increase in housing wealth (from eq. [5]) by an estimate of the government spending multiplier in equation (6).

Guren et al.'s idea to use fiscal multipliers to help identify other key parameters is very clever. The idea is related to some independent contemporaneous work (e.g., Wolf 2019a, 2019b; Auclert and Rognlie 2020). Guren et al. generalize the idea with both analytic results and a dynamic macro model of multiple regions with potentially incomplete markets. Their impressive analysis shows that it is a relatively robust approximation under numerous generalizations.

IV.   Alternative Ways to Estimate Micro Parameters

It is useful to step back and think about why macroeconomists might want to estimate the MPCH, which I have argued is a micro parameter. After all, the title of the paper is about what we learn in macroeconomics. I agree with them that knowing the MPCH is useful for macroeconomists: It may be a key micro parameter in DSGE models that estimate the aggregate effects of housing booms and busts.

However, I would suggest that there are more straightforward ways to estimate this key micro parameter. This statement ties to my point in the earlier section where I argued that Guren et al. mischaracterize this parameter as a partial equilibrium effect when in fact it is a micro parameter. I argue that although their method can be valuable in cases where there are no good micro data, in most cases there are better ways to estimate these types of parameters. These alternatives exploit rich household data and do not require a host of auxiliary assumptions. To demonstrate my point, consider two fine studies of the effect of changes in household wealth on household consumption.

The first study is by Campbell and Cocco (2007) who use UK household-level data and create a synthetic panel. They estimate a regression of changes in consumption on changes in house prices, controlling for household income, leverage, and other demographic variables. Thus, their regression is analogous to Guren et al.'s equation (2) and their estimate of the effect of housing wealth on consumption is exactly the micro MPCH, Guren et al.'s parameter C_p. Campbell and Cocco's estimates are not confounded by endogenous changes in income in a city because their estimate is from a household-level regression that nets out city effects with a constant term and that furthermore controls for the household's income. Thus, the error term in the regression is entirely due to idiosyncratic factors of the household, not the endogenous city-level feedbacks that confound Guren et al.'s estimates. Campbell and Cocco find that elasticity of nondurable consumption to housing wealth varies from 0 for renters (as we would expect) to 1.7 for older homeowners. The average elasticity is 1.2, which roughly translates to an MPCH of 0.077.

The second excellent household-level study is by Aladangady (2017), who uses rich Consumer Expenditure Survey (CEX) data linked to confidential geographic detail to link household-level consumption to changes in household wealth in the United States. His regression also controls for household income and other characteristics. He estimates an MPCH of 0 for renters and of 0.047 for homeowners.

But could household-level income be endogenous as well due to the local general equilibrium effect of house prices on income? In theory this is possible, but in practice there is no bias in most applications. There are two factors that eliminate the bias. First, the idiosyncratic components of household income swamp any common city components. For example, I estimate that city-fixed effects explain only 0.4% of the variation in household income in data from the 2000 Census. Second, the low estimates of marginal propensities to consume out of housing wealth mean that exogenous house prices are a minor source of variation in city-level income. My Monte Carlo simulations based on the simple Keynesian cross model verify this intuition. I find that although estimates of the MPCH based on a city-level regression of consumption on exogenous house prices are biased upward (by approximately the assumed government spending multiplier of 1.5), the estimates of the MPCH based on a household-level regression of consumption on both exogenous city-level house prices and household income show no bias.

Thus, data-rich and well-implemented household-level estimates solve the problem of the feedback from consumption to income in local GE that confounds cross-city estimates. The household-level approach obtains the estimates in one step. In contrast, consider how Guren et al. obtain the estimates in this paper and their companion paper. First, they estimate an elasticity of consumption to house prices of 0.072, based on a log difference specification using annual data on a panel of cities, instrument for housing prices. As they argue, this estimate includes the local GE effects. Thus, they must move to step 2, which is to convert the elasticity to a local GE MPCH = 0.033 by dividing by the average housing wealth-to-consumption ratio from 1985 to 2016, which was 2.17. Finally, in step 3 they purge this estimate of local GE effects by dividing by Nakamura and Steinsson's (2014) estimated state-level government spending multiplier of 1.5. Their final answer is that MPCH = 0.022.

But the previous review of two leading household-level studies highlights a further challenge to Guren et al.'s approach. The micro evidence shows us that there is important heterogeneity in the MPCH. For obvious reasons, it is much higher for homeowners than renters. Thus, Guren et al.'s estimate of MPCH purged of local GE effects confounds the household-level response with the fraction of renters versus homeowners in the average city; that is,

$$\text{MPCH}_{\text{city}} = \lambda\, \text{MPCH}_{\text{homeowners}} + (1 - \lambda)\, \text{MPCH}_{\text{renters}}$$

where λ is the fraction of households that are homeowners. Because their baseline estimates do not weight cities by population, the λ implicit in their MPCH estimate is not necessarily nationally representative. Furthermore, it seems that calibrated DSGE models of housing would need separate estimates of the MPCH conditional on owning a home and the fraction of renters versus homeowners in the economy.

V. Other Challenges to Implementing Guren et al.'s Method

Guren et al. consider many generalizations of their model. They are very upfront in showing that the approximation errors can be large for reasonable generalizations: the relative errors are often above 30%. In addition to the confounding of household MPCH with the fraction of renters that I discuss in the last section, there are other challenges to implementing their method. The main one is the reliance on the estimates of government spending multipliers.

As I discuss in an earlier section, dY/dG, the government spending multiplier, is the linchpin estimate for their approach. It is the government spending multiplier estimate that allows conversion of a local GE estimate to a micro parameter of use for a macro model. For an illustration of their method, Guren et al. use estimates of the multiplier of 1.5 from Nakamura and Steinsson (2014).

When Nakamura and Steinsson (2014) was published, the techniques used were state of the art. However, technological progress has been so rapid in this literature that we have figured out how to improve upon some of the things we did just a few years ago.

They study the effects of defense contracts on state- or region-level output and employment in a panel of states annually from 1966 to 2006. To do this, they estimate the following regression:

$$\frac{Y_{it} - Y_{it-2}}{Y_{it-2}} = \alpha_i + \gamma_t + \beta \frac{G_{it} - G_{it-2}}{Y_{it-2}} + \varepsilon_{it}$$

where Y is per capita output in state i, and G is per capita military procurement spending in state i. State and time fixed effects are included, and β is the estimate of the multiplier. They consider two possible instruments: (i) an interaction of state dummies with aggregate procurement growth and (ii) a Bartik instrument that interacts state historical sensitivity to aggregate procurement spending with the aggregate change in procurement spending.

When they use their preferred interaction instruments, they obtain a multiplier estimate of 1.43 (standard error [s.e.] 0.36). However, these instruments have a low first-stage F-statistic, suggesting weak instruments. When they use the Bartik instrument, the multiplier is estimated to be 2.48 (s.e. 0.94), and the first-stage F-statistic is high. Substituting a multiplier of 2.5 rather than the 1.5 that Guren et al. use has a significant effect on the implied MPCH.

But there are other issues with the 1.5 multiplier estimate they import. First, the multiplier is not aligned on timing. Their city-level effects of house prices on consumption estimates are based on annual changes but the government spending multiplier estimates are based on biennial changes. To determine the impact of this timing, I used the Nakamura and Steinsson (2014) replication files to reestimate their model using annual changes rather than biennial changes and found that the interactive instruments multiplier estimate falls from 1.43 to 0.69 and the Bartik instruments multiplier estimate falls from 2.48 to 1.65. Thus, aligning the timing means that we should use a smaller multiplier estimate to back out the MPCH.

I discovered additional issues with Nakamura and Steinsson's estimates in the course of reestimating their model. First, I discovered that the instruments are serially correlated—that is, the correlation of the instrument (which is a 2-year difference) and the previous 2-year difference is 0.28. Because Nakamura and Steinsson (2014) did not include lagged Ys, Gs, and instruments as controls, it means that their estimates probably do not satisfy Stock and Watson's (2018) lead-lag exogeneity condition. Chen (2019) recognized this problem and tested for lead-lag exogeneity and rejected it for some states in the Nakamura and Steinsson data.

The best way to account for dynamics is to use the external instrument in a structural vector autoregression (SVAR) or in an instrumental variable (IV) local projection (i.e., Ramey-Zubairy 2018). Thus, I use the Nakamura and Steinsson data to estimate local projections using annual growth rates to align with the city data. I include two annual lags of the growth of output, government spending, and the Bartik instrument. It is important to include these additional lags. Chen (2019) also estimated local projections using 2-year growth rates but did not include lags of the endogenous variables and instrument in his specification. Thus, his instrument is not a shock because it can be forecasted from past values. See Stock and Watson (2018) and Alloza, Gonzalo, and Sanz (2019) for more discussion.

To estimate the integral multiplier at horizon h, I use the easy-to-implement, one-step IV local projection (see, e.g., Ramey-Zubairy 2018). This integral multiplier is the ratio of the integral of the output response up to horizon h to the integral of the government spending response up to horizon h. Figure 2 shows the multiplier at each horizon, along with 95% confidence intervals, which correct for heteroskedasticity and autocorrelation.

Several points are noteworthy about these estimates. The point estimates are 0.7 at 1 year, 0.75 at 2 years, and 1 at 3 years. Recall that the Nakamura and Steinsson static 2-year multiplier estimate using the Bartik instrument was 2.48. Thus, using the same instrument but modeling the dynamics results in a fall in the multiplier from 2.48 to 0.75. Second, the multiplier appears to become larger and larger as the horizon grows. My analysis of the underlying impulse responses shows that it is the output response that keeps growing. It is not clear what the source of the rise is.

These new estimates do not deal with another potential issue that might affect the multiplier estimate needed to implement Guren et al.'s procedure: the misalignment of geography. These government multiplier estimates are at the state level, but their housing wealth estimates are at

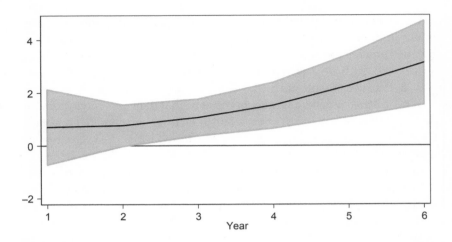

Fig. 2.   Local projection estimates of the multiplier on defense prime contracts by horizon.

the city level. Spillovers are more likely to be netted out by the intercept in
city regressions than at higher-level aggregation regressions, so this geographic misalignment could affect the procedure.

In sum, the Guren et al. method relies crucially on an estimate of the
government spending multiplier. The point of this section is to demonstrate that those estimates can vary quite a bit, not only with the instruments used but also with how dynamics are modeled, with the horizon
for the multiplier, and potentially with the geographic level.

VI.   Conclusions

Guren et al. have introduced a useful new tool for identifying microeconomic parameters from cross-city or cross-state local GE estimates. Although they illustrate their method in the context of estimating the micro-
level MPCH, it can potentially be used to identify micro parameters in
a wide array of applications. Even when rich data make household-level
estimation the superior method, it can serve as a useful check.

As I have illustrated in my discussion, although Guren et al. have offered a great new "recipe," the quality of the final product is only as good
as the ingredients. The two key ingredients of this recipe are local GE effects estimates and local government spending multiplier estimates. Thus,
high-quality estimates of these two ingredients are crucial.

Endnote

For acknowledgments, sources of research support, and disclosure of the author's material financial relationships, if any, please see https://www.nber.org/books-and-chapters /nber-macroeconomics-annual-2020-volume-35/comment-what-do-we-learn-cross-regional -empirical-estimates-macroeconomics-ramey.

References

Aladangady, A. 2017. "Housing Wealth and Consumption: Evidence from Geographically-Linked Microdata." *American Economic Review* 107:3415–46.

Alloza, Mario, Jesús Gonzalo, and C. Sanz. 2019. "Dynamic Effects of Persistent Shocks." Working Paper no. 1944, Banco de España, Madrid.

Auclert, A., and M. Rognlie. 2020. "Inequality and Aggregate Demand." Working paper, Stanford University.

Campbell, J. Y., and J. F. Cocco. 2007. "How Do House Prices Affect Consumption?" *Journal of Monetary Economics* 54:591–621.

Chen, Vince. 2019. "Fiscal Multipliers and Regional Reallocation." Working paper, Boston University.

Guren, Adam, Alisdair McKay, Emi Nakamura, and Jón Steinsson. Forthcoming. "Housing Wealth Effects: The Long View." *Review of Economic Studies.* https://doi.org/10.1093/restud/rdaa018.

Nakamura, E., and J. Steinsson. 2014. "Fiscal Stimulus in a Monetary Union: Evidence from US Regions." *American Economic Review* 104:753–92.

Ramey, Valerie A. 2019. "Ten Years after the Financial Crisis: What Have We Learned from the Renaissance in Fiscal Research?" *Journal of Economic Perspectives* 33 (2): 89–114.

Ramey, Valerie A., and Sarah Zubairy. 2018. "Government Spending Multipliers in Good Times and in Bad: Evidence from US Historical Data." *Journal of Political Economy* 126 (2): 850–901.

Saiz, A. 2010. "The Geographic Determinants of Housing Supply." *Quarterly Journal of Economics* 125:1253–296.

Stock, James H., and Mark W. Watson. 2018. "Identification and Estimation of Dynamic Causal Effects in Macroeconomics using External Instruments." *Economic Journal* 128 (610): 917–48.

Wolf, C. 2019a. "The Missing Intercept: A Demand Equivalence Approach." Working paper, Princeton University.

———. 2019b. "The Missing Intercept in Cross-Regional Regressions." Working paper, Princeton University.

Discussion

Greg Kaplan opened the discussion by inquiring about the goal of the estimation and the nature of the counterfactual exercises carried out in the paper. He expressed concern that the exercises that study the response of households to changes in prices are treating an equilibrium object—namely, house prices—as a parameter. Alisdair McKay responded that individual households treat house prices as exogenous. Thus, it is appropriate to treat house prices as a parameter in a partial equilibrium setting and study how sensitive household decisions are to that parameter. As a following step, it is then possible to aggregate housing decisions. He agreed that a real-world counterpart of this exercise is not immediate because it would consider an average of different housing parameters across individuals. Kaplan agreed on the scope of the exercise in the context of the model, but he pointed out that we need to believe that the assumptions made in the model also hold in the real world. He also emphasized the importance of clearly stating the relevant real-world counterfactual at the core of the analysis that is being carried out. Jón Steinsson argued that it was important to distinguish clearly between two separate objects. The first is what is measured in the data, which is clearly defined by the empirical specification. The second is the interpretation of the measured object. A theoretical model can provide an interpretation for the object measured in the data. He highlighted that housing is not exogenous in the model presented in the paper, yet it corresponds to the object observed in the data. Adam Guren further pointed out that the home price shock is similar to a foreign demand shock and that the effect of such a shock on consumption is instrumental to correctly calibrating the housing wealth effect in a general equilibrium model.

Robert Hall suggested that a useful research proposal in this area would include (i) writing a model with regions, (ii) assembling data on regions, (iii) estimating the model with econometric tools, and (iv) conducting policy analysis in the model. He expressed skepticism about the procedure introduced by the authors. Erik Hurst added that he explored the approach suggested by Hall in prior research and he argued that such an approach also has some weaknesses, such as being too dependent on modeling assumptions. Steinsson responded that their paper along with their earlier paper on housing contained many of the elements of Hall's proposal: they performed state-of-the art regional empirical analysis in the earlier paper and in this paper they had written down a state-of-the-art regional model to interpret their empirical results. He explained that the goal of their analysis was not normative. This meant that they did not conduct policy analysis. Instead, their goal was to introduce a dynamic micro-founded model that could correctly interpret the results of their regional estimates from their prior paper.

Esteban Rossi-Hansberg expressed skepticism about the lack of links between locations in the model, such as trade links or commuting networks. He specified that the use of a gravity equation, for example, could be a first step at introducing trade in the model. The authors responded that, through the lens of their model, trade matters because it makes the local multiplier smaller than the aggregate multiplier. They added that incorporating more realistic geography in the model would be an interesting direction for future research but is beyond the scope of the current paper, which focuses on the adjustment to local partial equilibrium effect.

Ricardo Reis followed up on the discussion about the links across locations in the model. He inquired about the persistence of the shocks and the relevant time horizon for the analysis. He conjectured that, under the appropriate assumptions, the model could generate no migration in the short horizon but some migration over a long enough horizon. McKay specified that the model is simulated at a quarterly horizon. He added that their results are robust to different values of the persistence of shocks. However, he acknowledged their analysis does not consider the role of migration.

In the last part of the discussion, the authors addressed some concerns raised by the discussants. First, Guren responded to a comment by Valery Ramey, who proposed to use individual-level data to directly estimate a partial equilibrium effect instead of regional-level data and then adjusting it to get the partial equilibrium effect. Guren agreed with Ramey that for some questions directly estimating the partial equilibrium effect using compelling individual-level variation is preferable. However, Guren observed that for some questions, individual-level data are either unavailable or have variation that is far less compelling for identification relative to regional variation. It is in these cases, he argued, that the methods in this paper are valuable. Guren pointed out that by definition, house prices are regional, so it is difficult to convincingly estimate a partial equilibrium effect using individual-level data when the variation is regional.

Second, Steinsson commented on the local projection technique discussed by Ramey. He highlighted that this approach progressively drops data from the analysis. Using a stable sample for the analysis delivered somewhat different results, he noted, such as a more pronounced response over time. Third, he pointed out that work by W. Chen ("Essays on Macroeconomics with Microeconomic Heterogeneity" [Mimeo, Boston University, 2019]) using the local projection method on regional variation had found a nontrivial response in population and construction. He indicated this to be a promising avenue for future research.

4

Innovative Growth Accounting

Peter J. Klenow, *Stanford University,* United States of America, *and NBER,* United States of America

Huiyu Li, *Federal Reserve Bank of SF,* United States of America

I. Introduction

Solow (1956) famously decomposed output growth into contributions from capital, labor, and productivity. Mankiw, Romer, and Weil (1992) further decomposed productivity into human capital versus residual productivity. We take this residual productivity, routinely calculated by the US Bureau of Labor Statistics (BLS), as our starting point. We attribute productivity growth to innovation and ask: What form does the innovation take, and which firms do most of the innovation?

Innovation can take the form of a stream of new varieties that are not close substitutes for any existing varieties (Romer 1990). Alternatively, growth could be driven by creative destruction of existing products as in Aghion and Howitt (1992). Examples include Walmart stores driving out mom-and-pop stores or Amazon stealing business from physical stores. Yet another possibility is that growth takes the form of existing producers improving their own products (e.g., successive generations of Apple iPhones or new car models). Even conditional on the form of innovation, growth could be led by entrants and young firms (e.g., Uber or Netflix) or by older and larger firms (e.g., Intel or Starbucks).

Figure 1 shows US productivity growth has been lackluster in recent decades, except for a decade-long surge from the mid-1990s through the mid-2000s.[1] At the same time, as shown in figure 2, plant and firm entry rates have fallen and reallocation of labor across incumbent firms has slowed—a phenomenon coined "declining business dynamism" by papers such as Decker et al. (2014). Large, established superstar firms have captured a bigger share of markets. Is this declining dynamism and rising

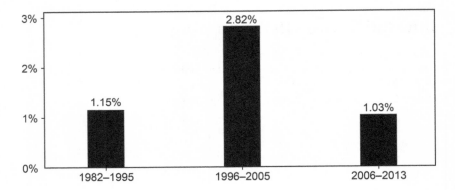

Fig. 1. US productivity growth rate. US Bureau of Labor Statistics (BLS) multifactor productivity (MFP) series. We calculate yearly productivity growth rate by adding research and development and intellectual property contribution to BLS MFP and then converting the sum to labor augmenting form. The figure plots the average productivity growth within each subperiod. The unit is percentage points. A color version of this figure is available online.

concentration responsible for the growth slowdown? Have superstar firms helped growth or hindered it?

We offer a new growth decomposition to shed light on these questions. We decompose growth into three types of innovation: creative destruction, brand-new varieties, and innovation by incumbents on their own products. We further decompose each of these sources into contributions by firm age and size.

We use firm and plant data on employment at all nonfarm businesses from 1983 to 2013 in the US Census Bureau's Longitudinal Business Database (LBD). We treat each plant as a unique product (or set of products). This

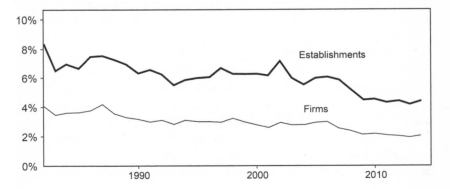

Fig. 2. Employment share of new plants and new firms, 1982–2013. Census BDS. A color version of this figure is available online.

enables us to observe the rate and importance of product entry and exit across firms. We rely on a model in which employment at a plant is iso-elastic with respect to the quality of products produced at the plant.[2] We use the size of entering versus exiting plants to gauge the quality of brand-new products and the quality improvements made through creative destruction. We assess quality improvements by firms on their own products using changes in employment over time at surviving incumbent plants. We also allow the lowest-quality products (plants) to exit due to obsolescence (i.e., inability to keep up with overall quality and variety growth) as in Hopenhayn (1992).[3]

We preview our findings as follows. Some 60% of growth on average comes from incumbent innovations on their own products, whereas about 27% comes from new varieties and 13% from creative destruction. Many exiting plants are quite small, suggesting much of exit is due to obsolescence rather than creative destruction. And new plants are smaller than incumbent plants on average, making us infer that most plant entry takes the form of new varieties rather than creative destruction.

We find that own innovation drove both the mid-1990s speedup and the mid-2000s slowdown of growth. Total factor productivity (TFP) growth averaged 1.15% per year from 1982 to 1995, then sped up to 2.82% per year from 1996 to 2005 before falling back to 1.03% per year from 2006 to 2013. Own innovation accounted for 148 of the 167 basis point acceleration, and 144 of the 179 basis point deceleration. Even though entry and job reallocation fell throughout the sample, growth from creative destruction accelerated modestly during the period 1996–2005 versus 1982–1995.

New firms in a given year account for about one-third of growth on average. New and young firms (ages 0–5 years) together contribute roughly one-half of all growth, despite employing less than one-fifth of all workers. Older incumbents (ages 6 and above) contribute the other half of growth. Such established firms played a bigger role in the speedup and slowdown of growth, however, accounting for 80% of the pickup and 70% of the dropoff.

The largest firms—those with 5,000 or more workers—accounted for only 11% of growth on average. This is less than half of their 25% share of employment. Small firms, with fewer than 20 employees, account for more than 60% of growth despite employing only 21% of all workers. This is very much in the spirit of Haltiwanger, Jarmin, and Miranda (2013), who emphasize the outsize contribution of young, small, fast-growing firms ("gazelles") to gross job creation.

The speedup and slowdown of growth occurred uniformly across the size distribution. In particular, firms with (1) less than 20 employees, (2) between 20 and 249 employees, (3) between 250 and 4,999 employees, and (4) 5,000 or more employees each produced a speedup and slowdown of around 40 basis points. Thus, in this accounting, superstar firms did not generate the bulk of the boom or bust. Focusing on the role of superstars in creating or hindering growth—at least directly—seems misplaced. It is possible, of course, that the rise of superstar firms discouraged innovation by other firms, as in Aghion et al. (2020).

The rest of the paper proceeds as follows. Section II relates our paper to the existing literature. Section III lays out the model we use to do innovation accounting. Section IV presents the mapping from model parameters to the moments in the LBD. Section V provides our main results. Section VI discusses further results and directions for future research. Section VII concludes.

II. Related Literature

The classic reference on creative destruction models is Aghion and Howitt (1992). Klette and Kortum (2004) developed potential implications of creative destruction for firm dynamics. Lentz and Mortensen (2008) formally estimated a generalization of the Klette-Kortum model using data on Danish firms. See Aghion, Akcigit, and Howitt (2014) for a survey of the literature on both models and evidence of creative destruction. Aghion et al. (2019) analyze how creative destruction can be missed in measures of aggregate productivity growth. Hsieh, Klenow, and Nath (2019) develop and calibrate a two-country version of the Klette-Kortum model.

Romer (1990) is the seminal paper on expanding variety models. Rivera-Batiz and Romer (1991) followed up with a two-economy version. Acemoglu (2003) and Jones (2016) provide two of many subsequent models built around variety growth. Chapter 12 of Acemoglu (2011) provides a textbook treatment. Feenstra (1994) and Broda and Weinstein (2006) estimate variety gains from imports. Broda and Weinstein (2006) estimate growth in the range of consumer products available.

Krusell (1998) was an early paper modeling innovation by incumbent firms on their own products. Lucas and Moll (2014) can be interpreted to be in this vein. See chapter 12 of Aghion and Howitt (2009) and chapter 14 of Acemoglu (2011) for models combining own innovation with creative destruction. Other papers with multiple types of innovation include Luttmer (2011), Akcigit and Kerr (2018), and Peters (2020). Atkeson and Burstein

(2019) analyze optimal policy in the presence of multiple innovation channels. They emphasize that the social return to creative destruction is smaller than to own innovation or to the creation of new varieties. From a policy perspective, therefore, we care about the importance of each type of innovation in overall growth.

A very large literature looks at research and development (R&D) spending or patenting to assess innovation inputs or outputs. A classic entry is Kortum (1997), who relates rates of patenting to productivity growth. More recent examples include Kogan et al. (2017) on patent counts and quality, Bloom et al. (2020) on R&D trends, and Acemoglu et al. (2018) on both patents and R&D. Such studies are clearly useful, but they are somewhat constrained by the propensity to patent (which is much higher in manufacturing) and the propensity to report formal R&D spending. Argente et al. (2018) illustrate the limits of patenting data even within consumer products manufacturing, where they find a much higher propensity to patent a new product by large firms compared with small firms. In comparison, an advantage of our indirect approach is that it can be applied to the entire nonfarm business sector, including firms and plants that do not patent or report any R&D spending.

Perhaps the closest paper to ours is Garcia-Macia, Hsieh, and Klenow (2019). They too use LBD data to infer the types of innovation behind US growth in recent decades. The key distinction is that they look only at firms. By using data on plants and assuming plants proxy for varieties produced by a firm, we are able to directly infer the sources of growth. Garcia-Macia et al. (2019) resort to indirect inference and also make simplifying assumptions such as that the step size of innovations is the same for own innovation and creative destruction. We are able to relax this assumption and even allow the step sizes to differ by the size and age of firms.

Our model also features the exit of the lowest-quality products due to obsolescence. Hopenhayn (1992) is a pioneering model with this feature. Hopenhayn, Neira, and Singhania (2018) applies this model to understand the falling entry rate. Akcigit and Ates (2019) and Peters and Walsh (2019) analyze the causes of both falling entry and falling growth. Other efforts to explain lackluster recent growth include Engbom (2019) and Liu, Mian, and Sufi (2019).

Our approach builds on Feenstra (1994), which infers quality and variety growth from a product's market share. Feenstra showed that one can back out underlying quality and variety using a constant elasticity of substitution (CES) demand elasticity and the market share of a product.

Hottman, Redding, and Weinstein (2016) follow the Feenstra approach, and they have the advantage of directly seeing products at a detailed level. They also observe prices and quantities, so they can adjust for markups when inferring a product's quality. Due to data constraints, we abstract from markup dispersion across products. The tradeoff is that we look beyond consumer-packaged goods to the entire nonfarm business sector.

With data on prices and quantities and products, one could adjust not only for markups but for other factors driving a wedge between a plant's employment and the quality and variety of its products. This includes adjustment costs, financial frictions, and capital intensity of production. One could focus more narrowly on US manufacturing and control for such factors. Following Foster, Haltiwanger, and Syverson (2008), one could separate quantity TFP (TFPQ) from revenue TFP (TFPR) by netting out the influence of markups, adjustment costs, factor intensity, and so on—and then apply our direct inference to TFPQ data to determine the sources of innovation. See Hsieh and Klenow (2009, 2014) and Eslava and Haltiwanger (2020) for efforts along these lines.

Just as growth accounting does not require that capital or labor be determined exogenously, our innovative growth accounting does not require that innovation rates be exogenous. For this reason, our accounting is not inconsistent with the literature arguing that innovation rates are sustained only because of growth in research efforts. See, for example, Jones (1995) and Bloom et al. (2017).

Less consistent with our approach are decompositions of productivity growth into within-firm, reallocation, and entry-exit terms by Baily, Hulten, and Campbell (1992), Griliches and Regev (1995), Olley and Pakes (1996), and Melitz and Polanec (2015). A prominent implementation is Foster, Haltiwanger, and Krizan (2001), and more recent versions are Decker et al. (2017) and Gutiérrez and Philippon (2019). Baqaee and Farhi (2020) show that such statistical decompositions are not derived from explicit general equilibrium models. Thus, although these decompositions provide useful moments that models should match, they do not provide a direct way to infer the sources of innovation and growth.

In particular, the above decompositions use growth in firm labor productivity to evaluate innovation within firms. Figures 3 and 4 compare growth in revenue per worker (labor productivity) to growth in employment for Walmart and Amazon based on Compustat data.[4] For Walmart, employment grew rapidly whereas labor productivity grew comparatively little. For Amazon, revenue productivity did grow markedly, but employment growth was much faster still. Figures A1–A5 cover Microsoft,

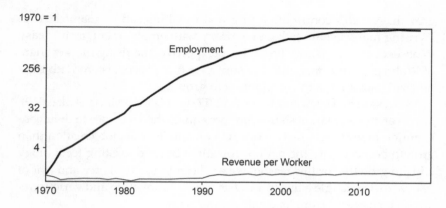

Fig. 3. Walmart. A color version of this figure is available online.

Google, Facebook, Apple, and Starbucks, respectively. For all of these famously innovative firms, employment growth dwarfed growth in revenue per worker. Perhaps these firms innovated by adding more markets and products with similar price-cost markups, thereby boosting their employment rather than their revenue productivity.[5]

In our simple framework, revenue productivity is actually the same across plants and firms, as each plant equates its marginal revenue product of labor to the common wage. In our setup, a firm's revenue productivity does not contain any information about a firm's contribution to

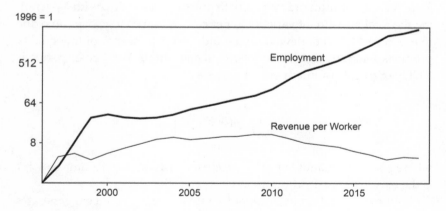

Fig. 4. Amazon. WRDS Compustat and BEA Table 1.1.9. Revenue per worker = "REVT/ (GDP Deflator × EMP);" Employment = "EMP;" Year = "FYEAR." The graph displays revenue per worker and employment relative to the first year when both series are available for the firm. A color version of this figure is available online.

growth. A firm's contribution to growth will instead be manifested in its rising market share (which we proxy with employment, as it is easy to observe and measure). From this perspective, the rising market share of Walmart, Amazon, and other superstar firms is consistent with their outsize innovation and contribution to growth.

As stressed by Hsieh and Klenow (2017) and Garcia-Macia et al. (2019), however, not all market share gains are equal when it comes to their contribution to growth. Creative destruction entails more job creation than growth because only the net improvement beyond existing technology adds to growth. For this reason, we are keen to use the entry and exit of plants to disentangle gains from a firm's own innovation and variety creation versus gains from its creative destruction.

III. Innovation Accounting

This section lays out a model wherein aggregate productivity growth comes from innovation by firms. The model connects a firm's growth contribution to the market share of its entering, surviving, and exiting products. The market share dynamics of its surviving products shed light, in particular, on the rate at which the firm improves its own products.

A. Final Goods Production

There is a continuum of intermediate products $i \in [0, N_t]$, with N_t denoting the total measure of varieties in period t. N_t can change over time due to the introduction of new varieties and the obsolescence of low-quality products. Omitting time subscripts, aggregate output Y in a given period is a CES aggregate of intermediate varieties:

$$Y = \left[\int_0^N [q(i)y(i)]^{\frac{\sigma-1}{\sigma}} di \right]^{\frac{\sigma}{\sigma-1}},$$

where $y(i)$ is the quantity of variety i and $q(i)$ is its quality. Parameter $\sigma > 1$ is the elasticity of substitution between varieties.

Profit maximization by competitive final goods producers generates the demand function for variety i:

$$y(i) = \left(\frac{P(i)}{P} \right)^{-\sigma} q(i)^{\sigma-1} Y, \tag{1}$$

where $P(i)$ is the price of variety i, and P is the aggregate price index

$$P = \left[\int_0^N \left(\frac{P(i)}{q(i)} \right)^{1-\sigma} di \right]^{\frac{1}{1-\sigma}}. \tag{2}$$

Let $p(i) := [P(i)/P]$ denote the relative price of good i. Demand for a product increases with its quality and decreases with its price.

B. Intermediate Goods Production

Each intermediate good i can be produced by a monopolistically competitive producer at a constant marginal cost equal to the competitive wage W. The profit-maximizing price given demand (eq. [1]) is the familiar constant markup over marginal cost:

$$P(i) = \mu \cdot W,$$

where $\mu := (\sigma/\sigma - 1) > 1$. The markup is lower when products are closer substitutes. We can also write the relative price as

$$p(i) = \mu \cdot w$$

where $w := W/P$ is the real marginal cost.

Substituting the aggregate price index (eq. [2]) and the profit-maximizing price into equation (1) yields the expenditure share (and employment share) of a product:

$$s(i) = \frac{P(i)y(i)}{PY} = \frac{l(i)}{L} = \frac{q(i)^{\sigma-1}}{\int_0^N q(i)^{\sigma-1} di}. \tag{3}$$

We can define an aggregate quality index as

$$Q := \left(\int_0^N q(i)^{\sigma-1} di \right)^{\frac{1}{\sigma-1}}.$$

Substituting this definition into equation (3), a product's market share can be written as

$$s(i) = \left(\frac{q(i)}{Q} \right)^{\sigma-1}$$

where the market share increases with relative quality with elasticity $\sigma - 1$.

Growth in this model is due to growth in the aggregate quality index
Q. Using $y(i) = s(i)L$ in the aggregate production function, aggregate
output is

$$Y = \left[\int_0^N (q(i)s(i))^{\frac{\sigma-1}{\sigma}} di \right]^{\frac{\sigma}{\sigma-1}} L = Q \cdot L.$$

We are interested in the growth rate of aggregate productivity Y/L:

$$g_t := \ln\frac{Y_t}{L_t} - \ln\frac{Y_{t-1}}{L_{t-1}} = \ln\frac{Q_t}{Q_{t-1}}$$

C. Innovation

We next describe the innovation process that drives the growth in Q.
We are interested in attributing growth to groups of firms or individual
firms. Let $\mathcal{M}_t$ denote the set of all firms in the economy in period t. The
set of firms can change over time from the entry of new firms and from
the exit of firms that lose all of their products. Let $\mathcal{E}_t$ and $\mathcal{X}_{t-1}$ denote
the set of firms entering and exiting between $t-1$ and t. Let $\mathcal{C}_{t,t-1}$ denote the set of continuing firms that operate in both t and $t-1$. By construction, the set of firms in t is the union of new and continuing firms
$\mathcal{M}_t = \mathcal{E}_t \cup \mathcal{C}_{t,t-1}$, and the set of firms in $t-1$ is the union of exiting and
continuing firms $\mathcal{M}_{t-1} = \mathcal{X}_{t-1} \cup \mathcal{C}_{t,t-1}$.

We denote the set of products produced by firm f in period t as $\mathcal{N}_{ft}$.
The complete set of products produced in t is therefore $\mathcal{N}_t = \{\mathcal{N}_{ft}\}_{f \in \mathcal{M}_t}$.
The set of products produced by a firm and the quality of those products
can change due to innovation. There are three types of innovation: (1) creative destruction, (2) own innovation, and (3) new varieties. With creative
destruction, the producer of an existing product is replaced by a better
producer. In own innovation, a producer innovates on its own products.
A new variety expands the set of products. We allow the arrival rate and
step size of each type of innovation to depend on the innovating firm. In
addition, products disappear due to obsolescence when their quality is below a threshold κ_t, which can rise over time.

Let $\mathcal{NV}_t$, $\mathcal{CD}_t$, $\mathcal{OI}_t$ and $\mathcal{O}_{t-1}$ denote the set of new varieties, creatively
destroyed products, products experiencing own innovation, and those
becoming obsolete between t and $t-1$, respectively. Let $\mathcal{S}_t$ denote the set
of products that are produced in t and $t-1$ with constant quality. The

set of products in t is $\mathcal{N}_t = \mathcal{NV}_t \cup \mathcal{CD}_t \cup \mathcal{OI}_t \cup \mathcal{S}_t$, whereas the set of products in $t-1$ is $\mathcal{N}_{t-1} = \mathcal{O}_{t-1} \cup \mathcal{CD}_t \cup \mathcal{OI}_t \cup \mathcal{S}_t$.

The timing of events in a period is as follows: firms produce, then obsolete products exit, then new varieties enter and existing products are creatively destroyed, and finally own innovation occurs on surviving incumbent products. Quality levels after innovation apply to production in the next period. Our assumption that obsolete products exit before innovation ensures that firms only carry out innovation on products that are not obsolete.

Let $\tilde{x}_{f,t-1}^O$ denote the share of products of firm $f \in \mathcal{M}_{t-1}$ that exit due to obsolescence:

$$\tilde{x}_{f,t-1}^O = \frac{\int_{i \in \mathcal{N}_{f,t-1}} \mathbf{1}\{q_{t-1}(i) < \kappa_t\} di}{N_{f,t-1}} =: G_{f,t-1}(\kappa_t)$$

where $G_{f,t-1}(q)$ is the cumulative distribution of quality for firm f in period $t-1$.

After exit of obsolete products, each surviving firm and new firm $f \in \mathcal{M}_t$ brings in $\nu_{ft} N_{t-1}$ new varieties for production in period t. The quality of a new variety is drawn from the distribution of nonobsolete varieties in period $t-1$ with a step size V_{ft}. These firms may also replace existing producers of $\delta_{ft} N_{t-1}$ nonobsolete products by improving on the quality of those products by step size Δ_{ft}. If the firm f was active in period $t-1$, then it loses some of the products it produced in $t-1$ to creative destruction and obsolescence. For the products it keeps, it randomly innovates on share $\tilde{o}_{ft}$ with step size O_{ft}.

Let $\mathcal{NV}_{ft}$, $\mathcal{CD}_{ft}$, and $\mathcal{OI}_{ft}$ denote the set of products of firm f that are new varieties, were acquired through creative destruction, or underwent own innovation, respectively. Let $\mathcal{X}_{f,t-1}^{CD}$ and $\mathcal{X}_{f,t-1}^O$ denote the set of products that firm f loses through creative destruction and obsolescence, respectively. Finally, let $\mathcal{S}_{ft}$ denote the set of products that f produces in both t and $t-1$ with constant quality. The set of products f produces in t is therefore $\mathcal{N}_{ft} = \mathcal{NV}_{ft} \cup \mathcal{CD}_{ft} \cup \mathcal{OI}_{ft} \cup \mathcal{S}_{ft}$, whereas the set it produces in $t-1$ is $\mathcal{N}_{f,t-1} = \mathcal{X}_{f,t-1}^{CD} \cup \mathcal{X}_{f,t-1}^O \cup \mathcal{S}_{ft}$. A firm exits the market when it does not have any products.

Thus, the share of products in $t-1$ that is subject to creative destruction is

$$\delta_t := \int_{f \in \mathcal{M}_t} \delta_{ft} \, df.$$

Similarly, the rate of arrival of new varieties between $t-1$ and t is

$$\nu_t := \int_{f\in M_t} \nu_{ft}\, df.$$

We need to specify how firms lose their products to creative destruction. Let $\tilde{x}_{f,t-1}^{CD} N_{f,t-1}$ be the number of products a firm active in $t-1$ loses between $t-1$ and t due to creative destruction. In equilibrium, the arrival rate of creative destruction equals the sum of the rate of product exit due to creative destruction. That is,

$$\delta_t = \int_{f\in M_{t-1}} \tilde{x}_{f,t-1}^{CD} \left(\frac{N_{f,t-1}}{N_{t-1}}\right) df = \int_{f\in M_{t-1}} x_{f,t-1}^{CD}\, df,$$

where $x_{f,t-1}^{CD} := \tilde{x}_{f,t-1}^{CD}(N_{f,t-1}/N_{t-1})$. For simplicity, we assume creative destruction is random so that all firms lose the same fraction of nonobsolete products, denoted by $\hat{\delta}_t$.[6] This implies that, for all firms in $t-1$,

$$\tilde{x}_{f,t-1}^{CD} = \hat{\delta}_t\left[1 - G_{f,t-1}(\kappa_t)\right].$$

Therefore, the share of products of a firm in $t-1$ that are not produced by the firm in t is

$$\tilde{x}_{f,t-1} = \tilde{x}_{f,t-1}^{O} + \tilde{x}_{f,t-1}^{CD} = G_{f,t-1}(\kappa_t) + \hat{\delta}_t\left[1 - G_{f,t-1}(\kappa_t)\right],$$

and the aggregate exit rate of product from producers at the end of $t-1$ is

$$x_{t-1} = \int_{f\in M_{t-1}} \tilde{x}_{f,t-1} \frac{N_{f,t-1}}{N_{t-1}}\, df = G_{t-1}(\kappa_t) + \hat{\delta}_t[1 - G_{t-1}(\kappa_t)].$$

The net growth rate in the number of varieties N_t is the difference between the rate of new variety arrival and the rate of obsolescence:

$$N_t = [1 + \nu_t - G_{t-1}(\kappa_t)] \cdot N_{t-1}.$$

Recall that $\tilde{o}_{ft}$ is the fraction of the products that survive both creative destruction and obsolescence which experience own innovation by incumbent firm f. The share of products of firm f that experience own innovation is

$$\tilde{o}_{ft} \cdot (1 - \tilde{x}_{f,t-1}^{CD} - \tilde{x}_{f,t-1}^{O}) = \tilde{o}_{ft} \cdot (1 - \hat{\delta}_t) \cdot \left[1 - G_{f,t-1}(\kappa_t)\right]$$

and the share of all products in $t - 1$ that experience own innovation is

$$(1 - \hat{\delta}_t) \int_{f \in \mathcal{M}_{t-1}} \tilde{o}_{ft} \left[1 - G_{f,t-1}(\kappa_t)\right] \left(\frac{N_{f,t-1}}{N_{t-1}}\right) df.$$

D. Aggregate Productivity Growth

Having laid out the innovation process, how does this process translate into aggregate productivity growth? Using $\mathcal{N}_t = \mathcal{N}\mathcal{V}_t \cup \mathcal{CD}_t \cup \mathcal{OI}_t \cup \mathcal{S}_t$, we can decompose growth $g_t = \ln(Q_t/Q_{t-1})$ into innovation types:

$$e^g = \left(\frac{\int_{i \in \mathcal{N}_t} q_t(i)^{\sigma-1} di}{\int_{i \in \mathcal{N}_{t-1}} q_{t-1}(i)^{\sigma-1} di}\right)^{\frac{1}{\sigma-1}}$$

$$\quad \quad (4)$$

$$= \left(\frac{\int_{i \in \mathcal{N}\mathcal{V}_t} q_t(i)^{\sigma-1} di + \int_{i \in \mathcal{CD}_t} q_t(i)^{\sigma-1} di + \int_{i \in \mathcal{OI}_t} q_t(i)^{\sigma-1} di + \int_{i \in \mathcal{S}_t} q_t(i)^{\sigma-1} di}{\int_{i \in \mathcal{N}_{t-1}} q_{t-1}(i)^{\sigma-1} di}\right)^{\frac{1}{\sigma-1}}$$

The first term on the right-hand side captures new varieties. Because the quality of new varieties is drawn randomly from the distribution of nonobsolete products (plus a firm-specific step size), this term simplifies to

$$\frac{\int_{i \in \mathcal{N}\mathcal{V}_t} q_t(i)^{\sigma-1} di}{\int_{i \in \mathcal{N}_{t-1}} q_{t-1}(i)^{\sigma-1} di} = \frac{\int_{f \in \mathcal{M}_t} \nu_f N_{t-1} \frac{(V_f \hat{Q}_{t-1})^{\sigma-1}}{N_{t-1}} df}{Q_{t-1}^{\sigma-1}} = \left(\int_{f \in \mathcal{M}_t} \nu_f V_f^{\sigma-1} df\right) \left(\frac{\hat{Q}}{Q}\right)^{\sigma-1},$$

where $\hat{Q}^{\sigma-1} := N_{t-1} \mathbb{E}_{G_{t-1}}(q^{\sigma-1} | q \geq \kappa_t)$ is the aggregate quality of nonobsolete products. Because $\hat{Q} \geq Q$, a given arrival rate of innovation (ν_t) generates more growth when the innovation happens on nonobsolete products. Hence, we will refer to

$$\int_{f \in \mathcal{M}_t} \nu_f V_f^{\sigma-1} df$$

as the growth contribution of new varieties and refer to

$$\left(\int_{f \in \mathcal{M}_t} \nu_f V_f^{\sigma-1} df\right) \left(\left(\frac{\hat{Q}}{Q}\right)^{\sigma-1} - 1\right)$$

as the contribution of obsolescence to growth. This Hopenhayn term is the interaction of selection and innovation.

With the assumption that creative destruction is random, we can simplify the second term in equation (4) to

$$\frac{\int_{f\in\mathcal{M}_t}\Delta_f^{\sigma-1}\int_{i\in CD_{ft}}q_{t-1}(i)^{\sigma-1}di\,df}{Q_{t-1}^{\sigma-1}}=\left(\int_{f\in\mathcal{M}_t}\delta_f\Delta_f^{\sigma-1}df\right)\left(\frac{\hat{Q}}{Q}\right)^{\sigma-1}$$

The third term in equation (4) is due to incumbent own innovation and therefore only applies to continuing firms. It is equal to

$$(1-\hat{\delta}_t)\int_{f\in\mathcal{C}_{t,t-1}}\tilde{o}_{ft}O_f^{\sigma-1}\int_{i\in\mathcal{N}_{ft-1},q_{t-1}(i)\geq\kappa_t}\frac{q_{t-1}^{\sigma-1}(i)}{Q_{t-1}^{\sigma-1}}di\,df$$

$$=(1-\hat{\delta}_t)\left(\frac{\hat{Q}}{Q}\right)^{\sigma-1}\int_{f\in\mathcal{C}_{t,t-1}}\tilde{o}_{ft}(1-G_{f,t-1}(\kappa_t))O_f^{\sigma-1}\frac{N_{f,t-1}\mathbb{E}_{G_{f,t-1}}(q^{\sigma-1}|q\geq\kappa_t)}{Q_{t-1}^{\sigma-1}}df$$

$$=\left(\frac{\hat{Q}}{Q}\right)^{\sigma-1}\int_{f\in\mathcal{C}_{t,t-1}}o_{ft}O_f^{\sigma-1}\frac{\mathbb{E}_{G_{f,t-1}}(q^{\sigma-1}|q\geq\kappa_t)}{\mathbb{E}_{G_{t-1}}(q^{\sigma-1}|q\geq\kappa_t)}df$$

where $o_{ft}:=\tilde{o}_{ft}(1-\hat{\delta}_t)(1-G_{f,t-1}(\kappa_t))(N_{f,t-1}/N_{t-1})$ denotes the arrival rate of own innovation by f relative to the total number of products in $t-1$.

The fourth term in equation (4) contains products that survive creative destruction and obsolescence but do not experience own innovation. This term is equal to

$$(1-\hat{\delta}_t)\int_{f\in\mathcal{C}_{t,t-1}}(1-\tilde{o}_{ft})\int_{i\in\mathcal{N}_{ft-1},q_{t-1}(i)\geq\kappa_t}\frac{q_{t-1}^{\sigma-1}(i)}{Q_{t-1}^{\sigma-1}}di\,df$$

$$=\left(\frac{\hat{Q}}{Q}\right)^{\sigma-1}(1-\hat{\delta}_t)\int_{f\in\mathcal{C}_{t,t-1}}(1-\tilde{o}_{ft})\left[\frac{(1-G_{f,t-1}(\kappa_t))N_{f,t-1}}{N_{t-1}}\right]\left[\frac{\mathbb{E}_{G_{f,t-1}(\kappa_t)}(q^{\sigma-1}|q\geq\kappa_t)}{\mathbb{E}_{G_{t-1}}(q^{\sigma-1}|q\geq\kappa_t)}\right]df.$$

The third and fourth terms in equation (4) combined equals the net change in quality of products that are produced by the same producer in t and $t-1$:

$$\left(\frac{\hat{Q}}{Q}\right)^{\sigma-1}\int_{f\in\mathcal{C}_{t,t-1}}o_{ft}(O_f^{\sigma-1}-1)\left[\frac{\mathbb{E}_{G_{f,t-1}}(q^{\sigma-1}|q\geq\kappa_t)}{\mathbb{E}_{G_{t-1}}(q^{\sigma-1}|q\geq\kappa_t)}\right]df$$

$$+\left(\frac{\hat{Q}}{Q}\right)^{\sigma-1}(1-G_{t-1}(\kappa_t)-\delta_t)$$

where the second line comes from

$$\delta_t = \int_{f\in\mathcal{M}_t} \delta_{ft}\, df = \hat{\delta}_t \int_{f\in\mathcal{M}_{t-1}} \left[1 - G_{f,t-1}(\kappa_t)\right] \left(\frac{N_{f,t-1}}{N_{t-1}}\right) df.$$

Combining our derivations for the right-hand-side terms of equation (4), we can express aggregate growth in terms of arrival rates and step sizes.

$$
\begin{aligned}
e^{g(\sigma-1)} = 1 &+ \int_{f\in\mathcal{M}_t} \nu_f V_f^{\sigma-1} + \delta_f(\Delta_f^{\sigma-1} - 1)df + \int_{f\in\mathcal{C}_{t,t-1}} o_{ft}(O_f^{\sigma-1} - 1)\left[\frac{\mathbb{E}_{G_{f,t-1}}(q^{\sigma-1})}{\mathbb{E}_{G_{t-1}}(q^{\sigma-1})}\right] df \\
&+ \left(\int_{f\in\mathcal{M}_t} \nu_f V_f^{\sigma-1} + \delta_f(\Delta_f^{\sigma-1} - 1)df\right)\left(\left(\frac{\hat{Q}}{Q}\right)^{\sigma-1} - 1\right) \\
&+ \int_{f\in\mathcal{C}_{t,t-1}} o_{ft}(O_f^{\sigma-1} - 1)\left[\frac{\mathbb{E}_{G_{f,t-1}}(q^{\sigma-1}|q \geq \kappa_t) - \mathbb{E}_{G_{f,t-1}}(q^{\sigma-1})}{\mathbb{E}_{G_{t-1}}(q^{\sigma-1})}\right] df \\
&- \left(1 - \left(\frac{\hat{Q}}{Q}\right)^{\sigma-1}\left[1 - G_{t-1}(\kappa_t)\right]\right).
\end{aligned}
$$

(5)

The first line of the right-hand side of equation (5) is the sum of the growth contributions from new varieties, creative destruction, and own innovation. The second and third lines on the right-hand side of equation (5) are positive contributions from obsolescence through selection, whereas the last line is the negative contribution based on the market share in $t - 1$ of varieties lost to obsolescence.

E. Firm Contribution to Growth

In addition to decomposing growth into types of innovation and obsolescence, we are also interested accounting for the contribution of firms or groups of firms. Define the contribution of firm $f \in \mathcal{M}_t \cup \mathcal{X}_{t-1}$ to growth

$$
\begin{aligned}
g_f :=\ &\nu_f V_f^{\sigma-1} + \delta_f(\Delta_f^{\sigma-1} - 1) \\
&+ o_f N_{t-1}(O_f^{\sigma-1} - 1)\mathbb{E}_{G_{f,t-1}}[s_{t-1}] \\
&+ o_f N_{t-1}(O_f^{\sigma-1} - 1)(\mathbb{E}_{G_{f,t-1}}[s_{t-1}|q \geq \kappa] - \mathbb{E}_{G_{f,t-1}}[s_{t-1}]) \\
&+ \left(\int_{j\in\mathcal{M}_t} \nu_j V_j^{\sigma-1} + \delta_j(\Delta_j^{\sigma-1} - 1)dj\right)\left(\left(\frac{\hat{Q}}{Q}\right)^{\sigma-1} - 1\right)\left[\frac{G_{f,t-1}(\kappa)N_{f,t-1}}{G_{t-1}(\kappa)N_{t-1}}\right] \\
&- \mathbb{E}_{G_{f,t-1}}[s_{t-1}|q < \kappa]G_{f,t-1}(\kappa)N_{f,t-1},
\end{aligned}
$$

(6)

where s_{t-1} is the market share of a product in $t-1$ and we abbreviated the subscript t. The first two lines on the right-hand side of equation (6) are firm f's contribution through new varieties, creative destruction, and own innovation. The third line is the positive contribution from own innovation focusing on nonobsolete products. The fourth line captures the contribution of obsolescence through improving the quality distribution that new varieties and creative destruction build upon. To attribute the aggregate contribution of obsolescence to individual firms, we multiply the fourth line by firm f's share of obsolete products. The final line is firm f's negative contribution to growth from losing its obsolete varieties.

For new firms, g_f simplifies to their contributions from new varieties and creative destruction, respectively:

$$g_f = \nu_f V_f^{\sigma-1} + \delta_f(\Delta_f^{\sigma-1} - 1).$$

Firms that exit, meanwhile, contribute only through obsolescence:

$$g_f = \left(\int_{j \in M_t} \nu_j V_j^{\sigma-1} + \delta_j(\Delta_j^{\sigma-1} - 1)dj \right) \left(\left(\frac{\hat{Q}}{Q} \right)^{\sigma-1} - 1 \right) \left[\frac{G_{f,t-1}(\kappa)N_{f,t-1}}{G_{t-1}(\kappa)N_{t-1}} \right]$$
$$- \mathbb{E}_{G_{f,t-1}}[s_{t-1}|q < \kappa]G_{f,t-1}(\kappa)N_{f,t-1}$$

Using $\ln(1 + x) \approx x$, we can approximate the growth rate by

$$g = \frac{1}{\sigma - 1} \ln \left(1 + \int_{f \in M_t \cup X_{t-1}} g_f \, df \right) \approx \frac{1}{\sigma - 1} \int_{f \in M_t \cup X_{t-1}} g_f \, df.$$

This allows us to define the share of growth coming from firm f as

$$c_f := \frac{g_f}{\int_{f \in M_t \cup X_{t-1}} g_f \, df}.$$

Similarly, we define the contribution of a group of firms $\mathcal{F} \subset (M_t \cup X_{t-1})$ as

$$c_{\mathcal{F}} := \frac{\int_{f \in \mathcal{F}} g_f \, df}{\int_{f \in M_t \cup X_{t-1}} g_f \, df}.$$

IV.   Calibration

In the previous section, we laid out our model of how product innovation contributes to growth. In this section we will describe how to relate the arrival rates and step sizes of innovation to moments we observe in the data.

Let k be any nonnegative number. For a set of products $\mathcal{P}$, the kth noncentered moment of market share is

$$S_{\mathcal{P}t}^{\{k\}} := \int_{i \in \mathcal{P}} s_t(i)^k \, di = \int_{i \in \mathcal{P}} \left(\frac{q_t(i)}{Q_t} \right)^{k(\sigma-1)} di \,.$$

If $\mathcal{CD}_{ft}$ is the group of products that firm f creatively destroyed between $t-1$ and t with step size Δ,

$$
\begin{aligned}
S_{\mathcal{CD}_{ft}}^{\{k\}} &= \int_{i \in \mathcal{CD}_{ft}} \left(\frac{\Delta q_{t-1}(i)}{Q_{t-1}} \frac{Q_{t-1}}{Q_t} \right)^{(\sigma-1)k} di \\
&= \left(\frac{\Delta}{e^g} \right)^{(\sigma-1)k} \int_{i \in \mathcal{CD}_{ft}} \left(\frac{q_{t-1}(i)}{Q_{t-1}} \right)^{(\sigma-1)k} di \\
&= \left(\frac{\Delta}{e^g} \right)^{(\sigma-1)k} \int_{i \in \mathcal{CD}_{ft}} s_{t-1}(i)^k \, di \\
&= \delta_{ft} \left(\frac{\Delta}{e^g} \right)^{(\sigma-1)k} \mathbb{E}_{G_{t-1}} (s_{t-1}^k | q \geq \kappa_t) N_{t-1}
\end{aligned}
$$

The second-to-last equality holds because, conditional on nonobsolescence, the arrival of creative destruction innovation is independent of $q_{t-1}(i)$.

For $\mathcal{NV}_{ft}$ the set of new varieties introduced by firm f,

$$S_{\mathcal{NV}_{ft}}^{\{k\}} = \nu_{ft} \left(\frac{V_{ft}}{e^g} \right)^{(\sigma-1)k} \mathbb{E}_{G_{t-1}} (s_{t-1}^k | q \geq \kappa_t) N_{t-1} \,.$$

Let $\mathcal{EF}_t$ be the set of new products introduced by a group of firms $\mathcal{F}$ with the same arrival rate and step size for creative destruction and new varieties. Applying the above derivations, we map the kth moments of the employment share of these products to

$$S_{\mathcal{E}_{\mathcal{F}t}}^{\{k\}} = S_{\mathcal{N}\mathcal{V}_{\mathcal{F}t}}^{\{k\}} + S_{\mathcal{CD}_{\mathcal{F}t}}^{\{k\}}$$

$$\frac{S_{\mathcal{E}_{\mathcal{F}t}}^{\{k\}}/E_{\mathcal{F}t}}{\mathbb{E}_{G_{t-1}}(s_{t-1}^k | q \geq \kappa_t)} = \left(\frac{N_{t-1}\nu_{\mathcal{F}}}{E_{\mathcal{F}t}} \left(\frac{V_{\mathcal{F}}}{e^g} \right)^{(\sigma-1)k} + \frac{N_{t-1}\delta_{\mathcal{F}}}{E_{\mathcal{F}t}} \left(\frac{\Delta_{\mathcal{F}}}{e^g} \right)^{(\sigma-1)k} \right), \tag{7}$$

where $\mathcal{E}_{\mathcal{F}t}$ is the *number* of new products introduced by $\mathcal{F}$.

Equation (7) says the noncentered kth moment of entering products of firm group $\mathcal{F}$ relative to the noncentered kth moment of all nonobsolete products in the previous period is equal to the average step size of these products' innovation relative to the aggregate growth rate. A group of products that have higher innovation step size has higher relative kth moment. This relationship holds for all k. We will use data on g (the aggregate TFP growth rate) and on S^k moments for $k = 0, 1, 2, 3$, plus the restrictions $V_{\mathcal{F}} > 0$ and $\Delta_{\mathcal{F}} > 1$, to infer $\nu_{\mathcal{F}}$, $V_{\mathcal{F}}$, $\delta_{\mathcal{F}}$, and $\Delta_{\mathcal{F}}$.

To estimate the contribution of an incumbent's own innovation, let $\mathcal{P}_f$ be the set of products that f produces in both $t-1$ and t. The market share growth for these products is

$$\frac{S_{\mathcal{P}_{ft}}}{S_{\mathcal{P}_{f,t-1}}} = \frac{\int_{i \in \mathcal{P}} q_t(i)^{\sigma-1} di}{\int_{i \in \mathcal{P}} q_{t-1}(i)^{\sigma-1} di} \left(\frac{Q_{t-1}}{Q_t} \right)^{\sigma-1}$$

$$= \frac{(1 + \tilde{o}_f(O_f^{\sigma-1} - 1))(1 - \hat{\delta}_t) \int_{i \in \mathcal{N}_{f,t-1}, q_{t-1}(i) \geq \kappa_t} q_{t-1}(i)^{\sigma-1} di}{(1 - \hat{\delta}_t) \int_{i \in \mathcal{N}_{f,t-1}, q_{t-1}(i) \geq \kappa_t} q_{t-1}(i)^{\sigma-1} di} \left(\frac{Q_{t-1}}{Q_t} \right)^{\sigma-1} \tag{8}$$

$$= \frac{1 + \tilde{o}_{ft}(O_f^{\sigma-1} - 1)}{e^{g(\sigma-1)}}.$$

The market share of the firm's continuing products grows if their realized average quality improvement exceeds the aggregate growth rate.

To estimate the negative contribution of obsolescence, we need to distinguish product exits due to obsolescence from product exits due to creative destruction. The share of firm f's products that it loses to obsolescence or creative destruction is

$$\frac{x_{f,t-1}N_{t-1}}{N_{ft-1}} = \hat{\delta}_t \left[1 - G_{f,t-1}(\kappa_t) \right] + G_{f,t-1}(\kappa_t). \tag{9}$$

The share of firm f's sales that belong to products it loses to obsolescence or creative destruction is

$$\frac{S_{x_{f,t-1}}}{N_{f,t-1}\mathbb{E}_{G_{f,t-1}}(s_{t-1})} = \hat{\delta}_t\left[1 - G_{f,t-1}(\kappa_t)\right]\left[\frac{\mathbb{E}_{G_{f,t-1}}(s_{t-1}|q \geq \kappa_t)}{\mathbb{E}_{G_{f,t-1}}(s_{t-1})}\right]$$
$$+ G_{f,t-1}(\kappa_t)\left[\frac{\mathbb{E}_{G_{f,t-1}}(s_{t-1}|q < \kappa_t)}{\mathbb{E}_{G_{f,t-1}}(s_{t-1})}\right] \qquad (10)$$

Because creative destruction is random while obsolescence is selected, the share of firm f's sales belonging to products it loses is smaller than the share of products it loses when it loses some its products to obsolescence. The gap increases with the share of exit that is obsolescence. This relationship helps us to distinguish between creative destruction and obsolescence.

Summing the exit rates across firms and summing the exiting product market shares across firms yield the aggregate exit rate and aggregate market share of exiting products:

$$x_t = \int_{f \in M_{t-1}} \left[\hat{\delta}_t + (1 - \hat{\delta}_t)G_{f,t-1}(\kappa_t)\right]\left(\frac{N_{f,t-1}}{N_{t-1}}\right)df = \hat{\delta}_t + (1 - \hat{\delta}_t)G_{t-1}(\kappa_t) \qquad (11)$$

$$S_{X,t-1} = \hat{\delta}_t \int_{i \in N_{t-1}, q_{t-1} > \kappa_t} s_{t-1}(i)\, di + \int_{i \in N_{t-1}}^{\kappa_t} s_{t-1}(i)\, di. \qquad (12)$$

Using equation (11), the exit rate can be rewritten as

$$\hat{\delta}_t = \frac{x_t - G_{t-1}(\kappa_t)}{1 - G_{t-1}(\kappa_t)}.$$

Substituting this expression into equation (12) yields

$$S_{X,t-1} = \frac{x_t - G_{t-1}(\kappa_t)}{1 - G_{t-1}(\kappa_t)} \int_{i \in N_{t-1}, q_{t-1} > \kappa_t} s_{t-1}(i)\, di + \int_{i \in N_{t-1}}^{\kappa_t} s_{t-1}(i)\, di. \qquad (13)$$

Holding fixed the exit rate, increasing κ_t lowers the market share of products exiting due to obsolescence or creative destruction. Instead of randomly replacing a fraction of the producers, increasing κ_t removes products with the smallest market share. Conditional on $\hat{\delta}_t$, we can use equation (9) to back out $G_{f,t-1}(\kappa_t)$.

Because the $t - 1$ market share of a firm's continuing products is

$$(1 - \hat{\delta}_t)\left[1 - G_{f,t-1}(\kappa_t)\right]N_{f,t-1}\mathbb{E}_{G_{f,t-1}}(s_{t-1}|q \geq \kappa_t),$$

we can use data on the $t-1$ market share of a firm's continuing products and equation (10) to infer the market share of obsolete products of firm f and hence calculate the negative contribution to growth from the firm.

We also need $\hat{Q}/Q$ to calculate the positive contribution of obsolescence. This term can be rewritten as

$$\frac{N_{t-1}[1 - G_{t-1}(\kappa_t)]\,\mathbb{E}_{G_{t-1}}(s_{t-1}|q \geq \kappa_t)}{1 - [G_{t-1}(\kappa_t)]} \tag{14}$$

This is none other than the market share of nonobsolete products divided by the share of nonobsolete products. This can be calculated using $\hat{\delta}_t$, $G_{t-1}(\kappa_t)$ and data on the $t-1$ market share of incumbent firms continuing products.

A. Measuring Products

We calibrate the model to the LBD plant-level data from the Census Bureau. To make progress, we assume that each plant produces one product and that all new varieties and creative destruction occur through new plants. This enables us to use plant entry and exit to measure the arrival rate of new varieties and creative destruction within firms.

We partition firms in each period into groups. For example, a group can be new firms (age 0) with fewer than 20 employees. Then the set of new and exiting products by the firm group, $\mathcal{E}_{\mathcal{F},t}$ and $\mathcal{X}_{\mathcal{F},t-1}$ respectively, maps into the set of new and exiting plants of the firm group in the data. The set of all products $\mathcal{N}_t$ maps to the total set of plants in the data. The arrival rates in the model map to the arrival rate of plants in the data. The market share of products map into to the employment shares of plants in the data. Table 1 summarizes the parameters for calibration and the data targets.

We carry out calibration in four steps. First, we use equation (8) plus the change in the employment share of surviving plants to calibrate the own innovation parameters relative to the aggregate growth rate. Given g and σ, these moments map directly into the composite arrival rate and step size of own innovation by a group of firms: $(1 + \tilde{o}_{\mathcal{F}}[O_{\mathcal{F}}^{\sigma-1} - 1])/e^{g(\sigma-1)}$. Second, we calibrate the arrival rate and step size of new varieties and creative destruction $\{v_{\mathcal{F}}, \delta_{\mathcal{F}}, V_{\mathcal{F}}/e^{g}, \Delta_{\mathcal{F}}/e^{g}\}$ to fit the employment share moments of entering plants in equation (7) for $k = 0, 1, 2, 3$.[7] Third, we sum the calibrated $\delta_{\mathcal{F}}$ across $\mathcal{F}$ to arrive at the aggregate rate of creative destruction δ. We substitute δ into the aggregate exit rate, and exiting plant employment share equations (11) and (13) to back out the

Table 1
Parameters and Data Targets

	Calibrated Parameters
$\nu_{\mathcal{F}}$	Arrival rate of NV by firm group $\mathcal{F}$
$V_{\mathcal{F}}$	Step size of NV by firm group $\mathcal{F}$
$\delta_{\mathcal{F}}$	Arrival rate of CD by firm group $\mathcal{F}$
$\Delta_{\mathcal{F}}$	Step size of CD by firm group $\mathcal{F}$
$o_{\mathcal{F}}(O_{\mathcal{F}}^{\sigma-1} - 1)$	Contribution of OI by firm group $\mathcal{F}$
κ	Cutoff quality of obsolescence
δ	Total rate of creative destruction

	Assigned parameter
σ	Elasticity of substitution

	Data targets
$\frac{\mathcal{E}_{\mathcal{F}t}}{N_{t-1}}$	Number of new plants by firm group $\mathcal{F}$
$\frac{X_{\mathcal{F},t-1}}{N_{t-1}}$	Number of exiting plants by firm group $\mathcal{F}$ in $t-1$
$S_{\mathcal{E}_{\mathcal{F}t}}$	Employment share of new plants by firm group $\mathcal{F}$ in t
$S_{X_{\mathcal{F},t-1}}$	Employment share of exiting plants by firm groups $\mathcal{F}$ in $t-1$
$\frac{S_{C_{\mathcal{F}t}}}{S_{C_{\mathcal{F},t-1}}}$	Growth in employment share of continuing plants by firm group $\mathcal{F}$
$S_{\mathcal{E}_{\mathcal{F}t}}^{\{2\}}$	2nd moment of employment share of new plants by firm group $\mathcal{F}$ in t
$S_{\mathcal{E}_{\mathcal{F}t}}^{\{3\}}$	3rd moment of employment share of new plants by firm group $\mathcal{F}$ in t
$S_{N_{t-1}}^{\{k\}}$	kth moment of employment share of all plants in $t-1$ for $k=0,1,2,3$
g	TFP growth rate

Note: $S_{\mathcal{P}t}^{\{k\}} \equiv \int_{\mathcal{P}} s_t^k(i)\, di$. CD = creative destruction; NV = new varieties; OI = own innovation; TFP = total factor productivity.

rate of obsolescence and the employment share associated with obsolescence. Fourth and finally, we recover the level of step sizes by multiplying the relative step sizes by the measured aggregate TFP growth rate in the data. When a resulting step size violates a minimum boundary condition—for example, when it is negative or when $\Delta_{\mathcal{F}} < 1$—we set that particular step size to the minimum. We check the validity of our estimates by comparing the fit of the model to the growth rate.[8]

V. Results

A. Data

We use the LBD data from the Census Bureau to calculate moments related to firms. We use the BLS multifactor productivity series to calculate productivity growth. We have access to the LBD data from 1976 to 2013. We partition the firms into age and size bins, where age is the number of years since the first plant of the firm enters the data set and size is the total

employment across all of plants of the firm in the previous year.[9] The age
bins are 0, 1–5, 6–10, and 11+, and the size bins are 0, 1–19, 20–249, 250–
999, 1,000–4,999, 5,000–9,999, and 10,000+. New firms are in the age 0 and
size 0 bin.

To observe firms aged 6+, the earliest year we can start is 1982. Productivity growth in the United States surged from 1996 to 2005. We divide the years into the prior period (1982–1995, average 1.15% growth
per year), the burst period (1996–2005, 2.82% per year), and afterward
(2006–2013, 1.03% per year). We target averages of entry, exit, productivity growth, and so on over each subperiod.

Table 2 presents some of the key data moments from the LBD that we
use to estimate arrival rates and step sizes. For conciseness, we average
them across all years in the table. The moments shown include the plant
entry rate, the employment share of new plants, and the employment
share of continuing plants in the current year relative to their share in
the previous year. Size 0 plants are those of new firms.[10]

Table 2
Data Moments by Age-Size Groups, 1982–2013

Age	Size	Entry Rate	Entry Emp. Share	$\frac{S_E^2}{S_N^2}$	$\frac{S_E^3}{S_N^3}$	Survivor Growth
0	0	8.99	3.10	2.54	3.52	NA
1–5	1–19	.12	.06	.04	.05	1.15
1–5	20–249	.11	.10	.02	.01	1.00
1–5	250–999	.04	.06	.02	0	.97
1–5	1k–4999	.03	.04	.04	.02	.95
1–5	5k–9999	.01	.02	.05	.08	.86
6–10	1–19	.11	.05	.09	.17	.99
6–10	20–249	.07	.06	.02	.02	.91
6–10	250–999	.04	.04	.01	0	.90
6–10	1k–4999	.03	.04	.04	.04	.91
6–10	5k–9999	.01	.02	.01	.01	.89
6–10	10k+	.01	.02	.04	.05	.89
11+	1–19	.26	.18	.39	.74	.98
11+	20–249	.18	.14	.07	.10	.91
11+	250–999	.15	.15	.06	.09	.91
11+	1k–4999	.23	.26	.19	.21	.91
11+	5k–9999	.13	.14	.15	.22	.91
11+	10k+	.58	.76	.72	.87	.90

Source: Census LBD.
Note: Firm size is the sum of employment across all of its plants. Firm age is the difference
between the year of observation and the birth year of the firm's first plant. "Entry rate" =
number of new plant divided by lagged total number of plants; "Entry emp. share" = employment share of new plants; "S_E^l/S_N^k" = new plant kth moment relative to all plants. Units
are %. "Survivor growth" = continuing plants employment share in t over employment
share in $t - 1$; Emp. = employment.

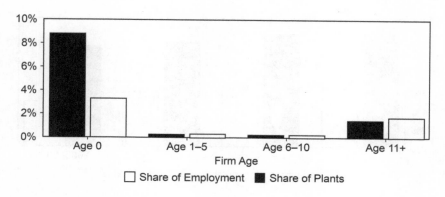

Fig. 5. Employment and plant share of new plants by firm age (%). Census LBD. A color version of this figure is available online.

Figure 2 in the introduction showed the generally declining employment shares of new plants and new firms over our 1982–2013 sample. Figure 5 illustrates that new plants at new firms are generally smaller than the average new plant; their share of new plant employment is less than half their share of all new plants. Figure 6 similarly shows that the new plants of smaller firms are typically smaller than the new plants of larger firms. Figure 7 indicates that exiting plants are smaller than surviving plants, as their employment share is about one-half as big as their share of plants. Figure 8 demonstrates that the employment share of continuing plants grew modestly in all three subperiods.

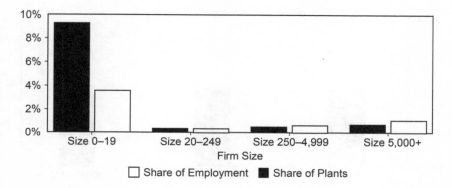

Fig. 6. Employment and plant share of new plants by firm size (%). Census LBD. A color version of this figure is available online.

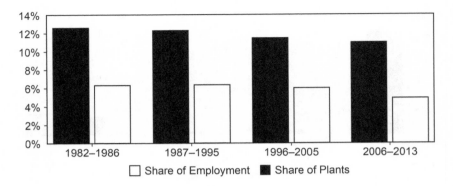

Fig. 7. Employment and plant share of exiting plants (%). Census LBD. A color version of this figure is available online.

B. Results: Parameter Estimates and Model Fit

Table 3 presents the parameters we estimate based on the moments in table 2. As above, the lower cases are arrival rates and upper cases are step sizes. The table provides these statistics by age-size group.

In table 4 we compare the growth rate in the data to that in our model. When we do not hit any corners, our calibration strategy fits the growth rate by construction. The table shows that we deviate slightly from the actual growth rates. This is because some parameters hit corner values (such as step sizes being no lower than 1 for creative destruction). Overall, the deviation is small, and the model fits the data well. The largest deviation is in the 1982–1986 period.

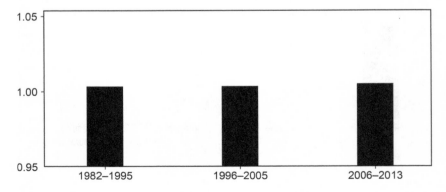

Fig. 8. Growth rate of employment share of continuing plants. Census LBD. A color version of this figure is available online.

Table 3
Calibrated Innovation Parameter by Age-Size Groups, 1982–2013

Age	Size	v_f	V_f	δ_f	Δ_f	$\tilde{o}_f(O_f - 1)$
0	0	.081	.602	.009	1.184	0
1–5	1–19	.001	.657	0	1.032	.213
1–5	20–249	.001	.985	.001	1.009	.056
1–5	250–999	0	1.113	0	1.116	.027
1–5	1k–4999	0	1.210	0	1.211	.013
1–5	5k–9999	0	.916	0	1.351	0
6–10	1–19	.001	.301	0	1.193	.123
6–10	20–249	.001	.929	0	1.046	.039
6–10	250–999	0	1.071	0	1.070	.027
6–10	1k–4999	0	1.202	0	1.102	.033
6–10	5k–9999	0	1.297	0	1.184	.014
6–10	10k+	0	.956	0	1.259	.017
11+	1–19	.002	.028	.001	1.232	.104
11+	20–249	.001	.943	.001	1.222	.036
11+	250–999	0	.994	.001	1.020	.037
11+	1k–4999	0	1.183	.002	1.059	.037
11+	5k–9999	0	1.280	.001	1.039	.035
11+	10k+	0	1.164	.006	1.119	.029

Source: Census LBD.
Note: Firm size is the sum of employment across all of its plants. Firm age is the difference between the year of observation and the birth year of the firm's first plant.

C. Results: Types of Innovation

We first decompose growth by innovation type over the entire 1982–2013 period in table 5. We estimate that, on average, 60% of growth comes from own innovation, whereas new varieties contribute about 27% and creative destruction the remaining 13%.

Table 4
Fit of Model

Period	Data g	Model g
1982–1986	1.25	1.33
1987–1995	1.10	1.13
1996–2005	2.82	2.83
2006–2013	1.03	1.03

Source: US Bureau of Labor Statistics (BLS) multifactor productivity (MFP) series.
Note: Percentage points of average yearly productivity growth within the specified period. Yearly growth is the sum of research and development and IP contributions to BLS MFP growth, converted into labor augmenting form.

Table 5
Growth by Innovation Type, 1982–2013

g	CD	NV	OI
1.64	.21	.38	1.06
	13.0%	27.2%	59.8%

Source: US Bureau of Labor Statistics (BLS) multifactor productivity (MFP) series.
Note: Percentage points of average yearly productivity growth within the specified period. Yearly growth is the sum of research and development and IP contributions to BLS MFP growth, converted into labor augmenting form. All other variables are calculated using the Census LBD. CD = creative destruction; NV = new varieties; OI = own innovation (incumbents improving on their own varieties).

Looking at subperiods in table 6, we see that own innovation generated 50% of growth in the slow-growth periods (1982–1995 and 2006–2013) and 70% of growth in the high-growth middle period (1996–2005). Table 7 shows that all three sources of growth rose in the 1996–2005 period and fell back again afterward. But the bulk of the acceleration (91%) and the subsequent slowdown (82%) were due to innovation by incumbent firms on their own products. This finding may be surprising in light of figure 8, which showed that the growth of continuing plants did not accelerate in the period 1996–2005 or decelerate afterwards. Growth of all surviving plants is not a sufficient statistic, however, for the contribution of own innovation to growth. Consider a hypothetical wherein the arrival rates of all types of innovation increase by the same proportion. The market share of innovating plants who survive stays the same, whereas the market share of noninnovating plants who survive shrinks more rapidly. The market share of all continuing plants is the combined market share of those who innovated and those who did not innovate. This combined market share declines even though the share of growth

Table 6
Growth by Innovation Type, Subperiods

Period	g	CD	NV	OI
1982–1995	1.15	.16	.42	.57
1996–2005	2.82	.33	.41	2.09
2006–2013	1.03	.13	.28	.62

Source: US Bureau of Labor Statistics (BLS) multifactor productivity (MFP) series.
Note: Percentage points of average yearly productivity growth within the specified period. Yearly growth is the sum of research and development and IP contributions to BLS MFP growth, converted into labor augmenting form. All other variables are calculated using the Census LBD. CD = creative destruction; NV = new varieties; OI = own innovation (incumbents improving on their own varieties).

Table 7
Share of the Change in TFP Growth from Innovation Types

Period	Δg	CD (%)	NV (%)	OI (%)
1982–1995 versus 1996–2005	1.67	9.8	−.5	90.8
1996–2005 versus 2006–2013	−1.79	11.0	7.1	81.9

Source: US Bureau of Labor Statistics (BLS) multifactor productivity (MFP) series.
Note: Percentage points of average yearly productivity growth within the specified period. Yearly growth is the sum of research and development and IP contributions to BLS MFP growth, converted into labor augmenting form. All other variables are calculated using the Census LBD. CD = creative destruction; NV = new varieties; OI = own innovation (incumbents improving on their own varieties).

from own innovation stays the same in this hypothetical. By comparison, the fact that the market share of continuing plants in the data stayed constant during the speedup and slowdown suggests own innovation contributed disproportionately to the speedup and slowdown.[11]

D. Results: Firm Age Groups

Table 8 displays the contribution of each firm age group to growth. Age 0 firms, who are in their first year of operation, contribute almost one-third of growth on average despite employing only 3% of workers. Firms ages 1–5 and 6–10 generate similar amounts of growth as their share of employment. Firms age 11+, in contrast, contribute much less growth (41%) than their share of employment (72%).

The high share of growth from new firms in table 8 can be better understood with three additional points. First, as the final row in the table shows, new firms are responsible for almost 60% of all employment at new plants. Second, as reported by Hsieh and Klenow (2017), new and young firms account for 50% of all gross job creation. Third, the employment

Table 8
Growth by Firm Age Groups, 1982–2013

	Age 0 (%)	Age 1–5 (%)	Age 6–10 (%)	Age 11+ (%)
% of growth	30.3	18.9	9.7	41.1
% of employment	3.3	13.4	11.2	72.1
% of firms	10.7	31.1	18.5	39.6
% of new plant emp.	58.8	5.4	4.5	31.2

Source: Census LBD.
Note: Average growth rate over the entire period is 1.66%. Firm age is the difference between the year of observation and the birth year of the firm's first plant. Emp. = employment.

Table 9
Growth by Firm Age Groups, Subperiods

Period	g	Age 0	Age 1–5	Age 6–10	Age 11+
1982–1995	1.15	.45	.25	.10	.35
1996–2005	2.82	.52	.47	.31	1.51
2006–2013	1.03	.31	.17	.09	.46

Source: US Bureau of Labor Statistics (BLS) multifactor productivity (MFP) series.
Note: Percentage points of average yearly productivity growth within the specified period.
Yearly growth is the sum of research and development and IP contributions to BLS MFP
growth, converted into labor augmenting form. All other variables are calculated using the
Census LBD. Firm age is the difference between the year of observation and the birth year
of the firm's first plant.

gains associated with new varieties contribute more to growth than identical employment gains associated with creative destruction. This is because only the net change in employment reflects the net improvement
brought by creative destruction.

Table 9 looks at growth contributions, in percentage points per year,
for firm age groups by subperiod. All age groups contributed to the acceleration of growth in the periods 1982–1995 to 1996–2005, as well as
the subsequent deceleration over 2006–2013. But, as displayed in table 10,
older firms drove the speedup (70%) and the slowdown (59%). These
fractions are still smaller than their share of employment, but much larger
than their share of growth in the slow-growth periods. The growth slowdown did not stem from a falling rate of innovation by entering and young
firms, but rather by older established firms.

The modest contribution of new and young firms to the 1996–2005
growth acceleration may seem surprising in light of the initial public offering
boom in the late 1990s. But such high valuations may have reflected a stream

Table 10
Share of the Change in TFP Growth by Age Group

Period	Δg	Age 0 (%)	Age 1–5 (%)	Age 6–10 (%)	Age 11+ (%)
1982–1995 versus 1996–2005	1.67	4.4	13.4	12.6	69.6
1996–2005 versus 2006–2013	−1.79	11.8	17.0	12.3	58.9

Source: US Bureau of Labor Statistics (BLS) multifactor productivity (MFP) series.
Note: Percentage points of average yearly productivity growth within the specified period.
Yearly growth is the sum of research and development and IP contributions to BLS MFP
growth, converted into labor augmenting form. All other variables are calculated using the
Census LBD. Firm age is the difference between the year of observation and the birth year
of the firm's first plant.

Table 11
Growth by Firm Size Groups, 1982–2013

	Small (0–19)	Medium (20–249)	Large (250–4,999)	Mega (5,000+)
% of growth	62.2	15.0	12.2	10.7
% of employment	21.4	26.3	26.9	25.4
% of firms	88.0	11.2	.8	.03

Source: Census LBD.
Note: Average growth rate over the entire period is 1.66%. Firm size is the sum of employment across all of its plants.

of expected future innovations by these firms, not just the innovations by these firms during this window.

E. Results: Firm Size Groups

Table 11 displays the contribution of each size group to growth. Size is based on employment in the previous year. Size 0 firms are hence new firms. The table shows four firm size groups, each with roughly one-fourth of all employment: those with 0–19 employees in the prior year, 20–249 workers, 250–4,999 workers, and 5,000+ workers. The smallest firms account for more than 60% of growth on average. Each of the other size groups account for about one-half as much growth as they do employment.

In table 12 we show that small firms play an outsize role in all sub-periods. All size groups accelerated and decelerated along with aggregate TFP. In fact, each size group contributed more or less equally to the speedup and slowdown in table 13. Thus the performance of mega firms does not directly explain the rise and fall of growth.

Table 12
Growth by Firm Size Groups, Subperiods

Period	g	Small (0–19)	Medium (20–249)	Large (250–4,999)	Mega (5,000+)
1982–1995	1.15	.85	.14	.08	.08
1996–2005	2.82	1.30	.55	.51	.46
2006–2013	1.03	.63	.15	.14	.10

Source: US Bureau of Labor Statistics (BLS) multifactor productivity (MFP) series.
Note: Percentage points of average yearly productivity growth within the specified period. Yearly growth is the sum of research and development and IP contributions to BLS MFP growth, converted into labor augmenting form. All other variables are calculated using the Census LBD. Firm size is the sum of employment across all of its plants.

Table 13
Share of the Change in TFP Growth by Size Group

Period	Δg	Small (0–19) (%)	Medium (20–249) (%)	Large (250–4,999) (%)	Mega (5,000+) (%)
1982–1995 versus 1996–2005	1.67	27.0	24.7	25.5	22.7
1996–2005 versus 2006–2013	−1.79	37.5	22.2	20.2	20.1

Source: Census LBD.
Note: Firm size is the sum of employment across all of its plants.

Tables 14 and 15 focus on the prominent role played by new firms versus small young firms—and, for contrast, small old firms. Here we define young as ages 1–5 and small as having 1–19 employees. Small young firms contribute twice as much to growth relative to their share of employment. Older small firms also contribute more to growth than their share of employment, but the difference is much less pronounced. This is reminiscent of the finding by Haltiwanger et al. (2013) that, even conditional on size, young firms grow faster than old firms.

F.   Results: Innovation Type for Each Age and Size Group

We know from table 8 that new firms contribute disproportionately to growth relative to their employment share. And we know they do no own innovation, by definition. But they do contribute via creative destruction or new varieties? Table 16 says that new firms mostly enter with new varieties. This seems intuitive in that it might be hard for new firms to eclipse existing products. At the other extreme, older firms

Table 14
Contribution of New, Young-Small, and Old-Small Firms, 1982–2013

	New	Young-Small	Old-Small
% of growth	29.9	14.1	11.6
% of employment	3.3	6.1	8.3
% of firms	10.7	28.8	32.0
% of new plant emp.	58.8	1.1	3.5

Source: Census LBD.
Note: "New" = age 0, "Young" = age 1–5, and "Small" = employment 1–19. Firm age is the difference between the year of observation and the birth year of the firm's first plant. Firm size is the sum of employment across all of its plants. Emp. = employment.

Table 15
Contribution of New, Young-Small, and Old-Small Firms by Period

Period	New	Young-Small	Old-Small
1982–1995	37.9	17.1	10.8
1996–2005	18.5	10.9	11.3
2006–2013	30.1	12.8	13.2

Source: Census LBD.
Note: "New" = age 0, "Young" = age 1–5, and "Small" = employment 1–19. Firm age is the difference between the year of observation and the birth year of the firm's first plant. Firm size is the sum of employment across all of its plants.

(age 11+) contribute 40% of average growth, and more than three-fourths of this comes from their efforts to improve their own products. They do comparatively little creative destruction and variety creation. The picture that emerges is that old firms improve their own products, and new firms introduce new varieties. Creative destruction is more evenly split among entrants and older firms.

Table 17 breaks the growth contribution of each age group into each innovation type for each subperiod. Old firms were evidently responsible for the bulk of the growth acceleration and slowdown. In table 18 we assess the type of innovation pursued by each firm size group. For every group other than entrants—from firms with 1–19 up through 10,000 or more employees—their main source of growth is own innovation. Table 19, which gives contributions by innovation type and size groups in subperiods, reveals some interesting patterns. The surge in own innovation from 1996 to 2005 occurred in firms with 20 or more employees. Even though young firms typically do a lot of own innovation, this increased relatively little in this fast-growth subperiod.

Table 16
Growth by Innovation Type for Each Age Group, 1982–2013

Age	CD	NV	OI	Total	% of Emp.
0	7.2	23.0	0	30.3	3.3
1–5	.7	1.2	17.1	18.9	13.4
6–10	.7	.9	8.1	9.7	11.2
11+	4.4	2.1	34.6	41.1	72.1

Source: Census LBD.
Note: CD = creative destruction; NV = new varieties; OI = own innovation (incumbents improving on their own varieties); Emp. = employment. Firm age is the difference between the year of observation and the birth year of the firm's first plant.

Table 17
Growth Contribution by Innovation Type and Age Groups, Subperiods

Period	Age	CD	NV	OI	Total	% of Emp.
1982–1995	0	7.8	31.0	0	38.8	3.9
	1–5	.9	1.9	19.0	21.8	15.5
	6–10	.4	1.5	7.2	9.1	12.1
	11+	5.1	1.9	23.4	30.4	68.5
1996–2005	0	5.1	13.4	0	18.5	3.1
	1–5	.8	.1	15.9	16.8	12.7
	6–10	1.0	.6	9.5	11.2	11.1
	11+	4.6	.4	48.5	53.5	73.0
2006–2013	0	8.9	21.2	0	30.1	2.5
	1–5	.1	1.2	15.3	16.6	10.6
	6–10	.7	.4	8.0	9.1	9.5
	11+	2.9	4.5	36.9	44.2	77.3

Source: Census LBD.
Note: CD = creative destruction; NV = new varieties; OI = own innovation (incumbents improving on their own varieties); Emp. = employment. Firm age is the difference between the year of observation and the birth year of the firm's first plant.

G. Obsolescence

As we described, our model features the exit of the lowest-quality products in each period. In the data, we observe both the exit rate of plants and the average employment of exiting plants. We can calculate these moments separately by firm age and size as well.

How do we distinguish the rate of creative destruction—which also produces plant exit—from obsolescence? The key is our assumption that creative destruction is undirected, or just as likely for low- and high-quality

Table 18
Growth Contribution by Innovation Type for Each Size Group, 1982–2013

Size	CD	NV	OI	Total	% of Emp.
0	7.2	23.0	0	30.3	3.3
1–19	1.3	.6	30.0	31.9	18.1
20–249	.1	2.8	12.1	15.0	26.3
250–999	.4	.5	4.9	5.8	12.8
1k–4999	.8	.1	5.5	6.4	14.1
5k–9999	.5	.1	1.9	2.5	5.8
10k+	2.6	.1	5.5	8.2	19.6

Source: Census LBD.
Note: CD = creative destruction; NV = new varieties; OI = own innovation (incumbents improving on their own varieties); Emp. = employment. Firm size is the sum of employment across all of its plants.

Table 19
Growth Contribution by Innovation Type and Size Groups, Subperiods

Period	Size	CD	NV	OI	Total	% of Emp.
1982–1995	0	7.8	31.0	0	38.8	3.9
	1–19	.5	1.2	33.5	35.2	19.0
	20–249	.1	3.7	8.1	11.9	25.8
	250–999	.5	0	2.5	3.0	12.0
	1k–4999	1.0	.1	2.9	4.0	13.5
	5k–9999	.7	.1	.8	1.5	5.8
	10k+	3.6	.2	1.8	5.6	19.9
1996–2005	0	5.1	13.4	0	18.5	3.1
	1–19	1.8	.1	25.9	27.8	17.8
	20–249	.1	.6	18.8	19.5	26.9
	250–999	.6	0	7.7	8.4	13.2
	1k–4999	1.1	0	8.5	9.6	14.3
	5k–9999	.3	.3	3.0	3.6	5.8
	10k+	2.6	.1	10.0	12.7	18.9
2006–2013	0	8.9	21.2	0	30.1	2.5
	1–19	2.2	.2	28.9	31.4	17.0
	20–249	.1	3.9	10.7	14.7	26.3
	250–999	.1	1.8	5.4	7.3	13.4
	1k–4999	.4	0	6.3	6.7	15.0
	5k–9999	.2	0	2.5	2.7	5.8
	10k+	.7	.1	6.3	7.1	19.9

Source: Census LBD.
Note: CD = creative destruction; NV = new varieties; OI = own innovation (incumbents improving on their own varieties); Emp. = employment. Firm size is the sum of employment across all of its plants.

products. For this reason, creatively destroyed plants should be of average size. In the data, in contrast, exiting plants are smaller on average than plants operating in the previous year. As a result, we can infer obsolescence from the difference between the average size of exiting plants and all plants.

From the point of view of our accounting, these are "lost varieties" that detract from growth.[12] We do not subtract this obsolescence from any particular innovation channel, but instead from all channels in equal proportion to their contribution to growth. Table 20 provides our estimates of the fraction of plants exiting due to obsolescence, and their share of employment. We infer that 3%–4% of employment is at the 9%–10% of plants that will exit due to obsolescence in the next year. These rates show no clear trend across subperiods.

Tables B1 and B2 trace the obsolescence to plants of varying ages and sizes. There is no obsolescence among entering plants (age = 0, size = 0) by construction. Roughly one-half of obsolescence occurs at plants 6+ years

Table 20
Obsolescence

Period	% of Emp.	% of Plants	Contrib OB
1982–1995	4.15	10.34	−1.06
1996–2005	2.93	8.53	−.29
2006–2013	2.83	9.01	−.84

Source: Census LBD.
Note: Entries are percent of all employment or percent of the overall number of plants. Emp. = employment; Contrib = contribution; OB = obsolescence.

old, and the other half at plants 1–5 years old. Not surprisingly, most of obsolescence involves the smallest plants, with 1–19 employees.

VI.   Further Results and Future Applications

A.   Treating All 0–5 Year Old Firms as Entrants

In table 16, we show that new firms mostly contribute by introducing new varieties, whereas young firms aged 1–5 contribute mostly through own innovation. In the presence of adjustment costs, however, what we infer as own innovation by young firms may actually be the dynamics of accumulating inputs and acquiring customers. We therefore check the robustness of our findings to treating age 1–5 firms as new firms. Doing so reinterprets the growth of young firms to come from creative destruction and new varieties rather than own innovation. Table 21 displays the results. We find that new firms (aged 0–5) now account for 49% of all growth, up from 30%. The contribution of own innovation falls

Table 21
Treating All Firms 0–5 Years Old as Entrants

Age	CD	NV	OI	Total	% of Emp.
0–5	12.0	37.2	.0	49.2	16.7
6–10	.7	.9	8.1	9.7	11.2
11+	4.4	2.1	34.6	41.1	72.1
Total	17.1	40.2	42.7		

Source: Census LBD.
Note: CD = creative destruction; NV = new varieties; OI = own innovation (incumbents improving on their own varieties); Emp. = employment. Firm age is the difference between the year of observation and the birth year of the firm's first plant. Entries are percent of all employment or percent of the overall number of plants.

from 60% to 43%. That from creative destruction increases from 13% to 17%, whereas the contribution from new varieties increases from 27% to 40%.

B.   Contribution of Superstar Firms

One advantage of our method is that it can be used to quantify the contribution of individual firms to aggregate growth. Because we cannot reveal the identity of individual firms in the Census data, we apply our method to the National Establishment Time-Series (NETS) Database, which ranges from 1990 to 2014. The unit of observation is an establishment. As in the Census, we define entry of an establishment as the first time an establishment is observed in a location in the data. We define exit as when an establishment ceases to operate in a location. For each establishment, we observe its employment and, mostly importantly, the identity of its headquarter plant and therefore its firm identity.[13] Finally, we restrict the time period to 1996–2005 because this period is comparable to the high growth period in our calculations with the Census data, and the post-2005 NETS data displays large swings in the entry and exit of plants that are inconsistent with the Census data.

As a demonstration of our method, we used the NETS 1996–2005 data to calculate the contribution of Amazon and Walmart. We find that although both companies grew during this window, their contribution to overall growth was quite modest. Amazon accounted for only 0.0041% of growth (less than 1% of all growth), and Walmart contributed 0.80% (closer to 1% of all growth, or more than 2 basis points of annual TFP growth). Nonetheless, Amazon's contribution was three times its employment share, whereas Walmart's growth contribution was twice its employment share.

C.   Future Applications

Our innovation accounting is distinct from gross job creation, gross job destruction, or net job creation. It can therefore be helpful to contrast our results to these statistics, which have garnered substantial attention. For example, young fast-growing firms—so-called gazelles—are responsible for a notable fraction of gross and net job creation. How much growth do they generate on average? And how much of gross job destruction is due to creative destruction, as opposed to obsolescence?

We could carry out several important robustness checks. We could follow Aghion et al. (2019) and distinguish between measured and true growth. They argue that measured growth mostly captures own innovation by incumbents and misses most growth from new varieties and creative destruction. We could reestimate parameters under this hypothesis.

For manufacturing, the Census has data on revenue and capital as well as labor at the plant level. Thus for manufacturing we could back out underlying productivity rather than assume sales are proportional to employment and the absence of adjustment costs and distortions. We could apply our innovation accounting directly to this underlying productivity measure to see how our inference compares to that with employment alone.

Future work could implement our approach to assess the contribution of locations (states, cities) to aggregate growth. It could also decompose growth within industries such as information and communications technology or retail. One could also look at which cohorts of entering firms have contributed the most to growth. Our method does not mechanically count firm employment growth due to mergers and acquisitions as contributing to growth. But one could investigate whether targets of M&A activity become more innovative after they are taken over. This could obtain results at odd with existing analyses, which focus on revenue productivity.

VII.   Conclusion

We used US Census data on employment at plants across all firms in the nonfarm business sector from 1982 to 2013. We traced aggregate TFP growth to the innovation efforts of firms by their size and age. We arrived at three main findings. First, young firms (ages 0–5) generate one-half of growth, roughly three times more than their share of employment might suggest. Second, large firms are at the other end of the spectrum, contributing notably less to growth than their share of employment. Third, a majority of growth takes the form of quality improvements by incumbents on their own products. New varieties and creative destruction contribute less, but they are still important. Such own innovation accounts for the bulk of the growth speedup and slowdown in the middle of our sample.

Our study comes with many caveats that we hope future work, with better data, can address. We used a plant as a proxy for a product. With more detailed data on products sold within plants, this can be relaxed. See, for example, Bernard, Redding, and Schott (2010) on manufacturing and Hottman et al. (2016) on packaged consumer goods.

We gauged a plant's size by its employment rather than its sales and combined plants with a CES aggregator. Though they are highly correlated in manufacturing, where we can see both, some innovation surely tilts toward capital and away from labor (automation). And a richer analysis could place industries into CES nests and entertain non-CES aggregation.

Even under CES aggregation, a plant's sales are a perfect reflection of its underlying productivity only in the absence of adjustment costs and distortions such as markups, markdowns, and financial frictions. Adjustment costs could include those for inputs or acquiring a customer base. We could be overstating the importance of young firms for innovation (overall and by incumbents on their own products) if their fast growth is due, in part, to adjusting their inputs and stock of customers.

We assumed that creative destruction was untargeted. That is, higher-quality products are just as likely to be creatively destroyed as lower-quality products. One can think of a priori reasons why creative destruction would target higher-quality products (more sales to gain) or lower-quality products (perhaps easier to improve upon).

We made the arrival rates and step sizes of innovation depend only on the size and age of innovating firms. Studies such as Akcigit and Kerr (2018) have argued that innovation by new and young firms generates bigger spillovers. This would reinforce our conclusion that younger firms punch above their weight class in terms of growth.

Our innovation accounting is silent on the determinants of arrival rates and step sizes of innovation. Knowing the structural parameters that drive these variables is vital for drawing policy lessons (see Atkeson and Burstein 2019). One key question for future research is whether creative destruction is a strategic complement or substitute for own innovation by incumbents. If they are substitutes, as in Peters (2020) and Akcigit and Ates (2019), then a falling rate of creative destruction may be offset by a rising rate of own innovation. If they are complements, however, then perhaps the threat of creative destruction spurs innovative efforts by incumbents. This is the spirit of the model in Aghion et al. (2005), in which the threat of being overtaken by followers or entrants leads to more innovation by leaders.

Appendix A

Revenue Productivity versus Employment Growth

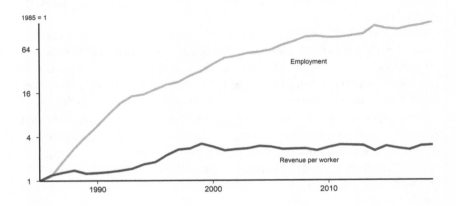

Fig. A1.   Microsoft. A color version of this figure is available online.

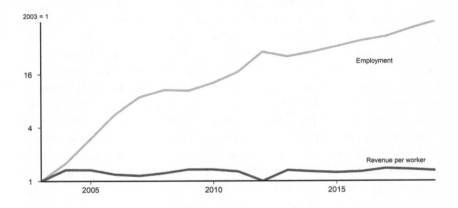

Fig. A2.   Google. WRDS Compustat and BEA Table 1.1.9. Revenue per worker = "REVT/ (GDP Deflator × EMP)," Employment = "EMP," and Year = "FYEAR." The graph displays revenue per worker and employment relative to the first year when both series are available for the firm. A color version of this figure is available online.

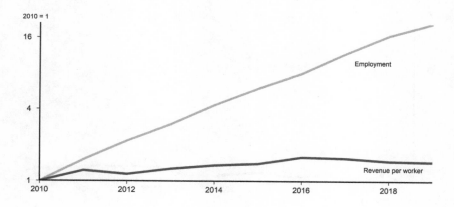

Fig. A3. Facebook. A color version of this figure is available online.

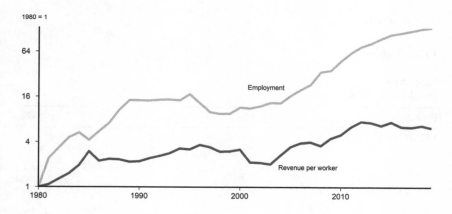

Fig. A4. Apple. WRDS Compustat and BEA Table 1.1.9. Revenue per worker = "REVT/ (GDP Deflator × EMP)," Employment = "EMP," and Year = "FYEAR." The graph displays revenue per worker and employment relative to the first year when both series are available for the firm. A color version of this figure is available online.

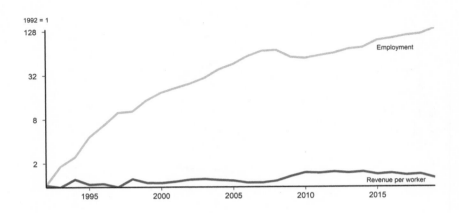

Fig. A5. Starbucks. WRDS Compustat and BEA Table 1.1.9. Revenue per worker = "REVT/(GDP Deflator × EMP)," Employment = "EMP," and Year = "FYEAR." The graph displays revenue per worker and employment relative to the first year when both series are available for the firm. A color version of this figure is available online.

Appendix B

Extra Tables

Table B1
Obsolescence by Age Groups

Period	Age	% of Emp.	% of Plants	Contrib OB
1982–1995	0	0	0	0
	1–5	2.1	5.8	–.5
	6–10	.7	1.7	–.2
	11+	1.3	2.9	–.3
1996–2005	0	0	0	0
	1–5	1.3	4.4	–.1
	6–10	.5	1.4	–0
	11+	1.1	2.8	–.1
2006–2013	0	0	0	0
	1–5	1.5	4.6	–.4
	6–10	.6	1.5	–.2
	11+	.8	2.9	–.2

Source: Census LBD.
Note: Firm age is the difference between the year of observation and the birth year of the firm's first plant. Units are percent of total employment or total number of plants. Emp. = employment; Contrib = contribution; OB = obsolescence.

Table B2
Obsolescence by Size Groups

Period	Size	% of Emp.	% of Plants	Contrib OB
1982–1995	0	0	0	0
	1–19	2.6	9.2	−.7
	20–249	.9	.3	−.2
	250–999	.1	.1	−0
	1k–4999	.1	.2	−0
	5k–9999	.1	.1	−0·
	10k+	.4	.4	−.1
1996–2005	0	0	0	0
	1–19	1.5	7.4	−.2
	20–249	.6	.2	−.1
	250–999	.1	.1	−0
	1k–4999	.1	.2	−0
	5k–9999	.1	.1	−0
	10k+	.5	.6	−0
2006–2013	0	0	0	0
	1–19	2.0	8.3	−.6
	20–249	.7	.1	−.2
	250–999	0	0	0
	1k–4999	0	.1	0
	5k–9999	0	.1	0
	10k+	.2	.5	−0

Source: Census LBD.
Note: Firm size is the sum of employment across all of its plants. Units are percent of total employment or total number of plants. Emp. = employment; Contrib = contribution; OB = obsolescence.

Table B3
Contribution by Age-Size Groups, 1982–1995

Size	Age	CD	NV	OI	Total	% of Emp.
0	0	7.6	30.3	0	37.9	3.9
1–19	1–5	.1	.7	16.4	17.1	7.2
1–19	6–10	.3	.4	6.1	6.8	4.2
1–19	11+	.4	0	10.4	10.8	7.7
20–249	1–5	0	1.1	2.2	3.4	5.6
20–249	6–10	0	.8	1.3	2.1	4.6
20–249	11+	.1	1.6	4.4	6.1	15.5
250–999	1–5	.3	0	0	.3	1.3
250–999	6–10	.2	0	0	.2	1.4
250–999	11+	.1	0	2.5	2.6	9.3
1k–4999	1–5	.2	0	0	.2	.9
1k–4999	6–10	.4	0	.2	.6	1.1
1k–4999	11+	.6	.1	2.6	3.4	11.5

Table B3
Continued

Size	Age	CD	NV	OI	Total	% of Emp.
5k–9999	1–5	.2	0	0	.2	.5
5k–9999	6–10	.2	0	0	.2	.3
5k–9999	11+	.4	0	.7	1.2	5.1
10k+	6–10	1.4	0	0	1.4	.4
10k+	11+	3.5	.2	1.7	5.4	19.5

Source: Census LBD.
Note: CD = creative destruction; NV = new varieties; OI = own innovation (incumbents improving on their own varieties); Emp. = employment. Firm size is the sum of employment across all of its plants. Firm age is the difference between the year of observation and the birth year of the firm's first plant.

Table B4
Contribution by Age-Size Groups, 1996–2005

Size	Age	CD	NV	OI	Total	% of Emp.
0	0	5.1	13.4	0	18.5	3.1
1–19	1–5	0	.1	10.8	10.9	5.6
1–19	6–10	.4	0	5.1	5.5	3.6
1–19	11+	1.3	0	10.0	11.3	8.5
20–249	1–5	.1	0	4.1	4.2	4.6
20–249	6–10	0	.6	2.9	3.5	4.2
20–249	11+	0	0	11.8	11.8	18.0
250–999	1–5	.2	0	.7	.9	1.2
250–999	6–10	.1	0	.7	.8	1.3
250–999	11+	.3	0	6.4	6.6	10.7
1k–4999	1–5	.3	0	.3	.6	.8
1k–4999	6–10	.2	0	.6	.8	1.1
1k–4999	11+	.6	0	7.7	8.2	12.4
5k–9999	1–5	.2	0	0	.2	.4
5k–9999	6–10	.1	0	.1	.2	.3
5k–9999	11+	.1	.3	2.9	3.3	5.0
10k+	6–10	.2	0	.2	.4	.5
10k+	11+	2.4	.1	9.8	12.3	18.4

Source: Census LBD.
Note: CD = creative destruction; NV = new varieties; OI = own innovation (incumbents improving on their own varieties); Emp. = employment. Firm size is the sum of employment across all of its plants. Firm age is the difference between the year of observation and the birth year of the firm's first plant.

Table B5
Contribution by Age-Size Groups, 2006–2013

Size	Age	CD	NV	OI	Total	% of Emp.
0	0	8.9	21.2	0	30.1	2.5
1–19	1–5	0	.2	12.6	12.8	4.8
1–19	6–10	.2	0	5.2	5.4	3.2
1–19	11+	2.1	0	11.1	13.2	9.0
20–249	1–5	0	.9	2.4	3.3	4.0
20–249	6–10	.1	.4	1.8	2.3	3.7
20–249	11+	0	2.5	6.6	9.1	18.6
250–999	1–5	0	0	.3	.3	1.0
250–999	6–10	.1	0	.5	.6	1.2
250–999	11+	0	1.8	4.5	6.3	11.2
1k–4999	1–5	.1	0	0	.1	.6
1k–4999	6–10	.1	0	.4	.4	.9
1k–4999	11+	.2	0	5.9	6.2	13.6
5k–9999	1–5	0	0	0	0	.3
5k–9999	6–10	.1	0	0	.1	.2
5k–9999	11+	.1	0	2.5	2.6	5.3
10k+	6–10	.2	0	.1	.2	.3
10k+	11+	.5	.1	6.3	6.9	19.6

Source: Census LBD.
Note: CD = creative destruction; NV = new varieties; OI = own innovation (incumbents improving on their own varieties); Emp. = employment. Firm size is the sum of employment across all of its plants. Firm age is the difference between the year of observation and the birth year of the firm's first plant.

Appendix C

Directed Creative Destruction

The benchmark model assumes creative destruction innovation is random in that all existing products have the same probability of being creatively destroyed. This appendix lays out an extension of the model where creative destruction can be directed to certain ranges of quality. That is, we allow the probability of being creatively destroyed to depend on whether the quality of the incumbent product is above a quality cutoff. Creative destruction is random, conditional on whether the quality is above or below the cutoff. The benchmark model is a special case of this extension with the cutoff equal to the obsolescence cutoff. We use one cutoff here for illustration. The model can be extended in the same way for multiple cutoffs.

Suppose new producers of a product take over $\delta_{ft}^H N_{t-1}$ nonobsolete products with quality above q_t^H by improving on the quality of those products by step size $\Delta_{ft}^H > 1$ and $\delta_{ft}^L N_{t-1}$ nonobsolete products with quality below q_t^H by improving on the quality of those products by step size

$\Delta_{ft}^{L} > 1$. Thus, the share of products in $t - 1$ that is subject to creative destruction is

$$\delta_t := \int_{f \in \mathcal{M}_t} \delta_{ft}^{H} + \delta_{ft}^{L} \, df.$$

We need to modify how firms lose their products to creative destruction. Let $\tilde{x}_{f,t-1}^{CDH} N_{f,t-1}$ and $\tilde{x}_{f,t-1}^{CDL} N_{f,t-1}$ be the number of products a firm active in $t - 1$ loses between $t - 1$ and t due to high- and low-quality creative destruction, respectively. In equilibrium, the arrival rate of creative destruction equals the sum of the rate of producers' exit from a product due to creative destruction. That is,

$$\delta_t = \int_{f \in \mathcal{M}_{t-1}} (\tilde{x}_{f,t-1}^{CDH} + \tilde{x}_{f,t-1}^{CDL}) \left(\frac{N_{f,t-1}}{N_{t-1}} \right) df = \int_{f \in \mathcal{M}_{t-1}} x_{f,t-1}^{CD} \, df,$$

where $x_{f,t-1}^{CD} := \tilde{x}_{f,t-1}^{CD}(N_{f,t-1}/N_{t-1})$. For simplicity we assume both high- and low-quality creative destruction innovation are random, conditional on the type of destruction. This implies all firms lose the same fraction of high-quality and low-quality nonobsolete products, denoted by $\hat{\delta}_t^{H}$ and $\hat{\delta}_t^{L}$, respectively. However, unlike the benchmark model, firms with a different composition of high- and low-quality products will have a different average probability of losing a product if $\hat{\delta}_t^{H} \neq \hat{\delta}_t^{L}$. Hence for all firms in $t - 1$,

$$\tilde{x}_{f,t-1}^{CDH} = \hat{\delta}_t^{H}(1 - G_{f,t-1}(q_t^{H})), \quad \tilde{x}_{f,t-1}^{CDL} = \hat{\delta}_t^{L}(G_{f,t-1}(q_t^{H}) - G_{f,t-1}(\kappa_t)),$$

the share of products of a firm in $t - 1$ that are not produced by the firm in period t is

$$\tilde{x}_{f,t-1} = \tilde{x}_{f,t-1}^{O} + \tilde{x}_{f,t-1}^{CD} = G_{f,t-1}(\kappa_t) + \hat{\delta}_t^{H}(1 - G_{f,t-1}(q_t^{H})) + \hat{\delta}_t^{L}(G_{f,t-1}(q_t^{H}) - G_{f,t-1}(\kappa_t)),$$

and the aggregate exit rate of products from producers at the end of $t - 1$ is

$$\begin{aligned} x_{t-1} &= \int_{f \in \mathcal{M}_{t-1}} \tilde{x}_{f,t-1} \left[\frac{N_{f,t-1}}{N_{t-1}} \right] df \\ &= G_{t-1}(\kappa_t) + \hat{\delta}_t^{H}(1 - G_{t-1}(q_t^{H})) + \hat{\delta}_t^{L}(G_{t-1}(q_t^{H}) - G_{t-1}(\kappa_t)). \end{aligned}$$

The extension affects the quality distribution of products experiencing own innovation. Recall that $\tilde{o}_{ft}$ fraction of the products that survive both creative destruction and obsolescence experience own innovation by the incumbent produce. With the extension, the share of products of firm f that experience own innovation is

$$\begin{aligned} \tilde{o}_{ft} \cdot (1 - \tilde{x}_{f,t-1}^{CD} - \tilde{x}_{f,t-1}^{O}) = \tilde{o}_{ft} \cdot [1 - G_{f,t-1}(\kappa_t) - \hat{\delta}_t^{H}(1 - G_{f,t-1}(q_t^{H})) \\ - \hat{\delta}_t^{L}(G_{f,t-1}(q_t^{H}) - G_{f,t-1}(\kappa_t))], \end{aligned}$$

and the share of all products in $t-1$ that experience own innovation is

$$\int_{f\in\mathcal{M}_{t-1}} \tilde{o}_{ft}\cdot[1-G_{f,t-1}(\kappa_t)-\hat{\delta}_t^H(1-G_{f,t-1}(q_t^H))-\hat{\delta}_t^L(G_{f,t-1}(q_t^H)$$
$$-G_{f,t-1}(\kappa_t))]\left(\frac{N_{f,t-1}}{N_{t-1}}\right)df.$$

Having shown how the extension modifies the innovation process, we next show how the extension affects the expression for aggregate productivity growth. Recall that we can decompose growth into innovation types

$$e^g = \left(\frac{\int_{i\in\mathcal{N}_t} q_t(i)^{\sigma-1}\,di}{\int_{i\in\mathcal{N}_{t-1}} q_{t-1}(i)^{\sigma-1}\,di}\right)^{\frac{1}{\sigma-1}}$$

$$= \left(\frac{\int_{i\in\mathcal{NV}_t} q_t(i)^{\sigma-1}\,di + \int_{i\in\mathcal{CD}_t} q_t(i)^{\sigma-1}\,di + \int_{i\in\mathcal{OI}_t} q_t(i)^{\sigma-1}\,di + \int_{i\in\mathcal{S}_t} q_t(i)^{\sigma-1}\,di}{\int_{i\in\mathcal{N}_{t-1}} q_{t-1}(i)^{\sigma-1}\,di}\right)^{\frac{1}{\sigma-1}}$$

The first term is not affected. The second term becomes

$$\left(\int_{f\in\mathcal{M}_t} \delta_f^H \Delta_f^{H\sigma-1}\,df\right)\left(\frac{\hat{Q}^H}{Q}\right)^{\sigma-1} + \left(\int_{f\in\mathcal{M}_t} \delta_f^L \Delta_f^{L\sigma-1}\,df\right)\left(\frac{\hat{Q}^L}{Q}\right)^{\sigma-1}$$

where

$$\hat{Q}^H := N_{t-1}\cdot\mathbb{E}_{G_{t-1}}(q^{\sigma-1}|q\geq q_t^H) \tag{15}$$

$$\hat{Q}^L := N_{t-1}\cdot\mathbb{E}_{G_{t-1}}(q^{\sigma-1}|\kappa_t\leq q < q_t^H) \tag{16}$$

The third term changes to

$$\int_{f\in\mathcal{C}_{t,t-1}} \tilde{o}_{ft} O_f^{\sigma-1}\left[(1-\hat{\delta}_t^L)\int_{i\in\mathcal{N}_{ft-1},q_t^H\geq q_{t-1}(i)\geq\kappa_t} \frac{q_{t-1}^{\sigma-1}(i)}{Q_{t-1}^{\sigma-1}}\,di\right.$$

$$+\left.\left(1-\hat{\delta}_t^H\right)\int_{i\in\mathcal{N}_{ft-1},q_t^H<q_{t-1}(i)} \frac{q_{t-1}^{\sigma-1}(i)}{Q_{t-1}^{\sigma-1}}\,di\right]df$$

$$= \left(\frac{\hat{Q}^H}{Q}\right)^{\sigma-1}\int_{f\in\mathcal{C}_{t,t-1}} o_{ft}^H O_f^{\sigma-1}\left[\frac{\mathbb{E}_{G_{f,t-1}}(q^{\sigma-1}|q\geq q_t^H)}{\mathbb{E}_{G_{t-1}}(q^{\sigma-1}|q\geq q_t^H)}\right]df$$

$$+ \left(\frac{\hat{Q}^L}{Q}\right)^{\sigma-1}\int_{f\in\mathcal{C}_{t,t-1}} o_{ft}^L O_f^{\sigma-1}\left[\frac{\mathbb{E}_{G_{f,t-1}}(q^{\sigma-1}|\kappa_t\leq q\leq q_t^H)}{\mathbb{E}_{G_{t-1}}(q^{\sigma-1}|\kappa_t\leq q\leq q_t^H)}\right]df$$

The fourth term contains products that survive creative destruction and obsolescence but do not experience own innovation. This term changes to

$$
\int_{f \in \mathcal{C}_{t,t-1}} (1 - \tilde{o}_{ft}) \left[(1 - \hat{\delta}_t^L) \int_{i \in \mathcal{N}_{ft-1}, q_t^H \geq q_{t-1}(i) \geq \kappa_t} \frac{q_{t-1}^{\sigma-1}(i)}{Q_{t-1}^{\sigma-1}} di \right.
$$

$$
+ \left(1 - \hat{\delta}_t^H \right) \int_{i \in \mathcal{N}_{ft-1}, q_t^H < q_{t-1}(i)} \frac{q_{t-1}^{\sigma-1}(i)}{Q_{t-1}^{\sigma-1}} di \right] df
$$

$$
= (1 - \hat{\delta}_t^H) \left(\frac{\hat{Q}^H}{Q} \right)^{\sigma-1} \int_{f \in \mathcal{C}_{t,t-1}} (1 - \tilde{o}_{ft})(1 - G_{f,t-1}(q_t^H)) \left[\frac{N_{f,t-1} \mathbb{E}_{G_{f,t-1}}(q^{\sigma-1} | q \geq q_t^H)}{\hat{Q}_{t-1}^{H\sigma-1}} \right] df
$$

$$
+ (1 - \hat{\delta}_t^L) \left(\frac{\hat{Q}^L}{Q} \right)^{\sigma-1} \int_{f \in \mathcal{C}_{t,t-1}} (1 - \tilde{o}_{ft})(G_{f,t-1}(q_t^H) - G_{f,t-1}(\kappa_t)) \left[\frac{N_{f,t-1} \mathbb{E}_{G_{f,t-1}}(q^{\sigma-1} | q_t^H \geq q \geq \kappa_t)}{\hat{Q}_{t-1}^{L\sigma-1}} \right] df
$$

Combining the terms we derived so far, we can write the aggregate productivity growth rate as

$$
e^{g(\sigma-1)} = 1 + \int_{f \in \mathcal{M}_t} \nu_f V_f^{\sigma-1} df + \int_{f \in \mathcal{M}_t} \delta_f^H (\Delta_f^{H\sigma-1} - 1) \left(\frac{\hat{Q}^H}{Q} \right)^{\sigma-1} df
$$

$$
+ \int_{f \in \mathcal{M}_t} \delta_f^L (\Delta_f^{L\sigma-1} - 1) \left(\frac{\hat{Q}^{LL}}{Q} \right)^{\sigma-1} df
$$

$$
+ \left(\frac{\hat{Q}^H}{Q} \right)^{\sigma-1} \int_{f \in \mathcal{C}_{t,t-1}} o_{ft}^H (O_f^{\sigma-1} - 1) \left[\frac{\mathbb{E}_{G_{f,t-1}}(q^{\sigma-1} | q \geq q_t^H)}{\mathbb{E}_{G_{t-1}}(q^{\sigma-1} | q \geq q_t^H)} \right] df
$$

$$
+ \left(\frac{\hat{Q}^{LL}}{Q} \right)^{\sigma-1} \int_{f \in \mathcal{C}_{t,t-1}} o_{ft}^L (O_f^{\sigma-1} - 1) \left[\frac{\mathbb{E}_{G_{f,t-1}}(q^{\sigma-1} | q \leq q_t^H)}{\mathbb{E}_{G_{t-1}}(q^{\sigma-1} | q \leq q_t^H)} \right] df
$$

$$
+ \left(\int_{f \in \mathcal{M}_t} \nu_f V_f^{\sigma-1} df \right) \left(\left(\frac{\hat{Q}}{Q} \right)^{\sigma-1} - 1 \right)
$$

$$
+ \left(\int_{f \in \mathcal{M}_t} \delta_f^L (\Delta_f^{L\sigma-1} - 1) df \right) \left(\left(\frac{\hat{Q}^L}{Q} \right)^{\sigma-1} - \left(\frac{\hat{Q}^{LL}}{Q} \right)^{\sigma-1} \right)
$$

$$
+ \int_{f \in \mathcal{C}_{t,t-1}} o_{ft}^L (O_f^{\sigma-1} - 1) \left[\frac{\mathbb{E}_{G_{f,t-1}}(q^{\sigma-1} | \kappa_t \leq q \leq q_t^H) - \mathbb{E}_{G_{f,t-1}}(q^{\sigma-1} | q \leq q_t^H)}{\mathbb{E}_{G_{t-1}}(q^{\sigma-1})} \right] df
$$

$$
- \left(1 - \left(\frac{\hat{Q}}{Q} \right)^{\sigma-1} (1 - G_{t-1}(\kappa_t)) \right)
$$

where

$$
\hat{Q}^{LL} := N_{t-1} \cdot \mathbb{E}_{G_{t-1}}(q^{\sigma-1} | q < q_t^H)
$$

is the quality distribution from which low-quality creative destruction would have drawn had there been no obsolescence.

Finally, the expression for firm contribution to growth becomes

$$
\begin{aligned}
g_f &= \nu_f V_f^{\sigma-1} + \delta_f^H (\Delta_f^{H\sigma-1} - 1)\left(\frac{\hat{Q}^H}{Q}\right)^{\sigma-1} + \delta_f^L (\Delta_f^{L\sigma-1} - 1)\left(\frac{\hat{Q}^{LL}}{Q}\right)^{\sigma-1} \\
&+ \left(\frac{\hat{Q}^H}{Q}\right)^{\sigma-1} o_{ft}^H (O_f^{\sigma-1} - 1)\left[\frac{\mathbb{E}_{G_{f,t-1}}(q^{\sigma-1}|q \geq q_t^H)}{\mathbb{E}_{G_{t-1}}(q^{\sigma-1}|q \geq q_t^H)}\right] \\
&+ \left(\frac{\hat{Q}^{LL}}{Q}\right)^{\sigma-1} o_{ft}^L (O_f^{\sigma-1} - 1)\left[\frac{\mathbb{E}_{G_{f,t-1}}(q^{\sigma-1}|q \leq q_t^H)}{\mathbb{E}_{G_{t-1}}(q^{\sigma-1}|q \leq q_t^H)}\right] \\
&- o_{ft}^L (O_f^{\sigma-1} - 1)\left[\frac{\mathbb{E}_{G_{f,t-1}}(q^{\sigma-1}|\kappa_t \leq q \leq q_t^H) - \mathbb{E}_{G_{f,t-1}}(q^{\sigma-1}|q \leq q_t^H)}{\mathbb{E}_{G_{t-1}}(q^{\sigma-1})}\right] \\
&- \mathbb{E}_{G_{f,t-1}}[s_{t-1}|q < \kappa_t] G_{f,t-1}(\kappa_t) N_{f,t-1} \\
&+ \left\{\left(\int_{f\in\mathcal{M}_t} \nu_f V_f^{\sigma-1} df\right)\left(\left(\frac{\hat{Q}}{Q}\right)^{\sigma-1} - 1\right)\right. \\
&+ \left.\left(\int_{f\in\mathcal{M}_t} \delta_f^L (\Delta_f^{L\sigma-1} - 1) df\right)\left(\left(\frac{\hat{Q}^L}{Q}\right)^{\sigma-1} - \left(\frac{\hat{Q}^{LL}}{Q}\right)^{\sigma-1}\right)\right\}\left[\frac{G_{f,t-1}(\kappa_t) N_{f,t-1}}{G_{t-1}(\kappa_t) N_{t-1}}\right]
\end{aligned}
$$

Endnotes

Authors' email addresses: Klenow (Klenow@Stanford.edu), Li (tohuiyu@gmail.com). We thank Mark Bils, John Haltiwanger, Hugo Hopenhayn, Chang-Tai Hsieh, Erik Hurst, and Chad Jones for useful comments. We also thank Amber Flaharty and Gladys Teng for excellent research assistance. Any opinions and conclusions expressed herein are those of the author(s) and do not necessarily represent the views of the US Census Bureau or the Federal Reserve System. This research was performed at a Federal Statistical Research Data Center under FSRDC Project Number 1440. All results have been reviewed to ensure that no confidential information is disclosed. For acknowledgments, sources of research support, and disclosure of the authors' material financial relationships, if any, please see https://www.nber.org/books-and-chapters/nber-macroeconomics-annual-2020-volume-35/innovative-growth-accounting.

1. See Fernald (2015) for discussion on the timing of the productivity speedup and slowdown.

2. We model product heterogeneity as coming from quality differences, but these will be isomorphic to differences in process efficiency in our model setting.

3. We do not model the arrival rates and step sizes of innovation but rather back them out from data moments in the LBD. We allow them to vary over time and across firms. In this sense, we are not assuming these arrival rates and step sizes are exogenous. Instead, we are estimating and carrying out a model-based growth decomposition.

4. The Census LBD, which we use for almost all of our estimates, does not have data on revenue, and the US Census Bureau forbids us from revealing the identity of firms. Hence, we compare measures of revenue labor productivity with employment growth for select firms in Compustat.

5. The level of revenue productivity is high in these firms compared with the average firm. But their rapid growth did not bring down their revenue productivity, as one might expect if their employment growth was a drawn-out response to previous shocks due to adjustment costs.

6. See appendix C for an extension that allows targeted creative destruction.

7. We minimize the $L2$ distance between the kth moments in the data and that implied by equation (7) for $k = 0, 1, 2, 3$. We fit the $k = 0$ and $k = 1$ moments exactly while giving equal weight to $k = 2, 3$ moments. Note that equation (7) by itself is symmetric in the new variety and creative destruction parameters and hence only identifies a pair of values. That is, $\{v_{\mathcal{F}}, \delta_{\mathcal{F}}, V_{\mathcal{F}}/e^g, \Delta_{\mathcal{F}}/e^g\} = \{\bar{v}_{\mathcal{F}}, \bar{\delta}_{\mathcal{F}}, \bar{V}_{\mathcal{F}}/e^g, \bar{\Delta}_{\mathcal{F}}/e^g\}$ and $\{v_{\mathcal{F}}, \delta_{\mathcal{F}}, V_f/e^g, \Delta_{\mathcal{F}}/e^g\} = \{\bar{\delta}_{\mathcal{F}}, \bar{v}_{\mathcal{F}}, \bar{\Delta}_{\mathcal{F}}/e^g, \bar{V}_{\mathcal{F}}/e^g\}$ generate the same distance. Given the growth rate in the data, restrictions $\Delta_{\mathcal{F}} > 1$ and $V_{\mathcal{F}} > 0$ break the symmetry and help us choose between the two specifications. This identification does not work if both $\Delta_{\mathcal{F}}$ and $V_{\mathcal{F}}$ exceed 1. Then we use the aggregate exit rate for identification.

8. We fit the growth rate by construction when the boundary conditions are not violated. Any gaps between the model-implied growth rate and the growth rate in the data reflect the extent to which we run into corners.

9. We keep ownership of a plant to the firm that first owns the plant. We use employment in the previous year because the current-year employment is affected by innovation.

10. For period 1982–1986, we only observe age groups 0, 1–5, and 6+. We attribute the employment and plant shares of age group 6+ to age groups 6–10 and 11+ using their employment and plant shares in 1987–1995. We also assume the employment share growth of surviving plants of firms in age groups 6–10 and 11+ is the same as that of age group 6+.

11. This explanation has the testable prediction that the dispersion of employment growth should have increased (decreased) among surviving plants during the speedup (slowdown) due to the divergence between innovating and noninnovating survivors.

12. A structural model might feature overhead labor to explain such exit.

13. We do not use NETS sales data because it is imputed at the establishment level from establishment employment and firm-level sales. Also, as we did for the Census data, we remove mechanical effects from mergers and acquisitions by defining the owner of an establishment as the firm that owns the establishment at the time of entry.

References

Acemoglu, Daron. 2003. "Labor- and Capital-Augmenting Technical Change." *Journal of the European Economic Association* 1 (1): 1–37.

———. 2011. *Introduction to Modern Economic Growth*. Princeton: Princeton University Press.

Acemoglu, Daron, Ufuk Akcigit, Harun Alp, Nicholas Bloom, and William Kerr. 2018. "Innovation, Reallocation, and Growth." *American Economic Review* 108 (11): 3450–91.

Aghion, Philippe, Ufuk Akcigit, and Peter Howitt. 2014. "What Do We Learn from Schumpeterian Growth Theory?" *Handbook of Economic Growth* 2:515–63.

Aghion, Philippe, Antonin Bergeaud, Timo Boppart, Peter J. Klenow, and Huiyu Li. 2019. "Missing Growth from Creative Destruction." *American Economic Review* 109 (8): 2795–822.

———. 2020. "A Theory of Falling Growth and Rising Rents." Working Paper no. 26448, NBER, Cambridge, MA.

Aghion, Philippe, Nick Bloom, Richard Blundell, Rachel Griffith, and Peter Howitt. 2005. "Competition and Innovation: An Inverted-U Relationship." *Quarterly Journal of Economics* 120 (2): 701–28.

Aghion, Philippe, and Peter Howitt. 1992. "A Model of Growth through Creative Destruction." *Econometrica* 60 (2): 323–51.

———. 2009. *The Economics of Growth*. Cambridge, MA: MIT Press.

Akcigit, Ufuk, and Sina T. Ates. 2019. "What Happened to U.S. Business Dynamism?" Working Paper no. 25756, NBER, Cambridge, MA.

Akcigit, Ufuk, and William R. Kerr. 2018. "Growth through Heterogeneous Innovations." *Journal of Political Economy* 126 (4): 1374–443.

Argente, David, Salome Baslandze, Douglas Hanley, and Sara Moreira. 2018. "Patents to Products: Innovation and Firm Performance." In 2018 Meeting Papers no. 858, Society for Economic Dynamics, Minneapolis.

Atkeson, Andrew, and Ariel Burstein. 2019. "Aggregate Implications of Innovation Policy." *Journal of Political Economy* 127 (6): 2625–83.

Baily, Martin Neil, Charles Hulten, and David Campbell. 1992. "Productivity Dynamics in Manufacturing Plants." *Brookings Papers: Microeconomics* 4:187–267.

Baqaee, David Rezza, and Emmanuel Farhi. 2020. "Productivity and Misallocation in General Equilibrium." *Quarterly Journal of Economics* 135 (1): 105–63.

Bernard, Andrew B., Stephen J. Redding, and Peter K. Schott. 2010. "Multi-Product Firms and Product Switching." *American Economic Review* 100 (1): 70–97.

Bloom, Nicholas, Charles I. Jones, John Van Reenen, and Michael Webb. 2017. "Are Ideas Getting Harder to Find?" Working Paper no. 23782, NBER, Cambridge, MA.

———. 2020. "Are Ideas Getting Harder to Find?" *American Economic Review* 110 (4): 1104–44.

Broda, Christian, and David E. Weinstein. 2006. "Globalization and the Gains from Variety." *Quarterly Journal of Economics* 121 (2): 541–85.

Decker, Ryan, John Haltiwanger, Ron Jarmin, and Javier Miranda. 2014. "The Role of Entrepreneurship in U.S. Job Creation and Economic Dynamism." *Journal of Economic Perspectives* 28 (3): 3–24.

———. 2017. "Declining Dynamism, Allocative Efficiency, and the Productivity Slowdown." *American Economic Review* 107 (5): 322–26.

Engbom, Niklas. 2019. "Firm and Worker Dynamics in an Aging Labor Market." Working Paper no. 756, Federal Reserve Bank of Minneapolis.

Eslava, Marcela, and John Haltiwanger. 2020. "The Life-Cycle Growth of Plants: The Role of Productivity, Demand and Wedges." Working Paper no. 27184, NBER, Cambridge, MA.

Feenstra, Robert C. 1994. "New Product Varieties and the Measurement of International Prices." *American Economic Review* 84 (1): 157–77.

Fernald, John G. 2015. "Productivity and Potential Output Before, During, and After the Great Recession." *NBER Macroeconomics Annual* 29:1–51.

Foster, Lucia, John C. Haltiwanger, and C. J. Krizan. 2001. "Aggregate Productivity Growth: Lessons from Microeconomic Evidence." *New Developments in Productivity Analysis* 8:303–72.

Foster, Lucia, John Haltiwanger, and Chad Syverson. 2008. "Reallocation, Firm Turnover, and Efficiency: Selection on Productivity or Profitability?" *American Economic Review* 98 (1): 394–425.

Garcia-Macia, Daniel, Chang-Tai Hsieh, and Peter J. Klenow. 2019. "How Destructive Is Innovation?" *Econometrica* 87 (5): 1507–41.

Griliches, Zvi, and Haim Regev. 1995. "Firm Productivity in Israeli Industry 1979–1988." *Journal of Econometrics* 65 (1): 175–203.

Gutiérrez, Germán, and Thomas Philippon. 2019. "Fading Stars." *AEA Papers and Proceedings* 109:312–16.

Haltiwanger, John, Ron S. Jarmin, and Javier Miranda. 2013. "Who Creates Jobs? Small versus Large versus Young." *Review of Economics and Statistics* 95 (2): 347–61.

Hopenhayn, Hugo A. 1992. "Entry, Exit, and Firm Dynamics in Long Run Equilibrium." *Econometrica* 60 (5): 1127–50.

Hopenhayn, Hugo, Julian Neira, and Rish Singhania. 2018. "From Population Growth to Firm Demographics: Implications for Concentration, Entrepreneurship and the Labor Share." Working Paper no. 25382, NBER, Cambridge, MA.

Hottman, Colin J., Stephen J. Redding, and David E. Weinstein. 2016. "Quantifying the Sources of Firm Heterogeneity." *Quarterly Journal of Economics* 131 (3): 1291–364.

Hsieh, Chang-Tai, and Peter J. Klenow. 2009. "Misallocation and Manufacturing TFP in China and India." *Quarterly Journal of Economics* 124 (4): 1403–48.

———. 2014. "The Life Cycle of Plants in India and Mexico." *Quarterly Journal of Economics* 129 (3): 1035–84.

———. 2017. "The Reallocation Myth." Federal Reserve Bank of Kansas City Economic Policy Symposium on Fostering a Dynamic Global Economy.

Hsieh, Chang-Tai, Peter J. Klenow, and Ishan B. Nath. 2019. "A Global View of Creative Destruction." Working Paper no. 26461, NBER, Cambridge, MA.

Jones, Charles I. 1995. "R&D–Based Models of Economic Growth." *Journal of Political Economy* 103 (4): 759–84.

———. 2016. "Life and Growth." *Journal of Political Economy* 124 (2): 539–78.

Klette, Tor Jakob, and Samuel Kortum. 2004. "Innovating Firms and Aggregate Innovation." *Journal of Political Economy* 112 (5): 986–1018.

Kogan, Leonid, Dimitris Papanikolaou, Amit Seru, and Noah Stoffman. 2017. "Technological Innovation, Resource Allocation, and Growth." *Quarterly Journal of Economics* 132 (2): 665–712.

Kortum, Samuel S. 1997. "Research, Patenting, and Technological Change." *Econometrica*: 65:1389–419.

Krusell, Per. 1998. "How Is R&D Distributed across Firms? A Theoretical Analysis." Manuscript, Institute for International Economic Studies, Stockholm University.

Lentz, Rasmus, and Dale T. Mortensen. 2008. "An Empirical Model of Growth through Product Innovation." *Econometrica* 76 (6): 1317–73.

Liu, Ernest, Atif Mian, and Amir Sufi. 2019. "Low Interest Rates, Market Power, and Productivity Growth." Working Paper no. 25505, NBER, Cambridge, MA.

Lucas, Robert E., Jr., and Benjamin Moll. 2014. "Knowledge Growth and the Allocation of Time." *Journal of Political Economy* 122 (1): 1–51.

Luttmer, Erzo G. J. 2011. "On the Mechanics of Firm Growth." *Review of Economic Studies* 78 (3): 1042–68.

Mankiw, N. Gregory, David Romer, and David N. Weil. 1992. "A Contribution to the Empirics of Economic Growth." *Quarterly Journal of Economics* 107 (2): 407–37.

Melitz, Marc J., and Sašo Polanec. 2015. "Dynamic Olley-Pakes Productivity Decomposition with Entry and Exit." *RAND Journal of Economics* 46 (2): 362–75.

Olley, G. Steven, and Ariel Pakes. 1996. "The Dynamics of Productivity in the Telecommunications Equipment Industry." *Econometrica* 64 (6): 1263–97.

Peters, Michael. 2020. "Heterogeneous Mark-Ups, Growth and Endogenous Misallocation." *Econometrica* 88 (5): 2037–2073.

Peters, Michael, and Conor Walsh. 2019. "Declining Dynamism, Increasing Markups and Missing Growth: The Role of the Labor Force." 2019 Meeting Paper no. 658, Society for Economic Dynamics.

Rivera-Batiz, Luis A., and Paul M. Romer. 1991. "Economic Integration and Endogenous Growth." *Quarterly Journal of Economics* 106 (2): 531–55.

Romer, Paul M. 1990. "Endogenous Technological Change." *Journal of Political Economy* 98 (5, part 2): S71–S102.

Solow, Robert M. 1956. "A Contribution to the Theory of Economic Growth." *Quarterly Journal of Economics* 70 (1): 65–94.

Comment

John Haltiwanger, *University of Maryland,* United States of America, *and NBER,* United States of America

Understanding the determinants of innovation and productivity growth is a core open area of economics research. Although enormous progress has been made in theoretical models of innovation accompanied by an increasing use of firm-level data to quantify the nature of innovation and productivity, many challenges remain. A key challenge is that much of the research using firm-level data has focused on firms with observable measures of the inputs into innovation (e.g., research and development [R&D] expenditures) and direct measures of the success of innovations (e.g., patents). This approach focuses on a relatively narrow subset of firms and sectors where such observables are relevant. Most firms do not report R&D expenditures or patents. It is implausible that only the firms with these observable measures of innovation are responsible for the observed fluctuations in productivity growth from innovation. As evidence of this, a National Academy of Sciences report (Brown et al. 2005) highlighting the limitations of R&D data reported that one of the most innovative firms in retail trade, Walmart, reports no R&D expenditures in its 10-K reports.

This paper takes an indirect approach to identifying innovation activity that overcomes these limitations. Using an innovative growth accounting framework that is motivated by a quality ladder model of innovation, this paper uses data on the employment growth rate distribution for the universe of private sector, nonfarm (hereafter private sector for short) establishments to quantify the contribution of creative destruction (CD), own innovation, and new varieties. The authors accomplish this important objective by using the Longitudinal Business Database (LBD) that tracks the employment dynamics, including entry and exit, firm size, and firm age of the universe of private sector establishments and their parent firms. This paper uses the LBD for the period 1982–2013.

The quantitative analysis yields many interesting results. These are well described in the paper, so for the sake of brevity I highlight two of key results discussed in the abstract. First, the authors find that new and young firms punch more than their weight. Almost 50% of aggregate productivity growth over their sample period is accounted for by firms age <5 even though they account for only about 16% of employment. Most of this is coming from new variety introduction by startups and young firms. Second, in spite of this outsize role for young firms, the authors find that most of the surge in productivity in the mid-1990s and then slow-down thereafter is accounted for by older firms. Here the primary contributor is own innovation by older firms.

Quantifying the contribution of innovation to economic growth for the entire private sector is a major step forward. However, the authors' indirect approach using the LBD is implemented with a number of strong assumptions that are inconsistent with empirical evidence. Relatedly, the approach taken does not distinguish between the key distinct patterns in firm dynamics and productivity that vary by sector. These limitations imply that appropriate caution is needed in interpreting the quantitative results. The authors acknowledge many of these limitations and discuss addressing them as next steps. In the remainder of my comments, I discuss the evidence that implies that these limitations are likely quantitatively important. In turn, I discuss potential next steps in this promising research agenda.

To understand the limitations, it is helpful to review briefly the key assumptions of the framework and the accompanying identification approach. New products are identified through new establishments. New establishments are used to identify new varieties and CD. Own innovation is identified via the growth in employment of incumbent establishments. The framework and data permit heterogeneity in own innovation, arrival rate of CD, step size by groups of establishments classified by firm age, and firm size classes. A key strong assumption is that CD is random. That is, the rate of loss from CD is the same across all firm groups. Another key strong assumption is that there are no frictions that yield dispersion in marginal revenue products. Accordingly, in the simple framework used with employment as the only input, the model implies that there is no dispersion in revenue per worker across firms and establishments. Yet another strong assumption is that the framework treats all of the establishments and firms in the private, nonfarm sector as contributors to final output via a single constant elasticity of substitution (CES) aggregator across products.

The assumption that CD is random implies that when Walmart opens a new store in a specific geographic location, any implied CD loss applies to all incumbent establishments in all sectors and locations. The evidence on establishment entry and exit as well as studies of the effect of entry of establishments on incumbent establishments implies that CD is both sector and location specific.

Figure 1 shows tabulations from the Business Dynamic Statistics (BDS), which reflect public domain tabulations by the US Census Bureau from the LBD. The top panel shows the share of employment of entering establishments for the entire private sector (economy) and for selected broad sectors. The lower panel shows the share of employment for exiting establishments for the same sectors. These are two of the key moments used in the analysis in this paper (see, for example, table 2 of the paper). In these tabulations, the patterns reflect the combination of all firm age and size classes. The subperiods correspond closely to the subperiods used in this paper.[1] It is evident that the retail trade sector exhibits especially high entry and exit shares on average. This is consistent with the findings in Foster, Haltiwanger, and Krizan (2006) and Foster et al. (2016) that firm expansion and contraction is dominated by establishment entry and exit in retail trade. The industry-specific variation in entry and exit shares suggests that an entering establishment in, say, retail trade competes directly with other establishments in retail trade and not with establishments in other sectors. More direct evidence in Haltiwanger, Jarmin, and Krizan (2010) shows that when a new big-box store enters a local market, the effect is on other establishments in the same narrow retail trade sector and is very local. That is, establishments in the same narrow retail trade sector and in close proximity are adversely affected. Local establishments in complementary sectors like restaurants actually fare better upon such entry.

Figure 1 also shows that the decline in entry and exit in retail trade is more pronounced than in other sectors. Foster et al. (2006) and Foster et al. (2016) (and the cites therein) show that this reflects structural change in the retail trade sector away from single-unit establishment firms to large national chains. Single-unit establishment firms have a much higher pace of entry and exit than the establishments of large national chains, which accounts for the decline in the pace of entry and exit. This structural transformation is linked to globalization and advances in information technology that have enabled large national chains to develop global supply chains and efficient distribution networks. During this period of structural transformation, aggregate productivity (measured as real output

A. Entry Employment Share (Employment from Entering
   Establishments/Total Employment in Sector)

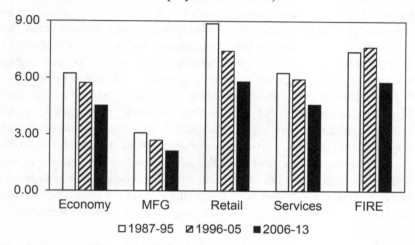

B. Exit Employment Share (Employment from Exiting
   Establishments/Total Employment in Sector)

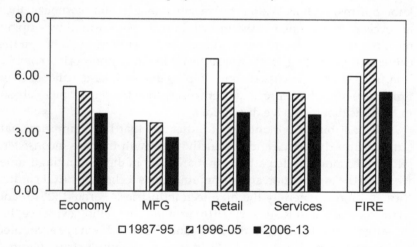

Fig. 1. Moments of establishment entry and exit share for selected sectors. A color version of this figure is available online.

per worker) according to the US Bureau of Labor Statistics (BLS) has exhibited especially robust growth (see Manser 2005). The approach taken in this paper does not enable capturing this industry-specific structural transformation.

A related issue for retail trade is that Foster et al. (2006) and Foster et al. (2016) show that revenue per worker for the entering establishments at large, national chains is about 30 log points larger than for the exiting establishments of the single-unit establishment firms that they are displacing within the same narrow sector. Such dispersion is at odds with the assumption of no dispersion in revenue per worker across establishments in the accounting framework in this paper.

The finding that revenue per worker exhibits considerable dispersion across establishments and firms within the same narrow sector is not unique to retail trade (see, e.g., Decker et al. 2020).[2] However, in retail trade the evidence exhibits a particularly systematic pattern with the structural change moving employment and sales away from low-revenue-per-worker single-unit establishments to high-revenue-per-worker establishments of large, national chains. Moreover, this reallocation at the establishment level is accompanied by rising revenue per worker at the detailed sectoral level within retail trade.

In the paper, the authors defend the strong assumption of no dispersion in revenue per worker across establishments and firms by presenting evidence (from publicly available information) that for individual well-known firms, such as Walmart, Amazon, Google, and Starbucks, their life-cycle patterns exhibit rapid growth in scale as measured by employment but relatively modest growth in revenue per worker. Although this evidence is interesting, it is not clear this is the most appropriate comparison. The evidence discussed above implies that such large national chain firms have much higher revenue per worker than the single-unit establishment firms that they have displaced.

A distinct but important set of industries that have empirical patterns of firm dynamics and productivity growth that are inconsistent with the economywide patterns that are used in the accounting framework are the information and communications technology (ICT) industries and more generally the high-tech industries.[3] Fernald (2015) and Byrne, Fernald, and Reinsdorf (2016) provide compelling evidence that the surge in productivity in the 1990s and the slowdown are accounted for by the ICT producing and ICT intensive using industries. Figure 2 shows the distinct firm dynamics for the high-tech industries. Unlike the overall economy and sectors like retail trade, the high-tech sectors exhibited a surge in firm entry in the 1990s, with the share of young firm activity growing substantially over this decade. In the post-2000 period, the share of activity accounted for by young firms declined through 2017. Further evidence that young firms in high-tech sectors exhibit distinct dynamics over this period is seen by tracking the cohort of initial public

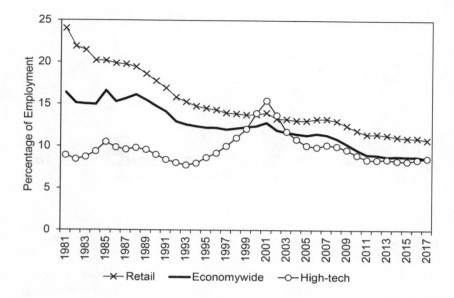

Fig. 2. Percent of employment at young (age < 5) firms by selected sectors. A color version of this figure is available online.

offerings (IPOs) in the period before the 1990s, during the 1990s, and in the post-2000 period (see fig. A6 of Decker et al. 2016 and Ritter 2016). The 1990s cohort is high-tech-intensive and rapidly becomes the dominate cohort in terms of the share of sales and employment that it accounts for among publicly traded firms.

Building on the findings in Fernald (2015) and Byrne et al. (2016), figure 3 presents the patterns of real labor productivity growth for the high-tech industries versus other industries from BLS over this period of time.[4] The surge in productivity in the high-tech sectors during the 1990s and the slowdown in the post-2000 period (especially post 2005) is evident.

Further evidence of potentially important connections between the firm entry and productivity surge in the 1990s in the high-tech industries is presented in Foster et al. (2019). Using four-digit NAICS industries that comprise high-tech and a difference-in-differences empirical specification, Foster et al. (2019) present evidence that the surge in productivity growth in a given high-tech industry is preceded by a surge in entry about 6–9 years before. Interestingly, they also find that following a surge in entry in a given high-tech industry, there is a substantial increase in revenue labor productivity dispersion initially (about 4–6 years after the entry surge). They argue that these patterns are consistent with

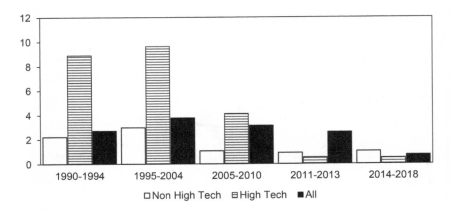

Fig. 3. Growth rate in output per hour (average annual for reported subperiods). A color version of this figure is available online.

the Gort and Klepper (1982) characterization of the important role of young firms in the experimentation phase of innovative activity. Gort and Klepper (1982) experimentation and learning are features missing from the current innovative accounting framework.

These patterns for high tech raise questions about the analysis in the paper that suggests the productivity surge and slowdown is due to an own innovation surge and slowdown amongst mature firms. These inferences are based on matching the economywide moments that show a steadily declining pace of entry during the period of the productivity surge and decline. However, the ICT (high-tech) industries exhibit both a surge in entry and productivity growth in the 1990s and a post-2000 decline in entry and productivity growth. Moreover, detailed industry-level data suggest that an entry surge precedes the surge in productivity growth. Because the ICT (high-tech) industries played a dominant role in the productivity surge and slowdown, these industry-specific patterns need to be considered for explaining economywide patterns. The current paper does not attempt to account for these ICT (high-tech) patterns. Another feature of the evidence related to ICT (high-tech) that raises questions about the inferences from the accounting framework used here is the evidence from Fernald (2015) and Byrne et al. (2016) that emphasizes the spillover effect of ICT on other sectors. The accounting framework used here does not readily permit innovation of a general-purpose technology like ICT that has such spillover effects.

Yet another reason that taking into account sectoral differences is likely important in this context is illustrated in figure 4A. An important structural transformation over this sample period is the well-known shift in economic activity away from goods-producing industries such as manufacturing toward service industries, including retail trade. This structural change is likely driven by forces (e.g., globalization) that are outside the scope of the accounting framework in this paper. However, such structural change

A. Employment Shares of Economy-Wide Employment
   by Selected Sectors and Subperiod

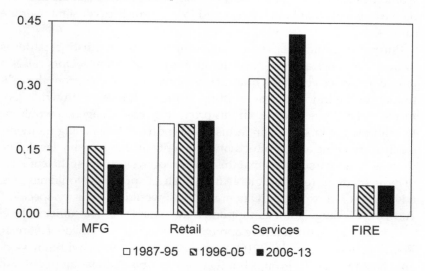

B. Employment Shares of Age 11+ Within Sectors

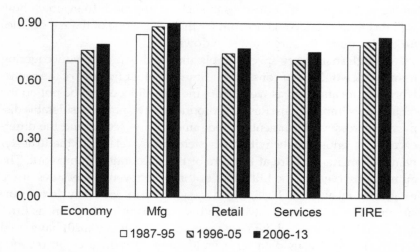

Fig. 4. Employment shares by sector and by age within sector. A color version of this figure is available online.

influences the targeted moments on establishment entry and exit dynamics by firm age and size that are used to quantify the respective contribution of different firm groups to economic growth. As can be seen in figure 4B, the share of employment at mature firms is much higher in manufacturing than services. This implies that the shift from goods to services dampens the increase in the share of activity at mature firms. It would be useful to consider the quantitative implications using firm dynamic moments that hold the composition of industries constant over the sample period.

Putting all of the pieces together, taking into account distinct patterns of firm dynamics and productivity growth by different sectors raises a variety of issues about the quantitative inferences drawn from the calibration of the innovative accounting framework to economywide moments. An obvious next step in this promising research agenda would be to calibrate the model on an industry-by-industry basis using moments on firm dynamic and productivity moments at the industry level. The discussion above suggests that this likely requires using a sufficient level of industry detail (e.g., 4-digit NAICS). Such an approach would have the advantage of making the CD nonrandom (it would be industry-specific).[5] Also, the CES aggregator assumption is more plausible at a sufficient level of industry detail. An attractive approach here would be to follow Hottman, Redding, and Weinstein (2016), who use a CES structure within reasonably narrow product groups but then use a Cobb-Douglas aggregator to aggregate across sectors. It would also be interesting to focus attention on the ICT (high-tech) industries in such an approach to evaluate how well this framework could account for the outsize role of these industries for the productivity surge and slowdown.

Although an industry-specific application of this innovative accounting framework would be of considerable interest, other features of the framework require attention as well before more confidence can be put on the quantitative implications. Revenue productivity exhibits considerable dispersion across establishments in the same narrow sector, and the differences in revenue productivity are systematically related to the firm dynamic moments that are at the core of this accounting framework. The authors observe that the LBD does not include revenue measures at the establishment and firm level, which is one of the reasons they do not pursue this line of inquiry. However, other options using the Census firm- and establishment-level data are feasible. Autor et al. (2020) have used the Economic Census data for a wide range of industries on revenue and employment. Although the frequency is only every 5 years, such an analysis is feasible for the last several decades with revenue and employ-ment at the establishment level. Moreover, the Economic Census data can be readily integrated with the LBD, so moments that take the firm age and firm size heterogeneity into account as in the current analysis are feasible.[6]

Finally, it would be of considerable interest to compare and contrast the inferences that emerge from this framework with the large literature that uses direct approaches (i.e., with R&D and patents) to quantify the contri-bution of the different components of innovation to economic growth. Yet another alternative and more direct approach is to track innovation as in Argente et al. (2018), using product entry and exit from item-level product data. To the authors' credit, they have developed a framework that en-ables exploring these issues on a much broader basis than the research, which uses a more direct approach. Finding some way of reconciling what we are learning from these alternative approaches would have consider-able value. In considering such potential reconciliation, one of the seeming limitations of the approach in this paper actually has some attractive fea-tures. In this paper, new products are captured by new establishments. At first glance, using direct measures of products would seemingly domi-nate. However, for many businesses, opening a new establishment in a specific location is a form of innovation (offering access to the products and services to consumers at this specific location). Keeping this location-specific feature that inherently is connected to establishment entry and exit should be part of the research agenda going forward.

Endnotes

Authors' email address: Haltiwanger (haltiwan@econ.umd.edu). For acknowledgments, sources of research support, and disclosure of the author's material financial relationships, if any, please see https://www.nber.org/books-and-chapters/nber-macroeconomics-annual -2020-volume-35/comment-innovative-growth-accounting-haltiwanger.

1. The first subperiod is 1987–1995 rather than 1982–1995 as in the analysis in this pa-per. The analysis in the paper considers three firm age groups: 0–5, 6–10, and 11+. The lat-ter two groups can only be defined directly from 1987 forward. The analysis in the paper relies on an imputation that decomposes those two age groups for the period 1982–1986. I don't think this imputation and the difference in the first subperiod is critical because the empirical patterns for the moments for subperiods I construct from the BDS that can be compared with those in the paper are broadly similar.

2. See figure 3b of Decker et al. (2020).

3. Here I am using the high-tech industry definition following Hecker (2005), which are the STEM-intensive sectors. These industries, so defined, encompass the ICT industries. The high-tech industries also include industries such as biotechnology.

4. Fernald (2015) and Byrne et al. (2016) provide evidence of the outsize role of ICT on total factor productivity (TFP) growth. Figure 3 shows the patterns for labor productivity growth for high tech and non–high tech. The patterns in figure 3 for labor productivity for high-tech

industries closely mimic the patterns for TFP for ICT. High-tech patterns are shown in figure 3 to correspond to the young firm share evidence in figure 2 for the high-tech industries.

5. The post-conference draft includes appendix C, which provides a framework that specifies nonrandom CD. This extension permits CD to be targeted to specific quality ranges. This is a step forward, but it has not been implemented empirically. Moreover, it is unclear that this approach will be suitable for capturing the core idea that CD is both industry and location specific (especially in sectors such as retail trade).

6. Decker et al. (2020) also use administrative revenue data at the firm level in a revenue-enhanced version of the LBD from the period 1996–2014. The administrative data provide revenue information only at the firm level, which would pose challenges for the approach taken in this paper. However, adding moments based on firm-level variation could provide more discipline on the quantification analysis.

References

Argente, David, Salome Baslandze, Douglas Hanley, and Sara Moreira. 2018. "Patents to Products: Innovation and Firm Performance." 2018 Meeting Papers no. 858, Society for Economic Dynamics, Minneapolis.

Autor, David, David Dorn, Lawrence Katz, Christina Patterson, and John Van Reenan. 2020. "The Fall of the Labor Share and the Rise of Superstar Firms." *Quarterly Journal of Economics* 135 (2): 645–709.

Brown, Lawrence, Thomas Plewes, and Marisa Gerstein. 2005. *Measuring Research and Development Expenditures for the U.S. Economy*. Washington, DC: National Academies Press.

Byrne, David, John Fernald, and Marshall Reinsdorf. 2016. "Does the United States Have a Productivity Slowdown or a Measurement Problem?" *Brookings Papers on Economic Activity* (Spring): 109–182.

Decker, Ryan A., John Haltiwanger, Ron S. Jarmin, and Javier Miranda. 2016. "Where Has All the Skewness Gone? The Decline in High-Growth (Young) Firms in the U.S." *European Economic Review* 86 (July): 4–23.

———. 2020. "Changing Business Dynamism and Productivity: Shocks vs. Responsiveness." Revised version of Working Paper no. 24236 (2018), NBER, Cambridge, MA.

Fernald, John. 2015. "Productivity and Potential Output Before, During, and After the Great Recession." In *NBER Macroeconomics Annual 2014*, vol. 29, ed. Jonathan A. Parker and Michael Woodford, 1–51. Chicago: University of Chicago Press.

Foster, Lucia, Cheryl Grim, John Haltiwanger, and Zoltan Wolf. 2019. "Innovation, Productivity Dispersion, and Productivity Growth." In *Measuring and Accounting for Innovation in the Twenty-First Century*, Studies in Income and Wealth, vol. 78, ed. Carol Corrado, Javier Miranda, Jonathan Haskel, and Daniel Sichel. Chicago: University of Chicago Press.

Foster, Lucia, John Haltiwanger, Shawn Klimek, C. J. Krizan, and Scott Ohlmacher. 2016. "Evolution of National Retail Chains: How We Got Here." In *Handbook on the Economics of Retailing and Distribution*, ed. Emek Basker. Northampton, MA: Edward Elgar.

Foster, Lucia, John Haltiwanger, and C. J. Krizan. 2006. "Market Selection, Reallocation and Restructuring in the US Retail Trade Sector in the 1990s." *Review of Economics and Statistics* 88 (4): 748–58.

Gort, Michael, and Steven Klepper. 1982. "Time Paths in the Diffusion of Product Innovations." *Economic Journal* 92 (367): 630–53.

Haltiwanger, John, Ron S. Jarmin, and C. J. Krizan. 2010. "Mom-and-Pop Meet Big-Box: Complements or Substitutes?" *Journal of Urban Economics* 67 (1): 116–34.

Hecker, Daniel. 2005. "High-Technology Employment: A NAICS-Based Update." *Monthly Labor Review* 128 (7): 58.

Hottman, Colin J., Stephen J. Redding, and David E. Weinstein. 2016. "Quantifying the Sources of Firm Heterogeneity." *Quarterly Journal of Economics* 131 (3): 1291–364.

Manser, Marilyn. 2005. "Productivity Measures for Retail Trade: Data and Issues." *Monthly Labor Review* (July): 30–38.

Ritter, Jay. 2016. "Initial Public Offerings: Updated Statistics." Mimeo.

Discussion

Erik Hurst followed up on a comment made by the discussant, John Haltiwanger. He posited that the increasing dispersion in revenue productivity across firms might arise because of differential shifts in the composition of the labor force based on human capital accumulation. Haltiwanger added that the source of dispersion in revenues per employee could also be the result of misallocation deriving from a learning process. The adoption of information and communications technologies across firms is a slow process, which would result in staggered revenue productivity gains across firms, he argued. The authors agreed that markup dispersion—the main source of productivity differentials according to their results—provides a good explanation, but it is not exhaustive. Other possible channels, like human capital, and the resulting misallocations are worth investigating, they said.

The authors also sympathized with the discussant's suggestion to extend their analysis to the sectoral level and to employ a nested CES production structure. They agreed that this methodology might be useful to shed more light on the role of big firms in driving aggregate productivity growth.

The discussion ended with a brief question by Haltiwanger on the surge of IPOs in the 1990s. He asked whether the authors had researched their role in contributing to subsequent growth. The authors answered that they did not perform the exercise but that their framework could be employed for answering the question.

5

The Glass Ceiling and the Paper Floor: Changing Gender Composition of Top Earners since the 1980s

Fatih Guvenen, *University of Minnesota,* United States of America, *Federal Reserve Bank of Minneapolis,* United States of America, *and NBER,* United States of America

Greg Kaplan, *University of Chicago,* United States of America, *and NBER,* United States of America

Jae Song, *Social Security Administration,* United States of America

I. Introduction

Since the late 1970s, the US earnings distribution has experienced profound changes. Among these changes, two of the most well-known are the increasing share of total earnings that accrues to top earners (i.e., individuals in the top 1% or top 0.1% of the earnings distribution) and the continued relative absence of women from this top-earning group.[1] This latter phenomenon is commonly referred to as the *glass ceiling*, the emergence of which has spurred both debate over the appropriate policy response as well as active research into its primary causes.[2] However, progress on both fronts has been hampered by the scarcity of empirical evidence from nationally representative data on the gender structure at the top of the earnings distribution.[3] Our goal in this paper is to provide this necessary empirical evidence on the glass ceiling, using newer and better data than have been previously available. In doing so, we also revisit several important questions about top earners of both genders: the dynamics of their earnings, their industry composition, their age and cohort composition, and the evolution of earnings for lifetime top earners.

Our interest in top earners is motivated by their disproportionately large influence on the aggregate economy. This influence operates through at least three channels. First, top earners are crucial economic actors. In the United States, individuals in the top 1% of the income distribution earn approximately 15% of aggregate before-tax income and pay about 40% of individual income taxes—more than one and a half times the amount paid by the bottom 90 percentiles—and 50% of all corporate income tax.[4] Because this group includes virtually all high-level managers and executives of US businesses (both public and private), top earners play a pivotal role in decisions about business investment, employment creation, layoffs, and international trade. Second, top earners are key political actors. Political scientists have argued that the increasing polarization of political discourse in the United States can be partly attributed to the rising influence of top earners, through political contributions that have in part been made possible by changes in campaign finance regulations since the 1970s (Barber 2013; Baker et al. 2014). Third, because top earners include a large fraction of the economy's top talent, understanding the distribution of top earners across gender, industries, and cohorts helps us to better understand the allocation of human capital in the economy.

The pivotal role of top earners has led to a burgeoning literature whose goal is to explicitly model the thick Pareto tail at the top end of the earnings distribution and then either evaluate alternative mechanisms that could give rise to top earners (e.g., Gabaix and Landier 2008; Jones and Kim 2018), study the allocation of top talent across occupations (e.g., Hsieh et al. 2019), or ask how to best design fiscal policy in the presence of influential top earners (e.g., Saez 2001; Badel and Huggett 2014; Guner, Lopez-Daneri, and Ventura 2014). Therefore, one goal of this paper is to provide the empirical evidence that this literature requires to address these issues—on gender differences, persistence, mobility, age, and industry composition, and on the life-cycle dynamics of top earners. The literature on optimal taxation of top earners has so far only considered the taxation of individuals; as this literature moves toward studying the taxation of families, evidence on gender differences among top earners of the type we provide will become essential.

Our data set is a 10% representative sample of individual earnings histories from the US Social Security Administration (SSA). Several features of these data are well suited for our goals. The large number of observations enables us to study earnings within the top 1%, including the earnings of those at the very top, the 0.1%, as well as the characteristics of female top earners, who constitute only a small subset of top earners. The panel nature of the data set enables us to track the same individuals over time and, hence, to perform our analysis using both 5-year average earnings as well as annual earnings. This is important because of the relatively low probabilities of top earners remaining in the top percentiles from year to year, as shown by Auten, Gee, and Turner (2013), and which we confirm and expand on. The presence of Employer Identification Numbers (EIN) from W-2 forms enables us to obtain detailed industry information about each worker's jobs, which we use to construct an industry breakdown that is informative about the types of jobs held by top earners. In particular, we separate workers in finance and insurance, health services, legal services, and engineering from executives in other service industries. The 32-year time span of our data and the absence of attrition both enable us to paint a sharper picture of how top earners' earnings evolve over their life cycles than has been possible in previous work.

Our findings on gender differences speak to three broad themes: (i) trends in top earnings over the last 3 decades, (ii) the persistence and mobility of top earners, and (iii) the characteristics of top earners.

First, regarding recent trends in top earnings, we find that although large strides have been taken toward gender equality at the top of the distribution, very large differences between men and women still remain. Since 1981, the share of women among top earners has increased by more than a factor of 3. Yet in 2012, the earnings share of women still comprised only 11% of the earnings of all individuals in the top 0.1%, and only 18% of the earnings of the top 1%. The glass ceiling is still there, but it is thinner than it was 3 decades ago. Moreover, among the top 0.1%, virtually all of the increase came in the 1980s and 1990s; the last decade has seen almost no further improvement. We decompose the rise in the share of women among top earners into a component that is due to changes in female participation in all parts of the distribution and find that these compositional effects play little role in explaining the observed trend. This finding reflects the fact that gender differences have narrowed much less in the bottom 99% of the distribution than in the top percentiles—the fraction of women in the bottom 99% increased from 43% in 1981 to 49% in 2012.

For top earners of both genders, after several decades of rising earnings, a leveling off has taken place during the last decade. Both the thresholds for membership and the average earnings of workers in the top percentiles have remained relatively flat since 2000. It is too soon to tell whether this represents a change in the increasing trend that has dominated the last half century (Kopczuk, Saez, and Song 2010) or whether it is a temporary flattening due to top earners suffering disproportionately large temporary falls in earnings during the 2000–2 and 2008–9 recessions (Guvenen, Ozkan, and Song 2014).[5]

Second, regarding persistence and mobility at the top of the earnings distribution, we find substantial turnover among top earners. The frequency with which workers enter and exit the top earnings groups sounds a cautionary note to analyses of top earners that use only data from annual cross sections. This high tendency for top earners to fall out of the top earnings groups was particularly stark for women in the 1980s—a phenomenon we refer to as the paper floor. But the persistence of top-earning women has dramatically increased in the last 30 years, so that today the paper floor has been largely mended. Whereas female top earners were once around twice as likely as men to drop out of the top-earning groups, today they are no more likely than men to do so. Moreover, this change is not simply due to women being more equally represented in the upper parts of the top percentiles; the same paper floor existed for the top percentiles of the female earnings distribution, but this paper floor has also largely disappeared. We use a decomposition to show that this change in persistence accounts for a substantial fraction of the increase in the share of women among top earners that we observe during the last 3 decades.

As the persistence of top-earning women was catching up with men during this period, the persistence of top-earning men was itself increasing, particularly after the turn of the twenty-first century. Throughout the 1980s and 1990s, the probability that a male in the top 0.1% was still in the top 0.1% 1 year later remained at around 45%, but by 2011 this probability had increased to 57%. When combined with our finding that the share of earnings accruing to the top 0.1% has leveled off since 2000, this implies a striking observation about the nature of top earnings inequality: despite the total share of earnings accruing to the top percentiles remaining relatively constant in the last decade, these earnings are being spread among a decreasing share of the overall population. Top earner status is thus becoming more persistent, with the top 0.1% slowly becoming a more entrenched subset of the population.

Third, regarding the industry composition of top earners, we find that the finance industry dominates for both men and women. In 2012, finance and insurance accounted for around one-third of workers in the top 0.1%. However, this was not the case 30 years ago, when the health-care industry accounted for the largest share of the top 0.1%. Since then, top-earning health-care workers have dropped to the second 0.9% where, along with workers in finance and insurance, they have replaced workers in manufacturing, whose share of this group has dropped by roughly half. Perhaps surprisingly, these changes in industry structure do not play much of a role in explaining either the level or the change in the share of women among top earners, because the industry composition of the top percentiles is very similar for men and women.

Fourth, to gain some insight into possible future trends for the glass ceiling, we also examine the age and cohort composition of top earners. Top earners are older than average and have become more so over time. In contrast with analyses of the gender structure of corporate boards (e.g., Bertrand et al. 2012), we do not find that female top earners are younger than male top earners. Entry of new cohorts, rather than changes within existing cohorts, account for most of the increase in the share of women among top earners. These new cohorts of women are making inroads into the top 1% earlier in their life cycles than previous cohorts. If this trend continues, and if these younger cohorts exhibit the same trajectory as existing cohorts in terms of the share of women among top earners, then we might expect to see further increases in the share of women in the overall top 1% in coming years. However, this is not true for the top 0.1%. At the very top of the distribution, young women have not made big strides: the share of women among the top 0.1% of young people in recent cohorts is no larger than the corresponding share of women among the top 0.1% of young people in older cohorts.

All of the findings described so far pertain to a relatively short-run perspective on identity of top earners, based either on annual earnings or 5-year average earnings. But for many questions about top earners, such as human capital accumulation or optimal taxation, a longer-run perspective based on lifetime earnings is more relevant. However, little is currently known about lifetime top earners partly due to the scarcity (until recently) of large and representative panel data sets on earnings with a long enough time span to compute lifetime earnings. Therefore, in the last part of the paper, we document new facts about lifetime top earners and examine how male and female lifetime top earners differ over the life cycle, where in the distribution these individuals start their working lives, and in which parts of the distribution they spend the majority of their careers. We find that within the top 1% of lifetime earners, men and women display distinct life-cycle patterns, so that the gender gap between these groups is inverse U-shaped over the life cycle, increasing substantially in the 30s (presumably when some females' careers are interrupted for family reasons) and then declining toward retirement.

Our results on the glass ceiling relate to a large and active literature. However, the bulk of the existing empirical evidence has been relatively indirect and pertains to somewhat specialized subsets of top earners, such as CEOs and other executives, members of corporate boards, the list of billionaires compiled by *Forbes* magazine, or master of business administration (MBA) graduates from a top US business school (e.g., Bell 2005; Wolfers 2006; Bertrand et al. 2010; Gayle et al. 2012). Although these analyses have revealed a wealth of interesting information, the extent to which their conclusions carry over to other top-earning women is unknown. For example, Wolfers (2006) reports that over a 15-year period starting in the early 1990s, only 1.3% of ExecuComp CEOs were women. This is about

10 times smaller than the share of women we find among the top 0.1% of earners in the 2000s.

Finally, this paper is also related to the literature initiated by Piketty and Saez (2003) that aims to understand the evolution of top earnings. More recently, Parker and Vissing-Jørgensen (2010) and Guvenen, Kaplan, and Song (2014) have studied the cyclicality of top earnings. Our focus is on long-run trends rather than the cycle. Kopczuk et al. (2010), Bakija, Cole, and Heim (2012), and Auten et al. (2013) are related papers that also use large representative samples of individual-level data to study the trends and characteristics of top earners. Brewer, Sibieta, and Wren-Lewis (2007) is a complementary paper that analyzes the characteristics of high-income individuals in the United Kingdom. However, these papers do not focus on the glass ceiling or the paper floor.

II. Data

A. Data Source

We use a confidential panel data set of earnings histories from the SSA covering the period 1981–2012.[6] The data set is constructed by drawing a 10% representative sample of the US population from the SSA's Master Earnings File (MEF). The MEF is the main record of earnings data maintained by the SSA and contains data on every individual in the United States who has a Social Security number (SSN). The data set contains basic demographic characteristics, including date of birth, sex, race, type of work (farm or nonfarm, employment or self-employment), employee earnings, self-employment taxable earnings, and the EIN for each employer, which we use to link industry information. Employee earnings data are uncapped (i.e., there is no top-coding) and include wages and salaries, bonuses, and exercised stock options as reported on the W-2 form (Box 1). The data set grows each year through the addition of new earnings information, which is received directly from employers on the W-2 form.[7] For more information on the MEF, see Panis et al. (2000) and Olsen and Hudson (2009). We convert all nominal variables into 2012 dollars using the personal consumption expenditure deflator. For an individual born in year c, we define their age in year t as $t - c$, which corresponds to their age on December 31 of that year.

To construct the 10% representative sample from the MEF, we select all individuals with the same last digit of (a transformation of) their SSN. Because the last four digits of the SSN are randomly assigned to individuals, this generates a nationally representative panel. The panel tracks the evolution of the US population in the sense that each year 10% of new individuals who are issued SSN numbers enter our sample, and those who die each year are eliminated (determined through SSA death records).

B. Sample Selection

For the analyses in Sections III–VI, in each year t we select all individuals in our baseline 10% sample who satisfy the following two criteria:

1. The individual is between 25 and 60 years old.

2. The individual has annual earnings that exceed a time-varying minimum threshold. This threshold is equal to the earnings one would obtain by working for 520 hours (13 weeks at 40 hours per week) at one-half of the legal minimum wage for that year. In 2012, this corresponded to annual earnings of $1,885.

We impose these selection criteria to focus on workers with a reasonably strong attachment to the labor market and to avoid issues that arise when taking the logarithm of small numbers. These criteria also make our results comparable to the literature on earnings dynamics and inequality, where imposing age and minimum earnings restrictions is standard (see, e.g., Abowd and Card 1989; Juhn, Murphy, and Pierce 1993; Meghir and Pistaferri 2004; Storesletten, Telmer, and Yaron 2004; Autor, Katz, and Kearney 2008).

The MEF contains a small number of extremely high earnings observations each year. To avoid potential problems with outliers, we cap (winsorize) observations above the 99.999th percentile of the distribution of earnings for individuals who satisfy the above two selection criteria in a given year. From 1981 to 2012, the mean and median 99.999th percentiles across years were both $11.5 million, and the maximum, which was in 2000, was $25.4 million.

We report results using two definitions of earnings: (i) annual earnings and (ii) 5-year average earnings. Annual earnings provide us with a snapshot of top earners in each year. But top earners in a given year include some workers whose high earnings were a one-off event such as the receipt of a large one-time bonus or other windfall. Such workers would not be considered as top earners when using 5-year average earnings, which focus on individuals with more stable membership of the top earnings percentiles.

For the analyses using annual earnings, in each year $t = 1981, \ldots, 2012$ we assign all individuals who satisfy the two selection criteria to a percentile group based on their earnings in year t. We focus mostly on the top 0.1%, second 0.9%, and bottom 99%, but we also report some results from finer groupings within the bottom 99.9%. For the analysis using 5-year average earnings, we construct a rolling panel for each year $t = 1983, \ldots,$ 2010 that consists of all individuals who satisfy the two selection criteria in at least three of the years from $t - 2, \ldots, t + 2$, including the most recent year $t + 2$. For each of these individuals, we compute their average annual earnings over the years $t - 2, \ldots, t + 2$ that they satisfy the selection criteria. We then assign individuals to percentile groups based on these 5-year average earnings. For both definitions of earnings, we keep all individuals in the top 1% of the distribution, and we take a 2% random sample of individuals in the bottom 99%.

In Section VII, we also analyze 30-year average earnings, which we refer to as lifetime earnings. For the analysis in that section, we restrict attention to cohorts of individuals from ages 25 to 54 and include individuals in the sample if they satisfy the two selection criteria above for a minimum of 15 years during that 30-year period. In appendix F, we also report results for cohorts of individuals from ages 30 to 59.[8]

III. Trends in Top Earnings

In this section, we study trends in top earners from three related angles. In Subsection III.A we analyze trends for top earners in the overall earnings distribution, without distinguishing by gender. Then, in Subsection III.B, we turn to gender-specific earnings distributions and define top-earning men and women relative to their ranking in the distribution of workers of the same gender. Finally, in Subsection III.C, we return to top earners in the overall distribution and analyze the gender composition of this group and how this composition has changed over time.

A. Top Earners in the Overall Earnings Distribution

In 2012, a worker had to earn at least $1,018,000 to be included in the top 0.1% of the overall earnings distribution and at least $291,000 to be included in the top 1%. During the last 5 years of our sample (2008–12), the analogous thresholds for being included in the top 0.1% and 1% based on 5-year average earnings were $918,000 and $282,000 respectively.[9] These thresholds are only 5%–10% lower than the annual thresholds, which suggests that top earnings are quite persistent. As we will see, this persistence is a recurring theme in our findings.[10]

Figures 1A and 1B show how these top-earning thresholds have changed over our sample period. We emphasize four points. First, the thresholds have risen substantially, reflecting the well-documented rise in top earnings. Second, the rise has not been in the form of a secular trend but was more episodic, with two large bursts (from 1981 to 1987 and from 1994 to 2000) interrupted by two periods when the thresholds were flat. The lack of an upward trend after the turn of twenty-first century is especially noteworthy against the general perception that top earnings have been continuing to rise at a very fast pace. Third, figure 1C, which plots the ratio of thresholds, shows that the thresholds have evolved almost in parallel fashion since 1987, suggesting that inequality *within* the top 1% has been largely stable in recent decades. This is also evident in figure 1D, which shows that the share of total earnings of the top 1% earned by top 0.1% has risen only slightly during this period.[11] Fourth, the thresholds for 5-year average earnings (solid black lines) are not only smoother than the annual

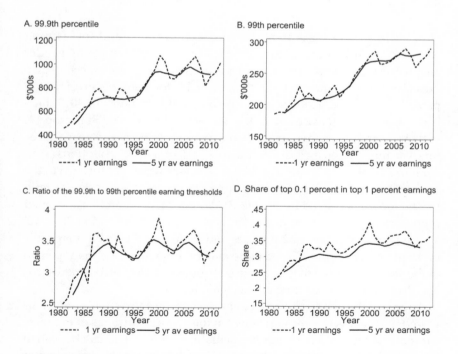

Fig. 1. Top earnings thresholds: (*A*) 99.9th percentile, (*B*) 99th percentile, (*C*) ratio of *A* to *B*, and (*D*) shares of top 0.1% and 1% earnings in aggregate earnings.

thresholds, but are also only slightly lower, reflecting the persistence of top earnings.[12]

These findings are not sensitive to the focusing on top-earnings percentile thresholds. In appendix B, we report the trends in the share of total earnings accruing to workers in various top percentiles (fig. B1A) and trends in average earnings within each percentile group (figs. B1B–B1D). These figures confirm the episodic nature of the rise in top earnings, the tapering off in the rise post-2000, and the parallel trends in the top 0.1% and second 0.9%.

Although the timing of earnings growth over this period was similar for other income groups, in particular the surge in earnings in the late 1990s with little to no growth after, the magnitude of this growth was much larger for top earners than the rest of the distribution. For example, focusing on 5-year averages, the growth in average earnings from the 1981–85 period to the 2008–12 period was 139% for the top 0.1% (fig. B1B), 63% for the top 1% (fig. B1C), and only 22% for the bottom 99% (fig. B1D).

B.   Top Earners in Gender-Specific Earnings Distributions

How different are these trends for top-earning men and top-earning women? To answer this question we split the overall sample by gender and define top earners of each gender relative to the gender-specific earnings distribution. Figure 2 shows the thresholds for membership of the top percentiles of these gender-specific earnings distributions. In 2012, men had to earn roughly twice as much as women to be included in the top 1% of their respective gender-specific earnings distributions and nearly three times as much to be included in the top 0.1% of their distributions.

Figure 2C shows the ratio of the top earnings threshold for men to the top earnings threshold for women. For 5-year average earnings, this ratio for the top 0.1% peaked in the late 1980s at around 4.1 and has declined monotonically since then to reach a level of 2.75 for the period 2008–12. This means that whereas 2 decades ago, a man at the 99.9th percentile of the male distribution earned more than four times as much as a woman at the same percentile of the female distribution, today such a man earns less than three times as much as such a woman.

Although the gender differences in top earnings thresholds have narrowed in recent years, the gap between the average earnings of top male earners and top female earners has actually widened. This can be seen in figure B2A, where we plot average earnings for the top 0.1% of men and the top 0.1% of women, and in figure B2B, where we plot average earnings

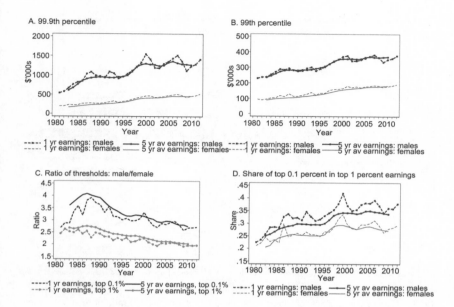

Fig. 2. Top earnings thresholds by gender: (A) 99.9th percentile, (B) 99th percentile, (C) ratios of gender-specific thresholds, and (D) share of top 0.1% earnings in top 1% earnings by gender group. A color version of this figure is available online.

for the second 0.9% of men and the second 0.9% of women. These two seemingly contradictory views of trends in the gap between the top ends of the gender-specific distributions—thresholds versus average earnings—can be reconciled by observing that inequality within the top 1%, as measured by the earnings share of the top 0.1% in the top 1%, is higher for men than for women and has remained relatively constant since the late 1990s (fig. 2D).

C. Gender Composition at the Top: Cracks in the Glass Ceiling?

We now return to top earners in the overall earnings distribution and analyze the gender composition of this group. Our findings are displayed in figure 3. The top left panel (fig. 3A) shows that the share of women among top earners has increased substantially since the early 1980s. For example, during the 1981–85 period, women constituted just 1.9% of the top 0.1% group and just 3.3% of the second 0.9% group based on 5-year average earnings (the solid lines). By 2008–12, the corresponding shares of women had risen to 10.5% and 17.0%, respectively.

The magnitude of this change is even more striking when expressed in terms of the number of men for every woman in the top percentiles,

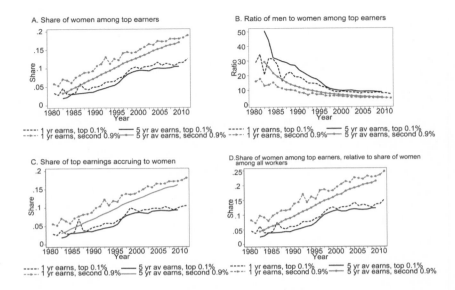

Fig. 3. Gender composition of top earners: (*A*) share of women, (*B*) ratio of men to women among top earners, (*C*) share of earnings accruing to women, and (*D*) share of women among top earners relative to share of women among all workers.

shown in the top right panel (fig. 3*B*). During the 1981–85 period, there were 50.6 men for every 1 woman in the top 0.1% group, whereas in 2008–12 this number had fallen to 8.5 men for every woman. A similar decline happened for the second 0.9% of earners, with the number of men per woman falling from 29.3 to 4.9 during the same period.

The rising fraction of women among top earners has also translated into a corresponding rise in the share of top earnings that accrues to women, shown in the bottom left panel (fig. 3*C*). In fact, the share of earnings has risen almost as rapidly as the rise in the population share of women in these groups, suggesting that the women who have entered the top percentiles are not disproportionately concentrated toward the bottom of the top earner groups.

When interpreting these trends, it is also important to consider that the gender composition of the overall labor force shifted toward women during this time, due to the rise in female labor force participation, which raised the female employment share in the lower 99% of the earnings distribution from 44% to 49.2% from the 1981–85 period to the 2008–12 period (see fig. B6 for the full time series). This means that part of the trends in figures 3*A* and 3*B* might be due to this broader trend. But comparing the share of women among top earners with the share of women among *all* workers suggests that this effect is small (fig. 3*D*).[13] The time series for the share of women among top earners is almost unchanged by adjusting for the increase in the share of women among all workers.

This conclusion is confirmed by a formal decomposition of the change in the share of women in top percentiles into a component that is due to the changing gender composition of the overall labor force and a component that is due to the changing gender composition of top percentiles beyond the change in the overall distribution. The equations underlying the decomposition are contained in appendix A. The results of the decomposition (table 1) imply that only 7%–9% of the total increase is due to changes in the overall female share of workers.

So far, the description of our empirical findings has painted a glass-half-full picture: Women have made substantial inroads toward gender equality at the top. Today a working female is more than four times more likely to be in the top 0.1% of the earnings distribution than a working female was 3 decades ago (fig. 3D). Yet, with the same data, it is also easy to paint a glass-half-empty picture of these trends: despite this dramatic transformation, women are still vastly underrepresented at the top. There has been almost no increase in the share of women among the top 0.1% of earners in the first decade of the twenty-first century (fig. 3A). Even in 2012, a working woman was only 12.2% as likely to be in the top 0.1% as a working man was (fig. 3D), and the shares of women in the top percentiles were below 15% for the top 0.1%, and below 20% for the second 0.9% (fig. 3A).

D. Changing Gender Composition outside of the Top 1%

We have so far focused on the gender composition inside the top 1% group, but how has the gender composition changed for other high earnings percentiles outside of the top 1%? Figure 4 shows the time series of

Table 1
Decomposition of Change in Share of Women among Top Earners

	Annual Earnings		5-Year Earnings	
	Top .1%	Second .9%	Top .1%	Second .9%
Total change in share	.09	.13	.09	.14
Fraction due to:				
Gender comp. of labor force (%)	7	9	7	7
Gender comp. of top percentiles (%)	93	91	93	93

Note: Change for annual earnings is from 1981 to 2012. Change for 5-year earnings is from the period 1981–85 to the period 2008–12. See appendix A for details of decomposition.

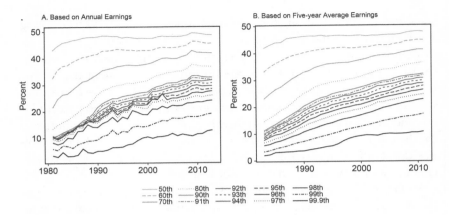

Fig. 4. Changing gender composition in various earnings percentiles based on (A) annual earnings and (B) 5-year average earnings.

the share of women in selected percentiles above the median of the overall earnings distribution. It is clear from this figure that the share of women has increased across the entire upper half of the earnings distribution, and especially strongly inside the top 10%. This is true not only for annual earnings (fig. 4A) but also for 5-year earnings (fig. 4B).

A related perspective on the convergence in labor market outcomes is to look at where female workers at a certain percentile of the female earnings distribution rank in the male earnings distribution. To answer this question, figure 5 shows the difference between the two gender-specific 5-year distributions (male's minus female's) for select percentiles above the median. Figure 5A shows the four deciles from the median to the 90th percentile, and the figure 5B shows the percentiles within the top

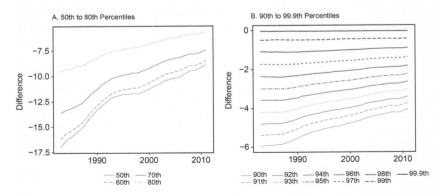

Fig. 5. Females in male earnings distribution: difference from male percentiles, 5-year earnings (A) between the median and 80th percentile and (B) between 90th and 99.9th percentiles.

10%. So for example, the dotted line in the left figure shows that women in the 80th–90th percentiles (9th decile) of the female distribution in the early 1980s would have been around 9 percentiles lower in the male distribution, whereas they were only around 5 percentiles lower in the male distribution by 2011.

Similarly, figure 5B shows that women in the 90th–91st percentile of the female distribution would have been around 6 percentiles lower in the male distribution in the early 1980s (i.e., in the 84th percentile), and 4 percentiles lower in the male distribution by 2011 (i.e., in the 86th percentile). A similar pattern emerges for annual earnings distributions (see fig. B3). Both figures 4 and 5 suggest that the convergence between genders was pervasive across the earnings distribution and not confined to the very top earnings groups only.

IV. A Paper Floor? Gender Differences in the Likelihood of Staying at the Top

In any given year, the members of a given earnings percentile are composed of newcomers (those who moved in since last year) and stayers (those who were in that percentile in the previous year). Hence, to understand the changes in the gender composition of top earners, it is important to understand how mobility patterns differ for men and women and how these patterns have changed over time. The persistence of top earner status is also relevant for a range of other economic questions, including the determinants of wealth concentration at the top, the earnings risk faced by top earners, and the optimal taxation of their labor earnings. The scarcity of representative panel data sets covering top earners—which is necessary to measure earnings mobility—has largely prevented the analysis of these dynamics in the existing literature.[14] In this section, we fill this gap. We start by examining the mobility of overall top earners, and we then examine gender differences in persistence and how these differences contribute to the trends shown in Section III.

A. Mobility of Overall Top Earners

We begin with a broad measure of mobility based on the transition probabilities in and out of three earnings groups—top 0.1%, second 0.9%, and bottom 99%—over 1-year and 5-year periods. Below we will also analyze transition between groups outside of the top 1%. We first analyze the mobility patterns in the most recent time period and then turn to how these patterns have changed since the early 1980s.

Table 2 reports the transition matrices for the most recent periods covered by our data. For annual earnings, these are 1-year transition probabilities between 2011 and 2012, and for 5-year average earnings these are transition probabilities between the 2003–7 period and the 2008–12 period.

The first question we are interested in is the mobility of top earners—the rates at which they enter, stay in, or exit a given top earner group. The top panel of table 2 reports the annual transition rates, which reveal substantial year-to-year mobility and suggest that top earnings status is far from a permanent state. For example, of all the workers in the top 0.1% in 2011, only 57% were still in the top 0.1% 1 year later, 31% had dropped to the second 0.9%, and 7% had dropped out of the top 1% altogether (panel A of table 2). In addition, 5% of workers left the sample, either through aging (turning 61) or by failing to meet the minimum earnings criteria. For workers in the second 0.9% in 2010, 69% were still in the top 1% (of which 4% had moved up to the top 0.1%) and 27% had dropped down to the bottom 99%.

The transition rates for 5-year earnings are very similar to those for annual earnings once the higher exit rate is accounted for. The probability of exiting through aging is higher because of the 5-year horizon and the fact that the top earners' age distribution skews older for 5-year earnings than for annual earnings. In panel B, the numbers in parentheses report the transition rates conditional on remaining in the sample (i.e., normalized by one minus the exit rate). Comparing these numbers to the annual rates in

Table 2
Transition Probabilities across Top Earnings Groups, Post-2000s

	A. Annual Earnings, 1-Year Transitions			
	Top .1%	Second .9%	Bottom 99%	Exit Sample
Top .1%	.57	.31	.07	.05
Second .9%	.04	.65	.27	.04
Bottom 99%	<.01	<.01	.91	.08
	B. Five-Year Earnings, 5-Year Transitions			
	Top .1%	Second .9%	Bottom 99%	Exit Sample
Top .1%	.40 (.59)	.22 (.32)	.06 (.09)	.32
Second .9%	.05 (.07)	.46 (.61)	.24 (.32)	.25
Bottom 99%	<.01 (<.01)	<.01 (<.01)	.72 (.96)	.27

Note: One-year transition probabilities refer to the period 2011–12. Five-year transition probabilities refer to the period 2003–7 to the period 2008–12. In panel B, numbers in parentheses are transition rates conditional on remaining in the sample (i.e., normalized by one minus exit rate).

panel A makes the similarities clear. For example, the probabilities of staying in the top two earnings groups after 5 years were 59% and 61%, respectively (versus 57% and 65%, respectively, in panel A). Thus, both annual and 5-year transitions reveal a significant amount of turnover at the top. An important corollary of this turnover is that drawing conclusions about top earners from cross-sectional data is fraught with danger because one-third of the individuals in these groups are different from one year to another. We return to this point in Section VII, where we study top earners over 30-year periods.

Before moving forward, a cautionary remark is in order. Although it might seem plausible at first blush, this large turnover at the top does *not* imply that the earnings of top earners display a lot of mean reversion. Nor is there a straightforward mapping between the transition probabilities reported in table 2 and the persistence parameter of a first-order autoregressive (AR[1]) earnings process.[15]

We next turn to the evolution of these mobility patterns over time. Figure 6 plots the time series of the transition probabilities between the same

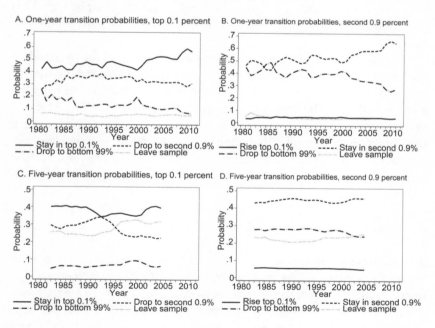

Fig. 6. Transition probabilities in and out of top percentiles, all sample. These figures show the probability that an earner in the top 0.1% group (*A*, *C*) or the second 0.9% group (*B*, *D*) transitions to other parts of the distribution. The top panels show 1-year ahead transitions based on annual earnings and the bottom panel shows 5-year ahead transitions based on 5-year average earnings.

groups as in table 2. The overall pattern we see here is that mobility was higher—alternatively, the top earner status a less stable state—in previous decades. For example, during the 1980s and 1990s, the annual probability of staying in the top 0.1% group was fairly stable at about 45%. Since 2000, this probability has steadily risen, reaching more than 57% in 2011 (fig. 6A).

The pattern is similar for the second 0.9% group, with a fairly stable probability of staying put of around 50% during the first 2 decades, a 5% probability of moving upward into the top 0.1%, and a 40% chance of falling out of the top 1% group. Since then, the probability of staying has risen to nearly 70%, mostly accounted for by a large reduction in the probability of moving down to the bottom 99% group, from 40% to under 30% (fig. 6B). Transition probabilities for 5-year average earnings over 5-year horizons, which are displayed in figures 6C and 6D, show similar qualitative trends to the 1-year transition probabilities based on 1-year earnings over the second half of the sample, but the magnitude of the changes is smaller. In figure B7, we report analogous figures for the time path of transition rates conditional on not leaving the sample, for which the trends in 1-year and 5-year transition probabilities are even more similar.

The rising stability of top earner status after the turn of the twenty-first century sheds light on the leveling off of the annual top-earning thresholds and annual top earner shares during this period, shown in figures 1 and B1. Although the share of earnings accruing to the 0.1% and top 1% groups has not shown an upward trend during this period, the declining mobility at the top implies that top earners are slowly being entrenched, because the group shows less turnover than before. This observation highlights the benefits of studying top earners through the lens of individual panel data.

B.   Gender Differences in Mobility

Behind these mobility patterns for top earners in the overall population are important differences by gender. In the early 1980s, there was a distinctive paper floor for top-earning women, by which we mean that they faced a very high probability of dropping from either of the two top-earning groups to the bottom 99% from one year to the next. For example, in 1981, this probability was 64% and 74%, respectively, for women in the top 0.1% and second 0.9% groups. By comparison, these probabilities were much lower for men: 24% and 43%, respectively, for the same two groups. This is the essence of the paper floor: not only were women vastly underrepresented among top earners in a given year, but even those who did have high earnings were much more likely than men to drop out of the top earnings groups within a year.

However, the last 3 decades have seen a steady mending of the paper floor. This mending can be seen clearly in figure 7, which shows the time path of transition probabilities separately for men and women in the top percentiles of the overall earnings distribution. The overall picture that emerges from the four panels in this figure is that the gender gap in persistence has almost disappeared. For example, in 2011, the annual probability of dropping from the top 0.1% to the bottom 99% was 8.1% for women compared with 6.6% for men; Similarly, the analogous probability of dropping down from the second 0.9% was 32% for women compared with 26% for men. During the same time frame, there have been similar improvements in upward mobility. For example, the transition rate of women from the second 0.9% up to the top 0.1% has more than doubled, from 1.2% in 1981 to 3.2% in 2011, but has increased much less for men, from 3.4% to 4.1%.

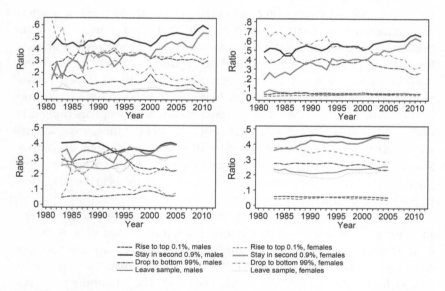

---- Rise to top 0.1%, males   ---- Rise to top 0.1%, females
——— Stay in second 0.9%, males   ——— Stay in second 0.9%, females
—·—·— Drop to bottom 99%, males   — – — Drop to bottom 99%, females
——— Leave sample, males   ········· Leave sample, females

Fig. 7. Transition probabilities in and out of top percentiles over time, by gender. These figures show the probability that a top earner based on average earnings over the period $t-2, \ldots, t+2$ is a top earner based on average earnings over the period $t+3, \ldots, t+7$, separately for male top earners (darker shades of each line style) and female top earners (lighter shades of each line style). A color version of this figure is available online.

One potential explanation for the mending of the paper floor is that top-earning women may have become more evenly distributed within the top 0.1%—rather than being bunched just above the top 0.1% threshold. If true, then mean reversion in earnings would be pushing fewer of them below the top 0.1% threshold, increasing the persistence of top-earnings status for women. However, two pieces of evidence suggest that this was not a major factor. First, the persistence of top earner status has also risen significantly when we define it relative to the gender-specific earnings distributions (see app. C). Persistence defined in this way has risen significantly for women but not for men, both at an annual and 5-year horizon. Second, the ratio of the earnings share of women in the top 0.1% to the population share of women in top 0.1% has barely changed over this period (see fig. 3C), suggesting that there has not been a dramatic change in the average position of women within the top 0.1%. In fact, for both annual and 5-year average earnings, the gender gap within the top 0.1% (as measured by the ratio of average earnings of women to men) has been flat over the last 30 years, whereas the same ratio calculated within the second 0.9% group has declined.

The dramatic increase in the persistence of female top earners has been an important factor in accounting for the rise in the share of women among top earners. To understand the contribution of changes in transition rates, we decompose the change in the gender composition of each top-earning group into a component that is due to *different trends* in the transition probabilities in and out of the top percentiles for men versus women and a component that is due to *preexisting* differences in the same transition probabilities. We describe our procedure for implementing this decomposition in appendix A. The former component measures the contribution of changes in persistence to the overall change in gender composition, whereas the latter component measures the change in gender composition that would have taken place absent any changes in the transition probabilities over this period.[16]

The decomposition, which is reported in table 3, shows that 33% of the increase in the share of women among the top 0.1%, and 41% of the increase among the second 0.9%, is due to the fact that women are now less likely to drop out of the top percentiles than they were in the past and so receive high earnings for longer periods of time. The remainder of the increase is due to preexisting differences in the fraction of men and women in the top percentiles, and changes in the probability of new women entering the top-earning percentiles.

So far we have focused only on transition rates out of the top 1% into the bottom 99%, but it is also useful to know where in the bottom 99%

Table 3
Decomposition of Change in Share of Women among Top Earners

	Annual Earnings	
	Top .1%	Second .9%
Change in female share	.097	.136
Fraction due to:		
Existing differences and persistence (%)	56.5	42.4
Change in transition probabilities (%)	43.5	57.6
Due to change in inflow (%)	10.2	16.3
Due to change in outflow (%)	33.3	41.3

Note: The change in female share is for the period 1982–2012 rather than 1981–2012 because the decomposition requires an initial period to compute the initial transition probabilities. See appendix A for details.

those workers dropping out of the top 1% are actually dropping to. Figure 8 offers an answers to this question. The top two panels show annual transition rates out of the second 0.9% group into each of the four deciles from the median to the 90th percentile, and into each percentile within

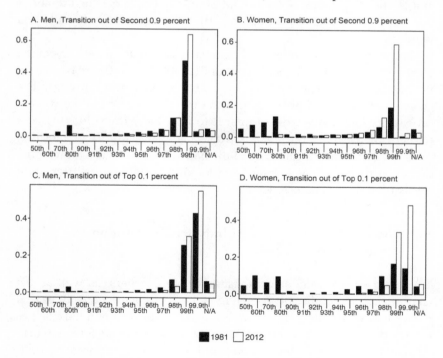

Fig. 8. Changes in annual transition probabilities out of top percentiles into finer percentile groups, by gender: (*A*) men, transition out of second 0.9%; (*B*) women, transition out of second 0.9%; (*C*) men, transition out of top 0.1%; and (*D*) women, transition out of top 0.1%.

the top decile, in 1981 and 2012 for men (fig. 8A) and women (fig. 8B). The figures illustrate clearly the large increase in the probability of staying in the second 0.9% from 1 year to the next, with a much bigger increase in this probability for women so that the probability of staying in these two groups has nearly converged to the probability of staying for men.

However, for both genders this increase in staying in the top percentile groups is not due to a decline in transition rates to nearby percentiles, but rather is a due to a decline in transition rates to percentile groups much lower down the distribution. This finding is particularly stark for women. In 1981, a woman had only had a 20% chance of staying in the second 0.9%, and those who fell out of the top 1% had an almost 40% chance of falling out of the top decile, and more than a 25% chance of dropping out of the top 20%. Thus, for women in 1981, dropping out of the top 1% meant a very large drop in earnings. This has changed dramatically. By 2012, the probability of staying in the second 0.9% had increased from about 20% to 60% (as seen in fig. 7B), and importantly, this increase came as a result of a decline in the probability of large falls in earnings. For example, the 40% chance of falling out of the top decile declined to about 5% and the 25% chance of dropping out of the top 20% declined to less than 2%.

Figures 8C and 8D show that a similarly dramatic change has taken place for transition probabilities out of the top 0.1%. In figure B9, we report analogous 5-year transition rates, based on 5-year earnings. The changes are smaller, but the conclusion that the increase in the staying probability for women is due primarily to a decline in transitions to lower parts of the distribution remains true. This analysis of finer transition rates suggests that the mending of the paper floor is a more robust phenomenon than one could infer from looking at only overall transition rates out of the top percentiles.

V. Where Is the Glass Thinner? Industry Composition of Top Earners

The trends in the gender composition of top earners, as well as the changes in the mobility of women in and out of the top percentiles that have partly fueled these trends, may in part be due to differential changes in the observable characteristics of male workers versus female workers over this period. In this section and the next, we examine gender differences in two potentially important characteristics that are observed in our data: the industry in which individuals work and the individual's age. Our goal is to ascertain whether there are certain industries in which women have made greater inroads into the top percentiles and how much of the increased female share of top earners is due to an increased presence of women in industries that have higher representation at the top of the distribution, as opposed to an increased share of women among the top earners within given industries.

To address these questions, we use the Standard Industrial Classification (SIC) code assigned to the EIN that is associated with each worker's main source of earnings. Based on these SIC codes, we construct the 13 industry groups listed in table 4. Our logic in combining SIC codes into industry groups in this way is to group together businesses in which top-earning workers are likely to perform similar tasks, despite their potentially disparate SIC codes. Typically, SIC codes are grouped based on 1-digit or 2-digit classifications. But such classifications are intended to group industries by the type of goods they produce rather than by the type of work that their employees do. For example, the 1-digit SIC classification places a computer hardware company (such Apple, Dell, or Hewlett-Packard) under Durable Manufacturing (SIC 357: Industrial machinery and equipment), whereas placing a computer software company (such as Google, Microsoft, or Oracle) under Business Services

Table 4
Aggregating Industries

	Aggregated Industry	Included SIC Codes
1	Engineering	7370–79, 3570–79 (computers) 8711 (engineering services)
2	Health Services	80
3	Legal Services	81
4	Management, Accounting, Business Consulting	3660–69, 8700, 8712–29, 8741–49
5	Other Services	7000–8999 Except 737, 80, 81, 87
6	Finance, Insurance	60, 61, 62, 63, 64, 66, 67
7	Wholesale Trade	50, 51
8	Retail Trade	52–59
9	Transportation, Communication	40, 41, 42, 43, 44, 45, 47, 48
10	Durable Manufacturing	24, 25, 30, 31, 32, 33, 34, 37, 38, 39 35 (except 357), 36 (except 366)
11	Nondurable Manufacturing	20, 21, 22, 23, 26, 27, 28
12	Construction and Real Estate	15, 16, 17, 65
13	Commodities and Mining	2911, 46, 49, 10, 11, 12, 13, 14

Note: SIC codes 781–84 and 79 correspond to "Hollywood, Artists, and Professional Sportsmen." We include workers in this category as part of "Other Services" to avoid privacy issues.

(SIC 737: Computer programming, data processing, and other data-related services) and an engineering consulting company under Engineering, Accounting, Research Management, and Related Services (SIC 8711: Engineering services). Under our classification, workers at the businesses listed above are all included as part of engineering, and top-earning workers at these firms likely have similar roles. Thus, our industry grouping should be interpreted as lying somewhere between an industry and an occupational classification, when compared with the typical SIC industry classification. Table 4 contains a full crosswalk between SIC codes and our 13 industry groups. In appendix D we report the SIC codes of selected large US companies.

We assign each individual to the industry that corresponds to the SIC code of their main employer in year t (i.e., the employer that contributes to the largest share of their annual earnings). For 5-year average earnings, we define their industry as the SIC code of their main employer in the most recent year $t + 2$. To minimize the number of figures in the main text, in this section we only report results based on 5-year average earnings. The analogous figures using annual earnings can be found in appendix D, and they yield similar conclusions.

A.   Industry Composition of All Top Earners

Finance and insurance is by far the most highly represented industry among the highest earners. For the 5-year period 2008–12, 31% of individuals in the top 0.1% worked for employers in the finance and insurance industries, and these workers received 32% of the earnings of all individuals in the top 0.1%. Among the second 0.9% of workers, health services is the most highly represented industry, in terms of both numbers of workers and share of earnings, with finance and insurance a close second. Together these two industries accounted for 33% of workers in the second 0.9% in 2008–12 and accounted for 34% of the earnings of the second 0.9%. The population shares and earning shares of each of the 13 industry groups among top earners in 2008–12 can be seen as the gray bars in figures 9A and 9C (top 0.1%), and in figures 9B and 9D (second 0.9%).

Interestingly, the industry share of top earners has not always looked this way. In the early 1980s, employers in the health services industry represented a larger share of top earners than finance and insurance, in terms of both number of workers and total earnings. In addition, employers in manufacturing, particularly those in durable manufacturing, had a very strong presence at the top of the earnings distribution. Hence,

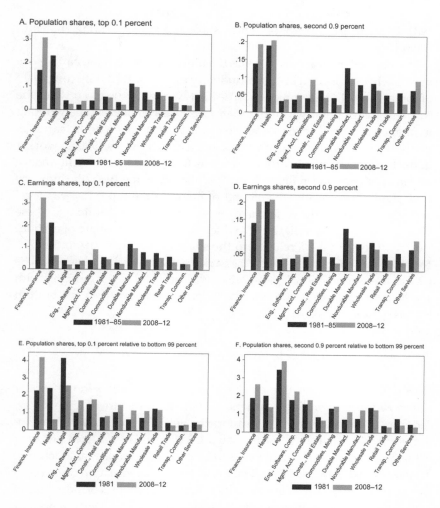

Fig. 9. Industry composition of top earners, 5-year average earnings population shares for (*A*) top 0.1% and (*B*) second 0.9%; (*C*) earnings shares of top 0.1% and (*D*) second 0.9%; and (*E*) population shares of top 0.1% relative to bottom 99% and (*F*) population shares of second 0.9% to bottom 99%.

over the last 3 decades, the major change in the industry composition of top earners has been the rise in earnings in the finance and insurance industry, offset by a relative decline in the earnings of the highest paid doctors and, to a lesser extent, a relative decline for the highest earners employed by manufacturing firms. These changes can be seen in the panels of figure 9 by comparing the solid black bars, which show the population and earnings shares of each industry group among top earners in

1981–85, with the gray bars, which show the corresponding shares in 2008–12.

Finance and insurance not only is the industry in which top earners are most likely to work, but also is the industry that is most heavily composed of top earners. For example, in 2008–12, a worker in the top 0.1% of the earnings distribution was more than four times as likely to be working in finance and insurance as a worker in the bottom 99% of the earnings distribution. This too was not always the case: in the early 1980s, a worker in the top 0.1% was only around twice as likely to be working in finance and insurance as one in the bottom 99%. Instead, in the 1980s the industry with the highest relative likelihood of being in the top 0.1% was legal services, for which the ratio has dropped from 4.2 to around 2.6. These changes can be seen in figure 9E, which shows how the share of each industry in the top 0.1% relative to the share of that industry in the bottom 99% has changed between the period 1981–85 and the period 2008–12. For the second 0.9%, legal services was, and still is, the industry with the highest representation relative to its representation in the bottom 99% (fig. 9F).

B. Gender Differences in Industry Composition

Surprisingly little variation can be seen across industries in the gender composition of overall top earners. In 2008–12, the share of women varied from 6% in health services to approximately 15% in nondurable manufacturing and retail trade for the top 0.1% (fig. 10A), and from just over 10% in construction and real estate to 24% in nondurable manufacturing for the second 0.9% (fig. 10B). Thus, although some variation can be seen across industries, today there is no single industry, or subset of industries, in which top-earning women are disproportionately absent. Thirty years ago, however, the share of women among top-earning workers in retail trade and other services was substantially higher compared with other industries.

The similarity across industries in terms of the gender composition of top earners suggests that the large increase in the overall representation of women at the top of the earnings distribution is not due to women disproportionately moving into high-earning industries like finance and health services. Moreover, the industry composition of top earners in the most recent 5-year period 2008–12, shown in figures 10C and 10D, is almost identical for men and women, suggesting that the remaining gender differences among top earners are not due to an underrepresentation of women at the top of any one industry but rather are an across-the-board phenomenon.

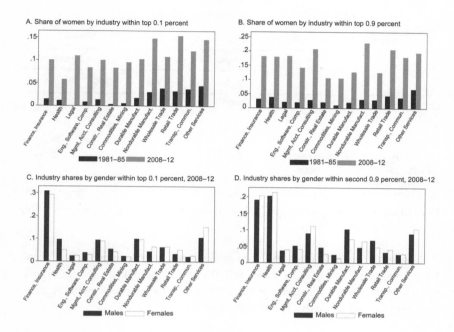

Fig. 10. Industry composition of top earners, 5-year average earnings: share of women by industry (*A*) within top 0.1% and (*B*) within second 0.9%; industry shares by gender (*C*) within top 0.1% and (*D*) within second 0.9%. A color version of this figure is available online.

The conclusion that gender differences in industry shares do not play a role in understanding changes in the gender composition of top earners is confirmed by a formal decomposition. In appendix A, we explain our procedure for decomposing the change in the gender composition of top earners into (i) a component that is due to changes in the industry composition of working women across the entire earnings distribution, (ii) a component that is due to changes in the industry composition of top earners of both genders, and (iii) a component that is due to changes in the gender composition of top earners within industries. The results of the decomposition, which are reported in table 5, show that industry composition plays no role whatsoever in accounting for the increased representation of women at the top of the distribution. In fact, the contribution of the first two components is negative, suggesting that on average over this period there was a shift of the industry composition of working women toward industries that are slightly underrepresented in the top percentiles, and a shift of the industry composition of top earners toward industries with less female representation.

Table 5
Decomposition of Change in Share of Women among Top Earners

	Annual Earnings		5-Year Earnings	
	Top .1%	Second .9%	Top .1%	Second .9%
Change in share	.09	.14	.09	.14
Fraction due to:				
Industry comp. of women in labor force (%)	−3	−2	−1	0
Industry comp. of top earners (%)	5	5	5	6
Female share of top earners within industry (%)	98	97	96	94

Note: Change for annual earnings is 1981–2012, and change for 5-year earnings is 1983–2010 (centered 5-year groups).

Although the last 3 decades have seen significant changes in the industry composition of top earners overall, these changes have been relatively similar for men and women and do not account for the changes in the gender structure of top earners over this period.

VI. Looking Upward? Gender Differences in Top Earnings by Age

Because earnings growth at young ages is a key driver of earnings later in life, we can gain insight into possible future paths for gender differences among top earners by examining how top-earning gender gaps vary by age. Hence, in this section we divide the population of 25- to 60-year-olds into 5-year age groups and study both the age distribution of top earners as well as the composition of top earners among individuals of a given age. Our goals are to ascertain whether top-earning gender gaps already exist at the time of entry into the labor market or whether they emerge slowly as a cohort ages, and to measure how much of the increase in the share of women among top earners is due to shifts in the gender composition of recently entered cohorts versus changes that have occurred within older cohorts. To keep the presentation of the results manageable, in this section we only report our findings for 5-year average earnings. The analogous figures for annual earnings lead to similar conclusions and are contained in appendix E.[17]

A.   Age and Gender Composition of Top Earners

Relative to the average age of the workforce, top earners are old and have become more so since the 1980s. For earnings over the 5-year period 2008–12, 58% of the individuals in the top 0.1% were ages 47–58 in 2010 (we measure an individual's age in the middle of the 5 years used to construct average earnings), and 21% were ages 27–41. By contrast, for earnings over the 5-year period 1981–85, only 48% of individuals in the top 0.1% of the earnings distribution were ages 47–58 in 1983, and more than 31% were below 40. This aging of top earners can clearly be seen in figure 11A, which shows the fraction of top earners in each 5-year age bin for these two 5-year periods. A similar pattern and trend is evident among the second 0.9% of earners (fig. 11B), as well as for the share of top earnings that accrues to individuals of different age groups.

This large change in the age composition of top earners is a possible source of changes in the gender composition of top earners. Because top earners overall have become older, if female workers were on average initially older than male workers, then this would generate an increase in the share of women among top earners. In 1981–85, working women were indeed slightly older than men, although the difference is small. The aging of the labor force over this period was more pronounced for women than men, which could also generate an increase in the share of women among top earners (see app. E for figures illustrating these features of the data). Thus, a plausible conjecture is that part of the increased share of women among top earners is due to compositional effects related to the aging of the workforce.

Indeed, a formal decomposition confirms that around 12%–17% of the increased share of women among top earners is due to age differences across men and women. In appendix A, we explain our procedure for decomposing the change in the gender composition of top earners into (i) a component that is due to changes in the age composition of top earners relative to the age composition of the bottom 99%, (ii) a component that is due to differential changes in the age composition of men and women among workers in all parts of the earnings distribution, and (iii) a component

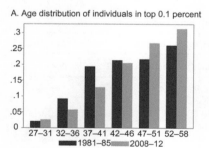
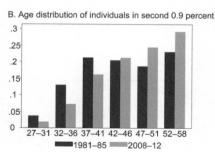

Fig. 11. Age distribution of workers (A) in top 0.1% and (B) in second 0.9%, based on 5-year average earnings. Age labels in figures refer to center year of 5-year age ranges. For example, 27–31 refers to the 5-year age ranges 25–29, 26–30, . . . , 29–33.

that is due to changes in the fraction of women among top earners in a given age range. The results of the decomposition, which are reported in table 6, indicate that 6%–11% of the increase is due to the first component, 6%–8% is due to the second component, and 83%–88% is due to the third component.

B. Gender Composition of Age-Specific Top Earners

Because there are so few young workers among the overall top earners, it is perhaps more informative to study the gender composition of top earners at each age, both for learning about the way in which top-earning gender gaps evolve over the working life and for making guesses at the future path of top-earning gender gaps.

The thresholds for membership in the top percentiles of each age-specific earnings distribution are much higher for older workers than for younger workers. For the 5-year period 2008–12, workers who were ages 27–31 in 2010 would have needed to earn an average of at least $303,000 per year to be included in the top 0.1% of their age group, and workers who were ages 52–58 in 2009 would have needed to earn an average of at least $1,153,000 over the same period to be included in the top 0.1% of their age group. For membership in the top 1%, these thresholds were $136,000 for ages 27–31 and $342,000 for ages 52–58.

Since the early 1980s, these thresholds for membership in the age-specific top percentiles have increased for all age groups but have increased more sharply for older workers. The ratio of the 99.9th percentile of the 5-year average earnings distribution for workers ages 52–58 to the 99.9th percentile for workers ages 27–31 was 3.0 in 1981–85 and had increased to 3.8 by 2008–12. See appendix E for the full time series of top-earning thresholds for each age group.

Table 6
Decomposition of Change in Share of Women among Top Earners

	Annual Earnings		5-Year Earnings	
	Top .1%	Second .9%	Top .1%	Second .9%
Change in share	.09	.13	.09	.14
Fraction due to:				
Age comp. of top earners (%)	10	6	11	6
Age comp. of women in labor force (%)	6	8	6	6
Top earners within women given age (%)	84	86	83	88

Note: Change for annual earnings is 1981–2012, and change for 5-year earnings is 1983–2010 (centered 5-year groups).

The share of women among the top 0.1% and second 0.9% of earners in a given age group, shown in figure 12*A* and 12*B*, respectively, is substantially higher for younger workers. However, in recent years, the share of women among the top 0.1% of young workers has increased substantially less than the share of women among the top 0.1% of older workers. This is in contrast to the second 0.9%, for which there has been a steady increase in the share of women among top earners of all age groups. Hence, the data show very different trends for the gender composition of young workers in the second 0.9% versus those in the top 0.1% of the earnings distribution. Whereas the share of women among the second 0.9% of workers ages 27–31 increased by more than one-third between the period 1993–97 and the period 2008–12 (from 22% to 29%), the share of women among the top 0.1% of workers ages 27–31 barely changed over the same period (from 12% to 14%).

Viewing these same trends from a cohort perspective rather than an age perspective reveals a striking observation about the source of the increased female share of top earners: almost all of the increase has come from the entry of successive cohorts with higher proportions of women among top earners at all ages, rather than from an increase in the female

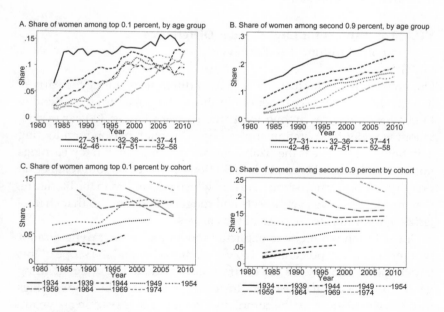

Fig. 12.   Female population shares by age group and cohort, 5-year average earnings. By age: share of women among (*A*) top 0.1% and (*B*) second 0.9%; by cohort: share of women among (*C*) top 0.1% and (*D*) second 0.9%.

share within existing cohorts. This can be seen most clearly for the second 0.9% in figure 12D, which plots the same data as in figure 12B, but connects the data for individuals from the same birth cohorts rather than individuals of the same age. Almost no increase has occurred in the share of women among the second 0.9% of workers within cohorts, and the female shares for the more recent cohorts have actually declined as these cohorts have aged. However, a striking increase has occurred in the gender composition of top earners across cohorts. The same trends are evident for the top 0.1% (fig. 12C), with the exception of the 1949 and 1954 birth cohorts, which were unique in that the female share increased as these cohorts aged.

If new cohorts continue to follow life-cycle trends for top earner gender shares that are similar to those cohorts just older than them, then these figures imply that we may expect to see a continued increase in the share of women in the second 0.9% of earners in the next decade but perhaps a leveling off of the share of women in the top 0.1%. On the other hand, if these younger cohorts turn out to have trajectories for top earnings shares that mirror more closely those of the baby boomer cohorts, the share of women may continue to rise even at the very top of the earnings distribution.

VII. Top Earners for Life? Gender Differences among Lifetime Top Earners

Our analysis has so far focused on gender differences among top earners in a given 1-year or 5-year period. In this section, we turn our attention to gender differences among top earners over a longer 30-year period, whom we refer to as lifetime top earners. Our main reason for adopting a lifetime perspective is the sizable transitory component in top earnings implied by the mobility analysis in Section IV. Moreover, our reliance on first-order Markov transition matrices, which is standard in the literature, may mask richer life-cycle effects and longer-run dynamics that characterize the earnings trajectories of top earners.

One solution would be to explicitly model the earning dynamics for workers in the top percentiles. However, this is beyond the scope of this paper and would take us too far from our main goal of understanding gender differences in top earners. Instead, by measuring lifetime earnings directly, we can observe the cumulative impact of these earnings dynamics and life-cycle trends with a single statistic. Our goals in this section are thus (i) to measure the fraction of lifetime top earners that are female,

(ii) to understand how lifetime top earners differ from others in terms of the life-cycle evolution of their earnings, and (iii) to examine how the timing of earnings over the life cycle differs between male and female lifetime top earners. Because of the need for data on the full earnings histories of top earners for this type of analysis, the existing literature offers little in the way of answers to these questions.

We categorize people based on their earnings over the 30 years between ages 25 and 54. Because our data cover the period 1981–2012, we have lifetime earnings information for three cohorts of workers.[18] We have chosen to focus on 30-year earnings because this length balances the objectives of a long horizon that approximates a working life with the need to combine multiple cohorts to have a sufficiently large number of individuals in the top 0.1% of lifetime earners. To construct lifetime earnings for the 25–54 age range, we first select all individuals from the 1956, 1957, and 1958 birth cohorts who satisfy the minimum earnings criteria described in Section II for a minimum of 15 years.[19] We then compute each individual's total earnings over this age range and classify these individuals as in either the top 0.1%, the second 0.9%, or the bottom 99% of the distribution of lifetime earnings for individuals in these cohorts.

A.   Lifetime Top Earners Overall

For the 1956–58 cohorts, the threshold for membership in the lifetime top 0.1% was just over $19.1 million (see table 7). This is equivalent to average annual earnings of around $635,000, which is smaller than the average threshold for membership in the top 0.1% based on annual earnings over the same period, $812,000. The threshold for membership in

Table 7
Lifetime Earnings Top Earnings Statistics

	Top .1%	Second .9%	Bottom 99%
30-year earnings thresholds:			
99.9th percentile ($'000s)	19,052		
99th percentile ($'000s)		6,459	
Mean 30-year earnings ($'000s)	33,874	9,552	1,197
Median 30-year earnings ($'000s)	26,524	8,625	969
Mean no. working years	27.9	28.3	25.7
Mean fraction of working years in age-specific:			
Top .1% (%)	33	4	0
Second .9% (%)	36	38	0
Bottom 99% (%)	31	58	99

the lifetime top 1% was $6.5 million, equivalent to average annual earnings of $215,000, which is smaller than the average annual threshold of $242,000.

Lifetime top earners have high total earnings both because they work for a greater number of years and because they have faster earnings growth than workers in the bottom 99%. The top 1% of lifetime earners work an average of 2.5 years longer than the bottom 99%, but those in the top 0.1% work on average half a year less than those in the second 0.9% (table 7).[20] However, these differences in the number of years worked are insignificant when compared with the differential average earnings growth experienced by the three earnings groups conditional on working, shown in figure 13A. The higher average earnings growth for individuals in the top percentiles takes place entirely between the ages of 25 and 43, after which average earnings are constant for all three groups of workers. Hence, lifetime top earners tend to be workers who experience particularly high earnings growth over the first half of their careers.[21]

How closely related are lifetime top earners to annual top earners? This question is important, because although cross-sectional earnings data are

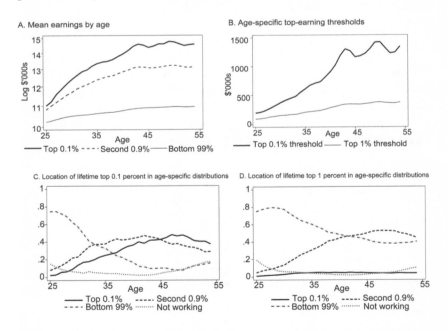

Fig. 13. Age profiles by 30-year top-earning groups: (A) mean earnings by age, (B) age-specific top earning thresholds; location in age-specific distribution of lifetime (C) top 0.1% and (D) top 1%. Figures refer to individuals from the 1956, 1957, and 1958 birth cohorts. Age-specific top-earning thresholds and groups are computed using only these three cohorts.

more readily available than data on lifetime earnings, for many economic questions lifetime earnings are a more relevant statistic. As we explained in Section VI, the age distribution of top earners is strongly skewed toward older ages (see figs. 11A and 11B). This means that very few lifetime top earners have earnings in the top 1% of the annual earnings distribution during the first half of their careers. Hence, to track the earnings paths of lifetime top earners, it is useful to ask whether they are top earners with respect to their own cohort in a given year, rather than with respect to all workers in that year.

To this end, in each year that he or she is working, we categorize each worker as in either the top 0.1%, second 0.9%, or bottom 99% of the age-specific distribution of earnings for workers in these three cohorts. The thresholds for membership in each of these groups at each age are displayed in figure 13B, and show that the gap between the top 0.1% and the rest of the top 1% starts out relatively small and then widens from ages 25–43.

When compared with members of their own cohort, lifetime top earners and annual top earners are two very different groups. Typical members of the lifetime top 0.1% spend nearly one-third of their working years in the bottom 99% of their cohort's annual earnings distribution. The remaining two-thirds of their working years are on average split evenly between the top 0.1% and the second 0.9% of earners. The second 0.9% of lifetime earners spend more than half of their working years as members of the bottom 99% of annual earnings and only 4% of their time in the top 0.1%. The average breakdown of working years for lifetime top earners in each annual earnings group is shown in the bottom three rows of table 7.

The disconnect between annual top earners and lifetime top earners is particularly salient early in the working life. This can be seen in figures 13C and 13d, which show, respectively, the fraction of the lifetime top 0.1% and second 0.9% at each age that are in the within-cohort annual top 0.1%, second 0.9%, and bottom 99%, as well as the fraction that are not working. At young ages, well over half of both groups of lifetime top earners are in the bottom 99%, and even during the peak earnings years during the mid-40s, around 40% of the second 0.9% of lifetime top earners are in the bottom 99% of their within-cohort distribution. This pattern of earnings growth—starting low and rising rapidly—is consistent with the predictions of models of human capital accumulation in the presence of heterogeneity in abilities (see, e.g., Ben-Porath 1967; Guvenen and Kuruscu 2010; and Huggett, Ventura, and Yaron 2011). Consequently, identifying individuals as annual top earners may give at best a very noisy signal about their long-term prospects as lifetime top earners.

B.   Gender Differences in Lifetime Top Earners

Because the individuals in the top percentiles of the earnings distribution based on short horizons are possibly a very different group of individuals compared with those that are in the top percentiles based on lifetime earnings, gender differences among annual or 5-year top earners may or may not be informative about gender differences among lifetime top earners. In this section, we investigate these differences by measuring gender differences among lifetime top earners directly. Analogously to our analysis of gender differences in Section III, we approach the measurement of lifetime top earner gender gaps from two perspectives. First, we compare men and women in the top percentiles of the overall lifetime earnings distribution. Second, we compare men and women classified as top earners with respect to their gender-specific lifetime earnings distribution.

For the 1956–58 cohorts, about 12% of the top 0.1% of lifetime earners were women (panel A of table 8). This compares with an average female share of the top 0.1% of annual earners for this period of 8%. The fraction of the second 0.9% of lifetime earners who were women was 13%, which was also the average female share of the second 0.9% of earners over this period.

Within the top 0.1%, average lifetime earnings are higher for men than women: There is a 17 basis point difference in the log mean and a 7 basis point difference in the log median. For the second 0.9%, these differences are both around 5 basis points. In figure 14A, we plot the gender gap based on annual earnings at each age for the overall lifetime earning groups. For example, the solid line shows the difference between the log of mean annual earnings for men in the top 0.1% of the lifetime earnings distribution

Table 8
Gender Differences among Lifetime Top Earners

	Top .1%	Second .9%	Bottom 99%
A. Overall Top Earners			
Female worker share (%)	12	13	48
Female earnings share (%)	10	12	38
Log mean gender gap	.17	.05	.43
Log p50 gender gap	.07	.06	.46
No. working years gender gap	.45	−.05	1.09
B. Gender-Specific Top Earners			
Male threshold ($'000)	24,471	8,387	
Female threshold ($'000)	9,324	3,838	
Log mean gender gap	1.08	.85	.48
Log p50 gender gap	.99	.83	.47
No. working years gender gap	−.19	−.21	1.13

and the log of mean annual earnings for women in the top 0.1% of the lifetime earnings distribution. The figure clearly illustrates that the gender gap among top earners is largest during the 30s. This finding is consistent with the hypothesis explored in Bertrand et al. (2010) that career interruptions for family reasons explain a substantial portion of the top-earning gender gap.

The thresholds for membership in the top 0.1% and top 1% of male lifetime earners are more than twice as large as those for membership in the corresponding percentiles of female lifetime earners (panel B of table 8). Moreover, the gender gaps between the tops of the respective lifetime earnings distribution are large: around 100 basis points in the log mean for the top 0.1%, and around 85 basis points in the log mean for the second 0.9%. These compare with a gap of under 0.5 for the bottom 99%. These large gender gaps at the top are not driven by a few top-earning men, because the gaps in the log median lifetime earnings are very similar to the gaps in the means. Nor are the gaps being driven by women spending more time not working: in fact, on average the lifetime top-earning women have a slightly higher number of working years than the lifetime top-earning men. Figure 14B shows that these large gender gaps evolve gradually over the first half of the working life. At age 25, the average gender gap in the top percentiles is actually slightly lower than in the bottom 99%, but the gap gradually rises and remains constant after around age 35.

VIII. Conclusions

Although we have intentionally remained relatively descriptive in this paper, our findings potentially have important implications for a number of aspects of the US economy. Therefore, rather than concluding with a

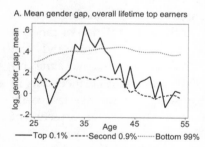 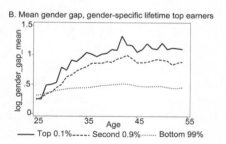

Fig. 14. Gender gap among 30-year top earners by age. Mean gender gap by age for (*A*) overall lifetime top earners and (*B*) gender-specific lifetime top earners. Figures refer to individuals from the 1956, 1957, and 1958 birth cohorts. Age-specific top-earning thresholds and groups are computed using only these three cohorts.

summary of our findings (for that, we refer readers to the introduction), we will conclude by mentioning some areas in which our empirical observations suggest the need for complementary theoretical work and further empirical analysis using other data sources.

We found that although the share of women among the top 1% has increased steadily over the last 30 years, the fraction of women in the top 0.1% has barely increased during the last decade, and the gender composition of both top-earning groups is still very different from the composition of the bottom 99%. These findings reinforce the need for research into the factors that can account for both the glass ceiling and the paper floor. Our analysis of lifetime top earners revealed that the timing of the emergence of the top-earning gender gap is consistent with the hypothesis that career interruptions may be an important consideration. Our finding that industry composition plays very little role in explaining either the level or the change in the top-earning gender gap suggests that in this respect, selection into particular firms or jobs may be more important than selection into particular industries. Unfortunately, the SSA data lack many of the important variables that would be required for a more complete answer to this question: children, marital status, and work hours.

The large temporary component in top earners' earnings, the increasing persistence of top earner status, and the relatively weak relationship between annual top earners and lifetime top earners all suggest the need for a comprehensive analysis of the dynamics of top earnings. Although an extensive literature has proposed and estimated various statistical models that provide a good fit to the dynamics of earnings for the bulk of the distribution, little is currently known about how well this class of models fits earnings dynamics for top earners.

On the theory side, our findings suggest the need for progress in at least two areas. First, there is the need to understand how and why the earnings distribution is characterized by a Pareto tail. Most existing theories of Pareto-generating mechanisms, such as the accumulation of random returns over long periods of time, can be adapted to explaining right-tail inequality in the wealth distribution, which is accumulated over time and passed down across generations. But for explaining right-tail inequality in earnings, new theories are necessary, because human capital is less easily transmitted across generations and, as we have shown, a large fraction of top earnings is accrued within a lifetime, often in just a few years.

Second, the rise of the finance and insurance industry in accounting for top earners of both genders suggests a need for better theories of labor compensation in this sector. Why is such a large share of labor earnings concentrated in a single industry? Does this reflect the extraordinarily high productivity of this industry? Or do these earnings reflect rents? And if so, rents to what? A useful starting point would be to study the top of the distribution of earnings across and within firms, within industries.

Appendix A

Details of Decompositions

In this appendix, we provide details of the methodology underlying the decompositions presented in tables 1, 3, 5, and 6.

We start by establishing some notation. Let G_{it} be the gender of individual i who is included in our sample in year t, with the convention that $G_{it} = 1$ for a female and $G_{it} = 0$ for a male. Let p denote a percentile range (e.g., top 0.1%, second 0.9%, or bottom 99%), and let D_{it}^p be an indicator variable that takes the value 1 if individual i is in the percentile range p of the earnings distribution in year t. Let σ_t^p be the fraction of top earners that are female.

$$\sigma_t^p = E_t[G|D^p = 1] \tag{A1}$$

Let E_t denote a moment of a time t distribution and let P_t denote a probability based on the time t distribution.

A.1. Decomposition for Changing Gender Composition
of the Labor Force (Table 1)

The goal is to measure how much of the observed change in σ_t^p is due to changes in the share of women in the labor force $E_t[G]$. Using Bayes's rule we can decompose σ_t^p as

$$\sigma_t^p = \frac{P_t[D^p = 1|G = 1]P_t[G = 1]}{P_t[D^p = 1]} \tag{A2}$$

$$\sigma_t^p P_t[D^p = 1] = E_t[D^p|G = 1]E_t[G] \tag{A3}$$

$$\Delta(\sigma_t^p P_t[D^p = 1]) = E_t[D^p|G = 1](\Delta E_t[G]) + (\Delta E_t[D^p|G = 1])E_{t-1}[G] \tag{A4}$$

The term on the left-hand side of equation (A4) is the change in the fraction of the workforce that are female and in percentile group p. The first term on the right-hand side of equation (A4) is the component of this change that is due to changes in the share of women in the labor force. The second term on the right-hand side is the component that is due to changes in the fraction of women that are in percentile group p. We implement this decomposition for each pair of consecutive years using sample analogues of the moments in equation (A4) and then summing the components over all years to get the total decomposition.

In principal $P_t[D^p = 1]$ is constant for all t, because it is simply the fraction of the population in percentile group p. However, because we take different size random samples for the top percentile groups compared with the bottom 99%, in practice there are small year-to-year fluctuations in our sample estimates of this moment. If $P_t[D^p = 1]$ were constant then the fraction of $\Delta \sigma_t^p$ that is due to changes in the gender composition of the labor force would be given by

$$\frac{E_t[D^p|G = 1]\Delta E_t[G]}{P_t[D^p = 1]\Delta \sigma_t^p}. \tag{A5}$$

With our decomposition the fraction is given by

$$\frac{E_t[D^p|G = 1]\Delta E_t[G]}{P_t[D^p = 1]\Delta \sigma_t^p + \sigma_{t-1}^p \Delta P_t[D^p = 1]}. \tag{A6}$$

Because the term $\sigma_{t-1}^p \Delta P_t[D^p = 1]$ is very small relative to $P_t[D^p = 1]\Delta \sigma_t^p$, this sampling variation has a negligible effect on the results of the decomposition.

A.2. Decomposition for Changing for Age and Industry Composition (Tables 5 and 6)

The goal is to measure how much of the observed change in σ_t^p is due to a changes in the distribution of an observable characteristic X_{it}. We consider only characteristics that take a discrete set of values such as age and industry. Analogously to the decomposition above, we can write

$$\sigma_t^p P_t[D^p = 1] = E_t[D^p|G = 1]E_t[G = 1]$$

$$= \sum_x E_t[D^p|G = 1, X = x]P_t[X = x|G = 1]E_t[G]$$

$$= \sum_x E_t[D^p|G = 1, X = x]E_t[G|X = x]P_t[X = x] \tag{A7}$$

$$\Delta(\sigma_t^p P_t[D^p = 1]) = \sum_x E_t[D^p|G = 1, X = x]\Delta E_t[G|X = x]P_t[X = x]$$

$$+ \sum_x \Delta E_t[D^p|G = 1, X = x]E_{t-1}[G|X = x]P_t[X = x] \tag{A8}$$

$$+ \sum_x E_{t-1}[D^p|G = 1, X = x]E_{t-1}[G|X = x]\Delta P_t[X = x]$$

The term on the left-hand side of equation (A8) is the change in the fraction of the workforce that are female and in percentile group p. The first term on the right-hand side is the component of this change that is due to changes in the gender composition of different categories (i.e., industries or age groups). The second term on the right-hand side is the component that is due to changes in the fraction of women in each category that are in percentile group p. The third term on the right-hand side is the component that is due to changes in the fraction of the overall labor force in each category of X.

A.3. Decomposition for Changes in Mobility (Table 3)

The goal is to measure how much of the observed change in σ_t^p is due to changes in the transition probabilities in and out of the percentile group p. Let D_+^p be an indicator variable that takes the value 1 if an individual was in percentile group p in year $t + 1$. Because gender is constant over time, $G_t = G_{t-1}$, we can decompose σ_t^p using the relationship that

$$\sigma_t^p P_t[D^p = 1] = E_t[D^p|G = 1]E_t[G = 1]$$

$$= \sum E_{t-1}[D_+^p|G = 1, D^q = 1]E_{t-1}[D^q|G = 1]E_{t-1}[G = 1] \quad \text{(A9)}$$

$$= \sum E_{t-1}[D_+^p|G = 1, D^q = 1]E_{t-1}[G|D^q = 1]E_{t-1}[D^q].$$

Then taking first differences yields

$$\Delta(\sigma_t^p P_t[D^p = 1]) = \sum_q E_{t-1}[D_+^p|G = 1, D^q = 1]\Delta E_{t-1}[G|D^q = 1]E_{t-1}[D^q]$$

$$+ \sum_q \Delta E_{t-1}[D_+^p|G = 1, D^q = 1]E_{t-2}[G|D^q = 1]E_{t-1}[D^q] \quad \text{(A10)}$$

$$+ \sum_q E_{t-2}[D_+^p|G = 1, D^q = 1]E_{t-2}[G|D^q = 1]\Delta E_{t-1}[D^q].$$

The term on the left-hand side of equation (A10) is the change in the fraction of the workforce that are female and in percentile group p. The first term on the right-hand side is the component of the change that is due to changes in the female share of top percentiles in the previous period at the prevailing levels of persistence. The second term on the right-hand side is the component of this change that is due to changes in the transition probabilities into the top pth percentile. The third term is due to sampling variation and is a negligible component of the overall change; we present the decomposition for the change net of the effects of this term.

The idea behind this decomposition is that any one-time change in transition probabilities will lead to continued changes in the fraction of women in the top percentiles in subsequent years, even if there are no further changes in the transition probabilities. Hence any observed change is partly due to the effects of changes in the transition probabilities in the past as the system moves toward its new stationary distribution and is partly due to new changes in the transition probabilities. The first term captures the former effect, the second term captures the latter effect.

Appendix B

Top Earner Trends and Mobility Additional Figures

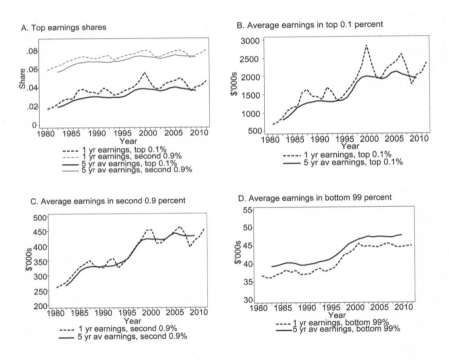

Fig. B1.   Average earnings among top earners

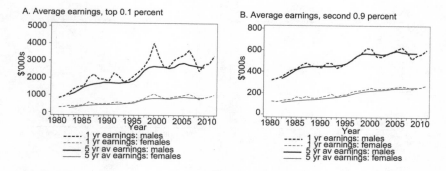

Fig. B2. Top-earning men versus top-earning women (based on gender-specific earnings distributions). A color version of this figure is available online.

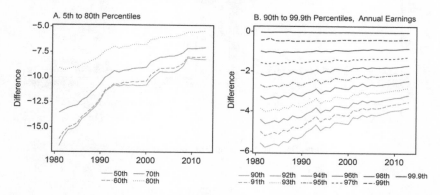

Fig. B3. Females in male earnings distribution: counterpart of figure 5 for annual earnings

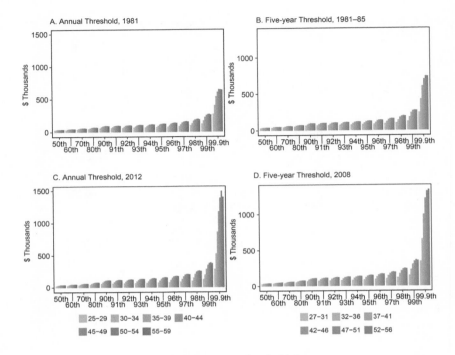

Fig. B4. Top-earning thresholds by age

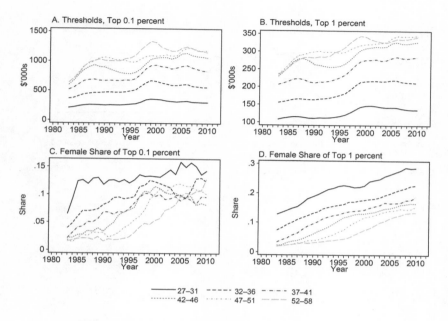

Fig. B5. Top-earning thresholds by age and gender, 5-year earnings

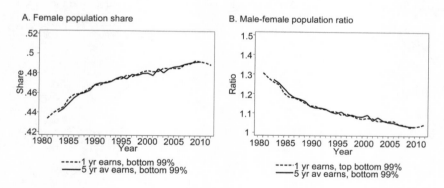

Fig. B6. Gender composition of overall top earners, bottom 99%. Time trend for the female population share and the male-female population ratio, for the bottom 99% of the earnings distribution.

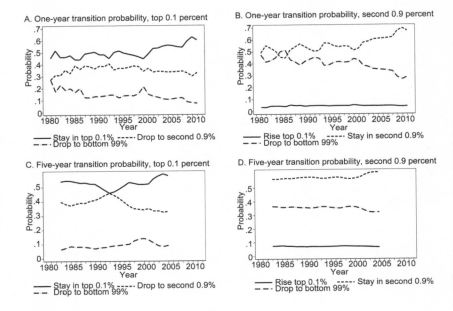

Fig. B7. Transition probabilities in and out of top percentiles, conditional on not leaving sample. These figures show the probability that a top earner based on average earnings over the period $t - 2, \ldots, t + 2$ is a top earner based on average earnings over the period $t + 3, \ldots, t + 7$.

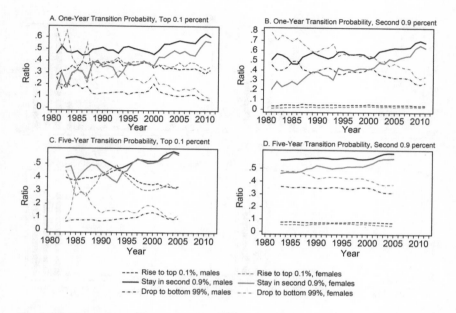

Fig. B8. Transition probabilities in and out of top percentiles over time conditional on not leaving sample, by gender. These figures show the probability that a top earner based on average earnings over the period $t - 2, \ldots, t + 2$ is a top earner based on average earnings over the period $t + 3, \ldots, t + 7$, separately for male top earners (darker shades of each line style) and female top earners (lighter shades of each line style). A color version of this figure is available online.

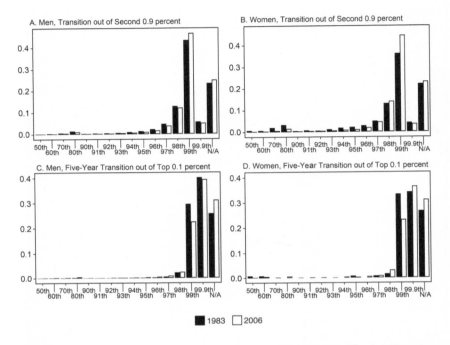

Fig. B9. Changes in 5-year transition probabilities out of top percentiles into finer percentile groups, by gender.

Appendix C

Mobility within Gender-Specific Distributions

This appendix reports figures that are analogous to those in Section IV, but in which individuals are defined as top earners based on their position in their gender-specific earnings distribution rather than the overall earnings distribution.

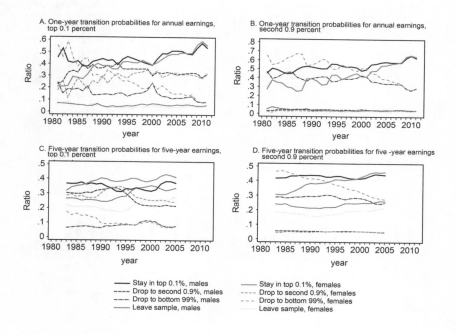

Fig. C1. Transition probabilities in and out of top percentiles of earnings distribution, by gender. These figures show the probability that a top earner based on average earnings over the period $t - 2, \ldots, t + 2$ is a top earner based on average earnings over the period $t + 3, \ldots, t + 7$, separately for male top earners (darker shades of each line style) and female top earners (lighter shades of each line style). Individuals are classified as top earners based on gender-specific earnings distributions. A color version of this figure is available online.

Appendix D

Industry Analysis Further Figures

This appendix contains figures that are analogous to those in Section V, but which are constructed using annual earnings rather than 5-year average earnings.

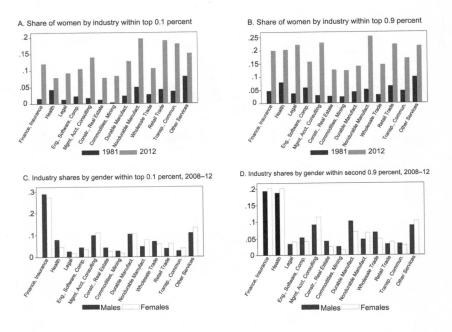

Fig. D1. Top earners by industry and gender, annual earnings. A color version of this figure is available online.

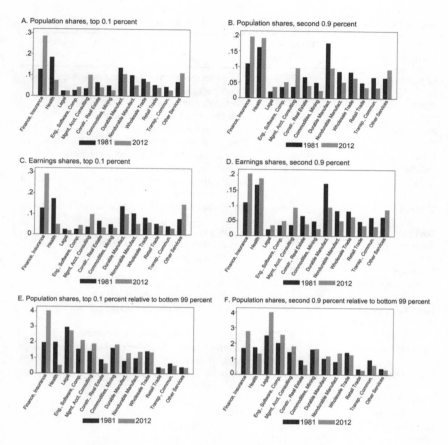

Fig. D2. Industry composition of top earners, annual earnings

Table D1
Selected US Companies and Associated (Primary) SIC Codes

Company Name	Primary SIC Code	Descriptions
Google	7370	Computer programming, data processing, and computer services
Apple, Dell	3571	Electronic computers
HP	3570	Computer and office equipment
Microsoft	7372	Prepackaged software
IBM	7371	Computer programming services
Intel	3674	Semiconductors and related services
Oracle	7372	Prepackaged software
Cisco	5045	Wholesale-computers and peripheral equipment and software
Qualcomm	3663	Radio and TV broadcasting and communication equipment
Boeing	3721	Aircraft and parts
Amazon.com	5961	Retail-catalog and mail-order houses
3M	3291	Abrasive products
Walmart	5331	Retail-variety stores
Exxon, Chevron, BP	2911	Petroleum refining
Total SA	1211	Crude petroleum and natural gas
Ford, GM, Tesla	3711	Motor vehicles and passenger car bodies
Berkshire-Hathaway, State Farm	6331	Fire, marine, and casualty insurance
General Electric	3600	Electronic and other electrical equipment except computers
Cargill Inc.	5153	Grain and field beans; domestic transportation of freight
Bank of America, JP Morgan	6021	Banks
Goldman Sachs	6022	Investment bank
Morgan Stanley	6199	Investment bank
MetLife	6311	Life insurance

Note: Some companies listed here have further SIC codes associated with them. For example, Microsoft: 7371, 7372, 7379 (prepackaged software, primary), 3944 (electronic games), and 3861 (photographic equipment). And similarly, Cargill Inc.: 5153 (grain and field beans), 4424 (deep-sea domestic transportation of freight), 6221 (commodity contracts brokers and dealers), and 2041 (flour and other grain mill products).

Appendix E

Age Analysis Further Figures

This appendix contains figures that are analogous to those in Section VI, but which are constructed using annual earnings rather than 5-year average earnings, and additional figures that are referenced in Section VI.

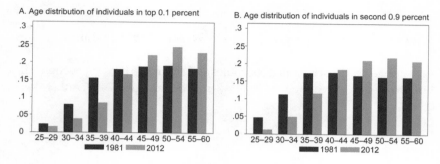

Fig. E1. Age distribution of workers, annual earnings

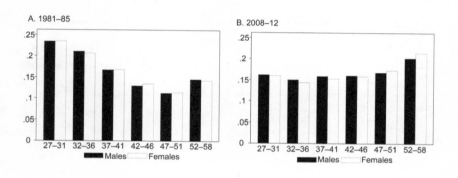

Fig. E2. Age distribution of workers by gender, overall distribution, 5-year average earnings. A color version of this figure is available online.

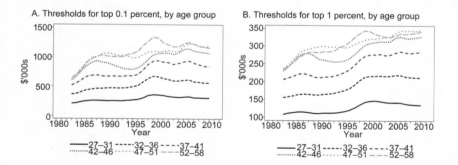

Fig. E3. Top-earning thresholds within age groups, 5-year average earnings

Appendix F

Lifetime Earnings Analysis for 30- to 59-Year-Old Age Range

This appendix reports analogous tables and figures to those in Section VII, but where the 30-year age range is taken to be the ages 30–59, rather than 25–54.

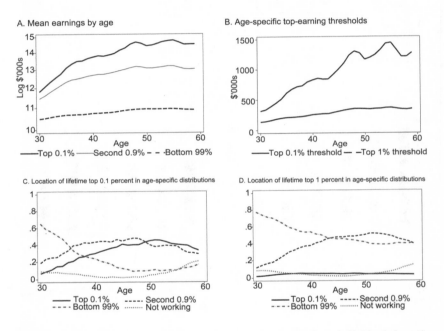

Fig. F1. Age profiles by 30-year top-earning groups. Figures refer to individuals from the 1951, 1952, and 1953 birth cohorts. Age-specific top-earning thresholds and groups are computed using only these three cohorts.

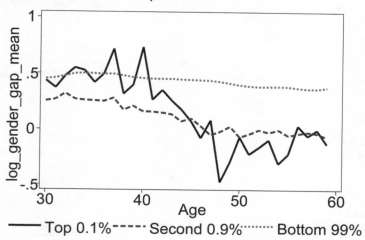

A. Overall lifetime top earners

B. Gender-specific lifetime top earners

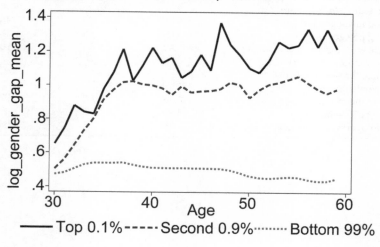

Fig. F2. Gender gap among 30-year top earners by age. Figures refer to individuals from the 1951, 1952, and 1953 birth cohorts. Age-specific top-earning thresholds and groups are computed using only these three cohorts. Figures show mean gender gap in each part of the earnings distribution.

Table F1
Lifetime Earnings Top Earnings Statistics

	Top .1%	Second .9%	Bottom 99%
30-year earnings thresholds:			
99.9th percentile ($'000s)	20,704		
99th percentile ($'000s)		7,043	
Mean 30-year earnings ($'000s)	38,092	10,545	1,276
Median 30-year earnings ($'000s)	29,467	9,443	1,043
Mean no. working years	27.9	28.3	25.6
Mean fraction of working years in age-specific:			
top .1% (%)	35	5	0
next .9% (%)	40	42	0
bottom 99% (%)	25	53	100

Table F2
Gender Differences among Lifetime Top Earners

	Top .1%	Second .9%	Bottom 99%
A. Overall top earners:			
Female worker share (%)	9	11	49
Female earnings share (%)	9	10	38
Log mean gender gap	−.01	.06	.46
Log p50 gender gap	−.05	.05	.48
No. working years gender gap	.40	.20	.90
B. Gender-specific top earners:			
Male threshold ($'000)	27,512	9,320	
Female threshold ($'000)	9,487	3,828	
Log mean gender gap	1.18	.97	.52
Log p50 gender gap	1.16	.96	.49
No. working years gender gap	−.19	−.01	.94

Appendix G

Including Self-Employment Income

This appendix contains deleted figures from the main text, constructed using a definition of income that includes both wage and salary earnings, and earnings from self-employment income.

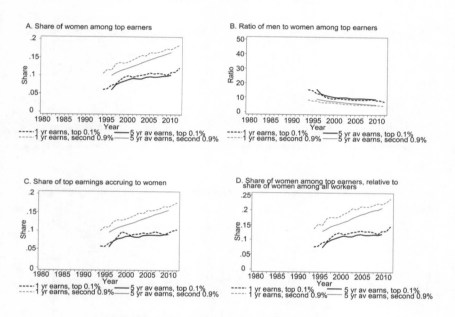

Fig. G1. Gender composition of top earners

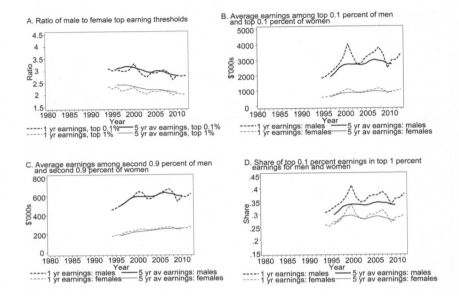

Fig. G2. Male top earners versus female top earners. A color version of this figure is available online.

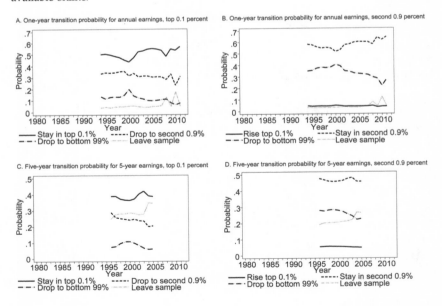

Fig. G3. Transition probabilities in and out of top percentiles of earnings distribution. These figures show the probability that a top earner based on average earnings over the period $t-2, \ldots, t+2$ is a top earner based on average earnings over the period $t+3, \ldots, t+7$.

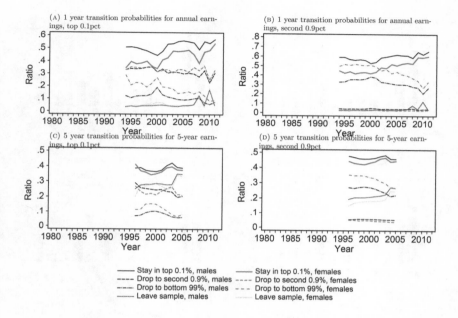

Fig. G4. Transition probabilities in and out of top percentiles of earnings distribution, by gender. These figures show the probability that a top earner based on average earnings over the period $t - 2, \ldots, t + 2$ is a top earner based on average earnings over the period $t + 3, \ldots, t + 7$, separately for male top earners (darker shades of each line style) and female top earners (lighter shades of each line style). A color version of this figure is available online.

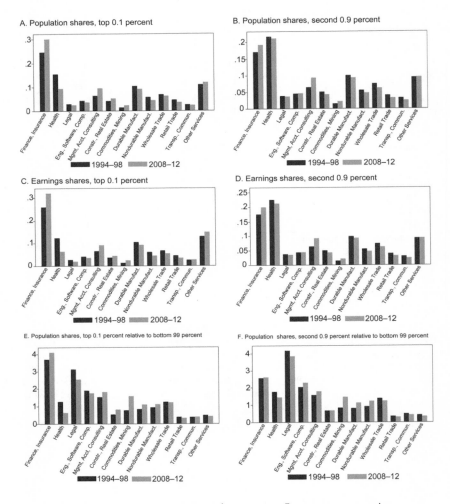

Fig. G5. Industry composition of top earners, 5-year average earnings

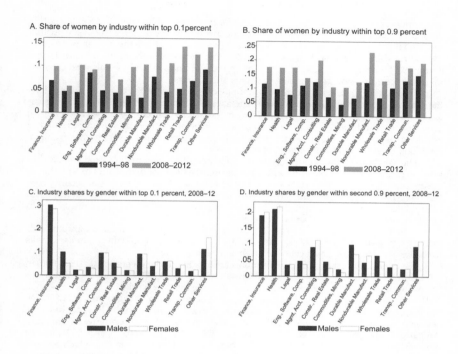

Fig. G6. Top earners by industry and gender, 5-year average earnings. A color version of this figure is available online.

Endnotes

Author email addresses: Guvenen (guvenen@umn.edu), Kaplan (gkaplan@uchicago.edu), Song (jae.song@ssa.gov). This paper uses confidential data supplied by the Social Security Administration. The views expressed herein are those of the authors and not necessarily those of the Social Security Administration, the Federal Reserve Bank of Minneapolis, or the Federal Reserve System. For acknowledgments, sources of research support, and disclosure of the authors' material financial relationships, if any, please see https://www.nber.org/books-and-chapters/nber-macroeconomics-annual-2020-volume-35/glass-ceiling-and-paper-floor-gender-differences-among-top-earners-1981-2012.

1. See Bertrand, Goldin, and Katz (2010) and Gayle, Golan, and Miller (2012) for recent attempts to measure the gender composition of top earners.

2. The term "glass ceiling" was coined in the 1980s and is typically defined as an "unseen, yet unbreachable barrier that keeps minorities and women from rising to the upper rungs of the corporate ladder, regardless of their qualifications or achievements" (see, e.g., Federal Glass Ceiling Commission 1995).

3. Existing evidence typically relies on data from nonrandom samples, such as CEOs and top executives, billionaires from Forbes 400 lists, and MBA graduates, among others. We review this evidence below.

4. Statistics are for 2010 from table 3 in Congressional Budget Office (2013).

5. See Guvenen and Kaplan (2017) for a reconciliation of this finding with results from other data sources and different samples that show a continued increase in the income share of the top 0.1% over this period. The difference in these findings is not due to our focus on

wage and salary income as opposed to a broader measure. In Guvenen and Kaplan (2017), we show that the slowdown in the growth of top incomes is present for total income (including capital gains), except at the very top of the distribution (above the 99.99th percentile). Instead the difference in findings is mainly due to differences in the implied trends for the bottom 99% that arise because of the different units of analysis: individuals who satisfy a minimum earnings and age restriction, versus all tax units.

6. The data set contains earnings information going back to 1978. However, prior to 1981 the data are of poorer quality due to inconsistencies in complying with the switch from quarterly to annual wage reporting by employers, mandated by the SSA (see Olsen and Hudson 2009; Leonesio and Del Bene 2011). For large parts of the population, most of these reporting errors can be corrected. However, these methods do not work well for very high-earning individuals, who are the focus of this paper.

7. The MEF also contains earnings information on self-employment income for sole proprietors (i.e., income reported on form Schedule SE; see Olsen and Hudson [2009] for more information); however, these data are top-coded at the taxable limit for Social Security contributions prior to 1994. Because of this top-coding, we focus our main analysis on wage and salary data. In appendix G, we verify the robustness of our findings to the inclusion of self-employment income for the period 1994–2012.

8. To avoid possible privacy issues, we do not report any statistics for demographic cells (e.g., a given industry/gender/year/income group) with fewer than 30 individuals. Thanks to the large sample size, such cells are rarely encountered.

9. For comparison, mean (median) annual earnings in our data were $51,000 ($35,000) in 2012, and mean (median) 5-year average earnings were $53,000 ($38,000), which illustrates the well-known vast gap between top earners and the average worker.

10. As explained in Section II, our earnings data comprise only wage and salary income reported on W-2 forms. According to Statistics of Income data from the Internal Revenue Service, wage and salary income in 2011 accounted for 45.6% of total income (excluding capital gains) for the top 0.1% of taxpaying units, 62.3% for the second 0.4%, and 77.0% for the next 0.5%. The next biggest component of income is entrepreneurial income, which consists of profits from S corporations, partnerships, and sole proprietorships (Schedule C income). In 2011, this accounted for 28.6% of income for the top 0.1% of tax units, 28.4% for the second 0.4%, and 16.7% for the next 0.5%.

11. For annual earnings there was an isolated peak in 2000, most likely due to payouts related to the information technology boom pushing up earnings at the very top of the distribution. Consistent with this hypothesis, the 2000 peak in annual earnings for the 99.9th percentile is particularly prominent in the engineering sector (which, according to our definition, includes technology companies; see Section V) and is much less prominent in other sectors.

12. The lack of a continued increase in top-earnings thresholds post-2000 is not specific to the particular measure of income (wage and salary earnings) or sample we use. In Guvenen and Kaplan (2017), we use data from aggregate tax records and show that the same tapering off happens for various measures of income, including capital and private business income. The only exceptions are the incomes above the top 0.01% threshold, which show an upward trend driven almost entirely by private business income.

13. We define individuals to be working if they satisfy the age and minimum earnings criteria described in Section II.

14. Two notable exceptions are Kopczuk et al. (2010) and Auten et al. (2013), who also document transition rates among top percentiles. However, neither of these papers studies gender differences in mobility nor mobility within the top 1%.

15. There are three reasons for this. First, holding the variance of earnings fluctuations fixed, the transition probabilities discussed here depend on the size of the earnings group we define (e.g., a 0.1% group versus a 10-percentile-wide group). The smaller the group, the higher the mobility in and out. Second, an empirically plausible earnings process also features permanent differences across workers, as well as transitory shocks. The transition rate is a function of the variances of these different disturbances. So, for example, simulating an AR(1) process for earnings with a persistence parameter of $\rho = 0.99$ and Gaussian shocks generates annual and 5-year transition rates for the top 0.1% of around 0.7 and 0.5, respectively. However, we can generate the same transition rates by adding a fixed effect whose unconditional variance matches that of the AR(1) process and reducing ρ to 0.85. Third,

and less obviously, the right tail of the earnings distribution is closer to Pareto than Gaussian. This implies that the gap between two percentiles of *log* earnings at the top end widens as we move up in the distribution. So if the variance of shocks to log earnings is the same for all workers, it will move fewer workers down to lower percentiles by virtue of this widening gap between earnings levels.

16. Conceptually, the fraction of women in the top percentiles can change even if the transition matrix stayed constant, simply because of an earlier change in the transition matrix and the fact that it takes time for the implied Markov process to reach its new stationary distribution. In addition, the fraction of women can change because of further changes in the transition matrix relative to the transition matrix for men. We perform this decomposition only for 1-year transition probabilities using annual earnings, because the overlapping nature of the 5-year analysis makes an analogous decomposition for 5-year earnings difficult.

17. We analyze 5-year earnings for 5-year age groups. We denote each group by their age in the middle of the 5-year period. So, for example, the 27–31 age group over the period 2008–12 refers to average earnings during this period for individuals who were ages 27–31 in 2010.

18. In appendix F, we report analogous figures and tables for average earnings over the 30 years from ages 30 to 59. Those results yield essentially the same conclusions as those for the 25- to 54-year-old age range.

19. Recall that the threshold for satisfying the minimum earnings criterion is equal to the earnings one would obtain by working for 520 hours (13 weeks at 40 hours per week) at one-half of the legal minimum wage in that year.

20. Here, we define individuals as working in a given year if they meet the minimum earnings criterion in that year. Due to our imposed selection criteria, all individuals in the sample worked for a minimum of 15 out of the 30 years.

21. Because we follow workers from only three cohorts, the age patterns that we document naturally confound time and age effects. We have also examined gender gaps in lifetime earnings for individuals in the full distribution of earnings using a smaller 1% sample that goes back to 1957. In those data, we can observe multiple cohorts and hence separate out time and age effects. The results of that analysis lead us to believe that these patterns are more likely to reflect age effects than time effects.

References

Abowd, J. M., and D. Card. 1989. "On the Covariance Structure of Earnings and Hours Changes." *Econometrica* 57 (2): 411–45.

Auten, G., G. Gee, and N. Turner. 2013. "Income Inequality, Mobility, and Turnover at the Top in the US, 1987–2010." *American Economic Review, Papers and Proceedings* 103 (3): 168–72.

Autor, D. H., L. F. Katz, and M. S. Kearney. 2008. "Trends in U.S. Wage Inequality: Revising the Revisionists." *Review of Economics and Statistics* 90 (2): 300–323.

Badel, A., and M. Huggett. 2014. "Taxing Top Earners: A Human Capital Perspective." Working paper, Georgetown University.

Baker, S. R., N. Bloom, B. Canes-Wrone, S. J. Davis, and J. A. Rodden. 2014. "Why Has U.S. Policy Uncertainty Risen since 1960?" *American Economic Review, Papers and Proceedings* 104 (5): 56–60.

Bakija, J., A. Cole, and B. Heim. 2012. "Jobs and Income Growth of Top Earners and the Causes of Changing Income Inequality: Evidence from U.S. Tax Return Data." Working paper, Williams College.

Barber, M. 2013. "Ideological Donors, Contribution Limits, and the Polarization of State Legislatures." Technical report, Brigham Young University.

Bell, L. A. 2005. "Women-Led Firms and the Gender Gap in Top Executive Jobs." Discussion Paper 1689, Institute for the Study of Labor (IZA), Bonn.

Ben-Porath, Y. 1967. "The Production of Human Capital and the Life Cycle of Earnings." *Journal of Political Economy* 75 (4): 352–65.

Bertrand, M., S. Black, S. Jensen, and A. Lleras-Muney. 2012. "Breaking the Glass Ceiling? The Effect of Board Quotas on Female Labor Market Outcomes in Norway." Working paper, University of Chicago.

Bertrand, M., C. Goldin, and L. F. Katz. 2010. "Dynamics of the Gender Gap for Young Professionals in the Financial and Corporate Sectors." *American Economic Journal: Applied Economics* 2 (3): 228–55.

Brewer, M., L. Sibieta, and L. Wren-Lewis. 2007. "Racing Away? Income Inequality and the Evolution of High Incomes."

Congressional Budget Office. 2013. "The Distribution of Household Income and Federal Taxes, 2010."

Federal Glass Ceiling Commission. 1995. "A Solid Investment: Making Full Use of the Nation's Human Capital." Technical report, US Department of Labor, Washington, DC.

Gabaix, X., and A. Landier. 2008. "Why Has CEO Pay Increased So Much?" *Quarterly Journal of Economics* 123 (1): 49–100.

Gayle, G.-L., L. Golan, and R. A. Miller. 2012. "Gender Differences in Executive Compensation and Job Mobility." *Journal of Labor Economics* 30 (4): 829–72.

Guner, N., M. Lopez-Daneri, and G. Ventura. 2014. "Heterogeneity and Government Revenues: Higher Taxes at the Top?" Working paper, Arizona State University.

Guvenen, F., and G. Kaplan. 2017. "Top Income Inequality in the 21st Century: Some Cautionary Notes." *Federal Reserve Bank of Minneapolis Quarterly Review* 38 (1). https://doi.org/10.21034/qr.3811.

Guvenen, F., G. Kaplan, and J. Song. 2014. "How Risky Are Recessions for Top Earners?" *American Economic Review, Papers and Proceedings* 104 (5): 148–53.

Guvenen, F., and B. Kuruscu. 2010. "A Quantitative Analysis of the Evolution of the U.S. Wage Distribution: 1970–2000." *NBER Macroeconomics Annual* 24:227–76.

Guvenen, F., S. Ozkan, and J. Song. 2014. "The Nature of Countercyclical Income Risk." *Journal of Political Economy* 122 (3): 621–60.

Hsieh, C.-T., E. Hurst, C. I. Jones, and P. J. Klenow. 2019. "The Allocation of Talent and U.S. Economic Growth." *Econometrica* 87 (5): 1439–74.

Huggett, M., G. Ventura, and A. Yaron. 2011. "Sources of Lifetime Inequality." *American Economic Review* 101 (7): 2923–54.

Jones, C. I., and J. Kim. 2018. "A Schumpeterian Model of Top Income Inequality." *Journal of Political Economy* 126 (5): 1785–826.

Juhn, C., K. M. Murphy, and B. Pierce. 1993. "Wage Inequality and the Rise in Returns to Skill." *Journal of Political Economy* 101 (3): 410–42.

Kopczuk, W., E. Saez, and J. Song. 2010. "Earnings Inequality and Mobility in the United States: Evidence from Social Security Data since 1937." *Quarterly Journal of Economics* 125 (1): 91–128.

Leonesio, M. V., and L. Del Bene. 2011. "The Distribution of Annual and Long-Run US Earnings, 1981–2004." *Social Security Bulletin* 71 (1): 17–33.

Meghir, C., and L. Pistaferri. 2004. "Income Variance Dynamics and Heterogeneity." *Econometrica* 72 (1): 1–32.

Olsen, A., and R. Hudson. 2009. "Social Security Administration's Master Earnings File: Background Information." *Social Security Bulletin* 69 (3): 29–46.

Panis, C., R. Euller, C. Grant, M. Bradley, C. E. Peterson, R. Hirscher, and P. Steinberg. 2000. *SSA Program Data User's Manual*. Baltimore: Social Security Administration.

Parker, J. A., and A. Vissing-Jørgensen. 2010. "The Increase in Income Cyclicality of High-Income Households and Its Relation to the Rise in Top Income Shares." *Brookings Papers on Economic Activity* 41 (2): 1–70.

Piketty, T., and E. Saez. 2003. "Income Inequality in the United States, 1913–1998." *Quarterly Journal of Economics* 118 (1): 1–39.

Saez, E. 2001. "Using Elasticities to Derive Optimal Income Tax Rates." *Review of Economic Studies* 68 (1): 205–29.

Storesletten, K., C. I. Telmer, and A. Yaron. 2004. "Cyclical Dynamics in Idiosyncratic Labor Market Risk." *Journal of Political Economy* 112 (3): 695–717.

Wolfers, J. 2006. "Diagnosing Discrimination: Stock Returns and CEO Gender." *Journal of the European Economic Association* 4 (2–3): 531–41.

Comment

Paola Sapienza, *Kellogg School of Management, Northwestern University,* United States of America, *and NBER,* United States of America

The paper by Guvenen, Kaplan, and Song provides many useful insights into the evolution of top earners' earnings and the dynamics of the gender gap at the top of the earning distribution. The authors have access to a representative sample of 10% of individual earnings from the US Social Security Administration (SSA) between 1981 and 2012. The panel structure of the data allows them to follow individuals over time, shedding light on the persistence of top earners and addressing some of the shortcomings of the literature that uses cross-sectional data.

They find several interesting results. First, in 2012, the share of women among the top 0.1% of earners is only 11% and among the top 1% only 18%. This gap was even larger earlier in the sample, suggesting a slow positive trend toward the reduction of the gender gap, with the majority of the gain concentrated in the 1980s and the 1990s. Second, the paper unveils a very large turnover over the life cycle among top earners, for both men and women, and highlights that gender improvements coincide with a larger persistence over time of women at the top of the income distribution. Although in the 1980s women were twice as likely as men to drop out from the top earners, in recent years the probability of men and women of dropping out has become similar. Third, industry and age variations provide further insights on the dynamics of the gender gap. The authors do not find any obvious relationship between the evolution of income across industries and the mitigation of the gender gap over time, whereas the distribution of age among top earners shows significant changes, with new cohorts of women making inroads into the top 1% earlier in their lifetime than previous cohorts (this results does not hold for the top 0.1% earners).

Overall, the evidence shows very slow progress of women among top earners and, although the paper remains descriptive, it has the merit to suggest several possible avenues of future research to study the causes of the persistence in the gender gap and its dynamics.

I. Excluded Income

The paper uses the best data available to make meaningful observations about the life-cycle evolution of top incomes. However, the SSA data also have some drawbacks. The most relevant limitation for this exercise is that the data studied in this paper contain only the information reported on Box 1 of the W-2 form. This information includes wages and salaries, bonuses, and exercised stock options for employees but does not contain several other measures of compensation such as interest, dividends, and rents. More importantly, unlike the Internal Revenue Service (IRS) data, it excludes all income that is reported on Schedule E, which includes compensation from partnerships and S corporations, as well as capital gains. Because compensation of top employees in certain industries (e.g., finance) has increasingly moved toward compensations of partnership contribution and carry (capital gains) and income from entrepreneurships has increased among top earners, it is possible that the SSA data overestimate the gains made by women, if women are less likely to hold nonsalaried jobs with very high compensations. An example of this trend is the evolution of the top jobs within the finance industry, where finance professionals increasingly receive nonsalaried compensation (Kaplan and Rauh 2013). Elite jobs in finance, real estate, and law firms are compensated with partnership compensation that does not appear in the SSA data. Using data from the IRS that contain information on income earned by pass-through businesses and capital gains, Bakija, Cole, and Heim (2012) show that, from 1979 to 2005, among taxpayers in the top 0.1% of the distribution of income, finance professionals increased from 11.2% to 17.7% and real estate professionals increased from 2.3% to 5.4%. Also, lawyers were 7.7% in 2005, an increase of 2.8% from 1979. Although within these groups there are several salaried employees, much of the growth over time has been concentrated in segments of these industries where employees are compensated with a percentage of the firm's profit and/or carried interests. These differences explain the discrepancies in the industry results between Bakija et al. (2012) and Guvenen et al. The increase of total compensation of top earners in these industries is due to both the increase in the number of individuals compensated with nonsalaried income and the growth in compensation in these categories. Kaplan and Rauh (2013) compare the average pay of the top 25 highest-paid hedge fund managers, every 2 years, from 2002 to 2012. They report that the average compensation for hedge fund managers was $537 million in 2012, up from $133.7 million in 2002. More importantly, several hedge fund managers ranked lower than 25 earned much higher compensation than in the previous decade and much higher than the total compensation of top corporate executives reported in the W-2. Bakija et al. (2012) show that the pay of closely held executives has also risen substantially as a share of the top 0.1% from 9% in 1979 to 22% in 2005. The exclusion of these incomes generates an important difference between the data of top earners from the IRS and those from the SSA. Guvenen and Kaplan (2017) report that the divergence between the IRS and SSA data increases over time starting in the 1980s, even without accounting for capital gains in the IRS data (fig. 1). Although wages between the two sources coincide, the exclusion of the other sources of income may deliver a substantially different picture regarding the evolution of the gender gap, especially among the very rich. *Institutional Investor's Alpha* magazine publishes a "rich list" that contains the names and compensation of the top 50 hedge managers by compensation. In 2016, for the first time, a woman made it into the list and was ranked 44th. Anecdotally, the industries and subfields in finance where Kaplan and Rauh (2013) identify the largest increase in nonwage compensation are also generally those where the proportion of women is the lowest. For example,

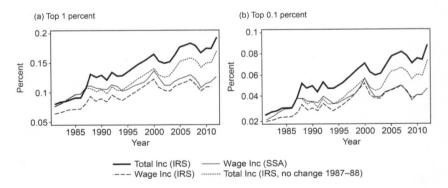

Fig. 1. Internal Revenue Service (IRS) data are for total income excluding capital gains from Saez (2012). US Social Security Administration data are from Guvenen, Kaplan, and Song (2014). The thin line is wage and salary income from W-2 forms. The dashed line is wage and salary income from IRS. The thick black line is total income excluding capital gains from IRS. Panel *a* presents the statistics for top 1 percent earners, while panel *b* for top 0.1 percent earners. Source: Guvenen and Kaplan (2017). A color version of this figure is available online.

in 2018 only 5.2% of women held seats representing private equity (PE) firms in portfolio companies (typically board seats are reserved to partners in the PE funds), suggesting that this segment of the finance industry has potentially a much higher gender gap than the industry that pays wages and bonuses. Thus, the reduction in the gender gap highlighted in the paper should be interpreted for the subset of salaried individuals, which over time contains fewer top earners, given the evolution of pay in the United States. This exclusion is likely to affect the interpretation of the results, especially for the 0.1% of top earners, as more top earners have moved toward nonsalaried income. It may also affect the interpretation of the paper floor. Evidence shows that successful entrepreneurs found companies later in life (Azoulay et al. 2020) and that there are fewer women among the most successful entrepreneurs. Similarly, many nonsalaried jobs in finance are the results of job transitions later in life. To study the evolution of income, Guvenen et al. require that each individual in the sample has a minimum annual earning every year. An interesting alternative exercise would be to study the transitions from salaried to nonsalaried high-income categories. If men leaving a top salaried category are more likely than women to enter into a higher-income category excluded from the SSA data, the effect of turnover is different for men and women, but it is hard to study with SSA data.

II. The Top versus the Very Top

Even with the caveat that the results are confined to the study of the trends among salaried individuals, one may worry about the interpretation of some of the results at the very top of this distribution. The literature has highlighted the fact that, in the past decades, the largest fraction of income increase has been concentrated at the very top of the distribution (Guvenen and Kaplan 2017). Guvenen et al. study the top 0.1% after winsorizing the observations above 99.999th percentiles. Although this choice may stem from the fact that the excluded incomes may be suspiciously high, the maximum of $25.4 million in their data is quite low when compared with the data provided by Kaplan and Rauh (2013), especially if considering that the demand for top talents is likely to affect salaried income at the very top. Given the objective of the paper, one could argue that it is important to show the unwinsorized results to study the gender gap evolution at the very top.

Using data from ExecuComp, which contains information on salary, bonuses, and exercised options for top executives (mostly CEOs and

CFOs) of publicly listed firms, I estimate the change over time for the average executive and for those with a compensation above the 99th and 99.9th percentile of the income distribution from 1992 to 2012. To calculate the top percentiles, I use the thresholds from the revised Piketty and Saez's (2003) IRS data, likely higher than the cutoffs used by Guvenen et al. because it includes incomes from pass-through entities.[1] The good news is that, after accounting for the fact that data for executives of publicly listed companies move much closer with the stock market, the trends in income over time in the ExecuComp data look remarkably similar to figure 1 in Guvenen et al. The income levels, however, are very different in this subset of highly paid individuals. In ExecuComp data, between 1992 and 2012, there are 1,114 executives with a compensation above the global maximum of $25.4 million in Guvenen et al. data; 1,094 (98.2%) are men and only 20 (1.8%) are women. One possibility for this large discrepancy could be due to potentially different ways of accounting for the exercised stock options in the two data sets. Yet, taking the most conservative approach and setting equal to zero the option values in the ExecuComp data, the number of executives with a compensation above $25.8 million drops to 32 and none of them is a woman. Given the large numbers of executives at the very top who exceed the maximum in the sample, it is certainly worth investigating the gender gap dynamics in this selected group. In figure 2, using the Piketty and Saez cutoffs for the top percentiles (0.1% and 1%) and ExecuComp data on salaries, bonuses, and stock options for executives, I plot the fraction of female executives who receive compensation above 0.1% and 1%. Although the trends are in line with Guvenen et al., the fraction of women at the very top are substantially lower every year in ExecuComp data. In 2012, there are 9% of women in the sample of executives, and the fraction of those above 0.1% and 1% are respectively 4.5% and 7.5%, 60% lower than the fraction obtained using the SSA sample.[2] Executives are not a representative sample of top earners, but these differences raise the question of how well the paper estimates the fraction of women at the very top.

III. Conclusions

Guvenen et al. have written an extremely helpful paper to study gender inequality at the very top. Their descriptive analysis does not make claims regarding the reasons of why women lagged behind, but the dynamics point us toward many interesting directions that are worth investigating further. They suggest that one reason for the relative gains

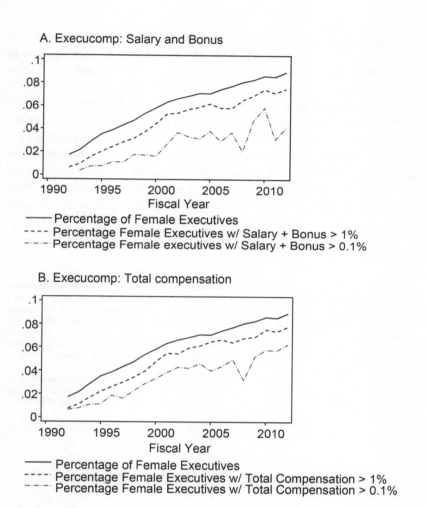

A. Execucomp: Salary and Bonus

——— Percentage of Female Executives
---- Percentage Female Executives w/ Salary + Bonus > 1%
—·—·— Percentage Female executives w/ Salary + Bonus > 0.1%

B. Execucomp: Total compensation

——— Percentage of Female Executives
---- Percentage Female Executives w/ Total Compensation > 1%
—·—·— Percentage Female Executives w/ Total Compensation > 0.1%

Fig. 2. The solid line is the proportion of women among executives. The dashed line is the fraction of women in the executive data who exceed the 1% income threshold, and the dash-dotted line is the fraction of women in the executive data who exceed the 0.1% income threshold. To calculate executive compensation in panel *a* the option values are set as equal to zero, while in panel *b* the option value used is as calculated in Execucomp. Calculation of the authors. Source: Execucomp data and Piketty and Saez (2003) data revised in 2018.

of women in recent years is the "mending the paper floor" phenomenon, as female turnover out of the top earners categories has decreased dramatically over time. This is a very interesting direction that is worth investigating further. They also highlight that the age when men and women first obtain a top earning position is correlated with the reduction in the gender gap. Both aspects of the analysis point to the importance of investigating this phenomenon with panel data, but further analysis of career interruptions and income trends would require studying income life progression combining information from IRS and SSA data. The integration of these data would allow not only to study the transitions from certain types of compensation to others, but it will enrich the analysis with the addition of various individual characteristics and economic and life decisions. For future research, data on the composition of the family, fertility choices, and spousal income, as well as family of origin background and resources, will be essential to make sense of the existence and persistency of the gender gap, not just at the top of the distribution but in every income bracket.

Endnotes

Author email address: Sapienza (paola-sapienza@northwestern.edu). For acknowledgments, sources of research support, and disclosure of the author's material financial relationships, if any, please see https://www.nber.org/books-and-chapters/nber-macroeconomics-annual-2020-volume-35/comment-glass-ceiling-and-paper-floor-gender-differences-among-top-earners-1981-2012-sapienza.

1. The thresholds for Guvenen et al. are not available in the paper, but given the differences in income data in the two data sets it is likely that the Piketty and Saez (2003) data have higher thresholds.

2. These numbers are calculated by setting the option values in the executive compensations equal to zero. When considering total compensation in ExecuComp (salary, bonus, and exercised options), the fraction of women exceeding the 0.1% and 1% thresholds of income is respectively 6.2% and 7.7%.

References

Azoulay, P., B. Jones, D. Kim, and J. Miranda. 2020. "Age and High-Growth Entrepreneurship." *American Economic Review: Insights* 2 (1): 65–82.

Bakija, J., A. Cole, and B. T. Heim. 2012. "Jobs and Income Growth of Top Earners and the Cause of Changing Income Inequality: Evidence from the U.S. Tax Return Data." Working paper, Williams College.

Guvenen, F., and G. Kaplan. 2017. "Top Income Inequality in the 21st Century: Some Cautionary Notes." *Federal Reserve Bank of Minneapolis Quarterly Review* 38 (1). https://doi.org/10.21034/qr.3811.

Guvenen, F., G. Kaplan, and J. Song. 2014. "The Glass Ceiling and the Paper Floor: Gender Differences among Top Earners, 1981–2012." Working Paper no. 20560, NBER, Cambridge, MA.

Kaplan, S., and J. Rauh. 2013. "It's the Market: The Broad-Based Rise in the Return to Top Talent." *Journal of Economic Perspectives* 27 (3): 35–56.

Piketty, T., and E. Saez. 2003. "Income Inequality in the United States, 1913–1998." *Quarterly Journal of Economics* 118 (1): 1–39.

Saez, E. 2012. "Striking It Richer: The Evolution of Top Incomes in the United States." Working paper, University of California, Berkeley.

Comment

Raquel Fernández, *New York University,* United States of America, *NBER,* United States of America, *CEPR,* United States of America, *and ESOP,* United States of America

This is a nice paper that uses data from the US Social Security Administration (SSA) to provide empirical evidence on gender differences in earnings. It focuses on differences in gender representation at the top 0.1% and the next 0.9% of the earnings distribution. It examines the persistence of an individual's presence in these top percentiles, how age and industry composition matter, and gives some feel for life-cycle dynamics, all the while contrasting the presence of women versus men.

The authors have access to a 10% representative sample of individual earnings histories from the SSA (constructed by selecting all individuals with the same last digit of a transformation of the social security number). This is a panel data set spanning 32 years: 1981–2012. There is basic demographic information available: age, sex, race, type of work (farm/ nonfarm, employment/self-employment), and earnings. The latter consists of wages and salaries, bonuses, and exercised stock options as reported in Box 1 on a W-2 form. For most of their analysis, they select from the 10% sample all individuals who in that year are between 25 and 60 years old and whose annual earnings exceed a minimum threshold (equivalent to 13 weeks, full-time, at one-half minimum wage).

Among the advantages of a panel set are that one can, for example, study earnings over a number of years to smooth out temporary fluctuations, ask questions about persistence, and examine measures of lifetime income. What this data set sacrifices, however, is any rich information about other characteristics of these individuals such as their education, marital status and children, spousal attributes, and occupation other than that captured by broad industry categories. This makes it virtually impossible to attempt to study what mechanisms are contributing to changes over time.

The paper's focus is on two findings: the increased female representation at the very top of the earnings distribution (the cracking of the "glass ceiling") and the higher persistence of this status over time (the mending of the "paper floor").

Turning first to the growth in the female share of top earners, whereas women constituted 1.9% of the top 0.1% in 1981–85, by 2008–12, this had grown to 10.5%. Their representation in the next 0.9% over the same time period also quintupled: from 3.3% to 17.0%. A closer look at their figure, reproduced here (see fig. 1) for convenience, shows that the dynamics of this increase have been different. The share in the top 0.1% has barely budged since the early 2000s whereas the share of women in the next 0.9% has kept steadily increasing. An extension of the data to more recent years would have been useful here to see whether both trends have continued. It is interesting to note that for other percentiles of the earnings distribution in the top 20%, the share of women has been increasing throughout, although women still make up less than 35% of these percentiles (see fig. 4A of the paper). More generally, it is useful to note that from 2004 onward, the median earnings of full-time working women has been more or less constant at around 81% of their male counterpart's (see fig. 2).

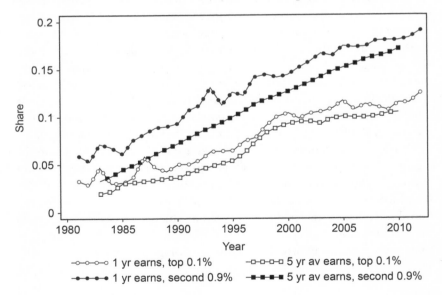

Fig. 1. Share of women among top earners. av = average. A color version of this figure is available online.

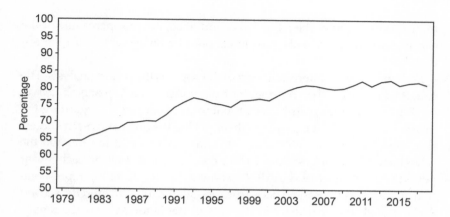

Fig. 2. Women's earnings as a share of male earnings. A color version of this figure is available online.

Can the increase in the female share of top earners be attributed to the growth in female labor force participation over this period? At least mechanically, the answer is no in the sense that the share of women at the very top has grown substantially more than the share of women in the labor force.

Turning next to the paper floor, the authors emphasize the greater propensity in recent times for women to stay in the top of the earnings distribution. Whereas in 1981, the probability that a man transited out of the top 0.1% to the bottom 99% was 24%, the comparable statistic for a woman was 67%. By 2011, the gender gap is almost closed and the persistence has increased for both: the probability of a woman transiting became 8.1% versus 6.6% for a man. The authors discuss another feature that I consider worthy of note. The 5-year transit probabilities depicted in the bottom panel of their figure 7 show that gender parity in permanence was reached quite early in the sample period. By 1994, both genders have essentially the same probability of remaining in the top 0.1%. A striking feature over this time period, however, is the initially large difference in the rate in which these top-earning females leave the sample as compared with males. In the mid-1980s, in fact, more than 20% of these women are exiting the sample. Is this the result of aging out (per the rules followed by the authors in sample construction) or because women are behaving differently, for example, taking earlier retirement or leaving to take care of a family member? The authors' data should allow them to answer the first part of the question but not, unfortunately, the mechanisms underlying differential behavior. It would also be of interest to know whether these women reenter the labor force, and, if so, at what percentile of the earnings distribution. This question should be answerable with the authors' data.

Perhaps the most interesting part of the paper is the cohort analysis. The cohort picture (fig. 3) graphs the share of women at the top of *their own cohort's* labor earnings distribution. It paints a mixed picture regarding the march toward gender equality at the top. One the one hand, each successive cohort is entering with a larger share of women at the top. On the other hand, the youngest three to four cohorts—those born in each 5-year period starting from 1934 to 1974—show a rapidly declining representation at the top as they age. This is true for both the top 0.1% and the second 0.9%, though less markedly in the case of the latter. Why is the female share of younger cohorts decreasing? A few possible explanations are (i) men are promoted more rapidly, (ii) men change jobs in an advantageous fashion more frequently (either because they obtain better offers or are more able to take advantage of the ones they receive), or (iii) women are exiting or reducing their hours as they age and take on a greater share of family responsibilities. This seems like a fruitful question to explore in greater depth in future work. In fact, it would have been interesting to have conducted the entire analysis from a cohort perspective.

Although the authors cannot observe occupations, they are able to use the SIC code to construct 13 industry groups. One unsurprising finding is that the representation of finance in the top 0.1% has increased markedly. Overall, there appears to be little variation across industries in the gender composition of the top earners during the latest set of years, 2008–12. This points at a common issue affecting the lack of women at

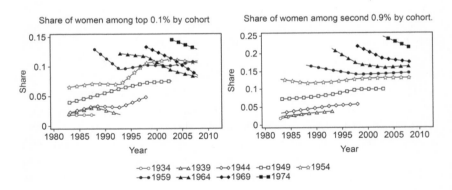

Fig. 3. Share of women in top 1% of cohort distribution. A color version of this figure is available online.

the top rather than their underrepresentation in particularly high-earning industries. This makes it even more important to understand the occupational structure by gender, as what may explain the underrepresentation of women at the top is a disproportionately higher employment in lower-earning occupations (e.g., if they are less likely to work, say, as a top executive in an industry).

It is instructive to end with some reflection on what factors might be responsible for the low representation of women in the top percentiles of the earnings distribution. As noted previously, although the authors focus on the very top, the underrepresentation of women is true for the top half of the distribution. Therefore there may be common factors that affect women generally rather than simply affect women at the very top of the labor earnings distribution.

A life-cycle perspective may be useful in terms of thinking about possible contributors. Although we have seen a significant reversal of the gender gap in education, the share of women at the top has been fairly stagnant over the 2000s. One contributor to this is likely to be their field of study, as this helps determine their occupation. Across OECD countries, on average boys score slightly better than girls in the PISA (Program for International Student Assessment) math test whereas girls on average score *much* better than boys in the reading test. Breda and Napp (2019) use 2012 PISA scores of 15-year-old students in OECD countries (a sample of around 300,000 students) as well as answers to questions regarding their intention to study math-intensive fields in the future. They show that both girls and boys seem to respond to their *relative* advantage in performance across fields, instead of their absolute advantage and the difference in relative rewards. This means that a girl who is good at math but even better in reading may favor the humanities because she perceives herself as a "verbal" person, leading girls to disproportionately opt out of mathematical fields. This response in high school contributes to the large STEM gender gap, which is then amplified in college and resulting choice of occupation.

Turning to the work stage of women's lives, studies by Gayle, Golan, and Miller (2012) on top executives in publicly traded firms and Bertrand, Goldin, and Katz (2010) on MBAs from Chicago Business School show that for these select high-earning groups there are large differences in exit rates from the labor force between women and men. Bertrand et al. use survey data to study the dynamics of wages of University of Chicago MBAs from the classes of 1990–2006. They find that a man in the 90th percentile of the male distribution earns more than $1 million at 10–16 years out as compared with $438,000 in the 90th percentile of the female distribution.

Even after accounting for loss in work experience and weekly hours worked, taking any time out of work results in a 23 log point reduction in annual earnings. Furthermore, it is not the case that women suffer a greater penalty for taking time away from work. In fact, the authors find that the reduction in earnings is even larger for men. The fraction of women, however, who take time out of work is much larger: 27% of women as opposed to 11% of men in their sample have a work interruption. Relatedly, recent work by Kleven et al. (2019) shows that, in general, women and men's earnings diverge when they have children. Using an event study methodology, they show that whereas men's earnings barely budge upon the birth of a child, women's earnings fall (presumably a combination of factors ranging from lower labor force participation, hours worked, and career consequences/choices), resulting in a child "penalty" of around 31%. These papers all point to the greater need to understand the interaction between family and work to identify the mechanisms responsible for the gender gap in labor earnings.

I conclude with two main suggestions. First, although the authors' SSA data do not allow them to study education, marital status, or fertility, they do have information on race and ethnicity. The paper would be greatly enriched if the study were broadened to include an analysis of minority groups at the top. How has the share of Blacks or Hispanics or Asians evolved over time? Within these groups, how do the results differ by gender or by area of the country? These seem like the sort of questions that the data are well suited to address. A second suggestion is to exploit more fully the panel nature of the data, which is where its strength lies. In particular, it would be great to look beyond 1-period transitions to paint a fuller picture of the labor earning dynamics of these top earners, especially by cohort. I look forward to seeing this work in the future.

Endnote

Author email address: Fernández (raquel.fernandez@nyu.edu). For acknowledgments, sources of research support, and disclosure of the author's material financial relationships, if any, please see https://www.nber.org/books-and-chapters/nber-macroeco nomics-annual-2020-volume-35/comment-glass-ceiling-and-paper-floor-gender-differ ences-among-top-earners-1981-2012-fernandez.

References

Bertrand, Marianne, Claudia Goldin, and Lawrence F. Katz. 2010. "Dynamics of the Gender Gap for Young Professionals in the Financial and Corporate Sectors." *American Economic Journal: Applied Economics* 2 (3): 228–55.

Breda, Thomas, and Clotilde Napp. 2019. "Girls' Comparative Advantage in Reading Can Largely Explain the Gender Gap in Math-Related Fields." *Proceedings of the National Academy of Sciences* 116 (31): 15435–40.

Gayle, George-Levi, Limor Golan, and Robert A. Miller. 2012. "Gender Differences in Executive Compensation and Job Mobility." *Journal of Labor Economics* 30 (4): 829–72.

Kleven, Henrik, Camille Landais, Johanna Posch, Andreas Steinhauer, and Josef Zweimuller. 2019. "Child Penalties across Countries: Evidence and Explanations." *AEA Papers and Proceedings* 109:122–26.

Discussion

The authors opened the discussion by addressing some concerns raised by the discussants. First, they addressed the limitations of the data used in the analysis. The data contain information about wage and salary income, leaving out other categories such as partnership income and capital income. Paola Sapienza noted in her discussion that the excluded categories might be particularly important for top income earners, and their omission might affect the results of the paper. The authors agreed that income categories beyond wage and salary are important. However, they argued that the omitted categories follow similar trends as wage and salary income, as they illustrated in another paper by F. Guvenen and G. Kaplan ("Top Income Inequality in the 21st Century: Some Cautionary Notes," *Federal Reserve Bank of Minneapolis Quarterly Review* 38, no. 1 [2017]: 2–15). They compared data from the Internal Revenue Service (IRS) on total income (labor income plus capital income) and individual-level micro data on labor income (wage and self-employment income) from the US Social Security Administration (SSA). Trends in income inequality at top 1% and 0.1% of income distribution revealed in the two data sets track each other very closely up to the year 2000. After 2000, IRS and SSA data reveal diverging patterns, but the gap is driven mainly by the group at the top 0.1%, they argued.

Second, the authors addressed concerns about winsorization of the data. Sapienza noted in her discussion that the authors used winsorized data, which might be misleading if there are many more men than women at the very top of the income distribution. As an example, she pointed out that the maximum earnings in the authors' data were $25.4 million in 2000. However, she reported from the ExecuComp database, which records data on compensation for CEOs at top firms, that a substantial number of individuals, mostly men, earned more than $25.4 million. The authors pointed out that CEOs at the top 1,000 firms are very different from the rest of individuals in the economy, and they account for a very small proportion of individuals at the top of the income distribution. In fact, there are about 1.4 million individuals in the top 1% and about 140,000 individuals in the top 0.1% of income distribution in the United States. Thus, the contribution of CEOs at the top 1,000 firms to trends in inequality at the top 1% or 0.1% is negligible, they claimed. In addition, the share of CEOs at the top 1% and 0.1% has been declining, as documented by J. Song, D. J. Price, F. Guvenen, N. Bloom, and T. von Wachter ("Firming Up Inequality," *Quarterly Journal of Economics* 134, no. 1 [2019]: 1–50).

The authors finally addressed a question from the discussion of Raquel Fernández about women's life-cycle patterns. They pointed out that the last section of the paper investigates individuals who are in the lifetime top 1% share of income distribution. For this group of individuals, the age-specific gender gap grows when individuals are aged 20–35, and then it declines. The authors interpreted this finding as evidence that women take time off when aged 20–35 for maternity leave, even if the data do not contain information to corroborate this interpretation. In addition, when considering individuals who are not in the lifetime top 1% income group, many women, especially in the finance sector, enter the top 1% group early in their career, but they subsequently drop out of the group and do not enter it again.

The authors concluded the discussion by arguing that the results of the paper suggest that, to find a solution to the problem of gender gap, future research should investigate the production function of an occupation at the micro level. Understanding how output is produced in different occupations can shed light on the reasons why, in sectors such as medicine, women are able to take some years off and come back at a high-ranked position, whereas in sectors such as finance, they do not enjoy a similar flexibility.

6

Sources of US Wealth Inequality:
Past, Present, and Future

Joachim Hubmer, *University of Pennsylvania,* United States of America

Per Krusell, *Institute for International Economic Studies,* Sweden, *NBER,* United States of America, *and CEPR,* United States of America

Anthony A. Smith. Jr., *Yale University,* United States of America, *and NBER,* United States of America

I. Introduction

The distribution of wealth in most countries for which there is reliable data is strikingly uneven. There is also recent work suggesting that the wealth distribution has undergone significant movements over time, most recently with a large upward swing in dispersion in several Anglo-Saxon countries (Piketty 2014; Saez and Zucman 2016). For example, according to the estimates in Saez and Zucman (2016) for the United States, the share of overall wealth held by the top 1% has increased from around 25% in 1980 to more than 40% today; for the top 0.1% it has increased from less than 10% to more than 20% over the same time period.

The observed developments have generated strong reactions across the political spectrum. In his 2014 book *Capital in the Twenty-First Century,* Piketty is obviously motivated by the growing inequality in itself, but he also suggests that further increases in wealth concentration may lead to both economic and democratic instability. Conservatives in the United States have expressed worries as well: Is the American dream really still alive, or might it be that a large fraction of the population simply will no longer be able to productively contribute to society? Given, for example, that parental wealth and well-being are important determinants of children's human capital accumulation, these are legitimate concerns regardless of one's political views. These concerns, moreover, have stimulated the proposal and discussion of a number of possible changes in policy. The primary aim of the present paper is, instead of focusing on policy changes, to understand the determinants of the observed movements in wealth inequality. This aim is basic but well-motivated in light of the policy discussion: to compare different policy actions, we need a framework for thinking about what causes inequality and for addressing how any particular policy influences not only inequality but also other macroeconomic variables.

In an effort to understand the movements in wealth inequality, Piketty (2014) and its online appendix suggest specific mathematical theories, and as part of the present study we examine those theories.[1] Our aim, however, is to depart instead from a more general, and by now rather standard, quantitative theory used in the heterogeneous-agent literature within macroeconomics: the Bewley-Huggett-Aiyagari model. This is a natural setting for the study of inequality. This model incorporates rich detail at the household level along the lines of the applied work in the consumption literature, allowing several sources of heterogeneity among consumers. It is based on incomplete markets and hence does not feature the "infinite elasticity of capital supply" of dynastic models with complete markets.[2] This model also involves equilibrium interaction: inequality is determined not only by the individual households' reactions to changes in the economic environment in which they operate but also by their interaction, such as in the equilibrium formation of wages and interest rates, two key prices determining the returns to labor and wealth, respectively. Our aim is to see to what extent a reasonably calibrated model can account for the movements in wealth inequality since the mid-1960s as a function of a number of drivers, the importance of each of which we then evaluate in separate counterfactuals.[3]

We build on the model studied in Aiyagari (1994); that is, we use the core setting of the recent literature on heterogenous agents in macroeconomics.[4] This kind of theoretical model is quantitative in nature: It is constructed as an aggregate version of the applied work on consumption. Moreover, inequality plays a central role in this model. We calibrate some key parameters of this model to match the wealth and income distributions in the United States in the mid-1960s and treat these distributions as representing a long-run steady state. In the 1960s, too, the dispersion of wealth was striking, and it is not immediate how to make the basic model match the data in this respect. In particular, the benchmark models in the literature do not readily produce long-run wealth inequality that is as striking as that observed: They do not produce wealth dispersion that goes much beyond earnings dispersion. The data shows, again wherever reliable data is available, a wealth Gini much above 0.5 (say, 0.8), whereas the earnings Gini is typically significantly below 0.5. In this paper we depart from the benchmark model by introducing portfolio heterogeneity across and within wealth groups. As we shall discuss in detail below, such heterogeneity has recently surfaced as a striking feature of households' investment patterns. In particular, register data in Norway and Sweden (see Fagereng et al. [2020] and Bach, Calvet, and Sodini [2019], respectively) have revealed, first, an average return that is increasing in the household's overall level of wealth, and, second, an idiosyncratic return component (because different households hold different types of assets) whose variance is also increasing in wealth.

Our first major finding is that, once portfolio heterogeneity, calibrated to the findings in Bach et al. (2019), is incorporated into the model, we replicate wealth inequality of the magnitude we see in the data. Thus, to match the agglomeration at the top, we do not need to consider discount-factor heterogeneity, as in Krusell and Smith (1998), or other mechanisms that raise the saving of the wealthiest.[5] Our model, which is fully nonlinear with household decision rules for saving whose slopes differ widely between the poorest and the richest, delivers a law of motion for wealth that becomes approximately linear in wealth for high wealth levels, with a random coefficient. It can thus be viewed as a microfoundation for the kind of models entertained in Piketty and Zucman (2015) (who simply assume linear laws of motion for wealth accumulation and either random saving propensities or random returns). A closely related setting is that in Benhabib, Bisin, and Luo (2019). These models, and by extension ours, generate a wealth distribution whose right tail is Pareto-shaped, a prominent feature in the data; we discuss this finding, and the relation to a number of other papers building on the same kind of reduced form, in detail in the paper.

With the resulting realistic starting wealth distribution, we then examine a number of potential drivers of wealth inequality over the subsequent period. One is tax rates: beginning around 1980 tax rates fell significantly for top incomes, so that tax progressivity in particular fell substantially. Thus, higher returns to saving in the upper brackets since that time can potentially explain increased wealth gaps between the rich and the poor. Another potential explanation for increased wealth inequality is the rather striking increases in wage/earnings inequality witnessed since the mid-1970s. Since at least Katz and Murphy (1992), it has been well-documented that the education skill premium has risen. Moreover, numerous studies have since documented that the premia associated with other measures of skill have also risen, as have measures of residual, or frictional, wage dispersion (Acemoglu 2002; Hornstein, Krusell, and Violante 2005; Quadrini and Rios-Rull 2015). In terms of the very highest earners, Piketty and Saez (2003) document significant movements toward thicker tails in the upper parts of the distribution. So to the extent that this increased income inequality has translated into savings and wealth inequality, it could explain some of the changes we set out to analyze. Moreover, and very importantly as it will turn out, we feed in fluctuations in asset returns like those observed in the United States and that, given the systematic portfolio heterogeneity across wealth groups, may imply dynamic movements of wealth inequality. Finally, the share of total income paid to capital has increased recently, potentially contributing to increased wealth inequality (see, e.g., Karabarbounis and Neiman 2014). We consider this factor as well in this study.

Thus, the overall methodology we follow is to attempt to quantify the mechanisms just mentioned and then to examine their individual (and joint) effects on the evolution of wealth inequality from the 1960s. For the time period considered, we find, first, that the benchmark model does account well for the net increase in wealth inequality over the period. The model is more or less successful depending on what aspect of the wealth distribution is in focus. The shares of wealth held by the top 10%, the top 1%, and the top 0.1% exhibit net increases that are very similar in the model and in the data, though for the top 0.01% the benchmark model does not deliver enough of an increase. For the bottom 50%, the model's fit is also good. Second, in terms of the dynamics, the model also proves to be successful in replicating the marked U-shape of wealth inequality. Furthermore, the model delivers a time path for the ratio of capital to net output that is similar to the one in the data.

Turning to which specific features explain the largest fractions of the increase in wealth inequality, the marked decrease in tax progressivity is by far the most powerful force for the cumulative increase in wealth inequality.[6] First, other things being equal, decreasing tax progressivity spreads out the distribution of after-tax resources available for consumption and saving. Second, decreasing tax progressivity increases the returns on savings, leading to higher wealth accumulation, especially among the rich for whom wages (earnings) are a smaller part of wealth. As for the dynamics, here swings in the returns of the different asset groups turn out to be crucial. In agreement with Kuhn, Schularick, and Steins (2020), we find that without portfolio heterogeneity, and without asset-price movements, we would not be able to understand the short- and medium-run movements in wealth inequality.

Wage inequality, on the other hand, has less clear-cut effects on wealth. As we argue in our paper, it can both increase and decrease wealth inequality, depending on the nature of the increased earnings risk and on what wealth-inequality statistics one looks at. In some aggregate sense—measured by the shares of wealth held by the richest households—the kind of earnings inequality we feed in on net contributes negatively to wealth inequality, taken together. We consider increases in earnings inequality of different kinds. We follow Heathcote, Storesletten, and Violante (2010) in modeling increased wage inequality as an increase in the riskiness of wage realizations around a mean. In a standard additive permanent-plus-transitory model of wages, we use the estimated time series in Heathcote et al. (2010) for the variances of the permanent and transitory shocks to wages. Both of those variances have increased over time, leading to a reduction in the share of wealth held by the richest for two reasons. First, increasing wage risk dampens the tendency of heterogeneity in returns or discount rates to drive apart the distribution of wealth.[7] In particular, as wage risk increases, poorer and less patient consumers—who are less well-insured against this risk through their own savings—engage in additional precautionary saving, compressing the distribution of wealth at the low end. Second, with more risk, aggregate precautionary savings increase, reducing the equilibrium interest rate and reducing the relative wealth accumulation of the rich, for whom wage risk is also not so important. In sum, the increasing riskiness of wages compresses the wealth distribution at both ends.[8] At the same time, these increases in earnings risk do induce higher inequality if one looks at the dispersion of wealth within the bottom part of the distribution rather than within the whole distribution.

In addition, we follow Piketty and Saez (2003) by adding a Pareto-shaped tail to the wage distribution so as to match the concentration of earnings at the top of the earning distribution; the standard wage process (as in Heathcote et al. 2010) does not match this extreme right tail well. Moreover, the right tail has thickened over this period, and accordingly we model this thickening as a gradually decreasing Pareto coefficient, based on the estimates in Piketty and Saez (2003). This element of increased wage inequality does generate more wealth inequality—because it occurs in a segment of the population where most workers are already rather well-insured through their own savings—but it is not so potent as to produce a net overall increase in wealth inequality from higher wage inequality. To allow for an increasing capital share over time, we conduct an experiment using a constant elasticity of substitution (CES) production function with a somewhat higher than unitary elasticity between capital and labor. We also consider an experiment using a Cobb-Douglas production function with time-varying coefficients, allowing us to exactly replicate the time series of observed factor shares. The resulting paths in these experiments differ only marginally from the baseline case with constant factor shares.

Given the role of portfolio heterogeneity and of asset-price movements, it is important to think more about the origins of these observations. In the present paper we take shortcuts in both these respects. First, we simply hard-wire the portfolio heterogeneity. The consumer making a saving decision knows, given the current level of wealth, what the return characteristics are (but has no choice but to accept them, i.e., cannot switch to holding different asset shares) and what they will be like henceforth. Because there is a higher average return as a function of wealth, the household therefore factors in this small amount of "increasing returns" to saving in setting the current saving rate. Interestingly, the household's choice of a saving rate is not very sensitive to the return characteristics, and hence a Solow-like constant saving rate comes close to approximating optimal behavior.[9] In particular, a model with myopic forecasts delivers very similar behavior to that in our benchmark (where agents have perfect foresight). Second, we do not attempt to solve for asset prices by clearing markets for each asset class. This would necessitate taking a stand on how to solve the equity premium puzzle and, more than that, also match returns for other asset classes—we incorporate houses and private equity as well, which are very important for the average household and the richest, respectively. The two shortcuts we take seem necessary at this stage; rather, we view our present paper as an important step forward in noting just how important portfolios and asset prices are for inequality. Taking the whole step forward in explaining them is one or two orders of magnitude more challenging, but these steps definitely seem worth taking now.

Whereas return premia are exogenous, the risk-free rate is an endogenous outcome in our model. Reassuringly, our model replicates the low-frequency variation in the risk-free rate very well, including the secular decline since the 1980s. We find that capital deepening, triggered by wealth accumulation at the top, decreases the marginal product of capital substantially. Moreover, rising return premia and rising wealth inequality mechanically depress the risk-free rate further in our setup.

What are the implications of our dynamic model of wealth inequality for the future? Quite strikingly, if the progressivity of taxes remains at today's historically low level, then wealth inequality will continue to climb and reach very high levels by, say, 2100: the top 10% will have an additional 10% of all of wealth, whereas the top 1% share will increase by more than 20%. Thus, decreasing the progressivity of taxes is a rather powerful mechanism for wealth concentration.

Our paper begins in Section II with a brief literature review, the purpose of which is to put our modeling in a historical perspective. We discuss the data on wealth inequality and its recent trends in Section III. We describe the basic model in Section IV and the implied behavior of the very richest in Section V. Section VI discusses the calibration in detail, and Sections VII and VIII the benchmark results for long-run wealth inequality and its historical evolution, respectively. A number of extensions are then included in Section IX. We conclude our paper in Section X with a brief discussion of potential other candidate explanations for the increased wealth inequality and, hence, of possible future avenues for research.

II. Connections to the Recent Macro-Inequality Literature

The study of inequality in wealth using structural macroeconomic modeling can be said to have started with Bewley (n.d.), though in Bewley's paper the focus was not on inequality per se.[10] Bewley's paper was not completed—it stops abruptly in the middle—and the first papers to provide a complete analysis of frameworks like his are Huggett (1993) and Aiyagari (1994). A defining characteristic of these models is that long-run household wealth responds smoothly to the interest rate, so long as the interest rate is not too high (higher than the discount rate in the case without growth).

In their early papers, neither Bewley nor Huggett nor Aiyagari focused on inequality per se but rather on other phenomena related to inequality (asset pricing and aggregate precautionary saving in the latter two cases, respectively). Soon after, however, the macroeconomic literature that arose from these analyses began to address inequality directly. There were several reasons for this development. One was the interest in building macroeconomic models with microeconomic foundations in which heterogeneity could influence aggregates—namely, cases that depart from the typical permanent-income behavior that characterizes the complete-markets model.[11] Another was an interest in wealth inequality per se and the challenge it posed: the difficulty that these models have in generating significant equilibrium wealth inequality. The difficulty is apparent in Aiyagari (1994), where the wage process is calibrated to Panel Study of Income Dynamics (PSID) data (as an AR(1) in logs): the resulting wealth distribution is slightly more skewed than the wage distribution the model uses as an input, but not by much. The Gini index for wealth, in the stationary distribution of Aiyagari's model, is only around 0.4, whereas it is around 0.8 in the data. The purpose here is not to go over the entire literature aiming at matching the wealth distribution but to acknowledge that several different extensions of the model have been proposed to match the data better. On some general level, successful paths forward involve introducing "more heterogeneity": typically in preferences (such as discount factors, as in Krusell and Smith 1998), in the wage/earnings process (as in Castañeda, Días-Giménez, and Ríos-Rull 2003), or in occupation (as in Cagetti and De Nardi [2006] or Quadrini [2000]).

More recently, a literature evolved that focuses on explaining the observed Pareto tail at the top of the wealth distribution. Benhabib, Bisin, and Zhu (2011) show analytically that the stationary wealth distribution in an overlapping-generations (OLG) economy with idiosyncratic capital return risk has a Pareto tail. Analogously, they provide analytical results for an infinite-horizon economy (Benhabib, Bisen, and Zhu 2015). In Benhabib et al. (2019), the authors conduct a quantitative investigation of social mobility and the wealth distribution in an OLG economy with idiosyncratic returns, which are fixed over a lifetime. In a stylized model, Gabaix et al. (2016) demonstrate that the random growth mechanism that can generate the Pareto tail in the wealth distribution (either through idiosyncratic capital return risk or random discount factors) implies very slow transitional dynamics. Furthermore, Nirei and Aoki (2016) consider a stationary Bewley economy with investment risk.[12] In that setting they find that decreasing top tax rates can explain the increasing concentration of wealth at the top.

Most of the literature on Bewley models has considered only the stationary (long-run) wealth distribution. A recent exception is Kaymak and Poschke (2016), who in line with our analysis here aim to quantify the contributions of changes in taxes and transfers and in the earnings distribution to changes in the US wealth distribution; we compare their results to ours in more detail below. Another recent paper of this sort is Aoki and Nirei (2017), which studies how a one-time drop in tax rates affects transitional dynamics in a setting with investment risk.

The present paper has three main characteristics that distinguish it from the just-discussed earlier work. The first characteristic is that, in contrast to all but a handful of studies, it addresses the long-run as well as short- and medium-run determinants of the wealth distribution. Second, our model is rather comprehensive, in two ways: (i) it considers all the main mechanisms that the literature discusses regarding the buildup in inequality, and (ii) it looks at the full distribution of wealth—that is, both the upper tail and at the bulk of the distribution. Our model generates a Pareto tail endogenously, because it delivers approximately linear saving dynamics for households—with a stochastic coefficient on wealth—as wealth grows large. The key measure of the fatness of the right wealth tail is the (inverse of the) Pareto coefficient. In the data, its value, as we elaborate on below and is also emphasized elsewhere, is significantly higher than that for the earnings distribution.[13] A model with earnings risk only will either not deliver a Pareto tail for wealth at all or, if earnings risk is itself Pareto, will deliver a Pareto tail for wealth of the same shape as for earnings (Stachurski and Toda 2019). To us, thus, stochastic returns to saving and/or stochastic discounting, which do deliver the correct right-tail shape of wealth, are essential for understanding the right tail of the wealth distribution in the long run. This sets our paper apart from other Aiyagari-based models. This includes Kaymak and Poschke (2016), which delivers a very nice account of the medium-run features of the bulk of the wealth distribution but which does not have its focus on, and does not fully account for, its right tail.[14] We have in common with Kaymak and Poschke (2016) that we also include a thorough discussion of the model's predictions for the middle and lower parts of the wealth distribution. We discuss how our transitional results differ from theirs in detail in Section VII below.

The third characteristic that sets our paper apart from, we believe, all of the above-mentioned literature and hence is the most novel, is that it incorporates portfolio behavior that differs across households. Wealthy households have portfolios with more risk and higher average return. In addition, there is a nonnegligible idiosyncratic return component at all wealth levels, with an accentuation for the wealthiest. These features are not free parameters in our model: We calibrate them to available micro data and, in particular, track the returns, by asset subgroup, over time. Because of the systematic differences in portfolio compositions and in the return to different portfolios over the period, we obtain predictions for the evolution of the wealth distribution, and it turns out that this allows us to match the short- and medium-run dynamics surprisingly well. In particular, there is a marked U-shape of the top wealth shares over the time period under study, and none of the other papers in the literature can generate this shape. We conclude that return heterogeneity—in particular, both the systematically different portfolios across wealth levels (which are important for wealth inequality dynamics) and the stochastic idiosyncratic component (which is important for understanding the right tail of the long-run wealth distribution)—is central to an understanding of wealth inequality and its evolution over time. We therefore now consider it crucial in this area to turn our attention toward understanding the deep determinants of all these features of observed portfolio decisions.

A final relevant literature connection is that to Piketty's $r - g$ theory: Our framework can be interpreted as giving support to an elaborate version of this theory. The elaboration involves (i) negligible emphasis on g; (ii) the interpretation of r as net of taxes; and (iii) the (crucial) recognition that r is heterogeneous across households and systematically different for different wealth levels, both because taxation is progressive and because portfolios are heterogeneous. It must be emphasized, however, that this theory primarily works for the right tail of the wealth distribution; for understanding the rest, the kind of analysis pursued by Kaymak and Poschke (2016), as well as that herein, seems necessary.

III.   Measuring Wealth Inequality over Time

Over the last century, the distribution of wealth in the United States has undergone drastic changes, and we briefly review data from some key studies here. Throughout the time period considered, wealth was heavily concentrated at the top. Figure 1 shows the evolution of the share of total wealth held by the top 1% and the top 0.1%, as measured using different estimation methods.

Considering all three methods jointly, top wealth inequality exhibits a U-shaped pattern in the twentieth century. At the same time, the magnitude of the increase in wealth concentration in the last 30 years differs substantially among estimation methodologies. We will calibrate the initial steady state of our model to the wealth shares estimated by Saez and Zucman (2016) and consequently compare the model transition to their estimates. Their estimates are especially useful for us as they allow for considering a group as small as the top 0.01%. Furthermore, they cover a long time period.

Even though the capitalization method that they use to back out wealth estimates does not suffer from the shortcomings of the US Survey of Consumer Finances (SCF) data (such as concerns about response-rate bias and exclusion of the Forbes 400), it is an indirect way of measuring wealth and as such has other drawbacks. For example, the tax data allows only for a coarse partitioning of capital income in asset classes,

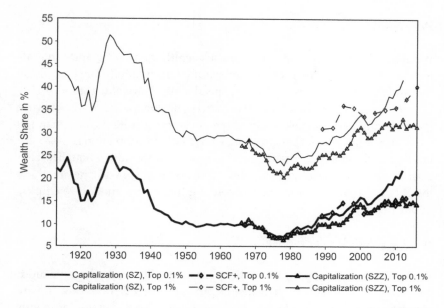

Fig. 1. Top wealth share measurements over time. The lines labeled "Capitalization (SZ)" display findings from Saez and Zucman (2016), who back out the stock of wealth held by a tax unit from observed capital income tax data. The lines labeled "Capitalization (SZZ)" display findings from Smith et al. (2020), who adjust the capitalization method for return heterogeneity within asset classes. The lines labeled "SCF+" refer to data from the Survey of Consumer Finances as reported by Smith et al., augmented with information on the Forbes 400, which are by design excluded from the US Survey of Consumer Finances. A color version of this figure is available online.

and within each class, returns are effectively assumed to be homogeneous. Because recent evidence based on both Norwegian and Swedish data (Fagereng et al. [2020] and Bach et al. [2019], respectively) shows significantly higher returns for high-wealth groups, the basic capitalization method suggests an overprediction of wealth levels for the richest group. Indeed, Smith, Zidar, and Zwick (2020) adjust the method of Saez and Zucman for heterogeneity within asset classes and find a smaller increase in wealth concentration that is comparable to survey data. Therefore, we will in addition contrast our findings to their estimates.[15]

Another takeaway from figure 1 is that the wealth distribution was quite stable in the 1950s and 1960s. In addition, some of the time series estimates we feed into our model start in 1967; we therefore take this year as the initial steady state in our model.

IV. Model Framework

What are the determinants of long-run wealth inequality, and what affects its dynamics? The present paper puts particular emphasis on these dynamics, but to understand them one also needs to take a stand on the longer-run drivers of wealth inequality. In particular, the framework we use for analyzing long-run inequality has important implications for dynamics, as we shall explain. As a background, let us first—in Subsection IV.A—very briefly recall some basic predictions for equilibrium wealth inequality from a set of standard models. In the subsequent sections, we will draw on these insights when formulating and interpreting the specific model we employ in our paper.

A. Long-Run Wealth Inequality: A Primer

Let us focus mostly on the predictions for inequality using dynastic models—that is, frameworks where agents put value on their offspring and are altruistic in that respect. At the very end, we will briefly make comments on alternative assumptions in this regard. We will, for simplicity, also abstract from age dependence of either preferences or income streams and simply regard household i's present-value utility as being $E_0 \sum_{t=0}^{\infty} \beta_i^t u_i(c_{it})$ and its income stream as a stationary process. Let us also consider a neoclassical production function $F(K_t, L)$, no technological change, and geometric depreciation of capital at rate δ.[16] That is, we have a standard optimizing growth model with more than one agent.

The Permanent-Income Model

Let us first consider a constant endowment stream. The consumer's budget constraint in our simplest setting is then $c_{it} + k_{i,t+1} = \omega_i w_t + (1 + r_t)k_{it}$, where w_t and R_t are the marginal products of labor and capital based on $F(K_t, L)$, and $r_t = R_t - \delta$; ω_i is agent i's endowment of labor in efficiency units. Let us also for illustration consider only two kinds of agents, A and B, with masses μ_A and μ_B, respectively. The key observation here is that if $\beta_A = \beta_B$, then any wealth distribution (k_A, k_B) is a steady state, so long as $\mu_A k_A + \mu_B k_B = K^*$, where K^* satisfies $\beta(1 + F_1(K^*, \mu_A \omega_A + \mu_B \omega_B) - \delta) = 1$, and neither $\omega_A w + (1/\beta - 1)k_A$ nor $\omega_B w + (1/\beta - 1)k_B$ is negative (which ensures nonnegative consumption for both agents). That is, given the unique level of capital consistent with steady state, any distribution of this capital will be a constant equilibrium where each individual just consumes the wage plus the interest on the capital. This case, including the associated transitional dynamics, is discussed in detail in Chatterjee (1994).[17] This model has no predictions for long-run wealth inequality other than to perpetuate whatever inequality initially prevails. This result is robust to adding a proportional tax on capital income (with lump-sum rebates).

Heterogenity in Critical Places

In contrast, assume that $\beta_A > \beta_B$. Then there is no steady state, but asymptotically there is extreme wealth inequality: Agent A owns the entire capital stock plus a claim on agent B such that the latter has zero consumption. Intuitively, the relatively impatient agent B borrows early on and then pays back later. Now, the model has predictions, and they are stark. The same stark outcome would hold asymptotically if the two agents had the same discount factors but different returns on their capital: $r_A > r_B$; we can assume that this is achieved by means of a proportional tax on agent B's capital income and lump-sum transfers of the proceeds. Again, agent A would hold all the wealth asymptotically.

Consider yet another case, where $\beta_A = \beta_B$ and $r_A = r_B$ but where there is a progressive tax rate on capital income. Assume first that this rate is strictly increasing in capital income. Then there is again a sharp prediction, but one with full equality: the only situation in which both agents' Euler equations can hold is that where they both have the same capital income and, therefore, the same levels of capital. A second case of interest obtains when the tax rate is weakly increasing in capital income, with flat sections. Then long-run inequality involves a unique total capital stock in steady state but a range of distributions of this stock, such that both agents remain within the same tax bracket.

Risk

Relative to these results, let us consider stochastic earnings. First, consider the case where the total effective amount of labor is always constant but where all of the A agents receive the same shock and all of the B agents receive another shock; thus, by construction, there is perfect negative correlation between the shocks of the two agents. Under complete markets—that is, when agents can fully insure—we obtain the same predictions for wealth inequality as above—in all the different subcases. In other words, random incomes do not matter per se.

However, when earnings are not fully insured, this result no longer holds. In particular, in the Bewley-Aiyagari-Huggett settings, there is only one asset and a constraint on borrowing, and hence perfect consumption smoothing is not possible; there is, instead, "precautionary saving." Moreover, in all the cases discussed above—no heterogeneity, different discount factors, different returns, progressive income taxation—the model typically has a sharp long-run prediction: There is a unique, and nondegenerate, steady-state wealth distribution. Intuitively, given that future earnings are random and cannot be traded away unrestrictedly early on, relatively impatient consumers cannot end up in eternal poverty because their wage income will always bounce back, hence eliminating the extreme wealth inequality predicted under complete insurance/no earnings risk. Similar intuition applies in the other cases.

In the case with idiosyncratic, uninsurable risks, notice that partial-equilibrium analysis too becomes interesting. For example, a lowering of the risk-free interest rate at which agents save will have smooth effects on the average long-run wealth level held by a household, as well as on its ergodic distribution of wealth more generally. This contrasts with the "infinitely elastic" supply of household saving under complete markets/no earnings risk around the point where the interest rate equals the discount rate (where the long-run saving is zero [infinity] if the interest rate is lower [higher] than the discount rate by ever so little).

Comparative Statics under Idiosyncratic Risk and Incomplete Markets

A key purpose of the present subsection is to illustrate, with some examples, how the variance of earnings shocks can influence steady-state inequality in the incomplete-markets settings. In later sections, we will also comment on other types of comparative statics (e.g., with regard to the randomness in returns or in discount factors).

Suppose one departs from the case with a zero earnings variance and then increases it infinitesimally. How will steady-state wealth inequality then be affected? Under homogeneity in preferences and returns, long-run wealth inequality can go either up or down—depending on its starting position. If the starting position is the case with full equality, earnings volatility will necessarily increase wealth inequality in the long run, but if the starting position is at one of the extremes, wealth inequality will necessarily fall.

In the cases with either different discount factors or different person-specific returns, an increase in earnings volatility above zero must decrease wealth inequality in the long run. The result that more earnings risk can lower wealth inequality is perhaps not intuitive at first, but with more risk one is further from the frictionless outcome, which is always extreme inequality in these cases.[18] Of course, higher earnings inequality can also increase long-run wealth inequality in these models, mechanically or because taxation is progressive (where absent shocks there is long-run equality). Kaymak and Poschke (2016) do report this finding and their framework is precisely one without return or discount-rate heterogeneity.

Nondynastic Households

Finally, let us comment on how departures from dynastic models affect long-run inequality. The general answer is that it depends on what the bequest function looks like. If households derive utility from bequeathing, then if the associated function happens to look exactly like the value function in the associated dynastic household case—which would require it to also depend on any current idiosyncratic shock—then we have the same predictions as above, except insofar as we perform comparative statics.[19] If the bequest function, instead, is more or less curved than the associated value function, one would (heuristically) obtain less or more wealth inequality to be passed on from generation to generation; if the bequest function does not take the earnings state into account, one would limit precautionary saving (to within one's own life). Absent definitive microeconomic estimates of bequest functions, we consider the dynastic structure a reasonable middle ground. A limitation of our approach is that our model does not speak to demographic shifts in the population; relatedly, it does not speak to the expansion of transfers to the elderly in the form of Social Security and Medicare.[20]

In the next sections, we describe our model economy. As advertised, the basic building block is the framework in Aiyagari (1994), on top of which we add several layers of complexity to account for the empirical evidence on earnings and return heterogeneity. The earnings process centers around a persistent and temporary component, augmented by a Pareto tail. The return on capital is stochastic. Both the mean and the dispersion of returns depend on the level of accumulated assets, a specification that can be interpreted as the reduced form of a full model of portfolio choice. Furthermore, the benchmark model also features stochastic discount rates. As we demonstrate below, this framework generates cross-sectional variation in the key consumer choice, saving, that is broadly in line with empirical evidence. Let us now describe each component separately.

B.   Consumers

Time is discrete, and there is a continuum of infinitely lived, ex ante
identical consumers (dynasties).[21] Preferences are defined over infinite
streams of consumption with von Neumann-Morgenstern utility in constant relative risk aversion (CRRA) form:

$$u(c) = \frac{c^{1-\gamma}}{1-\gamma}. \tag{1}$$

In period t, a consumer discounts the future with an idiosyncratic stochastic factor β_t that is the realization of a Markov process characterized
by the conditional distribution $\Gamma_\beta(\beta_{t+1}|\beta_t)$, giving rise to the following
objective:

$$\max_{(c_t)_{t=0}^\infty} \left\{ u(c_0) + \mathbb{E}_0 \left[\sum_{t=1}^\infty \prod_{s=0}^{t-1} \beta_s u(c_t) \right] \right\}. \tag{2}$$

Labor supply is exogenous. Each period t, a consumer supplies a stochastic amount $l_t = l_t(p_t, \nu_t)$ of efficiency units of labor to the market that
depends on a persistent component $p_t \sim \Gamma_p(p_t|p_{t-1})$ and a transitory com-
ponent $\nu_t \sim \Gamma_\nu(\nu_t)$. Taking as given a competitive wage rate w_t, her earnings are $w_t l_t$.

Asset markets are incomplete, and consumers cannot fully insure
against idiosyncratic shocks. In the model, the only endogenous choice
is the overall level of savings a_t. The gross return on it is

$$1 + \underline{r}_t + r_t^X(a_t) + \sigma^X(a_t)\eta_t, \tag{3}$$

where $\underline{r}_t$ is an aggregate return component, $r_t^X(\cdot)$ and $\sigma^X(\cdot)$ are functions
that control mean and standard deviation of excess returns, and η_t is an
i.i.d. standard normal idiosyncratic shock. The excess return schedule
should be viewed as the reduced form of an implicit portfolio choice
model, where the optimal choice is allowed to depend on the overall
wealth level, albeit not on other persistent state variables. In addition
to heterogeneity, this specification allows for a limited amount of return
persistence: in the cross-section of all agents in this economy, returns are
persistent because wealth is, but conditional on the level of wealth, returns are uncorrelated over time.[22]

The decision problem of the consumer can be stated in recursive form
as follows:

$$V_t(x_t, p_t, \beta_t) = \max_{a_{t+1} \geq \underline{a}}\{u(x_t - a_{t+1}) + \beta_t \mathbb{E}[V_{t+1}(x_{t+1}, p_{t+1}, \beta_{t+1})|p_t, \beta_t]\} \quad (4)$$

$$\text{subject to } x_{t+1} = a_{t+1} + y_{t+1} - \tau_{t+1}(y_{t+1}) + (1 - \tilde{\tau}_{t+1})\tilde{y}_{t+1} + T_{t+1} \quad (5)$$

$$y_{t+1} = (\underline{r}_{t+1} + r_{t+1}^X(a_{t+1}))a_{t+1} + w_{t+1}l_{t+1}(p_{t+1}, v_{t+1}) \quad (6)$$

$$\tilde{y}_{t+1} = \sigma^X(a_{t+1})\eta_{t+1}a_{t+1} \quad (7)$$

Given cash-on-hand x_t (all resources available in period t), the optimal savings decision and the resulting value function depend solely on the persistent component of the earnings process p_t and the current discount factor β_t. Conditional on (p_t, β_t), the expectation is taken over (p_{t+1}, β_{t+1}) as well as the transitory shocks to earnings v_{t+1} and the return on capital η_{t+1}. Ordinary gross income y_t is subject to a nonlinear income tax $\tau_t(\cdot)$, whereas there is a flat (capital gains) tax $\tilde{\tau}_t$ on the mean-zero idiosyncratic return component.[23] Each consumer receives a uniform lump-sum transfer T_t.

C. Production, Government, and Equilibrium

Firms are perfectly competitive and can be described by an aggregate constant returns to scale production function $F(K_t, L)$ that yields a wage rate per efficiency unit of labor $w_t = \partial F(K_t, L)/\partial L$ as well as an (average) market return on capital $r_t = (\partial F(K_t, L)/\partial K) - \delta$, where $\delta \in (0, 1)$ is the depreciation rate. Aggregate labor supply L is normalized to 1 throughout.

As in Aiyagari (1994), aggregate capital K_t equals the average of consumers' asset holdings a_t in equilibrium. Thus, the production side is rather standard, and aggregate capital income, net of depreciation, is $r_t K_t$. However, in case there is a nontrivial excess return schedule $r_t^X(\cdot)$, individual capital income is not proportional to asset holdings (i.e., not even the expectation of it). Thus, for capital market clearing, a second condition has to hold, namely that aggregate capital income equals the average over individual capital income. Both $r_t^X(\cdot)$ and $\sigma^X(\cdot)$ are treated as exogenous objects (that will be taken from the data), thus the scalar $\underline{r}_t$ is the second aggregate equilibrium object, beside K_t. Note that $\underline{r}_t$ is not solely a function of K_t but depends on the asset distribution as well.

The government redistributes aggregate income by means of a uniform lump-sum payment, which amounts to a constant fraction $\lambda \in [0, 1]$ of aggregate tax revenues. The remainder is spent in a way such that marginal utilities of agents are not affected. Because revenues from the flat capital gains tax net out to zero in the aggregate, we omit them from the government budget constraint for simplicity.

Given time-invariant excess return schedules $r^X(\cdot)$ and $\sigma^X(\cdot)$, a steady-state equilibrium of this economy is characterized by a market clearing level of capital K^*, an aggregate return component $\underline{r}^*$, and a lump-sum transfer T^* such that:

(i) factor prices are given by their respective marginal products $w^* = \partial F(K^*, 1)/\partial L$ and $r^* = (\partial F(K^*, 1)/\partial K) - \delta$;

(ii) given $\underline{r}^*$, w^*, and T^*, consumers solve the stationary version of their decision problem, giving rise to an invariant distribution $\Gamma(a, p, \beta, \nu, \eta)$;

(iii) the government redistributes a fraction λ of total tax revenues, that is,

$$T^* = \lambda \int \tau((\underline{r}^* + r^X(a))a + w^* l(p, \nu)) d\Gamma(a, p, \beta, \nu, \eta); \tag{8}$$

(iv) and capital markets clear, that is,

$$K^* = \int a d\Gamma(a, p, \beta, \nu, \eta), \quad \text{and} \tag{9}$$

$$r^* K^* = \int (\underline{r}^* + r^X(a) + \sigma^X(a)\eta) \, a d\Gamma(a, p, \beta, \nu, \eta). \tag{10}$$

In the benchmark perfect-foresight transition experiment, we start the economy in period t_0 in some initial steady state, described by a parameter vector θ^* and by the equilibrium objects $(K^*, \underline{r}^*, T^*)$. The vector θ^* parametrizes the tax schedule, the excess return schedule, and the earnings process. Agents are fully surprised and learn about a new exogenous environment $(\theta_t)_{t=t_0+1}^{t_1}$ that will prevail over some transition period $t = t_0 + 1, t_0 + 2, \ldots, t_1$. From t_1 onward, the exogenous environment will once again be constant and equal to θ_{t_1}. In a perfect-foresight equilibrium, agents are fully informed about future equilibrium objects $(K_t, \underline{r}_t, T_t)_{t=t_0+1}^{\infty}$ too and optimize accordingly. Capital markets clear, and the fraction of tax revenues λ that is redistributed is fixed.

In an alternative myopic transition experiment, agents are surprised about the new exogenous environment and equilibrium prices every period. That is, in period $t = t_0, t_0 + 1, \ldots, t_1 - 1$, given a distribution $\Gamma_t(x_t, p_t, \beta_t)$, they choose a savings decision rule, $a_{t+1} = g_t(x_t, p_t, \beta_t)$, assuming that both θ_t and $(\underline{r}_t, w_t, T_t)$ will prevail forever. In period $t + 1$, they are accordingly surprised, one, that the exogenous environment has changed to θ_{t+1}; and two, that equilibrium factor returns $(\underline{r}_{t+1}, w_{t+1})$ and transfers T_{t+1} result from capital-market clearing and government-budget balance in period $t + 1$.[24]

These two informational structures are, of course, extreme. We chose them because we expect them to bracket a range of informational assumptions. Given that the results, as will be reported below, turn out to be very similar across the two structures, we are confident that our findings are robust to other variations in this dimension.

V. The Right Tail of the Wealth Distribution: Approximately Pareto

In this section, we briefly explain the main mechanism that leads to a "fat" Pareto-shaped right tail in the wealth distribution. The same mechanism is at play in the much simpler stochastic-β model originally proposed in Krusell and Smith (1998).

Formally, we make use of a mathematical result on random growth by Kesten (1973): consider a stochastic process

$$a_t = s_t a_{t-1} + \varepsilon_t, \tag{11}$$

where s_t and ε_t are (for our purposes positive) i.i.d. random variables. If there exists some $\zeta > 0$ such that $\mathbb{E}[s^\zeta] = 1$ as well as $\mathbb{E}[\varepsilon^\zeta] < \infty$, then a_t converges in probability to a random variable A that satisfies $\lim_{a \to \infty} \text{Prob}(A > a) \propto a^{-\zeta}$—that is, the right tail of the stationary distribution has a Pareto shape.[25]

In a setup like ours, it turns out—as we discuss in some more detail below—that s is the asymptotic marginal propensity to save out of initial-period asset holdings. Moreover, this propensity is random, whence it obtains a time subscript. In a basic model with only discount-factor randomness, s varies precisely with β; this turns out to be a property already of the model in Krusell and Smith (1998) designed to match the wealth distribution, though the β-distribution there is quite stripped down. In the present somewhat augmented model, s_t also varies with the idiosyncratic return to wealth, η_t. Random earnings appear in the linear approximation through the error term ε_t. Crucially, in this class of models, optimal saving decisions are asymptotically, with increasing wealth, linear in economies with idiosyncratic risk and incomplete markets.[26]

Assuming a fixed discount rate, Carroll and Kimball (1996) prove in a finite-horizon setting that the consumption function is concave under hyperbolic absolute risk aversion, which comprises most commonly used utility functions (e.g., CRRA). Hence, the savings rule is convex. However, as household wealth increases, the convexity in the savings rule becomes weaker and weaker.[27] Intuitively, as wealth grows large, consumers can smooth consumption more and more effectively. Moreover, with CRRA preferences, decision rules are exactly linear in the absence of risk (or with complete markets against such risk). The slope is then larger (smaller) than one as the discount rate is smaller (larger) than the interest rate. In the recent literature on the Pareto tail in the wealth distribution, either saving rates or returns to capital (or both, as in this paper) are assumed to vary randomly across consumers. Saving rules are then asymptotically linear with random coefficients: Benhabib et al. (2015) show analytically that in this case the unique ergodic wealth distribution has a Pareto distribution in its right tail.

Figure 2*a* shows the marginal propensity to save out of capital holdings (denoted k in the figure) arising from the stochastic-β model under study in the present paper.[28] As discussed above, the marginal propensity to save increases in wealth, holding earnings constant, and asymptotes to a constant that depends on the consumer's discount factor. Panel (*b*) displays the tail behavior of the stationary wealth distribution. In line with the theoretical results in Benhabib et al. (2015), the logarithm of its counter-cumulative distribution function becomes linear in the logarithm of assets as assets grow large, indicating that the right tail of the distribution follows a Pareto distribution.

In light of this result, it is worth noting that the model in Castañeda et al. (2003)—which generates substantial wealth inequality using an earnings process featuring a low-probability but transient very-high-earnings state—does not deliver a Pareto tail in wealth. In this model, in which consumers have a common discount rate, marginal propensities to save do not vary but instead converge to the same constant, independently of the level of earnings, and as a result the steady-state distribution of wealth does not feature a Pareto tail. This model can deliver such a Pareto tail, however, if the earning process itself has a Pareto tail. In the absence of randomness in either discount rates or returns, however, the wealth distribution inherits not only the Pareto tail of the earnings distribution but also its Pareto coefficient. Because earnings are considerably less concentrated than wealth, the resulting tail in wealth is too thin to match the data in such an alternative model.

VI. Calibration

In this section, we describe how we calibrate our model economy. As indicated in figure 1, the US wealth distribution was roughly stable in the

(a) Marginal propensity to save

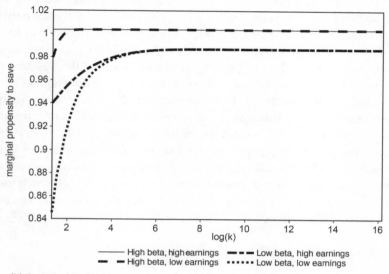

(b) Log wealth distribution

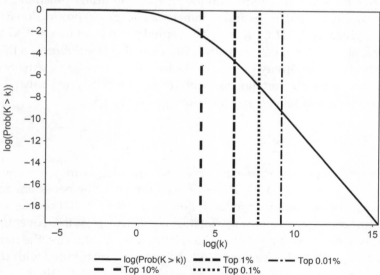

Fig. 2. Pareto tail of the wealth distribution. Panel *a* displays the marginal propensity to save as a function of log capital holdings for various values of the earnings and discount factor processes. Panel *b* displays the wealth distribution. A color version of this figure is available online.

1950s and 1960s, as was tax progressivity. This, together with the fact
that some of our time series estimates start in 1967, makes 1967 a natural
initial steady state. We set the model period to a year to conform to the
tax system. Overall, the strategy is to use observables to select the structural model parameters to the largest extent possible; the key observables are the earnings process, the tax system, and the households' portfolio and return structures. To the extent not all the wealth inequality
can be accounted for this way, we then calibrate the discount factor process to match the 1967 wealth distribution as completely as possible.
(Given the parsimonious process for discount factors and the multidi-
mensionality of the wealth distribution, a full match is of course not feasible.) As we shall see, we present two main cases, in one of which there
is no discount-factor heterogeneity at all (and the main results differ
only marginally between these two cases).

A. Basic Parameters

We parameterize the production technology and utility function using
standard functional forms and parameters. The (gross) production func-
tion is given by $F(K, L) = K^\alpha L^{1-\alpha}$. The capital share is set to $\alpha = 0.36$ and
depreciation to $\delta = 0.048$ annually. In an extension (see Subsection IX.A),
we check the sensitivity of our results to using a constant-elasticity-of-
substitution production function with (gross) elasticity greater than one.
The coefficient of relative risk aversion, γ, is set to 1.5.

B. The Earnings Process

The earnings process is based on the traditional log-normal framework
with $l_t(p_t, \nu_t) = \exp(p_t + \nu_t)$. That is, we assume that the persistent component p_t of the earnings process follows a Gaussian AR(1) process with
parameters (ρ^P, σ_t^P). The autocorrelation coefficient, ρ^P, is fixed over time,
whereas the innovation standard deviation varies. Likewise, the transi-
tory component ν_t is also assumed to be normally distributed with standard deviation σ_t^T. We use estimates by Heathcote et al. (2010) that span
the period 1967–2000 and assume that the time-varying variances of the
innovations are constant thereafter. The left panel of figure 3 displays
the resulting cross-sectional dispersion. The estimates show a significant increase in earnings risk for both components.

As is well-known, the resulting log-normal cross-sectional distribution of earnings understates the concentration of top labor income quite

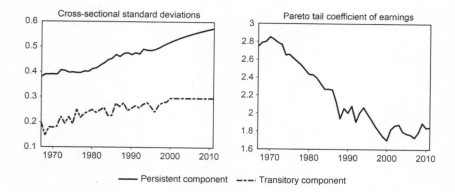

Fig. 3. Earnings process ingredients. Left panel: Cross-sectional standard deviation of temporary and persistent component of labor income from Heathcote et al. (2010). Right panel: Pareto tail coefficient for top 10% of labor income distribution; calibrated to replicate updated Piketty and Saez (2003) series. A color version of this figure is available online.

severely. Because the observed increase in top labor income shares is potentially an important explanation for the observed increase in wealth inequality at the top, we augment the framework for the top 10% earners in such a way that we can directly match the fraction of labor income going to the top 10%, top 1%, top 0.1%, and top 0.01%. In concrete terms, we posit $l_t(p_t, \nu_t) = \psi_t(p_t) \exp(\nu_t)$, where

$$
\psi_t(p_t) = \begin{cases} \exp(p_t) & \text{if } F_{p_t}(p_t) \leq 0.9, \\ F_{\text{Pareto}(\kappa_t)}^{-1}\left(\dfrac{F_{p_t}(p_t) - 0.9}{1 - 0.9} \right) & \text{if } F_{p_t}(p_t) > 0.9. \end{cases} \tag{12}
$$

$F_{p_t}(\cdot)$ is the cumulative distribution function (CDF) of p_t and $F_{\text{Pareto}(\kappa_t)}^{-1}(\cdot)$ the inverse CDF for a Pareto distribution with lower bound $F_{p_t}^{-1}(0.9)$ and shape coefficient κ_t. Effectively, we thus assume that top earnings are spread out according to a (scaled) Pareto distribution, whereas earnings for the majority of workers are distributed according to a log-normal distribution. The Pareto tail coefficient on labor income κ_t is then one additional free parameter to calibrate in each year. We use estimates on top wage shares from an updated series by Piketty and Saez (2003) spanning 1967–2011 as calibration targets. The right panel of figure 3 displays the calibrated Pareto tail coefficient κ_t, and figure 4 displays the resulting top labor income shares. That we can match top labor income shares very well using just a single parameter in each year (i.e., the tail coefficient) simply reflects the fact that the Pareto distribution is a very good description of the cross-sectional earnings distribution at the top.

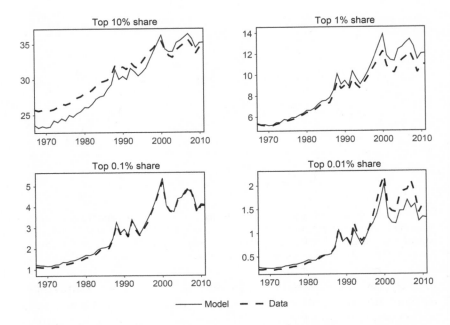

Fig. 4. Top labor income shares in percentage. Updated Piketty and Saez (2003) series. A color version of this figure is available online.

We do not explicitly model unemployment, voluntary nonemployment, or retirement. We do, however, introduce a zero-earnings state, occurring with probability $\chi = 0.075$ independently of (p_t, ν_t) and over time, reflecting both long-term unemployment and shocks that trigger temporary exit from the labor force. This probability is calibrated, together with a borrowing constraint amounting to roughly one yearly lump-sum transfer, so that the initial steady-state wealth distribution matches both the share of wealth held by the bottom 50% and the fraction of the population with negative net wealth.

C. Tax System

The progressivity of the US tax system has decreased substantially over the model period. To account for these changes, we use estimates on federal effective tax rates by Piketty and Saez (2007) for the period 1967–2000, keeping them constant thereafter. These comprise the four major federal taxes: individual income, corporate income, estate and gift, and payroll taxes.[29] Piketty and Saez (2007) calculate effective average tax rates for 11 income brackets, with a particularly detailed decomposition for top income groups (up to the top 0.01%). We translate this data to our model by means of a step-wise tax function $\tau_t(\cdot)$ with 11 steps. For each bracket, the threshold is set to match its income share in the data and the marginal tax rate such that the resulting average tax rate aligns with the data. Figure 5 shows that the US tax system has indeed become much less progressive over the model period.

In our model, taxes $\tau_t(y_t)$ are a function of total ordinary income y_t, defined as the sum of labor income and the deterministic part of capital income. A weakness of our calibration is that we do not have separate tax rates for different sources of income, but a strength is that we use effective tax rates, thereby accounting for tax avoidance and changing portfolio composition to the extent that these vary systematically with income.

The stochastic part of capital income is uncorrelated over time and equals zero in expectation for every agent. Especially at the top end of the (capital) income distribution, with sizable return risk and thus sizable year-to-year capital income fluctuations, agents have strong incentives to smooth reported capital income over time if the tax function is progressive. To avoid dealing with this issue in full detail, we use a time-varying flat tax $\tilde{\tau}_t$ for this part of capital income. In particular, we use an annual time series on the average effective capital gains tax.[30]

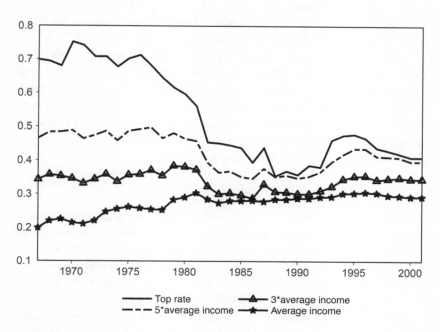

Fig. 5. Imputed marginal tax rates for selected total income levels. Piketty and Saez (2007). A color version of this figure is available online.

To account for government transfers, we introduce a social safety net in the simplest possible way by assuming that each agent receives an (untaxed) lump-sum transfer T_t every period, its size being a constant fraction $\lambda = 0.6$ of tax revenues.[31] The presence of a lump-sum transfer implies that the resulting net tax and transfer system is substantially more progressive than the gross tax system, as we show in appendix B.

Note that the income tax does not distort labor supply in our setting because we assume the latter is exogenous. This simplification is obviously not a good one for understanding the welfare consequences of changes in tax rates, but because our current focus is on wealth accumulation and its distribution in the population, we do not think that it is a major shortcoming.

D. Idiosyncratic Returns to Capital

The idiosyncratic return component depends on the overall wealth level a_t. In recent work, both Bach et al. (2019), using Swedish administrative data, and Fagereng et al. (2020), using Norwegian administrative data, document a strong relation between a household's overall wealth and return characteristics. These papers disagree somewhat in their conclusions as to whether differential returns can be fully explained by differential portfolio choice. The possibility that different households have different skills in finding returns (an interpretation made in Fagereng et al. 2020) is particularly radical relative to the traditional finance literature. Although we do not want to rule out this hypothesis as true, our calibration strategy is to follow the work of Bach et al. (2019). In particular, we calibrate the schedules of mean excess returns $r_t^X(a_t)$ and return dispersions $\sigma^X(a_t)$ such that they represent an approximation to the reduced form of an underlying portfolio choice model.[32]

The mean excess return schedule is computed as

$$r_t^X(a_t) = \sum_{c \in C} w_c(a_t)(\bar{r}_{c,t} + \tilde{r}_c^X(a_t)), \tag{13}$$

where $w_c(a_t)$ is the portfolio weight on asset class c, $\bar{r}_{c,t}$ is the aggregate excess return on asset class c, and $\tilde{r}_c^X(a_t)$ is an idiosyncratic component that accounts for within-asset class return heterogeneity. We consider four asset classes: a risk-free asset, public equity, private equity, and housing. The schedules for portfolio weights $w_c(\cdot)$ and within-asset class heterogeneity $\tilde{r}_c^X(\cdot)$ are fixed over time. We base them on data from Bach et al. (2019), who report a detailed breakdown up to the top 0.01%.[33] Aggregate excess returns $\bar{r}_{c,t}$ are time-varying and based on aggregate US data. In particular, for public and private equity, we use estimates from Kartashova (2014), who documents a premium for private equity over public equity.[34] For housing, we model the financial return as the sum of capital gains and imputed rent. For the capital gains term, we rely on the national Case-Shiller home price index.[35] In the initial and eventual steady states, we assume that house prices grow at the rate of overall inflation, in line with long-run evidence. We assume that the imputed rent term is fixed over time; we set it to 5.33%, the US time average reported in Jordà et al. (2019). Note that the level of the excess return schedule $r_t^X(\cdot)$ is irrelevant, as the endogenous aggregate return component r_t adjusts for market clearing. In other words, only differences in returns across asset classes, and within, are treated as exogenous.

The schedule of idiosyncratic return dispersion is computed as

$$(\sigma^X(a_t))^2 = \sum_{c \in C}(w_c(a_t)\tilde{\sigma}_c^X(a_t))^2,\qquad(14)$$

where the idiosyncratic standard deviation of the return on asset class c, $\tilde{\sigma}_c^X(\cdot)$, is fixed over time but allowed to depend on the wealth level. For private and public equity, we again rely on Bach et al. (2019). For housing, we set the standard deviation to 0.14 across the wealth distribution, based on the observed volatility of individual house prices in the United States (Piazzesi and Schneider 2016).

Figure 6 summarizes the excess return schedule in the 1967 steady state. Full details are relegated to the appendix (see table E1). As we

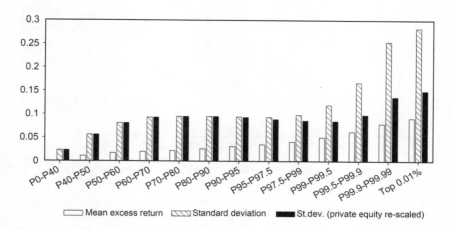

Fig. 6. Schedule of excess returns. Own computations based on Bach et al. (2019), Kartashova (2014), Jordà et al. (2019), Piazzesi and Schneider (2016), Case-Shiller home price index. A color version of this figure is available online.

explain below, using the unadjusted schedules results in too much wealth inequality at the very top. For this reason, in the benchmark model we scale down the standard deviation of private equity across the board by a factor $\phi = 0.52$. As can be seen in figure 6, this adjustment reduces in particular the volatility of the portfolio standard deviation for the top 1% of the wealth distribution, and consequently reduces the thickness of the extreme right tail to a level commensurate with data.

Over time, only aggregate returns by asset class $\bar{r}_{c,t}$ are varying. We use 10-year moving averages of realized aggregate returns for the transition, displayed in figure 7. These are expressed relative to the return on the base category, the risk-free asset.

E.   Idiosyncratic Discount Rates

We provide results for two model versions. In the first one, we do not rescale the standard deviation of private equity ($\phi = 1$) and we do not allow for preference heterogeneity. We refer to this as the single-β model. Thus, the only two free parameters to calibrate are then the borrowing constraint and the probability of the zero earnings state, which mostly affect the bottom end of the wealth distribution. Table 1 shows that, quite remarkably, the resulting invariant wealth distribution matches the data in 1967 quite well.[36]

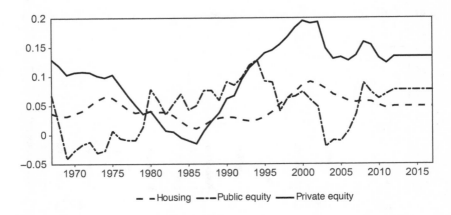

Fig. 7.   Aggregate excess returns. Own computations based on Kartashova (2014), Case-Shiller home price index. The series correspond to 10-year moving averages of realized excess returns over the federal funds rate. The initial steady state in 1967 is based on time averages over 1960–67. From 2012 onward (including the new steady state), we use time averages over 2007–17. A color version of this figure is available online.

Table 1
Matching the 1967 Wealth Distribution as a Steady State

Parameter	ρ^β	σ^β	ϕ		$\underline{a}$	χ (%)
Single-β model	n.a.	(0)	(1.0)		−.26	7.5
Benchmark model	.992	.0006	.52		−.22	7.5
Target	Top 10%	Top 1%	Top .1%	Top .01%	Bottom 50%	Fraction $a < 0$
Data (%)	70.8	27.8	9.4	3.1	4.0	8.0
Single-β model (%)	66.6	23.7	11.2	7.2	3.5	7.3
Benchmark model (%)	73.8	27.4	8.4	3.2	3.0	6.6

Source: Top wealth shares from Saez and Zucman (2016); bottom 50% and fraction of population with negative net wealth from Kennickell (2011) based on US Survey of Consumer Finances.

Although the single-β model reproduces the overall amount of wealth inequality, it overstates wealth concentration at the top end. To the extent that the wealth distribution has a Pareto tail to the right, this coefficient is pinned down by the ratio of the top 0.01% share to the top 0.1% share, or the ratio of the top 0.1% share to the top 1% share, both of which are roughly one-third in the data. In the single-β model, this ratio is increasing the further one moves out in the right tail and stabilizing at a value that is by far too high. These findings motivate the specification of the benchmark model—a model that in addition allows for discount factor (β) heterogeneity and rescales the standard deviation of private equity returns by a factor ϕ. Intuitively, the discount-factor distribution affects the entire asset distribution, including the Pareto tail. More heterogeneity creates more wealth inequality. The standard deviation of private equity returns, on the other hand, mostly affects the very right tail, and thus the tail coefficient.

We use an AR(1) structure for the discount factor. Thus, from the perspective of dispersion in the benchmark model we have three parameters to calibrate: the variance and persistence of β and the scaling factor ϕ. First, we select the persistence of the β process based on what seems a priori reasonable given a generational structure. Second, we target two wealth-distribution statistics to obtain the remaining two variance elements (σ^β and ϕ): the Pareto tail coefficient and the fraction of total wealth held by the 10% richest. This identifies our parameters. We now describe the details.

We posit that β follows a Gaussian AR(1) process:

$$\beta_t = \rho^\beta \beta_{t-1} + (1 - \rho^\beta)\mu^\beta + \sigma^\beta \varepsilon_t^\beta, \qquad \varepsilon_t^\beta \sim N(0, 1). \tag{15}$$

Importantly, all these parameters are fixed over time (by varying them freely, we could of course track the evolution of the wealth distribution at will). The mean discount factor determines the equilibrium capital-output ratio, and we set it to $\mu^\beta = 0.944$ to match a ratio of capital to net output of about 4 in the initial steady state. The calibrated stochastic-β parameters are $\rho^\beta = 0.992$ and $\sigma^\beta = 0.0006$, implying that the standard deviation of the cross-sectional distribution of discount factors, which does not vary over time, is 0.0050. Moreover, the choice of ρ^β implies that roughly one-third of the gap between a given discount factor and the average discount factor is closed within a generation.

To summarize the calibration of the benchmark model, table 1 lists the values of the five parameters (persistence and standard deviation of the discount rates; standard deviation of return shocks; the borrowing constraint; and the probability of zero income) calibrated to match six features of the initial steady-state wealth distribution as closely as possible: the shares held by the top 10%, the top 1%, the top 0.1%, the top 0.01%, and the bottom 50% as well as the fraction of the population with negative net wealth. The fit is excellent at both ends of the distribution. Compared with the single-β model, the benchmark model matches the Pareto tail coefficient in addition.

Two comments are in order. First, when solving the model numerically, we truncate the β and η distributions to ensure that the consumer's optimization problem is well defined (with finite present-value utility) and that a stationary distribution of wealth emerges. Unlike in a standard Aiyagari economy without heterogeneity in preferences or returns, in our model some agents temporarily have discount rates that are smaller than the rate of return, a necessary condition for generating a Pareto tail in the wealth distribution based on discount-rate or return heterogeneity alone (see the discussion in Section V). It follows that the support of the stationary wealth distribution is not bounded from above. In practice, we use a large enough upper bound in our numerical implementation that the resulting truncation error is negligible.[37]

Second, if our goal were solely to match the Pareto coefficient in the right tail of the wealth distribution, it would be excessive to calibrate as many as five parameters to match features of the wealth distribution. But the tail coefficient is not a sufficient statistic for wealth inequality unless the entire distribution is (counterfactually) Pareto-shaped: even if, say, the top 1% of the wealth distribution can be described exactly by a Pareto distribution, the tail coefficient determines only the distribution of wealth within these top 1% but not the fraction of total wealth held by the top 1%.

VII. Results I: Steady-State Wealth Inequality

A first and, we believe, important contribution of the present paper is its comprehensive breakdown of long-run wealth inequality, on which Subsection VII.B reports. Such a breakdown is also useful because it hints at what to expect from movements over time in some of the drivers of long-run wealth inequality—the subject of Section VIII. In Subsection VII.A, we first briefly relate to the relevant literature. Both of these sections draw on, and to some extent reiterate, the earlier discussions in Section II and Subsection IV.A.

A. Relations to the Literature on Long-Run Wealth Inequality

In the basic Aiyagari (1994) setting, where steady-state earnings inequality is calibrated as an AR(1) process to PSID data, very little wealth inequality is generated. Intuitively, the very highest earners are well insured, and the interest rate is not high enough to maintain their asset levels: It is below the discount rate, because it is depressed by the precautionary saving of less-well-insured households, and so they decumulate. Since then, the literature has thus had the challenge to come up with mechanisms that generate a greater accumulation, or maintenance, of wealth by the richest. Krusell and Smith (1998) propose discount-rate heterogeneity, so that the richest are rich because they choose to save at higher rates than others. Castañeda et al. (2003) propose a different earnings process, whereby there are extreme right-tail outcomes at the same time the risk of very large drops in earnings for the extreme earners is nonnegligible. Hence, precautionary saving operates in the right tail as well. Quadrini (2000) and Cagetti and De Nardi (2006) look at entrepreneurs (and occupational choice) specifically as a candidate richest group and argue that the returns to saving can be higher for high wealth levels. Relatedly, Campanale (2007) uses a return schedule that is simply increasing in wealth, motivated by the fact that wealthier households hold more stock. Giving the bequest function a low curvature can also help (see, e.g., Cagetti and De Nardi 2009). More recently, idiosyncratic return heterogeneity has been explored by a number of papers, as discussed in Section II.

We clearly view discount-factor heterogeneity as realistic, but, because we do not have fully reliable measurements of it, it plays only a residual role. We view the Castañeda et al. (2003) approach as interesting but somewhat problematic because it does not rely on independent, direct measurement of the earnings process—some features are selected to match wealth inequality—and the implied right-tail features of the earnings distribution are, in fact, too extreme compared with data. Moreover, as already discussed, it is not consistent with a Pareto-shaped right tail in wealth. Our table 1 above shows that, quite encouragingly, given the observables we use, it is no longer necessary to resort to residual explanations (such as preference heterogeneity or a nonaltruistic bequest function) to generate realistic wealth inequality.[38] In fact, the right tail of the wealth distribution is too thick relative to the data, so that, as explained in Subsection VI.E, we rescale the observed cross-sectional variation in returns to private equity and instead introduce a small amount of heterogeneity in discount factors to provide an even better fit to the entire distribution of wealth.

The next section will detail how each of the factors behind long-run wealth dispersion matter, but let us already emphasize that portfolio and return heterogeneity is key. What our present paper does not provide is a deeper theory either of portfolio choice or of return differences across assets. The latter have plagued the macrofinance literature since Mehra and Prescott (1985), but to understand the former is at least as challenging. One should therefore view our encouraging results here as far from satisfactory; rather, we now need to turn to household finance as a key area for understanding long-run wealth inequality.

B.   Decomposing Wealth Inequality in the Benchmark Model

How much does each of the various sources of heterogeneity contribute to wealth inequality in the benchmark economy? To answer this question, we start from the benchmark model, shut down one channel at a time, and report on the general equilibrium differences in table 2. These counterfactual exercises also give clues as to how the dynamics will work out, but of course they will not help us understand the speed of these dynamics.

The first row in the table corresponds to a counterfactual in which discount factor heterogeneity is removed ($\sigma^\beta = 0$). Then, for example, the top 10% wealth share decreases from 73.8% (the value in the benchmark model) to 65.0%. We interpret this as β-heterogeneity contributing +8.8% to the top 10% wealth share. Overall, discount factor heterogeneity does contribute positively to wealth inequality, but it is not the most important factor. Instead, differences in returns are crucial. Line 7 shuts down return differences across wealth levels ($r_t^X(\cdot) = 0$), line 8 returns risk ($\sigma^X(\cdot) = 0$), and line 6 combines the two modifications. Overall, differences in mean returns across wealth levels are far more important,

Table 2
Contribution of Various Channels for Steady State Wealth Inequality in the Benchmark Model

#		Top 10% (%)	Top 1% (%)	Top .1% (%)	Top .01% (%)	Gini
1	β-heterogeneity	8.8	7.7	3.8	2.0	.050
2	Earnings heterogeneity	−27.5	−17.8	−9.5	−6.4	−.173
3	Persistent	−5.0	−7.5	−4.2	−2.9	.009
4	Transitory	−11.6	−4.3	−1.7	−.9	−.109
5	Tax progressivity	−21.3	−61.8	−71.2	−67.1	−.148
6	Return heterogeneity	29.5	18.4	6.6	2.8	.192
7	Mean differences	25.8	16.7	6.0	2.6	.174
8	Return risk	.7	2.2	3.3	2.5	.004

though at the very top idiosyncratic return risk matters equally. Note that because model moments are highly nonlinear as a function of parameters, individual modifications do not add up.

A striking feature of table 2 is the fundamental importance of tax progressivity in keeping wealth inequality in check. Line 5 refers to a counterfactual that replaces the progressive income tax $\tau(\cdot)$ with a flat tax, such that aggregate tax revenues relative to output are unchanged. Wealth inequality is exploding. For example, the top 1% share increases from 27.4% to 89.2%. Why is tax progressivity so important? There are both partial- and general-equilibrium effects at work here. Starting with the latter, as we argued in Subsection IV.A, it is well-known in the context of complete-markets models without heterogeneity in returns, discount factors, or earnings that progressivity in the tax rate on saving is a strong force toward long-run equality, whereas mere proportional taxes are consistent with any distribution of wealth as a steady-state equilibrium.[39] The mathematical intuition behind the force of progressivity is particularly clear in a simple case where the marginal tax rate is strictly increasing in wealth. Here, because all consumers face the same market rate under complete markets (and have the same discount rates and wage incomes), they also need to have the same net of tax return if their consumption levels are all constant (or growing at a common constant rate); hence they need to have the same wealth in the long run. This mechanism is still present in a more general model such as the present one, which has incomplete markets and differences in wages, returns, and discount rates, though with less long-run poignancy: a strictly increasing marginal tax rate is still consistent with long-run wealth inequality.

Turning to the partial-equilibrium analysis, note that the marginal saving propensity for a well-insured consumer with power utility is approximately $\beta(1 + r(1 - \tau'(y)))$ raised to a positive power, where $\tau'(y)$ is the consumer's current marginal tax rate.[40] This tax rate varies with income, y, but it is persistent over time because income is persistent. Tax progressivity, therefore, generates persistent differences across consumers that act like persistent differences either in the consumers' after-tax rates-of-return, $r(1 - \tau'(y))$, or, equivalently, in consumers' discount factors. Consequently, decreases in progressivity have the same effect as increasing the dispersion in returns, a powerful force for generating higher wealth inequality.

Lines 2–4 in table 2 document that earnings heterogeneity reduces wealth inequality in the benchmark model. Line 3 shuts down heterogeneity in the persistent component, line 4 likewise in the transitory component, and line 2 removes all earnings heterogeneity. Overall, both components reduce wealth inequality, though the strength of each of these channels depends somewhat on the particular wealth distribution statistic one looks at. To understand this finding, note first that without return or discount factor heterogeneity, earnings dispersion would contribute positively to wealth inequality. Then why is the effect reversed in the benchmark model? As also noted in Subsection IV.A, heterogeneity in either discount factors (or returns) is a powerful force driving the wealth distribution apart: with permanently different discount rates and complete markets to insure against earnings risk, the most patient household would eventually hold all the economy's wealth. Earnings risk, then, is a friction, or glue, that keeps the distribution from flying apart altogether, as also in the work of Becker (1980) cited in Section I. This risk operates especially strongly at the low end of the wealth distribution, where poorer consumers save to move away from borrowing constraints when earnings risk is larger.

In our model, higher earnings risk also generates a thinner right tail in the wealth distribution because the resulting increase in aggregate precautionary savings drives down the equilibrium interest rate. This drop in the interest rate shifts the distribution of saving propensities to the left, particularly for the well-insured wealthy consumers for whom wage risk is largely immaterial and who therefore have essentially linear decision rules. As discussed in Section V, the Pareto tail coefficient, ζ, is defined implicitly by the equation $\mathbb{E}[s^\zeta] = 1$, where s is the (asymptotic) marginal propensity to save out of wealth. As s falls for all discount-factor types, ζ must increase to compensate, and the Pareto tail becomes thinner.[41]

Given that our model is replicating the wealth distribution very well, a related question is how our model-generated saving rates compare to the data. We find that our model generates a strong positive relation between household income and saving rates, comparable to US data (see app. D for details).

VIII.   Results II: The Evolution of the Wealth Distribution

In Section VII, we showed that our model framework, when properly calibrated, can replicate wealth heterogeneity, including the Pareto-shaped right tail, as well as other macroeconomic moments in the initial steady state. We proceed in this section to report on our second main result: the evolution of the wealth distribution in the benchmark model economy contrasted with the data. Subsequently, we employ counterfactual analysis to decompose those overall changes and identify the key drivers of movements in the wealth distribution.

A.   Benchmark Transition Experiment

Figure 8 displays the evolution of top wealth shares in the model (solid line) compared with the data as measured by Saez and Zucman (2016) using the basic capitalization method (dashed line; henceforth SZ). In addition, we augment the graphs with the estimates of Smith et al. (2020), who use a modified capitalization method approach that allows for return heterogeneity within asset classes (dash-dotted line; henceforth SZZ).[42] These shares display a pronounced U-shape, reaching the trough in the late 1970s to mid-1980s, followed by a sharp subsequent increase. The model economy matches both the initial decrease and the overall increase very well for the top 10% and the top 1%. Further in the tail, the model continues to capture the trend, though the increase is not quite as fast as estimated by SZ. In contrast, relative to SZZ, the model predicts a similar increase even for the very richest. As we discuss further in Subsection IX.C, the top wealth shares in the model economy continue to increase slowly over a long transition period before reaching the new steady state. This finding is consistent with Gabaix et al. (2016), who argue that the random growth mechanism that drives top wealth inequality tends to produce slow transitions (especially in the tails of the distribution).

Figure 9 displays the evolution of the capital-net output ratio and of the bottom 50% wealth share. The model's implications for aggregate wealth

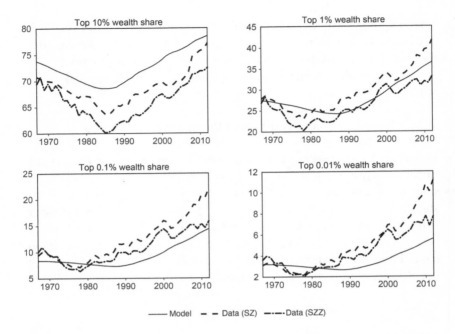

Fig. 8. Top wealth shares in percentage, 1967–2012. Dashed black lines refer to Saez and Zucman (2016; abbreviated as SZ); dash-dotted gray lines refer to Smith et al. (2020; abbreviated as SZZ). A color version of this figure is available online.

are broadly in line with the data, thus showing a steady rise, ignoring shorter-run movements. The bottom 50% have lost a little more than two-thirds of their already small share of aggregate wealth; the model accounts for about two-thirds of this decline in wealth.[43]

We also summarize the findings from our main experiment in table 3. As illustrated above, both model and data show strong increases in wealth concentration at the top.

Looking at the top 10%, top 1%, and top 0.1% wealth share, the model explains between one-half and three-quarters of the cumulated increase in inequality as measured by SZ. On the other hand, relative to the more moderate estimates by SZZ, the model overpredicts the rise in concentration by about one-third. In sum, although there is some ambiguity in the measurement of wealth inequality stemming from the lack of direct administrative data, the model is broadly in line with the data both qualitatively and quantitatively.

For the very richest, the model's performance is still qualitatively correct, but quantitatively it underpredicts the rise in wealth inequality.

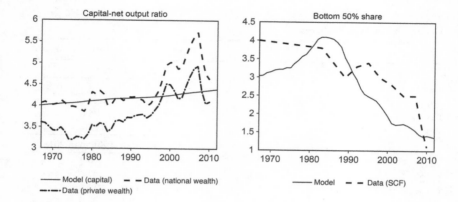

Fig. 9. Capital-net output ratio and bottom 50% share (in percentage), 1967–2012. Wealth-output ratios from Piketty and Zucman (2014); bottom 50% share from Kennickell (2011). SCF = US Survey of Consumer Finances. A color version of this figure is available online.

The model predicts an increase in the fraction of wealth held by the top 0.01% of about three-quarters, whereas in the SZ data set the increase is even larger, by more than a factor of three. Relative to SZZ, the model explains about two-thirds of the rise in wealth concentration.

Clearly, although—as suggested above—the basic capitalization method underlying the data may exaggerate the increases in wealth for the richest, this discrepancy is a major one unlikely to be solely due to mismeasurement, and it does not appear that the present model is fully adequate for capturing the bulk of how much the richest have gained. There is an obvious remaining candidate explanation: idiosyncratic return volatility has gone up over time. The measures of idiosyncratic return volatilities (across wealth classes) cover only a short period of time, so we have no direct measure of movements in these volatilities over time. The increasing share of private equity in household portfolios—the flipside of which is a smaller and smaller share in publicly traded stock—could be a source of increases in idiosyncratic return volatility. Moreover, Campbell et al. (2001) provide evidence of increased volatility of individual stock returns (by about a factor of two, as measured by its standard deviation), so that if households held similarly undiversified portfolios throughout the period, their portfolio returns would indeed display increasing idiosyncratic volatility. We have not systematically examined this channel, as it involves much guesswork, but we have arbitrarily run an experiment where the volatility of private equity returns is doubled over the period and it indeed increases top wealth inequality by the end period quite significantly

Table 3
Change in Top Wealth Shares

	Top 10%	Top 1%	Top .1%	Top .01%
	Model			
1967	73.8	27.4	8.4	3.2
2012	78.5	36.5	14.4	5.6
Change	4.7	9.1	6.0	2.4
Relative change (%)	6.4	33.2	72.2	75.4
	Data (Saez and Zucman 2016)			
1967	70.8	27.8	9.4	3.1
2012	77.2	41.8	22.0	11.2
Change	6.4	14.0	12.6	8.1
Relative change (%)	9.0	50.4	134.0	261.3
Fraction of relative change explained by model (%)	70.8	65.9	53.8	28.9
	Data (Smith et al. 2020)			
1967	69.4	26.9	10.0	3.6
2012	72.5	33.2	15.9	7.7
Change	3.1	6.3	5.9	4.1
Relative change (%)	4.4	23.5	59.0	113.3
Fraction of relative change explained by model (%)	144.1	141.4	122.2	66.6

Source: Data based on the capitalization method estimates of Saez and Zucman (2016) and Smith et al. (2020).
Note: Wealth shares are displayed in percentage points. For example, the top 1% controlled 27.8% of all wealth in 1967 according to Saez and Zucman (2016). By 2012, they controlled 41.8% of all wealth, an increase of 14 percentage points or 50.4% in relative terms. In the model, their share increased from 27.4% to 36.5%, an increase of 9.1 percentage points or 33.2%. Thus, the model explains a fraction 33.2/50.4 = 65.9% of the cumulative increase for this group.

to levels comparable to those in the data. This is all suggestive, but much more work is needed on this point.[44]

Rates of Return in Model and Data

By construction, our model replicates the time paths of return premia on various asset classes perfectly. However, the overall level of returns is endogenous. Hence, the resulting equilibrium path for the risk-free rate is another model outcome that can be compared with the data to assess the performance of the model. Figure 10 shows that the model calibration, which targets the capital-output ratio, results in a real risk-free rate that is comparable to the data in the initial steady state.[45] Interestingly, the model reproduces almost the entire long-run decline. What drives

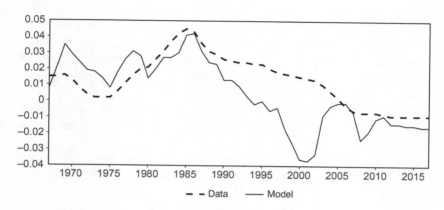

Fig. 10. The risk-free rate. A color version of this figure is available online.

the 2.4 percentage point decline in the model? The marginal product of capital falls by 0.9 percentage points in response to capital deepening, accounting for more than one-third of the overall decline. The remainder is—in about equal parts—due to both rising return premia and rising wealth inequality: a higher fraction of aggregate wealth is held by rich agents, whose risky portfolio weights are higher; this depresses the risk-free rate in our setup.

The model is not doing as well in reproducing all medium-run swings. Around 2000, the model, unlike the data, generates a pronounced slump in the risk-free rate. Mechanically, this is because realized return premia on housing and equity were high. Although in the data these high returns were largely driven by capital gains, in the model all capital income corresponds to the return on currently installed physical capital. Consequently, matching the return premia implies a counterfactually low risk-free rate.

B. Counterfactuals

Changes in four structural factors—earnings risk, top earnings inequality, tax progressivity, and excess returns—drive the transitional as well as long-run dynamics in the model economy. To assess which of these is the most important quantitatively, we conducted four experiments in which only one of the four structural factors is allowed to change, the other three being held constant instead at their values in 1967. Which of these changes is the main driver of increases in wealth inequality, particularly in the upper reaches of the distribution? As we shall see, the main driver of changes in the right tail of the wealth distribution is changes in taxes. Increases in earnings risk, on the other hand, reduce top wealth inequality, other things being equal. Changes in return premia account in particular for the shorter-run dynamics.

Table 4 summarizes the results of the four experiments, quantifying how much each of the factors contributes to the changes in the wealth shares over the time period 1967–2012.[46]

To understand the numbers in the table, focus on the share of total wealth held by the richest percentile. Saez and Zucman (2016) measure an increase in this share from 27.8% to 41.8% from 1967 to 2012. Over the same time period, allowing for changes only in earnings risk and keeping all other parameters fixed at their initial steady-state values, the model predicts a decrease from 27.4% to 24.5%. Changes in earnings risk therefore explain a fraction $[(24.5 - 27.4)/27.4]/[(41.8 - 27.8)/27.8] = -0.21$ of the actual change.[47] Again, the observed increases in earnings risk reduce inequality, moving it in the opposite direction from the observed changes! (Separate increases in either the persistent or transitory components of earnings risk also reduce inequality.) Instead, as can be seen for all the different distributional statistics, the main driver of the surge in wealth concentration is the changing US tax system. The increase in top earnings inequality (parameterized by changes over time in the Pareto tail coefficient κ_t on labor income) has worked in the same direction, although the effect of this channel is much smaller. Changes in return premia have also dampened the increase in wealth concentration on net, in particular explaining the initial dip.

Why does an increase in earnings risk reduce wealth inequality? As explained in Subsections IV.A and VII.B, in the presence of return or discount factor heterogeneity, earnings risk can be viewed as the friction that prevents the wealth distribution from exploding. Facing higher

Table 4
Fraction of Change in Wealth Shares Explained by Model: Decomposition by Channel

	Bottom 50%	Top 10%	Top 1%	Top .1%	Top .01%
Taxes	.49	1.57	1.15	.72	.36
Top earnings inequality	.42	.44	.14	.10	.06
Earnings risk	−.04	−.84	−.21	−.09	−.05
Return premia	−.03	−.58	−.28	−.13	−.08
Combined	.76	.71	.66	.54	.29

earnings risk, consumers seek to increase precautionary savings, more so at the lower end of the wealth distribution. In addition, in general equilibrium the interest rate decreases, slowing down wealth accumulation at the top.

Why have changes in the tax system induced such large changes in wealth inequality? Note first that the average tax rate (i.e., aggregate tax revenues as a fraction of net output) in our model increases from 0.23 to 0.27 over the period 1967–2012. An increase in average taxes tends to reduce effective earnings risk (because the tax is multiplicative), increasing inequality for the same reason (but in the opposite direction) that the observed increases in (pre-tax) earnings risk reduce inequality. This effect, however, is a small one unless the average tax rate changes dramatically. Much more important quantitatively is the dramatic decrease in tax progressivity, where even small changes have large effects on inequality, especially at the high end of the wealth distribution. As explained when discussing steady-state inequality, tax progressivity effectively reduces dispersion in returns or discount factors, two powerful forces for driving the wealth distribution apart. Consequently, the observed decrease in progressivity triggered a large increase in wealth concentration. In figure A3 we decompose the effects of progressivity into a direct effect—the (mechanical) compression of after-tax resources induced by changes in progressivity, holding behavior fixed—and an indirect effect—the change in marginal saving propensities induced by changing progressivity, excluding its effects on the compression of after-tax resources—by showing the effects of the latter only and the effects of the former only, along with the full equilibrium response. Clearly, the direct effect is most important for the very richest and hence for changes in top wealth inequality.

Changes in return premia are key to explain the U-shape of wealth shares. In particular, the time series of private equity, primarily important for the rich, exhibits a pronounced U-shape (displayed earlier in fig. 7). Likewise, the average return on the US stock market was quite low in the 1970s and 2000s. In contrast, house prices, particularly important for the middle class, have boomed until the Great Recession. Overall, changes in asset returns have reduced wealth inequality until about 1990 while contributing positively to increasing concentration subsequently.[48]

In sum, among the different drivers of wealth inequality considered in the benchmark experiment, it is clear that decreasing tax progressivity is key: It spreads out the resources available to consume and invest, and it increases the relative return of the rich on any given saving.

In a representative-agent model, the increase in average taxes would lead to a decrease in the capital-to-output ratio in equilibrium, but it does not in our heterogeneous-agent model for three reasons. First, the (smallish) increase in average taxes does not offset the even larger increase in the riskiness of pre-tax earnings, leading to more precautionary savings in the aggregate. Second, decreasing tax progressivity increases the returns to saving, a particularly powerful force for the rich. Third, the increasingly "thick" right tail in earnings provides the rich (who tend to be those with high earnings) with additional resources for saving. These three forces combine to generate a fairly large increase in the ratio of capital to net output over the period 1967–2012.

If one looks at the wealth holdings of the bottom 50% of the population, the bulk of the decrease is again accounted for by the decrease in tax progressivity as well as increases in top earnings inequality, whereas the movements in the aggregate capital-output ratio are mostly accounted for by the increase in earnings risk.[49] However, different measures can tell different stories. If one looks at the Gini coefficient for wealth within the bottom 50% or even within the bottom 90%, we find that the rise in earnings risk in our model does contribute positively to the increase in wealth inequality within this subgroup.

Let us now, finally, briefly compare our results to those in Kaymak and Poschke (2016). Their study emphasizes an increase in earnings inequality as a main driver of the increase in wealth inequality but also finds the decline in tax progressivity to be important. As for their main finding, the effect of the increase in earnings inequality in their model appears only after 1980, and after 1980 they consider only an increase in "top earnings" inequality—which is roughly similar to the top earnings inequality in our paper. Prior to 1980, they do not break down the effects on top wealth shares into a part that is due to changes in top earnings inequality and a part that is due to changes in earnings risk in the rest of the distribution. But, because wealth inequality is roughly constant before 1980 in their model, we conjecture that they go in opposite directions, just as they do in the present paper. Had we similarly considered only an increase in top earnings inequality after 1980, we would have obtained a positive effect of earnings inequality—as in their paper. Hence, overall, our models have similar predictions, with slightly different drivers, explaining the discrepancies in emphasis. As an important last remark, Kaymak and Poschke (2016) do not obtain the kind of U-shape in the evolution of inequality that we (and they) observe in the data; they do not consider the portfolio heterogeneity channel.

IX. Extensions

We now look at a number of robustness exercises and extensions. First, we examine whether the observed falling labor share contributed to rising wealth inequality. We find that this mechanism does not appear very promising for understanding the data at hand.

We then weaken the consumers' ability to predict changes in their environment. In particular, in our benchmark experiment we assume that consumers in 1967 could predict the future paths of the tax schedule, the degree of idiosyncratic earnings risk, and even the return premia. These are of course strong assumptions, so it is interesting to compare this case to one with more limited abilities to predict. Here, our finding is that a model with entirely myopic expectations (that the current policy/risk environment is expected to last forever) behaves almost like our benchmark environment.

Finally, we conclude the section with a cautious prediction for the long run. Barring any future changes, the main message is that the adjustment process of the economy to the new steady state is far from over.

A. Robustness to Falling Labor Share

The stability of the fraction of income accruing to labor, for a long time a central pillar of macroeconomic models, has recently been questioned. Karabarbounis and Neiman (2014), among others, document a visible (though not large) decline in the labor share. Using a production function with a CES, they estimate an elasticity of substitution between capital and labor of 1.25. To look into the possibility of a falling labor share, we use a standard CES production function,

$$F_{CES}(K_t, L) = A_{CES}(\alpha_{CES} K_t^{\frac{\sigma-1}{\sigma}} + (1 - \alpha_{CES}) L^{\frac{\sigma-1}{\sigma}})^{\frac{\sigma}{\sigma-1}}, \tag{16}$$

where A_{CES} and α_{CES} are chosen such that the initial steady state is identical to the Cobb-Douglas benchmark. Over time, there is capital deepening, leading to a lower labor share because the elasticity of substitution is above 1. We find, however, only very small differences as compared with the Cobb-Douglas benchmark (see table 5).[50]

Capital deepening leads to a smaller reaction of the interest rate, so the rise in the capital-output ratio is slightly larger in equilibrium, and the Gini coefficient on gross income increases a small amount more (relative to the benchmark). At the same time, we find that top wealth shares increase

Table 5
Robustness to Falling Labor Share and to Myopia

	Top 10%	Top 1%	Top .1%	Top .01%	Bottom 50%	$\frac{K}{Y}$	r
1967	73.8	27.4	8.4	3.2	3.0	4.00	5.93
2013:							
Benchmark	78.9	37.1	14.8	5.8	1.3	4.40	5.11
CES	78.6	36.7	14.6	5.7	1.3	4.45	5.20
Time-varying C–D	76.6	35.1	13.9	5.5	1.6	4.80	7.81
Myopia	76.9	34.9	14.1	5.7	1.4	4.42	5.07

Note: Wealth shares and the interest rate are reported in percentage. This table compares various statistics from the benchmark model transition to alternatives. In the benchmark transition experiment, the production technology is assumed to be Cobb-Douglas, and agents have perfect foresight. The row labeled "CES" reports results from a model with CES production technology. The row labeled "Time-varying C–D" reports results from a model with a Cobb-Douglas production function with time-varying coefficients, which we calibrate to match the time series of the US Bureau of Labor Statistics nonfarm business sector labor share. The row labeled "Myopia" reports results from a transition experiment in which agents are completely myopic about the future, assuming present prices, returns, and the parameters of the earnings process and the tax schedule will prevail. CES = constant elasticity of substitution.

more slowly; unlike for the decline in tax progressivity, higher equilibrium interest rates induce more savings across the whole wealth distribution. In other words, at least over the time frame considered, the saving of the poor tends to be more elastic with respect to the (pre-tax) interest rate than the saving of the rich. Overall, though, the quantitative effects of considering a different elasticity of substitution are very small.

Using this CES production function, the gross labor share falls by 1 percentage point over the period 1967–2013 in our model, and the net labor share increases slightly. To assess the robustness of our model predictions to a falling labor share more broadly, we also run a transition experiment with a time-varying Cobb-Douglas production function. Choosing the capital exponent α_t each year to match the labor share as measured by the US Bureau of Labor Statistics (BLS) for the US nonfarm business sector, the gross (net) labor share declines by 7 (14) points cumulatively. Qualitatively, our findings continue to hold. Quantitatively, the main message is that the falling labor share, although increasing income inequality, has a rather small dampening effect on wealth inequality over the transition period through the lens of our model.

B. Robustness to Agents' Abilities to Predict Policy, Risk, and Returns

It is surely bold to assume that agents have perfect foresight on the entire path of the tax schedule, the parameters governing the earnings process, excess returns, and the resulting equilibrium prices. To gauge the sensitivity of our findings to this assumption, we computed the transitional dynamics under complete myopia—that is, a polar opposite case in terms of agents'. ability to predict. That is, in every period, agents believe that the current environment will prevail forever, and accordingly, they are surprised to learn about their forecasting mistake in the subsequent period.[51] Table 5 shows the effects of myopia in the last row. Clearly, the differences are small. We conclude that the perfect-foresight assumption is not critically driving the results in the benchmark experiment. What is the reason for these results? One would perhaps particularly have guessed that being able to predict return movements would give rise to very different behaviors. Recall, however, that portfolio shares are hard-wired and hence the household's ability to act on the foreseen changes in returns is limited. The same goes for the other factors: any changes need to go through changes in saving rates, and these are rather robust.

C. The Long Run

We have focused so far on the transitional dynamics of the wealth distribution over the period 1967–2012, but what are the longer-run implications of the changes in earnings risk and, especially, tax progressivity that have occurred over this time period? In the calculations underlying these results, we have assumed no further changes in either earnings risk, taxes, or return premia after 2012.

Figure 11 illustrates a striking prediction: the model suggests that the adjustment to the new fundamentals is far from completion and that wealth inequality is likely to rise even more. As pointed out before, the wealth distribution is a slow-moving object, especially in a setting with random growth in which the right tail of the wealth distribution is Pareto-shaped. Changes in fundamentals (such as the structure of taxes) that influence the consumption-savings decision differently for consumers with different wealth levels are bound, then, to have long-lasting effects. The contrast between the behavior of the wealth distribution over the transitional period and the eventual long-run steady-state wealth distribution (assuming an unchanged environment going forward) underscores the hazards of looking solely at steady states when attempting to quantify how fundamentals affect wealth inequality.

Of course, we urge caution in interpreting figure 11 as a plain prediction for the future, because no doubt the economic environment will not remain unchanged going forward. Various exogenous impulses are

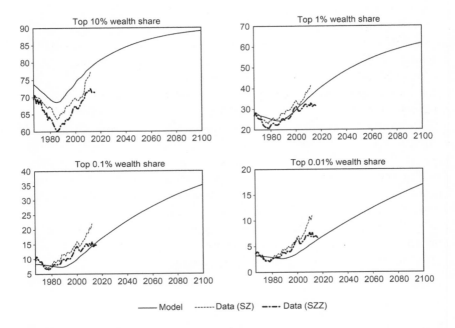

Fig. 11. Top wealth shares in percentage, long run. Dashed black lines refer to Saez and Zucman (2016; abbreviated as SZ); dash-dotted gray lines refer to Smith et al. (2020; abbreviated as SZZ). A color version of this figure is available online.

possible (e.g., external forces affecting the US interest rate, changes in demographics, and further change in earnings inequality). In addition, the model abstracts from plausible feedback mechanisms. For example, changes in wealth inequality could themselves, via the political process, lead to changes in the structure of taxes. In addition, accumulation of wealth in private equity by the richest could put downward pressure on its average return. Notwithstanding these points, the long-run analysis contained here does emphasize how powerfully tax progressivity can shape the wealth distribution, particularly in its right tail.

X. Concluding Remarks

The determinants of wealth inequality, in particular its developments over the last half a century, are much discussed recently, and a number of new hypotheses have been put forth. This paper takes a "first-thing-first" perspective and asks what established quantitative theory predicts based on the behavior of a number of plausible and observable factors over the same period. We thus use a macroeconomic general-equilibrium model with heterogeneous agents—the Bewley-Huggett-Aiyagari setting—to examine more closely a set of candidate explanations for the increase in US wealth inequality over the last 40 or so years. The method we follow is thus to (i) independently measure changes in the environment, such as in the tax code, the earnings processes facing individuals, and their portfolio returns; (ii) feed these into the model assuming that the economy is in a steady state in 1967; (iii) examine the resulting wealth distribution path; and (iv) conduct counterfactuals. We find that the model generates a path for inequality that is quite close to that observed, the main exception being that the rise in inequality at the very top of the distribution is underpredicted if one takes the Saez-Zucman capitalization method as providing the right characterization of how the top wealth shares have evolved; compared with SCF data or the modified capitalization method of Smith et al. (2020), we instead overpredict the changes. The satisfactory performance of the model in predicting the overall path for wealth inequality notwithstanding, the first main contribution is the conclusion that the most important factor—by far—behind the long-run developments is the significant decline in tax progressivity that began in the late 1970s.

Declining tax progressivity, together with increasing earnings risk and higher earnings inequality amongst top earnings, can also account for the rise in the capital-to-net-output ratio and at least some of the decline in the (gross) labor share when the elasticity of substitution between capital and labor is larger than 1, as in Karabarbounis and Neiman (2014). Our model thus provides an alternative to the central mechanism—declining growth rates—to which Piketty (2014) draws attention in attempting to connect these macroeconomic trends to rising inequality.

Our second major finding is that the key mechanism accounting for dynamics lies in heterogeneous portfolios across and within wealth groups, along with systematic return movements in the data.

Our third major finding, which is the one we discussed first in the paper, is the observation that to match wealth inequality in the beginning of the sample—which we do taking this year to represent a steady state—it is not necessary to add a "mop-up" explanation such as heterogeneous discount rates. Return heterogeneity is crucial here, giving a Pareto shape for the right wealth-distribution tail that significantly exceeds that for earnings.

Our findings merit several remarks. Although we find that tax progressivity has played a central role in increasing inequality, our model is designed primarily as a positive rather than a normative tool. To evaluate the pros and cons of, say, reversing the changes in tax progressivity, it is important to account for the distortions created by labor taxation; in the present setting, labor earnings are exogenous, and taxation is levied jointly on all incomes. We do not think that the introduction of distortionary labor taxation would change the model's predictions for wealth inequality measurably, but it would be central for understanding the welfare consequences of tax changes. Further research contrasting the larger distortions of increased tax progressivity with the accompanying reductions in inequality seems very promising.

Our emphasis on differences in portfolios and portfolio returns between households is reminiscent of Piketty's stylized $r - g$ theory emphasizing the rate of return on assets, r, as an important determinant of the relative growth rates of wealth (including human wealth, which grows at rate g) of the rich and the poor. The elaboration of this theory that we essentially propose is to attach less weight on g, to think of r as an after-tax return, and to recognize that r not only depends on household wealth (arising both from heterogeneous portfolio choices and progressive taxation) but also has a (stochastic) idiosyncratic component. This theory, moreover, mostly applies for the very richest; to understand the bulk and other side of the wealth distribution we side with Kaymak and Poschke (2016), who emphasize an increase in earnings inequality as a main driver of the increase in wealth inequality, but who also find the decline in tax progressivity to be important.

Regardless of one's normative views on wealth inequality, there are many reasons to care about its future course, as there are now many research contributions suggesting that the macroeconomy works quite differently when there is significant heterogeneity among consumers. This insight goes back at least as far as Krusell and Smith (1998), who showed that aggregate time series can depart significantly from permanent-income behavior in models in which wealth inequality matches the data. More recently, a growing body of research has demonstrated that both fiscal and monetary policy work differently too in models with proper microfoundations: for examples, see Heathcote (2005), Brinca et al. (2016), and McKay and Reis (2016) for fiscal policy, and McKay, Nakamura, and Steinsson (2016), Kaplan, Moll, and Violante (2018), and Auclert (2019) for monetary policy. The prediction from the present paper is that, barring reverses in the tax code, wealth inequality will go up even further, thus potentially strengthening the case for further research on the heterogeneous-agent approach to macroeconomics.

Finally, because so many of our findings rely on portfolio heterogeneity, we conclude by reiterating what we have stated repeatedly throughout the text: next, we need to understand households' portfolio choices better.

Appendix A

Additional Figures

This section contains additional figures and results referred to in the main text.

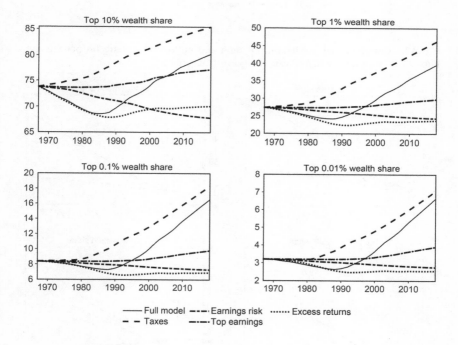

Fig. A1. Counterfactual top wealth shares in percentage, 1967–2012. A color version of this figure is available online.

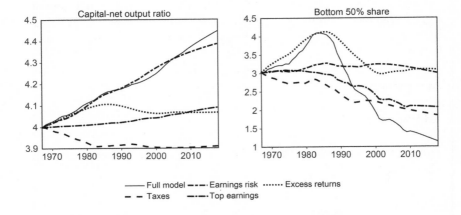

Fig. A2. Counterfactual capital-output ratio and bottom 50% share (in percentage), 1967–2012. A color version of this figure is available online.

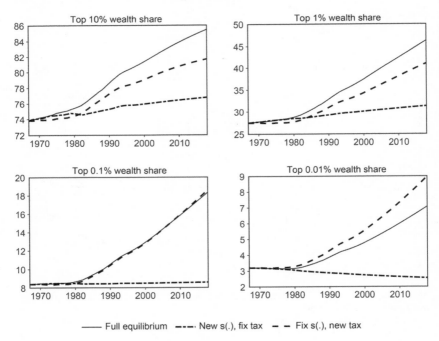

Fig. A3. Tax-change decomposition: top wealth shares. A color version of this figure is available online.

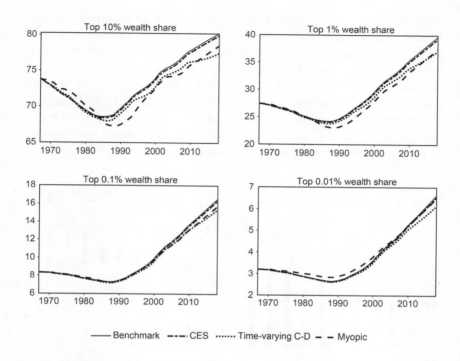

Fig. A4. Robustness to myopia and falling labor share. CES = constant elasticity of substitution. A color version of this figure is available online.

Appendix B

Progressivity in the Tax and Transfer System

In the main text, we calibrate the tax function $\tau_t(\cdot)$, which is levied on gross income in the model, to data on gross tax rates. Because the model features a lump-sum transfer T_t, the implied net tax and transfer rate is more progressive. In particular, for a household j with income y_{it} and gross tax rate $\tau_t(y_{it})$, the net tax rate $n_t(y_{it})$ is given by:

$$n_t(y_{jt}) = \tau_t(y_{jt}) - \frac{T_t}{y_{jt}}.$$

The left panel of figure B1 shows gross tax rates in our model, which reflect the estimates of Piketty and Saez (2007). The right panel shows the combined net tax and transfer rate by income group in 1967 and

2000. Because (pre-tax) income inequality is substantial, the lump-sum nature of our transfer implies that the net tax and transfer system is much more progressive than the tax system exclusive of transfers. This property of US taxes and transfers is highlighted by Auerbach, Kotlikoff, and Koehler (2019). Their estimates are not directly comparable, because we do not have a life cycle in our model, but in agreement with their findings our model also produces quite substantial net subsidies at the lower end of the distribution. At the upper end, the transfer effectively vanishes in relative importance—gross and net rates coincide.

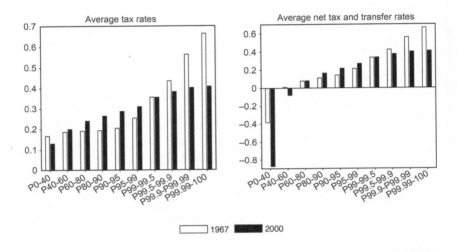

Fig. B1.   Progressivity in the tax and transfer system. A color version of this figure is available online.

Appendix C

Comparison to US Portfolio and Return Data

Is the resulting excess return schedule, which we constructed using detailed information on Swedish households adopted from Bach et al. (2019), comparable to data on US households? In an online appendix, Bach et al. (2019) use SCF data to show that overall return differentials by wealth group are remarkably similar in the United States and in Sweden. "For instance, the risk premium on gross wealth is 2.1% in the U.S. and 2.3% in Sweden on average for a household in the bottom decile;

3.7% in the U.S. and 3.8% in Sweden for the top 40%–50%; 5.3% in the U.S. and 5.6% in Sweden for the top 1%–0.5%. For the top 0.01%, however, a discrepancy arises: the risk premium on gross wealth is 6.6% in the U.S. and 7.5% in Sweden."[52] They argue that limited response rates and exclusion of the Forbes 400 are potentially an issue in SCF data (especially at the very top). Moreover, they document that when they impute excess returns in Swedish data, using only information that is comparably available in US survey and aggregate data, return heterogeneity across wealth groups is substantially dampened. For this reason, and because it allows for within-wealth-group heterogeneity, we prefer calibrating our model using their high-quality data.

Relatedly, how restrictive is the assumption of constant portfolio weights over time? Figure C1 displays portfolio weights from the US Distributional Financial Accounts (DFAs).[53] Panel (*a*) shows portfolio weights for the top 1% (no further disaggregation is provided within the top 1%). There is some time series variation. For example, the portfolio share of risky financial assets (including stocks) increases substantially in the 1990s. Presumably, households are not constantly rebalancing their portfolios (ceteris paribus, a boom in stock prices must necessarily increase the aggregate portfolio weight of public equity, and by extension the portfolio weight of most households in a value-weighted sense). However, what matters in our model is primarily differences in portfolio shares between wealth groups.[54] Panel (*b*) of figure C1 plots differences between the portfolio shares of the top 1% and the middle class (P50–90). These differential portfolio shares are relatively constant over time. It is in this sense that we are confident that our assumption of constant portfolio weights does not substantially affect our quantitative findings.

(a) Top 1% portfolio shares

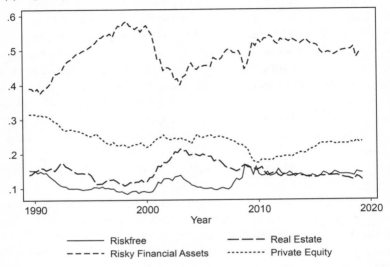

(b) Top 1% − middle class portfolio shares

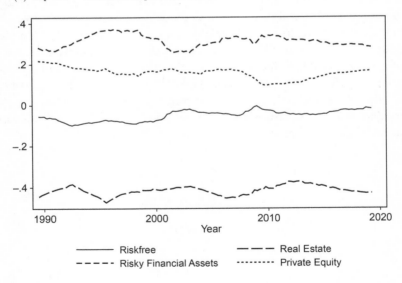

Fig. C1. US household portfolio shares 1989–2019. Panel *a* displays the portfolio shares of the top 1% of the wealth distribution over time. Panel *b* shows the difference between the portfolio shares of the top 1% and the ones of the middle class (defined as percentiles 50–90). US Distributional Financial Accounts. A color version of this figure is available online.

Appendix D

Saving Rate Heterogeneity

Empirical evidence suggests substantial cross-sectional heterogeneity in saving rates. For example, Dynan, Skinner, and Zeldes (2004) document a strongly increasing relation between household income and the saving rate: going from the bottom to the top income quintile, the average saving rate increases by about 15 percentage points (without capital gains) and by about 30 percentage points (with capital gains). Figure D1 reports average saving rates by income decile in our model. Abstracting from the lowest decile that contains negative income observations (due to negative portfolio return realizations), the saving rate increases from −0.3 for households with the lowest incomes to +0.2 for the top income decile. This represents an increase of about 45 percentage points across income quintiles. Thus, our model, which can be thought of as including capital gains through the return process, is qualitatively in line with US data and actually produces slightly too much cross-sectional heterogeneity in saving rates.

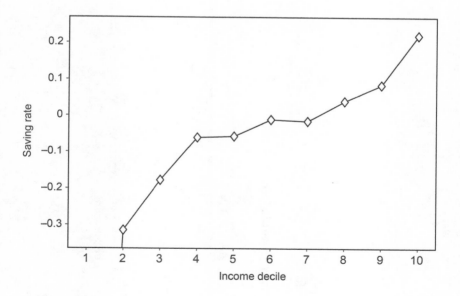

Fig. D1. Saving rates in the model. A color version of this figure is available online.

Appendix E

Excess Return Schedule Details

Table E1
Details of Excess Return Schedule

	P0–P40	P40–P50	P50–P60	P60–P70	P70–P80	P80–P90	P90–P95	P95–P97.5	P97.5–P99	P99–P99.5	P99.5–P99.9	P99.9–P99.99	Top .01%
Fixed portfolio weights:													
Risk-free	.722	.412	.248	.182	.156	.134	.115	.102	.090	.079	.071	.051	.029
Housing	.162	.394	.580	.662	.678	.674	.658	.626	.572	.482	.363	.253	.155
Public equity	.113	.189	.165	.147	.153	.170	.189	.207	.219	.232	.230	.185	.179
Private equity	.002	.005	.007	.009	.013	.021	.038	.065	.118	.207	.336	.511	.637
Difference from aggregate return on asset class:													
Risk-free	0	0	0	0	0	0	0	0	0	0	0	0	0
Housing	0	0	.002	.004	.005	.007	.009	.010	.010	.011	.010	.010	.011
Public equity	0	0	.001	.002	.003	.005	.008	.012	.014	.015	.016	.016	.016
Private equity	0	0	-.019	-.030	-.054	-.055	-.049	-.066	-.064	-.063	-.063	-.059	-.060

Standard deviation of return
on asset class:

Risk-free	0	0	0	0	0	0	0	0	0	0	0	0	0
Housing	.140	.140	.140	.140	.140	.140	.140	.140	.140	.140	.140	.140	.140
Public equity	.035	.035	.031	.031	.031	.031	.032	.033	.035	.038	.042	.046	.053
Private equity	.664	.664	.621	.595	.544	.525	.518	.480	.474	.470	.474	.492	.443
Private equity (rescaled)	.345	.345	.323	.309	.283	.273	.269	.249	.246	.245	.246	.256	.230
Excess return schedule in 1967:													
Mean excess return	0	.011	.017	.020	.022	.026	.031	.035	.041	.050	.062	.079	.091
Standard deviation	.023	.056	.081	.093	.095	.095	.094	.093	.098	.119	.167	.254	.283
Standard deviation (private equity rescaled)	.023	.056	.081	.093	.095	.095	.093	.089	.086	.085	.098	.136	.149

Note: Portfolio weights by wealth group are adopted from Bach et al. (2019). The risk-free asset refers to bank account balances and money market funds. Housing refers to residential and commercial real estate. Public equity refers to risky financial assets in their data (financial assets minus risk-free assets). Private equity refers to shares of unlisted companies. Differences from aggregate returns on a particular asset class by wealth group are also taken from Bach et al. (2019). The standard deviation of returns by asset class and wealth group is also taken from Bach et al. (2019) (and corresponds to idiosyncratic risk only); except for housing, where we use an estimate for individual house price volatility in the US from Piazzesi and Schneider (2016). The resulting excess return schedule is then computed as described in the main text (using in addition aggregate excess returns by asset class from US data).

Endnotes

Author email addresses: Hubmer (jhubmer@sas.upenn.edu), Krusell (per.krusell@iies .su.se). For helpful comments and suggestions, the authors would like to thank Chris Carroll, Marty Eichenbaum, Ben Moll, Jim Poterba, Paolo Sodini, Harald Uhlig, Owen Zidar, and seminar participants at the 2015 SED Meetings, the 2015 Hydra Workshop on Dynamic Macroeconomics, the Seventh Meeting of the Society for the Study of Economic Inequality, the 2017 NBER Summer Institute, the 2019 NTA Conference, the 2020 NBER Macroeconomics Annual, Bern, ECB, Johns Hopkins, Indiana, M.I.T., Oslo, Penn State, University of Pennsylvania, SOFI, and Yale. A previous version of this paper circulated as NBER Working Paper no. 23011 under the title "The Historical Evolution of the Wealth Distribution: A Quantitative-Theoretic Investigation." For acknowledgments, sources of research support, and disclosure of the authors' material financial relationships, if any, please see https:// www.nber.org/books-and-chapters/nber-macroeconomics-annual-2020-volume-35/sources -us-wealth-inequality-past-present-and-future.

1. The appendix is available here: http://piketty.pse.ens.fr/files/capital21c/en /Piketty2014TechnicalAppendix.pdf. See also Piketty (1995, 1997), which develop theories of the dynamics of the wealth distribution.

2. This elasticity refers to the long-run response of a household's savings to a change in the interest rate: in particular, with infinitely lived consumers and complete markets, the equilibrium interest rate is pinned down by the rate of time preference.

3. We do not specifically study Piketty's "Second Fundamental Law," which is not a theory about inequality per se but about the aggregate capital-output ratio and which has also been extensively examined in Krusell and Smith (2015).

4. The first application in this literature was one to asset pricing (the risk-free rate): Huggett (1993). Aiyagari (1994) addresses the long-run level of precautionary saving, whereas Krusell and Smith (1998) look at business cycles.

5. In our benchmark model we do in the end incorporate heterogeneity in discount factors, in part because the cross-sectional variance of returns for the wealthiest is so large that the shape of the right tail of the wealth distribution is, in fact, thicker than in the data. As explained in Subsection VI.E, we therefore adjust this variance and compensate by introducing a small amount of discount-factor heterogeneity. Although we do not explicitly calibrate our model to it, the empirical micro literature provides abundant support for such heterogeneity; see, for example, Cronqvist and Siegel (2015).

6. These conclusions are in line with two studies of France and the United States: Piketty (2003) and Piketty and Saez (2003).

7. As Becker (1980) shows, if discount rates are permanently different and there is no wage risk at all, then in the long-run steady state, the most patient consumer owns all of the economy's wealth.

8. Similar forces are at play in Krusell et al. (2009), but in the opposite direction: they find that reductions in wage risk that accompany the elimination of business cycles lead to higher wealth inequality.

9. Bach et al. (2019) document striking "stickiness" in individuals' portfolio choices. This is consistent with our saving rates being quite insensitive to the return characteristics.

10. This model is of course not the first one with theoretical implications for inequality. An early example is Stiglitz (1969) who, building on his 1966 PhD dissertation, studies the dynamics of the distributions of income and wealth in a neoclassical growth model with exogenous linear savings functions. A defining characteristic of the literature in focus here is that consumers face problems much like those studied in the applied consumption literature: they are risk-averse and choose optimal saving in the presence of earnings shocks for which there is not a full set of state-contingent markets.

11. See, e.g., Krusell and Smith (1998) and Guerrieri and Lorenzoni (2017) for this line of work.

12. See also Toda (2014), which also studies a stationary economy with investment risk, and Toda (2018), which studies a Huggett-like economy with random discount factors.

13. For an illuminating recent discussion, see Benhabib, Bisin, and Luo (2017).

14. In Kaymak and Poschke (2016), the long-run wealth distribution does not have a Pareto tail. Moreover, the fraction held by the top group in the study is as high as in the data only because the earnings inequality is assumed to be more extreme than what the available micro data suggests.

15. See also Kopczuk (2015) and Bricker et al. (2016) for a detailed comparison of different measurement methods. In addition to the series presented here, Kopczuk and Saez (2004) use observed estate tax data to make inferences about the distribution of wealth. The resulting top wealth share series roughly confirm the Saez and Zucman (2016) findings until about 1980; afterward, there is hardly any increase. This discrepancy has been linked to differential evolution of mortality rates across wealth groups (Saez and Zucman 2019). Furthermore, Piketty, Saez, and Zucman (2018) and Saez and Zucman (2019) present revised capitalization method estimates that show a slightly smaller but comparable increase relative to Saez and Zucman (2016).

16. The consideration of technological change gives slightly different results but does not materially affect the key discussion in what follows.

17. Notice that $u_A(\bullet)$ need not equal $u_B(\bullet)$ for this result to hold.

18. As an example, Krusell et al. (2009) shows that the removal of aggregate risk, which also involves a lowering of idiosyncratic risk, raises long-run wealth inequality quite significantly. (This is because in that framework, different households have different discount factors, so the removal of idiosyncratic risks takes us closer to the no-risk, extreme long-run inequality outcome.)

19. The bequest function not depending on the current idiosyncratic shock amounts to not letting bequests be influenced by the future income (shocks) faced by the offspring.

20. We note that, in principle, a dynastic framework can address these channels as well by including age as a state variable, possibly with stochastic transitions as, e.g., in Castañeda et al. (2003).

21. To save on notation, we drop household subscripts from now on.

22. Fagereng et al. (2020) and Bach et al. (2019) find not only heterogeneity but persistence in idiosyncratic asset returns. However, especially Bach et al. (2019) find that a good portion of this persistence stems from richer consumers bearing more aggregate risk, which we do not model here. Furthermore, we find below that we can replicate the wealth distribution in 1967, even in its remotest tails, quite accurately without genuine persistence in idiosyncratic returns.

23. In the presence of a progressive income tax, sophisticated agents would seek to smooth capital income over time. For tractability reasons, instead we impose a flat tax on the mean-zero stochastic capital income component.

24. That is, (r_{t+1}, w_{t+1}) are the marginal products of the net production function $F(K_{t+1}, 1) - \delta K_{t+1}$, where

$$K_{t+1} = \int g_t(x_t, p_t, \beta_t) d\Gamma_t(a_t, p_t, \beta_t, \nu_t, \eta_t),$$

$\underline{r}_{t+1}$ is given by

$$\underline{r}_{t+1} = r_{t+1} - \frac{1}{K_{t+1}} \int (r_{t+1}^X(a_{t+1}) + \sigma^X(a_{t+1})\eta_{t+1})a_{t+1} d\Gamma_{t+1}(a_{t+1}, p_{t+1}, \beta_{t+1}, \nu_{t+1}, \eta_{t+1}),$$

and

$$T_{t+1} = \lambda \int \tau_{t+1}((\underline{r}_{t+1} + r_{t+1}^X(a_{t+1}))a_{t+1} + w_{t+1}l_{t+1}(p_{t+1}, \nu_{t+1}))d\Gamma_{t+1}(a_{t+1}, p_{t+1}, \beta_{t+1}, \nu_{t+1}, \eta_{t+1}),$$

where Γ_{t+1} is the distribution in period $t + 1$ generated by the period-t distribution Γ_t and the decision rule g_t.

25. The exact conditions and a very accessible treatment can be found in Gabaix (2009).

26. In fact, the decision rules are almost linear for all but the very poorest agents, i.e., those close to the borrowing constraint. For this reason, approximate aggregation as introduced in Krusell and Smith (1998) typically works very well.

27. A direct proof for a two-period problem can be found in Krusell and Smith (2006); Carroll (2012) proves the asymptotic linearity of the savings rule in a finite-horizon problem as the horizon grows large.

28. The graphs in this section are derived from a simplified model with a flat tax, to focus on the main mechanism.

29. Given that our model abstracts from the life cycle, it is appropriate to include the estate tax in the tax on total income, thus effectively smoothing out the incidence of this tax over the life cycle. Ignoring the estate tax would mean omitting a major source of decreasing tax progressivity. Piketty and Saez (2007) assume further that the corporate income tax burden falls entirely (and uniformly) on capital income. The authors argue that this is a middle-ground assumption (regarding the resulting tax progressivity) between assuming that the tax falls solely on shareholders at one extreme and is effectively born by labor income at the other extreme.

30. The time series is published in US Department of the Treasury (2016). This is a slight approximation to the actual, historical, US tax schedule for capital gains, which features rates that vary across asset categories, amount of time the asset was held, and overall income. The capital gains tax schedule has been slightly progressive as well, though much less so than the one on ordinary income.

31. About 60% of total federal outlays are mandatory spending, the bulk of it on Social Security, Medicare, Medicaid, and income security programs (CBO 2015). The remainder is spent on the Department of Defense and other government agencies as well as on interest payments.

32. In a fully rational portfolio choice model, optimal allocations would depend not only on the wealth level but also on our other persistent states (in particular, the persistent component of earnings). The data we use does not allow for this level of detail.

33. In appendix C, we argue that US data is comparable, to the extent that it is available. We also demonstrate that relative portfolio differences across wealth groups are quite stable over time.

34. Because corporate taxes are included in the federal effective tax rates we are using, these equity premia would ideally correspond to returns before corporate taxes to avoid double counting. In practice, we found this correction difficult to implement.

35. The series is accessible at http://www.econ.yale.edu/~shiller/data/Fig3-1.xls.

36. The data on top wealth shares in table 1 is from Saez and Zucman (2016), who use a capitalization method to calculate them. Because this method is unreliable for a breakdown of the bottom 90%, the other data moments are based on survey data (SCF and precursors); see Kennickell (2011).

37. The accompanying online appendix describes in detail our numerical procedure. Briefly, we use a version of the endogenous grid point method to solve the household's dynamic program. To track the distribution of wealth across households, we follow Huggett (1993) and Castañeda et al. (2003) in using linear interpolation on a fine grid of points to approximate the CDF, which we then update numerically.

38. One can view a departure from the dynastic structure, by "freeing up" the bequest function, as an alternative very similar to discount-factor heterogeneity.

39. Total wealth is of course pinned down so that the return to saving equals the discount rate, abstracting from consumption growth.

40. With $u(c) = (c^{1-\sigma} - 1)/(1 - \sigma)$, the power is $1/\sigma$.

41. Nirei and Aoki (2016) observe the same effect.

42. As illustrated in Section III, their findings align closely with those from the SCF.

43. The method of Saez and Zucman (2016) unfortunately does not allow for a breakdown of the bottom 90% into subgroups.

44. Atkeson and Irie (2020) investigate precisely this channel in the context of family firms.

45. The data is heavily smoothed (using 10-year moving averages) and refers to the effective federal funds rate minus consumer price index inflation.

46. The dynamics are graphed in figures A1 and A2.

47. Note that the fractions generally do not add up to the fraction explained when feeding in all observed changes at the same time, as in our benchmark experiment. The remainder is due to interaction effects in general equilibrium.

48. Relatedly, Kuhn et al. (2020) assemble a long-run SCF data set for the postwar United States and show in an accounting framework that differential exposure to asset price movements—due to differences in portfolio shares across wealth groups—accounts for a significant fraction of medium-run wealth inequality dynamics.

49. Figure A2 displays these results.

50. Figure A4 shows the time series.

51. See Subsection IV.C for an exact description of how this experiment is conducted.

52. See https://sites.google.com/site/laurentbach/AppendixRichPickings.pdf, p. 52–4.

53. The DFAs are a new data product harmonizing SCF household data with aggregate data from the Financial Accounts. See Batty et al. (2019). We aggregate assets in asset classes that are comparable to the classification in Bach et al. (2019), which we use to calibrate our model. The risk-free class consists of checkable deposits and currency, time deposits and short-term investments, and money market funds. The risky financial asset class consists of corporate equities and mutual fund shares (69.2%), debt securities (20.1%), and other loans and life insurance reserves (10.7%). Private equity refers to equity in noncorporate business. We exclude consumer durables and pension entitlements.

54. To see this, consider a uniform increase in the risky asset share (and a corresponding decrease in the risk-free asset share). Provided the risk premium $\bar{r}_{c,t}$ is positive, the mean excess return $r_t^X(a)$ increases for all wealth levels. In turn, market clearing in our setup requires a corresponding decrease in the common component $\underline{r}_t$, such that the expected return $\underline{r}_t + r_t^X(a)$ is unchanged. Because our setup also features heterogeneity within asset classes across wealth groups (and within wealth groups), such a uniform shift in portfolio weights would nevertheless have a small effect on returns.

References

Acemoglu, D. 2002. "Technical Change, Inequality, and the Labor Market." *Journal of Economic Literature* 40 (1): 7–72.

Aiyagari, S. R. 1994. "Uninsured Idiosyncratic Risk and Aggregate Saving." *Quarterly Journal of Economics* 109 (3): 659–84.

Aoki, S., and M. Nirei. 2017. "Zipf's Law, Pareto's Law, and the Evolution of Top Incomes in the United States." *American Economic Journal: Macroeconomics* 9 (3): 36–71. http://www.aeaweb.org/articles?id=10.1257/mac.20150051.

Atkeson, A. G., and M. Irie. 2020. "Understanding 100 Years of the Evolution of Top Wealth Shares in the U.S.: What Is the Role of Family Firms?" Working paper, University of California, Los Angeles.

Auclert, A. 2019. "Monetary Policy and the Redistribution Channel." *American Economic Review* 109 (6): 2333–67. http://www.aeaweb.org/articles?id=10.1257/aer.20160137.

Auerbach, A. J., L. J. Kotlikoff, and D. Koehler. 2019. "U.S. Inequality and Fiscal Progressivity—An Intragenerational Accounting." Working paper, University of California, Berkeley.

Bach, L., L. E. Calvet, and P. Sodini. 2019. "Rich Pickings? Risk, Return, and Skill in the Portfolios of the Wealthy." *American Economic Review* 110 (9): 2703–47.

Batty, M., J. Briggs, K. Pence, P. Smith, and A. Volz. 2019. "The Distributional Financial Accounts." FEDS notes. Washington, DC: Board of Governors of the Federal Reserve System. https://doi.org/10.17016/2380-7172.2436.

Becker, R. A. 1980. "On the Long-Run Steady State in a Simple Dynamic Model of Equilibrium with Heterogeneous Households." *Quarterly Journal of Economics* 95 (2): 375–82.

Benhabib, J., A. Bisin, and M. Luo. 2017. "Earnings Inequality and Other Determinants of Wealth Inequality." *American Economic Review* 107 (5): 593–97. http://www.aeaweb.org/articles?id=10.1257/aer.p20171005.

———. 2019. "Wealth Distribution and Social Mobility in the US: A Quantitative Approach." *American Economic Review* 109 (5): 1623–47. http://www.aeaweb.org/articles?id=10.1257/aer.20151684.

Benhabib, J., A. Bisin, and S. Zhu. 2011. "The Distribution of Wealth and Fiscal Policy in Economies with Finitely Lived Agents." *Econometrica* 79 (1): 123–57.

———. 2015. "The Wealth Distribution in Bewley Economies with Capital Income Risk." *Journal of Economic Theory* 159 (part A): 489–515. http://www.sciencedirect.com/science/article/pii/S0022053115001362.

Bewley, T. n.d. "Interest Bearing Money and the Equilibrium Stock of Capital." Manuscript, Yale University.

Bricker, J., A. Henriques, J. Krimmel, and J. Sabelhaus. 2016. "Measuring Income and Wealth at the Top Using Administrative and Survey Data." *Brookings Papers on Economic Activity* 41 (Spring): 261–331.

Brinca, P., H. Holter, P. Krusell, and L. Malafry. 2016. "Fiscal Multipliers in the 21st Century." *Journal of Monetary Economics* 77:53–69.

Cagetti, M., and M. De Nardi. 2006. "Entrepreneurship, Frictions, and Wealth." *Journal of Political Economy* 114 (5): 835–70.

———. 2009. "Estate Taxation, Entrepreneurship, and Wealth." *American Economic Review* 99 (1): 85–111.

Campanale, C. 2007. "Increasing Returns to Savings and Wealth Inequality." *Review of Economic Dynamics* 10 (4): 646–75. https://ideas.repec.org/a/red/issued/04-102.html.

Campbell, J. Y., M. Lettau, B. G. Malkiel, and Y. Xu. 2001. "Have Individual Stocks Become More Volatile? An Empirical Exploration of Idiosyncratic Risk." *Journal of Finance* 56 (1): 1–43. https://onlinelibrary.wiley.com/doi/abs/10.1111/0022-1082.00318.

Carroll, C. D. 2012. "Theoretical Foundations of Buffer Stock Saving." Working paper, Johns Hopkins University.

Carroll, C. D., and M. S. Kimball. 1996. "On the Concavity of the Consumption Function." *Econometrica* 64 (4): 981–92.

Castañeda, A., J. Días-Giménez, and J.-V. Ríos-Rull. 2003. "Accounting for the U.S. Earnings and Wealth Inequality." *Journal of Political Economy* 111 (4): 818–57.

CBO (Congressional Budget Office). 2015. "The Budget and Economic Outlook: 2015 to 2025." Technical report, Congressional Budget Office, Washington, DC.

Chatterjee, S. 1994. "Transitional Dynamics and the Distribution of Wealth in a Neoclassical Growth Model." *Journal of Public Economics* 54 (1): 97–119. https://ideas.repec.org/a/eee/pubeco/v54y1994i1p97-119.html.

Cronqvist, H., and S. Siegel. 2015. "The Origins of Savings Behavior." *Journal of Political Economy* 123 (1): 123–69. https://doi.org/10.1086/679284.

Dynan, K. E., J. Skinner, and S. P. Zeldes. 2004. "Do the Rich Save More?" *Journal of Political Economy* 112 (2): 397–444. https://doi.org/10.1086/381475.

Fagereng, A., L. Guiso, D. Malacrino, and L. Pistaferri. 2020. "Heterogeneity and Persistence in Returns to Wealth." *Econometrica* 88 (1): 115–70. https://ideas.repec.org/a/wly/emetrp/v88y2020i1p115-170.html.

Gabaix, X. 2009. "Power Laws in Economics and Finance." *Annual Review of Economics* 1 (1): 255–94.

Gabaix, X., J.-M. Lasry, P.-L. Lions, and B. Moll. 2016. "The Dynamics of Inequality." *Econometrica* 84 (6): 2071–111. https://doi.org/10.3982/ECTA13569.

Guerrieri, V., and G. Lorenzoni. 2017. "Credit Crises, Precautionary Savings, and the Liquidity Trap." *Quarterly Journal of Economics* 132 (3): 1427–67. https://ideas.repec.org/a/oup/qjecon/v132y2017i3p1427-1467.html.

Heathcote, J. 2005. "Fiscal Policy with Heterogeneous Agents and Incomplete Markets." *Review of Economic Studies* 72 (1): 161–88.

Heathcote, J., K. Storesletten, and G. L. Violante. 2010. "The Macroeconomic Implications of Rising Wage Inequality in the United States." *Journal of Political Economy* 118 (4): 681–722.

Hornstein, A., P. Krusell, and G. Violante. 2005. "The Effects of Technical Change on Labor Market Inequalities." In *Handbook of Economic Growth*, vol. 1, ed. P. Aghion and S. Durlauf, 1275–370. Amsterdam: Elsevier.

Huggett, M. 1993. "The Risk-Free Rate in Heterogeneous-Agent Incomplete-Insurance Economies." *Journal of Economic Dynamics and Control* 17 (5–6): 953–69.

Jordà, Ò., K. Knoll, D. Kuvshinov, M. Schularick, and A. M. Taylor. 2019. "The Rate of Return on Everything, 1870–2015." *Quarterly Journal of Economics* 134 (3): 1225–98. https://ideas.repec.org/a/oup/qjecon/v134y2019i3p1225-1298.html.

Kaplan, G., B. Moll, and G. L. Violante. 2018. "Monetary Policy According to Hank." *American Economic Review* 108 (3): 697–743. http://www.aeaweb.org/articles?id=10.1257/aer.20160042.

Karabarbounis, L., and B. Neiman. 2014. "The Global Decline of the Labor Share." *Quarterly Journal of Economics* 129 (1): 61–103.

Kartashova, K. 2014. "Private Equity Premium Puzzle Revisited." *American Economic Review* 104 (10): 3297–334. http://www.aeaweb.org/articles?id=10.1257/aer.104.10.3297.

Katz, L. F., and K. M. Murphy. 1992. "Changes in Relative Wages, 1963–1987: Supply and Demand Factors." *Quarterly Journal of Economics* 107 (1): 35–78.

Kaymak, B., and M. Poschke. 2016. "The Evolution of Wealth Inequality over Half a Century: The Role of Taxes, Transfers and Technology." *Journal of Monetary Economics* 77 (C): 1–25.

Kennickell, A. B. 2011. "Tossed and Turned: Wealth Dynamics of U.S. Households 2007–2009." Finance and Economics Discussion Series 2011–51, Board of Governors of the Federal Reserve System, Washington, DC.

Kesten, H. 1973. "Random Difference Equations and Renewal Theory for Products of Random Matrices." *Acta Mathematica* 131 (1): 207–48.

Kopczuk, W. 2015. "What Do We Know about the Evolution of Top Wealth Shares in the United States?" *Journal of Economic Perspectives* 29 (1): 47–66.

Kopczuk, W., and E. Saez. 2004. "Top Wealth Shares in the United States, 1916–2000: Evidence from Estate Tax Returns." *National Tax Journal* 2 (part 2): 445–87.

Krusell, P., T. Mukoyama, A. Şahin, and A. A. Smith, Jr. 2009. "Revisiting the Welfare Effects of Eliminating Business Cycles." *Review of Economic Dynamics* 12:393–404.

Krusell, P., and A. A. Smith, Jr. 1998. "Income and Wealth Heterogeneity in the Macroeconomy." *Journal of Political Economy* 106 (5): 867–96.

———. 2006. "Quantitative Macroeconomic Models with Heterogeneous Agents." In *Advances in Economics and Econometrics: Theory and Applications, Ninth World Congress*, Econometric Society Monographs 41, ed. R. Blundell, W. Newey, and T. Persson, 298–340. New York: Cambridge University Press.

———. 2015. "Is Piketty's 'Second Law of Capitalism' Fundamental?" *Journal of Political Economy* 123 (4): 725–48.

Kuhn, M., M. Schularick, and U. I. Steins. 2020. "Income and Wealth Inequality in America, 1949–2016." *Journal of Political Economy* 128 (9): 3469–519.

McKay, A., E. Nakamura, and J. Steinsson. 2016. "The Power of Forward Guidance Revisited." *American Economic Review* 106 (10): 3133–58.

McKay, A., and R. Reis. 2016. "The Role of Automatic Stabilizers in the U.S. Business Cycle." *Econometrica* 84 (1): 141–94.

Mehra, R., and E. C. Prescott. 1985. "The Equity Premium: A Puzzle." *Journal of Monetary Economics* 15 (2): 145–61. http://www.sciencedirect.com/science/article/pii/0304393285900613.

Nirei, M., and S. Aoki. 2016. "Pareto Distribution of Income in Neoclassical Growth Models." *Review of Economic Dynamics* 20 (1): 25–42.

Piazzesi, M., and M. Schneider. 2016. "Housing and Macroeconomics." In *Handbook of Macroeconomics*, vol. 2, ed. J. B. Taylor and Harald Uhlig, 1547–640. Amsterdam: Elsevier. https://ideas.repec.org/h/eee/macchp/v2-1547.html.

Piketty, T. 1995. "Social Mobility and Redistributive Politics." *Quarterly Journal of Economics* 110 (3): 551–84.

———. 1997. "The Dynamics of the Wealth Distribution and the Interest Rate with Credit Rationing." *Review of Economic Studies* 64:173–89.

———. 2003. "Income Inequality in France, 1901–1998." *Journal of Political Economy* 111 (5): 1004–42.

———. 2014. *Capital in the Twenty-First Century.* Translated by Arthur Goldhammer. Cambridge, MA: Belknap.

Piketty, T., and E. Saez. 2003. "Income Inequality in the United States, 1913–1998." *Quarterly Journal of Economics* 118 (1): 1–41.

———. 2007. "How Progressive Is the U.S. Federal Tax System? A Historical and International Perspective." *Journal of Economic Perspectives* 21 (1): 3–24.

Piketty, T., E. Saez, and G. Zucman. 2018. "Distributional National Accounts: Methods and Estimates for the United States." *Quarterly Journal of Economics* 133 (2): 553–609. https://ideas.repec.org/a/oup/qjecon/v133y2018i2p553-609.html.

Piketty, T., and G. Zucman. 2014. "Capital Is Back: Wealth-Income Ratios in Rich Countries 1700–2010." *Quarterly Journal of Economics* 129 (3): 1255–310.

———. 2015. "Wealth and Inheritance in the Long Run." In *Handbook of Income Distribution*, vol. 2, ed. A. B. Atkinson and F. Bourguignon, 1303–68. Amsterdam: Elsevier.

Quadrini, V. 2000. "Entrepreneurship, Saving, and Social Mobility." *Review of Economic Dynamics* 3 (1): 1–40.

Quadrini, V., and J.-V. Rios-Rull. 2015. "Inequality in Macroeconomics." In *Handbook of Income Distribution*, vol. 2, ed. A. B. Atkinson and F. Bourguignon, 1229–302. Amsterdam: Elsevier.

Saez, E., and G. Zucman. 2016. "Wealth Inequality in the United States since 1913: Evidence from Capitalized Income Tax Data." *Quarterly Journal of Economics* 2:519–78.

———. 2019. "Progressive Wealth Taxation." Brookings Paper on Economic Activity. https://www.brookings.edu/bpea-articles/progressive-wealth-taxation/.

Smith, M., O. Zidar, and E. Zwick. 2020. "Top Wealth in the United States: New Estimates and Implications for Taxing the Rich." Working paper. http://ericzwick.com/wealth/wealth.pdf.

Stachurski, J., and A. A. Toda. 2019. "An Impossibility Theorem for Wealth in Heterogeneous-Agent Models with Limited Heterogeneity." *Journal of Economic Theory* 182 (C): 1–24. https://ideas.repec.org/a/eee/jetheo/v182y2019icp1-24.html.

Stiglitz, J. E. 1969. "Distribution of Income and Wealth among Individuals." *Econometrica* 37 (3): 382–97.

Toda, A. A. 2014. "Incomplete Market Dynamics and Cross-Sectional Distributions." *Journal of Economic Theory* 154 (C): 310–48. https://ideas.repec.org/a/eee/jetheo/v154y2014icp310-348.html.

———. 2018. "Wealth Distribution with Random Discount Factors." *Journal of Monetary Economics* 104:101–113. http://www.sciencedirect.com/science/article/pii/S0304393218305592.

US Department of the Treasury. 2016. "Taxes Paid on Capital Gains for Returns with Positive Net Capital Gains, 1954–2014." Technical report, Office of Tax Analysis, US Department of the Treasury, Washington, DC.

Comment

Owen Zidar, Princeton University, United States of America, *and NBER,* United States of America

Hubmer, Krusell, and Smith use a heterogeneous agent model to quantify the sources of wealth inequality in the United States since 1960. They find that the substantial decline of US tax progressivity is a key driver of wealth inequality in the United States. Two other key model features are (1) allowing for heterogeneous returns and (2) portfolio heterogeneity.

My comments focus on the three main determinants that Hubmer et al. emphasize, which I agree are quite important, and then discuss a few other drivers of wealth inequality that strike me as first order and worthy of more analysis and discussion in future work.

I. Discussion of Main Determinants in Hubmer et al.

My assessment of the evidence is that the three forces that Hubmer et al. emphasize—tax progressivity, portfolio heterogeneity, and return heterogeneity—are important drivers of wealth inequality in the United States. This section will describe and discuss each of these drivers in light of evidence in the literature.

A. Tax Progressivity

One of the most striking features of US tax policy is the decline in tax progressivity during the last half century (Saez and Zucman 2019). Although there is some disagreement about the exact magnitudes of this decline, it is quite clear that top income groups pay much lower taxes than they did in the first part in the postwar period. Quantifying how this decline in tax progressivity has fueled wealth inequality is a valuable contribution of Hubmer et al. According to their calculations in table 2 of the

Table 1
Contribution of Various Channels for Steady-State Wealth Inequality in Hubmer et al. Benchmark Model

#		Top 10% (%)	Top 1% (%)	Top .1% (%)	Top .01% (%)	Gini
1	β-heterogeneity	8.8	7.7	3.8	2.0	.050
2	Earnings heterogeneity	−27.5	−17.8	−9.5	−6.4	−.173
3	Persistent	−5.0	−7.5	−4.2	−2.9	.009
4	Transitory	−11.6	−4.3	−1.7	−.9	−.109
5	Tax progressivity	−21.3	−61.8	−71.2	−67.1	−.148
6	Return heterogeneity	29.5	18.4	6.6	2.8	.192
7	Mean differences	25.8	16.7	6.0	2.6	.174
8	Return risk	.7	2.2	3.3	2.5	.004

Note: Sourced from table 2 of Hubmer et al.

paper (reproduced below as table 1; see line 5), tax progressivity has played a considerable role.

However, there are a few considerations about the decline of US tax progressivity that are worth noting. One substantial force driving the decline as measured by Saez and Zucman (2019) is falling corporate tax revenues. McGrattan and Prescott (2005) argue that declines in taxes on corporate income and corporate distributions can account for much of the growth in US stock market value relative to gross domestic product since 1960. Indeed, Sialm (2009) finds that the declines in investor tax burden are capitalized into equity prices.

It is not clear how well Hubmer et al.'s calibration of the tax system captures both these aspects of capital taxation and the implications for the growth in equity prices. First, the marginal condition that uses after-tax rates of return $\beta(1 + r(1 - \tau'(y)))$ may not be the relevant tax rate for the decision to invest another dollar in practice. Dividends and capital gains taxes seem more relevant and the time series looks a bit different (see fig. 2 in Sialm [2009]) than marginal tax rates on earnings in Hubmer et al.'s figure 5. I would suspect that a key if not more important role of declining progressivity of the personal tax system (outside of its effects via private business growth as in Smith et al. [2020]) is that high-income individuals have more after-tax resources that can be saved and grow more rapidly through compounding. It would be helpful for Hubmer et al. to clarify these two different channels through which tax progressivity affects wealth inequality: (1) affecting after-tax returns in the Euler equation versus (2) higher resources after taxes for those with high income. Second, Hubmer et al. use a somewhat outdated series that stops in year 2000 and then is assumed to be flat thereafter, but in practice there have been substantial declines in tax progressivity since 2000 (Zidar and Zwick 2020), including the 2001 income tax cuts, the 2003 dividend tax cut, the 2001 estate tax cuts, the reduction in capital gains taxes in the early 2000s, and a range of cuts in the 2017 tax reform. Third, from a macro perspective, incorporating the multiple layers of capital taxation may change the level, evolution, and implications of the change in tax rate progressivity (see, e.g., fig. 1 of Acemoglu, Manera, and Restrepo [2020] and fig. 7 of Cooper et al. [2016]). Fourth, the rise of pensions, non-profits, and foreigners is a key development for the role of taxes in asset markets. Large pools of capital no longer face the marginal rates Hubmer et al. show in figure 6. Rosenthal and Austin (2016) estimate that the share of US corporate stock held by taxable shareholders has declined from roughly 90% in 1965 to about 25% in 2016.

Overall, in terms of taxes, my main two recommendations are (1) to compare the tax series set forth by Hubmer et al. to those in more recent studies that account for income that adds up to national income (Piketty, Saez, and Zucman 2018; Auten and Splinter 2019; Smith, Zidar, and Zwick 2020) and (2) to consider ways to incorporate the link between asset prices and tax policy that reflects some of the aforementioned issues.

B. Portfolio Heterogeneity

I completely agree with Hubmer et al. that portfolios vary substantially across the wealth distribution, and that this heterogeneity can be an important aspect of understanding wealth growth. Among the bottom 90%, pension wealth, social security wealth, and housing are the main forms

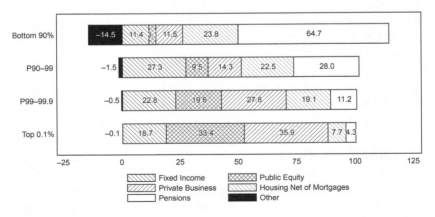

Fig. 1. Portfolios vary across the wealth distribution. Smith, Zidar, and Zwick (2020). A color version of this figure is available online.

of wealth. Among top wealth groups, private and public equity become more important. For example, figure 1 illustrates that two-thirds of the top 0.1%'s wealth is in the form of public and private equity according to estimates from Smith, Zidar, and Zwick (2020). It would be helpful for Hubmer et al. to clarify how pension wealth is treated given its importance in the bottom and middle of the income distribution.

C.   Heterogeneous Returns

Equation (13) in Hubmer et al., which characterizes how returns increase across and within asset classes as a function of wealth, is a key part of the model. The authors argue that this characterization is a reduced-form way to capture an underlying model of portfolio choice. Although I agree that heterogeneous returns along the wealth distribution, due in part to heterogeneous portfolio choices, are a key aspect of modeling wealth, I'd encourage Hubmer et al. and future researchers to unpack the sources of this underlying heterogeneity, especially for private equity.

It is useful to consider the four asset classes in Hubmer et al.: risk-free assets, private equity, public equity, and housing. For fixed-income assets, Smith, Zidar, and Zwick (2020) show that fixed-income portfolios vary substantially along the wealth distribution. Most households in the United States hold primarily low-yielding deposits, but richer households have fixed-income portfolios that have larger shares of higher-yielding bonds and fixed-income mutual funds that have different risk and duration than the typical fixed-income portfolios. Figure 2a uses data from the Survey of Consumer Finance (SCF) from Smith, Zidar, and Zwick (2020) to illustrate the consequences of these different portfolios for returns on fixed-income assets. Most households earn very low returns on fixed-income assets, but going further into the tail shows that the rich hold much higher yielding securities. Smith, Zidar, and Zwick (2020) compare fixed-income flows to stocks in both SCF data and estate tax data to establish this result. In short, in terms of fixed income, using a heterogeneous portfolio model to capture the essence of underlying heterogeneity is well founded.

Heterogeneous returns from private equity holdings, however, are more complicated to interpret and could benefit from a richer model. Smith et al. (2019) use the change in firm performance following premature deaths of private business owners to estimate that 75% of business profits of closely held firms in the United States represent the returns to human capital recharacterized as profits for tax purposes. Therefore, interpreting the heterogeneity in private equity returns in the United

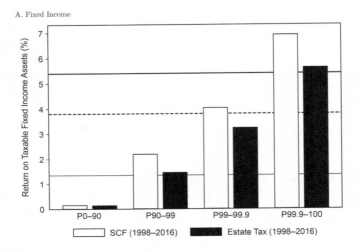

A. Fixed Income

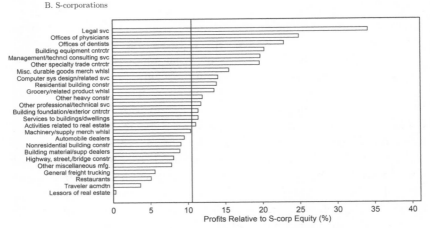

B. S-corporations

Fig. 2. Returns vary within asset classes. SCF = Survey of Consumer Finance. Smith, Zidar, and Zwick (2020). Panel *a* shows variation in returns to fixed claims assets across the interest income distribution; the top line is the Moody's Aaa yield, the middle is the US Treasury 10-year yield, and the bottom is the deposit rate (sourced from Drechsler, Savov, and Schnabl [2017]). Panel *b* shows variation in returns to S-corporation equity by industry. A color version of this figure is available online.

States requires grappling with a large role for human capital and expanding beyond a portfolio choice model. Figure 2*b* plots estimates from Smith, Zidar, and Zwick (2020) on the return on equity of S-corporations. It shows that some human-capital intensive firms like legal services, physician and dentist offices, and other consultancies that tend to rely heavily on human capital inputs generate substantial business income, which is often characterized as "profit" for tax purposes, relative to equity. Recognizing this empirical fact and feature of the US tax system suggests that doctors and dentists are not necessarily the most skilled at portfolio allocation. Moreover, some industries like auto dealers can generate substantial profits and exhibit considerable market power in local areas, which can lead to considerable heterogeneity in returns within the industry.

Finally, there has been substantial regional divergence in house price growth. Coastal cities have tended to exhibit more growth than in wealth than other locations (Smith, Zidar, and Zwick 2020). Thus, the portfolio choice aspect of housing reflects in part a location choice, which then reflects regional income growth and housing regulation and supply conditions, and can lead to meaningful heterogeneity across places and thus across people.

II. Discussion of Other Determinants

Although heterogeneous returns and tax considerations are clearly important, Hubmer et al.'s discussion of the underlying drivers of wealth inequality could put more emphasis on other factors that strike me as first order: (1) life-cycle and demographic trends, (2) falling interest rates and concomitant asset price growth, and (3) inherited wealth and family firms.

A. Life-Cycle and Demographic Trends

The combination of an aging population and wealth accumulation over the life cycle plays a central role in capital accumulation and wealth dynamics. Auclert et al. (2020) present a compelling analysis of this issue. First, they document a striking rise in the share of people who are aged 50 or older across countries. Figure 3a shows that this share is projected to more than double in many countries. For example, in China, 15% of the population was aged 50 or older in 1975, and the most recent data shows the share at roughly 30%. Moreover, some countries are even further along: Italy, for example, now has about 45% of its population aged 50-plus and is on track to have half of its population aged 50-plus by 2025. In the United States, this panel suggests, about one in three individuals is currently aged 50 or older. And this share is projected to increase steadily over the next century.

One reason these demographic trends matter is that there is a pronounced life-cycle profile in wealth accumulation. Figure 3b shows this profile for pension wealth, which is one of the largest components of household wealth, and figure 3c shows overall wealth among the rich

A. The world is getting much older

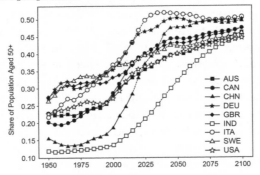

B. Pension wealth over the lifecycle

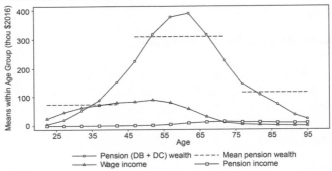

C. Top wealth over the lifecycle

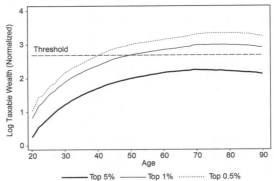

Fig. 3. Wealth, demographic trends, and life-cycle profiles. (*a*) Auclert et al. (2020). (*b*) Smith, Zidar, and Zwick (2020). (*c*) Jakobsen et al. (2020). A color version of this figure is available online.

over the life cycle. Figure 3*b*, which is from Smith, Zidar, and Zwick (2020)'s work with SCF data, shows an inverse U–shape pattern of pension wealth in which the young start accumulating wealth for retirement and then begin deaccumulating around retirement in their early-to-mid 60s. Figure 3*c*, which is from administrative wealth data in Denmark from Jakobsen et al. (2020), shows a similar accumulation process for the wealthy in their working years but interestingly does not find much role for deaccumulation after retirement. Jakobsen et al. (2020) rationalize this behavior by putting wealth in the utility function, which can be a stand-in for a large bequest motive or other force that explains why the rich don't tend to die with less wealth than they had at the start of retirement. In any case, the main point is that the combination of aging and these life-cycle patterns is that we now have more people who are further up their inverse U–shape life-cycle pattern, which means aggregate wealth will be much higher relative to income. Indeed, Auclert et al. (2020) do a simple shift-share exercise to estimate how much higher wealth accumulation is and will be due to a larger share of people being at a more advanced part of the life-cycle profile. They find that this compositional shift can explain much of the rise in wealth-to-income ratios and corresponding decline in real interest rates that we have seen in recent years. In terms of wealth inequality, these findings matter because many people at the top of the wealth distribution are older (Smith, Zidar, and Zwick 2020), so capturing these life-cycle dynamics and demographic trends strikes me as first order both for explaining current and past levels of wealth inequality and, especially, for making predictions about the future of wealth inequality in the United States and the world.

B.   *Falling Interest Rates and Asset Price Growth*

As Auclert et al. (2020) point out, these demographic trends and life-cycle patterns contribute to falling interest rates. And the decline in interest rates has been an important force driving asset price growth, which plays a key role in rising wealth-to-income as well as wealth-inequality trends. Figure 4 plots wealth as a share of national income in the United States along with the yields on US Treasury 10-year bonds. Although there have been some cyclical fluctuations in the wealth-to-income ratio, such as during the Great Recession, lower rates tend to be associated with higher wealth to income. There is considerable recent evidence that asset price growth plays a key role in understanding recent wealth growth and savings behavior (Fagereng et al. 2019; Mian, Straub, and Sufi 2020; Smith, Zidar, and Zwick 2020).

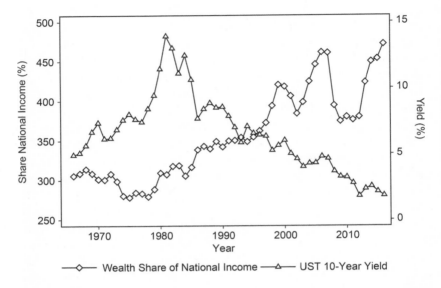

Fig. 4. Interest rate declines contribute to asset price and wealth growth. Smith, Zidar, and Zwick (2020). A color version of this figure is available online.

Another implication of the importance of falling rates and rising asset prices is that the portfolio heterogeneity that Hubmer et al. emphasize can play a leading role in wealth inequality because the responsiveness of an individual's portfolio to these asset price changes can vary considerably depending on how much exposure they have to stocks and other risky assets.

C. *Inheritance*

A classic debate in public finance is the share of inherited wealth in total wealth (see, e.g., Kotlikoff and Summers [1981] versus Modigliani [1986]). Although the exact magnitudes are debated, it is clear that inheritance plays a key role in wealth inequality in the United States. Figure 5 presents recent estimates from Alvaredo, Garbinti, and Piketty (2017) that suggest that the inherited wealth may represent a majority of wealth in the United States in recent years. The importance of inheritance also interacts with Hubmer et al.'s key point about the decline of tax progressivity and the life-cycle patterns of the rich highlighted in Jakobsen et al. (2020). As tax progressivity has declined and the wealthy die with more wealth, it seems clear that inheritance should play a key role in the analysis of wealth inequality. And one of the striking contributors to the decline of

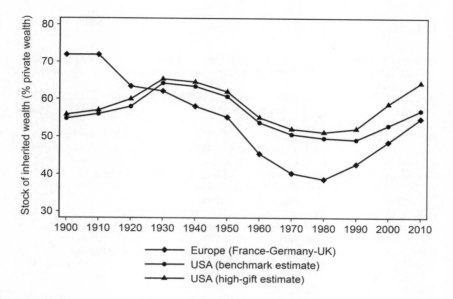

Fig. 5. Inherited wealth can be a substantial share of total wealth. Alvaredo et al. (2017). A color version of this figure is available online.

tax progressivity has been the material reductions in estate taxation in recent decades (see Kopczuk [2013] for a review and Zidar and Zwick [2020] for a sense of how much policy change there has been since 1997).

III. Conclusion

Although these other components—demographics, life-cycle patterns, inheritance, family firms (see, e.g., Atkeson and Irie [2020] for a recent analysis)—are important to consider in future work, I congratulate Hubmer et al. for putting together an insightful analysis that contributes to our understanding of the drivers of wealth inequality, the importance of declining tax progressivity, and the future of wealth inequality in the United States.

Endnote

Author email address: Zidar (ozidar@princeton.edu). This discussion is for the 2020 Macro Annual NBER conference. For acknowledgments, sources of research support, and disclosure of the author's material financial relationships, if any, please see https://www.nber.org/books-and-chapters/nber-macroeconomics-annual-2020-volume-35/comment-sources-us-wealth-inequality-past-present-and-future-zidar.

References

Acemoglu, Daron, Andrea Manera, and Pascual Restrepo. 2020. "Does the U.S. Tax Code Favor Automation?" *Brookings Papers on Economic Activity* (Spring): 231–300.

Alvaredo, Facundo, Bertrand Garbinti, and Thomas Piketty. 2017. "On the Share of Inheritance in Aggregate Wealth: Europe and the USA, 1900–2010." *Economica* 84 (334): 239–60.

Atkeson, Andrew, and Magnus Irie. 2020. "Understanding 100 Years of the Evolution of Top Wealth Shares in the US: What Is the Role of Family Firms?" Working paper, NBER, Cambridge, MA.

Auclert, Adrien, Hannes Malmberg, Frédéric Martenet, and Matthew Rognlie. 2020. "Demographics, Wealth, and Global Imbalances in the Twenty-First Century." Working paper, NBER, Cambridge, MA.

Auten, Gerald, and David Splinter. 2019. "Income Inequality in the United States: Using Tax Data to Measure Long-Term Trends." Working paper, US Department of the Treasury, Office of Tax Analysis, Washington, DC.

Cooper, Michael, John McClelland, James Pearce, Richard Prisinzano, Joseph Sullivan, Danny Yagan, Owen Zidar, and Eric Zwick. 2016. "Business in the United States: Who Owns It, and How Much Tax Do They Pay?" *Tax Policy and the Economy* 30 (1): 91–128.

Drechsler, Itamar, Alexi Savov, and Philipp Schnabl. 2017. "The Deposits Channel of Monetary Policy." *Quarterly Journal of Economics* 132 (4): 1819–1876.

Fagereng, Andreas, Martin Blomhoff Holm, Benjamin Moll, and Gisle Natvik. 2019. "Saving Behavior across the Wealth Distribution: The Importance of Capital Gains." Working Paper no. 26588, NBER, Cambridge, MA.

Jakobsen, Katrine, Kristian Jakobsen, Henrik Kleven, and Gabriel Zucman. 2020. "Wealth Taxation and Wealth Accumulation: Theory and Evidence from Denmark." *Quarterly Journal of Economics* 135 (1): 329–88.

Kopczuk, Wojciech. 2013. "Taxation of Intergenerational Transfers and Wealth." *Handbook of Public Economics* 5:329–90.

Kotlikoff, Laurence J., and Lawrence H Summers. 1981. "The Role of Intergenerational Transfers in Aggregate Capital Accumulation." *Journal of Political Economy* 89 (4): 706–32.

McGrattan, Ellen R., and Edward C. Prescott. 2005. "Taxes, Regulations, and the Value of U.S. and U.K. Corporations." *Review of Economic Studies* 72 (3): 767–96.

Mian, Atif R., Ludwig Straub, and Amir Sufi. 2020. "The Saving Glut of the Rich and the Rise in Household Debt." Working Paper no. 26941, NBER, Cambridge, MA.

Modigliani, Franco. 1986. "Life Cycle, Individual Thrift, and the Wealth of Nations." *American Economic Review* 76 (3): 297–313.

Piketty, Thomas, Emmanuel Saez, and Gabriel Zucman. 2018. "Distributional National Accounts: Methods and Estimates for the United States." *Quarterly Journal of Economics* 133 (2): 553–609.

Rosenthal, Steve, and Lydia Austin. 2016. "The Dwindling Taxable Share of US Corporate Stock." *Tax Notes* 151 (6): 923–934.

Saez, Emmanuel, and Gabriel Zucman. 2019. *The Triumph of Injustice: How the Rich Dodge Taxes and How to Make Them Pay*. New York: Norton.

Sialm, Clemens. 2009. "Tax Changes and Asset Pricing." *American Economic Review* 99 (4): 1356–83.

Smith, Matthew, Danny Yagan, Owen M. Zidar, and Eric Zwick. 2019. "Capitalists in the Twenty-First Century." *Quarterly Journal of Economics* 134 (4): 1675–1745.

———. 2020. "The Rise of Pass-Throughs and the Decline in the Labor Share." Working paper, NBER, Cambridge, MA.

Smith, Matthew, Owen M. Zidar, and Eric Zwick. 2020. "Top Wealth in America: New Estimates and Implications." Working paper, NBER, Cambridge, MA.

Zidar, Owen, and Eric Zwick. 2020. "A Modest Tax Reform Proposal to Roll Back Federal Tax Policy to 1997." Working paper, NBER, Cambridge, MA.

Comment

Benjamin Moll, *London School of Economics,* United Kingdom, *and NBER,* United States of America

I. Overview

Hubmer, Krusell, and Smith provide the best quantitative assessment to date of a number of plausible drivers of the rise in wealth inequality in the United States. To this end, they synthesize 30 years of macroeconomic research on wealth distribution into a benchmark heterogeneous-agent model with many "frontier ingredients." The paper's main finding is that this benchmark model is surprisingly successful in accounting for many US wealth inequality trends. The key model ingredient for achieving this remarkable feat is a rich stochastic process for idiosyncratic asset returns, empirically disciplined by estimates from a number of recent studies. My overall evaluation of Hubmer et al.'s paper is very positive, and partly for this reason I take the opportunity here to comment on what I see as important avenues for future work on wealth inequality dynamics. All of these relate in some way to a point that Hubmer et al. make repeatedly and that I agree with, namely, "just how important portfolios and asset prices are for inequality" and that "next, we need to understand households' portfolio choices better."

My comment has two parts. First, I discuss the need for theories of wealth distribution with endogenous asset returns and how these may affect the authors' conclusions on the drivers of US wealth inequality. Second, I discuss the role of asset prices in driving wealth inequality and, in particular, the question: If a large fraction of the increase in wealth inequality is due to changing asset prices, should we care?

II. Needed: Theories of Asset Returns

Hubmer et al. find that idiosyncratic asset returns are key to accounting for the evolution of US wealth inequality.[1] But return premia in their model are exogenous in both the time series and the cross-section. This suggests that future work should develop theories of wealth distribution in which these asset returns are endogenously determined in equilibrium.

Endogenous return premia also raise the possibility that some of the authors' conclusions about the main drivers of US wealth inequality may change. For example, they find that the falling labor share falls short of accounting for the data. But because asset returns are exogenous, this finding does not take into account that there may be a link from the labor share to asset returns. This is precisely the possibility considered in Moll, Rachel, and Restrepo (2020), who argue that on the flip side of a declining labor share (e.g., due to automation) are increasing returns and return premia for owners of capital. The point is more general though: one can envision many drivers of secular changes in advanced economies as also affecting return premia, and given Hubmer et al.'s findings, all of these are therefore candidate drivers of wealth inequality.

Theories of wealth distribution with endogenous asset returns are therefore a promising avenue for future research. Of course, a number of such theories already exist, for example, theories with entrepreneurship (e.g., Quadrini 2000; Cagetti and Nardi 2006). But future work should link returns more closely to their deep underlying drivers (technology, market structure, and so on) as well as bringing to the table more of the recently available high-quality empirical evidence on such returns.

III. Asset Prices, Wealth Inequality, and Welfare Inequality

I now pick up on Hubmer et al.'s observation "just how important portfolios and asset prices are for wealth inequality," briefly discuss some other work that reaches the same conclusion, and flesh out some of this finding's implications. My main point is that asset-price changes are not merely pesky "valuation effects" to be treated as residuals but that they are empirically important for understanding wealth inequality dynamics and also raise some interesting conceptual issues regarding the welfare consequences of rising wealth inequality.

A.   *Empirical Importance of Asset-Price Changes for Wealth*
     Accumulation and Distribution

The authors' theoretical finding about the importance of portfolio choice
and asset prices for wealth accumulation and distribution is consistent
with an emerging empirical literature on these topics (e.g., Fagereng et al.
2019; Feiveson and Sabelhaus 2019; Martínez-Toledano 2019; Kuhn,
Schularick, and Steins 2020). Figure 1 uses data from Kuhn et al. (2020)
to demonstrate the importance of asset-price changes for the evolution
of wealth inequality in the United States. The solid black line plots the
evolution of the top 10% wealth share from 1971 to 2016. The dotted-and-
dashed red line plots a counterfactual version of the same series under
the assumption that stock prices were constant at their 1971 level. Similarly, the dashed blue line plots the series with constant house prices.[2]
The figure shows that asset-price changes play a large role in accounting

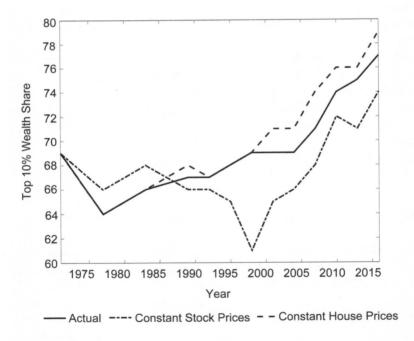

Fig. 1.   Asset-price changes account for a large share of US wealth inequality changes.
Kuhn et al. (2020). See their paper for an exposition of the accounting procedure used
to calculate the counterfactuals with constant stock prices and constant house prices. A
color version of this figure is available online.

for the evolution of the top 10% wealth share. For instance, in the absence of stock price changes, the top 10% wealth share would have been 3 percentage points lower in 2016 (71% rather than the observed level of 74%) and an entire 8 percentage points lower in 1998 (61% rather than 69%). That is, increasing stock prices have tended to increase wealth inequality as measured by the top 10% wealth share. In contrast, increasing house prices have tended to *decrease* wealth inequality as measured by the top 10% wealth share. This is because the top 10% hold relatively less housing and relatively more equity than the bottom 90%. Kuhn et al. (2020) term these differential effects the "race between housing and stock markets in shaping the wealth distribution, p. 3471." Motivated by such empirical findings, an emerging theoretical literature constructs models of wealth distribution with endogenous asset prices. Examples include Garleanu and Panageas (2017), Gomez (2018), Cioffi (2020), and Gomez and Gouin-Bonenfant (2020).

B.   Do Asset-Price Changes That Increase Wealth Inequality Also Increase Welfare Inequality?

If a large fraction of the increase in wealth inequality is due to asset-price changes, should we care? Do those whose wealth increases due to rising asset prices also benefit in welfare terms? Or are such capital gains just "paper gains"? In a nutshell, do asset-price changes that increase wealth inequality also increase *welfare* inequality?

In the remainder of my discussion I consider this question through the lens of standard economic theory. The question about the welfare effects of asset-price driven wealth inequality is closely related to a somewhat simpler question: How does an asset-price change affect an asset owner's welfare? In what follows I think through both of these questions using a simple two-period model. To be clear, both questions are distinct from Hubmer et al.'s positive question asking why wealth inequality has increased and their important progress toward answering it.

My analysis is heavily inspired by existing work, in particular Auclert (2019). It also draws on work analyzing the consumption and welfare effects of house-price changes (Glaeser 2000; Sinai and Souleles 2005; Campbell and Cocco 2007; Berger et al. 2018) an older literature on capital gains taxation (Paish 1940; Whalley 1979) and even a blog post (Cochrane 2020). Some of the results I derive are "folk knowledge" or exist in dispersed form, but I nevertheless thought it useful to derive them explicitly here using simple theory and to present them in a unified fashion.

The discussion is organized around three exercises in this simple two-period model. The first exercise considers the welfare effects of simple exogenous asset-price increases. The second exercise endogenizes asset prices and examines different sources of these increases. The third exercise considers house-price changes.

Exercise 1: Exogenous Asset-Price Changes

An asset owner has utility over consumption in two time periods, $u(c) + \beta u(c')$, where a prime superscript denotes a variable in the second period. Period utility u is strictly increasing and concave. She receives exogenous income flows y and y' in the two periods. She can transfer income across periods by saving in an asset that trades at price p and pays dividend D. This asset is the only saving vehicle. She has an initial asset endowment k and decides how many assets k' to carry into the second period. Summarizing, the individual's problem is

$$V(y, y', D, p) = \max_{c, c', k'} u(c) + \beta u(c') \quad \text{s.t.}$$

$$c + pk' = y + pk, \tag{1}$$

$$c' = y' + Dk',$$

where V denotes her welfare as a function of model parameters. The individual's initial wealth is pk so that an increase in the asset price p makes her wealthier. But does it also make her better off? The answer is simple and follows straight from the envelope condition

$$\frac{\partial V}{\partial p} = -\lambda(k' - k) \quad \text{where} \quad \lambda = u'(c). \tag{2}$$

Importantly, what matters for the welfare effect of an asset-price change is not the level of asset holdings k but the planned change in asset holdings $\Delta k = k' - k$, what is sometimes called "net" or "active saving." Intuitively, a rising asset price is good news if you are planning to sell, $\Delta k < 0$, and bad news if you are planning to buy, $\Delta k > 0$. As usual for an application of the envelope theorem, these statements are correct to first order and ignore second-order welfare effects due to the asset owner reoptimizing her asset holdings k', a point I return to below. A particularly interesting case is an individual who, without the asset-price change, was content to just consume her income each period and whose net saving was thus zero $c = y$, $c' = y' + Dk$, and $\Delta k = 0$. For such an individual, a small asset-price increase $dp > 0$ does not change welfare at all and is indeed just a "paper gain."[3]

The situation is depicted in figure 2. Figure 2A plots the individual's welfare V as a function of the asset price p, and figures 2B and 2C do the same for net saving Δk and consumption in the first period c. Consider first the solid blue lines. They depict an individual whose planned net saving at a baseline price p_0 (the dashed vertical line) is exactly zero; see figure 2B. Figure 2A shows that welfare is a U-shaped function of the asset price and that the welfare effect of a small asset-price increase $dp > 0$ is zero, exactly as expected from equation (2). It is worth noting that the welfare effect is zero despite the fact that her consumption increases in response to the rising asset price, in line with most empirical evidence on marginal propensity to consume out of asset-price changes. That is, it would be erroneous to conclude from the fact that the asset owner consumes out of her capital gains that her welfare must increase. This is because the welfare effects of such consumption changes are second order.[4] This also explains the U-shape of welfare: the second-order effects from reoptimization are always positive regardless of whether the price increases or decreases. Intuitively, because the individual always has the option to simply keep consuming her income flow, the option to reoptimize means she has to be at least as well off as without the price change. Next consider the dashed red lines, which depict an asset owner who was planning on selling, $\Delta k < 0$. When the asset price increases, she is better off, again as expected from equation (2).

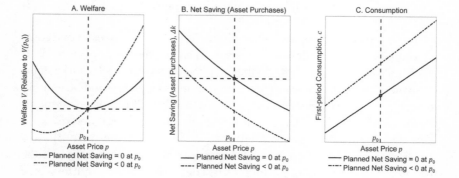

Fig. 2. Effect of asset-price change on (A) Welfare, (B) Net Saving (Asset Purchases), and (C) Consumption. A color version of this figure is available online.

Exercise 2: Different Sources of Asset-Price Changes

The previous exercise with an exogenous asset price raises the question, Where do such asset-price changes come from? I now endogenize this price in a simple fashion. In particular I introduce another asset, namely a bond b with an interest rate R set by monetary policy.[5] Using the same notation as in equation (1), the individual's problem becomes

$$V(y, y', R, D, p) = \max_{c,c',b',k'} u(c) + \beta u(c') \quad \text{s.t.}$$

$$c + pk' + b' = y + pk, \tag{3}$$

$$c' = y' + Dk' + Rb'.$$

There is now a portfolio choice between bonds b' with return R and assets k' with return D/p. In equilibrium, the price p adjusts so that the two returns are equalized

$$p = \frac{D}{R}, \tag{4}$$

that is, the asset price is the present discounted value of dividends. There are thus two sources of rising asset prices: rising dividends D and a declining discount rate R.

Returning to my main question about the welfare effects of asset-price changes, I now additionally ask, Do these depend on the source? To answer this question, I fully differentiate equation (3) while taking into account the dependence of the asset price p on dividends D and the discount rate R. After a bit of algebra[6]

$$\frac{dV}{\lambda} = k\frac{dD}{R} + (b' + pk' - pk)\frac{dR}{R} \quad \text{where} \quad \lambda = u'(c). \tag{5}$$

This is the key expression in my discussion. It summarizes in one compact equation the answer to the question: What are the welfare effects of an asset-price increase, and how do they depend on its source? To understand it, consider two polar cases: in one extreme, an asset price could be entirely driven by rising dividends $dD > 0$ and $dR = 0$; in the other extreme, it could be entirely driven by a declining discount rate $dR < 0$ and $dD = 0$.

In the first case of rising dividends $dD > 0$ only, we have $dV/\lambda = kdD/R > 0$. That is, if the source of rising asset prices is higher dividends, then welfare unambiguously increases. The intuition is straightforward: the increase in dividends expands the individual's budget set, which has an unambiguously positive effect.

The second case of declining discount rates is more subtle. When $dR < 0$ we have

$$\frac{dV}{\lambda} = (b' + pk' - pk)\frac{dR}{R}, \tag{6}$$

which could be either positive or negative. The logic is the same as in equation (2): what matters is net saving $b' + pk' - pk$—that is, the change in the individual's asset position, not the level. (As an aside, Auclert [2019] refers to this term as "unhedged interest rate exposure" precisely because it determines the individual's response to interest rate changes.) An immediate corollary is that if the asset owner just consumes her income stream so that $b' + pk' - pk = 0$, then an asset-price increase due to declining interest rates does not affect her welfare $dV = 0$. An example by Cochrane (2020) provides the intuition and is worth citing in full: "Suppose Bob owns a company, giving him \$100,000 a year income. Bob also spends \$100,000 a year. The discount rate is 10%, so his company is worth \$1,000,000. The interest rate goes down to 1%, and the stock market booms. Bob's company is now worth \$10,000,000. Hooray for Bob! But wait a minute. Bob still gets \$100,000 a year income, and he still spends \$100,000 a year. Absolutely nothing has changed for Bob! The value of his company is 'paper wealth.'"

However, we can also see from equation (6) that, even when a falling discount rate is the only source of rising asset prices, this may affect welfare. In Cochrane's example, if Bob dissaves, say by selling some of his shares from time to time, then he will benefit in welfare terms from a stock market boom. In the notation of equation (6), when $b' + pk' - pk < 0$, $dR < 0$ implies $dV > 0$.

Returning to the key expression (eq. [5]), the answer to the question "What are the welfare effects of an asset-price increase?" can thus be summarized as follows. First, the source of capital gains matters: when dividends increase, the resulting asset-price increase unambiguously benefits the asset owner; in contrast, when the discount rate decreases, the resulting asset-price increase has ambiguous welfare effects. Second, individuals' investment plans matter: if the asset owner just consumes her dividend stream, then an asset-price increase stemming from a declining discount rate has no effect on her welfare; in contrast, if the asset owner tends to dissave, a declining discount rate increases her welfare. Which of these cases is most relevant? This is, of course, an empirical question, and I hope that future work will aim to answer it.

The argument that the source of capital gains matters is also related to a debate in the public finance literature whether capital gains should be taxed on realization (as is common in practice) or on accrual (as under a Haig-Simons income concept). See Paish (1940) and, in particular, Whalley (1979) who provides a beautifully clear graphical analysis of a two-period model similar to the one above.

Housing

Housing differs from financial assets such as stocks in two dimensions. First, housing is not only an asset but also a consumption good. Second, housing is indivisible and subject to substantial adjustment costs. Economists often emphasize the consumption aspect of housing, and intuition suggests that this aspect may, by itself, change how to think about asset-price changes. As Glaeser (2000) puts it: "A house is both an asset and a necessary outlay, p. 147. [. . .] When my house rises in value, that may make me feel wealthier, but since I still need to consume housing there in the future, there is no sense in which I am actually any richer. And because house prices are themselves a major component of the cost of living, one cannot think of changes in housing costs in the same way as changes in the value of a stock market portfolio."

I here revisit the welfare effects of house-price changes through the lens of an extension of the simple two-period model above. My main argument is that, as far as the welfare question is concerned, there is to first order no conceptual difference between housing and other assets. The model is identical to equation (3) with one difference: I replace the asset k by housing h, which generates a utility flow and depreciates at rate δ. The asset owner's problem becomes

$$V(y, y', R, p) = \max_{c, c', h', b'} u(c, h) + \beta u(c', h') \quad \text{s.t.}$$

$$c + ph' + b' = y + ph,$$

$$c' = y' + Rb' - \delta h'.$$

In this formulation without indivisibilities or transaction costs, the only difference between housing and a financial asset is that housing pays a utility dividend $\tilde{D}(c', h') := u_h(c', h')/u_c(c', h') - \delta$ rather than a financial dividend D. I now briefly repeat the two exercises I conducted in the model with a financial asset. First, analogously to equation (2), the effect of an exogenous house-price change is $\partial V/\partial p = -\lambda(h' - h)$ with $\lambda = u_c(c, h)$. As before, a rising house price is good news if you were planning to sell, $\Delta h < 0$, bad news if you were planning to buy, $\Delta h > 0$, and it leaves welfare unchanged if you were planning to do neither. Similarly, the source of house-price changes matters for their welfare effects.

Analogously to equation (4), in equilibrium the house price adjusts so that the returns on housing and bonds are equalized, and hence $p = \tilde{D}(c', h')/R$. The house price can thus again rise for two reasons: first, because interest rates fall and, second, because individuals' preferences for housing increase. To understand the two effects, we consider a small interest rate perturbation $dR < 0$ as well as a small perturbation to the utility dividend $d\tilde{D}(c', h') > 0$.[7] Analogously to equation (5),

$$\frac{dV}{\lambda} = h\frac{d\tilde{D}}{R} + (b' + ph' - ph)\frac{dR}{R} \quad \text{where} \quad \lambda = u_c(c, h)$$

To first order, the welfare analysis is thus exactly analogous to the earlier one. First, the source of the house-price change matters, and a house price increase driven by a declining interest rate has ambiguous effects. Second, investment plans matter: if the house's owner is not planning on moving, then a house-price increase stemming from a declining interest rate has no effect on her welfare; in contrast, if she is planning on selling, then a declining interest rate increases her welfare. It is worth briefly relating this analysis back to the passage from Glaeser (2000) cited above: as far as welfare is concerned and to first order, one actually *can* think of changes in housing costs in the same way as changes in the value of a stock market portfolio. However, this does not invalidate Glaeser's statement—or rather, it only "invalidates it to first order"—because the second-order welfare effects of asset-price changes will generally differ for housing and financial assets. Housing also has other features besides the consumption aspect—for instance, that it is indivisible and entails substantial transaction costs, which further complicate a full welfare analysis of house-price changes.

Main Takeaways: Asset Prices, Wealth Inequality, and Welfare Inequality

Let me return to my motivating question: Do asset-price changes that increase wealth inequality also increase welfare inequality? Through the lens of standard economic theory, the answer is a resounding "it depends." The first lesson is that the source of capital gains matters: to take a concrete example, if the booming stock prices that have increased observed wealth inequality in figure 1 are primarily due to rising dividends, then higher wealth inequality likely also translated into higher welfare inequality; in contrast, if they are primarily due to falling discount rates, then things are more complicated. The second lesson, which applies precisely in this more complicated case, is that investment plans matter. Whether investors benefit from an asset-price boom depends not on the amount of assets they own but on whether they intend to buy, sell, or keep their portfolios unchanged (as in the example of Cochrane [2020]). Finally, I show that the situation is (to first order) the same if a prime reason for rising wealth inequality is rising house prices.

IV. Conclusion

Hubmer et al. have produced a state-of-the-art quantitative evaluation of the drivers of US wealth inequality and should be applauded. There are two main takeaways from their work and from my comments. First, the wealth inequality literature needs better theories of idiosyncratic asset returns. Second, it should pay more attention to asset-price changes as a driver of wealth inequality. Both are important features of the data.

Endnotes

Author email address: Moll (b.moll@lse.ac.uk). I thank Adrien Auclert for useful comments and Moritz Kuhn for sharing the data used in figure 1. For acknowledgments, sources of research support, and disclosure of the author's material financial relationships, if any, please see https://www.nber.org/books-and-chapters/nber-macroeconomics-annual-2020-volume-35/comment-sources-us-wealth-inequality-past-present-and-future-moll.
1. On this point see also the excellent survey by Benhabib and Bisin (2018) and the references cited therein.
2. See Kuhn et al. (2020) for a description of the data and the counterfactual exercise.
3. A complementary intuition starts from the question, How can an increase in wealth pk be ambiguous for the individual's welfare? The answer is that asset-price changes have another offsetting effect: at the same time as her wealth pk increases, the asset return D/p decreases.
4. Why does rising consumption after an asset-price increase not translate into first-order welfare gains? The intuition can be seen from writing out equation (2) without using the envelope theorem to drop terms:

$$\frac{\partial V}{\partial p} = \underbrace{\left(u'(c) - \beta \frac{D}{p} u'(c') \right)}_{=0} \frac{\partial c}{\partial p} - u'(c)(k' - k).$$

So there is indeed a term $u'(c)\partial c/\partial p$ that captures the intuition that a rising asset price increases consumption and hence welfare. But this term is offset by a decrease in consumption and marginal utility in the future.
5. The analysis is thus not one of full general equilibrium. Some readers may prefer to reserve the term "endogenous" for such analyses. The point that the source of asset-price changes matters would be the same.
6. We have

$$dV = \frac{\partial V}{\partial p} \left(\frac{\partial p}{\partial D} dD + \frac{\partial p}{\partial R} dR \right) + \frac{\partial V}{\partial D} dD + \frac{\partial V}{\partial R} dR.$$

As before, the partial derivatives of V follow from the envelope theorem. In addition, from equation (4), we have $\partial p/\partial D = 1/R$ and $\partial p/\partial R = -D/R^2 = -p/R$.

7. The perturbation to the utility dividend $d\bar{D}(c', h')$ should be thought of as a perturbation to a preference parameter. For example, with separable utility $u(c, h) = U(c) + \theta V(h)$, this utility dividend is $\bar{D}(c', h') = \theta V'(h')/U'(c') - \delta$, and a small change $d\theta$ leads to a small change $d\bar{D}(c', h') = V'(h')/U'(c')d\theta$.

References

Auclert, A. 2019. "Monetary Policy and the Redistribution Channel." *American Economic Review* 109 (6): 2333–67.

Benhabib, J., and A. Bisin. 2018. "Skewed Wealth Distributions: Theory and Empirics." *Journal of Economic Literature* 56 (4): 1261–91.

Berger, D., V. Guerrieri, G. Lorenzoni, and J. Vavra. 2018. "House Prices and Consumer Spending." *Review of Economic Studies* 85 (3): 1502–42.

Cagetti, M., and M. D. Nardi. 2006. "Entrepreneurship, Frictions, and Wealth." *Journal of Political Economy* 114 (5): 835–70.

Campbell, J. Y., and J. F. Cocco. 2007. "How Do House Prices Affect Consumption? Evidence from Micro Data." *Journal of Monetary Economics* 54 (3): 591–621.

Cioffi, R. 2020. "Wealth Inequality and Asset Prices: The Role of Heterogeneous Exposure to Aggregate Shocks." Working paper, Princeton University.

Cochrane, J. 2020. "Wealth and Taxes, Part II." Blog post. https://johnhcochrane.blogspot.com/2020/01/wealth-and-taxes-part-ii.html.

Fagereng, A., M. B. Holm, B. Moll, and G. Natvik. 2019. "Saving Behavior across the Wealth Distribution: The Importance of Capital Gains." Working Paper no. 26588, NBER, Cambridge, MA.

Feiveson, L., and J. Sabelhaus. 2019. "Lifecycle Patterns of Saving and Wealth Accumulation." Finance and Economics Discussion Series 2019-010, Board of Governors of the Federal Reserve System, Washington, DC.

Garleanu, N., and S. Panageas. 2017. "Finance in a Time of Disruptive Growth." Discussion paper, UCLA Anderson School of Management.

Glaeser, E. L. 2000. "Comments on 'Real Estate and the Macroeconomy.'" *Brookings Papers on Economic Activity* 2000 (2): 146–50.

Gomez, M. 2018. "Asset Prices and Wealth Inequality." Working paper, Columbia University.

Gomez, M., and É. Gouin-Bonenfant. 2020. "A Q-Theory of Inequality." Working paper, Columbia University.

Kuhn, M., M. Schularick, and U. I. Steins. 2020. "Income and Wealth Inequality in America, 1949–2016." *Journal of Political Economy* 128 (9): 3469–519.

Martínez-Toledano, C. 2019. "Housing Bubbles and Wealth Inequality." Working paper, Paris School of Economics.

Moll, B., L. Rachel, and P. Restrepo. 2020. "Uneven Growth: Automation's Impact on Income and Wealth Inequality." Working paper, London School of Economics.

Paish, F. W. (1940): "Capital Value and Income," *Economica* 7 (28): 416–418.

Quadrini, V. 2000. "Entrepreneurship, Saving and Social Mobility." *Review of Economic Dynamics* 3 (1): 1–40.

Sinai, T., and N. S. Souleles. 2005. "Owner-Occupied Housing as a Hedge against Rent Risk." *Quarterly Journal of Economics* 120 (2): 763–89.

Whalley, J. (1979): "Capital Gains Taxation And Interest Rate Changes: An Extension of Paish's Argument." *National Tax Journal* 32 (1): 87–91.

Discussion

Greg Kaplan opened the general discussion with a remark about asset return heterogeneity. In the authors' model, a sufficient degree of dispersion in asset returns guarantees a well-defined equilibrium wealth distribution. Removing asset return heterogeneity would not imply a counterfactually low degree of wealth inequality but rather a degenerate wealth distribution with a mass point at infinity, he said. The authors clarified that their model is able to generate a Pareto tail in the wealth distribution by adding capital return heterogeneity to a standard S. R. Aiyagari ("Uninsured Idiosyncratic Risk and Aggregate Saving," *Quarterly Journal of Economics* 109, no. 3 [1994]: 659–84) model with labor income inequality. In their calibration, the mean asset return is below the discount rate, but introducing sufficient dispersion in asset returns allows the model to generate the Pareto tail in the wealth distribution observed in the data, they argued.

The rest of the discussion focused on a single topic: the importance of modeling the tax system and measuring the effective tax rate correctly. Frederic Mishkin noted that the effective tax rate can be influenced by tax avoidance. Actual tax collection from high marginal-income tax brackets in the 1960s and 1970s, for example, was likely impaired due to widespread avoidance, he argued. The authors agreed that accounting for tax avoidance is crucial. They emphasized that their paper employs estimates of the effective tax rate from T. Piketty and E. Saez ("How Progressive Is the US Federal Tax System? A Historical and International Perspective," *Journal of Economic Perspectives* 21, no. 1 [2007]: 3–24), which takes care of this issue. James Poterba offered two comments related to the measurement of the effective tax rate on capital income. Such estimates are typically low, Poterba argued, because of two features of the US tax system: the deferral of taxation until capital gains are realized and the "step-up in basis" upon inheritance. He asked the authors whether these characteristics, combined with a stable statutory tax rate, would be consistent with the paper's finding of an increase in capital gain taxation. In addition, Poterba recalled how the decline in corporate income tax is the main driver of the overall decrease in effective tax rates, as shown by empirical estimates in Piketty and Saez (2007). When calibrating return processes, one should then look at the after-tax return available to investors rather than the pre-tax return to investment, he argued. The authors sympathized with this concern and admitted that the after-tax measure of equity returns would in principle be superior to the pre-tax measure. They added that the concern is partially mitigated by the fact that asset price movements only account for medium-run fluctuations in inequality, but they are relatively less important in explaining overall wealth dynamics over the past 50 years.

The authors concluded the general discussion with a comment on the nature of their results, which was pointed out by the discussants. Asset returns in their model are assumed exogenous. As a consequence, they clarified, their framework allows for a positive analysis of the determinants of wealth inequality but is not suitable for normative analysis. They also conceded that their model does not encompass all possible channels behind the increase in wealth inequality, but they highlighted its ability to match the observed path of wealth distribution. A more careful analysis of the origins of returns is warranted if one wants to answer normative questions related to the increase in wealth inequality, they concluded.